THE WORLD OF THE IMAGINATION

Supported by a grant from the National Endowment for the Humanities, an independent federal agency.

THE WORLD OF THE IMAGINATION

Sum and Substance

by

Eva T. H. Brann

Rowman & Littlefield Publishers, Inc.

ROWMAN & LITTLEFIELD PUBLISHERS, INC.

Published in the United States of America
by Rowman & Littlefield Publishers, Inc.
4720 Boston Way, Lanham, Maryland 20706

British Cataloging in Publication Information Available

Library of Congress Cataloging-in-Publication Data

Brann, Eva T.H.
The world of the imagination : sum and substance / Eva T.H. Brann.
p.   cm.
Includes index.
1. Imagination (Philosophy) 2. Imagination (Philosophy)—History.
3. Imagination.   4. Imagery (Psychology)   5. Imagination in
literature. I. Title.
B105.I49B72   1990
153.3—dc20   90-48616 CIP

ISBN 0-8476-7650-1 (cloth : alk. paper)
ISBN 0-8476-7776-1 (pbk. : alk. paper)

Printed in the United States of America

 The paper used in this publication meets the minimum requirements of
American National Standard for Information Sciences—Permanence of
Paper for Printed Library Materials, ANSI Z39.48–1984.

To Barry and Gretchen Mazur,
for moments of being

PARTS

Contents

Preface and Introduction

Preface

A book as long as this calls for a concise statement of the motives behind it, the thesis within it, the approach taken, the topics discussed, and the format employed.

Motives. The intellectual perplexity that drives this inquiry defined itself as I was studying philosophical texts. In the Western tradition the imagination is assigned what might best be called a pivotal function. It is placed centrally between the faculties and intermediately between soul and world. Thus it both holds the soul together within and connects it to the objects without. Yet the treatment given this great power even by habitually definitive authors like Aristotle or Kant is tacitly unfinished, cursory, and problematic. The imagination appears to pose a problem too deep for proper acknowledgment. It is, so to speak, the *missing mystery* of philosophy. It was both the mystery and its neglect that first drew me to the subject.

Second, my strong curiosity was aroused by the recently burgeoning investigations of imagery in cognitive psychology. Here seemed to be an entirely novel possibility for getting the imagery function and its internal field to reveal their nature through non-introspective, experimental means. It turned out that the intricate and passionately argued methodological problems attendant on this enterprise were almost as interesting as the results. In the course of my reading I found, furthermore, that in tandem with this new science, exploiting its findings while suspecting its spirit, there had arisen a large, amorphous "imagery movement." It seemed worthy of attention as a revealing example of the contemporary revolt against the dominion of rationalism, and it proved interesting not so much for its independent discoveries as for the light that the very fact of its existence throws on the current intellectual status of the imagination.

Third, I was moved by a life-long love of fiction, especially of all novels, most children's literature, and this or that poem. Like any lengthy love, this one has developed its recurrent, naggingly absorbing problems: Concerning the texts themselves, *how* is the read word actually imagined—which means, primarily, transformed into visual images? And concerning their fictive figures and scenes, *why* should beings and settings so actual to the receptive soul be consigned to "nonexistence" in sober discourse? These conundrums, felt even while the fiction is working its enchantment, led, oddly enough, straight to logic. There a certain limited kind of help is to be found in formulating the problem. It may be viewed in terms of the actuality attributable to "nonexistent objects," to the first originals that the verbal and visual images represent. In logic, too, is carried on the inquiry into the common nature of those most fascinating of ontic structures after which the imagination itself is named, namely images, be they natural, artificial, or mental.

The last and most encompassing motive was the doubly and triply enigmatic magic of the imaginative life. In my reckoning, by far the largest share of our psychically active life, far more than in perceiving, is spent in various sorts of imagining. We while away our time in desirous daydreaming and floating reveries; in remembering past scenes, envisioning future sights, and projecting mental images onto present perceptions; in disciplined fictionalizing; and above all in that nocturnal dreaming (said to take fifty-four months of an average life) in which our daily places undergo a sea-change from the indifferently familiar to the intimately strange. The sober questions induced by these ethereal human activities concern the existence and the character of the psychic field in which they take place. What is wanted is a delineation of the inner space into which mental imagery is, as it were, painted, and a theory of its reflection in the material images of the arts, particularly in paintings.

Finally, besides these pervasive, continual, and common activities, the imagination seems to have its intermittent and exceptional moments, its "moments of being," when it suddenly gathers the mundane appearances into an imaginative world dense with meaning. As it turns out, for all the delicate intensity of such epiphanies, they too have a tradition and a literature which relieve the burden imposed by their privacy.

All these motives flowed together into a plan to write a "Praise of the Imagination," a labor of love which would pay its dues by omitting no appropriate pedantry, a review of the imagination both as a human experience and as a subject of study, as detailed and comprehensive as I could make it. The result may, I hope, serve in three capacities: as a book to read for the attraction of its matter, as a compendium to consult for information, and perhaps as a text to adopt for a course or a seminar. I believe no other effort of this sort exists.

Thesis. Thus this book is frankly written *parti pris*. It has a multiple thesis. Its parts are these: There is an imagination; it is a faculty or a power; specifically it is a faculty for internal representations; these representations are image-like; therefore they share a certain character with external images; in particular, like material images, they represent absent objects as present; they do so by means of resemblance. This thesis is in varying formulations pursued in every part of the book. I doubt that without some such driving thesis anyone would have the heart to undertake a comprehensive study of so boundless a subject.

I can assure the reader fresh to the subject, to whom these articles may seem pretty obvious, that each is hotly contested, and that the debate is often of great intellectual interest and sometimes of fundamental human significance. I shall try to give fair accounts of the sophisticated counter-arguments. Though I find the imagistic position first and last more persuasive, I must say that I have not proven my case and cannot do so without a remainder of doubt. The case consists, in fact, of scores of related opinions, attendant inclinations, and pertinent preferences that I strive merely to make plausible by whatever means, plain or fancy, may be at hand. Sometimes they are confirmed mainly by their human consequences.

Among these opinions are the following: There is first the unfashionable conviction, reinforced at all the junctures of this inquiry, that the problems of the imagination could scarcely have the poignancy they do, if we did not have a soul. There is, secondly, a sense of the magnificent rightness of our tradition in articulating levels of life by discriminating, usually through the imagination, amongst its heights, depths, and shallows. Finally, there is the persuasion that, when food and shelter are assured, nothing matters to feeling and intellect, to private happiness and public well-being, as do well-stocked memories—which means that the past is of the essence.

In fact, so little is the possibility of formulating problems in terms guaranteed to make them soluble a part of the thesis of this book—which is dedicated (a more embattled project than one might imagine) to the salvage of the obvious, of ordinary experience and its naive convictions—that I shall actually argue explicitly for the imagination as being ultimately a mystery, indeed one of the great mysteries. Naturally I do not wish to use the term to short-circuit the inquiry, since it has always seemed to me that one must have looked very deeply indeed into a subject to declare that "it hath no bottom." By a mystery I mean not an intellectual conversation-stopper, but an ever-compelling perplexity that is not resolved just by being increasingly clarified.

Approach. In casting about for the best way to marshal the sum of information and the substance of argument about the imagination, I soon realized that the organization would have to be by disciplines. Most of the available investigations are specialized and enmeshed in intra-disciplinary debate, so it was only natural that related studies be considered together. I worried that there might be a danger of being entrapped in pre-decided categories, but instead the approach seemed to offer a bonus. It provided a detailed object lesson in the unavoidable—and indeed principled—skewing of the subject matter which is inherent in each discipline. Besides, there really was no choice. The one possible alternative was to approach the imagination through its contents. But since it contains whatever has appeared under the sun or has walked by night, to propose to order its matter is to try to tabulate the world.

Topics. As the main thesis articulated above is pursued through the various disciplines, it yields the following chief topics and sub-theses:

In *philosophy* the recurrent topic is the cognitive nature of the *imagination*. The final claim is that the imagination is the soul's one and only representational faculty, that it functions as the interface of world and mind, and that it has the nature of a pivot between sense and intellect.

In *psychology* the chief topic of debate pits "propositionalists" against "imagists." The former deny the cognitive efficacy and even the existence of mental *imagery*, attributing all knowledge-functions to symbolic reason, while the latter have, I think successfully, attempted to make a function of visual images reveal itself experimentally.

In *logic* the *image* is analyzed as a peculiar amalgam of being and nonbeing, and an argument is made for the actuality of the nonexistent, that is, fictional objects which are imaged in so many internal and external images, such as dreams and paintings.

In the study of *literature* the conversion by *imagining* of verbal texts, both of descriptive prose and of figurative poetry, is the topic, and the effect of figurative language is explained in terms of the superposition of mental images.

In the part concerning *depiction*, there is established and delineated an internal theater wherein *imaging* takes place, that is to say, an inner space. Furthermore, in opposition to the claim that pictures are not "resemblance-representations," the scenes and figures of this inner space are put forward as the originals imitated in the visual arts.

In the last part the imagination is considered as it works in various *worldly* ways—not as a vague manner of speaking, but in accordance with specific, traditionally established powers for informing the world. In *theology* it is recognized as triply at work: It is a source of wicked worldly designs; it is a way to gain other-worldly knowledge; and it is a divine power for world-creation. In *politics* the utopian imagination appears as the faculty for *imaginary* civic world-making. In *inner life* the feeling imagination acts as a capacity for *imaginative* world-making, a capacity which draws the sprawl of appearance into humanly informed, significant wholes.

Format. Instead of footnotes I have adopted the usage of many scientific journals: Author and date are cited right in the text. The full reference is given in the bibliography at the end of each chapter. Page numbers are given only where ten seconds' work with the respective indices would fail to raise the reference. When I have used specific facts or ideas, the source is cited next to these. More generally useful treatments are cited on a separate line at the bottom of the paragraph. Finally, all the burden of precise internal cross-referencing has been thrown on the Index.

★ ★ ★

It remains to express my thanks. The National Endowment for the Humanities has supported my studies materially with a year's grant. People too numerous to name have given me, on purpose or incidentally, bibliographical tips and food for thought. I feel a great sense of obligation to my school. The imagination thrives—or so it seems to me—on oblique attention; it never stirs so magically as when the intellect is austerely absorbed in worthy inquiries. At St. John's College, a true community of learning, I have for thirty years had the opportunity and the duty to think and talk and teach in this way, unencumbered by academic protocol and supported by a program prescribing studies that proved to be indispensable to this enterprise.

To one of my colleagues, Elliott Zuckerman, who gave the manuscript a first editorial reading, I owe a particular debt of gratitude. By his sterling intolerance for my stylistic deviations and his discerning attentiveness to my intended meaning, he imparted to the text whatever polish it may possess. I thank Carole Cunningham, Class of '88, for the patient intelligence she has invested in the production of the manuscript, and I thank my colleague, Beate Ruhm von Oppen, for her expert copy-editing.

Finally, and above all, I feel ever-fresh thankfulness to my adopted country, which, with its overlay of convenience upon a terrain of beauty, offers continual incitement to the critical intellect and abundant nourishment to the dreaming imagination.

Annapolis, 1989

Introduction

By way of beginning I want to enumerate the exclusions (A) and to account for the emphases (B) that shape this survey of the imagination's sum and substance. I will then go on to review the developing usages of terms concerning the imagination, as well as the major definitions of the imagination itself (C).

A. Exclusions

Certain aspects of imagery study that loom large in the literature and even in human experience were omitted regretfully, others with unregenerate glee.

1. A first exclusion applies to a development in the history of the imagination that is temporally very close to but intellectually rather remote from the tenor of this inquiry. The *"postmodern"* movement is, in one of its aspects, a response—though a response in the mode of a demission—to the image-flood now generated by the mass media. One characteristic element of our "civilization of the image," distinct from its mere massiveness, particularly prompts the postmodern turn from the image. It is the fact that in current life the traditional precedence of original over image, both in time and in dignity, is perturbed: We tend to see the images of people and things before the originals and to have our views preshaped by the former. Indeed, the latter are often unavailable, unattainable, or even quite nonexistent.

Kearney, in *The Wake of Imagination* (1988), has delineated the postmodern response not only to the contemporary image-condition but also to the philosophical tradition. From this perspective three phases or paradigms, admittedly schematic, are discernible (33). The first is the premodern tendency to repress human creativity in order to safeguard the "copyright" of an elevated original. Next, in the modern paradigm the autonomous author, in his infinite originality, is emphasized. This wave culminates in narcissistic Romanticism, and breaks in an Existentialist reversal which, in its discovery of human finitude, insists on the unreality of the imagination and the nothingness of its images.

Finally the postmodern paradigm dismisses traditional attempts to ground the imagination philosophically and dismantles it as a category: The image is an outdated vestige of humanism, for it requires the notion of a nuclear human self. Consequently the imagination is deprived of the definite article; the operative postmodern term is "the imaginary," which denominates the illusional contrivance of a false individual or social self (Lacan, Althusser, 256). Moreover, the imagination requires for its exposition concepts of truth such as meaning and reference, which are exploded in postmodernism. Thus the philosophy of truth and of the imagination, which once stood together, now fall together.

Accordingly, the image, too, disappears. It dissolves into "parody," a reflexive, labyrinthine play of mirrors, in which the multiplying reflections are not anchored in any original. "Resemblance," the traditional re-presentational mode, is distinguished from "similitude" (Foucault), which abandons the notion of reference with its hierarchy of original and imitation (270). The copy parodies itself in a series of "lateral repetitions." The representational intention is deliberately unsettled. A paradigmatic work of imaginal postmodernism is Magritte's picture of a pipe with a curved stem. It is a slickly painted, hard-edged representation on a plain ground with a legend, in cursive French: "This is not a pipe." The picture leaves us in a representational vertigo: Do the words make the Platonic point that the image of a pipe is not truly a pipe, or do they say that the ground is not the object, or do they signify that the writing is not the pipe?

The theses of the present inquiry are formed in continuity—if not in agreement—with a multitude of vigorous contemporary studies which endeavor to deal with the enigmas of the imagination not by playing with them but by making an effort in good faith to unravel them. Hence a decent respect for the opinions of one's contemporaries does not absolutely require the inclusion of this postmodern imaginal *trahison des clercs*.

2. I determined from the beginning to confine this study to the Western tradition, omitting—not quite, but nearly completely—the imaginative worlds and works of the *Near* and *Far East*. I made this exclusion from a sense of inadequacy, not merely of space but of understanding. Just because I adhere to the currently embattled view that nothing human—or at least no high civilization—is quite alien to me, I mistrust quick excursions into strange traditions. Hence I have omitted the powerful visualization tradition of Buddhism. And I refrained from even trying to comment on, say, the representative mode of a religion about which it has been suggestively said that "images are to the Hindu worshipper what diagrams are to the geometrician" (Rao 1914), or to do justice to the imaginative premises of an art out of which comes an anecdote that goes straight to the secret heart of this book:

> The Chinese painter Wu Tao-tzu painted on a palace wall a glorious landscape, with mountains, forests, clouds, birds, men, and all things as in Nature, a veritable world-picture; while the Emperor his patron was admiring this painting, Wu Tao-tzu pointed to a doorway on the side of a mountain, inviting the Emperor to enter and behold the marvels within. Wu Tao-tzu himself entered first, beckoning the Emperor to follow; but the door closed, and the painter was never seen again. [Coomaraswamy 1934]

3. I exclude with no regret at all imaginations that arise from *artificial material stimulation*, that is, from hallucinogenic drugs, except for a few paragraphs, mainly under the heading of the "evil imagination." First, I cannot write whereof I have no experience and, then, I despise the dangerous "recreational" trifling with that doctrine of our Western tradition which gives it at once its integrity and its grandeur, namely the belief that both the inner and the outer world have a natural state and are worth facing in a sober condition. There are, to be sure, tribal cultures that make serious, regulated ritual use of psychedelic drugs like mescaline; those I respectfully bypass.

4. From similar lack of empathy I omit treatment of *occult imaginations*, though they probably preempt quite as enormous a portion of human attention as do the various "altered states of mind." Just as the inducing of "artificial paradises" through hashish-smoking betokens a certain emptiness of mind, so do the illicit solicitations of a demon world by magical practices mark a salaciousness of soul which does no honor to the human power to call up the spirit. Again, there are old and serious traditions, such as the Cabbala, that attempt to draw down transcendence and to master its uncanniness, but even their venerable imagery is to the non-initiate at once grotesque and dull.

5. I omit the field of modern *image-manipulation* as practiced in commercial and political advertising because of the sheer contemporary enormousness—and, one might say, enormity—of the phenomenon. In itself it is nothing new. In the fourth century B.C. Plato paints a comically contemporary figure of a political community enslaved to opinion-makers. The people sit together in an artificial underground vault, as if glued to their places, chained so as to face away from the natural light of the entrance toward a screen in the back. Behind them there are artificial lights in front of which a crew of image-manipulators carry all sorts of talking or silent effigies. Their projected shadows are viewed on the screen by the captive audience. Plato assigns to the educator the great task of releasing at least some of these people and of turning them around, of literally "converting" them to the possibility of looking at the world directly (*Republic* VII).

In our day two new elements have been added to Plato's acutely recognizable picture by the advent of television, which means literally "far sight." Our images are manipulated more remotely, centrally, and expertly. Moreover, the viewing takes place mostly at leisure and at home. Thus the liberating turn is far more in the hands of the individual viewers than of the teachers. One might say that image-savvy is a major requirement of contemporary citizenship: I mean being alive not only to hidden motives and motifs—for example, the religious symbolism pervasively insinuated into commercial advertising—but to the spatial and temporal deceptions inherent in the medium. An aesthetic-symbolic primer of the television imagery, and indeed of all moving images, that now largely shape the opinions of adults and the sensibility of children (the two most important of all civic factors) ought to be a part of a study like this (*Daedalus* 1985). However, it was not only the lack of space that prevented the consideration of television and film, but also the deliberate bias of this study toward the "stills" of the imagination.

There is certainly a growing literature of analysis and warning about the flooding of the contemporary consciousness with media-mediated images passed through the filter of commercial interest. One early work of affectionate concern about the illusionism of American life is Boorstin's "how-not-to-do-it book," *The Image* (1961). More recent, and more rabidly sophisticated, is the "semiological guerilla warfare" against the ominous image-invasion mounted by Eco (in Kearney 1988), which begins at the point of reception with all individual viewers' freedom to interpret the image as they, not the system, will.

Against these sometimes apocalyptic anxieties for the stock and the operations of the human imagination one might urge certain commonsensical notions: The quantity of the images undermines the quality of the viewer's attention. Moreover, shallow sights tend to take shallow roots in memory. So it may well be that ordinarily sensible adults are far less vulnerable to the phantasmagoric invasion than intellectuals fear. The safety of the children is a different matter.

6. The bypassing of *non-visual imagery* is the most serious and problematic omission. If for present purposes we accept the standard definition of imagery—namely, that it is the internal representation of a sensory object in the absence of a corresponding sensory stimulus—then there are as many possible imageries as there are perceptual modalities: hearing, smell, taste, touch, and the senses of heat, gravity, posture (Buddenbrock 1958), and probably some others. However, the deliverances of the last three of those named often do not even rise to consciousness, and it would be hard to say what their specific imagery might be. They are, as it were, "all-over" senses, without a focused object.

Taste, smell, and touch do have local stimuli which can, moreover, be vividly recalled. One's mouth can water with a remembered meal, a stench can haunt one's nostrils, and one's skin can re-feel a welcome presence. Furthermore, these stimuli share with visual objects a capability that is, I shall argue, crucial to the understanding of any imagery: They can themselves be simulacra, imitations. Just as sight can be fooled by a *trompe l'oeil* painting, so taste, for example, can be fooled by substitutes, like aspartame for sugar. Yet these so-called "inner" senses are not imagistic in the most complete meaning of the word. Their activity delivers immediate qualities or feels, not the apprehension of complex objects confronting the subject over intervening distances. Thus the sense-memories of taste, smell, and touch seem to lack the triadic structure of optical and auditory imagery, which consists of the mind's eye or ear, of the internal field, and of the visible or audible object located within it. That is probably why there are practically no studies of their imagery, though there are interesting investigations into the senses themselves and into their social significance. (For example: taste, Brillat-Savarin 1825; touch, Montagu 1971; smell, Corbin 1986, who points up the "narcissism" of this sense as well as its special power to rouse visual memory.) Strictly speaking, then, these three are imageless, though they are powerful triggers or releasers of visual imagery. The classic testimony is Proust's *Remembrance of Things Past*, which takes off from the memory-visions called up by the taste of that famous madeleine steeped in herb tea, and culminates in visual recollections brought on by the tactile feel of an uneven pavement.

No one denies, on the other hand, that there are sound-images, differentiated mental object-wholes. Music, for example can be very effectively heard by the mind's ear:

Heard melodies are sweet, but those unheard
Are sweeter . . .

It is, however, a matter of debate whether auditory representations are ever purely mental in the sense of being strictly products of the "inner ear," as visual imagery is of the inner eye. It may be that auditory imagery is often an actual performance, a voiceless exercise of the larynx, a physiological, not just a neurological event.

But what distinguishes sound from vision imagery is, above all, its ultimately non-mimetic character. The musical image copies its physical original, to be sure, but that original does not ordinarily imitate anything, though it may, of course, express or signify something—just what is a subject of infinite argument. It is a commonplace that music, the premier temporal art, is not what painting, the principal spatial art, has traditionally been taken to be: an art of correspondence and resemblance. Indeed it is a main theme of this book that images in the strictest sense are always spatial and often atemporal.

Now sound, especially music, is certainly also spatial, indeed thrice spatial: It has aspects of a spatial structure, it informs perceptual space, and it animates space psychically. As to the first, there are many studies concerned with the significance of spatial terms in music—terms such as "high" and "low" for tones, "up" and "down" for beats, "long" and "short" for notes, "small" and "large" for intervals—and also with their physical bases (Zuckerkandl 1956, Morgan 1980). The second spatial aspect, the sound-field of perception and imagination that music fills with its "volume," has been only slightly studied (Ihde 1970), while the third has been mostly a preoccupation of literary or essayistic sensibility, of which a passage from Nietzsche's *Birth of Tragedy* may serve as an example:

> When a music sounds in fitting accord with any scene, action, event, environment, it seems to unlock its most secret sense and appears as the most correct and distinct commentary on it.

So auditory imagery shares with visual imagery the crucial feature of spatiality (Part Five, Ch. I C).

There are other suggestive parallels. For example, as visual imagery is without scale so musical imagery tends to be without key, at least for a listener not gifted with absolute pitch. Again, as a visualizer can summon an image by palpable ocular effort, so the internal auditor can, and evidently often does, perform the music laryngeally, though it may possibly also come to the mind's ear unproduced, from inner space.

I have nonetheless omitted auditory imagery not only for fear of ranging too wide and being drawn into enigmas yet more intricate than those attending visual imagery, but also because the available studies of the former are rather scanty compared to the rich mass of the latter.

7. Finally, I must omit the psychodynamics of images, the endeavor to bring particular images under laws of *image-formation* and image-concatenation, or to classify them according to their motives and contexts, though there will be passing references to the associationist and the Freudian theory. Global systems of image classification have indeed been attempted (Neuman 1978), but these taxonomies seem at once too slight, too rigid, too coarse-grained, and too idiosyncratic for the teeming worlds they are intended to regiment. In any case none have succeeded in establishing themselves, and my guess is that none ever will.

B. Emphases

This book is devoted mostly to the visual imagination for two related reasons. In the Western tradition the sense of sight occupies a distinct though continually scrutinized position of preeminence, and consequently visual imagery elicits by far the most sharply defined and complexly differentiated debate.

1. The Excellence of Sight. Since imagery goes by modalities of sense, the choice of visual imagery really acknowledges the primacy of sight. People form parties revealing their most intimate natures around their preference for the three great senses: touch, the sense of immediate contact; hearing, whose stimulus comes to its transducing organ mediated by a material pressure wave; and sight, the sense of pure distance whose stimulus travels through a sometimes immense immaterial vibrating field.

In our tradition, touch is the sense for instinctive, hands-on, *in-medias-res* practice and for the warmth of physical contact, while hearing is the sense for pointed communication, the sense through which a personal divinity compels attention: "*Hear*, O Israel!" Sight, on the other hand, is the sense which furnishes figures for objective knowledge: Thus the Greek word for "I know" is literally "I have seen" (*eidon*), and we too say "I see." Sight is valued as the sense which gives the distance and scope necessary to cognitive contemplation.

On these and related grounds testimonials to sight as the aristocrat among the senses are legion. Addison's opening paragraph to the series of papers on the "Pleasures of the Imagination" (1712)—a work which for all its famous demureness of style is among the most startlingly original treatments ever accorded to the imagination—is a good compendium of praises. Sight, he says, is the most perfect and delightful of the senses, most various, comprehensive, delicate, least easily tired or satiated, and most able to reach its object at the greatest distance.

A more recent and more extensive analysis of "The Nobility of Sight" (Jonas 1982) lists the following desirable features to account for the perennial primacy of vision: First, seeing is essentially simultaneous, since even if scanning takes place sequentially, this temporal order is accidental; while all the other senses, especially hearing, essentially register change, sight can apprehend an atemporally instantaneous or static manifold. Second, vision is the spatial sense *par excellence*; not only must the eyes maintain distance to see an object, but that distance itself enters into the view as part of the visual field; thus vision supplies us with the important notion of object-shapes placed in an indefinite visual background. Third, sight can be contemplative in the sense that it need not enter into material or force relations with its object; it is "dynamically neutral." Hence it can be more truly and more effortlessly objective than the other senses. Above all, it can separate the form of objects from their causally active matter—the soaring of spires, for example, from the heavy mass of their material. Since sensory form without real matter is precisely what defines an image, sight is the image-generating sense *par excellence*.

It is only fair to mention here that there is a serious current opposition to the tradition of visual primacy that is defended in this study.

2. The Primacy of the Inquiry into the Visual Imagination. The chapter bibliographies of this book testify to the overwhelming interest the visual imagination has drawn to itself. Nothing remotely comparable could be compiled for the other modalities.

The reason lies in the multiplicity of intellectually sharp problems and of humanly poignant questions to which the power of interior vision gives rise. Yet, multitudinous as these are, the solutions and answers proposed far outnumber them. That is, of course, what keeps the enterprise alive. As an example of the claims and counterclaims that abound in any imagery topic, take children's imagination: There is experimental evidence that children visualize more slowly and imperfectly than adults, and there is also a widespread conviction that they imagine more richly and vividly. There are observations to the effect that juvenile imagery is comparatively derivative, and there is also a conviction that it is more spontaneous than that of adults. There are old pedagogues who fear moral corruption from a lively

imagination, and also new educators who preach its stimulation. And so the debate goes on, see-saw fashion.

The open questions concerning fundamentals as well as the more constrained problems posed within a given conceptual frame arise when the characteristics of sight mentioned above are compounded with the interiority of consciousness—when, that is to say, the imagination is considered as a power of internal vision. Let me summarize them here, in a sort of multidimensional spectrum of inquiry:

How is a visual imagination *possible*? What is the psychic and somatic constitution of a being that can take into itself the looks of the world without its stuff? This is, of course, the question of questions concerning the imagination.

It is specifiable into problems that are more technically focused. Here is a survey of issues, together with the extremes delineating the ranges of proposed resolutions:

What kind of *power* is the imagination? It is a unitary faculty.—It is a set of operations.

What is the nature of its specific *representations*? They are discrete symbols.—They are quasi-spatial analogues.

What is the source of its *materials*? They are perceptual memories.—They are free creations.

What is the scope of its *effects*? It produces only idle epiphenomena.—It synthesizes all experience.

What is the nature of its *functioning*? It is a brain function.—It is a non-material consciousness.

What is its chief human *use*? It is for mundane practical orientation.—It serves to de-familiarize the ordinary world.

What is its moral *value*? It incites corrupting passions.—It prefigures paradise.

What is the proper *approach* to its study? It is a problem for experimental science.—It is a metaphysical question.

Finally, it must be emphasized once more that the primacy of the visual imagination in the intellectual tradition derives not only from the variety and intricacy of the issues it raises, but from the fact that these issues are amenable to treatment in terms of the sensory modality of vision. In other words, the imagination is most accessible as an inner visual space. This study is meant to be a testimonial to that approach.

C. Meanings

To fix the sphere of discourse it is in order to give a brief survey of (1) the principal terms and their usages, (2) the common definitions of the imagination, and (3) some representative appreciations of its importance and worth.

1. Usages of Terms Concerning the Imagination. Our names for the imaginative functions are clustered around two words. One, "fantasy" (b), is a word of Greek origin. In the course of a fascinating development it has yielded up all serious business to its Latin counterpart "imagination" (a), which is now the primary term.

a. *Imagination* is formed on the word "image" (from *imaginem*, acc. of Latin *imago*). Thus the imagination is originally the faculty for having or making images, a point that will be pushed in this book, somewhat against the intellectual mainstream. The term is, furthermore, cognate with the Latin word *imitatio*. Thus the mimetic or copying aspect of the imagination, also brought forward here against considerable current opposition, has etymological support. Of course, this means only that the imitative, representational function of the imagination must once have exercised a great fascination. It seems to be unknown which of the related roots preceded the other or what the prefix "im" signifies.

From "image" are derived numerous terms: nouns, gerunds, adjectives, verbs, participles. I have used the chief of these in entitling the six parts of this study.

Imagination. The psychic faculty or power—the philosophical problem of whose existence and nature looms large—of forming internal images and of employing these, it will be argued, to shape external images. "Imagination" is sometimes used for the image-object.

Imagery, mental. The representational contents of the mind taken collectively from the point of view of their common elements and structures; the definition of the specific imaginal character of imagery is a preoccupation of cognitive psychology. Literary imagery is figurative speech, especially similes and metaphors.

Image. The individual mental as well as material product of the imagination, and also any natural reflection; whether images are essentially mimetic is a major issue in this book. "Imaginal" means having the features of or pertaining to an image.

Imagining. The activity of forming fictional image complexes or imaginal worlds; in this book especially, the verbal versions of a fact or a fiction that by inviting translation into visual imagery raise the problem of the convertibility of word and image. "Imaginable" here means "capable of being envisioned."

Imaging. The activity of forming visual image-products in inner and outer space that raises problems of mental spatiality and representational resemblance. "Imageable" here means capable of being mimetically imaged.

Imaginary. Here used to characterize images of unreal or inactual originals; the status of these originals is a preoccupation of this book.

Imaginative. Here used for a way of informing and rectifying the actual world through the imagination, a theme of never-ending charm.

Words in the vocabulary of the imagination generally have the broadest imaginable usage—including the meaning "conceivable" as in this very sentence. They can be exclamations of surprise or approbation as in "Imagine!" and "Fantastic!"; or imperatives such as "Imagine!" and "Imagine that!"—intended to elicit incredulity, or moral sympathy, or free speculation of the sort that does not require mental imaging for compliance (Morstein 1974)—though imaginative souls will be apt to produce it. Sometimes imagination-terms are applied to quite unimaginable unrealities, such as the imaginary space of Leibniz or the imaginary number expressed by the root of a negative quantity among the mathematicians. However, the most common use is that of the verb to cover any uncertain or vaguely pictorial mentation concerning absent, unlikely, counter-factual, or impossible objects or situations. This extended use for guessing, conjecturing, and supposing, now universal, could in Dickens's time still raise the hackles of picky people:

"Do you imagine—" Mr. Lorry had begun, when Miss Pross took him up short with:
"Never imagine anything. Have no imagination at all."
"I stand corrected: do you suppose—you go so far as to suppose sometimes?"
"Now and then," said Miss Pross. [*A Tale of Two Cities*]

In the analytic tradition the "supposal" use is regarded as standard and taken very seriously (Furlong 1961). It occurs in various constructions. One may suppose a proposition ("imagine that x") or a direct object ("imagine x") or one may suppose adverbially ("thinking imaginatively"). Moreover, each of these uses may involve either what is called after Russell "knowledge by description" or "knowledge by acquaintance," the former corresponding to the ability to give a verbal account, the latter, in this context, to having something like an image. These usages, however, are not of much relevance to this study.

"Imagination" occurs probably most often in the language of literary criticism, where I.A. Richards (1924) distinguishes the following six connotations. The imagination is a capacity for the production of vivid, usually visual, images; for the employment of figurative language; for empathy; for inventiveness; and for the ordering of disparate experiences in art or science. Finally, it is Coleridge's capacity for unifying, intensifying, and idealizing the appearances. One might add as a seventh meaning that of sensibility. The vocabularies of other disciplines have similar spreads. Again, it is the first sense, the capacity for visual images, that will be put forward as central.

"Imagination," "image" and "imaging" are ubiquitous in every region of contemporary language, in newly favored expressions as well as in brand-new applications. "Imagination" is a great word for book titles, usually meaning a sphere of associated notions or mores, a "world-view." Thus there exist books called "The Democratic, [or Liberal, Melodramatic, Redemptive, Gothic, Romantic, Educated, Feminized] Imagination," and similarly titles like "The Imagination of X," where X is a writer or a painter or composer. I do not know the origin of this fashion.

The word "image," on the other hand, is most frequently used in the areas of public relations and self-improvement. A literal example of the former are the pseudo-events and photo-opportunities, happenings engineered to be visually recorded (Boorstin 1961). Again, however, the term is mostly taken figuratively. It refers to how persons or institutions look to others or to themselves, and the impression and associations they convey, which of course often involves actual picturing. Thus there are political, professional, personal, and self-images. This use is often connected with the deliberate manipulation of appearances, be they those that institutions present to the public, or those that persons present to themselves. Sometimes "image" is applied to the world-picture individuals construct for their own cognitive orientation (Boulding 1956).

"Imaging," too, has vast new uses having to do, for example, with the explosion of all sorts of investigative techniques. Hospitals, for example, now have Departments of Imaging.

In sum, the imaginative power and its image-products pervade contemporary speech to just the same extent as do the uneasily paired interests of catering to public opinion and establishing a distinctive personal domain.

b. *Fantasy*, from the Greek word *phantasia*, is the earliest, and was once the weightiest, term. Indeed, "imagination" comes late into Latin use, perhaps first established by Augustine in the fifth century A.D. The normal Latin translation of *phantasia* is plain *visum* (thing seen) or *visio* (sight):

"What the Greeks call 'phantasies' we rightly term 'sights,' through which the images of absent things are so represented in the mind that we seem to discern and have them present," says Quintilian (*Institutio Oratoria* VI 2), giving the full meaning of "imagination" without using the term.

Phantasia is a verbal noun that is ultimately derived from the verb *phainesthai*, which means "to bring to light," "to make shine out," "to appear," especially "to make appear before the soul"; and more immediately from *phantazesthai* (whence "phantasm"), a verb used specifically for the having of memories, dreams, and hallucinations. It is fairly synonymous with *phainomenon*, "appearance," and is eventually used for the faculty of entertaining appearances.

Thus *phantasia* supplies the original notion to which the Latin characterization of the imagination as an imitative power is the complement. Phantasia-imagination is a capacity for inner appearances, that is to say, for internal sense presentations, which resemble external perceptions. Ancient and medieval texts concerning *phantasia* will be discussed in Part One.

Here I want to give a brief account of the loss of dignity the word has obviously suffered over time. In current usage there are quite a few derivative forms, all tainted with frivolity. Here is a sample:

Fancy. As noun, a whimsical notion or the mental faculty responsible for it; as adjective, the property of being pretentiously fine; as verb, the pursuit of a frivolous preference. In some texts fancy is the specific faculty whose product is the fantastic.

Fantasy. The illusionistic mode of the imagination and the literary or visual genre that is its product. "Phantasy" should perhaps be the spelling used when a somewhat more elevated or visionary power is intended (Deutsch 1957).

Phantasm. A hallucinatory image.

Fantasia. A musical composition of no fixed form.

How did this decline and fall, or rather this reversal, come about? In Latin texts up into the seventeenth century the Greek and Latin terms were used concurrently and more or less interchangeably, as, for example by Kilwardby (Part One, Ch. II A); but *imaginatio*, because of its mimetic associations, carried a sense of plodding fidelity, while a high freedom was assigned to *phantasia* (Engell 1981).

The denigrating usage is, to be sure, found earlier. In the sixteenth century, for example, Paracelsus says of fantasy that it is "not *Imaginatio* but the cornerstone of fools" (*An Explanation of Astronomy as a Whole*); and Shakespeare has Mercutio speak of dreams

> Which are the children of an idle brain
> Begot of nothing but vain fantasy. [*Romeo and Juliet*, I iv]

On the other hand, in the seventeenth century Milton still refers to fancy straightforwardly as the physiological seat of visualization:

> Mine eyes he closed, but open left the cell
> Of fancy, my internal sight . . . [*Paradise Lost* VIII 461],

and as subservient to reason insofar as

> of all external things,
> Which the five watchful senses represent,
> She forms imaginations, aery shapes. [V 102]

But then, under the influence of seventeenth-century rationalism, "fantastical or chimerical ideas" begin to be more consistently distinguished from "real ideas . . . such as have a foundation in nature" (Locke, *Essay* 1690 II xxx). Soon this sort of discrimination affects ordinary speech. Toward the end of the eighteenth century "imagination" has settled in as the term of dignity for a cognitively and poetically productive power. At this time there arises, especially in Germany, a flood of descriptive analyses of a faculty felt by philosophers and poets alike to be central in human consciousness. In this literature fantasy is standardly defined as a lower level or mode of the imagination. The culmination of this subordination is Coleridge's influential treatment in his *Biographia Literaria* (1817). Here the imagination is presented as the vital power for idealizing and unifying perception, while the

> *Fancy*, on the contrary, has no other counters to play with but fixities and definites. The Fancy is indeed no other than a mode of Memory emancipated from the order of time and space. [I xiii]

Thus the fancy is reduced to a mere memory-mode that operates at once randomly and rigidly.

The term has never quite recovered, though there have been repeated efforts at rehabilitation in this century. T.S. Eliot, for example, mindful that memory is the Mother of the Muses, argued against the separation

Coleridge effects between memory and the imagination proper (Irwin 1982).

An addendum on the phrase "the mind's eye," which will be often used below in a quasi-literal sense, is in order. It appears in *Hamlet*, said of the ghost:

A mote it is to trouble the mind's eye. [I 112]

It may well have come thence into common use, the more welcome since the monocularity it attributes to the imaginative sight fits neatly in with the sizelessness and the aperspectivity that are so often observed in internal vision.

2. Definitions of the Imagination. Mere definitions, ripped from the background of thought and opinion of which they are distillations, are hardly helpful. At the same time it is necessary to get a first handle on the subject matter, and that is what preliminary definitions are good for. Once launched, this inquiry will be concerned not so much with defining the imagination as with articulating its nature as a many-faceted but coherent whole.

The definitions to be considered arise in several ways. Some express the crux of a personal experience; others represent an effort to extract the core of a common usage, or to provide a compact enunciation of a current sphere of problems and of a system of thought.

It is, furthermore, sometimes argued that "imagination" is really an "onomatoid," that is, a namelike word which in fact designates nothing because it signifies too broadly. At best, this objection goes, terms of the imagination might be said to have a family of applications, though Strawson (1969), for example, considers even that claim to consanguinity too strong. Instead he distinguishes four vaguely related areas of application. First, the imagination is linked with having a mental image, such as a picture in the mind's eye or a tune running in one's head. Second, it is associated with invention, originality, or insight. Bentham, for example, in his *Essay on Logic*, defines invention as "imagination directed in its exercise to the attainment of some particular end," and imagination as a faculty by which "a number of abstracted ideas . . . are compounded . . . into one image"; his is clearly a non-visual understanding. One might add that in this capacity it is often defined as a faculty for finding analogies. Third, it has to do with false belief, delusion, and mistakes of memory. To this set of meanings might be added deliberate pretending and make-believe. Those authors who prefer this last group of meanings, above all Ryle, do not believe that the imagination is a distinct faculty to begin with, let alone that it has to do with internal images. Finally, the term imagination is applied to the transcendental power for structuring perceptual cognition (Kant). One might add a group of allied aperçu-definitions, in which the imagination is tagged as a capacity for seeing similarity in difference (Shelley), for experiencing the familiar as unfamiliar (Stevens), or for making a conscious adjustment between the new and the old (Dewey).

In spite of these objections to attempts at essential definition, repeated and surprisingly consistent efforts have been made to articulate the core-meaning of the word imagination. The resultant *sensus communis* is the background against which are formulated the many alternative understandings reported in this study. This articulated definition is couched alternatively in philosophical and psychological terms.

In philosophy, the core-definition of the imagination is that it is a power mediating between the senses and the reason by virtue of representing perceptual objects without their presence.

In psychology, the preference is for defining the class of representations, that is, the mental imagery, rather than the faculty. Mental imagery is a quasi-sensory or quasi-perceptual experience which occurs in the absence of the usual external stimuli and which may be expected to have behavioral consequences different from those attendant on their sensory counterpart (Furlong 1961).

In ordinary discourse, finally, the imagination is most likely to be defined straightforwardly as a capacity for seeing things in one's head—the aforementioned "mind's eye." Two random testimonials will serve here. When nearly a century ago the famous actor Beerbohm Tree lectured to the Royal Institution on the imagination (1893), he referred to it quite naturally as the mind's eye; and if nowadays you ask a class of students to define it they are apt to say exactly the same thing. This common and perennial figure of speech expresses the crux of the mystery attending the imagination: the mystery of non-organic sight.

There are, in addition, numerous attempts to catch hold of the imagination by classifying its images according to their modes. Just as external images can be stick figures, diagrams, paintings, collages, solids, sculptures, or holograms, so mental imagery can be classified according to number of dimensions, degree of detail, or intensity of color, with the hope that such descriptive analyses of imagery will help to define the constituent functions of imagination. Alternatively, the imaginative consciousness can be classified in terms of its intentional frame—the way in which the imagining subject participates. Thus in imagining an activity, one can simply attend to it, or one can intend to imagine oneself participating in it, or one can deliberately visualize someone else doing it (Wollheim 1970).

Again, instead of intentionally, mental images can be typed psychologically, according to the format in which they are experienced. At least a couple of dozen such types have been distinguished, among them: memory-images, imagination-images, thought-images, illusions, after-images, déjà-vus, entoptic images, dreams, hypnagogic images, hallucinations (Horowitz 1970). Such classifications are the unavoidable though swampy approaches to a summary definition.

3. Lauds and Praises. Finally, there is a good-sized corpus, distinctive in purpose though multifarious in genre, varying from brief essays to long poems, which addresses itself not so much to defining the nature as to praising the works of the imagination. It includes charming meditative prose as well as dreadful exclamatory poetry. A fair sample of the latter is given by the opening lines of Tennyson's poem "Imagination":

> Perennial source of rapturous pleasure, hail!
> Whose inexhaustive stores can never fail;
> Bright as the sun and restless as the main, . . .

The most famous and influential laudations are the two "Pleasures of the Imagination," one a series of essays by Addison (1712) and the other a long didactic poem by Akenside (1744), both of which will be taken up later.

From among the scores of lesser essays, let me mention an assortment of typical efforts. Montaigne's "Of the Power of the Imagination" (1580) dwells on the devastating power of the empathetic imagination to induce psychosomatic symptoms, especially the erotic ability or disability of "the honorable member." James Russell Lowell's "The Imagination" (1855) praises the power through metaphor, terming it the "wings of the mind," as the understanding is its feet. One of Santayana's two essays entitled "Imagination" (1922) presents the imagination as epiphenomenal upon latent instinctual processes and without power of its own. The other, posthumous, essay propounds in the literary sphere a parallel thesis, one that is to become prominent in cognitive psychology. The body, when soaked "in the subtle but manifold emanations" from natural objects, enacts what it is thus imbued with, so that it is precisely physical mimesis that is the essence of the artist's activity: "Nothing could be more false or superficial than to suppose that the given images govern the work," for the conscious imagination only registers the epiphenomenal images that attend the artistic enactment.

There are, furthermore, dozens of contemporary essays identifying the imagination as the source of a more inspired science, or as the agency for saving the environment, or as the means to counteract contemporary rationalism, or as the power by which our most recalcitrant problems will be resolved. It is, of course, an injustice to these efforts to lump them all together in such a fashion that all the insights cancel each other and leave an inert mass. The point is simply that both the power and the products of the imagination seem to elicit, over and over, the desire to praise it in poetry or in prose. The present inquiry is, after all, conceived in this same vein:

> Man consists of body, mind and imagination. His body is faulty, his mind untrustworthy, but his imagination has made him remarkable. In some centuries, his imagination has made life on this planet an intense practice of all the lovelier energies. [John Masefield, *Shakespeare and Spiritual Life*]

Finally, I should cite the three contemporary general works in English that precede the present book in doing homage to the imagination by treating it as a many-faceted but definable theme, one that is humanly vital yet endangered. The first is Mary Warnock's *Imagination* (1976), which traces the imagination from Kant to Wittgenstein through the unifying concept of the capability for creating mental images. The second is Denis Donoghue's *The Sovereign Ghost: Studies in Imagination* (1976), a collection of essays on the poetic imagination containing a multitude of aperçus on texts and issues important to this book. The third is Richard Kearney's *Wake of Imagination* (1988), mentioned above, which traces the decline of the imagination in postmodernism through the failure of faith in the image as an authentic expression.

Bibliography

Beerbohm Tree, Herbert. 1893. *The Imaginative Faculty*. London: Elkin Mathews and John Lane. [Lecture delivered at the Royal Institution.]

Boorstin, Daniel. 1961. *The Image: A Guide to Pseudo-Events in America*. New York: Atheneum (1982).

Boulding, Kenneth E. 1956. *The Image*. Ann Arbor: University of Michigan Press.

Brillat-Savarin, Jean. 1825. *The Physiology of Taste; or Meditations on Transcendental Gastronomy*. New York: Dover Publications (1960).

Buddenbrock, Wolfgang von. 1958. *The Senses*. Ann Arbor: University of Michigan Press.

Coomaraswamy, Ananda K. 1934. *The Transformation of Nature in Art*. New York: Dover Publications (1956).

Corbin, Alain. 1986. *The Foul and the Fragrant: Odor and the French Social Imagination*. Cambridge: Harvard University Press.

Daedalus. Fall 1985. *The Moving Image*.

Deutsch, Babette. 1957. *Poetry Handbook: A Dictionary of Terms*. New York: Grosset and Dunlap.

Donoghue, Denis. 1976. *The Sovereign Ghost: Studies in Imagination*. New York: Ecco Press (1990).

Engell, James. 1981. "Distinctions between Fancy and Imagination." Chapter 13 in *The Creative Imagination: Enlightenment to Romanticism*. Cambridge: Harvard University Press.

Furlong, E. J. 1961. "Uses of the Term 'Imagination'." Chapter 2 in *Imagination*. New York: Macmillan Co.

Horowitz, Mardi J. 1970. *Image Formation and Cognition*. New York: Appleton-Century-Crofts.

Ihde, Don. 1970. "Auditory Imagination." In *Phenomenology in Perspective*, edited by F. I. Smith. The Hague: Martinus Nijhoff.

Irwin, W. R. 1982. "From Fancy to Fantasy: Coleridge and Beyond." In *The Aesthetics of Fantasy Literature and Art*, edited by Roger C. Schlobin. Notre Dame: The University of Notre Dame Press.

Jonas, Hans. 1982. "The Nobility of Sight." In *The Phenomenon of Life: Toward a Philosophical Biology*. Chicago: The University of Chicago Press.

Kearney, Richard. 1988. *The Wake of Imagination: Toward a Postmodern Culture*. Minneapolis: University of Minnesota Press.

Montagu, Ashley. 1971. *Touching: The Human Significance of the Skin*. New York: Columbia University Press.

Morgan, Robert P. 1980. "Musical Time/Musical Space." In *The Language of Images*, edited by W.J.T. Mitchell. Chicago: The University of Chicago Press.

Morstein, Petra von. 1974. " 'Imagine'." *Mind* 88:228–247.

Neuman, Matthias, O.S.B. 1978. "Towards an Integrated Theory of Imagination." *International Philosophical Quarterly* 18:251–275.

Rao, T.A.G. 1914. *Elements of Hindu Iconography*. Madras: Law Printing House.

Richards, I. A. 1924. "The Imagination." Chapter 32 in *Principles of Literary Criticism*. London: Routledge and Kegan Paul (1960).

Richardson, Alan. 1969. "Defining Mental Imagery." Chapter 1 in *Mental Imagery*. New York: Springer Publishing Company.

Strawson, Peter F. 1969. "Imagination and Perception." In *Freedom and Resentment and Other Essays*. London: Methuen and Company (1974).

Warnock, Mary. 1976. *Imagination*. Berkeley and Los Angeles: University of California Press (1978).

Wollheim, Richard. 1970. "Imagination and Identification." In *On Art and Mind*. Cambridge: Harvard University Press.

Zuckerkandl, Victor. 1956. "Space." In *Sound and Symbol: Music and the External World*, Volume 44 in the Bollingen Series, translated by Willard R. Trask. Princeton: Princeton University Press (1973).

Part One

Philosophy: The Nature of the Imagination

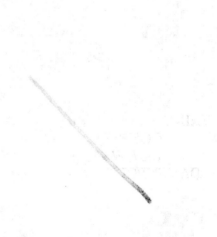

Part One

Philosophy: The Nature of the Imagination

Philosophy abounds in inquiries concerning the nature of things, and above all concerning the nature of human powers, their workings and their objects. So anyone proposing to study the imagination would do well to go first to the philosophical texts, or if not first—for first and last is the unaided attempt to think about the matter directly—at any rate, early on.

To start with philosophy means, however, to start with a bias. Since philosophical writers are, according to the very name of their activity, moved by the desire to know, they deal with every power, not excluding the imagination, only insofar as it helps or hinders knowledge, that is to say, cognitively. The other perspective on the imagination, the inside view as it were, is relegated to those who profess the imaginative life, the producers of poetry and painting, who are allowed to be lovers of reveries and dreams. Their writings are, to be sure, often informed by an acute and articulate intelligence, but in principle they are not works of consequential, coherent, and fundamental thought. The poets' mode is instead a sort of musing, a way of meditating, of eschewing the contortions of intellectual self-consciousness while developing the possibility of a pre-rational (though not, *nota bene*, an ir-rational) kind of direct imaginative insight. This possibility and the testimonials to it are the concern of the later parts of this book, particularly the end of Part Six.

The rivalry was recognized very early in the life of philosophy, though late in that of poetry. What Plato calls "a certain primeval difference between philosophy and poetry" (*Republic* 607 b) was, naturally, a quarrel picked by the late-comer philosophy against a far better established adversary. The difference is primeval only in the sense of being deeply rooted in the nature of things. Once recognized, the rift poses this immense double-pronged question: Whose truths are ultimate and whose insights better to live by? The division has run in our tradition for millennia and preoccupied individual lives for decades. Now and then it seems startlingly and satisfyingly mended and just as soon suddenly once more agape. Some think the opposition should never have been articulated and seek to compose it by means of shallow confusions—to no avail, for although the rift may not be insuperable, it must be recognized and appreciated to become tractable.

An avowed principle of this study is never to force resonant enigmas into the form of soluble problems, nor, on the other hand, to turn away from them. In this spirit the severe and distant rationality of the philosophical treatments will serve above all as the protecting charm with which later to face the enchantments of the imagination on its own territory. But philosophy is not only a protection from the overly passionate claims of the imagination. It also promotes them, for it is a fact of experience that nothing invigorates the imagination more than a spell of sharp thinking.

The difficulty, however, is that even the merely cognitive imagination is what I called above a "missing mystery" in philosophy. This does not mean that the subject is hard to identify in the texts. On the contrary, by means of the preliminary notion of a faculty concerned with inner appearances, and with the aid of the terms *phantasia* or *imagination*, it is easy to locate the salient and usually brief passages—though there are illuminating exceptions, in the form of texts that are implicitly about the imagination but use none of the identifying terms. It is rather that, when these passages are studied in their contexts, the imagination emerges as an unacknowledged question mark, always the crux yet rarely the theme of inquiry. It is the osmotic membrane between matter and mind, the antechamber between outside and inside, the free zone between the laws of nature and the requirements of reason. It is, in sum, the pivotal power in which are centered those mediating, elevating, transforming functions that are so indispensable to the cognitive process that philosophers are reluctant to press them very closely. In the minuscule section on the function of what is *the* central faculty of the *Critique of Pure Reason*, Kant's passing words are emblematic. The imagination, he says, is "a hidden art in the depths of the soul whose true devices nature will scarcely let us divine and spread exposed before our eyes" (B 181).

It is not until our century that the imagination finally obtains thematic treatment, but with the partial effect that its existence is thrown in doubt. Thereupon the subject migrates to experimental cognitive psychology, there to gain new life, as reported in Part Two.

To be sure, there were numerous long thematic treatments of the imagination from the eighteenth century on, but they went along descriptive lines and were frankly derivative in a philosophical respect. There has been, furthermore, a perennial flow of variations on the grand image-theories. I have, however, chosen to review here only those texts in which great or influential new departures are made. I will try to present interpretations that, while succinct, preserve enough of the grand context in which theories of the imagination are inevitably enmeshed not to reduce them to unmotivated schemata. For mere compendia of theories are a crime against the texts they pretend to represent.

Here is the place to say in general why a recapitulation of the tradition is called for at all, especially in view of the fact that quite a few contemporary writers on the imagination set it so resolutely aside. Ignoring the tradition seems to me to exact a price. It has about it an air of brilliant barbarism. On the one hand its products display the sort of racy novelty that is achieved by cutting loose from the past; while on the other hand they show the raw narrowness, the unwitting surrender to current convention, that usually comes from temporal self-isolation. For although in principle a truly original theory of real scope and depth should be a human possibility, in fact it just does not seem to happen. On the contrary, those unwilling to enlarge their view by riding pickaback on the wisdom of predecessors— even if only to proclaim their errors—consign themselves to pygmy stature.

My arrangement will be chronological. (For precise dates, see the chapter bibliographies.) The given temporal sequence of writers represents, after all, the minimal ordering hypothesis. It is a bonus that by tracing the imagination in this way one comes to a realization which is all the more valuable because its burden is sophisticatedly denied in contemporary writing. The realization is that we truly live in an intellectual tradition. I mean not only that discernibly identical subjects, with their enduring complex of problems, keep turning up, albeit in forms adapted to what looks to hindsight like a developing intellectual continuum. I also mean that every specific view ever held about such a perennial subject can be revived at any time, either by a deliberate recovery or through an accidental reduplication. It seems to be this fact, that few theories are permanently laid to rest, that there is no accepted progress of paradigms, that distinguishes philosophy from science (Kuhn 1962). Thus Kant's imagination as a power conflating sense and thought has a fairly precise precursor in Plato's *phantasia*, and as a field for geometric inscription it is recognizably anticipated in Plotinus. Hobbes's formula for the imagination as "decaying sense" is lifted straight from Aristotle; Hume's impression-imagination is a plain borrowing from the Stoics. And so on.

The happy conclusion is that the imagination in philosophy has no linear development—happy because that marks it as a genuine philosophical topic. Its preliminary shaping is an early achievement of philosophy, and its development brings accessions of perspectives, possibilities, and formulations but no lasting resolutions. Only if philosophy itself is to end can the enigma of the imagination be worn out or bypassed.

In the last chapter of this first part, I shall nevertheless venture to argue for the following conclusion: The imagination is indeed a faculty; it is a faculty of representations; it is moreover the only such faculty; and its proper objects are quasi-visual images. I hope that at the end this quadripartite thesis will seem less obvious, just as natural, and far more significant.

Chapter I

Ancient Writers

Among the ancients six writers and schools appear to me to present the most significant theories of the imagination: Plato, Aristotle, the Stoics, the Epicureans, the Neoplatonists, and Augustine.

Plato gives the name *eikasia*, literally "image-agency," to a distinctive power of the soul for recognizing images as images. Aristotle, in a first thematic treatment of *phantasia*, argues that it is not a power but a process by which sensation presents itself to the intellect as inner appearance. The Stoics understand the same terms as an affection or a "presentation," which comes into the soul from the external object and provides the only available access to it; when properly "affirmed" it is incorrigible. The Epicureans regard mental images as material films. The Neoplatonists extend the scope of the sources feeding the imagination from sensation upward, so that its images may also reflect objects proper to the higher parts of the soul. Augustine introduces the will into the process of imaginative cognition.

A. Plato: The Power of Image-Recognition

No philosopher in our tradition is more fascinated by and more embattled with images than Plato, and no major group of texts is briefer about the imagination. The first fact largely accounts for the second: Plato's great effort went into the inquiry concerning the being of images, which is reviewed in Part Three. The balance of the explanation lies in his understanding of appearance itself as being image-like. The world is a spatial and visible reflection of a non-spatial and invisible structure of thought-like originals. The plausibility of this view it is not my business to discuss here (Brann 1980). These originals are, figuratively, viewed with the eye of the soul (*Republic* 508 d, *Phaedrus* 250 b). That is to say, unlike images, they are not seen *in* the soul but *by* the soul. In other words, the simile for intellectual vision preempts the figurative room that will later come to be occupied by the imaginative "mind's eye" and its intra-psychic images.

Images do, on the other hand, turn up often and crucially in the Socratic dialogues. There are occasional references to precisely those objects that are later called mental images—picture-like inner visions, sensory and colorful. Second, there are important mentions of those minimally sensory images for rational use, namely geometric diagrams. And third, there are many crucial passages about external images both natural and artificial.

The mental pictures, which will later preoccupy psychologists, are merely slipped into the dialogues without much elaboration. There is a reference to inner "painted phantasms" that occur in wishful daydreams, as when a man has visions of himself rejoicing in his gold (*Philebus* 40 a). As it happens, this passage is preceded by a vivid figurative presentation of the psychic experience which will haunt contemporary psychology as the "propositionalist-imagist" dichotomy (Part Two, Ch. II C). The soul, Socrates says, resembles a book, and sensation and memory combine to inscribe the propositions into it. Both are needed because sensation must be referred to some sort of pre-knowledge in order for propositional apprehension to arise. The cognitive scribe is followed by "a second craftsman," an inner painter, who draws illustrative images to accompany the propositional text in the soul. In other words, the verbal judgments are converted into mental images, which are true or false according to their originating propositions. Derrida (1972, 189) interprets this psychic paint-ing as supplementing the psychic writing with a "direct intuition or an immediate vision," such that the mental image is a visual appearance of the intelligible form. However, no such contemplative function of the workaday imagination is ever made explicit in the dialogues. In fact, such a function would assign to the imagination a separate cognitive access to being, whereas the lines in question seem to lean toward the propositionalist view that the imagination is a mere accompaniment to rational cognition.

There is yet more of the future in the Socratic passage. For here is prefigured in passing the issue of translation of perceptions into verbal representations and their retranslation into visual images (Part Four, Ch. I). In the *Timaeus* (71 b) Socrates is given, by way of entertainment, the sort of material explanation of this process that he always finds comic. It is the liver, he is told, which as a shiny organ is contrived to receive verbal propositions and to reflect them as images, the better to control the nearby irrational belly. That seems to be the sum of Plato on mental imagery.

The most distinctive treatment is accorded to geometric images, images for the use of thought (Part Five, Ch. I C). The power dealing with these is called *eikasia*, a term literally close to "imagination," but in meaning more like "image-recognition." It is a noun formed from a denominative verb *eikazein*, meaning to do something about a likeness, an *eikon*. Thus *eikasia* can mean both the likeness itself and a claim that something is "likely," a conjecture. It is a word rare in general usage, and Plato lets Socrates use it in only one context, in the sixth and seventh book of the *Republic* (511 e, 534 a). But this use is central to Platonic psychology.

The context is the grand center of all Socratic dialogues, the series of similitudes presenting to Plato's brother Glaucon a preview of the path to be taken and the summit of knowledge to be scaled by the caretakers of the best political community. The end of all learning, called here the Idea of the Good, is described by Socrates as being to the intelligible world as the sun is to the visible world. As the sun is the source both of growth and of the visibility by whose light the bodily eyes perceive, so the Good is the principle both of being and of the intelligibility by whose illumination the soul's eye sees. The figure is confirmed and justified in a diagrammatic simile, the Divided Line, through the proportions of whose sections the visible world as a whole is represented as imaging the intelligible realm in the same way as the two sub-regions of these major realms respectively image each other. Finally, to each realm and sub-region of objects is matched the power (*dynamis*) of the soul by which it becomes accessible.

Eikasia is the name given to the power proper to the very lowest sub-region, in which Socrates places natural and, presumably, artificial images, such as shadows, reflections, and paintings. The upper region of the visible world contains all the objects of nature themselves, and its proper power is called "trust" (*pistis*)—that is, the unconscious familiarity with which we move in the surrounding world.

The divided line is meant to read from the top down, so that *eikasia*, although the lowest, is by no means the most primitive power. It is understandable only from a higher ground. Its exercise marks the complex beginning of all Platonic philosophy, which involves the ability to recognize images *as* images, to distinguish between copy and genuine original (Klein 1965).

In the upper end of the non-visible, intelligible realm are placed the ultimate originals, the invisible forms or ideas, which serve as the sources and principles of the lower realm. These are never to be seen as mere images (*Phaedo* 100 a); they are intellected as things in themselves. In contemplating them the soul meets with true steadfast "knowledge" (*epistēmē*). Their sub-region, the first shadows they throw, is the realm in which occurs "thinking through" (*dianoia*), or discursive thinking. Such thinking runs downward through the deductions to be made from the principles of knowledge without reflecting on those high beginnings. This is the realm of all ordinary logic and mathematics, though it also harbors other pertinent functions.

The dianoetic power picks up natural shapes as well as diagrammatic drawings and interprets them as images (511 c). This is what mathematicians do when they use material models and sketches as inexact representations of geometric figures. Moreover, this power also draws down the intellectual ideas from their invisible heights by giving them a sort of spatiality and visibility. Socrates does not specify this imaging function, which is exemplified in all sorts of model-making. The Neoplatonic writers will feel entitled to infer it.

Thus the *dianoia* is an "inbetween" power (511 d), since it mediates between mere opinion, which is the epistemic status of the lower realms, and knowledge, that of the higher realm. It has a triple work to do: It reasons. It engages in a kind of higher image-recognition, seeing through sensory things to their mathematical originals. It images the intellect. It is therefore a kind of imagination, the intellectual imagination.

Besides natural and geometric images there is also the artificial kind, produced in painting and poetry. The position of poetry, so brilliantly practiced and so utterly undermined, is *the* paradox of the Platonic writings. No set of texts will ever be more poignantly preoccupied by that "certain primeval difference between philosophy and poetry."

Among artificial images, two kinds are distinguished, the "iconic" and the "phantastic" (Part Three, Ch. I A). The former are at least correct copies; the latter are not only copies but deceitfully illusionistic to boot. Iconic poetry, as a true image of truth, is just barely permissible for pedagogic purposes. Presumably the Platonic myths themselves are such allowed images (Part Four, Ch. IV A). But there is no positive independent psychic power of poetry. What will much later be called the "creative imagination" is just a species of deceit, and the poets who practice it naturally fall into all sorts of other corruptions (*Republic* III).

A yet more radical attack on image-making is directed against painting: Indeed painting is the paradigm of all representational arts, and poetry is thrice compared to it (*Republic* 377 e, 601 a, 605 a). Both arts are understood as being mimetic or imitative, which is to say that they engage in deliberate imaging. In the symmetric architecture of the *Republic* the critique of mimetic poetry precedes the central discussion of the work, in which the order of being is shown to have an image-character, whereas the critique of painting follows the central discussion. The critique of poetry centers on its characteristic content, while that of painting concerns its ontic status. Paintings are twice removed from truth, for they are not only imitations, they are imitations of imitations (X). Since it is late at night, Socrates

humorously gives the example of a painted bed, which is at second remove
from genuine being since it is copied from the sensory bed, which is in turn
only an image of the ideal bed. Therefore painting appeals to the lowest
part of the soul, which, unless it is under strong discipline, is given to silly
sentiment and dangerous excitation (605 c). In sum, poets and painters are
generically concerned with the superficial looks of things.

Socrates' example is particularly felicitous for us, since by mere chance
there exist wonderfully specific paintings that might be cited as a direct
counter-example to Socrates' claim that not even the most artful representation of mere sensory appearance can ever give it revelatory force. They
are van Gogh's paintings of his bed in Arles (1888). In the ensuing argument
about the "primeval quarrel" between art and thought, it seems to me that
one becomes competent to defend the former only by having at some time
come to grips with Socrates' brave and engaged resistance to the worship of
art-images. So much for the Platonic treatment of images.

Plato does also have something to say about *phantasia*, the term that in
Greek texts was soon to mean imagination in the usual sense. It is cognate
with "phenomenon" and therefore means "something having to do with
appearance," sometimes even appearance itself. In the Platonic context it
might most accurately, if awkwardly, be rendered as "the capacity of being
appeared to" (Lycos 1964).

Thus, whereas *eikasia* is the power of recognizing images as images,
phantasia is a capacity for taking in an appearance and for apprehending and
affirming it as appearance. Correspondingly, whatever appears in the world
can become problematic in two ways. Just as images are either "iconic" or
"phantastic," so appearance can fail to be the genuine article and be in fact
a mere image, or it can misrepresent itself as other than it is and become a
sort of illusion. Because appearance can be delusive, taking it in involves a
moment of judgment, a brief internal dialogue along the lines: "What is
that standing yonder? It appears to be a man" (*Philebus* 38 c). More
precisely: There is, says the visiting interlocutor in the *Sophist* (264 a), a
sort of internal speech of the soul with itself, a type of thinking (*dianoia*),
which involves affirmation and denial and is therefore called judgment.
When it involves sensation it is rightly called *phantasia*. So when we judge
that "it appears to be x" we are mixing together sensation and judgment.

Phantasia, then, is a "mixing" or "connection" (*Theaetetus* 195 d) of
sensation and rational judgment, a power for forming composites, which
seems to function as follows: Sensation makes some sort of impression on
the soul (193 b). Thereupon an identifying memory is pulled up, and its
congruence with the sense-impression is checked by the familiar power of
rational image-recognition that also makes judgments, the *dianoia*. It issues

a quick, tacit affirmation or denial, and we say: "It appears to be a man."
That is what it means "to be appeared to." It would not be too far off to
say that Platonic *phantasia* turns sensation into perception by means of
rational affirmation. Not for nothing is the German word for perception
Wahrnehmung, "taking something in as true." The point of interest is that
for Plato perception works from the inside out, for appearance arises only
when sensation is judged by thought. This is the juncture at which Plato
pre-figures Kant, as well as the host of writers who assign to the cognitive
imagination a "taking in" function. Thence being humanly perceptive also
comes to be identified with having imagination. As one of Henry James's
formidably articulate young heroines shrewdly observes to her dinner
partner:

> You're familiar with everything, but conscious, really of nothing. What I mean
> is that you've no imagination. [*The Wings of the Dove*]

Naturally neither Plato's notion that worldly appearances are images nor
his view of the genesis of cognition is acceptable to Aristotle. In defending
the substantial nature of physical individuals, and by separating *phantasia*
from judgment, he will start the tradition on its way to a notion of the
imagination that is a distinct, full-blown faculty.

B. Aristotle: The Process of Appearance-Presentation

This way will, however, begin with a step backward, for Aristotle is at
pains to show that *phantasia* is not an independent power. It is rather an
activity of sensation, a psychic process. The process is nonetheless indispensable to cognition, since its function is to present to the intellect that
interpreted sensation without which there is no thought.

Aristotle's theory of the imagination is a prize example of what I have
called the "missing mystery." It endows the imagination with pivotal
functions but accords it only brief, scattered, negative, and apparently
contradictory treatment. The question, "What is the imagination?" (*ti esti*)
is asked, appropriately, in the essay *On the Soul* (III 3), a short text that is
long in perplexities. The following account is consequently heavily interpretative, and I should say right now that many passages I cite are contradicted by others, though several of these can, in turn, be explained away.
Furthermore, it must be said that Aristotle uses the phrase "I have a
phantasia" just as we use "I imagine"—that is to say, with a wide range of
casual meanings such as "it appears to me" and "I have the impression."

The two crucial sentences on the nature of the imagination are these:

> If *phantasia* is that according to which we say that a *phantasma* comes to be in us (and if we don't speak in a metaphor), is it a power or a condition by which we judge and are correct or incorrect? [428 a]

> If then all has been said, *phantasia*, as has been told, will be a motion proceeding from sensation as it goes on actively . . . . Concerning *phantasia* what it is and why it is let so much be said. [428 b]

The first passage is here rendered as a question rather than a statement (Hamlyn 1968). The latter reading is grammatically possible but makes no sense, since the discussion between the passage and the concluding thesis is largely devoted to showing that *phantasia* is not the judging-power nor indeed a power at all. I therefore understand Aristotle to say that those who call it a power speak of it metaphorically. The demonstration that *phantasia* is distinct from the various judging powers, which comprise sensation, opinion, knowledge, and intellect, includes arguments such as these: *Phantasia* is not sensation, since it can occur when there is no actual sensation. All sensations are true, that is, incorrigible, but imagination is often false, and the same distinction holds for knowledge and intellection. We do not say "it *appears* to be a man" except when sense is functioning inaccurately; which is to say that *phantasia* comes into play precisely when sensation fails. Animals have *phantasia*, though not the judging powers. And above all, imagination is a voluntary activity with respect to content, but how judgments come out is not a matter of will.

The passage culminates in the direct criticism of Plato's claim that *phantasia* is a conjunction of sensation and judgment, on the grounds that the two faculties are often obliged to oppose each other.

Aristotle's energetic distancing of his notion of *phantasia* from Plato's is an index and a consequence of their deepest differences. For Plato the appearances delivered by sensation are themselves image-like and constitutionally deceptive, so that their very apprehension requires judgment. For Aristotle, in contrast, sensation is activated by a world of individual, physical substances which require some function that will properly present them to the intellect. *Phantasia* will not so much perform as *be* that function (Wedin 1988).

For *phantasia*

> seems to be a kind of movement [*kinesis*] and not to come about without sensation and only in those who are sensing and only of those things that are

sensible. And since movement comes about by the activity of sensation, it is necessarily similar to sensation. [428 b]

As it turns out, it is more than similar; it is, in a manner of speaking, as a faculty identical:

> The *phantasia*-faculty [*phantastikon*] is the same with the sense faculty, but the being [*i.e.*, the theoretical account] of *phantasia* and sense differ. [*On Dreams* 459 a]

In other words, *phantasia*, if you insist on speaking of it as a faculty, is sensation, but when it comes to explanation, it is not the same but only a certain movement in the process of sensation.

Let us see what *phantasia* and sensation in fact have in common. They are both capable of being true or false, though, being incorrigible, they are not, as has been pointed out, powers of being right or wrong, that is, of affirmation or denial (432 a, Engmann 1976). Sensation, Aristotle says, is "that which is receptive of sensible forms without their matter" (*On the Soul* 424 a); to see something is to get hold of the shape of the thing without its body. Imagination too, takes place in the physical absence of the thing. Aristotle connects these two absence-presentations when he says that because the sense organ can receive the sensed object without its matter, "therefore sensations and imaginations are present in the sense organs even in the absence of the sense-object" (425 b). So the imagination is, as it were, a second degree of absence. In sensing, the object itself is present to the senses, though only its form is received, whereas in imagining the object itself is also absent. That would seem to be their chief difference. Imagination is sensation prolonged past the presence of the object, a motion of the soul set in train by the activity of sensation.

Now in respect to cognitive importance the secondary process of imagination seems to exceed by far the primary power of sensation. Sensation, Aristotle says in the chapter on imagination, can be true or false in three stages (427 b, 418 a). The sensation of sensibles proper, like white or warm, is always true in the sense of being incorrigible. Next there is the "incidental" sensation, which tells us that this white sensible is this or that thing, and it may be false. And finally there are the sensations of common attributes like motion, magnitude, and shape, which are least immediate and therefore most subject to error.

The context of this passage implies that in the last two stages sensation has in fact turned into imagination. Indeed insofar as the three stages are practically simultaneous it is present from the first. For these stages surely describe not sensation so much as what we call perception, the active taking in of sensed things rather than the passive reception of mere sense-properties. The implication is that the imagination, as the process peculiarly capable of error (as opposed to unfalsifiable sensation), is the first interpreter of sensation (Nussbaum 1978, 257), and is indeed by itself performing the function Plato assigned to tacit judgment. Above all, in the last stage, in the cognition of "common sensibles," the imagination is practically identical with the "common sense," which is unquestionably a power for interpreting sensation.

That observation brings us finally to the *phantasma*, the mental image which "comes to be" through the imagination. First it must be said that these images are not for Aristotle pre-existent objects on which the imagination-faculty is trained, but rather a kind of result it achieves (Philippe 1971). Mental images are treated in the wonderful little work *On Memory and Recollection*. Here an image is said to appear as an affection (*pathos*) of the "common sense" (Beare 1906). Though Aristotle seems reluctant to interpose the imagination as an independent faculty between sense and intellect, he makes the common sense do work analogous to that which two millennia later will have evolved into the "synthetic" function of Kant's productive imagination. This work involves, besides distinguishing and comparing the deliverances of the special senses, the perception of the common sensibles, among which are shape and time. Beyond that, it is in common sense that consciousness originates, for it first makes us aware of having sensations at all (*On the Soul* 425 b). But most important for present purposes, it receives the traces left by the *phantasia*-movement, and these affections are a kind of picture, an imprint of the sensation impressed physically on the bodily organ of the common sense, as from a seal ring (*On Memory* 450 a).

These stored affections are the same images that, after some time has passed, can be recollected as memories. For "memory belongs to that part of the soul to which imagination belongs." Thus all imaginable things are also, incidentally, memorable (*On Memory* 450 a).

There follows the most remarkable paragraph in antiquity on the nature of mental images (450 b), remarkable not only because it prefigures the modern notion of intentionality (Ch. IV A), but also because it presents a series of the subtlest questions that can be asked about memory. When memory occurs, Aristotle wonders, is it the present affection or its original cause that is remembered? When we have an internal picture of someone, how is it that we perceive this picture as a picture of something else and not simply as this present sense-impression? How can we remember what is not present? For, Aristotle observes, this is just what does happen: "As a

picture painted on a panel is at once a living being and an image" and the
two are one and the same, although their rational account is not the same,
so the *phantasma* within can be at once an object of contemplation in itself
and a mental image of something else. In the former case it is a mere mental
object (*noema*). In the latter it is a copy and a "souvenir" (*mnemoneuma*, Ross
1906). Here begins the philosophical double life of the mental image as an
object of the mind's eye in its own right and as an image referring to an
original, that is, as a mental representation intending an absent object. The
dual aspect of the mental image as a quasi-thing and as a picture of sorts
will become a preoccupation of modern inquiries.

It hardly needs saying by now that Aristotle has throughout treated
phantasia as primarily visual, since sight is for him the chief sense (429 a).

To conclude, let me briefly sketch the relation of Aristotle's *phantasia* first
to knowledge, then to passion, and finally to poetic production.

The first relation is direct. "When one contemplates [that is, intellects],
it is necessary at the same time to contemplate some mental image." For
what the intellect ultimately deals with are forms that have an independent
existence only in sensible objects. Sensation and then imagination pass these
objects up, as it were, to the intellect, purifying them in turn first just of
their matter and then of the very sense of their presence (432 a, 431 a). It is,
of course, not the spatiality and temporality attaching to mental images
that characterize them as products of the common sense that is necessary to
thought. The intellect does not use common sensibles as such, just as a
geometer makes no use of the determinate magnitude of his diagram
(Lachterman 1989, 83). Why the presence of these spatial and temporal
continua should nonetheless be necessary to the process of thought is, as
Aristotle himself says, another question (450 a). I do not know that any
explicit answer is forthcoming until Kant shows that thinking that functions
without space and time is empty. But such thinking is so remote from
Aristotelian intellection that the explanation is hardly transferable; so the
question remains unresolved for Aristotle.

Next let me take up briefly the relation of imagination to appetite and
desire, a subject discussed more extensively in Part Six. For Aristotle
imagination in itself has a certain emotional neutrality. In imagining we are
like spectators looking, say, at something frightening without necessarily
being afraid (427 b). However, imagining initiates movements of desire
(*Movement of Animals* 702 a) and induces pleasurable feelings (*Rhetoric* II 2).
Animals move themselves insofar as they have the capacity to desire, but
they cannot desire without imagination (*On the Soul* 433 b). Evidently the
imagination, which is connected either with sensation or thought, has to
present the object, be it sensory or rational, to any animate being before

that animal can feel desire and is moved to act (Nussbaum 1978, 233). The fact that for Aristotle desire is possible only through the imagination marks him, one might say, as classical. He does not acknowledge the diffuse, indeterminate, and objectless emotionality of romantics (Part Six, Ch. III B). For Aristotle, to desire is to desire something. Hence the imagination precedes the passions. The reverse order as a human possibility worthy of consideration is in the future.

Finally, the relation of imagination to poetry must be considered. In Aristotle's *Poetics*, *phantasia* plays no role, because that work is not about the psychology of producing poetry but about its nature. It seems to me nevertheless that for him the making and understanding of poetic imagery as well as of poetry in general require the exercise of *phantasia*.

For poetry is considered by Aristotle, as by Plato, to be imitative, "mimetic," and the making and apprehension of mimetic images does indeed depend on the imagination. What is new is the cognitive and ethical value Aristotle attaches to *mimēsis*. Poetry is natural to human beings, who, from childhood on, both enjoy and learn through imitation. Looking at accurate likenesses of even painful things is enjoyable, and as we look we learn, for we infer repeatedly that "that man is so and so." All human beings, "not only philosophers," love this sort of learning (iv). What Aristotle is describing here is, of course, precisely the appearance-presenting *phantasia* at work. Furthermore, the types presented in poetry have a certain universality, which prefigures the "concrete universal" of modern poetics (Part Four, Ch. IV A). This fact makes poetry more serious and more philosophical than history (ix). The governing feature in Aristotelian mimesis is thus its double effect. Whatever is re-presented mimetically is, as it were, actually present, yet not with the accidents of its ordinary phenomenal existence. Rather it recurs as a singular and significant re-appearance (Gadamer 1965, II i b).

Finally, the grandest images of poetry, those of tragedy, effect a purification or readjustment of the passions (vi). For Plato poetry diverts us from truth by presenting mere image-particulars, and diverts us from virtue by inducing excessive excitation. For Aristotle, in contrast, it aids learning by presenting imitations that have a universal character, and improves character by giving the passions a cleansing workout. These differences are all the more fascinating when one recalls that it is Plato who philosophizes in poetic figures and Aristotle who strives for prosaically literal exposition. The tolerance of the philosophers for the poets seems to begin at the moment when poetry, along with the imagination, has been given a distinct function and standing.

I should add that the mimetic theory of poetry and of painting is at present under thoroughgoing attack (Part Five, Ch. III A), though there are also attempts to reinstate it (Boyd 1985). These attempts recognize the possibility that mimesis is dependent on a "realistic" metaphysics, on the doctrine that the world is really and objectively given so that it can be more or less faithfully re-presented.

C. Stoics: The Affection of Appearance-Apprehension

The Stoics pick up one of the ordinary casual uses of the term *phantasia*: "I have a *phantasia*," literally "I have an appearance," is often, as was mentioned, used in Greek to mean "I have an impression. . . ." Such an impression-appearance presents itself as an affection of the soul. The Stoics say that it only needs to be embraced in assent to become the sole criterion of truth.

This bare-bones listing of the terms involved in the Stoic theory of the imagination can give no idea of the importance the theory acquires. It is the single element of ancient philosophy that captured a school, and the most popular one at that, of early modern philosophy, namely empiricism. Unfortunately, since many of the original texts bearing on Stoic *phantasia* are lost, while the surviving accounts, aside from being often hostile, are scattered and fragmentary (Arnim 1924), a review must be either very long or, like this one, sketchy. The doctrines here mentioned are mostly those of the Early Stoa, whose chief figures are Zeno, Cleanthes, and Chrysippus. Their views are reported mainly by Cicero (*Academic Questions*), Sextus Empiricus (*Against the Logicians*), and Diogenes Laertius (*Zeno*).

The Stoic theory of the *phantasia* belongs to Stoic logic, which is to say that the *phantasia* is considered as an element in truthful thinking. The Stoics are preoccupied with the "criterion of truth," that is, with the ways of obtaining the certainty of having it. This is a preoccupation that will dominate modern rationalism from Descartes on. The consequence, then as later, is a concentration on the contribution of what would come to be called the knowing "subject." This emphasis leaves the object itself outside and essentially inaccessible, though as the source of sensation still a necessary element of experience.

If the *phantasia* is the "criterion" or standard of truth it cannot well be a faculty. It is rather an occurrence, an affection, in fact an affection of the "ruling" or rational part of the soul (*hegemonikon.*) To have a *phantasia* is to have in the soul something belonging to the object. In the Stoic context the word is often translated as "presentation." *Phantasia* is the presence of the object as an internal appearance, its showing up in the soul. How, technically, *phantasia* takes place was the matter of a debate lasting generations. Zeno says it is some sort of impression (*typōsis*), Cleanthes says it is literally a seal imprint, and Chrysippus says that it is just an "alteration."

The existent external object is said to impress its *phantasia* "according to itself." That, however, as was intimated above, cannot be more than a hope. The soul has no outside coadjutator between the thing and its impression. Yet since it is undeniable that some sense-impressions are unfalsified, there has to be a further aspect to having a *phantasia*. Accordingly, complete sensation is both the impress of a *phantasia* and its ability to capture the assent of the soul.

Such a sensation is called a "graspable presentation," a *phantasia katalep-tikē*. It is noteworthy that Cicero, who translates this last term as *compren-dibile*, reports that Zeno was the first to use terms of manual grasping cognitively (I xi). The Stoics are thus responsible for the replacement of terms of vision with terms of contact in much of modern philosophy.

A presentation that has this quality of being comprehendible had better be given assent. This is the juncture where there is room for error and foolishness, namely in rejecting a cataleptic, or assenting to an acataleptic, presentation. The latter is one that is somehow unpersuasive, unclear, or contrary to experience and reason.

It follows that there must, in addition to the "graspableness" of the *phantasia*, be interior criteria, such as the "common ideas" of reason, which either are distilled from the "memories" left by previous *phantasiai* or preexist as "innate anticipations."

Stoic *phantasia* is, it follows, scarcely imagination in the sense pursued in this book. It is rather an elaborate construct satisfying a dual desire which proves to be unquenchable through the millennia: to make the incorrigible, adventitious sensory presence of the existing object the standard of truth while keeping the criterion of certainty within the control of the rational soul.

Yet the imagination proper is not ignored in Stoic theory. According to Chrysippus, the cause of *phantasia*—namely, the white or red out there which affects the soul through sight—is called the *phantaston*, explained as that which legitimately "makes" the *phantasia*. But there is also an analogue of the *phantaston*, termed *phantastikon*, an affection that comes from nothing, a "vain drawing." It is underlain by nothing. The vain void this "fantastic" affection draws us into is called a *phantasma*, a phantasm. Examples are hallucinations and dreams (Arnim 1924, II 54,55). What is remarkable in this scheme is the implication, which will be seriously revived early in this century by Meinong, that we have positive mental representations of nothing, or of nonexistent objects. This idea, so important to the logic of mental images, will be taken up in Part Three (Ch. III).

D. Epicureans: Subtle Simulacra

The Epicureans, a school beginning about the time of the early Stoa, think that all being is comprised in hard atoms and their configurations. Their account of imagining and mental images is plain and simple. It stands and falls—falls, in fact—with materialism as a whole.

The most, indeed the only, beautiful exposition of this curiously long-lived simplification is by Lucretius, who seems to expound Epicurus's crabbedly expressed doctrines fairly faithfully (Dalzell 1974). In Book IV of *On the Nature of Things*, he explains in "songs so clear on things obscure" how the vision (*visum*) of mythical monsters and dead men comes to haunt our minds. The mind and soul is itself only a collection of extremely subtle and motile atoms. Things give off filmy simulacra composed of particles, which move through the air and, being thin and fragile as a spider's web, sometimes unite with each other so as to form monsters. When they enter the body's interstices they "awake the thin substance of the mind." What so simplifies the account is that mental images are in principle the same as the material visions that "take possession of the eyes"; this curious phrase, *percipiunt oculos*, confirms that for Lucretius perception and imagination is not an activity—what would it be an activity of?—but a condition of being invaded, penetrated, or irritated (729). This account simply bypasses in its violent purity whatever is perplexing in the experience of having images.

E. Plotinus: Internal Mirror

There is no thematic discussion of the imagination in Plotinus's huge work, the *Enneads*. Yet in scattered passages are to be found certain novel ideas which, as it seems now, were bound to emerge. The three that are most closely and significantly connected are: the conception of two distinct imaginations, one directed upward and the other downward; the notion of an imagination specific to the rational soul; and a theory of representative art which obviates the imitation of sensible appearance (IV 3, 29 ff; I 4,10; V 8,1; Bundy 1927).

As a Neoplatonic, Plotinus naturally elaborates and systematizes the Platonic image-structure of being. From the One, his systematic version of the Idea of the Good, emanate downward, in image-fashion, Being, the

Intellectual World, the Soul and Nature, and Matter, the last a mere substratum with no independent form or being. Nature, brutish at the bottom, is characterized by having no *phantasia* at all (IV 4, 13), no power to receive intimations from above and none to reach into matter below. For nature knows nothing and transmits forms blindly to her productions.

The *phantasia* that appears first in this hierarchy is the capacity for representing sensation, a very inferior function belonging to the lower, passive soul. It is responsible for an animate being's enslavement to the passions and so for its depravity (VI 8, 3).

The problem now becomes how to save the imagination for those higher tasks which it ought to have in a system whose very genesis is based on imaging. The solution is to have two imaginations, an idea suggested by Aristotle when he says that a *phantasia* may be due either to thought or to sense (*Movement of Animals* 702 a). Conveniently, the soul itself has a rational part and an irrational sensory part, and a memory both for its own rational movements and for the forms of sensory objects. Memory, however, belongs to *phantasia* as a super-sensory capacity for holding the images of bodies in their absence. So, the argument runs, if there are two kinds of memories, there are two imaginations. The reason we do not notice the difference between them is that when they are in harmony one of the two leads the other, and, when at odds, one eclipses the other. *Phantasia* is thus saved by having a higher rational double.

This higher *phantasia* has a function which will be of crucial importance in modern philosophy. It spatializes thought. Taken as one, the Plotinian *phantasia* is Janus-faced. It looks below to receive images of matter, and above to receive images of thought. Discursive reason, when developing, literally explaining, the depth of intellectual thought, "makes it pass from the state of thought to that of image, spreads it out, as it were, in the mirror for our phantasy" (IV 3, 30). The Neoplatonic Proclus will quite naturally apply this notion to the geometric figures (Part Five, Ch. I C).

To explain how the *phantasia* works Plotinus turns to serious account the passage from the *Timaeus* cited above, which presents the *phantasia* as a mirror. The Intellect, he says, has an upward tendency, but its lower part, close to the life of the soul, "is, so to speak, flung down again and becomes like the reflection resting on the smooth and shining surface of a mirror" (I 4,10). So, if the soul is at peace and the mirror is smooth, the intellective act is attended by *phantasia*. Otherwise it goes unpictured. Thus, it seems, serenity is required for figural thinking, an observation that has psychological truth.

Finally, if the *phantasia* is open to figures from above, it follows that representational arts can be imitative without turning to sensation for their originals. For example, a stone can become beautiful by reason of the form introduced into it by the sculptor. This form is in his soul before it ever enters the stone and is not necessarily derived from sensory experience. In the stone its original beauty is seen only in a derivative and lesser form. "Therefore, although the images are sensory, the arts are not to be slighted on the grounds that they employ imitation of natural objects. . . ." For it is not really nature they are imitating: Phidias wrought his Zeus from no sensory model "but by apprehending the form Zeus must take if he chose to become manifest to sight" (V 8,1). The modern culmination of this aspect of Neoplatonic aesthetics will be in Schopenhauer's theory that the visual and verbal arts represent the Ideas in sensory form (Ch. III E).

There is, however, still an old Platonic element in the Plotinian theory: Though the form is from above, in the work it has descended into matter, where its original beauty is much weakened. No work of art can equal its envisioning thought (Panofsky 1924).

F. Neoplatonists: Autonomous Phantasy

The later Neoplatonic writers, in their eclectic way, drive to the limit the dual notion of the imagination as open to infusions from above and as liable to corruptions from below. But the latter theme, the drag exercised by the sense-burdened imagination and the dangers arising from manic phantasy, is more preponderant. This tradition of the "evil imagination" will be taken up in Part Six (Ch. I).

(Bundy 1927.)

On the other hand, there are authors, such as Porphyry and Iamblichus, who insist on the imagination as a faculty for receiving inspiration from above, as a place where divine possession manifests itself in, for example, divination and prophecy. Furthermore, as part of the Neoplatonic legacy to modernity, Proclus salvages imaginative activity in the arts from the total condemnation of the *Republic* by putting to work the Platonic distinction between "phantastic" and "imagistic" imitation. Recall that the former seeks to please illusionistically while the latter tries to tell the truth faithfully. This distinction, which is the direct counterpart of the important modern differentiation between fancy and imagination, helps to save the imagination only if truth is imageable. And indeed, as was shown above, the Neoplatonists insist that the supra-sensible is sensibly representable. Thus the Neoplatonist Synesius, Augustine's pagan contemporary, speaks of a *phantasticon pneuma*, an "imaginary spirit," which mediates between matter and spirit, and performs the marvelous, paradoxical act of entering human dreams and visions to show the world beyond.

The boldest notion, and the one that most directly speaks to the great enigma of the imagination, is advanced by Nebridius in a friendly epistolary debate with Augustine (Bundy 1927). Nebridius contends that there is *phantasia* without memory, though not the reverse. That, however, implies that the imagination has images that come only from itself by itself, acting autonomously (Ch. II A). The senses can arouse it, but there are also images within it that have no perceived originals. Though some people claim that such original images are the result of sensory experiences, that explanation implies that some bodily organ frames phantasy-impressions. Then why, Nebridius asks, is it impossible to share these dreams and visions—presumably by allowing another to observe one's internal sensory organ? This apparently arcane puzzle is really an early statement of a problem that preoccupies present-day brain-studies: Is there any sort of observable isomorphism between brain-process and experienced image? (Part Two, Ch. II D).

Augustine contests Nebridius's ideas energetically. First, he says, not all memories are derived from former sensation. There are non-imaginal memories and these may be the reflections of the eternal "images of reason," such as mathematical truths. On the other hand, there are no image-like memories that come to us except through the senses (Moore 1947). One might almost say that as a Christian, Augustine seeks to forestall the notion that will indeed one day, for some people, supplant Christian faith, namely the Romantic idea of an autonomously *creative* imagination.

G. Augustine: Mediating Imagination

Augustine meditates on the memory in the *Confessions* and theorizes on the imagination in *On the Trinity*. The former contains the finest description in literature of our treasury of images; the latter adds to the imagination a crucial missing element, the will.

Augustine's inquiries in the *Confessions* have a serene urgency which is the result of his spiritual situation. He has the comfort of faith already found, but he is still driven by the hot desire to know better the God whom he has gained. The tenth book is, accordingly, a long meditation moved by the happy anxiety to know whether the God he loves is to be found in memory (6). The conclusion will be that God is not in memory except insofar as Augustine has learned about him (26). Thus God himself is not to be reached by Platonic recollection. In the course of this discovery,

Augustine explores and praises the "fields and spacious palaces of memory," where he finds both the world and himself, where the "earth and sea are in readiness" with all that he has ever perceived within them and all he has forgotten, and where he meets himself and all his bygone life. In the lovely Watts translation of 1631:

> Great is the force of memory, excessive great, O my God; a large and an infinite roomthiness [sic]: who can plummet the bottom of it? Yet is this a faculty [vis] of mine and belongs unto my nature. [Loeb, 8]

He wonders at the enormousness of the mind's contents and about the place of the mental container: Where can that be which cannot contain itself? And he wonders at the manner in which memory-images are present. For while he is speaking of the vast ocean, of mountains, rivers, and stars, he does not see them with his eyes; yet he could not speak of them unless

> I saw [them] inwardly in my memory, yea, with such vast spaces between them as if I verily saw them abroad. Yet did I not swallow them into me by seeing, whenas with my eyes I beheld them. Nor are the things themselves now within me, but the images of them only.

Here is the most precise and vivid description of the experience of image-memory: its enormousness, its spatiality, its presence-in-absence—the very preoccupation of this book.

In the next book of the *Confessions* (XI) the memory will provide Augustine's solution to the problem of time. One way to see the beauty of this solution is to recall an explanation Aristotle gives in *On Memory* (ii). Memories are time-involved images, and accordingly we must have a faculty by which to judge time. However, to make a long story short, Aristotle cannot explain how we preserve internally the temporal distances along which memories are situated. To this problem Augustine has an answer, one which will have a powerful influence in modern times, above all in Husserl's work on internal time-consciousness: Time itself is nothing but the "stretching" (*distentio*) of the soul. It is in fact the "roomthiness" of memory. For present, past, and future "are indeed in our soul and elsewhere I do not see them. The present of what has gone by is memory; the present of what is present, eyewitness; the present of what is future, expectation" (20). A long time past is merely a "long memory," thickly stacked with images, as it were. The soul, one might say, is the space of time, the place where all times are co-present, exhibited in the spatial sequence of co-present memory-pictures. Thus the image-memory is responsible for human temporal awareness (Brann 1983).

On the Trinity (XI), finally, is a book of triads, and here the imagination is accorded, with novel explicitness, the mediating middle position that it had always implicitly held.

The guiding schema is the reappearance of the Trinity in man as the image of God. The powers of knowledge in particular have a trinitarian structure. The cognitive triad has as its lower extreme visual sensation and at its highest end intuitive mind. Both produce knowledge. In the middle there is imagination, which serves as mediator, bringing the extremes together (Gilson 1961, 216).

Vision, which belongs to the outer man, in turn consists of a sub-triad including the visible object, the act of seeing, and the intention that keeps the eye attentively trained on the object. The result is an "image impressed on the sense" (ii). Intuition, which belongs to the innermost man, involves these three elements: first, memory which stores the images that inform the mind's eye, second, the mind itself, and finally the will which joins them. The result is a "form" wrought in the eye of the mind (vii).

In between comes the imaginative trinity (iii). When the corporeally perceived form of a body withdraws, it leaves a likeness remaining in memory. The inner vision (*acies animi*) is informed by the memory-image. The will, again a mediating third, holds them in close union.

There are three novel points: Augustine is the first to make a clear division between sense-image and memory-image, that is to say, between sense-impression and reproductive imagination. They belong to different trinities (Bundy 1927). Second and yet more important is the introduction of the will. All the soul's life is governed by the will, and all the passionate movements, desire, joy, fear, sorrow, are related to it (Gilson 1961, 132). Hence, when Augustine conjoins will with memory, he can begin to account for a fact that is by and large neglected in antiquity, namely the originally affective character of the imagination. Moreover, this union accounts for imaginativeness itself. For besides directing attention to memory-images, the will in its freedom can incite internal vision to transform memories, to add and subtract and recombine them (Part Six, Ch. III B).

The third new point is the insistence on an inner vision specific to the imagination. It is a power for seeing the absent, be it remembered or invented. It is distinct both from bodily sight and from intellectual insight. In the commentary on Genesis (*De Genesi ad Litteram* XII) Augustine states outright that there are three visions, one corporeal, another intellectual, and between the two a spiritual vision of the imagination, to which appear things that are absent but significant.

The elaborate differentiation of the cognitive structure, the inventive freedom of the middle power, and the establishment of an autonomous inner vision—these are all notions with a future. I should add that Augustine is probably the first author to eschew deliberately the use of the term *phantasia* in the sense of appearance-presentation or sense-impression (Bundy, 158). In putting this usage out of commission he helped to establish the word *imaginatio*, which will prevail in the Middle Ages.

Bibliography

Aristotle [384–322 BC]. *On Memory and Recollection* (i) [see Ross, 1906, and Sorabji, 1972]; *On the Soul* (III 3). [See Hamlyn, 1968].

Arnim, J. von. 1921–24. *Stoicorum Veterum Fragmenta*. New York: Irvington Publishers (1986).

Augustine [354–430]. *Confessions* [c. 400] (X); *On the Trinity* [c. 416] (XI) [See Haddan, 1873.]

Beare, John I. 1906. *Greek Theories of Elementary Cognition from Alcmaion to Aristotle*, Part III, "Sensus Communis." Oxford: The Clarendon Press, William C. Brown Reprint Library.

Boyd, John D., S.J. 1985. "A New Mimesis." *Renascence: Essays on Values in Literature* 37:136–161.

Brann, Eva. 1980. "Plato's Theory of Ideas." *The St. John's Review* 32:29–37.

———. 1983. "Against Time." *The St. John's Review* 34:65–104.

Bundy, Murray W. 1927. *The Theory of Imagination in Classical and Medieval Thought*. Champaign: The University of Illinois Press.

Chambliss, J. J. 1974. *Imagination and Reason in Plato, Aristotle, Vico, Rousseau and Keats: An Essay in the Philosophy of Experience*. The Hague: Martinus Nijhoff.

Clark, Gordon H. 1942. "*Phantasia* in Plotinus." In *Philosophical Papers in Honor of Edgar Arthur Singer, Jr.*, edited by F. P. Clarke and M. C. Nahm. Philadelphia: University of Pennsylvania Press.

Cornford, Francis M. 1934. *Plato's Theory of Knowledge: The* Theaetetus *and* Sophist *of Plato translated with a running commentary*. New York: The Liberal Arts Press.

Dalzell, A. 1974. "Lucretius' Exposition of the Doctrine of Images." *Hermathena* 118:22–32.

Demand, Nancy. 1975. "Plato and the Painters." *Phoenix* 29:1–20.

Derrida, Jacques. 1972. *Dissemination*. Translated by Barbara Johnson. Chicago: The University of Chicago Press (1981).

Engmann, Joyce. 1976. "Imagination and Truth in Aristotle." *Journal of the History of Philosophy* 14:259–265.

Gadamer, Hans-Georg. 1965. *Truth and Method*, 2d ed. Translated by Garrett Barden and John Cumming. New York: Seabury (1976).

Gilson, Etienne. 1961. *The Christian Philosophy of Saint Augustine*. London: Victor Gollancz.

Haddan, Arthur W., trans. 1873. *On the Trinity* [Augustine]. Edinburgh: T. and T. Clark.

Hamlyn, D. W., trans. and comm. 1968. *Aristotle's* De Anima: *Books II and III*. Oxford: Clarendon Press.

————. 1958. "EIKASIA in Plato's *Republic*." *Philosophical Quarterly* 8:14–23.

Hart, Ray L. 1965. "The Imagination in Plato." *International Philosophical Quarterly* 5:436–461.

Klein, Jacob. 1965. *A Commentary on Plato's Meno*. Chapel Hill: The University of North Carolina Press.

Kuhn, Thomas S. 1962. *The Structure of Scientific Revolutions*, 2d ed., International Encyclopedia of Unified Science. Chicago: The University of Chicago Press (1970).

Lachterman, David. 1989. *The Ethics of Geometry: A Genealogy of Modernity*. New York: Routledge.

Lucretius [c. 94–55 BC]. *On the Nature of Things* (IV).

Lycos, K. 1964. "Aristotle and Plato on 'Appearing'." *Mind* 73:496–514.

Moore, Kate G. 1947. "Aurelius Augustine on Imagination." *The Journal of Psychology* 23:161–168. [Contains paras. 4–7 of the letter on the imagination to Nebridius.]

Nussbaum, Martha C. 1978. *Aristotle's* De Motu Animalium: *Text with Translation, Commentary, and Interpretive Essays*. Princeton: Princeton University Press.

Panofsky, Erwin. 1924. *Idea: A Concept in Art Theory*. Translated by Joseph J. S. Peake. Columbia: University of South Carolina Press (1968).

Philippe, M. D. 1971. "*Phantasia* in the Philosophy of Aristotle." *The Thomist* 35:1–42.

Plato [c. 429–347 BC]. *The Republic* (508 ff., 595 ff.), *The Sophist* (264), *Philebus* (38 ff).

Plotinus [205–269]. *The Enneads* (I 4,10; IV 3, 29 ff.; V 8,1). Translated by Stephen MacKenna. Revised by B. S. Page. London: Faber and Faber, 1962.

Ross, G.R.T. 1906. *Aristotle, De Sensu and De Memoria: Text, Translation, Commentary*. New York: Arno Press.

Sorabji, Richard. 1972. *Aristotle on Memory*. Providence: Brown University Press.

Thayer, H. S. 1970. "Plato on the Morality of the Imagination." *The Review of Metaphysics* 30:594–618.

Thomas Aquinas [c. 1271]. *Aristotle's* De Anima, *in the version of William of Moerbeke and the Commentary of St. Thomas Aquinas*. Translated by Kenelm Foster and Sylvester Humphries. New Haven: Yale University Press (1959).

Wedin, Michael V. 1988. *Mind and Imagination in Aristotle*. New Haven: Yale University Press.

Chapter II

Medieval Writers

Contrary to common opinion, the texts concerning the imagination which fall between the Ancients and the Moderns are not poor but excessively rich. The length of this review is thus in inverse ratio to the offerings of that intervening millennium. The excuse is that the medieval texts are of a particular sort. They are rich in acute and interesting distinctions, the kind brought about by a subtle and steadfast application to the matter and by a reverently refined reading of the received texts. But they are poor in revolutionary new departures. This character makes it almost impossible to report them in gist.

For present purposes the Renaissance is treated as an appendix to the Middle Ages.

A. Mainstream: *Vis Imaginativa* and Its Sources

The treatment of the imaginative power or *vis imaginativa* in medieval texts is largely descriptive (Bundy 1927), for such is the style of the prevailing "faculty psychology." It seeks to distinguish and enumerate the powers of the soul and to locate them physically in the cells or ventricles of the brain. One might say that medieval faculty psychology is the unsuccessful forerunner of contemporary attempts to identify brain-functions. Obviously, then as now the attempt to pinpoint the powers of the soul physically and the effort to distinguish them intellectually are complementary.

Of tinkering with the roster of faculties, of making new distinctions or conflating old ones, there is no end. But by and large the two strains discernible in antiquity continue. They might be called the top-down and the bottom-up school respectively. Of these the latter is the more prevalent. The top-down school, which goes back to the Neoplatonists, considers the imagination to be open to divine, spiritual, or intellectual influences from above. The bottom-up school, which proceeds under the aegis of Aristotle and Augustine, supposes that nothing is in the imagination which does not come up from sense.

The various enumerations of powers have this much in common: They are all hierarchical. A hierarchy is an ordering which, while assigning to each element a lower or higher place, also gives it its proper dignity. That is exactly how the *vis imaginativa* fares in faculty psychology. Where it is properly subordinated to reason it is thought to perform a vital cognitive function (Minnis 1981), but when it acts out of control it is vitiated and open to demonic influences. Nevertheless, in a few schemes the localization of the imaginative power assigns this faculty a seat so far from the higher functions that it loses its participation in thought. In this separation is prefigured the later sharp opposition of imagination and reason (Bundy 180).

Descriptive schemes go back to the fourth century, to Nemesius of Emesa, for example, and they culminate in the thirteenth century with Thomas Aquinas. Avicenna produces a listing typical in approach but of special interest in its results. The imagination is located in two cells and has several functions. It is placed in the front of the head, along with common sense, as the power for retaining absent sensibles, and it occurs in the middle, where it performs two different functions related to the will. As *virtus imaginativa* it is responsible for events like dreams that are imperfectly under the control of the will, and as *phantasia* it produces deliberate imaginary compounds and divisions.

The most representative and most full-blown faculty psychology, of great importance to Thomas, is that of his contemporary Albertus Magnus. In this scheme there are two basic sets of organs, those of comprehension, that is, of conceptual thought, and those of apprehension, that is, of reception and retention. We are concerned here with the latter, for they are collectively called now imagination, now *phantasia*. In this group is found, first, the common sense, which receives, compares, and retains sensation with matter. Next there is the imagination proper, which retains sensation without matter, and is called *formalis*, or formal, with reference to its retention of matterless shape, *species*, or ideal, with reference to its spiritual side, and *thesaurus* or treasury with reference to its retentive power. Third there is the *vis aestimativa* or opinion, the "esteeming power," which adds to the essentially neutral images of the imagination feelings of joy and grief leading to action. Fourth there is memory, which retains the estimative "intentions" but adds a sense of time. Last comes phantasy, which does with images what the common sense does with sensation, comparing, dividing, and uniting them.

Here phantasy is almost-reason. It is the "excogitative" power, the focus of the internal sense, functioning simultaneously as a discerning and a recombining power. To be cognitively useful it must be under the control of reason; for on its own it is susceptible to illusion and error. Thus it has a curious double character that epitomizes the cognitive problems surrounding the imagination. They are mirrored in Albertus's terminology. His Latin translation of the Stoic term *phantasma*, the empty fabrication of the soul, is *phantasia*, while he translates the Greek term *phantasia* as *imaginativum*, as in *vis imaginativa*. So Albertine *phantasia* is the fancy-free faculty of cognitively empty imaginative play. Yet in its old sense it is the indispensable empowering function of the whole imagination-complex. This shifting, idiosyncratic terminology mirrors dilemmas which will be conceptually fixed in modern times, though never resolved.

A concluding observation: The consideration of the imagination in the Middle Ages is almost entirely a matter for philosophy. The poets, though it turns out that they have plenty to say about it (Kelly 1978, Minnis 1981), invariably follow philosophical categories. In the old quarrel between philosophy and poetry, the poets have yet to learn to talk back in their own terms, as the Romantics will. However, it appears that the production of poetry is well accounted for by faculty psychology. Poetic "*imaginatio*," says one poet, occurs, "when through a certain remembrance of sensibles to which the sense has gone out, the soul inscribes for itself a memory-example within, as it were. Thus the whole conceptual power [*intentio*] of the soul, away from the presence of the sensibles about which it thinks, seems to be suspended in a comparative mode over the imagination of them" (Kelly 48). Poetry is here plausibly defined as beginning with a kind of comparative brooding over mental images. It is of course the genesis of metaphor or simile that is being described.

The view of the poetic imagination as a rational power attentively scanning its images to find likenesses puts it directly in the service of philosophy and theology. For the philosophers by and large agree that the only positive way to God, as opposed to the intellectual *via negativa*, is through imaginative likenesses. "Incorporeal beings, of which there are no phantasms, are known to us by comparisons with sensible bodies of which there are phantasms" says Thomas (*Summa Theologica* I 84, 8). It is the poets who supply these figures and allegories. When "Ymaginatif" speaks out in Langland's *Piers Plowman*, that is just what he will claim (Minnis 1981).

Finally, a note on visions: The text exerting the most pervasive influence on the medieval theory of mystical visions is Augustine's passage on the triple sight, mentioned in Ch. I (G). Of these three visions, the corporeal, the spiritual (or "imaginary"), and the intellectual, it is the last with which "the truth of the mysteries" is apprehended (Minnis 1981). Accordingly, the medieval mystics deprecate, though they do not altogether condemn, the imagination as yielding only a second best vision and not direct insight. The middle vision, though necessary, is at best ancillary. As Rachel had her children first through her handmaid Bilhah, so it is sweet to have in the imagination what one cannot yet attain by reason, writes Richard of St. Victor (*Benjamin Major*, in Bundy 1927). Nevertheless, the imagination is but a garrulous menial which the virginal contemplative, Rachel, can neither live with nor live without (Kearny 1988). The lesson to the student is that the sensual visions gotten from reading are not to be accepted literally. Instead "a mystical meaning is sought."

The *visio imaginaria* includes not only dreams but also the influences of spiritual beings, good and bad angels. Thomas Aquinas carefully analyzes such extra-mental sources and concludes that imaginary visions can indeed be so formed. True knowledge of future events can come through the ministry of good angels, and deception through demons. However, "an angel changes the imagination, not by the impression of an imaginative form in no way previously received by the senses" but physiologically (I 111, 3). In other words, Thomas protects the imagination from direct extra-mental influence. Even the angels have access to humans only through the senses (Part Six, Ch. I B).

★   ★   ★

Let this moment of leaving medieval faculty psychology serve as an opportunity to engage in the useful exercise of tabulating all the possible sources for the images in the imagination, anywhere, at any time.

There happens to be a work of unknown title by a contemporary of Thomas's, Roger Kilwardby, which offers a good occasion for such a summary. It is a treatise on the imagination as the lower part of the human spirit or soul. The author, naming the part for the whole, calls it the *spiritus fantasticus*. Kilwardby is largely concerned with the sources of its images. He defends the Augustinian-Aristotelian thesis that the imagination has neither any original images nor any source for corporeal and sensual images other than the senses. Question I (5–33) asks precisely whether the *spiritus fantasticus* originates sensible images for itself or acquires them from the senses. Only the first five, most telling, arguments are reported here and the *items*, *contras*, and *responsios* are conflated:

(1) If, Kilwardby argues, the *spiritus fantasticus* had images by itself, a man could imagine sensible things before the use of his senses. But the

blind, for example, cannot give accounts of colors. (2) Nor can the human soul answer questions about such arts as pertain to sensibles without use of the senses. (3) Again, if the *spiritus fantasticus* contained original images they could be aroused by mere words, so that one need only hear "Rome" to see it in the imagination. Now people do of course imagine what they have never seen, but that is because there is indeed an innate power of diminishing, increasing, changing, and compounding sensory images which makes it possible to imagine, for instance, a centaur. (4) Furthermore, if the *spiritus fantasticus* did have images antecedent to sense, it would, pointlessly, contain a double set of images, original and acquired. (5) Moreover, by the same reasoning by which some innate images of corporeal things were thought to be present, all must be present; yet that would be redundant in this life and in the next.

However, since the authorities, especially Augustine, seem to indicate that we do have in memory some images that have not been drawn in through the senses, namely those pertaining to the intellectual disciplines, Kilwardby deals with the possibility that the intellect might be a second source for the imagination. In Question II (33–40), he interprets Augustine to mean this: As the soul struggles to understand intelligibles such as mathematical objects, to see, for example, how a point can be without parts or a line without breadth, "thought [which is] still imaginative" (*cogitatio adhuc ymaginaria*) undergoes a sort of "illumination by reflection" (*resplendentiam*) from the intellect above—but not before the use of the senses, only after.

Finally, Kilwardby also touches, evasively, on a second, supernatural mode of imagination, which is in fact without the use of the senses but does not concern bodies and sensibles (39); presumably it is a spiritual vision of non-corporeal figures.

★   ★   ★

Images, then, may arise through the upward deliverance of the senses (Aristotle), or through the downward mirroring of intellectual objects (Neoplatonists), as well as through the spatializations of thought. (The last are what Augustine calls "images of reason.") They may come from visions of quasi-sensory spiritual regions. (This is poetic inspiration.) They may have their origin in the influence of extra-mental spirits, either directly—Bonaventura speaks of *phantasiae protervae*, "shameless apparitions," implanted by demons right into the purely spiritual imagination (Bundy 1927, 209)—or through corporeal stimulation (Thomas). Images, further, come about through recombinations worked by the kind of imagination eventually called "fancy" (Avicenna). And finally, images come into being through the autonomous activity of the creative imagination (modern Romantics).

That seems to me to be the complete list of possible originations of the images in the imagination (as distinct from the processes of their production). It is presented without prejudice, but it does force questions which cannot help but haunt this study: What, in truth, are the sources of the imagination's images? Can they all be said to image *something*? Is it even sensible to ask such questions? (Part Three, III C).

B. Culmination: Thomas Aquinas

In regard to the imagination, as in much else, Thomas presents a summation of previous thought in such a way as to revivify subtle internal problems and to broach deep ultimate questions. The subtlest and most difficult problem is the function of the imagination's "phantasm" in cognition, and the deepest question concerns the significance of the fact that the human being is imaginative (*Summa Theologica* I, Ques. 78, 85, 87).

As always, the imagination, or rather its images, have a middle status between the being proper to a form in matter and the being proper to a form that has come into the intellect through abstraction from matter. The being of a form in the imagination is without matter but not without material conditions, namely its sensory origin (I 55, 3). The faculty for images belongs to the "interior senses" (78, 4), of which there are four, familiar from previous descriptive psychology: common sense, imagination, the estimative sense, and memory. Criticizing Avicenna's listing of a fifth faculty, *phantasia*, Thomas argues that its power for combining and dividing imaginary forms, which is in play when, for instance, a golden mountain is imagined, is found only in humans and might as well be assigned to the imagination itself (Lisska 1976).

There are diverse powers because a power or faculty is—here we get, for once, a definition of this central term—"the proximate principle of the soul's operation," meaning the factor immediately responsible for the function. The specific rule of a faculty psychology is therefore: different actions, different powers. The definition and the rule together give the justification for positing faculties. The faculty hypothesis, long held in disrepute in modern psychology, has recently been revived in cognitive psychology (Part Five, Intro.).

The common sense is the common root of all five external senses. To it all the deliverances of the individual senses, for example, the sensibles white and sweet, are referred for discernment. It is also responsible for the fact that sensing of sensing itself is going on, as when someone sees that he sees—in short, has sense-awareness. Next, the estimative power is the "particular reason," which forms non-universal rational conceptions. It has the place to which the ancients assigned "opinion." Memory is the storehouse of all such rational intentions and is therefore strictly conceptual in this scheme, just as in Albertus's ordering the estimative and the memorative powers are all-but-rational.

It is the imagination, according to Thomas, that functions as the storehouse of forms received through the senses. But it does much more (84, 4, 6, 7). The intellect cannot understand without images or "phantasms." We know this from our own experience. We form mental images when we think, and we teach by concrete examples. There is also the fact that when the senses are disordered, thought is often impaired. But a reason of a deeper order is the very fact that we have bodies. Why would we have corporeal senses if the intellect could act alone on autonomous intelligible forms (*species*)? For that matter, why should we have souls if bodies were known by bodies, as Democritus says? Human beings are essentially composite. Therefore they are initially turned toward bodies, toward the outside, where God, their first cause, acts. Concordantly, the beings in the external world also have to be by their very nature corporeal, because to be is to be an individual, and that means a body.

Since, however, nothing corporeal can make an impression on anything incorporeal, the intellect has to work a transformation of the sensory phantasm. It illumines the images of interior sense and makes them fit for "abstraction." The intellect abstracts intelligible species from their individual conditions (85, 1). Abstraction is an arcanum of metaphysics which will be pursued only a short distance in the paragraphs following.

The ultimate answer, then, to the question why we need images in order to know is: because we are human beings and, as such, beings composed of body and soul. But Thomas also has an answer to the narrower question why it is images in particular that help us know. He introduces the answer by asking: Why, if the intellect is so noble, is it continually dependent on the presence of images, even though the inferior faculty of the imagination can often function independently of the presence of the sense-objects that are its inferior source? He answers that the image is itself a *likeness*, and so it does not require the presence of the "further likeness" of the individual sensory original itself. The intellect, however, whose proper objects are not themselves individual likenesses, does need the presence of an image that looks like the individual the intellect intends to think about (84, 7).

Now it is "universally admitted that like is known by like" (84, 2), or "the thing known is in the knower by its own likeness" and "the likeness of the thing understood is the form of the intellect" (85, 2). That likeness is the intelligible species. But, as we have just seen, it is clearly no likeness in a straightforward sense; there is, in later terms, no "primary isomorphism." So it is not the identical form that was in the phantasm that wanders into the intellect (85, 1). For it is not necessary that the form should be in the knower in the same way as it is in the known.

What distinguishes imaginative from intellectual cognition, therefore, is precisely that in the imagination the object does have the same form as it has in the sense-object, namely that of an extended spatial likeness. That is why the imaginal object has a certain self-sufficiency, and does not need a present sensory source. That, too, is what it means for the imagination to be an interior sense that is necessary to the intellect: From its sense-like images the intellect can simultaneously extract the intelligible nature of things while it yet has them sensorily present on its own, non-material, terms—for "it understands these natures in phantasms." The images of the imagination keep the great cognitive principle "like is known by like" from becoming a mere manner of speaking. However the intellect may operate, the human soul as a whole knows by harboring likenesses of—that is to say, becoming like—the things it is intent upon.

Thomas himself, having previously called the common sense, by which space and time are sensed, the root of all external senses, also calls it the root of imagination and memory. Hence an acute modern interpreter suggests applying the term imagination to the whole intimately involved triad of common sense, imagination, and memory, and understanding the complex as a "pure intuition of spatiality" and an "*a priori* sensibility" (Rahner 1957, 106). These are, of course, anachronisms, being Kant's terms for his transcendental imagination. Yet it is surely the case that Thomas strongly prefigures them.

Thomas's exposition of the intellect's need to "turn to the phantasm" (84, 7), that is to say, of the "conversion" to the image that it must undergo, is elaborated by Rahner into a theology of the imagination. This subject is touched on in Part Six (Ch. I B). Enough to say here that for Thomas human beings are bound to enter the world, which is for him the sole source for the images of the imagination. They must become worldly because to know anything at all they must always turn toward an image.

C. Renaissance: Pico della Mirandola, Charron, Bacon

Renaissance writers do not, by and large, expend the same theoretical ingenuity on the imagination as do their predecessors. Instead they attend to its practice. I shall briefly review three texts: Pico della Mirandola's *On the Imagination* (last quarter of the 15th cent.), because it is the one accessible thematic work of the period; Charron's *On Wisdom* (1601), because it is a kind of compendium of humanist opinion; and Bacon's *On the Advancement of Learning* (1605), because it presages things to come in a pricelessly pithy and fresh style.

The pleasure in Pico's essay lies in its zestful pedantry. It heaps up authors and opinions, though its main reference is Aristotle's *On the Soul*. Thus when Pico comes to say what the imagination is, he adopts all the definitions at once: It is a power that follows upon sensation and precedes intellection, a motion, and a force related to all the other powers. Its source is present sensation, though it produces images even of things "that cannot be brought to light by nature." Pico bypasses certain questions that "trouble and torment" others, such as whether the imagination is distinct from memory, common sense, and the estimative power; or where its physical seat is—whether in the heart as in Aristotle, the brain as in Galen, or somewhere between these as in Averroes. For the imagination as a "medium" that joins corporeal and uncorporeal nature is, as Synesius says, difficult to grasp by philosophy. Some separate phantasy and imagination as Avicenna does, but reputable philosophers have exploded the distinction; there is no phantasy into which supernatural forms descend, as claim the Platonists. The life of action, "as we have learned from Aristotle as well as experience itself," depends on the imagination. Thus phantasy may be irrational and devoid of correct judgment, or it may be guided by reason. If the latter, it beatifies man; if the former, it is responsible for the depravity and evil that Holy Writ reminds us we are prone to. The dignity in which man is created and placed requires that he look toward the light of his inborn intellect, which Pico identifies with the light of faith in God rather than with man's perverse imagination and its false phantoms.

Here the most diverse strands of the tradition are eclectically twisted together to make one humanistic whole. Its gist is that visible pictures of the imagination must be seen in the interpretative light of the believing intellect if they are not to be mere seductive illusion.

In Charron's *On Wisdom* (XII, XIV, XVI) "the philosophical *Summa* of humanism" (Sabré)—and, incidentally, a work deeply admired by Jefferson, the man of the Enlightenment—the faculty of the imagination is described as capable of presenting to mind and thought images so strong and lively that it "does the very same to the understanding now which the object itself did, by the first and freshest impression heretofore." The imagination is not, however, a distinct faculty. For "the mind of man, including its intellectual part, is a dark and deep abyss, an intricate labyrinth, full of corners and crooks," whose essence is all one even though its operations are separable. Thus the imagination, along with understanding, discourse, penetration, judgment, wisdom, and resolution, is only one of "so many several methods by which the same mind moves and exerts itself." In particular it plays the role of apprehension within the intellect, the role of "barely receiving and apprehending images and simple ideas." Yet its power is exceedingly great: "Almost all the clutter or disturbances we feel are owing to it." Indeed all the intimations, enthusiasms, and fancies people experience, as well as the apparitions and demons they see, are due to their own imagination.

Charron's view of the human mind is that of an infinitely complex whole, ever active in affections and "inventions" (by which he means primarily the optical contrivances of the visual arts), incapable of attaining the truth, but well nourished on doubts and difficulties. Here the fixed-faculty imagination has become fluid. It is now a method of the mind and a mode of operation. Here is modernity in the making.

Finally, Bacon's *Advancement of Learning* (II xi–xii) treats of the imagination as the faculty specifically devoted to poetry. It plays the role of messenger from sensation to understanding as well as from reason to appetite. Thus sensation refers its deliverances to the imagination before reason judges, and reason refers its judgments to imagination before action takes place:

> Saving that this Janus of Imagination hath different faces: for the face towards Reason hath the print of Truth, but the face towards Action hath the print of Good.

Nor is the imagination just a messenger,

> but [it] is invested with, or leastwise usurpeth no small authority in itself, besides the duty of the message. . . . For we see that, in matters of Faith and Religion, we raise our Imagination above our Reason.

Bacon calls such an extreme use of the imagination "fascination," a term that will later be used not so dissimilarly by Sartre. It names the act of an imagination intent upon seeing the invisible, and so exalted by its own power as to meddle with miracle-working. The imaginative ceremonies of the Roman church imply such a magical use of the imagination for working extra-corporeal wonders, as do "the operations of a pretended natural magic," of the kind practiced by the school of Paracelsus. ("Natural magic" is the pre-modern name for the attempt to turn the secrets of nature to practical account. It is the precursor of technology.)

What Bacon enunciates in his vigorous formulations is the revolutionary notion that both religion and poetry are specifically imaginative—as opposed to rational—enterprises. This understanding obviously differs *toto caelo* both from the medieval reliance on imagery for reaching a suprasensible divinity and from the ancient condemnation of poetry as dealing in fictions. For it denigrates religion by consigning it to an inferior cognitive mode, and it emancipates poetry by assigning to it its own special faculty. No idea will have more widespread repercussions in modern times. It will be echoed and amplified in the Enlightenment, in Romanticism, and in their magnified contemporary aftermath (Part Four, Ch. II A).

Bibliography

Bacon, Francis [1561–1626]. 1605. *The Advancement of Learning*. Edited by G. W. Kitchin. London: Everyman's Library (1915).

Bundy, Murray W. 1927. *The Theory of Imagination in Classical and Medieval Thought*. Champaign: The University of Illinois.

Charron, Pierre [1541–1603]. 1601. *Of Wisdom*. Translated by George Stanhope. London: J. Tonson (1729).

Kearney, Richard. 1988. *The Wake of Imagination: Toward a Postmodern Culture*. Minneapolis: University of Minnesota Press.

Kelly, Douglas. 1978. *Medieval Imagination: Rhetoric and Poetry of Courtly Love*. Madison: The University of Wisconsin Press.

Kilwardby, Robert, O.P. [d. 1279]. Probably late 1250s. *On Time and Imagination: De Tempore, De Spiritu Fantastico*. Edited by P. Osmund Levy, O.P. Oxford: Oxford University Press (1987). [Not translated.]

Lisska, Anthony J. 1976. "A Note: Aquinas' Use of PHANTASIA." *The Thomist* 40:294–302.

Minnis, Alastair J. 1981. "Langland's Ymaginatif and late-medieval theories of imagination." *Comparative Criticism* 3:71–102.

Pico della Mirandola, Gianfrancesco [1463–1494]. After 1475. *On the Imagination*. Translated by Harry Caplan. New Haven: Yale University Press (1930).

Rahner, Karl. 1957. *Spirit in the World*. Translated by William Dych. New York: Herder and Herder (1968).

Thomas Aquinas [1225–1274]. 1254–1272. *Summa Theologica* (I Questions 78, 84, 85). In *Basic Writings of Saint Thomas Aquinas* I, edited by Anton C. Pegis. New York: Random House (1945).

Chapter III

Modern Writers

In the thinking of the Moderns about the imagination there are surely some elements—few in number but stupendous in their consequences—that are radically, revolutionarily new. For the most part, however, the Moderns are the recognizable, if rebellious, progeny, more remotely of the Ancients, especially of Aristotle and the Stoics, and more immediately of the Medieval writers. The exact gauging of the debt is an ever-instructive and never-conclusive effort.

One element is new, indeed almost definitive of the most characteristically modern "Moderns," who get their name from *modo*, "just now," a coinage of the sixth century A.D. In those days it was intended to distinguish, uninvidiously, contemporary from older, "antique" books. Later it announces the will to be rid of the burden of the textual tradition. The moderns want to start anew, to escape the domination of the old texts with their sophistications and complexities. For they see these as designed to preoccupy the intellect contemplatively, thus keeping it from the practical mastery of physical and human nature. The first consequence of this rejection is a great baring of the bones of reason, an almost rabid simplification. However, as the untenable consequences of this paring of terms emerge, the imagination becomes re-enmeshed in metaphysical systems every bit as abstruse and as deep as were the classical philosophical developments. Consequently it is impossible to specify one peculiarly modern result, except to observe that the old questions re-emerge in new contexts, driven by new motives and methods.

To summarize the main treatments: Descartes requires an imagination that can act as interface between a new interior and a new exterior substance, functioning to represent the latter, extension, to the former, mind (A). Hobbes, Locke, and Leibniz, each in different ways, sacrifice the imagination to their simplification of the cognitive process (B). Hume reinstates it along Stoic lines as the single representational faculty of impressions and images alike (C). Kant introduces the new notion of the imagination as a "transcendental" faculty, meaning that it participates in the constitution of experience by projecting the functions of thinking into the field of sensation, working deep below consciousness (D). For Fichte the imagination is the power of the absolute originating ego to posit for itself any other, to represent to itself a confronting world (E). Finally, Hegel, positioned with respect to the Moderns somewhat as Thomas is to the Medievals, presents a conspectus of the imaginative functions arranged as a dialectic development (F). A number of writers of the mid- and late-nineteenth century, who treat the imagination rather incidentally, are included as harbingers of yet another new era in imaginative study (G-K).

A. Descartes: The Interface of Extension and Mind

With respect to the imagination more than to any other topic, Descartes is the first of the moderns in time and stature. The new departure he initiates has two premises. First, he arches back over the whole tradition so far reviewed to return to Plato insofar as he excludes the imagination from the human essence. Consequently its position becomes both more complex and more problematic. Second, while up to his time being had been identified either with body only (Democritus), or with intelligible form only (Plato), or with the individual composite of these (Aristotle), Descartes posits two confronting substances, namely thinking being and extended being. As a result, the imagination will have a new object before it and a new mediation to perform.

There is a curious effect with which one must come to terms in reading Descartes. It is particularly strong in his treatment of the imagination. Almost all the terms and distinctions, taken at face value, are old, borrowed from Aristotle, the Scholastics (Gilson 1951) and, above all, the Stoics. Yet the whole context and intention is altogether new. This circumstance marks Descartes not only as a modern but as the paradigmatic innovator. For it seems to be the rule that serious novelty always insinuates itself in ancient guise.

The exposition of the imagination in Descartes's writings, taken mostly from Rules XII and XIV of the *Rules for the Direction of the Mind* (1628) and from Meditations II and VI of the *Meditations on First Philosophy* (1641), falls quite naturally into four parts: first and second, brief sections respectively on the thinking substance as the essential self and the extended substance as the natural world; third, the main section on the joining of self and nature through the imagination; and last, a discussion concerning the significance to the imagination of Descartes's new departure.

Mind, the thinking substance, and extension, its antithesis, between them define the nature and function of the imagination. Mind turns up as the first-fruit of Descartes's method of inquiry. This method aims not at the traditional contemplation of being, but at the new discovery of one indubitably existent thing on which to found an absolutely certain knowledge. Radical doubt, which is, as an initial position, the diametric opposite of Socrates's spontaneous, *in-medias-res* philosophical wonder, disallows the existence of everything that has not been proved indubitably to exist. In particular it begins by "feigning" the non-existence of bodies. Thereupon one indubitably existent thing—which the method has indeed been devised to produce in the first place—does turn up. It is the thinking self, or rather the proposition "I am a thinking thing." Neither the connection of the first indubitable truth, that where there is doubting there is thinking, with the existence of a thinking thing, nor the interpretation of this thing as a self, are logical inferences. They are intuitions, the immediate insights of the mind when it is directed on itself. They are certified by the Cartesian criteria of truth, namely the clarity and distinctness of their presence to the mind. Intuitions can be both bright and sharp because the mind is comparable both to an eye and to a light.

Though this thinking thing is the first being to be established with certainty, it is not first in the hierarchy of beings. Prior to mind and extension is a third substance, God their creator, who is the guarantor of their coordination. God is more veritably a substance than the two created things. For a substance is defined as "an existent thing which requires nothing but itself in order to exist." But the problem how the substantiality of the mind in fact differs from that of God is not so pertinent to the theory of the imagination as is the question about the substantiality of mind itself.

For Descartes, to be a substance is to be a thing, and to be a thing is to be the kind of existent which has one primary characterizing attribute. For the mental thing that attribute is that it thinks, that it is a thinking thing, *res cogitans*. But it is also a self, a being that says "*I* think" (*cogito*) and finds implicit in that proposition another, "I am" (*sum*), which asserts its existence as a self.

More than any other notion, the conception of a thinking thing which is a self marks Descartes as the thinker pivotal between the old and the new dispensation. The classical intellect is separable and self-sufficient, but since it is pure activity it is not a thing, and since its fulfillment is not through volition it is not a person. The post-Cartesian—for example, the Kantian—reason characterizes a spontaneous, autonomous subject that is not a thing either, though it is certainly a person. The thinghood of mind, the specific Cartesian factor, will of course shape a highly peculiar imaginative function.

Let me complete the account of the thinking thing (*res cogitans*). Its defining attribute, thinking, encompasses all awareness and consciousness: knowledge, ignorance, willing, doubting, affirming, denying. Among these, willing, of which the last three are only modes, is preeminent. Thus cognition and will are the two basic kinds of awareness. Of the two, willing is the wider. Indeed it is in a certain respect infinite, for it reaches into the limitless region beyond what is clearly and distinctly before the mind. That is how it becomes the cause of error. The disposition of the will is what most truly pertains to humanity. Hence it is presumably the possession of a will which makes the thinking thing a self.

Besides the mental operations of volition and cognition, which the mind knows by a certain "inborn light unaided by any corporeal image," it also knows its innate ideas, which are, as Descartes inconsistently says, few or innumerable. Among them are "the idea of God, mind, body, triangle, and generally all which represent any true, immutable and eternal essences." Not that these ideas are "in some way different from the faculty of thinking." Indeed they are not actually present in the mind except as its propensity to think them. Descartes can claim at one and the same time that the mind knows only its own operations and that it knows the different essences innately; he does so by relying on a scholastic notion, namely that thoughts are all the same insofar as they are modes of mind, and yet differ insofar as they contain diverse ideal essences (Med. III).

(Smith 1952, Caton 1973.)

The crux of the foregoing sketch of the Cartesian thinking self is that it is the essence of man, that it can exist "entirely and absolutely distinct from body," and that it can know itself by itself, without the mediation of the imagination. It is a thinking thing rather than a rational animal. To the strange conception of the thinghood of the mind is thus added the unprecedented notion of a human self divorced from the imagination.

The extended thing (*res extensa*), the second substance, confronts the thinking thing antithetically. Since this non-thinking, non-incorporeal thing is essentially other than the self, it will for that very reason turn out to *be* as it is *known* to mind.

Its existence, certified in a brief quasi-proof, marks the culmination of the method of doubt. Although nothing belongs to my essence as an unextended thing but thinking, yet I have, Descartes argues, a clear and distinct idea of bodies. That alone does not prove their existence, but it does assure their possibility. However, I also find in myself certain powers, such as those of locomotion. These, together with the fact that God, who is no deceiver, has given me a very great inclination to believe that the ideas of sense I have come from no other than corporeal objects, guarantees to me that "we must allow that corporeal objects exist."

What is this extended substance that is here identified with body? *Res extensa* is divisible body as it presents itself to indivisible *res cogitans*. Extension, the identifying attribute of body, as thinking is of mind, is not the set of sensible qualities we perceive, such as heat and color. These are not bodies but only powers that bodies have to set our nerves in motion. Through them we, who have a body, sense bodies though we do not know them, for we do not clearly and distinctly intuit them. When all sense-qualities are discounted, what remains is extension in length, breadth, and depth. Sense-qualities, figure, motion, cannot be conceived without dimensionality, though the converse is possible.

Extension conceived as dimensionality is nothing but space. Therefore the corporeal substance, body, is different from space only by a purely conceptual distinction of our understanding. "Hence we announce that by extension we do not here mean anything distinct and separate from the extended object itself; and we make it a rule not to recognize those philosophical entities which really cannot be presented to the imagination" (Rule XIV).

Thus the imagination is ordained as the guarantor of the extension/space/body identity. What the mind, and only the mind, can intuit is not space or body, but spatiality and corporeality, that is to say, the essence of body (Med. II). Accurately speaking, that is just what extension is.

The imagination in which the extended substance is to be represented has its seat in a corporeal organ—according to Descartes, the pineal gland. (In contemporary brain studies this structure is, as it happens, suspected of being involved in seasonal mood-swings). This corporeal imagination has to be conceived as a genuine part of the body, of sufficient magnitude to allow its different parts to assume shapes distinct from one another (Rule XII). The images imprinted on the imagination-organ are "corporeal ideas," a notion that goes back to the early Stoics. Descartes's understanding of the term "idea" is not consistent in this context, since he sometimes denies that ideas are corporeal (Macintosh 1983). However, a bodily "idea" is not a contradiction in terms if one remembers that the Greek word means "look" or "aspect."

.This organ is truly Janus-faced. It can receive imprints from the inside, from the mind. Descartes calls such inside-out ideas "factitious," that is, contrived. Naturally, it can receive external impressions from the outside, from other bodies. He calls such outside-in ideas adventitious, that is, by chance. Whether contrived or fortuitous, the ideas or "figures" of the imagination are some sort of corporeal configuration. How and why does the mind impress ideas on the body? How does the body present itself to the mind?

The imagination is indeed the interface between mind and corporeal world. That much is already clear, as is the fact that this organ-faculty is well and truly corporeal and represents external bodies by some sort of extensional, that is, spatial, isomorphism. Hence the corporeal ideas are the precursors of more recent, though now superseded, notions such as engrams. There is a lively contemporary effort, analogous to Descartes's, to find a form of isomorphism which will preserve the experience of mental imagery and fit in with the neurophysiology of the brain (Part Two, Ch. II D). The mind is well and truly incorporeal, but it turns to the pineal gland, its own corporeal brain organ, in order to know bodies.

Human beings know of their mind by their mind alone, of their body by mind and imagination together, but of the union of their mind and their body, which is as ultimate as each of its elements, they know "by relying exclusively on the activities and concerns of ordinary life, and by abstaining from metaphysical meditation" (*Letter to Princess Elizabeth* 1643). Evidently the union of mind and body is fundamental, given *de facto*, and not philosophically provable.

There we have a bold statement of that infamous mind/body problem which haunts Cartesianism into the present. The two substances are together in fact and yet are in their essence incommensurable. This condition can be put specifically in terms of the imagination: There is no mental faculty of the imagination, and no "inner space" for quasi-sensory phantasms. Therefore there are no mental images by way of which bodily species or looks are transmitted to the mind or transmuted into intellectual species or essences.

So once again, how does the imagination work? The answer is fascinating, albeit technical. To begin with, the mind or consciousness is one agency with several modes, such as those named above. These are faculties in the traditional sense, for faculties are defined by having their peculiar objects (Caton, 166). Hence mental "imagination . . . is nothing but a certain application of the faculty of knowledge to the body which is immediately present to it." This mode, in which consciousness turns toward bodies and images them, is also called the *ingenium*, "natural capacity." Having attended to bodies, it, as was said, "either forms new ideas in the imagination, or attends to those already formed" (Med. II).

The imagination-organ in its sensory mode is called the *sensus communis*. To it the special senses communicate their passively received shapes mechanically and isomorphically (Rule XII). By means of their immediate presence,

the ideas that imaginative consciousness finds in the *sensus communis* persuade it, again as above, of the existence of corporeal things. However,
aside from being adventitious, these images are often quite indistinct. A
thousand-sided figure is indistinctly imagined, though sharply enough
conceived (Med. VI). What these externally received ideas contribute to
knowledge is only the idea of existence and actuality. Understanding, the
application of conceptions whose logical possibility is certified by their
clarity and distinctness, comes from within (Caton, 170). This remarkable
cognitive movement from mind to imagination (a notion which, incidentally, goes back to the Neoplatonists) is now to be reviewed.

But first it should be noted that Descartes also takes account of ordinary
imaginative fictions, such as enchanted castles, and of dreams. The former
are perceptions projected into the imagination by acts of the will; the latter
are passions produced by disturbances in the intra-bodily animal-spirits.
Both sorts are usually more aimless and less vivid than perceptions of really
existent objects (*Passions of the Soul* I xx-xxiii).

The sensory particular ideas represented in the *sensus communis* are obscure
and confused enough to make us think that they do not represent corporeal
things very truly. They have, however, an aspect which is conceived clearly
and distinctly, namely whatever about them may become the object of pure
mathematics (Med. VI).

The objects of pure mathematics are precisely the figures and shapes
belonging to extended substance, that is, dimensional, measurable, spatial
magnitudes. Hence it does no harm—it is, in fact, exceedingly helpful—to
re-present in the imagination all merely sensible aspects of body by means
of figured magnitudes. For example, it is advantageous for the understanding to abstract from every feature of color and to re-present different colors
in terms of diverse geometric figures. All other sensible differences can be
expressed in the same manner. The advantage Descartes keeps emphasizing
is this: The mind is able to view with intuitive evidence not only itself but
also those ideas clearly re-presented in the imagination. Mathematical
imaginative re-presentation leads to certain knowledge.

Since the actual illustrative diagrams given by Descartes in Rule XIII are
so unspecific, examples of what he is prophecying can be supplied by
opening the color chapter of any physics textbook. There will be found,
for instance, spectral-distribution and color-mixture diagrams. These exemplify precisely the mathematical re-presentation of color qualities which
Descartes is demanding. Indeed, the basic measured representable quantities
of physics are termed "dimensions."

Furthermore, the mind can, as it were, escalate its representational
activity. What it intuits are its own operations, which are, taken objectively,

the essences of things. The essence of body is extension, or better, extensionality. Extensionality involves not this or that continuous or discrete magnitude, but magnitudinousness as such, magnitude in general. When the mind abstracts yet further from the particular mathematical lengths and figures or from the specific numbered multitudes in the imagination, these are what it obtains: general magnitudes in which numbers and extensions are no longer distinguished. Indeed, they cannot be distinguished, for the mind cannot contain extended substance in either discrete or continuous configurations. The science of magnitude taken generally, or better, the science of general magnitude, is called by Descartes "universal mathematics" (*mathesis universalis*, Rule IV). It is, in effect, algebra with a Cartesian grounding. General magnitudes are conventionally represented by letters for knowns and unknowns, for example, a, b, x, y. The point of such letters is that they symbolize indiscriminately geometrical magnitudes and numerical quantities.

Now comes the crux: The mind may find it convenient to project these general magnitudes which it has generated by abstraction from the imagination back into the imagination. As imaginative tokens they are then precisely what we call symbols (Klein 1936, 208). Descartes is thinking primarily of analytic geometry, insofar as it employs spatially displayed equations and graphs. Such equations and loci are not meant to present the shapes of actual bodies or paths. Rather they re-present symbolically the relations of general magnitudes, plotted in a Cartesian coordinate system. The theory of imaginative symbolic re-presentation has had deep and long repercussions. Among those taken up in this book are the question of the "intuitivity" of the diagrams of physics and the issue of the spatialization of mental operations (Part Five, Ch. II B). Both are lively current topics.

Thus the cognitively most valuable inscriptions the corporeal imagination receives are re-presentations sent down from the imaginative mode of the mind, not sent in from external bodies. That is a way of saying that they are mathematical rather than physical representations. The difference between mathematical and physical objects is, after all, only that between the possible and the actual (*Conversations with Burman*, Gaukroger 1980). Therefore the science of physics may begin with an imagined, hypothetical world. This is indeed the way of the *Principles of Philosophy*, Descartes's significantly titled work on the world of bodies. Thus in physics external, adventitious ideas serve only to raise the questions and to set the limit-conditions on the solutions by supplying the particular data. An actual example of this procedure is to be found in Newton's *Philosophiae Naturalis Principia Mathematica* (1687), also significantly titled. In that book the different possible laws of gravitational force for any number of orbital figures are worked out mathematically from a few given axioms of motion. For example, an elliptical orbit with a sun at one focus implies an inverse square law for planetary motion. This particular force law is then picked out on the basis of actual astronomical data, and the focal ellipse of our celestial planetary orbit falls out in turn. So the Cartesian procedure of imaginative retro-projection is compatible with observational science.

For all its ostensible importance, however, Descartes continually speaks of the symbolic imagination as a mere convenience, leaving open the possibility of a mind bright enough to operate entirely without re-presentation. Such a mind would have a mathematical intuition in need neither of imagination nor paper, nor even, perhaps, of data.

In sum, body, corporeal imagination, and imaginative thought are mathematicized with a vengeance. Nevertheless, these elaborate preparations for mutual cooperation notwithstanding, it remains a total mystery how unextended mind can influence extended body, or the reverse. Ultimately *res extensa* and *res cogitans* can have no intelligible interface.

What, finally, is the significance both in itself and for the future of the Cartesian theory of the imagination? First, since imagining is the mode in which mind meets corporeal nature, Descartes's insistence that imagination "is in no way a necessary element in my nature, or in my essence" (Med. VI) means that humanly speaking their meeting is purely adventitious. Neither is the human being necessarily of or in the world, nor do other beings reveal themselves to him through their own cognizable individual natures. The external world confronts mind as non-mind and is taken in only in the mathematical mode. Thus the imagination deals only with one, unitary, colorlessly non-sensual, extended thing. This disjunction of the imagination from an essentially mental humanity, and, in turn, of this humanity from the world, will eventually raise the Romantic and Existential revolt. Both will be bent on reinstating in a modern mode the necessary connection between the sensuous world and the human being.

At the same time it is hard to see how science in the modern sense, the mathematical inquiry into an essentially external nature, can be more candidly or more revealingly grounded. The exposition is candid insofar as the corporeal convenience of science—Descartes thinks of medicine as the end of his scientific efforts—does not obscure its irrelevance to human salvation and self-knowledge, for the self is not imageable. It is revealing because it shows precisely how body comes to be knowable by mathematics and only by mathematics. Descartes's demonstration makes the imagination the mode of physics, not in the loose inspirational role it is often given in contemporary writings, as a field for suggestive mental imagery, but very precisely, as the interface between space and mind.

The thinking self is, in the end, the Cartesian crux and thus the first object of criticism. It is its insight (*intuitus*), its viewing (*inspectio*), and its light (*lumen naturale*), that by their easy naturalness and immediacy usurp the traditional place of the imaginative phantasm in inner life. Classical contemplative illumination was thought to come at the end of a long, thoughtful process. It was not for those who had not accomplished it to say that intellectual insight was impossible. Cartesian intuition is proposed as a general human prerogative. Therefore it can be attacked on the basis of ordinary rational experience. And that experience seems to be that such immediacy, clarity, and distinctness as people enjoy in their mental operations almost always come with the assistance of mental imagery. This circumstance implies that the next phase in the modern project must be to save the scientific function of the imagination without pitting it so radically against an intuitive intellect. Kant will undertake just this task.

B. Hobbes, Locke, Leibniz, Berkeley: The Imagination Displaced

Meanwhile, for the following three writers, the imagination plays a small role, since they posit cognitive processes that are in no need of a mediating power.

Hobbes. Philosophers with the starkest views often write the most elegant prose. Hobbes's account of the imagination in the *Leviathan* (I 2) is as reductionist in theory as it is supple in style. The chapter begins with a statement of the law of inertia: "When a body is once in motion, it moveth, unless something else hinder it, eternally." It then makes the application to human sensation. The stimulus of the sense organs results in interior, physical motions that, like vibrations, cease only through diffusion, damping, or interference from new motions caused by newly presented objects. Hence

> after the object is removed, or the eye shut, we still retain an image of the thing seen, though more obscure than when we see it. And this it is, the Latins call *imagination*, from the image made in seeing; and apply the same, though improperly, to all the other senses. But the Greeks call it *fancy*; which signifies *appearance*, and is as proper to one sense, as to another. IMAGINATION therefore is nothing but *decaying sense*; and is found in men, and many other living creatures, as well sleeping, as waking.

Imagination then is "decaying sense" (a notion originating with Aristotle), while sense is the "seeming or *fancy*" resulting from motions passed on by the proper organ to the brain (I 1). Therefore the image as experienced is merely some sort of "consequence" of bare motion in matter. It is the same unexplained resultant that nowadays is called an "emergent" quality. When the sense is far decayed, "fading, old, and past," it is called memory, and "much memory, or memory of many things, is called *experience*." Compounds of imaginations, like centaurs, are called fictions of the mind. Apparitions and visions are all explicable as brief dreams or deliberate deceptions, for neither good nor evil thoughts are "blown (inspired) or poured (infused) into man" by God or the devil.

The "Train of Imaginations" (I 3), identical with the succession of thoughts or mental discourse, may be unguided, as in daydreaming, in which there is a certain mechanical dependence of each thought on the previous one. Or it may be regulated, driven by desire and design. Thus thoughts—for imagination is in fact thought and indeed the only thought there is—are concatenated either by a somewhat random inner association or by the direction of desire. James Mill, in his *Analysis of the Phenomena of the Human Mind* (1829), will pick up this description and define imagination as the unguided, purposeless train of conceptions proceeding according to principles of association. He will be emphatic that imagination is not a type of idea, nor even a faculty for forming new combinatory "creations," but merely an associative process. Imagination as a process thus has a Hobbesian root.

When, Hobbes says, imagination is raised verbally in man or in any creature endowed with the faculty of imagination, it is called understanding in general. When these thoughts are of the kind that connected speech was "constituted to signify," it is specifically human understanding.

Reason "is nothing but *reckoning*, that is adding and subtracting, of the consequences of general names agreed upon for the *marking* and *signifying* of our thoughts."

Thus the complex process of the older tradition, in which the object comes to be thought by the intellect through the mediation of the phantasm of the imagination, is now reduced to the marking of sensations in various stages of decay by conventional verbal counters, and to the calculation carried out with these symbolic counters. This theory is to have a great future (Part Two).

Locke. Next comes a simplification which, beginning with somewhat more sophisticated premises, arrives at a yet more radical reduction. Now the imagination becomes quite redundant. Of the two related premises the first is implicit. It is that sense-impression and image need not be distinguished, because all mental representations are on the same level of interiority. The second, explicitly stated, is that image and idea need not be distinguished because all representations are equally perceptual. Those few ideas that are not derived from sensation are the "ideas of reflection" with which experiences furnish the understanding. They are received from "the perception of the operations of our own minds within us, as it is employed about the ideas it has got." Thus the primary source of knowledge, sensation, and the secondary source, reflection, both supply their respective representations in the form of "ideas." These, regardless of origin, belong to a formally similar type of mental item, presented to the mind's "perception" to be operated on by it, somewhat in the way a collating machine sorts papers (*An Essay Concerning Understanding* II 1).

Locke remarks on his own use of the term "idea" that it stands for "whatever is meant by *phantasm, notion, species* or whatever it is which the mind can be employed about in thinking." He presumes that it will be easily granted that such items are to be found in the mind. The passage demonstrates the simplification. In the tradition, phantasms and species are distinct aspects of the cognitive process (though scientists like Roger Bacon had thrown them together even in the thirteenth century). The latter belong to the intellect, the former to the imagination. The Lockean mind lacks these fine distinctions, and consequently it lacks an imaginative power.

There is, however, a faculty of retention. It includes, first, "contemplation," by which Locke means the continuous actual maintaining of any ideas brought into the mind. (Contemplation is, *nota bene*, the ancient term for the highest intellectual intuition.) Memory is then the faculty for reviving ideas that have disappeared after "imprinting." In the second edition of the *Treatise* Locke added a paragraph to forestall any suspicion that the mind might store ideas that were not "actual perceptions." To lay up ideas in the repository of memory means nothing more than to be able to revive them together with the additional perception that the mind has had them before. But before they are revived, ideas are "actually nowhere." They are merely an ability in the mind, a somewhat mystical potentiality. Condillac, in the chapter on imagination in his *Essay on the Origin of Human Knowledge* (1756, I ii), faults Locke for supposing that every perception leaves an image or impression to be revived. There are, he claims, cases of merely verbal memory, when only names are recollected. This is a psychological issue for the future.

By the same token by which there is for Locke no role for the imagination, once the phantasm has been assimilated to the species (which is only the Latin translation of "idea"), it can just as well become the one and only umbrella-power. All it takes is for ideas to be assimilated to images. Hume will effect just that conflation.

Leibniz. The dimness of the role assigned to the imagination by Leibniz again has three causes. First, since cognizing beings are monads that "have no windows" (*Monadology* 7), there is no role for a receptive imagination proper. For monads are living mirrors of the universe, but not by means of a receptive sensibility and its sensory memory. Second, since for Leibniz space (like time) is a pure relation, namely the order of co-existent things, there is no place for an internal spatial medium such as the imagination is generally understood to be. Third, his search for a "universal characteristic," a symbolic language or algebra, is specifically intended to "economize" the imagination: "It makes us reason at little cost, putting characters in the place of things in order to ease the imagination." Thus Leibniz initiates the displacement of the concretely geometric imagination by symbolic logic which has dominated the teaching of mathematics into recent times.

To be sure, Leibniz speaks of an internal sense, also

called the *imagination*, which comprises at once the *concepts of particular senses*, which are clear but confused, and the *concepts of the common sense*, which are clear but distinct. And these clear and distinct ideas which are subject to the imagination are the objects of the mathematical sciences, namely arithmetic and geometry. [*Letter to the King of Prussia*, 1702]

Leibniz then completes the old triad by joining intellect to sensation and imagination: Intellect adds self-consciousness and other intelligible metaphysical concepts such as lie beyond the imagination. This passage shows that for Leibniz the objects of the imagination are characterized not by distinct spatial qualities but by their degree of clarity and distinctness, a middling degree. A monad's all-internal representations form a continuum along the lines of the latter criteria.

Berkeley. Berkeley will be considered again later on (Ch. IV B). Suffice it to say here that his chief contribution to the tradition of the imagination is the emphasis on the active nature of the imagination, namely its connection to the activity of the will as opposed to the passivity of sense: "This making and unmaking of ideas doth very properly denominate the mind active." But "the Spirit, the Active thing, that which is Soul or God, is the Will alone" (*Principles of Human Knowledge* 1710, paras. 25–30). Thus the imagination is linked to the creating will, an anticipation of Romantic imagination-theology. It is a concomitant of the active imagination, God's and ours, that the impressions and images themselves are inert, "visibly inactive," and have no power of mutual interaction. That is precisely what

Berkeley means by ideas, to which he grants only perceived or imagined being, dependent on an active, spiritual substance. Here Hume will differ radically. For him mind will not be an active host-substance, and therefore he must ascribe a motive power to the images themselves.

So Berkeley really no longer quite belongs with the foregoing group of those who displace the imagination, except that by emphasizing the active nature of the imagination he excludes its unconscious and passive depths.

C. Hume: The All-Inclusive Imagination

Hume's avowed way is "to leave the tedious lingering method" of previous philosophy. He intends to march right up to its capital and center, to human nature itself, and to take it by storm, charging ahead as far as experience and observation will take him. When he comes to the limits of what is thus explicable, he will "sit down contented" with the fact that we can give no reason for our most general and refined principles "beside our experience of their reality." This campaign, in which the imagination emerges as all-important, is carried out in the *Treatise of Human Nature* (1739, here cited by book, part, section) and its later abridged revision, the *Enquiry Concerning Human Understanding* (1751). The enlightenment effected by this brisk clearing of the space between the evident and the inexplicable is, to be sure, momentary. The questions that led to the scholastic clutter eventually prove insuppressible.

With respect to the imagination, Hume occupies, incidentally without acknowledgment, the same position among the moderns as the Stoics did among the ancients. The imagination as the faculty for sense-impressions and its derivations becomes the almost all-embracing power of representations. Descartes too borrows from the Stoics. But whereas he picks up their preoccupation with the certainty of comprehending assent and sets aside their reliance on internalized sense-impressions, Hume leaves the former and takes the latter.

The Humean imagination is most conveniently studied in three stages: First, the exposition of its implicit universality; then the explicit Humean description of the power; and finally the delineation of the more restricted faculty of metaphysical and poetic fictions. In other words, the Humean imagination presents itself in three descending degrees of inclusiveness.

The first Humean imagination, then, is the imagination in its largest compass. It must be established as much by inference from its functions as by tracing the term itself in the text. If imagination is the act of the mind by which it entertains representations with sensory qualities, then one may infer that for Hume the imagination is the mind's sole function or, as he says, "modification."

The famous first sentence of the *Treatise* runs: "All perceptions of the mind resolve themselves into two distinct kinds, which I shall call IMPRES-SIONS and IDEAS." Impressions appear when people are looking with open eyes, whereas ideas are the representations of visual (or any sensory) impressions when the eyes are shut. Thus "all the perceptions of the mind are double." The role of the imagination in distinguishing them will be treated below. For the moment suffice it to say that ideas are resembling-images, "copies taken by the mind" (I i 1). Hence ideas have originals whence they come, either as simple copies or as complexes combined from various originating impressions (I i 1). Impressions, on the other hand, have no originals except insofar as one might follow out the physiology of their production to a first stimulus. They make their appearance in the soul "without any introduction" (II i 1). Hume apologizes for their literal name, which is not meant to describe the manner of their production (I i 1, n. 1).

Perceptions then have no extra-mental originals. Indeed they are not perceptions *of* any object:

> For philosophy informs us, that everything, which appears to the mind, is nothing but a perception, and is interrupted, and dependent on the mind; whereas the vulgar confound perceptions and objects, and attribute a distinct continued existence to the very things they feel or see. This sentiment, then, as entirely unreasonable, must proceed from some other faculty than the understanding. [I iv 2]

That other faculty will, incidentally, be the third, most specialized, imagination. From the beginning Hume enforces the notion that neither an object nor its existence is distinct from the perception: ". . . to form the idea of an object and to form an idea simply is the same thing" (I i 7). "The idea of existence, then, is the very same with the idea of what we conceive to be existent" (I ii 6).

Perceptions are all that is ever present to the mind (III i 1). They are, as their name (which Hume does use deliberately) intimates, in varying degrees sensory, above all visual. Moreover, not only do impressions have this nature but so do ideas and even abstract ideas. They too are in fact not general but particular, that is to say, precisely determinate in quantity and quality. Their generality consists only in their being associated with a word that has been habitually used of many similar particulars (I i 7). Hume does not say how this association comes about. Here as everywhere he quite deliberately refuses to account for the "how" of the cognitive process he posits.

The mind's perceptions, then, have these two apparently inconsistent characteristics: First, as being particulars having quantity and quality, they are truly sensory. Second, as having no reference to externally existing objects, they are purely intra-mental. The sole "modification" to which the Humean mind is subject is thus descriptively parallel to the Stoic *phantasia*. For the latter is also an "affect" of the soul, that is, a sensory presentation quite divorced from outside causes.

In fact, a comparison of various Humean passages leads to the inference that Hume should have been quite ready to call this one and only act of the perceiving mind imagination outright. For in the vigorous pursuit of cognitive simplification, he reduces the three traditionally distinct faculties of the understanding, which are conceiving, reasoning, and judging, to one, the first (I iii 7, n. 1). Conceiving he in turn identifies, quite as a matter of course, with imagining (I ii 2). Indeed, he says explicitly and directly that understanding is nothing but the general and more established properties of the imagination (I iv 7). It follows that all thinking belongs to the imagination (Wilbanks 1986, 79). Moreover, since it will be shown that impressions are images, the imagination spans the whole cognitive spectrum from sense impressions to thinking.

However, one must not go so far as to say that the imagination *is* the mind, for the mind is no self-identical substance, thing, or subject. "What we call mind is nothing but the heap or collection of different perceptions, united together by certain relations" (I iv 2). It is a "kind of theatre" (I iv 6), but with nothing behind the scenes. It is really only the spectacle itself. The elements of this spectacle are themselves active, for they influence each other. But in fact the word "action" seems to convey too much meaning: It is enough to say that "modifications" of the mind occur (I iv 5). Of course it follows that there can be no impressions *of* the mind *in* the mind.

This imagination, which is nothing but the perceptual modification of the mind, might, like the Stoic *phantasia*, be said to be too undifferentiated for psychological interest, its epistemological scope notwithstanding. Yet the Humean imagination implies just that understanding of mental images (for that is exactly what the mind's perceptions are) which will eventually spark the specific criticism driving the most interesting twentieth-century treatment of the imagination.

This criticism goes under the title of the "illusion of immanence" (Cowley 1968). Perceptions or mental images have a purely intra-mental, and therefore evanescent, existence. They come and go as objects given to consciousness. Although when talking naturally Hume says he has an "idea *of*" an object, theoretically he denies that the idea alone is mental while its object is extra-mental. The object represented is rather "immanent" or resident in the representation itself, which is therefore a sort of idea-object. However, "a theory which, like Hume's, takes a mental image to be an entity, hypostatises a kind of consciousness of things, and makes this hypostasis what we are conscious of" (Cowley, 33). In other words, it takes ideas as the ultimate objects of consciousness. The three chief difficulties with immanence theories are these: First, they ignore the common experience of perceiving as being precisely the perceiving of objects existing externally. Second, they make impossible a principled distinction between *bona fide* perceiving and imagining. This is of course what I have just meant to show concerning Hume's notion of perception. Third, they make thoughts into things, ideas into objects. In sum, immanence theories lay themselves open to this question: To what purpose is it to say that "the mind has perceptions" rather than simply that "people see things"? All these difficulties will be taken up in contemporary philosophy (Ch. IV).

The second, more narrowly defined, Humean imagination emerges when the cognitive scope of the first is curtailed by cutting off from its spectrum impressions on one end and reasoning on the other.

Now this narrower imagination is specifically charged with converting impressions into ideas:

> We find by experience, that when any impression has been present with the mind, it again makes its appearance there as an idea; and this it may do after two different ways: either when in its new appearance it retains a considerable degree of its first vivacity, and is somewhat intermediate betwixt an impression and an idea; or when it entirely loses that vivacity, and is a perfect idea. The faculty, by which we repeat our impressions in the first manner, is called the MEMORY, and the other the IMAGINATION. 'Tis evident at first sight that the ideas of the memory are much more lively and strong than those of the imagination, and that the former faculty paints its objects in more distinct colours, than any which are employ'd by the latter. When we remember any past event, the idea of it flows in upon the mind in a forcible manner; whereas in the imagination the perception is faint and languid, and cannot without difficulty be preserv'd by the mind steddy and uniform for any considerable time. Here then is a sensible difference betwixt one species of ideas and another. [I i 3, also *Enquiry* II]

I have quoted this long passage because its chief claim becomes such a bone of contention in the later literature on the imagination. What is most notable is that when direct reference to the actual presence or absence of external objects before the senses is out of play, there really is no mark by which to distinguish perception from imagination or memory except what one might call the impressiveness of the impressions. And that is precisely what Hume means by their force and vivacity. In theories that admit an independent nature out there confronting the senses, the liveliness of impressions is due to the independent life of their source. For Hume it is simply an immanent characteristic of the mental presentation.

He knows perfectly well, however, that vivacity or its absence is not an unfailing or essential mark distinguishing perceptions. There are idea-images which grow to surpass their original impressions in force. Inversely, some impressions are at inception as weak as ideas (I iii 5, i 1). When all is said and done, a safe, though not a universal, criterion for distinguishing an impression from its idea as a cause from its effect is that the former precedes the latter in time (I i 1).

There are, moreover, ideas to which no impressions directly correspond, though such ideas are usually composed of impression-elements. There is even supposed to be a case where an idea arises originally. For we can supply the idea of a shade of a color, say blue, that is missing from our spectrum of impressions. Descartes makes a parallel claim explicable in terms of "imaginative projection." For him the color spectrum is a mathematical continuum, which is first thought and then projected back into the imagination as a geometric figure. But in Hume's scheme, the ability to originate an idea willfully is an ungrounded abnormality, a sign that an entirely non-originative imagination is not quite adequate to the range of inner experience. It is a live issue whether there are mental images that are not based on an exact perceptual prototype, whether sensory qualities can originate in the imagination. Psychologists with positivist tendencies have flatly denied the possibility—William James, for example, in his *Principles of Psychology* (1892, ch. XIX). So have novelists; as Elizabeth Bowen has said: "Physical detail cannot be invented." I will argue later that the originative power of the imagination appears in its wholes rather than in its elements (Part Six, Ch. III).

If the imagination as a faculty of idea-copies is thus—however dubiously—distinguished from the perception of impressions on the one hand, it is, on the other hand, marked off from reasoning as follows: When two objects are present to the senses together as contemporary impressions "we call *this* perception rather than reasoning." "All kinds of reasoning consist in nothing but a *comparison*," which yields the discovery of *temporal*, that is to say, causal, relations between objects (I iii 2). Neither relations of identity nor relations of place are the results of reasoning, but they arise rather as immediate sensory presences. Hence there are ideas that are immediately perceived. As I have shown, Hume does not strictly maintain the distinction between imagining and reason. It is in fact made mainly to emphasize the—

unexplained—peculiarity of a mental operation that goes beyond present perception.

What remains when impressions and reasoning are subtracted is the imagination *par excellence.* It is that faculty by which impressions are represented "in their new appearance" so as to "retain virtually none of their first vivacity." Memory does the same, except that, unlike imagination, which "is not restrained to the same order or form with the original impressions" (I i 3), it merely preserves those originals. The ideas of memory are, in turn, "more *strong* and *lively* than those of the fancy." Later writers have been spurred on by the fallibility of Hume's criterion for distinguishing fantasy from recollection to find a better one. Urmson (1967) cuts the Gordian knot by claiming that such a criterion is to be found not at all in the image itself but only in the intention of the imager. If it matters to him that the event imaged should in fact have happened, he is fairly said to be recollecting. But again, he can find no direct mark of its factuality or accuracy which is internal to the memory-image.

However, there is a strong specification of the memory-imagination, though not an internal one. That is to say, the rememberer cannot identify the impression as a memory by its own feel, but needs an external criterion. This specific characteristic is that the memory has a certain freedom from the originals: The memory-imagination may re-associate them.

This ability to re-arrange the form and order of impressions is "guided by some universal principles," a "gentle force, which commonly prevails"— commonly only, for "nothing is more free than that faculty." The "universal principles" are therefore no more than fairly pervasive regularities. They are certainly not "inseparable" connections (I i 4). Indeed, in accordance with the fact that for Hume it is not the mind and its powers but only its perceptions that are entities, these linkages are not constitutive laws of the faculty at all, but are qualities of the perceptions themselves. Ideas associate *themselves* by resembling each other, or by being contiguous in time or space, or by standing in relation of cause and effect (I i 4, *Enquiry* V 2). This passage enumerating the connections of mental images became the founding reference for the various associationist psychologies, which, together with their modifications and refutations, dominated the field through the nineteenth century.

However freely ideas may autonomously associate, "*nothing we imagine is absolutely impossible*" (I ii 2). This assertion will turn into a fascinating problem of image-logic (Part Three, Ch. III). But for Hume it is simply a fundamental fact or "maxim" that whatever the mind clearly conceives includes the idea of possible existence. It is a maxim that would be more likely to seem obvious to someone like Hume, for whom conceiving meant having mental images. For what is imageable is at least possible as a spatial structure (Part Three, Ch. I B).

Here we come to the third Humean imagination, the imagination defined by the special function of making fictions. For although the ideas of the imagination are never impossible, they can certainly be artificial.

The fictions of the imagination in which Hume is philosophically interested (I iv) are primarily not works of imaginative art but metaphysical fabrications. As imagination is the source of such "feigning," it is also the ultimate judge of all systems of philosophy (I iv 4). In general the criteria by which it discriminates are two: Can the idea whose artificiality is in question be traced back to its impression? And is it in itself—imaginatively—conceivable? The first means that it is founded on evidence; the second that it is at least not impossible.

Why does the imagination undertake at all to make fictions of the sort that "the vulgar" entertain and that some philosophers see through? When the fictions are enumerated it becomes evident that they are all ways the mind invents to make itself comfortable. Its comfort lies in finding and objectifying sameness, persistence, completeness, and union (e.g., I iv 5). Thus the fictions, which can be classified into those regarding objects, those concerned with the subject itself, and those of "ancient" metaphysics, all serve just that purpose. They feign persistent external objects; they invent continuous self-identity; and they make up a host of metaphysical hypostases like substances, forms, accidents, and occult qualities (I iv 3). There is some question whether in these fictions the imagination is "supposing" picturelessly, or actually feigning weakly perceived ideas (Wilbanks 1968, 82, Yolton 1984, 173). Since the former use would be out of character with the fundamental perceiving function of the imagination, and since, moreover, introspection reveals that faint figures do attend the thought of metaphysical entities, the latter interpretation would seem to me to be preferable. The genuine philosophers are left with the anxious and melancholy business not so much of eradicating these philosophical fictions as of containing and restraining them. Compared to the feigning philosophers, poets are harmless "liars by profession" (I iii 10). I cannot resist pointing out that Hume, who hates the metaphysicians, demeans the poets with mild contempt, while Plato, who exalts philosophy, honors poetry with passionate opposition.

(Sokolowski 1968.)

In Hume's theory the imagination, though presented on three levels of specificity, is one power, the power of self-associating perceptions. This "magical faculty in the soul" (I i 7), though it is presented with an air of simple self-evidence and demystifying candor, seems to me as peculiar a product of philosophy as ever there was. It turns the world into inner appearances, but severely suppresses their relation to any causal being. It takes these appearances as mental modifications, but posits no mind to support them. It interprets these mental modification as perceptions, though it provides no mental process for appropriating them. It makes ideas have associative tendencies while it posits no necessary laws of connection. It calls for critical thinking but makes all ideas imaginal. In sum, it is a brilliant notion waiting for a philosophical ground. It will be Kant's project to supply such a foundation.

D. Kant: The Transcendental Meeting-Ground

Now the imagination goes underground. As the Humean imagination was all-embracing, the Kantian imagination, the submerged foundation of experience, becomes profound—one might even say abysmal—more so than ever before or since. That depth gives the Kantian imagination its enormous significance. What renders it unceasingly fascinating is that the novel specificity of its foundational functions is accorded so brief and sketchy an exposition. The two-thousand-year-old fate of the imagination is thus exemplified in Kant's treatment of the "transcendental product" of the imagination. In a work whose very grandeur stems from its satisfying thoroughness, *The Critique of Pure Reason*, he chooses to omit as a "dry and boring analysis," of all things, any extended account of the "schema," the peculiar and all-important product of the transcendental imagination. No element of the *Critique* underwent a more serious revision between the first and second editions of 1781 and 1786 (referred to as A and B) than the treatment of the imagination in its cognitive employment. The difference is in the approach, which is more psychological in the earlier and altogether logical or "transcendental" in the later edition (A 100–102, *115–124*, B 151–155, 160–162, *175–187*, 741 ff). The playful, aesthetic use of the imagination is at issue in the *Critique of Judgment* (1790, Intro vii; I para. 9 and end: "General Remark"). Finally, the description of its functions in ordinary human life is given in the *Anthropology* (1798, para. 28 ff).

"Transcendental" literally means "what goes beyond," that is, lies beyond and behind experience. "Transcendental" is whatever comes logically—not psychologically or temporally—before experience, as its condition and ground. The inquiry into the transcendental grounds of experience or material cognition is called "critique." By means of the critical enterprise the transcendental imagination is found to be a power responsible for knowledge not of empty logical forms but of experienced material things.

For Kant such knowledge is exactly what we now call science, above all classical physics, the mathematical science of matter in motion. The object of his first *Critique* is to give "the grounds of the possibility" of a sure and certain science. This science already exists, its mathematics discovered by Euclid anciently and its dynamics by Newton recently (B x ff).

The imagination is not only responsible but centrally responsible for knowledge, namely as the meeting-ground of the understanding and the sensibility; the first of these is by itself empty, the other, blind (B 75). The Humean imagination had worked magically, at once immanently and unaccountably. Kant endeavors, by analyzing the cognitive product, to uncover its imaginative ground. Unlike Hume, he has faith that something is gained by a critique of the powers necessary to the knowing "subject," the self. Yet such a critique cannot reveal either that subject or its objects as substances or things in themselves, Descartes notwithstanding. Therefore a second motive of the *Critique*, besides the grounding of science, is the critique—now in the usual sense—of the illusions by means of which cognitive reason overleaps its limits to claim to know such transcendent things.

Kant's critique has a third aim, incidental to the *Critique of Pure Reason* but perhaps central to Kant, namely to reveal an active subject, a self, possessing a practical reason—in fact, the will—which is different from cognitive reason only in employment, not in principle. The middle critique, the *Critique of Practical Reason*, then treats of the self insofar as it has a will and is therefore a "person," an autonomous, self-legislating subject, capable of freedom and morality. The first *Critique* shows how the subject gives laws to nature; the second how it legislates to itself. The latter work will treat of the transcendental imagination only once (I ii, "Of the Type of Pure Practical Judgment"). Thus Kant considers the imagination in turn with respect to Truth, Goodness, and Beauty, for these may, broadly, be said to be the respective topics of the three *Critiques*.

Just as in the case of Descartes it was necessary to sketch out the two opposing substances in order to show how the imagination mediates between them, so in the case of Kant it is necessary to describe the two utterly diverse faculties for which the imagination provides the meeting ground.

Understanding is the name of the thinking faculty concerned with experience. It is the cognitively effective part of the aforementioned Reason, which is the encompassing name for the higher powers of thought (B 863). Reason and its lower subdivision, understanding, are powers of a self, a subject. Unlike Descartes, Kant regards this "I" as a non-thing, as pure inwardness, which underlies its "representations" and is hidden behind them. Far from being what is best and most certainly known, it is not legitimately knowable at all. Yet it is always present as the implicit "I think," the steady "correlate" of all my thinking activity (A 123). Thus we can know about it only that it is, never what it is (B 157).

The subject has "representations." This unfortunate term, borrowed from Leibniz, means all things somehow present to the self (B 376). Among them are the thinking functions of the understanding. Of these there is indeed knowledge, albeit formal and empty. The understanding, or the subject by means of it, is known to function in a definite number of definite ways, called categories or concepts *a priori*. *A priori*, literally "from the very first," means effectively the same thing as "transcendental," for the concepts do not come from experience but, on the contrary, they first make experience possible. Some of these concepts will be named here as occasion arises. Suffice it to say that they are the laws of transcendental logic, which rule the organization of the multitudinous representations that are before the subject. They do one job with a double aspect. As the functions of one identical subject, they unify its sprawling representations so as to make them all its property; my representations are "mine." By the same token, they connect the representations to one another by combining or synthesizing them. What all the categories together effect is precisely an organization of all the multifarious representations into object-structures, for taken by themselves, without any fulfilling sensation, the categories function as "the concepts of an object in general" (B 128). Thus they lay the foundations for the ordinary judgments about objects of experience in which concepts are logically connected. For example, my making the empirical propositional judgment that "this stone is heavy" involves four elements. First, it is I who thinks it. Second, though it is my, the subject's, thought, I think it as objectively true, as being truly about a real object having a complete object-structure. Third, I am combining the concept of stone with the concept of heaviness by subordinating the former to the latter. And fourth, simply as a judgment it has a number of logical features, such as being singular and affirmative. All these aspects of articulated knowledge are made possible by the logically antecedent synthetic unification, or as Kant says, the "synthetic unity," effected by the subject through its understanding (B 130).

Now where does it come from, this field of unconnected and ununified representations, which the understanding has to pre-structure—this *manifold*, as Kant calls it?

At the lower end of the cognitive hierarchy our representational faculties become receptive and open up to intimations from outside the subject. Such intimations are, as in the tradition, called sensation. But Kant gives up the old paradoxical desire to believe that sensation represents to the subject inside the objects outside as they are in themselves. No more than the inner subject can be known to itself through thought can the true form of external objects be known through sensation. Consequently, the sensations that flow in are a mere indeterminate and adventitious material for cognitive shaping.

The faculty which is receptive to them is the sensibility (B 33). As thinking structures the manifold actively, the sensibility receives its material passively. But this is the most potent passivity that ever was, for the sensibility is formatively receptive. It imposes a form, or rather two forms, on its contents. Kant calls this formative sensibility "intuition" (*Anschauung*). The prefix "in" has nothing to do with *in*sight but is merely intensive; intuition is not a penetrating power. Nor is intuition what it used to be, reason's highest work, the direct contemplation of intelligible objects. Kant shows that thinking does not function by looking at thought-objects, and if it did, it would not yield knowledge. For the only objects of real, material knowledge are those we form from given sensation-material. So intuition has been consigned to the sensibility, and knowledge is now limited to experience.

The formative intuition is, I think, the most original and the most mind-wrenching element of the first *Critique*, since it requires us to invert our natural attitude toward the world. All appearances present themselves to us in spatial and temporal form. We must learn to think that spatiality and temporality do not originally belong to the appearances, but are forms imposed on them by our own receptive faculty. Objects and relations do not appear to us as they do because they are in space and time, but they are spatial and temporal because they appear to us. Kant gives a number of arguments for instituting this revolution. The most general one is that space and time show every sign of being *a priori* necessities of appearances. For we cannot begin to represent to ourselves objects that are not in space and time, but we can very well represent to ourselves empty space and time (B 38, 46). Kant calls empty space and time "pure intuitions." They are singular presentations, antecedent to sensation, "pure" structures that the sensibility can intuit *a priori* (B 38, 47). More is said of this pure spatial sensibility and its pure space-object in Part Five (Ch. I B). In sum, while the understanding functions discursively by running over and unifying a multiplicity of representations, the sensibility receives its matter intuitively into two singular, unique presentations, pure space and pure time.

The intuition, then, really consists of two "senses," which Kant calls the outer and the inner sense (B 37). The spatial form of sensibility is the "outer sense," or, better, the sense of externality. "Outer" here has less to do with going outside the subject than with the form of space itself. Space, as extended, is quintessentially that each of whose parts is outside of all the others. The inner sense, on the other hand, is the form of consciousness; it is time, the form in which our inner condition appears to us. The subject itself does not, of course, appear, but its functions do.

The two senses are not altogether cognitively symmetrical. In the remarkable "Refutation of Idealism," which Kant added to the second edition, he argues that there are real objects in outside space. His proof relies on the argument that the undeniable consciousness I have of myself in time is dependent on permanence in space (B 275). In order to become conscious of myself I also have to be immediately conscious of persistent things in space. Thus time can appear only through space. This priority of space for consciousness in general will be balanced by the primary importance of time to experience in particular (B 177, Brann 1979).

Kant calls the sense-filled formations of the intuition "appearances." The multifarious field of appearances within the intuition is the very same manifold, mentioned above, that the functions of the understanding were called to unify and synthesize. So the intuition from below provides the field over which the understanding functions from above. But such cooperation is more easily called for than accounted for. The sensibility and the understanding are totally diverse powers, opposed as "outermost extremes" (A 124). How can they ever come together?

It is the transcendental power of the imagination that will be the enabling ground on which they can interpenetrate each other. Logically, what the imagination makes possible is a judgment in which the sensible appearances are subsumed, or grasped in concepts. Therefore the account Kant gives of it is a doctrine of the faculty of judgment, the power in play when thinking and sensibility get down to their common concrete business (B 173). In order for the judgment-making imagination to do its work of connecting representations, they have to be of like kind. This requirement is obvious to Kant. The empirical concept of a plate, for example, can be subsumed under the purely geometric concept of a circle only because they share roundness, though it is conceived in the latter and intuited in the former (B 176). But the transcendental concepts of the understanding are, as was said, so diverse from the intuitions of the sensibility that they can never be met with *in* intuition.

Thus it is clear that there must be a "third" element which is similar enough to both understanding and intuition to make the application of the former to the latter possible; it must be both thought-like and sensible. This "third" something is "the transcendental schema of the understanding," which is a "product" of the imagination (B 177 ff.). Its name notwithstanding, it is not a sketch-like picture, though its psychological, empirical counterpart may be just that. Indeed, in the *Critique of Judgment* (para. 17) Kant describes just such a normative sketch, an averaging of mental images, as present-day cognitive psychologists hypothesize. However, the transcendental schema is rather the representation of a method to be used by the understanding, which Kant calls its "schematism."

This method is used by the understanding to prepare itself for interpenetration with the sensibility, and it works as follows (B 178): Time is the form of the inner sensibility. As such it shapes the sensible manifold of consciousness, which is therefore thoroughly imbued with time. Now if it were possible for the categories of the understanding to become temporally determined, then the sensible manifold and the thinking functions would have a common ground on which to get together.

And get together they must, if fulfilling, real, material knowledge, the kind Kant calls experience or science, is to occur. For the thought-functions by themselves are empty, unsubstantial graspings, and the sensible material alone is an indiscriminately heaped-up field. An object, a determinate, knowable thing, arises only when thought grasps sense.

So the categories must be time-determined, or "schematized." How, specifically, does the understanding schematize itself? Before I show the answer by examples, an observation about space and time is in order, especially since it is the bias of this book to see the imagination as primarily a spatial power. It was pointed out above that for Kant space is the ultimate condition of temporal consciousness. Now when it comes to experience, that is, to real knowledge, it must be admitted that Kant clearly gives time the priority. For time, as the form all objects have before consciousness, is, as it were, closer to thought than is space, which is turned toward sensation. Since the temporalization of thought is the product of the transcendental imagination, the power lying deep, presumably below all other cognitive powers, this is the faculty responsible for making us time-affected twice over. For our thinking is often about, and always in, time. From the *Critique* itself it is not at all clear that Kant attached great significance to his discovery that it is the temporalizing imagination that makes our existence temporal; but a later interpreter certainly will do so, namely Heidegger.

It will be useful to give examples of the temporal and spatial schemata of the imagination, though Kant treats the former cursorily and the latter scarcely at all.

Among the categories, some are transcendental rules for constituting objects in their necessary relations. They ensure that objects of experience are always related as substances and accidents, as causes and effects, and as standing in a reciprocal relation of agent and patient. When these three categorical relations are temporalized or time-determined, they ground, in succession, the conception of a sensible object that persists in time so that only its accidents change, of a sensible object that stands in a real, rule-governed, temporal succession of events, and of a sensible object that maintains relations of reciprocal causality with other objects (B 183). Anyone familiar with the Newtonian laws of motion (inertia, force, action and reaction) will recognize them here in logical embryo. Kant is providing the transcendental ground for the science of classical physics. The temporal schematism of the imagination is its crux.

The spatial schemata are more familiar. We have all experienced the sketchy imaginative schema which serves as a guide for drawing a generalized picture of, say, a dog. The transcendental schema is a "monogram," as it were, which makes such pictures possible to begin with. It is not itself a picture but it is a rule by which the imagination helps thought to synthesize the manifold of space. Again, among the categories are rules connecting all objects to quantity. Only when these are spatialized does it become possible for thought to structure space geometrically. Thus the spatial schematism grounds the science of geometry, which, after all, requires that spatial intuitions should be understood conceptually (B 154, 182, 741 ff). I skirt here two highly technical problems: whether all of Kant's categories can be schematized, and which of them are time- and which space-determined. Kant does not explicitly say (Woods 1983). Kant's spatial schema will be picked up in contemporary cognitive studies (Ch. IV A).

In sum, these schematized categories, or thought-functions "realized" in intuition, are concepts whose transcendental generality has been restricted by real conditions. They are sensible concepts, applicable to the sensation-filled manifold (B 186). This unifying synthesis of concept and intuition has been effected by the imagination. It supplies to the understanding the schematizing method. Ultimately it even *is* the understanding in its schematizing employment. For although in the course of his analysis Kant distinguishes two syntheses, one called "intellectual," which is the conceptual unification sketched above, and the other called "figural," which is the imaginative unification just reviewed (B 151), in the end they are identified. It is one and the same "spontaneity"—Kant's term for the ultimate, original activity of the subject—that shows itself in both syntheses, that of the understanding and that of the imagination (B 162 n.).

"Spontaneity" is in fact the term that helps to explain why it is, of all faculties, the imagination to which these deep activities are assigned. Kant's definition of the term "imagination" is traditional. It is "the faculty for representing an object even *without its presence* in the intuition" (B 151). Now since intuition is sensible, imagination must belong to the sensibility, where objects are passively represented. Since, on the other hand, the object that the imagination represents is not really, not sensorily, given, it must also be said to present its objects actively or spontaneously. Hence it is eminently suited to holding sensibility and thinking together.

Kant calls this transcendental and spontaneous power the "productive" imagination. We are indeed a long way from Aristotle's receptive *phantasia*. However, Kant also recognizes a reproductive imagination. It is simply the ordinary empirical imagination, which works according to the Humean laws of association and belongs not to philosophy but to psychology (B 152).

In the first edition, Kant had nevertheless included a prominent discussion of the psychological imagination at work (A 100–102, 115–124). He had described the cognitive progress towards full-blown experiential knowledge in three empirically separable genetic stages. Analogous phases still turn up in contemporary research on cognitive processes (Part Two, Ch. IV B).

The first stage is a kind of synoptic scanning by means of which the intuitive manifold is "taken up" into consciousness. Kant names it the synthesis of "apprehension"; it is in fact perception. The middle stage occurs when the reproductive imagination, which is just the memory, recalls the previously apprehended intuitions according to its empirical rules; this is the "association" of representations. Finally, the subject supplies the ground for the associability of intuitions through its understanding, which unifies intuitions conceptually; the result is their thoroughgoing "affinity" (A 120 ff). In the passage here summarized these stages are ultimately due to the transcendental synthesis of the imagination. The imagination is thus proclaimed as the underlying cognitive power (A 123).

In the preceding paragraphs (A 99 ff.) Kant had already named the grounding, or transcendental, counterparts of these merely empirical psychological stages. The "synthesis of apprehension," which is responsible for first taking the manifold into consciousness, goes by the same name as the corresponding empirical stage. The "synthesis of reproduction" is again the term for the transcendental stage responsible for association of memory-intuition. Only the final phase is given a separate name, the "synthesis of recognition." For the intuitions reproduced in transcendental memory are re-cognized, in the sense that the subject recognizes that what it thinks now is identical with what it thought before. Thus it grasps a sequence of intuitions in one conceptual representation.

Kant struck both the psychological and the transcendental developments from the second edition. The former account was obviously not strictly critical business. By the same token, the latter was really nothing but psychology with a transcendental prefix. That is, of course, precisely why it is this first exposition that best illuminates the actual functioning of the imagination. The account of the centerpiece in Kant's treatment of the imagination is now in outline complete. The review of the imagination as it fares in the second and third *Critiques* and in the *Anthropology* will be much briefer.

The *Critique of Practical Reason* contains a section, the "Typic of Pure Practical Judgment," that is the practical complement to the theoretical schematism in the first *Critique*, since it concerns the relation of intuitions to moral judgments. It is, however, mainly cautionary. Unlike the theoretical categories, the practical categories do not require the sensibility, since they are not sensually conditioned and are free from the laws of nature. Therefore moral reason is not mediated by the imagination. Nevertheless the imagination can, if correctly used, be helpful in providing a "typic" of the moral law, namely a method for giving concrete examples of such law at work. The idea of natural law itself provides such a "type": Imagine before each action whether you would wish the rule by which you have chosen to act to become a universal law of nature. Kant mentions suicide as an action whose morality may be tested by the "typical" imagination. Clearly a universal law of self-destruction gives results absurd to imagine.

The *Critique of Judgment*, which presents the grounds upon which judgments of taste rest, would seem to be the natural home of the imagination, both because it is indeed a faculty of judgment and because it is the faculty ordinarily concerned with aesthetic matters. However, the actual working of the imagination as a faculty is taken up only in passing in this *Critique*. The extreme brevity of exposition, compounded with an inherent embarrassment about its relation to beauty, make the Kantian aesthetic imagination as mystifying as it is fascinating. (Its relation to the sublime is referred to in Part Six, Ch. III A.)

As the faculty of intuitions, the imagination can represent sensory objects in the absence of real sensation. Now it may happen that these intuitions are, quite undesignedly, in agreement with the understanding, not through a law-bound process of cognition, but freely. If that occurs, there arises a pleasure which is quite subjective, in the sense that it has nothing to do with knowing a real object. Such pleasure proceeds from the "purposiveness" of the intuitive object. This is the sense that the object gives of being formed purposefully, even though any actual end or utility is absent. Whenever an intuitive object is thus judged by the faculty of taste to have been produced by the imagination in free conformity with the laws of understanding, it is called beautiful (Intro.).

This free, spontaneous conformity to law would seem to turn the imagination into an originally active agent, such as moral reason is. Not so, says Kant; only the understanding legislates. "Hence it is conformity to law without a law" that is being propounded, a merely subjective harmony of imagination and understanding, one not bound by any cognitive requirement ("General Remark"). The imagination and understanding are said to be in "a state of free play" (I 9). Nevertheless, in exercising the productive imagination (productive not in the transcendental but in the poetic sense), that is, in appreciating or making beauty, we may symbolize morality. For though the arena is aesthetic intuition rather than moral reason, yet the faculty of judgment here "gives the law to itself in respect to the objects of so pure a satisfaction"; such aesthetic feeling bears a strong resemblance to the self-satisfaction of well-used autonomous moral reason (I 59, Crawford 1982).

This analysis of the cognitive origin of beauty manages to be at once plausible and enigmatic. It introduces into the tight-knit architecture of the first *Critique* a loose joint, which will be more specifically discussed later (Ch. IV A). Thus poetic, or creative imagination appears to defeat this, as it does all, systems.

In the *Anthropology*, finally, a witty and observant work which reveals the humanity and even the humor of the man who wrote the *Critiques*, the imagination is treated descriptively, or "pragmatically" (paras. 28 ff.). The terms are partly critical, partly traditional. The poetic imagination consists of the powers of forming intuitions in space, of associating them in time, and of relating sensible thoughts according to their affinity. This productive imagination—productive again in the aesthetic sense of the third *Critique*, rather than in the cognitive sense of the first—is now said to be incapable of bringing forth a sensory representation that has never been in the sensibility. Yet it is a power for the "originating exhibition" of objects in the intuition. (Recall that the reproductive imagination is memory, or "derivative exhibition.") It provides all the material that the poetic productive imagination requires. On that account, Kant says, the original figures exhibited in the productive imagination should not be called "creative." For it is not infinitely original but it is limited by its dependence on memory (Sallis 1980). What it does contribute originally are, precisely, the original forms of space and time. I think Kant is here taking account of that strange characteristic of the poetic imagination which is particularly impressive in dreams and other kinds of involuntary production of images, the sort Kant calls "phantasy." Such imagery may seem utterly strange in the combinations of its sensory contents while yet preserving the familiar space and time of the waking world. The connective laws of sensation may, to be sure, be magically perturbed, but there is no gainsaying that even the most phantastic objects do appear in the general form of the originary intuitions, space and time. Thus, odd though it may seem, it is the reproductive memory that adds the elements of estrangement in the form of representations outlandishly rearranged, while the originary intuition contributes the abiding factors of phantasy. Kant comments that "we play with the imagination with enjoyment and frequency, but the imagination, as phantasy, plays with us just as frequently, and sometimes with much less enjoyment" (para. 31).

There are many other acute definitions and observations, especially concerning the role of imagination in desire. Since imagination is richer in representations than is sense, the absence of the desired object often enlivens passion more than its presence does. This sickness of longing as the effect of a poetic power of imagination is incurable—except through marriage. "For marriage is truth" (para. 33).

In sum, Kant's schema-producing imagination, that "hidden art in the depth of the human soul" (B 181), does the ancient work of bringing sense and thought together, but it does so in a new way, which is both newly complex and newly explicit. A new element is the location of space and time within the subject's sensibility. A future-laden effect of this relocation is that the imagination becomes intimately involved with time, the inner sense *par excellence*. A more general discovery, to which Kant himself points as a thought no psychologist has ever had before, is that perception, the first structuring of sensation, has imagination as a necessary ingredient (A 120 n). It will certainly dominate psychology in the future.

Kant's transcendental imagination is too deep to be easily recognizable as imagination in any ordinary sense (Schaper 1971). Goethe, having made a stab at studying the first *Critique*, came away with the notion that, since imagination is not listed with the three cognitive powers of sensibility, understanding, and reason, it is absent from the *Critique* (*Letter to the Grand Duchess Maria Paulowna* 1817). Of course it is not absent but is located deep beneath the other powers as their common root. For it is the aim of the critical enterprise to ground knowledge in the appropriate faculties, and the power of the imagination is the ground of this grounding.

★ ★ ★

As is generally the case with great works, Kant's critical discoveries had not only significant long-term effects, but a spate of early derivatives. A voluminous example is an *Essay on the Imagination* by Johann Maass (1797), which combines the Kantian distinction between concepts and intuitions with an attempt—no more successful than those of subsequent associationists—to assign to the imagination a certain original activity of its own and to formulate its specific principles in terms of the basic laws of association.

E. Fichte: The Ego's World-Producing Power

In Fichte's perfect idealism, the transcendental imagination reaches its ultimate range and function. His idealism is perfect insofar as the necessity of all that is and is known is meant to be deduced from one fundamental principle, which is itself a subject, an ego. It is not, of course, an individual phenomenal self but a universal activity, not a substance but Life itself, out of which individual selves are then differentiated. This universal ego is transcendental because it is beyond and before experience. The imagination is an ultimate power insofar as it is simply the ego's ability to produce for itself a non-I, a world.

The philosopher uncovers this ego by an intellectual intuition, a transcendental reflection yielding the fundamental proposition from which all else is deduced. It is this: The ego posits itself as being.

Now we are aware of things other than ourselves which confront us. More particularly, we distinguish between mental representations (*Vorstellungen*), which are before us in individual consciousnesses, and independent things, which are given to us collectively as nature. It therefore becomes a practical necessity of the deduction to account for this opposing, confronting other, this given nature, which appears to the individual, and to do so in terms of the originating subject, the universal ego.

Thus a non-ego is posited. The absolute original ego produces a non-ego, which, while opposing the former as a given world, is yet the ego's very own. (Of course, although this development is discovered by individual reflection, the deductive moment precedes individual consciousness). Both the non-ego and the ego are indeterminate and unlimited. Just as the ego is mere undifferentiated subjectivity, it posits the non-ego as mere undifferentiated objectivity. The two then delimit each other reciprocally. But they do so only partially, thereby revealing that both must be divisible. Thus a third proposition is deduced: that within the ego there is both a divisible ego and a divisible non-ego.

The ego's power to project the non-ego, to make for itself a world, is called "the power of the productive imagination." It is, of course, a preconscious or transcendental power.

Generally, the more grandiose the position assigned to the imagination within a system, the less interesting are its functions as a psychic power, since all its features are systematically predetermined. Consequently I shall treat the Fichtean imagination very succinctly, though it is a large and deep subject within its system (Inciarte 1970).

The account so far given derives mostly from the *Grundlage* or *Fundamental Basis of the Whole Doctrine of Knowledge* (1794). It gives the idealistic development from a Kantian point of departure. Its main theme is the transcendental imagination (Copleston 1963, Hohler 1982). Here is its summary delineation of the "imaginative power":

> This exchange of the ego in and with itself, wherein it posits itself as finite and infinite at once—an exchange which stands, as it were, in an opposition with itself and reproduces itself by the ego's attempt to unite the ununifiable, trying now to absorb [*aufnehmen*] the infinite in the form of the finite, and again, having been rebuffed, to posit this infinite outside that form, and in that very moment again trying to absorb it in the form of the finite—that is the capability [*Vermögen*] of the power of the imagination. [II 4]

What follows comes from a sequel, the *Grundriss*, or *Foundational Sketch of What Is Peculiar to the Doctrine of Knowledge* (1796). It deals with the fact introduced above, that we distinguish between representation and object. The ego spontaneously limits its own imaginative activity and posits itself as passive. Thus it becomes a sensing ego. But this state in turn becomes active and turns sensation into an object. The ego now becomes intuitive. With intuition arise representational images.

To make himself clear, Fichte introduces the example of an object, that is, a delimited part of the non-ego with differentiated characteristics. In a first intuition the ego is "lost in its object." It then reflects upon itself. (Such reflection is taken as an unimpugnably basic activity of the ego.) It finds itself, and in doing so differentiates itself from the object as, conversely, the object differentiates itself from the ego. But in this object everything is as yet commingled. Again the ego reflects on the individual characteristics of the object, its figure, size, and color. In each such reflection the ego is doubtful and unsettled, and so it hypothesizes arbitrary schemata of figure, size, and color. These then become increasingly determinate and precise through observation.

> Through this passage of an indeterminate product of the free power of imagination to its total determination in one and the same act, that which occurs in my consciousness becomes an image [*Bild*] and is posited as image. It becomes *my* product because I must posit it through absolute self-activity. [3]

When the ego posits this image as its product it must, of necessity, oppose something which is not its product. It must be something not merely determinable but already completely determined without any cooperation on the part of the ego. This is the actual thing that then guides the ego in its sketch of the image. Thus the transcendental imagination, having been first responsible for the production of the general, indeterminate non-ego, now re-produces the image of a determinate external thing while simultaneously shaping that thing.

As a condition, or better, a concomitant, of its production of determinate objects, the imagination is also responsible for space and time.

Space is simply the common region within which objects become distinct by excluding one another. The Fichtean imagination is, as Sallis puts it, "the power of spacing." It delimits a space of opposition:

> Imagination hovers in-between opposites so as to hold together the finite and the infinite, so as to hold together relation to a not-I and absolute self-positing. Imagination is the power of spacing those oppositions that can be neither dissolved nor eliminated from theoretical knowledge. Imagination is the spacing of truth. [1987, 64]

Physical space is only the determinate version of the speculative space delineated by Sallis, the room separating the differentiated extrusions of the productive imagination.

The production of time by the power of the imagination is "perhaps the most difficult but unquestionably the most important" part of the doctrine of knowledge. Whence comes the duration of moments? It arises when there is "an activity and *something which resists* it." (Fichte's term *das Widerstehende* means something that both resists and opposes what it confronts.) There must be a capability for unifying this contradiction (*das Widersprechende*). Again it is the power of imagination, which by hovering between opposing (*entgegengesetzten*) directions, originates temporal duration in the intuition (*Lectures on Logic and Metaphysics*, posthumous). What this means, roughly, is that the ego intuits the manifold aspects of the not-ego, the confronting world, while itself remaining in one and the same individual state, in one moment. Time arises, as it were, between this identity of the ego and the variety of its world, when the imagination synthesizes the one consciousness and its many intuitions. To say this is one thing, to grasp it another. The general intention, however, is clear. It is to derive time as the conjunction of the persistently identical ego and its ever-different world.

Perhaps no other system has ever seemed, particularly to its own author, to require so many new circumscriptions and approaches. Since Fichte's transcendental imagination is unusually inextricable from the whole system, any brief account must come to an arbitrary halt. Let me end by pointing out that the poets of his own time were more receptive to the notion of a world-producing imagination than were subsequent philosophers.

★ ★ ★

Two addenda: First, I shall present Schelling's theory of the divine creative imagination, which would fit in here chronologically, with that of Ibn Arabi in Part Six (Ch. I B). Second, I should not pass over Schopenhauer's *The World as Will and Representation* (1819) without a word. As the title shows, the book proposes an idealism in which the human being is presented as driven from within by a noumenal will and as confronting on the outside a phenomenal world. Its opening sentence is: "The world is my representation." Insofar as the power of internal sensory representation is the imagination, this proposition might be said to put the imagination at the center of the system, the more so because aesthetic contemplation plays a central role. The objects of this contemplation are the ideas, the natural species which are the archetypes of the visible world. In these the will "objectifies" itself most immediately, and this objectification is said to be the salvation from an enslavement to its incessant striving. Since these very ideas are imaged in the visual and verbal arts, and since the genius both to intuit and to express them in such works is exalted by Schopenhauer, the imagination might be said to be pivotal for him. However, he scarcely uses the word, perhaps because it has too much of a personal, individual connotation in a teaching whose end it is to overcome ego-centered striving.

F. Hegel: The Representational Stage of Spirit

Hegel's account of recollection, of the reproductive, associative, and productive imagination, and of memory occurs in the *Philosophy of Mind* (1830, paras. 451–64). It contains no new conceptions or terms. What makes it invaluable, particularly as a final conspectus of the imagination in systematic contexts, is that he treats these mental activities as flowing from one another, as phases in the development of the mind. They are not, of course, individual temporal stages but rather the logical self-realization of the Spirit, which proceeds dialectically, by the movements of reversal and return inherent in conceptual thought.

In the Hegelian system the imagination occurs, as always, in the middle— in fact in the middle of the middle of the stage called "mind." Mind or spirit (*Geist*) is here employed in a narrow sense. Spirit in the global sense used above is the divine Idea, the logical plan which reveals itself in the world's history. Mind in the more local sense appears as the first moment in the last large logical stage of the Idea. Here, having "gone outside itself" into external nature, it has returned within itself to become "subjective spirit." The spirit thus returned to itself is at first a dimly semiconscious being of sensation. Then it develops in turn consciousness, self-consciousness, and reason. Finally, in its last stage, it becomes fully subjective as intelligent theoretical mind. This is the point where the imagination appears.

Subjective Spirit, the inward mind, the first part of the triad of the Spirit, is then followed by Objective Spirit, the mind's realization in external worldly institutions. The triad culminates in Absolute Spirit, in which the inside and the outside are reconciled when the mind recognizes that all that is external is also its own.

So much for the systematic position of theoretical mind, which is the stage of imagination and whose study Hegel calls "psychology." The first phase of theoretical mind is "intuition." Here intuition is a low, not a high philosophical mode. It means about what it does in current language: having immediate and ungrounded feelings and insights. When intuition frees itself from outward reference and recognizes its intuitions as its own, it goes into the phase of "representation" (Stace 1923, 365, n. 1).

Representation is thus intuition made inward. Hegel calls this moment in the development *Erinnerung*, which ordinarily means "recollection," but literally "inwardization." In recollecting, intuition locates the content of its feeling in its own inwardness, its own inner time and space. The result is an inner picture. Hence mental images arise from the inward acknowledgement and appropriation of intuition.

But these pictures are transient. In particular, having lost their position in external time and space, they become indeterminate. In their indeterminacy they pass into the "dark mine-shaft" of the intelligence. There they exist virtually or potentially. Here the intelligence is an inward, unconscious, dark pit in which an infinite world of representations is stored in implicit form, devoid of distinctness, generalized. Hegel remarks that those who search for material loci of image-storage in the brain do not understand what potentiality is. One might well say that the unwillingness to accept so occult a notion is one motive that drives current cognitive science.

Hegel now considers the arrival of a new external intuition or sense impression. This fresh impression is held briefly and then subsumed under the generalized image (*Bild*) which intelligence already harbors and recognizes as its own. In turn the impression validates the inner image. This synthesis of mental image and inner, validated existence is "representation" proper. It occurs when inner pictures are once more remembered determinately enough to stand before the intelligence. Here Hegel clearly anticipates the distinction between short- and long-term memory, which is a central discovery of experimental psychology (Part Two, Ch. III A).

When the intelligence is active in this way it is called, first, the "reproductive power of the imagination." Its voluntary result is the emergence of pictures from the inwardness of the ego to stand before the intelligence. At first these pictures preserve something of their original temporal and spatial connection. At this point Hegel presents a critique of the spurious laws of associationism, for these loose and lawless associations are soon dissolved. The second, associative, imagination does not so much associate as subsume individual intuitions under those it had already made inward, by finding common features. It makes "concrete universals," a term of importance in poetics. It dissolves the empirical connections and substitutes its own. In particular it links intuitions in subjective ways and touches them with passion and feeling.

The inwardness of the reproductive imagination is that of a concrete and determinate subject. Here the intelligence works with a sort of subjective interest. It freely combines and subsumes its supply of images in its own peculiar ways. At this point arises the third imaginative activity, the "productive imagination" or "phantasy," which takes on in turn a symbolizing, an allegorizing, and a poetizing function. Its more or less concretely individual formations are syntheses of a subjective content with fresh adventitious intuitions.

In the phase of phantasy, intelligence has gone so far in self-intuition as to give an image-existence to a content originating with itself. At first this self-intuition is purely subjective. This is clearly the state of mere internal imagining. The next dialectical movement is to turn this internal formation into something that exists externally, namely a sign.

The sign-making phantasy is the "center in which the general and the existent, the own and the adventitious, the inner and the outer, are completely formed into one" (457). In this phase, phantasy is already Reason. Yet its content is, as such, unmeaning, since it still has adventitious shapes.

The phantasy's sign-making activity consists in giving its self-originated pictures external existence, that is to say, in expressing them. But the point about the real intuitable expressions is that in various degrees of freedom they represent not only what they resemble but also a meaning, an "alien soul" that has been injected into them by the subjective intelligence. Symbols, allegories, and figures of poetry are less free than phantastic products because their form is constrained by their meaning. The sign proper, on the other hand, need have no intuitive relation to its meaning at all. It is phantasy's most untrammeled, highest, and final product.

In the sign, the phantasy has produced an external intuition which represents something else than itself. An uttered vocal sign is a name. When it is made inward and used in place of an image, memory proper becomes possible. For Hegel, then, the term "memory" applies strictly to verbal memory. The possibility of internally "re-cognizing" the thing in a word, which is the possibility of language, leads to thinking. Thinking, in turn, determines the mind, bringing about willing and free choice. Here culminates and closes the development of the "theoretical mind," whose pivot point is the representational sign-making phantasy.

Such is the exposition of the imagination as a psychological moment within the system of the Spirit. Sallis (1987), who shows how truly Hegel has recapitulated the moments of the imagination established by Aristotle (and elaborated, one should add, by the tradition), intimates that he has failed, for all his dialectical pains, to reabsorb them into Reason without remainder. Something of that dark pit whence the imagination sets out, that place of absence and withdrawal, clings to phantasy even up to the rationalized end (ch. V).

Perhaps this notion of imaginative recalcitrance was not so alien to Hegel. For there is an earlier, propaedeutic activity—earlier both in date of discovery and in dialectic. It is made explicit in the final pages of the *Phenomenology of the Spirit* (1807) and convincingly brought forward by Verene (1985). Spirit, Hegel says, comes to know itself from two sides. Conceptually, it gains self-knowledge through a "science of the *coming into appearance of knowing*," that is, phenomenology. Historically, it appears to itself as a "gallery of pictures," imaging the "languid movement and succession of spirits." This wealth of spiritual riches is appropriated by the Spirit in conceptually grasped history, which is the recollection or "inwardization"—*Er-Innerung* (Hegel's hyphenation)—of that picture gallery. *Erinnerung* is, of course, the very word used as a narrower intra-systematic term for imaginative recollection. This "inwardization" reverses the exteriorization (*Entäusserung*) or alienation that the Spirit has undergone in space and time. The coming to self-knowledge of the Spirit is thus a path of formation (*Bildung*) through images (*Bilder*).

Image-recollection is not, in Verene's explication, a merely edifying loose notion. To be sure, lecture notes immediately preceding the publication of the *Phenomenology* show how passionately vivid was Hegel's sense of memory as the night of inner life shot through with sudden phantasmagorical presentations. But recollection is more than an imaginative experience. It is the strictly necessary access to speculative knowing, the kind of knowing Hegel regards as Life itself. Speculation begins when a representation or memory-image, a renewed past, is put before cognition. Conceptual thought, using this image as the basis of its own speculative motion, transforms its pictorial nature: It seizes the image, elevates it, preserves it, abolishes it, and indeed does everything included in the meaning of Hegel's untranslatable verb *aufheben*, which characterizes conceptual motion. The restless negativity, the ultimate desperate effort of this process, consists in the attempt to draw the concept from the picture in such a way as to rescue both from dumb togetherness while preventing their arid isolation. There is no assessment of the imaginative function in the work of knowing that is as grand and yet as just.

★ ★ ★

Here ends an epoch, the epoch of the grand modern systems centered on the imagination. For two-thirds of a century it will now go into philosophic eclipse. There is a complex of possible reasons. Interest in systematic epistemology had worn out. The Romantics had made the imagination the particular province of poetry. Similarly, the investigations of descriptive psychology, especially of the associationist school, had displaced philosophical theories about the imagination. The temporal/moral, rather than the spatial/representational, aspects of the soul were now the focus of interest. These are the circumstantial or historical reasons. But when all is said and done, the single most effective cause for the eclipse of the imagination was surely that no philosophical writer of stature found anything compelling to say about it. It is always an enigma whether thoughts run out because attention has waned, or attention wanes because no one has a galvanizing idea. At any rate, with the arrival of the twentieth century the old problems were invigorated by fresh solutions.

Yet four writers, though they treat the imagination only incidentally or extra-systematically, are such original harbingers of the themes that preoccupy this study that brief accounts are in order: Kierkegaard, Peirce, Meinong, and Bergson.

G. Kierkegaard: The Infinitized or Fantastical Imagination

In *The Sickness unto Death* (1849), writing on the spiritual sickness called Despair (I iii a), Kierkegaard characterizes the imagination as the faculty *instar omnium*, "worth all the others," since it is the "medium of the process of infinitizing." "Infinitizing" is the movement of the self away from its finite particularity toward God. The "despair" comes from the loss of self that results if this movement is not at the same time also a process in which the self finds its concretely individual human existence. The imagination is the faculty that can make this movement, since it is the power of self-conscious feeling, of knowledge, of will, of having a "counterfeit present-ment of the self," and of reflection in general. Its intensity is "the possibility of the intensity of the self." The Kierkegaardian imagination is the faculty of the self, simply. Never has this power been more subjectively conceived.

Now when the imagination goes fantastic the self becomes more and more volatized. Its feeling becomes an inhuman production which squan-ders the self. Its will, instead of being concrete and addressed to daily tasks, becomes abstract and remote. The religiously fantastic self has an isolated, lost, emptily inebriated existence. Anyone for whom the "God-relationship infinitizes" cannot endure even before God, not to speak of life, since, though he may look normal, he lacks a self.

This theological understanding of fantasy forms a serious counterpart to the more light-minded "infinitizing" of the imagination in the literary genre of fantasy, which is considered in Part Four (Ch. IV B).

H. Peirce: The Denial of Mental Images

Next there is a writer who must be mentioned because he so startlingly anticipates a claim about mental imagery which becomes dominant in the twentieth century. The writer is Peirce, and the claim is that there are no mental images. The empirical psychologists of the Würzburg school dis-covered imageless states of thought early in the century, and the "proposi-tionalists" of present-day cognitive studies try to show that the presence of imagery is an unnecessary hypothesis. But Peirce had already given a logical argument against mental images in an early essay (1868).

We have, he says, no power of introspection, no power of immediate intuition, and no power of originating cognitions, since every cognition is logically determined by preceding ones. Consequently, "every sort of modification of consciousness is an inference." Inferences, however, are general, while images are absolutely singular. "Singular" for Peirce means completely determinate, such that for every possible character either it or its negative must be true of a given singular object. Thus Locke's notion of a general image, such as the triangle that is neither scalene nor isosceles nor equilateral, should be considered a logical scandal discreditable to the "friends of images."

Now Peirce invites his readers to test by introspection whether we have any mental images about whose visible characteristics we can answer all possible questions. We surely have no such images. What we do have is a *"consciousness that we could recognize"* the color or shape in question if we saw its real counterpart again. Therefore the logical nature of imagery is in conflict with our experience. So we cannot be having images. Since we have no power of introspective intuition and cannot directly distinguish one internal mode from another, there is an easy explanation of our thinking that we have had an image-singular. It is that what we have taken for a picture was really a construction by the understanding from attenuated data.

This negation of the mental image is, to be sure, not entirely novel in the history of the imagination. Ockham, for example, had claimed that when one imagines a man one has seen, "this mental picturing is an act of thinking (*illa fictio est intellectio*) which refers to all men" (c. 1324). But then, Ockham is in certain respects as starkly modern as Peirce.

Indeed, Peirce argues, not even actual perception involves images. Vision does not involve seeing pictures. For if to see were to have images like pictures, we would be in possession of representations loaded with infinite information—a most uneconomical and idle hypothesis. Actual seeing is not an agglomeration of infinite detail but an impression of general features. This theory of perception has a contemporary ring.

Peirce's argument against images stands or falls with the notion, taken from Hume (*Treatise* I i 7), that images are determinate particulars. Later in this book the indeterminacy of mental images will be variously defended. They are not, it will be argued, either determinate or infinitely determinable, any more than they are hopelessly vague. Indeed, if the imagined schematic triangle is conceived in the manner of a cognitive process (Part Two)—not as a photographic still, but as a series of mental scanning events—its indeterminacy becomes quite intelligible (Langacker 1987, 137). Such a scanning chain might comprise three elements: a simple scanning of the three legs, (much like Kant's synthetic apprehension), a length comparison, and finally a judging of the shape as a whole. If this sequence were terminated at the first step, the resulting mental image would be precisely that of an indeterminate triangle. Furthermore, the possibility and reliability of immediate introspection will become a major issue of cognitive science in the twentieth century (Part Two, Ch. II A). Yet Peirce's thesis is admirably prescient.

I. Dilthey: Imagination as Lived Experience

Dilthey's *Imagination of the Poet* (1887) includes a theory of the imagination which casts loose both from the Kantian synthetic faculty and from Humean associationism. Although his views are proposed in a much less strenuously radical vein, he anticipates approaches of two major related theories of the twentieth century, those of Phenomenology and Existential-ism (Ch. IV A)—Dilthey was read and respected by both Husserl and Heidegger. The anticipations relevant here are Dilthey's non-naturalistic attention to the phenomena of psychic life, and his interest in the categories of a human existence as ungrounded in transcendental being.

The imagination is, then, for him not the transcendental faculty it was for Kant, but a structural configuration of traits that are especially highly developed in poets. The traits include intensity of sensory impressions and vivid clarity of memory; one kind of poet even has the ability to project memory-images into space. Further traits are intensity of passion, with the complementary ability to charge images with life and to saturate them with feeling, and, finally, the ability to unfold images freely beyond the bound-aries of reality. These image-traits are brought together in the concept of the "lived experience" (*Erlebnis*) that arises from a centrally informing feeling in which the whole temperament (*Gemüt*) cooperates. Dilthey distinguishes two types of poetic experience, the "objective," best exempli-fied by Shakespeare, who projects himself into external figures like an actor into a role, and the "subjective," as seen in Rousseau, who turns everything inward. In Goethe the types are said to have been balanced.

In contrast to the Kantian faculty, this complex of traits does not synthesize or unify the sensory manifold, but rather it articulates ordinary given experience into significant types (Makkreel 1975).

In contrast to the usual Humean laws of association, Dilthey enunciates three laws of transformation: First, images are transformed by exclusion, when elements are eliminated or drop out. Second, they expand or shrink in the intensity of their sensory effect under the impact of feeling. Third, they metamorphose structurally; if the previous laws had established a "nucleus" or core image, this is now penetrated and filled out by new memory material. These laws are meant to show not how images associate but how they achieve liveliness and life. For everywhere Dilthey is con-cerned to remain concrete, not allowing his psychological analysis to outstrip the lived experience of the human being.

J. Meinong: The Intuitivity of Imaginative Representations

Meinong, who is best known for his defense of nonexistent objects—which is taken up in Part Three under the logic of images—also wrote an essay on what might be called the philosophical psychology of imaginative representations ("Phantasie-Vorstellung" 1889). His aim is to establish a working definition of the productive imagination as opposed to memory and to explicate its terms. This definition will be:

Imagination is the capacity for a representational production which has intuitivity.

A capacity, as opposed to an act, is determined by its correlate, that for which it is the capacity, in this case the intuitive representations and their production. Meinong begins by showing that the two traditional laws of the reproductive or memorial imagination are applicable in expanded form also to imaginative imagination (*phantasia*). The first law, the law of image-matter, is that "nothing is in the imagination which was not previously in perception." Meinong argues that the productive imagination uses remembered perceptions, but in new complexes. The second law, of image-connection, is the association of images close in time or similar in content. Associative connections hold even in imaginatively new representations because they have an element of indeterminacy which allows some spontaneity.

But the main and original point is the attempt to find formal criteria for the "intuitivity" that is the specific difference of imaginal representations. Intuitivity (*Anschaulichkeit*) is to be distinguished from intuition (*Anschauung*), which is merely perceptual representation. The former is the peculiar quality of *visualizability* which images have. It will come to play a great role in the representational debate in atomic physics (Part Five, Ch. II B).

Meinong begins to examine what kinds of language and knowledge are visualizable, and how their translation into imagery takes place. (This is a main topic of Part Four.) For example, indirect or relational knowledge tends, he says, to be less visualizable than object-cognition. These observations prefigure the word/image experiments of cognitive psychology (Part Two, Ch. III A).

However, the main criterion of intuitivity is negative:

A complex representation has intuitivity insofar as it is in every direction free from incompatibility.

The logical inverse of this important rule, namely that no image is capable of self-contradiction, will also be discussed under the logic of images (Part Three, Ch. I B).

Finally, the two laws of the imagination are connected with intuitivity. The first law is *ipso facto* applicable insofar as imagination uses visual perception. The second is empirically corroborated, insofar as words and concepts that arise associatively tend to be visualizable, an observation again experimentally confirmed (Part Two, Ch. III A).

What distinguishes Meinong's essay is the pioneering attempt to analyze the tricky problems of the imaging-process and of image-constitution finely enough to make possible the kinds of close conceptual and experimental investigations that will be undertaken in the next century.

K. Bergson: The Image as Space-Time Intercept

The source for the following account is Bergson's *Matter and Memory* (1896). The most fascinating particular defect in this flawed yet admirable book is, as will become plain, that it is not about the imagination at all, though it is about images. Its general defect is its weakness in grounding its notions clearly and systematically. There is too little exposition of the whys and hows. Its virtue, the virtue of its vices, comes from Bergson's passionate desire to keep philosophy close to life, and from his fresh, not to say inchoate, presentation of old problems.

Images in two senses, which are never successfully merged, are the subject of this book. For images turn out to be crucial to memory as well as to matter, and it is Bergson's particular purpose here to solve the mind/body problem. He will fail to do so precisely because he lacks a theory of the imagination.

Images in the bodily sense comprise all reality whatsoever, all perceptible things. Bergson is not saying that perception is perception of mere appearances that image actual beings behind them. On the contrary, matter understood as the assemblage of images is all there is. Nor are these things images insofar as they are perceived and imaged in the perceiving consciousness. On the contrary, they remain fully images even when they are unperceived. Another way to put this is that perception takes place *at* the image in such a way that being and being perceived is not a difference in the nature of things but only a difference of degree. Consciousness has no correlate; it is simply a character of all reality, which is sometimes actual, sometimes virtual.

If the justification for these somewhat obscure claims is insufficient, there is something compelling about their intention: It is to carry perception into the world and to establish a community of mutual consciousness among any and all things.

Now among these many image-bodies there is one that is privileged—my own body. Here is the locus where certain images are cut out from all the others. These do indeed become re-presentations, though without being at all qualitatively modified. This pure perception is the taking-in of world-images, which are selected, stopped, and demarcated so as to fix their becoming. How such perception is accomplished is unclear. Here it is that we first miss an account of the faculty of the imagination. Sartre's critical version of Bergsonian perception is this: It is as if a person looked through a spy-glass at a landscape and then endeavored to carry off the glass with the vignette within it. At any rate, perception additionally involves spreading a kind of spatial web beneath the concrete indivisible diversity of image-things. Thus arises homogeneous, divisible space, a Kantian shade. The images so fixed are completely preserved with place, date, and circumstance.

Here memory comes in, or rather two memories. One is a sensorimotor memory, the learned habits of the body (which will become so important to Piaget's mimetic theory of cognition—Part Two, Ch. IV B). This memory asserts itself in the unself-conscious action of the present.

The other "pure" memory is temporal. It is pure duration, pure past. It is an indivisible unity of inner motion. Without going very far into this central Bergsonian notion, one can say only that pure memory is the temporality of the images, but it is not the images themselves. Remembering and picturing are not the same; memory is not imagination. For images can be both dateless and unconscious. (Here Bergson prefigures the coming interest in the unconscious.)

This pure memory is in fact spirit, *esprit*, usually translated as "mind." It is utterly different from matter. Consequently the memory-images it somehow stores cannot have a location in the brain. Bergson cites psychological studies of aphasia in order to show that memory is not destroyed by localized lesions; this is still a live question. The brain merely acts as inhibitor, allowing only memories relevant to action to enter bodily perception. For neither spatial bodily perception nor temporal spirit-memory ever exists in pure isolation. It is rather that the latter impregnates the former to give it depth and meaning. How?

Before coming to this crux of his theory of images, it should be said that Bergson is now able to make a fairly original philosophical point against associationism, the dominant theory of the nineteenth century, which had begun to come under serious psychological attack in the eighties. His motive is to preserve the spontaneity and fluidity of mental life. His argument is directed against the "capital error" of Humean associationism, namely its juxtaposition of atomic fixed psychic states that have no cognitive complexity or life. For when images and memories are understood as weak perceptions that are mechanically associated, the process has been absorbed into the product, and the fluidity of mental life is lost. There is therefore no way of explaining the transformation of perception into image and back again that Bergson posits.

Does Bergson do better? How does memory return its images to perception so as to shape action? The representational image is, so to speak, the space-time intercept, and stands at the intersection of body and mind. Here is the origin of actual consciousness, big with impending future action. Bergson illustrates this relation in a diagram (184, fig. 3) anticipating those in Husserl's studies of internal time-consciousness. The space line represents the world of objective things, which are assumed to exist indefinitely in their juxtapositions. The time line, orthogonal to it, stands for the unconscious memory images preserved for recollection. The origin expresses the crossing of the mind with matter, the point where images enter perception and conscious action takes place.

So the question concerning the recollection of representational images is identical with the mind/body issue. The clue to Bergson's solution is in the opposition of "extensity" to "extension." The former is precisely the indivisible diversity of the image-world. The latter is the safety net of the aforementioned homogeneous divisible space, which is strung beneath the manifold in perception. Embedded deep in memory, the world-images preserve their fluid indivisible extensity. As an image evolves out of memory into actuality, it assumes more and more the form of extensional spatiality. In the essay "On Intellectual Effort" in *Mind-Energy* (1919), Bergson will speak of a "dynamic schema" which guides the externalization of images. "It contains in a state of reciprocal implication what the image is to develop as parts external to each other."

The intention is to bring world-image and representational image back together for the sake of human action. However, the problem that then requires solution is, as ever, that of mental spatiality. Bergson provides what is surely a non-solution: The world-images in their extensity are first somehow imported into the spirit, and then again somehow metamorphose into spatial images as they are recollected into the extensional spread of consciousness in actuality, that is, externalized. Nothing is gained here but such problematic illumination as comes from an energetic meditation on a deep problem.

Consequently it is not surprising that Bergson's views exercised little concrete influence. He was original in too private a sense. Yet Sartre, in reviewing previous image theories (*Imagination* 1936), gives more room to a sharp though pertinent criticism of Bergson and the spirit he engendered than to any other author. He particularly scores Bergson's failure after all to overcome the prevailing associationism of the psychologists, understood as the doctrine that images interact. For Bergson, quite like any Humean before him, treats images as things, even as actively developing beings. Thus Bergson's theory of images, the last of the nineteenth century, draws to itself and focuses the dissatisfactions that then bring about the peripety of the twentieth: the revolt against the mental image and the vigorous assertions of its non-being.

Bibliography

Bergson, Henri [1859–1941]. 1896. *Matter and Memory*. Translated by Nancy M. Paul and W. Scott Palmer. London: George Allen and Unwin (1911).

Berkeley, George. 1710. *A Treatise Concerning the Principles of Human Knowledge* (paras. 25–30).

Brann, Eva. 1976. "An Appreciation of Kant's *Critique of Pure Reason*: An Introduction for Students." In *Essays in Honor of Jacob Klein*. Annapolis: St. John's College Press.

———. 1979. "What is a Body in Kant's System?" *Independent Journal of Philosophy* 3:91–100.

Caton, Hiram. 1973. *The Origin of Subjectivity: An Essay on Descartes*. New Haven: Yale University Press.

Copleston, Frederick, S.J. 1963. *A History of Philosophy* 7, 1, *Modern Philosophy*, Part. I, *Fichte to Hegel*. Garden City, N.J.: Doubleday and Co. (1965).

Cowley, Fraser. 1968. *A Critique of British Empiricism*. London: Macmillan.

Crawford, Donald. 1982. "Kant's Theory of Creative Imagination." In *Essays in Kant's Aesthetics*, edited by Ted Cohen and Paul Guyer. Chicago: The University of Chicago Press.

Descartes, René [1596–1650]. 1628. *Rules for the Direction of the Mind* (Rules XII, XIV, and XVI). In *The Philosophical Works of Descartes*, translated by Elizabeth S. Haldane and G.R.T. Ross (1911). New York: Dover Publications (1955).

———. 1641. *Meditations on First Philosophy* (Meditations II and VI). In *The Philosophical Works of Descartes*, translated by Elizabeth S. Haldane and G.R.T. Ross (1911). New York: Dover Publications (1955).

Dilthey, Wilhelm [1833–1911]. 1887. *Die Einbildungskraft des Dichters: Bausteine für eine Poetik* [The Imagination of the Poet: Elements for a Poetics]. *Gesammelte Schriften* VI, 3d ed. Edited by Georg Misch. Göttingen: Vandenhoeck und Ruprecht (1958).

Fichte, J. G. [1762–1814]. 1794. *Grundlage der gesamten Wissenschaftslehre* [Foundational Basis of the Whole Doctrine of Knowledge]. In *Werke* I (1792–1795), edited by Fritz Medicus. Leipzig: Felix Meiner Verlag (1908).

————. 1796. *Grundriss des Eigentümlichen der Wissenschaftslehre* [Foundational Sketch of What Is Peculiar to the Doctrine of Knowledge]. In *Werke* I (1792–1795), edited by Fritz Medicus. Leipzig: Felix Meiner Verlag (1908).

Fóti, Véronique M. 1986. "The Cartesian Imagination." *Philosophy and Phenomenological Research* 46:631–642.

Gaukroger, Stephen. 1980. "Descartes' Project for a Mathematical Physics." In *Descartes: Philosophy, Mathematics and Physics*, edited by Stephen Gaukroger. Totowa, N.J.: Barnes and Noble Books.

Gilson, Etienne. 1951. *Etudes sur le rôle de la pensée médiévale dans la formation du système cartésien*. Paris: Librairie Philosophique J. Vrin.

Hegel, G.W.F. [1770–1831]. 1830. *Philosophy of Mind*, Being Part Three of *The Encyclopaedia of the Philosophical Sciences* (para. 455). Translated by William Wallace. Oxford: Clarendon Press (1971).

Hobbes, Thomas [1588–1679]. 1651. *Leviathan, or the Matter Forme and Power of a Commonwealth Ecclesiastical and Civil* (I 2–3).

Hohler, T. P. 1982. *Imagination and Reflection: Intersubjectivity: Fichte's Grundlage of 1794*. The Hague: Martinus Nijhoff.

Hume, David [1711–1776]. 1739. *A Treatise of Human Nature* (I i 1–4, ii 1–2, iv; III 5–6; IV 7). Edited by L. A. Selby-Bigge. Oxford: Clarendon Press (1888, 1960).

————. 1751. *An Enquiry Concerning Human Understanding* (II–III, V 2).

Inciarte, Fernando. 1970. *Transzendentale Einbildungskraft: Zu Fichte's Frühphilosphie im Zusammenhang des Transzendentalen Idealismus*. Bonn: H. Bouvier and Co.

Kant, Immanuel [1724–1804]. *Critique of Pure Reason* [A ed. 1781; B ed. 1786] (A 115–124, B 175–187).

————. 1790. *Critique of Judgment* (Intro; I para. 9; "General Remark").

————. 1798. *Anthropology from a Pragmatic Point of View* (paras. 28–37). Translated by Mary J. Gregor. The Hague: Martinus Nijhoff (1974).

Kierkegaard, Soren [1813–1855]. 1849. *The Sickness unto Death*. Edited by Walter Lowrie. Princeton: Princeton University Press (1954).

Klein, Jacob. 1936. "The Concept of Number in Descartes." In *Greek Mathematical Thought and the Origin of Algebra*, translated by Eva Brann. Cambridge: The MIT Press (1968).

Langacker, Ronald W. 1987. *Foundations of Cognitive Grammar* I, *Theoretical Prerequisites*. Stanford: Stanford University Press.

Leibniz, G. W. [1646–1716]. "Letter to Queen Sophia Charlotte of Prussia." In *Philosophical Papers and Letters* II, translated by Larry E. Loemker. Chicago: The University of Chicago Press (1956).

Locke, John [1632–1704]. 1694. *An Essay Concerning Human Understanding*, 2d ed. (I 1, II 1, 10). Edited by A. S. Pringle-Pattison. Oxford: Clarendon Press (1960).

Maass, Johann G. E. 1797. *Versuch über die Einbildungskraft.* Brussels: Aetas Kantiana (1969).

Macintosh, J. J. 1983. "Perception and Imagination in Descartes, Boyle and Hooke." *Canadian Journal of Philosophy* 13:327–352.

Makkreel, Rudolph A. 1975. *Dilthey: Philosopher of the Human Studies.* Princeton: Princeton University Press.

Meinong, Alexius [1853–1920]. 1889. "Phantasie-Vorstellung und Phantasie." In *Gesammelte Abhandlungen I: Abhandlungen zur Psychologie,* edited by his students. Leipzig: Johann A. Barth (1929).

Ockham, William [born c. 1280]. c. 1324. *Quodlibeta septem* (I Q.1). In *Philosophical Writings,* edited by Philotheus Boehner. New York: Nelson (1957).

Peirce, Charles S. [1839–1914]. 1868. "Some Consequences of Four Incapacities." In *Philosophical Writings of Peirce,* edited by Justus Buchler. New York: Dover Publications (1955).

Sallis, John. 1980. "Imagination." Chapter 6 in *The Gathering of Reason.* Athens, Ohio: Ohio University Press.

―――. 1987. *Spacings—of Reason and Imagination in Texts of Kant, Fichte, Hegel.* Chicago: The University of Chicago Press.

Schaper, Eva. 1971. "Kant on Imagination." *Philosophical Forum* 2:430–445.

Smith, Norman Kemp. 1952. *New Studies in the Philosophy of Descartes: Descartes as Pioneer.* London: Macmillan.

Sokolowski, Robert. 1968. "Fiction and Illusion in David Hume's Philosophy." *The Modern Schoolman* 45:189–225.

Stace, W. T. 1923. *The Philosophy of Hegel: A Systematic Exposition.* New York: Dover Publications (1955).

Urmson, J. O. 1967. "Memory and Imagination." *Mind* 76:83–91.

Verene, Donald P. 1985. *Hegel's Recollection: A Study of Images in the* Phenomenology of Spirit. Albany: State University of New York Press.

Wilbanks, Jan. 1968. *Hume's Theory of Imagination.* The Hague: Martinus Nijhoff.

Woods, M. 1983. "Kant's Transcendental Schematism." *Dialectica* 37:201–219.

Yolton, John W. 1984. "Hume on Imagination: A Magical Faculty." Chapter 9 in *Perceptual Acquaintance from Descartes to Reid.* Minneapolis: University of Minnesota Press.

Chapter IV

Twentieth-Century Writers (with Debates and Developments)

The imagination had become the province of psychologists. Early in this century, however, with the advent of Behaviorism, their interest lapsed. The psychologists had ceased to believe in the imagination just when the philosophers were investing new energy in it—precisely because they too doubted its actuality. Therefore the tone the latter set, maintained as the mainstream opinion into the present day, is therapeutic: the expurgation of an age-old mistake.

As we come up to developments that are close to us and therefore naturally present themselves less in terms of canonical texts and more in terms of movements and debates, I shall give up the strictly chronological review by authors and proceed according to the schools that have emerged, taking, however, each development longitudinally. The first of these in time of origin is Phenomenology (together with Existentialism) which is the most international of movements (A). Next comes Analysis and Philosophy of Mind, which is largely English-speaking (B). Somewhat later again appears Neoromanticism, whose chief locus is France (C). A small spate of descriptive essays on the human significance of the imagination, leaning slightly on the Phenomenological school, forms a fitting coda (D).

The two schools that come first, the serious philosophical contenders in matters of the imagination, take their departure from brief but pregnant passages of Husserl and Wittgenstein respectively. Deeply opposed in philosophical method and human significance though they are, they have a common target, namely Hume's theory of mental representations, and therefore their conclusions look oddly alike. What the Phenomenologists oppose is the notion of immanence, namely the fact that for Hume it is the image that is imagined and not simply the object. For the Analysts the objection is to the inwardness of the imaginative process, the fact that it is

119

hopelessly private. Neither school manages to give satisfactory positive accounts of the imagination, but both sharpen and subtilize the debate beyond anything else in the two millennia of the tradition.

The Neoromantics, on the other hand, have no interest in clear conceptions—indeed they have an animus against them. By means of eclectic Romanticism, a new Romanticism that is shot through with various theories of the twentieth century, they raise imagination and the image to an all-dominating status.

A. Phenomenology and Existentialism: The Attack on Immanence

Phenomenology is, among other things, a response to the takeover of psychology by science in the nineteenth century, which resulted in the study of the soul as a piece of nature. It is, to begin with, a method, based on introspection or "direct self-apprehension," for giving an account of the phenomena of consciousness. It is therefore in starkest contrast to the other twentieth-century school that is deeply interested in the imagination, the school that engages in the analysis of concepts through the observation of language in social use.

There are two levels of phenomenal description, of which only the first and lower enters into this discussion. It is the level of descriptive psychology, in which the types and forms of consciousness are examined in order to comprehend the being of the soul. The higher (and later) preoccupation is a universal, a transcendental philosophy. It intends, once again, to establish the *a priori* conditions of knowledge by articulating the nature of subjectivity, the ego, for the Cartesian purpose of turning philosophy into a certain science.

The point of departure of phenomenological psychology is the understanding that the world is, before anything else, an object of experience. But since human beings live in this world unreflectively, its psychical, experiential aspect is drowned out. Therefore a special reflection is necessary, a phenomenological device. It is a position called "bracketing" or "abstention" (Greek: *epochē*), by means of which this natural attitude toward the world, especially the implicit acceptance of the independent existence of objects, is suspended. Consequently the world becomes a phenomenon, an appearance for consciousness. In the very notion of bracketing a special function for the imagination is already implicit.

The fundamental insight of phenomenology is that consciousness is constitutionally intentional. This means that it is always directed towards objects that are immanent to it. To think or to imagine, is always to think or to imagine something, and that thing, as a thing thought or imagined, abides within, or is immanent in, consciousness. The object is imagined and is thus within; but that very circumstance leaves no room for an immanent representation such as an image. Therefore the immanence attacked is that of re-presentations, since in Phenomenology the relation of thinking or imagining to its object is immediate and not through an intervening mental picture or symbol.

(Husserl 1929, Heidegger 1925.)

Intentionality as the distinguishing mark of the mental as opposed to the physical realm was first developed by Brentano and described by him in 1874 as "a reference to a content, a direction upon an object. . . . " At first his followers failed to draw the anti-imagist conclusion. For example, Twardowski compares having ideas with the act of painting, making the mental content analogous to, say, a landscape painting. Later he recognized that if mental contents were really related to their object as a canvas is to its scenic subject, they would have to possess some of the object's physical properties. This fact contradicts an important insight concerning intentionality, namely that a mental content has to be entirely mental.

Existentialism enters the picture in this study really only insofar as Sartre, the author of the very first full-scale theory of the imagination, incorporated certain existentialist elements into his essentially phenomenological account. These elements are, as will be seen, possibility and nothingness. They derive from the existentialist teaching that a human being has no natural given essence but exists as a being of possibility. Such a being forms itself by staunchly facing its own finitude, delimited at one extreme by the ungroundedness of its genesis, and at the other by the nothingness of its fatal end.

0. Heidegger: Imagelessness. Although he is the leader of the Existentialist school, Heidegger cannot figure in an account of the imagination as a power of quasi-visual and spatial imagining, because, as far as I can tell, such imagining plays no role in his work. There are several reasons, only superficially diverse. One is his way of thinking, the mode of his openness to being, which is, in his own words, "image-poor and charmless" ("Logos" 1951). Others are his resistance to all philosophical forms of non-engaged, comtemplative viewing; his understanding of works of art as revealing deep truth rather than correctly representing originals; and his emphasis on futurity, a notoriously imageless time-phase (Part Six, Ch. II C). Finally, in the broadest terms, comes his understanding of the human being as at the root temporal rather than spatial. It is a mark of this understanding that Heidegger's chief work, *Being and Time*, makes no explicit mention of the imagination.

The most direct example of Heidegger's displacement of the imagination is his reinterpretation of the Kantian faculty, set out in *Kant and the Problem of Metaphysics* (1951). There was, recall, some question whether, of the two faces of the sensibility that the imagination brings together with thinking, space or time is the more fundamental. Heidegger regards the synthesis worked by the imagination as temporal in all its phases and the transcendental power of the imagination as essentially time-forming (Sherover 1971). In particular he claims that Kant accords priority to the power of the imagination for forming anticipatory or futural images (Kearney 1988). Moreover, in explicating the figurative synthesis of the transcendental imagination, he takes special pains to show that the picture (*Bild*) Kant says it produces is not an image (*Abbild*) but an "aspect," a first sensualization of thought (*Logik* 1925, 366). This is undoubtedly so. It is the very thing that makes the Kantian imagination productive rather than reproductive. Yet it is a revealing point for Heidegger to insist on. It shows his determination to take the imagination as a time-grounding, and therefore not a space-manifesting, power.

Consequently Husserl and Sartre alone will figure in the following account.

1. Husserl: Fancy as Unposited Presentification. Husserl is apparently yet one more in the tradition of writers whose words do not match his deeds in the affairs of the imagination. While he is the most devoted advocate of rational cognition—Phenomenology is the "self-reflection" specifically of cognitive life—in his method he in fact gives imagining a central place. Yet, again, he all but ignores its productive aspect. His seems to be one more case of what a commentator calls "denial-cum-acknowledgement" (Casey 1976b). Perhaps, though, the disavowal is mostly appearance, since he calls the imaginative modification of consciousness an experience "of the highest importance which occupies a position all by itself" (*Ideas,* 109). I begin by dwelling on the ambivalence, because it pervades Husserl's theory.

Four texts will be considered, bearing on three themes. The first theme is the argument against mental images as constituting the meanings of expressions and against mental images as objects (a). The second theme is the imagination as a kind of consciousness that is distinguished from perception by a "neutrality modification," in which objects are made to be present or are "presentified" in consciousness without being "posited," or asserted as real existents (b). The last theme is the methodological role that imagining as "free variation" plays in a central aim of Phenomenology, the discovery of essences (c).

(Citations for the four texts bearing on the three themes are all by paragraphs: a. *Logical Investigations* 1900, I, Inv. I 171–78; *Ideas* 1913, 42–43; b. *L.I.* II, Inv. V 39–40; *Phenomenology of Internal Time-Consciousness* 1904– 10, App. II; *Ideas* 1913, 90, 99, 109–14; *Experience and Judgment* 1930, 37– 42; c. *Ideas* 4, 23, 70, 100–101, 140; *E.J.* 87–88.)

a. In the *Logical Investigations* the argument is not against mental images insofar as they are immanent but insofar as they confer meanings on expression; that is, it is against a picture-theory of meaning such as was at one time also held by Russell (Part Three, Ch. I B). Here Husserl does not deny that images sometimes accompany thought and speech, but, like Frege, he points out that they are hopelessly unfixed and diverse. Indeed, for abstract expressions they become quite indeterminate. Furthermore, a kind of thinking takes place that remains unfulfilled by any intuition; one may think of "red" without having anything in mental view. In addition, mental images are not only unregimented, they are also evanescent, whereas meaning is persistent. Moreover, one can think absurd meanings but one cannot illustrate them. Husserl cites Noneuclidean illustrations of, for example, two straight lines enclosing a space. No one thinks that these fudged figures actually picture the meaning. They are aids to thought, not representations of meaning. (Such diagrams are considered in Part Five, Ch. II A). Husserl emphasizes that he is not advocating mere nominalism. There certainly is a sense-giving operation of consciousness, but it is not a picture.

Of course, Husserl does not think of mental images, whose existence he does not deny, as objects. Neither, for that matter, are external objects known to us through Humean impression-images; they are directly perceived. Nor again are external objects regarded as images of things-in-themselves. For the notion of intentionality proscribes immanent mental objects, and requires that objects be directly intended, but intended *as* transcendent, as beyond consciousness and therefore not as mental (*Ideas* 42–43). What then would be the point of positing them as image-like? It is the objects we are conscious of directly, not their simulacra.

b. Then what kind of modification of perception—the activity Husserl regards as the straightforward base-line consciousness—*is* the imagination or the "fancy" (as Husserl's *Phantasie* is often rendered)? To answer this question it is necessary briefly to introduce two terms of the trade: "intuition" and "noema."

Intuition is the operation through which consciousness finds the plenitude or fullness mentioned above. The "principle of principles" of Phenomenology is that intuition is a source of authority for knowledge (*Ideas* 24).

A thought can reach for what it means but can fail to find it, as when one cannot attach a face to a familiar name. Husserl calls this unfulfilled reaching a merely signifying act. Or the thought can attain what it means, so that something becomes present to it intuitively as a source of truth.

There are two sub-modes of intuition: "presentation" and "presentification" (*Gegenwärtigung, Vergegenwärtigung*). They are respectively responsible for what is given as present and what is made to be present—not *in* or *to* consciousness but *as* a consciousness. Presentification is a neologism, but so is the German noun which it renders literally. It is often translated as "representation," but nothing could be more misleading. There is no sense of reiteration, of copying or imaging in the German word. Both terms refer to "objectifying acts," acts in which the things themselves are reached. The first refers to perception, the second will be connected to imagination. The ability to make things present to itself is a fundamental constituent of consciousness.

(Levinas 1963.)

Noema is the being that is immanent in consciousness. It is the correlate of any of the various acts of consciousness. (Husserl calls the act itself "noesis," Aristotle's term for both sensory and intellectual intuition.) The intuition-noema is what is intended by intuitive noesis, but it is not meant to be a representation. It is emphatically not an immanent, psychic, thing standing for an external thing. In fact, it is not an independent notion at all but is relative to phenomenological reflection. It is the object intended insofar as we become aware of it as a phenomenon of consciousness. It is the ordinary natural object seen from the phenomenological, the "bracketed" view. It is therefore not an object but the experience of an object—a subtle, typically phenomenological distinction. The object itself, which for Brentano was still internal, is for Husserl kept strictly transcendental, that is, beyond consciousness (*Ideas* 90). One important mark of transcendence is that the consciousness of an object includes a reference to as yet undisclosed properties whose eventual appearance may be anticipated. Thus the intentional object is fraught with anticipations.

Non-perceptual—or post-perceptual—intuitions, namely both memory and imagination, are, then, a kind of "making-present." They are, however, distinguishable from each other by their different relations to perception. Memory is more of a counterpart to perception than is imagination for two reasons. Memories, like perceptions, fit into a unitary time. They also have a sort of "closure," meaning that they are in fact completely given prior to the act of judgment upon them. Yet memory is also unlike perception insofar as it does not have the spatial simultaneity the latter may display. Its intuitions are all strung out in time (*Experience and Judgment* 37).

Imagination, on the other hand, has no unitary time. All imaginative worlds are in their own, different and non-coherent times. Such unity as they have comes from the fact that they are all experiences of one imaginer. Unlike the real world, the imagined worlds have no closure, no *de facto* givenness, but can be freely developed as they are judged. The only limit on the imagination is that it cannot represent logical impossibilities (*E.J.* 41; Part Three, Ch. I B). It is certainly not constrained by a requirement of unity across imagined worlds. The identity of an imaginary character in two worlds, say in two fairy-tales, makes no sense to Husserl, for individuation and identification in general require a unique, unitary, universal time (*E.J.* 37–40). A critique of the notion that the world of imaginary worlds is incoherent is given in Parts Three (Ch. III C) and Six (Ch. III A) on experiential and imaginative grounds. Husserl's insistence on it reveals a certain limiting logicism in his approach to "fancy."

There is, then, a deep difference between memory and imagination with respect to their temporality. Yet in one way of speaking memory is identified with "fancy," insofar as it is always apparitional, intuitively full and present (*Phenomenology of Internal Time-Consciousness* App. II). There are, moreover, several other modes of presentification. Casey has made a comparative classification of them all, from hallucination to imagination, using two marks: their temporal and their "thetic," that is, existence-affirming, positions (1976c).

So it is time to pass on to the central question of this section. What characterizes imaginative presentification? Husserl deals first with imagination in the sense of supposal, which will be very important for the analytic philosophers (*Logical Investigations* Inv. V 39–40). It is explained as that quality of the intention, that modification of the representing act, in which belief is changed into supposal in such a way that the intuition is not posited as having existence but is "non-thetic." All acts that hold something to be the case, all "doxic," or belief-modes, such as possibility, probability, questionableness, and negation, have imaginative, un-posited, non-thetic, counterparts. Doxic modes differ from the imaginative mode in yet another way: One can go into the latter from the former as into a new mode, but thereafter there is no way but back: For the undoing of the imaginative position leads to no further mode of consciousness, only back to belief.

Imagination proper is treated in *Ideas*. The characterization is the same as that of supposal, with a crucial provision added: that an intuition be involved. Thus imagination is essentially a modification of that mode of consciousness in which something is intuitively given, such that every doxic modality is disempowered (109). Husserl calls this mode a "neutrality-modification," for by it opinions of existence or reality are neutralized or made inoperative:

> . . . the process of fancy in general is the neutrality-modification of the "positing" act of presentification, and therefore of remembering in the widest conceivable sense of the term. [111]

In the last clause, Husserl is referring to the fact that in ordinary speech the German verb *vergegenwärtigen* means both reproducing in memory and seeing in the imagination. Nevertheless, memory-presentification proper is not actually a true neutrality-modification, because memories are posited as having once had existence, though they too can subsequently be treated as fantasies, that is, neutralized.

I do not think that Husserl is claiming that each particular act of imagination is bound to arise as a modification of a specific remembered perception (which, as we have just seen, is what a posited presentification is). Rather he is saying that imagination-consciousness comes about when the question of existence is set aside from memory in general.

While belief can be neutralized only once, imagination, once neutralized, can be modified *ad infinitum*, though consciousness always remains imaginative. Thus, in a fairy-tale, a secondary tale may be told which is to be regarded as imaginary in the context of the first tale, and so on.

Husserl chooses the viewing of a picture as an example of the neutrality-modification at work. He distinguishes these elements: There is first the picture-thing, say Dürer's engraving "Death and the Knight." Second, there is the perceptual intuition of the figures, the death-figure and the knight-figure. Finally, there are the objects attended to in aesthetic imaginative contemplation, namely the beings "in the picture" taken as if they were flesh and blood and bone characters, Death showing his hour-glass to an unheeding knight. What makes the last kind of consciousness specifically possible is the imaginative noesis applied to those engraved figures. Through it the *"depicting picture object* stands before us *neither as being nor as non-being,* nor in any *other positional modality."* Having undergone the neutrality-modification, it has a quasi-being (111). That is the sort of being "picture-objects," characters in paintings and stories, have for us.

This kind of noesis and its noematic correlates are not subject to any critique from reason; that gives them their freedom. It is a unique peculiarity of noetic acts that to every noema is correlated a shadow-noema, a modified consciousness. In other words, anything that is intuited can be imagined. And of course the thetic neutrality-modification changes nothing in the nature of things. Recall that such mere refraining or "suspension" from the affirmation of existence is just that *epochē* which lies at the heart of the phenomenological method.

c. So it is scarcely surprising that the imagination is assigned a major role in the methodical pursuit of Phenomenology:

Free fancies assume a *privileged position over against perceptions.* [70]

And again:

The element which *makes up the life of phenomenology as of all eidetic science* is "fiction." [70]

What is this "eidetic" science, this science of essences which is the life of Phenomenology? And how do the fancy-free fictions of the imagination contribute to it?

Essence, for present purposes, is what is invariant in experience over all the perceptions presented by an individual object taken as a type and over all the objects of a type. It is a new sort of pure object, obtained by "essential intuition." Husserl uses the Platonic-Aristotelian term *eidos*, form, for the intuitable aspect of essences. Thus he says: "*It belongs to the meaning of everything contingent that it should have essential being and therewith an Eidos to be apprehended in all its purity;* and this Eidos comes under *essential truths of varying degrees of universality*" (*Ideas* 2). As a contemplative, theoretical science, Phenomenology is in search of essences and what pertains to them, their being, hierarchy, necessity, relation to concepts, and other features on which this is not the place to dwell.

Since essences are invariants, they are intuited by the method of imaginative experimentation called "free variation." It brings to light a persistent, identical core of objects, namely their pure possibilities. They are "pure" in the sense of being freed from actual experience; they are "possibilities" because they are established in imagination, not in fact. In freely varying an object in the imagination the eidos is actually brought about, in the sense that it emerges as that which is inseparable from the object and necessary to its being that type of object. This variational play is meant to be not the alteration carried out on one individual so much as a variation over many individuals (*E.J.* 87).

Essential intuition is not empirical generalization. The latter cannot delimit the essences, for it has no way of discovering what variations are impossible because they would destroy the essence, the type itself. Moreover, an empirical generalization, such as the concept of "redness," is empty, unfulfilled, unintuitive. The eidos, on the other hand, is "seen" intuitively, directly and in itself (*E.J.* 88).

Although it is disclosed by imaginative consciousness, an essence is not an imagined object. But neither is it pre-existent, or even existent at all (*I.* 4). Unlike Plato's eidos, it is not discovered by intellectual recollection but brought about by conscious activity. It arises in phenomenological reflections as that without which an object cannot be thought (*E.J.* 87). It is coagulated, so to speak, as the transcendental or transpsychic *a priori* condition that makes the object apprehensible (Gurwitsch 1953, 187). Therefore when Husserl says that the eidos is seen, he means it is seen in the variations of the object.

(Sokolowski 1974.)

Let me end with an example of the process of free variation, which consists of such activities as removing unessential features, substituting possible alternatives, and producing novel ones (Casey 1977).

I might first say that the Chinese landscape painter Wu Tao-tzu of the anecdote told in the Introduction, who entered his own picture, was practicing imaginative variation. But the strictly geometric imagination is more obviously productive of essential insight than aesthetic imagining, the more so since the origin of geometric variation is not empirical. Hence it is paradigmatic for Husserl (*E.J.* 89, *I.* 4, *Crisis* 9 a). It seems to me that Pascal's reformation of the ancient theory of conic sections offers a perfect example. By intuitively varying the position of a section through a cone, disregarding inessential specific cases, imagining various limit-possibilities, and considering the novel possibility of including points at infinity, he discovered the parabola, the ellipse, the hyperbola, and their degenerate forms as perspectives of an essential invariant, the circle.

Debate. What Husserl has left unsaid is what imagination might be in its own right, for he understands it strictly relatively, as a modification of perceptual consciousness. This phenomenological reflection on the imagination in itself is exactly what Sartre will attempt (1936). As a prelude to the project he reviews Husserl's image-theory, distinguishing its achievements from its residual problems.

Chief among the achievements are two consequences of the intentional understanding of consciousness. First, although fictional beings, like a flute-playing centaur (*I.* 23), are actually nonexistent, they are not therefore intra-psychic things. Like any intended object, they are transcendental, only, as it happens, they are transcendental nothings. (The being of nonexistent objects is considered in Part Three, Ch. III A.) This analysis will be one point of departure for Sartre. The other is this: Husserl denies that mental images are needed for interpreting external pictures, on the grounds that such interpretation would start an infinite regress, for yet another mental picture will be needed to interpret the first one (*L.I.*, Inv. II 21). Sartre thinks that in doing so, he has made it once more possible fruitfully to compare internal and external pictures with respect to their structure. For when the internal picture is not regarded as the meaning of the external picture, they are actually put on a more equal, comparable footing.

Sartre's criticism is particularly acute. Ordinary perception and material picture-viewing are distinguishable by the kind of consciousness involved, but not by the sensory matter, the impressional stuff, present in both. Is this same sensory element, for which Husserl uses the term *hylē*, the Greek word for matter, also present in mental images? It would seem so. Memory-images, for example, are in Husserl's analysis only perceptions affected with a time-modification. But in that case he is caught in the old Humean problem of immanence, for then sense-impressions and mental images become indistiguishable. Especially after the phenomenological bracketing of existence, how will one tell the perceptual from the image-noema? Sartre suggests that a difference in intentionality is not enough. The *hylē* must also be different. Here his own theory begins.

My own doubts about the theory go further in this line: Is not the image-noema a crypto-representation after all, Husserl's disclaimers notwithstanding? For what is a modified noetic operation and its modified noema but a quasi-perception? And a quasi-perception is precisely the groping designation of a mental image.

The difficulty of speaking clearly in positive terms about imageless imagination-consciousness is indeed one of the marks of the phenomenological debate. Dufrenne (1953, 350), for example, says of the image that "it is not a piece of mental equipment in consciousness but a way in which consciousness opens itself to the object, prefiguring it from deep within itself as a function of its implicit knowledge." That is obscure precisely because it attempts to be faithful to phenomenological doctrine.

Sallis (1975) puts the matter another way. He observes that Husserl banishes the image from Phenomenology as a problem by allowing it no intrinsic character, no real predicates, such as having, say, this or that color. In sum, it has no essential "imaginality" (*L.I.* II, Inv. V 21), or, as Casey puts it, it has none of those "unique presentational features" without which images are reduced to second-order sensations (1970). Such an image has no revelatory power in its own right, and there is nothing much to be said about it. There is, in fact, no image. Now, Sallis says, "real" predicates are not the only predicates. The mental image may simply have more "delicate" predicates, namely those that make them apprehensible as images. (Nietzsche seems to me to ascribe such ethereality to the dream-image in the *Birth of Tragedy*, when he refers to "the glimmering intimations of its seeming.") On these terms the image can return as a central issue of Phenomenology. This outcome is the more desirable because the very object-structure worked out in phenomenological analysis has image-like aspects. For real objects are experienced in terms of the profiles and perspectives they offer. Hence insofar as an image-consciousness is characterized as one in which an original shows itself through its image-aspects, the perspectives through which objects show themselves are image-analogies.

This understanding, however, is implicitly at cross-purposes with an analysis by Kuehl (1970), who argues that image-objects are essentially non-perspectival. Whereas perceptual objects excite in perceptual consciousness anticipations of further views, the image-noema is absolute, without reference to further noemata. It is not the correlative of a process but a spontaneous achievement: "It is miraculous, for in one appearance the object intended as absent or unreal is absolutely present to consciousness, i.e., adequately and apodictically." I quote this sentence because it observes an image-feature often to be stressed in this book: the essentially momentary and episodic nature of the imaginative experience.

The fundamental difficulties of articulating what an imageless image-consciousness or an imaginal non-entity are, and how the latter is distinguishable from the perceptual object, arise all over again in accounting for the imaginative play of free variation. Imaginative variation works, as has been said, by reviewing what is non-essential in the various intuitive aspects of an object, so as to reveal the invariant. Now this review is authoritative because it is one of the fulfilled intuitive modes that bring the thing actually before us. For from presence there is no appeal (Sokolowski 1974, 84). And so, once again, the question arises: What is imagination that it can bring the object in its various aspects before us in the absence of its animating sensory presence? The question becomes particularly puzzling if the description of images given above as essentially episodic and unperspectival has something to it. Husserl's phenomenological description of the image-experience seems to stand in the way of an explanatory account.

Finally, Husserl's image-theory is criticized on the broadest human grounds. For Husserl the many imaginative and dream worlds are essentially non-coherent, and *the* world is the perceptual world with its unitary time and space. This naive, workaday world is the reference for the "multiple-realities" of imagination (Schuetz 1944). Therefore Kuspit faults Husserl for failing to appreciate the power of the inventive imagination when he considers it only as a modification of perceptions (1968). In

Husserl's defense, it must, however, be recalled that he surely does not mean that every particular imaginative consciousness is nothing but a neutralized specific perception.

Complementary to this preference for given perceptual presence is Husserl's unabashed and unreflective devotion to the theoretical search for essence, and this fact, too, meets with criticism: Phenomenology, as theory about given nature and carried on for the sake of theory, is motivated neither by concern for human existence nor grounded in a view of it (Levinas 1963, 157). Of course, one might reply in Husserl's behalf with the Socratic claim—nowadays regarded as scandalous—that the desire to know essence *is* the ground of human existence. This is, however, not the place to bring forward a notion so widely and deliberately eschewed in the current philosophical schools.

2. Sartre: Images as Posited Nothingness. Sartre's contribution to the theory of the imagination is epoch-making, if only because of the remarkable fact that he is the first major philosophical writer in its long history to devote a whole book—in fact two closely connected books—to the subject.

The earlier of these, called *Imagination: A Psychological Critique* (1936), is a preparatory review of previous theories as exemplifications of one pervasive error: the "naive ontology" that turns the mental image into a thing given to consciousness like any other thing. This thing is distinguished from a perception only by its inferiority, by its being, in some manner, a lesser thing. The common claim of ordinary people, that they see images in their imagination, is interpreted by Sartre as in fact a naively conceived theory rather than an experience (the kind of unreflective theorizing that contemporary cognitivists like to call "folk psychology"). The mistake is, however, shared by the great metaphysicians of the seventeenth and eighteenth centuries. As Sartre puts it, they confuse the identity of the essence of the image and its object with the identity of their existence. In other words, they think that because an image is in certain aspects the analogue of the object it images, it must itself be object-like in its being.

Sartre goes on to show the universal consequences of this "classical postulate" of the image-thing. Classical theorists have a hard time distinguishing between perception and imagination, despite the *ad hoc* criteria they invent. Differences in intensity, in context, in physiology, in probability—none of these really works. Similarly they cannot reliably distinguish imagination from thought, or decide whether the two are related as a continuum or a synthesis or an identity.

These unresolved difficulties, together with what he claims is a universal fact of introspection, namely that people spontaneously and invariably recognize their images *as* images, sets the problem for Sartre: to account for image-consciousness without resorting to the "naive ontology."

Imagination furthermore contains a concise critical account of the associationist school, a sprawling and not very profitable subject somewhat slighted in the present study. Sartre's book culminates in the critique of Husserl's theory reported above, which is his own technical point of departure.

The second Book, *L'Imaginaire* (1940), subtitled "A Phenomenological Psychology of the Imagination," expounds a theory intended to resolve the problem set in the previous book. It concludes with an appreciation of the function in human life of the "imaginary" or "irreal" world to which the title refers. In sum, one might say that Sartre takes over from Husserl the notion of the imagination as a mode of consciousness and that his own contribution is the development of the image as a materialization of non-being. The latter involves a humanly significant positing of nothingness, which will be explained below.

L'Imaginaire (*The Imaginary*) is divided into two parts. First comes a short but crucial phenomenological reflection, a conscious introspection provocatively called "The Certain"—Sartre is a Cartesian in regarding self-intuition as infallible. The long second part is headed "The Probable." Here experimental psychology is called in for the purpose of reaching hypothetical conclusions. Needless to say, the distinction between certainty and probability is imperfectly observed.

The results of the first book provide the beginning of the second: The "illusion of immanence" is to be overcome by treating the imagination as "a consciousness." Hence the following definition is basic to the book:

> In the woof of consciousness there appear at times structures which we shall call imaginative consciousness. They are born, develop and disappear with laws proper to them. [8]

These structures have four characteristics: The first is precisely that the image is not *in* consciousness but *is* a consciousness. For consciousness is transparent to itself, is consciousness through and through. Therefore an image-picture in consciousness would be an opaque intrusion. By an image one ought to mean at most the relationship of consciousness to an object.

The second characteristic of the image-structures of consciousness is a certain immediate completeness. They intend objects, but not in the same way as do the two other possible types of consciousness, perception and conception. The perceived object "slowly serves its apprenticeship," since it is learned from an infinity of perspectival observations. The conceived object is thought all at once in its essence, but it can then be unpacked progressively. An image, however, does not reveal itself progressively by observation as does a perception, nor can it be developed as can a conception. It is there all at once, and the judgment that it is an image is immediate and final. Nor does it teach anything, for one cannot learn something new by looking at one's mental image. (This claim is, of course, disputable— Part Two.) An image is essentially impoverished. A perceptual object overflows consciousness, or, in phenomenal language, it is transcendent with respect to consciousness, and this overflow is precisely the margin left for observation. Images, in contrast, give opportunity only for quasi-observation, such as yields no materially new information.

The third property of image-structures is their intentionality. Images are always images *of* something. Now by means of phenomenological reflection one may recover the features of non-reflective image-consciousness before it has construed itself as an image-object. What emerges then is the "thetic" or positional character of the act, namely that it posits its intentional object in four negative ways: as nonexistent, as absent, as elsewhere, and as neutral with respect to existence. The last of these is, of course, recognizable as Husserl's neutrality-modification. It is this negated character of the image-object that makes it subject to the quasi-observation mentioned above.

The fourth property is spontaneity. Imagining is, unlike perception, not passive. The imagining consciousness appears to itself as creative, though without positing the object of its creation as existent. This spontaneity is a vague and fugitive quality, an undefinable counterpart to the nothingness of the object. It is not necessarily willful: It is merely somehow active. The image may have certain inert, passive characteristics, but imagining itself is an act, an intentional act, of consciousness.

This list of image-properties leads to a definition of the having of an image. It is

an act which envisions an absent or nonexistent object as a body, by means of a physical or mental content which is present only as an "analogical representative" of the object envisioned. [26]

The definition, including as it does physical images, raises the question of how far internal images are comparable to external images—anything ranging from portraits to faces seen in a fire. Recall that Sartre had credited Husserl with making this comparison possible to begin with. The two types of images, Sartre now says, are the same with respect to their intentionality, but they differ in material. He had already intimated this distinction in his earlier critique of Husserl.

The material of the portrait is perceivable—there are real brush strokes on the real canvas. But these brush strokes are not themselves the aesthetic object, the image. That is evident in the fact that one may train a light on a a canvas without necessarily brightening up its picture (275). The canvas is a "material analogue" which is, as it were, "visited" by the object intended. When the viewer takes the imaginative attitude, he goes into the image-mode of consciousness and sees the picture *as* an image. This analysis, incidentally, implies that a picture is not an externally realized, objectified, mental image. For the material analogue is imaginal by a direct act of consciousness that is not a projection upon, but an apprehension of, the canvas.

Different external images differ in their "thetic" character. With faces in the fire or figures in clouds, neither is the material posited as representational nor the object posited as existing. The Sartrean theory has the great advantage over that of the Analysts (B) that it easily includes reveries, dreams, and hallucination—types of images the latter cannot accommodate. Sartre assigns to them a special, strange sort of spontaneity. It is "fascination," the willing bondage of consciousness before the image (64). In dreams, consciousness is taken in, spontaneity is spellbound. Yet dreaming does not contravene "that great law of the imagination: *there is no imaginary world*" (242). Therefore Descartes is wrong in presenting the dream as a possible alternative reality. The dream is a mere fiction, albeit one to which we somehow accede.

The next step is to delineate the conceptual transition from external to mental image. The analogon-material of a portrait is the embodiment of a quasi-face, an individual, unique in time and space. As the image rises in the spectrum toward the merely internal, its material becomes increasingly impoverished, its more specific qualities drop out, and it approaches ideality (73). Luminosity, for example, supercedes specifiable color, and symbolic movements substitute for forms; the material plays a lesser role, and intuition is that much the more stimulated by knowledge. Yet there is a mental content that stands as analogue to a real object; it is a material, representative content that is "already constituted as an object for consciousness" from the first, and therefore has what Sartre now calls transcendence.

Sartre is groping here, in order to avoid the "naive ontology" of mental image-objects without giving up the image-material. The material of mental imagery, he admits (77), is almost beyond introspective description, because one cannot focus on it as separate. When image-consciousness is bypassed, the transcendent element is simultaneously lost. The critical debate will, rightly, center on this aspect of Sartre's theory. Not the least difficulty with it is that the transcendence of the image-analogon-material is not what is usually called transcendence in Phenomenology, namely that "overflow" of consciousness which makes anticipations of fresh observations possible. Sartre is very firm about the fact that images offer no such anticipations.

For the evidence on which to base his more hypothetical conclusions, Sartre now goes to reports of psychological "experiments." Here begins the "probable" part. Much of this introspective, descriptive material is now a little dated (Part Two, Ch. II A), and therefore the account will be abbreviated.

Two subjects amenable to empirical treatment are the relations of the cognitive as well as of the affective consciousness to image-consciousness.

The "imageless" school of psychology may have discovered that there is thought without imagery, but, Sartre contends, there is no imagining without thinking. Once more he gropes for a description of their relation. The image is like: an incarnation of non-reflective thought, a spatialized thought, thought become a thing, a judgment appearing as an indeterminate image (160–162). Psychologists have shown, Sartre says, that knowledge, when it enters an image, is radically modified, not just fulfilled, as Husserl claims. The birth of an image involves what Sartre calls the debasement of knowledge. By debasement he means that such knowledge is no longer "pure," that is, purely relational. Rather it envisions relations concretely in terms of the sensory qualities of things. Examples are, I would guess, the colors and feelings some people report as their intuitions of logical terms— syncategorematics like "and," "but," and "if." In sum, when constituting the unreal, knowledge is drawn to the role of perception (200). It turns itself into intuition.

Affective consciousness is so close to imaginative consciousness as to be on occasion identical, especially where desire is involved. Both are intentional, and both posit their object as absent in its very presence in consciousness (104). In desire this sense of absence-in-presence is particularly prominent. (Sartre's theory of emotion is considered in Part Six, Ch. III B.)

This complexity is partly responsible for the common naive error of positing image-objects. People are, for a moment, possessed by the presence of the absent object. Because absent presence is repugnant to common sense, they posit internal objects, and do so undeterred by the utterly different mode of appearance that divides the internal objects from the real.

This peculiar mode of internal images includes features that are the empirical fleshing-out of the properties established earlier: The image is unitary and undifferentiated and inexact. Thus it appears as a qualitative whole that does not have extensionally articulated parts such as can be distinctly observed and counted. (This is a claim belied in recent experiments—Part Two, Ch. II B.) In sum, imaginative space has no coordinates and is more qualitative than extensional. The same goes for imaginative time: It is an annihilation of real time; it is absent time (186).

Moreover, the imaginary object is powerless or has only a negative power, and it is without consequence. It always receives and never gives. It has, as it were, the shape of a cavity, and it can concentrate but never satisfy desire. (This appears to me a manifestly false observation. Imaginary objects can on occasion satisfy, and satisfy solidly, all sorts of desire.) The affective dialectic of imagination, says Sartre, feeds on itself. It is a tension without repose. It induces a tenderness lacking in "sincerity," "docility," and richness (205). Imagination absorbs debased feeling, as before it incorporated debased thought. As the object is, so is the act: Imagining is a magical incantation intended to produce an object of thought and desire for the purpose of possession. It is an object seen from no particular situational perspective, but, as it were, from beyond, as a whole, all at once. Consequently the imaginary life is a congealed, formalized, denatured life. A preference for it is a form of pathology, whose extremes are seen in persons suffering from hallucinations.

These observations show that by their very nature "the real and the imaginary cannot coexist," and that the imaginary is debased and impoverished. (This conclusion will be countered later on in this book by distinguishing between the imaginary and the imaginative.) Nevertheless, by a not quite intelligible turnabout, Sartre will now present the imagination as both essentially perspectival and essentially necessary to human existence.

In his conclusions, then, he considers the deepest questions concerning the role of imaginative consciousness in human existence. If consciousness in general is constitutive of the world—this is the phenomenological presupposition—what specifically characterizes a consciousness capable of imagining? What is it to posit an object as nothingness, be it absent or nonexistent or neutral? Or, more arrestingly, is a non-imagining consciousness—a consciousness totally absorbed in its intuitions of the real—even conceivable?

The "imaginative act is at once *constituting, isolating* and *annihilating*." It is isolating in concentrating or focusing on certain absences implied by the present world. It is annihilating in grasping these as being nothing for the self, in positing them as a nothingness, as negating the world through different degrees of negativity. The understanding of an image as a "nothingness" will be the second major point for criticism.

For consciousness to be imaginative it must be able to posit the world in its synthetic totality, and it must be able to posit the imagined object as being out of reach of this synthetic totality. Imaginative consciousness must, in a word, be able not only to posit the image as a nothing but also the world as nothingness in relation to the image.

It follows from the world-negating nature of the imagination that a consciousness incapable of imagining would be a purely positive consciousness, one driven deterministically by the real world. Conversely, only the consciousness that is able to withdraw from the world and to see it in perspective can engage in imagining. This ability to posit reality as a whole, and oneself as free from it, is for Sartre freedom itself. "Thus to posit the world as a world or to 'negate' it is one and the same thing. In this sense Heidegger can say that nothingness is the constitutive structure of the existant" (267). Since freedom is always freedom from a specific reality, consciousness has to be situated in the world in order to deny it. Moreover, so situated, it cannot help but deny the world: "The unrealizing function" is present in all conscious determination (Altieri 1971). The nothingness itself is, of course, not intuitable. The intention of imagination is always the negative of something, and nothingness presents itself only "as infrastructure of something" (271). "The imaginary thus represents at each moment the implicit meaning of the real," insofar as it comes about by a setting aside of the real world which is both specific to that world and free from it:

> In order to imagine, consciousness must be free from all specific reality, and this freedom must be able to define itself by a "being-in-the-world" which is at once the constitution and the negation of the world; the concrete situation of the consciousness in the world must at each moment serve as the singular motivation for the constitution of the unreal.

Here, in capsule form, is the high function of the imagination as an essential element of consciousness *per se*: It at once determines the world and holds it at bay. It *is* human freedom. Since this determining function also binds the imagination far more closely to the real world than seems warranted by the antecedent theory, it becomes a third focus of criticism in the debate.

Sartre ends *L'Imaginaire* with a brief consideration of the imaginary world as it appears in works of art. His main thesis is completely coherent with the preceding argument, though he elaborates and emends it later on. It is that a work of art, material analogue aside, is wholly and radically unreal: out of time and out of reach. Aesthetic contemplation is an "induced dream," and passing back into reality is an awakening attended by the "nauseating disgust" that characterizes all consciousness of reality. The real is never beautiful, for beauty is a value applicable only to the imaginary world, the negation of reality. And so "it is stupid to confuse the moral with the aesthetic," real action with aesthetic contemplation.

By way of a coda it should be said that in *What is Literature?* (1948) this harsh but consequential separation is modified, at least with respect to novels, though only because they are not pure art. For novelistic language can be used not so much to create a material analogue of life as to communicate reality, to elucidate rather than to escape the world. Novels are not, like expository prose, for the presentation of ideas, nor are they for the enjoyment of the language itself. Instead they present the feeling of certain ideas in such a way that the scene of their enactment is recalled even when the specific language is forgotten. To achieve this interpretative purpose, the novelist must situate himself in the world and combine his negativity—that is, his imaginative consciousness, which is here understood in terms of resistance to the social *status quo*—with a project for a better future order (Altieri 1971). The curious impetus behind Sartre's modification of his own aesthetic theory is the wish to adapt the unrealizing function of the imagination to revolutionary purposes. This self-contradictory project of combining "the sovereign nothingness of an isolated imagination and the affirmation of collective commitment to revolutionary action" represents for Kearney (1988) the "defiant death-rattle" of the modern humanist era. It is the harbinger of the postmodern demise of the imagination, which also spells the end of man (Introduction A).

Debate. Criticism of Sartre's phenomenological psychology of the imagination has been plentiful and pertinent. The vigor of this critique is, incidentally, in remarkable contrast to the practical immunity accorded to Wittgenstein, the contemporaneous founder of the second great image-theory of the century. The main issues will be those named above: First, Sartre's equivocation concerning the mental *hylē*, that is to say, the material analogon; second, his neglect of precisely what is ordinarily called the "imaginary," namely the products of the imagination in its positively inventive capacity; and third, his insistence on the negative character of the image, on its essential nothingness.

These three do seem to be the main, and ultimately the decisive, critical issues. I have one broad observation to add. It applies, as it happens, equally to the analytic writers, and I mention it here somewhat reluctantly because it has a certain *ad hominem* air about it. I mean that for all his descriptive flair and piquant language, Sartre's assessments of the imaginative life are somehow strained and off the mark, as if he felt compelled to disesteem his own imaginative world at one and the same time for its riches and for its poverty. Indeed, Casey (1981), whose sympathetic critique of Sartre is also the most comprehensive, emphasizes his faulty descriptions and calls attention to the project's underlying anti-Romantic rationalism. Moreover, he interprets Sartre's retreat from "The Certain" to "The Probable" as an abandonment of the introspective descriptive method on the grounds that it is impossible; he claims that Sartre in fact turns to a conceptual analysis that brings him close to Wittgenstein. Actually, of course, Sartre does not find the descriptive line logically impossible so much as psychologically uncongenial, though his valuation of the imagination as cognitively empty does coincide with that of the analytic tradition. In short, Sartre forces his phenomenological case in his condemnation of the imaginative mode.

Before the consideration in summation of the careful technical points of Hannay, Casey, and J. Furlong, two further criticisms should be mentioned concerning this Sartrean undervaluation of the imagination. Dufrenne (1953) asserts that the imagination is much more than a world-denying power. It is our power for reforming the real and for bearing its vision within us, a power of the "prereal," without which reality would be a spectacle lacking depth and duration, a power for surpassing the real so that we may return to it (355). Taylor (1981) argues more pointedly against Sartre that the imagination is in fact a source of fresh knowledge and judgment. For by suppositions and visualizations we can induce "trial experiences" which have a potent practical cognitive function in, for example, anticipating outcomes. Similarly, the quasi-observations of imagined situations are important in aesthetic appraisals, such as deciding how objects will look in certain settings. And finally, the imagination provides us with affective knowledge, experience of our own emotional states and those of others.

Hannay (1971, ch. VI) provides a close logical analysis of Sartre's text and finds a multitude of imprecisions. The chief set of problems is this: On the widest plane, Sartre introduces two assumptions that are insufficiently warranted. First, he works with a transcendent object, borrowed from Husserl, understood as an extra-mental intention which is capable of further determination. He simply assumes that when consciousness intends an object in this sense, it in fact has hold of an object, though there can be no logical guarantee of this. Because of this assumption, Hannay calls his chapter "Sartre's Illusion of Transcendence." Second, Sartre unwarrantedly assumes that consciousness, imaginative consciousness in particular, is fully and transparently self-aware, since consciousness is generically self-conscious.

As Hannay shows, a first dilemma facing Sartre is that the object of imagining must be one of two things. Either it is something totally immanent which must be related to the transcendent object externally, that is, not through its own nature. Or it is that transcendent, intentional, object itself and must therefore be mediated by an immanent image (104). Sartre escapes the difficulty by positing an image-medium that "conjures" up the object—in other words, re-presents it—not in a resembling sense but by bringing it before us in person, so to speak. This medium presents the object as a genuine member of the class of ways an object can appear before us, for example, in the way of incompleteness: An imaginary object is not an incomplete object but an object of which the consciousness is incomplete or "impoverished." Thus the imaginary and the transcendent object are one and the same, though not in a material sense. This is, as will be pointed out again and again, Sartre's principal equivocation. Therefore "full disjunctive force" is lacking in Sartre's claim that imaging consciousness is not a perceptual relation to a special object but a *sui generis* relation to an ordinary object. Somehow an intermediary "medium" seems to have slipped in.

The "object" notion, together with the nihilating function of the imagination, is the source of more problems. Sartre implies that not every correlative of consciousness is an object; indeed, objects are said to be outside consciousness. Yet images are supposed to be posited as negated objects. How can a nothing, a thing without essence, be posited? How can an image be imagined on those terms?

Moreover, as Hannay points out, Sartre gives no strong argument why images should not be objects. In the light of the ambiguity of the term "object," the argument that consciousness is transparent to itself really shows no more than that it never confuses its modes, never mistakes images for perceptions. But this claim is itself at least debatable. Sartre, incidentally, invoking the question-begging assumption that an image is an image and not a perception, calls absurd Perky's classical experiments proving the contrary (1940, 75, Part Two, Ch. VI A). Alternatively, Sartre supports himself by an extreme dualist position in which consciousness (being-for-itself) is sharply opposed to thinghood (being-in-itself). Thus not only can no object having physical-analogue properties appear in consciousness, but consciousness itself, being through and through activity, has no product-like effects, appearances, or correlates. This argument, found principally in *Being and Nothingness*, would throw totally in doubt the notion of the image as in any way distinct from the imaging act.

For all these equivocations, Hannay credits Sartre's theory with a double advantage over that of the analytic school, an advantage deriving from his dual proposal. The first part of Sartre's proposal is that imaging is an act of consciousness which aims at something in the world and qualifies it in the imaginative mode. The second part is that this qualifying unfolds spontaneously in the visual mode such as to make the qualification entirely the imaginer's act, though not a willful or deliberate one. The relations of image to world and of image to will are indeed unsolved problems in the analytic image theory (Part Six, Ch. III B).

Casey (1981) begins by emphasizing certain salient ingredients in Sartre's theory of the image: The two great attitudes of consciousness, perception and imagination, are not reducible to each other. The imagination has a paradigmatic position in the "unmotivated upsurge" of freedom. The effect of the imaginative act is doubly nihilating, once as it posits objects as not-being, and again as it sets the world at naught.

In this context Casey mounts three essential criticisms: The first concerns the analogue or analogon, the "Achilles' heel" of Sartre's analysis. The psychical analogon was intended to stand as proxy for sensation, as an equivalent of perception. This kind of analogon-representation requires resemblance. Thus the psychical analogon must somehow support just that sort of physical quality; it must somehow be a spatial, sensory quasi-thing. This lands Sartre in the "illusion of immanence." Indeed, Sartre's language does slip into immanence, for he denies that the "transcendence" of the material of intentional objects implies its externality, and he calls the mental image an "interposed object." The external, physical analogon of pictures is no more acceptable, for it implies that in viewing a picture we take the painted canvas as a mere cue, a reminder or *medium quo*, of the intended object. (However, for a defense of this "cue" function, see Part Five, Ch. III A.)

Second, Sartre's presentation of the image as nothingness is unintelligible, or at least contradictory. The image as intuited cannot be mere nothingness. It must have some sort of positivity, since it has some sort of existence. Again, Sartre repeatedly and sharply separates the world of perception and the world of the imaginary as utterly incompatible, yet they are also said to be constituted by the same objects. Thus the difference between the worlds seems to be sometimes merely "thetic," sometimes inherent.

Third, there is a problem with Sartre's account of the relation between imagination and knowledge. Sartre falls into the "intellectual illusion," the belief that imagination is an inferior form of intellection. (This type of denigration is taken up in Part Six, Ch. I A.) Sartre claims that in imagination the image determines thinking to the detriment of intellectual autonomy, that imagination degrades the purity of thought by its sensory concreteness, and that imagining teaches nothing. Thus the reputed arch-irrationalist in fact turns to purvey rationalist prejudices.

J. Furlong (1982) tries to come to grips with Sartre's equivocation about the existence of mental images. For Sartre imagination–consciousness intends the same object as perception does, but in specified different ways. Is the outcome that mental images do or don't exist? Sartre seems to embrace nonexistence but then stops short. He states that there are no images, yet constantly names them. Indeed, he claims to dignify the mental image by retrieving it from the fate of being a reborn sensation and turning it into a *sui generis* structure, the imaginary or "irreal" object. Furlong's question is: How can its function be described so that one might say whether it is or is not an entity?

Warnock and Hannay's interpretation is that Sartre views the image as a *medium quo*, an analogue which is a means or tool for visualization. Furlong points out that this interpretation seems to be contradicted by the Sartrean understanding of "appearing as an image" in terms of a consciousness of nothingness. Such a consciousness is not easily construable on an instrumental view.

Another explanation cited by Furlong is given by Snoeyenbos and Sibley (1978), again to the effect that the image is an analogue. There are three distinct elements in a picture: the physical material of the analogue, the thought-constituted analogue itself, and the intentional object. In mental images the first is missing. The analogue is not seen as a picture would be, but it is that which makes the intention be the intention of that particular object. Furlong objects—again—that the nature, and indeed the function, of this thought-analogue is unclear and implausible. What is needed is a recognition, absent in Anglo-Saxon literature, of how closely Sartre in fact follows Husserl. This requires an analysis of Husserl's intentionality in the terms relevant to Sartre, namely with particular respect to content.

The intentional act has, according to Furlong, three moments. Suppose, for example, one sees a friend in a crowd. One experiences him as perceived, as opposed to imagined; this is the quality of the intentional act. One sees him as this determinate person and no one else; this is the reference of the act. Finally, one sees him by means of certain sensory qualities; this is the content of the act. Note well that these sensory qualities are not themselves perceived. It is the friend who is perceived.

Now the same content occurs also in the imaginative act, except that it is viewed with a different act-quality. It is no more an impression than it was in the perceptual act; instead it is an experience, a consciousness lived through as part of the intentional act of imagining. Although belonging to the experience, the content is not its aim. So if the question is put to Husserl: Do mental images exist? the answer is: There is no immanent mental object aimed at in the imaging experience; it does not exist. But there is a kind of content.

Now Furlong can elucidate Sartre's apparent equivocation. Mental images are not objects, but one cannot quite say that such events do not occur. In a sense the intended object appears, and just insofar as it does not appear as present, is it said to appear as an image, as *not* there. It appears not as a medium *by* which the object is seen (a material substrate), nor as the image *of* the object (a pictorial copy), but as an appearance *as* which the object is in imaginative consciousness (an experienced nothing). This is for Furlong the ultimate difficulty with the phenomenological view of mental images: The role of the image is somehow idle when it is reduced to being a part of an experience in which it nevertheless does not participate as imaging the intentional object. What is an image that is purely phenomenal and not intentional? Furlong's unease is really an oblique objection to the image as nothingness.

The next question is whether the above-defined content is representational: Does it appear as a resemblance? For Furlong Hannay's understanding of the material analogue as a resemblance-shaped "content" or as a representational *hylē* is a misconceived reading of Husserl. (However, I think it is what Sartre does mean, and this is the very point on which he criticizes and emends Husserl). In fact Hering very early (1947) picked out this Sartrean project of providing the hyletic analogon and criticized it as misconceived. Furlong cannot save Sartre from the consequent suspicion of surreptitiously introducing immanent representational images.

Finally, Furlong draws the important conclusion that the phenomenological-intentionalist image-theory is not so easily collapsible into that of the analytic school as is often claimed. There is one telling difference: For the Analysts the nonrepresentational properties of mental images—those that belong to them not as features of the object imaged but in their own, imaginal, right, for example fleetingness and fuzziness—are a continual bedevilment to be explained or explained away. The intentionalists have obviated this difficulty. These features are qualities of the intentional act, not of its product, for the image is not separable from imaginative consciousness.

3. Developments. If for Sartre the perceptual and the imaginary realms are irreconcilable, Merleau-Ponty, though he often cites Sartrean formulations concerning the latter, actually sets out a diametrically opposed view. The two realms are not only continuous, but the imaginary is entirely an adumbration of the real. In his critique of empiricism (1945), he argues against the role of memory-images in perception. The theory that gaps in sense-data are filled out by a projection of memories is untenable, he says, because perceptions could not arouse memory-images were they not from the first understood in the light of past experience. The order that the empiricists think is supplied by the imagination is, on the contrary, already immanent in the perceptual object. The wholeness of an object, including its hidden, invisible parts, its whole presence for us, is not compacted of perceptions plus watered-down sensations (that is, Humean images). Nor is an object merely a permanent set of possibilities of sensation. It is rather a part of the original structure of the perceived world.

The same holds for imaginative external images, which Merleau-Ponty takes up in "Eye and Mind" (1961). Paintings offer to sight "the inward traces of vision, the imaginary texture of the real." Accordingly a painter, immersed in the visible world through his visible body, does not appropriate what he sees in terms of immanent mental images, which leave the world lying outside, inertly "in-itself." There is a continuity between the seeing human body and the world. That is why so many painters curiously declare that things look at them. A " 'visible' of the second power" appears to them. It is not a faded copy but what Merleau-Ponty calls an "icon," an external shape which is not where the medium is but is also not elsewhere, since it never breaks from its material moorings: "It is more accurate to say that I see according to it, or with it, than that I *see it*." The source of the icon is the painter's perception: "The world has at least once emblazoned in him the ciphers of the visible." Yet the fictional icon does lack the full transcendent otherness of an actual object. Thus it expresses the "carnal" structure of the object in isolation from its actuality. With this icon Merleau-Ponty gets pretty close to an immanent image-noema (Mallin 1979). The mental image in painting is again taken up in Part Five.

Casey's complement to his critique of Husserl and Sartre is a phenomenological image-theory of his own, whose two chief tenets are these: first, imaginative autonomy, which is the irreducible independence of the imagination from perception; and second, imaginative freedom, which is the "possibilizing power" of the imagination—in Casey's words: *"the conscious projection and contemplation of objects posited as pure possibilities"* (1970). These views are fully set out in *Imagining: A Phenomenological Study* (1976a), one of the few full-length books on the philosophy of the imagination.

Casey's method is phenomenological in two senses. First, imagination is taken as intentional, which means that it can be analyzed into two phases. There is an "act-phase," which includes several interwoven kinds of imagining: imaging or visualization, imagining that, imagining how. There is, second, an "object-phase," which includes an imaginal content: that in an image which can be verbally described. This content, further, has its own imaginal space and time which determines its world-frame, an "imaginal margin" that surrounds, almost unnoticed, every image without exactly being part of it. Finally the object-phase refers to the image itself, to the total imaginative presentation in its givenness.

Secondly, the phenomenological approach means that there is an effort to discover the essential traits of the imagination through the analysis of introspective examples. The method yields three pairs of traits, which are at first advanced tentatively and then amplified:

a. Spontaneity and controlledness are a pair of traits related as alternatives. Images often arise unsolicitedly, effortlessly, surprisingly, and instantaneously. But alternatively one may induce and guide and break off an imagining sequence. These two traits not only clash but also complement each other. The one not in force is always felt by the imaginer to be a possibility. There are three limitations constraining imaginative spontaneity and controlledness. Logically, one cannot imagine the conceptually impossible; ontologically, one cannot bring about existence by imagination; and empirically, there are personal limits to the imaginative power.

b. Self-containedness and self-evidence are not alternatives but are co-necessary to every imaginative experience. The first trait means that no imagination-episode calls for completion by further experiences. It is all there, self-sufficient and monadic; the experience is self-delimited as the imaginer's own activity. It is discontinuous both with other types of conscious acts and with other imaginative episodes. It is not even explorable, since it does not give a sense of interiority, the expectation that its frontal perspective might be penetrable. The second trait, closely allied to the first, is self-evidence. It means that every such experience is pellucidly, unquestionably, incontrovertibly what it is. It is both incorrigible and unquestionable. Consequently, although imagination has to do with possibility, it comes in the form of certainty.

c. Indeterminacy and pure possibility are the final eidetic traits, and they are neither mutually exclusive nor jointly exhaustive but mutually facilitating. The more indeterminate the image, the more it presents itself as purely possible, with respect to both content and states of affairs. The content tends to be vague, inconstant, and lacking in regional detail. The states tend to be *tableaux vivants* strangely suspended in time, lacking continuity and direction. (In Part Six, I associate the propensity of the imagination for *tableaux* with its special relation to places. There too Casey's phenomenology of place-memory is taken into account—Ch. III A.) So also the imaginal margin has no precise perimeter and, indeed, cannot be brought into focus without losing the central image. The margin displays not mere indeterminacy but a spectacularly variable indeterminacy.

Of all six traits, Casey regards pure possibility as the most critical and essential but also as the most controversial. For while it constitutes the thetic character of the imaginative object phase, its essentiality is not obvious.

Recall that the thetic character of the object is the imputation of an existential status to it. If imagining is sheer supposal or "self-entertainment," the object imagined, insofar as it is imagined, is posited as purely possible, even if it is in fact real. Casey distinguishes pure possibility from hypothetical possibility, which is viewed as a means for the realization of some ulterior end. Pure possibility is possibility entertained for its own sake. The imaginal content is viewed as purely possible, but above all the mode of its givenness is so viewed. The image is actual enough, but it is experienced as infintely free and variable, as only one of the many ways a describable content might be given.

Casey admits continuities as well as discontinuities between perceiving and imagining. In fact, he categorizes traditional image-theories by means of the degree to which they place perception and imagination in a continuum. Concerning the content of imagination, some theories claim that it may overlap and some that it must coincide with perception. Casey himself argues that there may be genuine similarity of specific content, and even more, that there can be "sortal," merely generic, continuity, which may in fact drive perception and image apart by slow degrees (a point elaborated for dreams in Part Six). Also, one may in imagination supplement and extend perception continuously, as when visualizing the backs of given objects. Particularly during aesthetic experience, for example during a play, the imaginer extends the given perception continuously beyond the present spectacle. Finally, Wittgensteinian "seeing-as" is a type of continuity between perceiving and imagining. All these continuities may, but needn't, come into play.

The discontinuities are, however, more distinctive. First, arguments against discontinuity are discounted. *Contra* Sartre, Casey contends that imagining and perceiving can go on simultaneously, though they cannot be of the same thing. Against Perky's experiment purporting to show that a subject may fail to discriminate between image and percept, Casey argues precisely that it is based on the false assumption that one can imagine and perceive the same thing at the same time. (This is, I think, a tricky argument, on account of the visual indeterminacy of image-contents that are descriptively the same. For that indeterminacy makes the term "same" ambivalent.)

The true discontinuities are, for Casey, the following: The mode of approach to imaged objects is leap-like and discrete and unhindered by interposing volumes, while the objects themselves loom and retreat suddenly. Perceptual things, on the contrary, must be approached through continuous space. Next, imagined objects do not have either "external" or "internal horizons" in the way that perceived objects have them. The external horizon is the context in which the object of attention is set: the whole perceptual field subtending it and the other things with it and around it. No perceptual field undergirds and outlasts the image, and image-objects do not possess stable and determinable relations with each other. The internal horizon is constituted by the aspects of the objects presently perceived, together with the potentially discoverable features that are predelineated in the present appearance, as a facade implies a certain type of back. Internal horizons are *ipso facto* absent in bizarre, fantastic objects. But even the imagined facade of perceptually faithful things gives no sure basis for projecting a back at all. Finally, images are apprehended with certainty and cannot be mistaken. One cannot mis-imagine, whereas it is in the nature of percepts to rebuff one's expectations, to deceive judgment, to prove illusory, and to change character.

Casey also enumerates the essential discontinuities between imagining and remembering (1977): We posit the former existence of what we recall, and we have a sense of familiarity with it. Neither of these conditions holds for what is imagined. Moreover, while imagining comes only in the three act-forms of imaging, imagining that, and imagining how, remembering has their analogues and several more: remembering to do, remembering the occasion of, even remembering to remember.

Casey (1976a) concludes that the relation between imagining and perceiving is, in sum, that "*imagination is phenomenologically self-sufficient but epistemologically non-self-sufficient.*" He means that, as experienced, imagining is quite independent of perception, but that from the point of view of causes and conditions imagining presupposes perception. Casey's dictum defines the freedom or autonomy of the imagination.

Here autonomy does not mean Kantian self-legislation, the imposition of laws by the imagination on itself or on other psychic agencies. Nor does it mean a Romantic predominance over them stemming from a monopoly on creativity, since not all creativity is of the imaginative sort and imagining is not always creative. There is no hierarchy of faculties implied in the freedom of the imagination. The autonomy of the imagination is "thin," that is to say, it is disconnected from the robust world of deeds, although much imagining goes on in parallel with practical involvement. The imagination is essentially independent of specific perceptual causes, of contexts and surroundings, of particular experienced contents, and of pressing applications. Balancing this disengagement from the perceptual and practical world is a weightier aspect of imaginative autonomy. It represents mental self-sufficiency, the carrying out of a psychic project by the mind on its own. In fact, each of the six essential traits, from spontaneity to pure possibility, displays a facet of this mental freedom. As Casey puts it, mind is most free when engaged in imagining independently of the world and performing the "autonomous act proper," which is to range over a wide field of possible variations.

In conclusion the human significance of imaginative autonomy is brought out, as it appears in the fields of art, psychology, and philosophy. Casey finds that both representational and expressivist theories of art demote the possibilizing imagination, the former by insisting on the isomorphism of picture and original, the latter by concentrating on purely affective states. What they omit, with respect to both the conception and the experience of a work of art, is its radical openness at any point, in its genesis as well as in its contemplation: Anything within the limits of conceivability may yet happen. Thus a painter in successive sketches might have taken any direction, and a reader might expect any turn in a plot.

In philosophical method, despite the habitual denigrations of the imagination, the imagination has traditionally played an enormous role (as corroborated throughout Part One). In logic it is at work in the projection of possible worlds (Part Three, Ch. III A), for such inventions cannot be solely the work of pure intellection. In metaphysical speculation Casey cites Whitehead as paradigmatic for a metaphysical use of the possibilizing imagination. For Whitehead the freedom of the imagination establishes "the *principle of possibility* of diverse actual entities," which means that the imagination mediates between the finitude of actual objects and the infinitude of possibilities inherent in eternal objects.

This summary of Casey's *Imagining* has omitted a wealth of well-observed detail. The book shows how rich, how lucid, and how unidiosyncratic phenomenological, introspective analysis can be. This fidelity to experience, born of sympathy, is what the Analysts, for all their superiority in precision, will turn out frequently to lack.

Casey's characterization of the imagination as phenomenologically free and only epistemologically conditioned by perception seems to me to be a good formulation of its curiously sense-bound inventiveness. Similarly persuasive is his description of the imagination as psychically self-sufficient, as a sort of self-entertainment disengaged from the cares of the world, though here I must register a first reservation. It is addressed to Casey's assertion (already qualified above) that one cannot perceive and imagine the same thing at the same time. This claim seems to me not only difficult to fix but descriptively not quite right. I shall argue in the Conclusion of this book that imagination furnishes just such a second sight, that perceptual and imaginal visions of the world—the *same* world—do occur simultaneously, and that it is precisely by reason of this double vision that the imagination is very much engaged with the world. Its autonomy, I would therefore say, is far from being "thin" and disconnected from life. It is about as robust as any human mode can be.

A more central reservation concerns the essentiality of "pure possibility" to imagining. As Casey recognizes, the characterization of the imagination as the power of the possible pursued for its own sake is bound to be controversial. It does seem admirably to catch what people ordinarily call "having imagination": the ability to see possible comparisons in a situation, to make the most of the possibilities in what is at hand, to play possibilities to their limit. But it seems to say nothing about what actually goes on when one uses the imagination. Therefore, one's first inclination might be to think that what is dubious in the definition is the mere formality of the trait: It says something only about the logical mode of imaginative activity and nothing about its substantial nature. It omits, in short, saying what the image-object actually is. But on second thought, the problem seems to lie in the descriptive inadequacy of possibility as the thetic mode of imagining—even when balanced by the experienced certainty of image-apprehension. (I leave aside the harder question whether any thetic aspect entering into the imagination is not actually the business of reason rather than imagination. Can any but a formal agency posit possibility?)

Take Casey's own example, Picasso's succession of sketches for *Guernica*. Rather than exemplifying the openness of the imagination, doesn't the series illustrate its advancing closure, its closing in on *the* intended image? Take another case from literature. There is extant a cancelled chapter of *Persuasion*. Its replacement came to Jane Austen overnight, as a relief from a period of depression brought on by the tameness of the original. One sees immediately that the new version, with its neatly devised situations and its bubbling undercurrent of restrained feeling, is the one right telling of the "revolution" that initiates the heroine's happiness. Does it not seem that in literary invention the moment of open possibility is a passing, anxious phase? Who would sustain it for its own sake?

Perhaps the following compromise contains the truth. Reveries, daydreams, and mental play of all sorts are indeed under the aegis of a possibilizing imagination, but the perfect images, the grand visions, the "big dreams," present themselves not as possible but as compellingly actual—not as a playing with shifting variations but as a being possessed by abiding figures.

Here I must mention an article by Ricoeur (1976) on the philosophy of the imagination, since for all its eclecticism its central reference is phenom-enological. It adverts, however, not to Husserl's theory of the imagination, but to his idea of inter-subjectivity, as set out in the fifth *Cartesian Medita-tion*. Ricoeur is concerned with the role of the imagination in writing history and in acting socially. He begins with a critical schematization of all previous theories in terms of two skewed axes. One represents an object-dimension, whose two extremes are the Humean image as a weak impres-sion of a present object and the Sartrean image as a consciousness of an absent object. The other is a subject-axis, with one pole assigned to the believing imager who credits the image as real and the other to the non-believer who, capable of critical self-consciousness, takes the image as image. The whole diagram is said to display by its complex of possibilities the impasse of contemporary theory, which Ricoeur intends to break by shifting from the traditional understanding of the imagination as a phenom-enon of visualization to a novel view of the imagination as a linguistic phenomenon. He is not exactly proposing another type of propositional-ism, the cognitive theory that images are completely reducible to verbal processes (Part Two). But he is advancing the priority of language in the imaginative process. His version is meant to give new access to the image-phenomenon: "to say that our images are spoken before being seen" is to renounce the false claim that an image is essentially a scene displayed before a mental theater, or that it is the mental stuff in which we dress our abstract ideas.

Images as derived from language are best studied in metaphor. Metaphor is not a matter of using individual nouns deviantly but of a shift in semantic outlook. In employing "impertinent predicates" a new "predicative perti-nence" is produced, which results in a "restructuring of semantic fields on the level of predicative usage." (Simply put, things are given a new significance.) The bearing of this view of metaphor on the philosophy of the imagination is that it ascribes to the imagination a distinct cognitive function. The imagination is the agency that offers its specific mediation at the moment when a new significance arises from the "ruins of the literal predication." Imagination is the sudden vision of a new pertinence, the abolition of the distance between remote semantic fields, the assimilation of significance that engenders the "semantic shock" of figurative speech. Ricoeur here appeals both to Kant's schematism of the imagination, which, as a method for providing an image for a concept, is, he claims, an operation for seizing resemblances, and to Wittgenstein's notion of "seeing-as." Visualization with its Bachelardian "reverberations" (see C, below) then follows on these essentially verbal processes. Ricoeur merely asserts that this process always begins verbally. The assertion is, I think, probably false. No one, however, would deny the general point that the capability of making and apprehending metaphors is to be assigned to the imagination, though its relation to metaphor will be analyzed quite differently in Part Four (Ch. III).

According to Ricoeur, the imagination proceeds to become practical in a number of modes that serve to break through the impasses reached by the tradition (Gerhart 1979). Most important of these is the "social" imagination, which mediates the experience of history by means of analogy: The temporal fields of my contemporaries, predecessors, and successors are all analogous, in the sense that I am historically linked to others through a resemblance that makes possible an intersubjective empathy. The special task of this imagination is to battle "the terrifying entropy in human relations," which ossifies institutions and turns this "we" into a "they."

There are a number of imaginative practices that make accessible the analogical link that binds me to others by resemblance. The chief among these devices are "ideology" and "utopia." The ideological imagination mediates between authority and the beliefs of the individual and is a pacifying instrument of social integration, while the literary utopia provides rousing images of excessive authority, of subversion, and of social alternatives. Ricoeur proceeds here, it seems to me, by abrupt intimations rather than consequential exposition. The utopian imagination will be more extensively taken up in Part Six (Ch. II B).

I must conclude this section by considering a very recent and very encouraging work. It is, as an enterprise, phenomenological, since it begins with careful observation of actual experience and uses phenomenological insights; but the style is analytic, because it works with precise logical distinctions and employs analytical terms. This book, Mark Johnson's *The Body in the Mind* (1987), is, moreover, the first attempt to construct a theory of specifically imaginative meaning, and one that saves the natural spatial functions of the imagination.

The basic notion of the book is the "image schema." It is an adaptation, made in the light of contemporary work, of Kant's schematism of the imagination. In Johnson's use, the schema is no longer a transcendental method, that is, pre-experiential, but itself emerges from experience, though it in turn interprets the environment. This use of "schema" will not be entirely identical with the various usages of the term in cognitive science in Part Two.

The "image schema" or "embodied schema" falls between the structures of reason and what Johnson calls the "rich image," the particular mental picture. The schema invites diagrammatic representation, though it is "abstract" in the sense of not being limited to visual properties. The operations performed with image schemata are analogues of spatial operations but they are influenced by general knowledge in a way that a particular mental picture is not. For example, if subjects are shown two circles connected by a straight line, they will draw it from memory differently, according to the cue given to them. If it is for "eyeglasses" they will tend to curve the connecting line, but for "dumbbells" they will draw it straight. The schema is thus cognitively loaded.

In sum, the schema is an organizing pattern, shape, or regularity for ordering everyday activities, evidently an attenuated mental picture or an embodied concept. Its salient, operative feature is that it has "entailments." For example, an important schema is that of "containment," by which is meant boundedness or "in-and-out orientation." The experience of containment typically entails protection from external forces and restraint of movement within the container (for example, a house), as well as relative fixity of location; also, containment is transitive.

The image schema serves to overcome "objectivism." For Johnson the principal opponent is not recent cognitive propositionalism so much as it is a more philosophically conceived attitude. It is said to be deeply rooted in the Western tradition, evidently as revealed of late in the analytic tradition. The objectivist theory of meaning has these chief marks: Meaning is an abstract relation between symbolic representations, verbal or mental, and objective reality; the mental representations involve general, logical entities or concepts that are divorced from perceptual experience; an objectivist theory of meaning must give the general conditions under which a state of affairs can be specified such as would make a sentence true; it requires that the mental representations be literal, univocal concepts which map onto definite, fixed real objects and relations.

What objectivism ignores, according to Johnson, is the essentially metaphorical structuring of experiences. "Metaphors" here are not conscious literary devices but operate at a deeper cognitive level. They are not figurative ways of speaking in which the categories of objective reality are confounded, such as can be set straight in literal speech. They are rather extensions or elaborations or projections of image schemata and are thus constitutive of experience. An exemplary case is the metaphor of balance as experienced, say, in a drawing of a black dot within a frame. Gestalt theorists have long pointed out that such configurations give a sense of balance or unbalance which has no objective dynamic cause. The picture seems to have a hidden experiential structure.

This structure is here attributed to the image schema. It in turn works metaphorically or by metaphorical projection. For we experience balance in terms of a schematic metaphor, on the analogy of visually apprehended weight and force. The balance metaphor is very pervasive. It structures not only visual perception but our understanding of rational processes such as the logical notions of symmetry, transitivity, and reflexivity. (Here Johnson's exposition comes close to Johnson-Laird's "mental models"—Part Five, Ch. II B.) Since, as the title indicates, one of the purposes of the book is to show how the body enters essentially into understanding, the structuring metaphors considered are those in which mental terms are somatically or physically presented.

The process of "metaphorical projection" is explicated through Kant's device for allowing the imagination to have interplay not only with cognitive understanding but also with regulative reason. This device is "presentation," set out in the *Critique of Judgment* (I 59). Through presentation, structures of one domain are projected onto another. If one wishes to speak of an idea of reason, such as immortality, that has no physical instantiation, one represents it through "an analogy . . . in which the judgment exercises a double function." It first brings the concept to bear on the empirical intuition and then, reflecting on, or playing over, the representation, finds an understanding which it applies to a different object, one for which the first intuition is now the symbol. "Presentation" is clearly a metaphorical operation, one which allows the imagination to exhibit sensually a supersensible idea of reason. Kant himself mentions such philosophical metaphors as "ground," "consequence," "flowing," and "substance."

Johnson's largest project, which is to initiate a philosophical theory of imaginative meaning, again begins with an acute assessment of Kant, this time of the theory of the imagination, adumbrated in the same *Critique*. Johnson points out that the reflective judgment mentioned above—in effect the free play of the imagination, as restricted by conceptual rules, in search of significant structures—is not a strictly subjective activity. It has elements of objective, communicable meaning. Consequently in the third *Critique* the imagination itself has the function of a faculty of understanding, that of effecting a structuring such as gives significance and leads to shared meaning. This imaginative preconceptual rationality is not really explicable within the terms of Kant's distinction between the understanding and the imagination. Indeed, it undermines the strict separation of faculties and suggests a specifically imagination-based theory of cognition, one that would overcome the gulf between the faculties.

The theory of meaning with which Johnson works is one that essentially involves the understanding subject. Yet its understandings are not private. Image schemata are generally human, since the somatic underpinning is generic, and the metaphorical projections are culturally shared. More specifically, meaning is taken as having two features. It involves human intentionality, and it is essentially dependent on a background structure. This background is already part of the meaning, because it is permeated by the image-schematic structures and their metaphoric elaborations. The image schemata in turn emerge interactively from the skilled bodily performances of daily life. They are characteristically somatic "presentations" of psychic or logical conditions. Hence the title of the book. These schemata have a continuous "analogue" character, and yet by virtue of their own internal structure they can connect with propositions. Although the image schemata do not have logical truth conditions in the correspondence-sense, they do give rise to meaning insofar as they too support some sort of fit. Such a fit occurs when a situation is grasped as instantiating a certain schema.

To turn this outline into a full-fledged theory of imaginative meaning it would be necessary, Johnson points out, to present first a theory of categorizations, which will supply a clue to the basic classifications within which experience is organized. The second requirement is a survey of the principal image schemata and an explanation of their modes of adaptation to novel situations. The third requirement is a description of the possible kinds of metaphorical projections, as well as of other figurative structurings.

This is certainly a hopeful project, one on which can be brought to bear the techniques of both phenomenological observation and cognitive-psychological experimentation. Nothing, it seems to me, could be more welcome than this new resistance to the habit of opposing reason and imagination—a habit which is rabid among rationalists and romantics alike (Conclusion). Nothing is more needed at this juncture than a theory of meaning that essentially includes the human imagination without falling into subjectivity and relativism. Nothing could be more in tune with the present book than a theory of the imagination that saves the analogue functions of the imagination and details how the imagination gives significance to the world.

Nevertheless, there are three sorts of misgivings I want to register, not criticisms so much as apprehensions concerning the premises of the project.

The first is this: Suppose that traditional reason is confirmed as fixed in the role of an untenable element-and-rule rationalism that is locked in hopeless opposition to a loose imagination. It may then deserve to be completely supplanted by Johnson's imaginative rationality, which interacts with the physical habitat through spatial schemata. Then our very powerful experience of having distinct faculties that are to each other as dreaming night and sober day, as receptive space and active structure, even as female and male principle—an experience that plays so great a role in philosophy and poetry—will, as so many deep human tropes have done, go out of style. At the same time the effort to rediscover a way of thought that is neither somatic nor operational will be—I think, unfortunately—obviated. Moreover, though the image schema rightly supplies the middle ground upon which reason and imagination can operate, it is not clear how such an explanatory construct could in any case come about unless the faculties were first apprehended as distinct. If a theory should preserve rather than subvert its constituent beginnings, then there is a danger in favoring the amalgam over its elements.

Johnson does, of course, recognize that approach to the old enigma of how space is mastered by thought is best made in terms of human understanding. He premises a pragmatist, interactive, environmental, and evolutionary understanding. In that vein, he gives a very narrow account of idealism as an imposition of concepts on a malleable reality, even though the grand idealisms do not, after all, regard the ontic structures of nature as being *our* imposition. And similarly he gives no account at all of the cause for the objectivist preoccupation with fixed reality, even though it has a good reason, namely the experience that sometimes some things seem to be objectively so. Otherwise why would some designs work better than others? Grant, for instance, that the "basic-level category," that is, the middle-level natural class such as "cat" (superordinate: animal; subordinate: Manx) is "the highest level at which a single mental image can reflect the entire category" (Lakoff 1988). If it is also true that this is "the level at which category members have similarly perceived overall shapes," then how does a thoroughgoing anti-objectivist account for the fact that the external world offers itself to us in just this way?

The third difficulty I see, has directly to do with the metaphorical theory of imaginative understanding. In metaphoric projection the basic image schema, which is itself spatial or physical, is projected onto various domains, most interestingly onto non-somatic ones, such as soul or reason. It is not clear—nor probably can it be at this early stage—what kind of mental process "projection" actually is, or how metaphorical fits or failures are in fact "grasped." So Kant's reflective judgment is not yet really elucidated, though the problem is certainly advanced—as a problem—by its translation into terms that are technically somewhat more precise.

Furthermore, this metaphorical projection seems itself to call for a cognitive base. Just as successful operation in the world requires some reliance on a literal, objectively given world, so does the mere recognition of a metaphor as a metaphor require not only basic categorizations—as Johnson certainly admits—but it would seem to need also prior beliefs about the nature of things, acknowledged or unacknowledged.

This precondition of having a conscious intention is of the essence, it seems to me, in making and grasping philosophical metaphor, whatever may be true of the culturally shared, more conventional, sort of figure. To begin with, it is one philosopher's literal truth that is branded as mere metaphor by another. But even the grasping of a philosophical metaphor that is intended as metaphor—be it the Heraclitean river, the Platonic "invisible vision" (*aeides eidos*), Hegelian "innerization" (*Erinnerung*), or Heideggerian "thrownness"—requires a special attitude. Like the theological *via negativa*, the way of analogy depends on the tension arising from the non-fit between the literal and the figural domain. To grasp such an unconventional metaphor is therefore not only to see a fit but simultaneously to see it as false. In most imaginative philosophical expositions bodily metaphors are not meant to be a resting place for the reader but to be kicked away like a ladder ascended. The aptest illustration of this claim is provided in Plato's *Timaeus*. There "the body in the soul" is actually and quite precisely the figure for the cosmos, and the physical world is depicted as wrapped in psychic bonds. But the reader's assimilation of the metaphorical image as cosmology is not the dialogic aim. That aim is somehow to make us understand that there can be no body without the soul. Similarly, the title metaphor of Johnson's book is more honored in the doubting than the believing.

B. Analytic Philosophy and Philosophy of Mind: The Attack on Inwardness

The most closely reasoned debate concerning the imagination, or rather mental imagery, was initiated by two terse texts, one by Wittgenstein and the other by Ryle. These writers are the chief representatives in imagery matters of the Analytic Method and of one of its specific applications, the Philosophy of Mind. Analytic philosophers reject the intuitive and introspective leap to first principles that is found in classical metaphysics and psychology because they think it results in vague and unmeaning talk. They insist on careful analysis of the language in which thinking goes public, as well as on clear evidence of what the language claims to be about. In the Philosophy of Mind this method is applied to the language concerning mental phenomena. The aim is to give accurate and unfuzzy descriptions and classifications of mental conduct without resorting to unwarranted and unnecessary hypostases of mental faculties and objects. Philosophers of Mind are therefore wary of being betrayed into these hypostases by unanalyzed ways of speaking. Chief of such unanalyzed terms for present purposes is the word "imagination" itself, which, because of its etymological connection to imaging, is commonly and uncritically taken to warrant talk of the images imagined. The writers of this school, then, mount a bold show-me attack on mental imagery. This challenge will be taken up by contemporary cognitive psychologists (Part Two). If their results tend to refute the Analysts' biases, so much the more to the Analysts' credit. Being falsified is one index of having actually said something.

1. Wittgenstein: Imagination as Aspect-Seeing. The two chief sequences on which the analytic image critique is founded are from Part II of the *Philosophical Investigations* (1947–49, xi, pp. 193–c.214), which comprises posthumously edited material Wittgenstein might or might not have fitted into the main work, and a collection of manuscript fragments, also posthumous, called *Zettel*, "Slips" (1945–48, nos. 621–c.646). These texts, especially the first, together with some other paragraphs in the *Investigations* (nos. 370, 388–400), have had an understandably pervasive influence. Not the least reason is that if a pregnant apothegm is memorable, a suggestive question is enthralling. There is no easy release from the grip of Wittgenstein's probings.

Whereas the sequence in the *Investigations* suggests, in the mode of indirection and analogy, what the imagination is, by analyzing its role in visual perception, the *Zettel* passages tell what imagination is not, by distinguishing it from perception. I shall start by setting out these distinctions as culled from the *Zettel*, then go to the section on "seeing-as" in the *Investigations*, and only last come to the main task, which is to discern from sporadic paragraphs the reason why questions about the imagination are raised by Wittgenstein in the first place.

But first it is only fair to make a preliminary remark on the reading of these texts, or rather on my reading of them. In studying these passages it is as if one were entering a world dominated by a taboo, a novel taboo, instituted, as it were, out of an honorable anxiety not to propitiate the Unseen. In this world it becomes a deadly serious matter, a matter of integrity, to maintain a gulf between the public and the private, the inner and the outer, the sayable and the unsayable. Wittgenstein is the most austerely elegant exponent of an all-inclusive duality that becomes a dominant strain of contemporary life: Whatever is not speakable thought must be consigned to ineffable subjectivity (Langer 1942, 87). This harsh dichotomy requires a certain overlooking of image-experiences, a certain image-blindness. For, as I will try to show, the answers invited by the bias of Wittgenstein's probings into the actual event of imagining do not fall out as he intimates they will. In almost every particular, experiment and experience contradict the response he implies.

The burden of the *Zettel* is to distinguish visual representations (*Gesichts-vorstellungen*) from visual impressions. (Various contexts show that it will be safe to write "image" for "representation.") The distinction is not between these two experiences directly. To eschew that direct approach is one of Wittgenstein's driving motives in all matters of mind, as will be shown below. The distinction is rather between their concepts. These concepts can be gathered from the distinct "language games" associated with the inner events, where by a language game is meant the set of rules which speech about them seems to embody.

The salient peculiarity of mental images is that what is imaged has the same description as what is seen (621, 637). Both may even on occasion be described as pictures. But the contexts for the use of image and the use of impression are utterly different. Images and impressions are connected, to be sure, but they are not similar (625). Indeed so diverse are they that finally nothing could be more false than to speak of them as different. It would be as if someone were to say that moving a piece and losing a game in chess were different activities (645). They don't, for example, differ by Humean vivacity. These activities are not confusable, for no one who wanted to be understood would say that he didn't know whether he was imagining or seeing a tree, unless he merely meant that he was "just fancying" that there was a tree there (634). Nor, consequently, can they be simultaneous; one cannot have an image of an object while seeing it (621). In sum, imagining and perceiving are not coordinate and are therefore in certain ways incomparable.

But they are not entirely incomparable, since Wittgenstein differentiates them under four headings:

a. Subjection to Will. Imagining is subject to the will (621). Its concept is that of doing; it might be called a creative act (637). Seeing, on the other hand, is receiving; we learn its concepts by describing what we see. What is imagined is not observed. An image-picture isn't something that happens to us; it does not surprise us (632). We can chase it away, unlike an impression, of which we say neither that we can nor that we can't drive it off (633). Listening or looking is connected with listening to, or looking at, whereas imaging a sound or sight is not. That is why listening and imaging may be said to occupy a different space (622). The two activities also involve different imperative language: when trying to get someone to see, "Look closely!"; when trying to get someone to imagine, "Close your eyes!" (626). Yet it doesn't make sense to say that images are internal pictures similar to my visual impressions, except that they are subject to the will. It isn't, after all, clear what the command to imagine now this, now that, would mean, even to someone who had learned to report these sights. For what does it mean to follow the order, say, to move an image by mere will? Could one report failure, as with physical acts? (642–43).

b. Cognitive Inefficacy. Because images are subject to the will, they teach us nothing about the independent external world (621, 627).

c. Inaccessibility. There might be people who never spoke of seeing something before their inner eye or who denied having mental images, just as most people affirm it; but what value, either for or against mental images, should one attach to these reports? (624). The claim that images resemble impressions is purely private, known only from personal experience, for voluntarily forming images is not like making overt movements (641). The similarity becomes manifest only in the expressions people use, not in something the expressions are used to say (630–31).

d. Picture-unlikeness. Mental images are not pictures (621), nor is a visual impression a picture. This is not a matter of their different genesis. It is that neither of them are picture-concepts (637). One may, to be sure, answer the question "What are you imagining?" with a picture, since both impression and image have a connection with pictures, though each has a different connection (638). "An image is not a picture though a picture can correspond to it" (*Philosophical Investigations* no. 301). But which object I am representing to myself is not to be discerned by means of the similarity of my image to it (621).

Here are my reservations, item by item:

a. Some imaging is surely involuntary. In arguing the subjection of imaging to the will, Wittgenstein wants to make sure that this subjection is not tied to quasi-physical making and moving, whose concept includes success or failure. Failure, however, is in fact a common event in imaging. To try to raise, say, the face of a distant love and to get nothing—the whole pathos of absence lies in this failure. Moreover, imagining is only very partially voluntary. The adventitiousness of imagery, with its delightful or disturbing surprises, which are not a poet's prerogative alone, is an excellent reason for assimilating imagination to seeing. Seeing, on the other hand, aside even from the fact that the attention is voluntarily focused, is not so obviously involuntary. "See it this way!" (as Wittgenstein knows better than anybody) is a perfectly sensible order.

To make his point, Wittgenstein explicitly excludes hallucinations, that is, compulsive imagining, from mental imagery. Why? The continuity of the image-spectrum will assert itself against him over and over again in experience (Parts Two and Six).

Voluntariness is, then, not a good mark of mental images.

b. The cognitive relevance of images will be tested experimentally, with results contrary to Wittgenstein's claim (Part Two). But such results aside, one might ask, first, questions of fairly shallow draft: Why isn't it learning something about the outside. world to recover an image of what is absent and gone? Or if communicableness is at stake, in what way is what one sees internally more incommunicable than what one sees externally? After all, the possibility of pointing, which is indeed what distinguishes communication about internal and external vision, doesn't really guarantee that the one sees what the other meant him to see. Again, why isn't it learning something about the external world to see how one's imagination deals with it? And finally a deeper question: Would there be an external world at all were there not internal images?

c. Whether imagery is in principle inaccessible to any process but introspection, though not in itself empirically resoluble, again becomes a practical problem for cognitive scientists. Wittgenstein himself observes that imagining seems to be attended by some sort of genuine duration (624), and that precisely is the point of departure for actual experiments. However, the better question is: Why should an introspective protocol be a weaker testimonial to its object than any other descriptive report of things we can't possibly see ourselves? In both cases the description fails to achieve the perfect communication of a fully determinate given.

d. Still, all these counter-arguments float a little above Wittgenstein's project, because they tend simply to impugn his image-awareness. But response to the fourth and most famous feature of mental images can touch bottom: Being picture-like does, I think, belong to the concept of a mental image, Wittgenstein to the contrary.

First it should be said that his claim about visual impressions and visual images, namely that they are not similar enough in category to be contrasted, is somewhat belied by the differences he himself lists. At least it is a judgment call whether being sometimes voluntary, possibly uninformative, and in some ways inaccessible makes mental images un-perceptions, hence comparable to and therefore not utterly unlike perceptions. But if it must be admitted that mental images are somehow like perceptions, then there might be a use for talk about objects of inner seeing as there is of outer vision. Now experimental evidence does tend at least to show that images are both temporally and physiologically connected to parts of the perceptual process, and that, *pace* Wittgenstein, people even do sensibly speak of confusing them (see Perky, Index).

Consequently, images might yet be picture-like objects, and their content like objects in a picture (I shall so argue in Part Three, Ch. II B). For if imagining is after all like perceiving, then it follows that images might be like their perceptual originals. At least this is the inference Wittgenstein accepts, though he wants to block its conclusion.

Wittgenstein's most pertinent and deepest question concerning mental images is:

What makes an image of him an image of him?

and the famous answer is:

Not the similarity of the picture.

The same question can, he says, be asked of the expression "I now see him vividly before me." And again, Wittgenstein claims that nothing lies in the expression or "stands behind it" that can be held responsible, certainly no likeness. To the question "How do you know it is him you see?" the imager's description is the decisive and sufficient answer. It can take the place of the image (*Philosophical Investigations* p. 177).

Can it, though? Perhaps for us it would be sufficient (though if his description, as is conceivable, turned out to be duller when and only when he said he had no mental image, this would surely strike us as needing an explanation). But surely for him it would be quite insufficient, especially if he was trying hard to describe his image with precision. There are reported cases of people who have lost the ability to image and feel it as a loss. A description they might compose doesn't take the place of an image for them. There are, conversely, famous morons, numerical *idiots savants*, who give practical evidence of having enormous and intricate interior landscapes of which one must somehow get a glimpse in order to do justice to their dumb genius (Sacks 1987).

How do we tell whom or what we are imagining? Oddly, or, as it seems to me, naturally enough, the ordinary answer is just the same as to the question whom or what are we seeing. "It is so and so," we say. "What makes you say it?" we are asked. "It looks like him; it has his air, a similar silhouette, even the coloring matches," we answer. The reason this is not nonsensical is that one can inspect one's mental image. One can be puzzled by the identity of a mental image and attempt to look hard at it or wait for it to reveal itself. Such image-episodes—in which a mysterious figure suddenly turns round, and behold! it is so and so—happen, to be sure, mostly in dreams, and dreams, like hallucinations, Wittgenstein would, unjustifiably, exclude from the image rubric. At any rate, he himself observes that I may have an unidentifiable face hover before me, and may even draw it (*Philosophical Investigations*, p. 177). Thus he admits that even in fully conscious imagining a figure is not *ipso facto* and always who I intend it to be or say it is. My conceptual intention can misconnect and summon the wrong picture or a blur. The intention is not perfectly congruent with the image.

These experiences, of course, speak only for the possibility of recognition by similarity, that is to say, of finding internally some visual features like those observed externally. Moreover, though resemblance may after all identify an image (Part Five, Ch. III A), it does not yet constitute a picture. For that there have to be further features, such as a medium. They too are indeed discernible in mental images (Part Two, Ch. II B). However, Wittgenstein does not raise that issue here.

If being an image is not yet being a picture, being a picture may now no longer involve being similar to an original. In that case, even if mental images existed to begin with, and even if they were picture-like, they might not represent by similarity. Wittgenstein implies this, the ultimate blow to the literal imaginal character of mental "images," in the *Blue Book* (p. 32), where he asks the same question of portraits as he later asks of images: What makes this portrait a portrait of Mr. N? It is clear to Wittgenstein that similarity does not constitute the essence of a portrait, for a good likeness might be a bad portrait. This is, of course, disputable or at least equivocal. He himself, when impugning anyone's claim to have an image of another's feelings, say a toothache, argues that "the sense in which an image is an image is determined by the way in which it is compared with reality. This we might call the method of projection" (p. 53). What can this method of projection, mentioned in the *Tractatus*, be but the search for similarity? So he must think images do represent by resemblance.

Nevertheless, the answer he prefers is, for all its complications, that what makes the portrait a portrait of N is the painter's intention. This intention is not so much what the painter aims at as what he has in mind, what he is thinking of. Such intention is, of course, much less elusive in the case of a material artifact than of a mental image. Wittgenstein's intimation that similarity or resemblance might not be the essence of a representational picture is the germ of a radical, new notion in contemporary aesthetics. It is reviewed and criticized in Part Five.

In the much-studied section on "aspect-seeing" or "seeing-as" of the *Philosophical Investigations* (xi), Wittgenstein suggests certain positive functions of the imagination. The following review is, of course, very much an interpretation. For one thing, Wittgenstein is not fond of connective parti-

cles, and so it becomes the reader's responsibility to discern the logical relations among his observations. For another, from this rich text I have picked out those remarks that seem to me to throw a light on the imagination, oblique as that light may be.
(Hallet 1977, 662 ff.)

Wittgenstein points out that one object seen in an identical viewing may yet appear under diverse categories. One may see a face or the sadness in the face. Or one object may have two aspects: One may see a duck in the picture when the two long loops play the role of a bill, or a rabbit when, turned through a quadrant, they are a pair of ears. Or a wedge-shaped outline drawing may be seen as a triangular hole, a triangular body, a geometric diagram, a semi-parallelogram, a mountain, an arrow, or a pointed body fallen over.

Normally we just see things. We don't see a picture-rabbit but a rabbit. We do not see a face as a face, but we see just a face. Seeing-as is therefore a special phenomenon. Eventually it will become an issue whether Wittgenstein can maintain his strong separation of seeing-as from perception (*P.I.*, p. 197). Perhaps he must be taken to imply that ultimately any seeing, from the merest glancing to aesthetic seeing (Aldrich 1958), is aspect-seeing or seeing-as, and that there is no merely perceptual seeing. Strawson (1970) will argue that Wittgenstein makes too much of the sudden unexpected "flashing" of an aspect, and that when Kant rightly posited a productive imagination which commingled thought and sense, he had in effect already turned all seeing into seeing-as. Wittgenstein himself does distinguish the "steady seeing" of an aspect from its sudden "dawning." At any rate, he is here interested in this "noticing of an aspect" in its concept and its position among other concepts of experience.

Of his three examples, neither the noticing of affects expressed in a figure, nor the perspectival flipping of figures deliberately designed to be optical illusions (which may be all but completely determined by physiology, Part Two, Ch. VI A) is as pertinent as the third case. This is the situation where it is not so much hard as impossible to point to that element in the figure which is the cause of a particular interpretation. For example, take the above-mentioned triangle picture. One points to a summit angle and the base line both when describing it as a wedge and as a mountain. This is the case of aspect-seeing which "requires the power of imagination" (*Vorstellungskraft*, p. 207).

Wittgenstein speaks in two ways of the dawning of an aspect. On occasion he observes that it is "half visual experience, half thinking" (p. 197), "the echo of a thought in sight" (p. 212). But more prominently—and this equivocation is never explicitly resolved—he says:

The concept of an aspect is akin to the concept of an image. In other words: the concept "I am now seeing it as . . ." is akin to "I am now having *this* image."

Doesn't it take imagination to hear something as a variation on a particular theme? And yet one is perceiving something in so hearing it. [p. 213]

Seeing-as somehow involves taking a perception as a picture or image. That is why the notion is useful in aesthetics (Ch. IV B). As an act of imagination it differs from "imagining that" in being more of a spontaneous transformation of a given perception, whereas the latter involves elements of deliberate supposal and hypothesis (Hannay 1971, ch. VII). Nevertheless, Wittgenstein insists, the concept of an "inner picture" is misleading, a confusion arising from an unwarranted analogy of inner image to outer picture. The drawing I can point to certainly doesn't render what a visual impression is, and "neither is it anything of the same category, which I carry within myself" (p. 196). And Wittgenstein repeats warnings not to try to analyze one's own inner experience but to ask instead what one may know about someone else (p. 207, 206).

Now one should ask what the kinship between aspect-seeing and image really is. Wittgenstein uses the latter to elucidate the former, but the reverse also works, so that one may delineate the image from aspect-seeing. They seem to me to have the following factors in common. First, both are subject to the will (p. 213). Second, they give rise to similar linguistic expressions, such as "I see a mountain in the wedge figure," and "I see a mountain in my mind's eye" (Ishiguru 1967). Third, they engender similar practices insofar as in both cases merely trying to point to the object ends in frustration. So Wittgenstein's concept of the imagination, established in analogy to aspect-seeing, would seem to amount to this: It is the assertion of seeing coupled with an inability to point to an object. This differs from aspect-seeing only insofar as the latter is parasitic on some sort of primary perception. Further explications are given below by Scruton and Furlong.

Can this sparse result check for good, as Wittgenstein means it should, our desire to inquire into the inner objects of the imagination? He himself gives what is to my mind the most perceptive description of imaginative seeing anywhere to be found. It happens also to be the one most apt to the project of this book (Conclusion). He says:

. . . it is as if an *image* came in contact with the visual impression and for a time stayed in contact with it. [p. 207]

But what illumination can this notion of contact cast on imaginative vision—for that is what aspect-seeing taken narrowly is—unless the image is precisely some sort of inner picture projected onto an external perception? It is as if here Wittgenstein's philosophical austerity had been counter-manded by his visual sensibility.

How does Wittgenstein's treatment of images fit into his primary enter-prise? Early, in the *Tractatus*, he had held a "picture-theory" of propositions (discussed under the logic of images, Part Three, Ch. I B). It was highly compatible with mental images. In the *Philosophical Investigations* "imagin-ability" no longer ensures the sense of a proposition. Having an image is as unnecessary to understanding a proposition as is drawing a sketch from it (395–96). Nor, conversely, does a drawing, besides representing an object to the viewer, also represent the image of the imaginer (280). What makes Wittgenstein now deny the need for a mental image hypothesis? That is the question.

At this moment we find that the point is really not so much whether we have mental images, or what the marks of that experience are. Perhaps we do have such internal viewings—but our private experiences don't matter much. That is why a critique directed to Wittgenstein's image-observation may seem to be a bit off-center. Here, however, is the central point, in unequivocal language:

> One ought to ask, not what images are or what happens when one imagines anything, but how the word "imagination" is used. But that does not mean that I want to talk only about words. For the question as to the nature of the imagination is as much about the word "imagination" as my question is. And I am only saying that this question is not to be decided—neither for the person who does the imagining, nor for anyone else—by pointing; nor yet by a description of any process. The first question also asks for a word to be explained; but it makes us expect a wrong kind of answer. [370]

The wrong kind of answer is the one in terms of inner objects and processes. The right kind may seem to be an answer about words, but it is really a new way of talking about the nature of things. The new way is in terms of the analysis of their concepts, that is to say, of the language sensibly used of these things and the practices ordinarily associated with that language.

In sum, Wittgenstein is providing all sorts of therapy against the explan-atory misuse both of image-pictures and of the speculatively philosophical imagination. Let me give one last example of each (nos. 388–90). First, he ridicules mental images as causes of our ability to recognize say, colors, by showing that such likenesses would have to be regarded as super-pictures, closer to the object color than any possible actual picture. And, second, he derides what he calls "image-mongering" (*Vorstellerei*), the fantastic flight in a vacuum which characterizes certain kinds of free philosophical speculation, such as the imaginative hypothesis that a stone has consciousness. This attack on the speculative imagination is later taken up by Aldrich (1962) in a distinction he makes between "imaging," which means having mere speculative fantasy pictures, and "image-management" or "imagining," which means using the imagination with respect to verifiable actual or logical possibilities. Fear of image-mongering might be said to have fatally infected the contemporary philosophical imagination (Part Four, Ch. IV A).

Debate. In mounting a book-length defense of mental images, Hannay (1971) criticizes Wittgenstein's attack on them in the context of his wider intentions. Wittgenstein's intentions, Hannay says, are not merely to show that accounts in image-terms are neither necessary nor sufficient for understanding what someone who speaks of images means, or that their claimed presence is redundant and their absence not significant (ch. VI). In insisting that "an inner process stands in need of outward criteria" (*P.I.* 580), Wittgenstein is precisely guarding against a danger to our belief in a mind, namely against behaviorism. For if we talk vaguely of inner processes or objects, we are sure to commit ourselves thoughtlessly to an unwarranted physical analogy between them and bodily processes, because that analogy may seem our only hope of learning about them. Then, when that fails to get us anywhere, we will be pushed into denying inner processes altogether and left with mere behavior—"And naturally we don't want to deny them" (*P.I.* 308).

So here Wittgenstein says outright that it is not his intention to deny activities like imagining and having mental images. On the contrary, he wants to save them for ordinary discourse. Yet, Hannay goes on to show, Wittgenstein's actual observations drive explicity or implicitly toward the denial of mental images. It is the notion of an outward criterion that makes images redundant, for it amounts to substituting their descriptions for the images themselves. Indeed, "the mental picture is the picture which is described when someone describes what he imagines" (*P.I.* 367)—an apothegm which is all of propositionalism *in nuce.* And in general, his various denials that psychological terms have or need private references, and that if they did have them, they would be processes or objects, and that imagining can be correlated to outward behavior sufficiently to make imagination-expressions possible—all these add up to a denial of mental images.

And so, finally, the Wittgensteinian texts must be accepted as equivocal about mental images. A bolder spirit, Ryle, will draw starker conclusions.

Wittgenstein has been practically immune from attack in the imagery debate. Most analytic writers have built on and developed his insights. Even Hannay's long critique poses what is really only one objection, though it is a broad one: Wittgenstein's concept-finding is carried on from too close a perspective. It is sometimes necessary to go beyond ordinary contexts in order to see the nature of the thing and to maintain a theoretical interest in it. Terms such as image, process, and object are perhaps not fully fixed by ordinary use, and an authoritative meaning may one day be found in a sphere as yet unexplored (233). Hannay's chief defense of mental images is really a call to reconsider their possibility: In view of the failure of anti-image theories, it would be better to give these ubiquitously recognized phenomena a chance, rather than to prejudge the case of mental images for the sake of a doubtful theory of mind.

2. Ryle: Imagination as Pretending. Where Wittgenstein wields an insidiously questioning scalpel, Ryle hammers pertinently away at error. The *Concept of Mind* (1949), hard-hitting though it is in its attack on purported dogma, is yet curiously approximate and unperspicacious in its positive claims. For example, its main solution to the problem of imagining, that it is a form of pretending, is hard to fix in meaning and, on the face of it, implausible. Indeed, the *Concept of Mind* acquaints the reader with an invigorating pleasure. It is the opportunity to produce counter-claims to all its observations of psychic fact as well as linguistic usage, and to offer reasonable resistance to almost all its explanatory formulations. Yet the enormous influence of the book is well-warranted. In trying to shatter, as if by a mere hard look, the most ordinary sense of what imagination is, it initiates an acute debate regarding the human claim to inner experiences.

The general purpose of Ryle's book is to expose the falsity or even the absurdity of the "official doctrine," purportedly stemming from Descartes, which Ryle, "with deliberate abusiveness," calls "the dogma of the Ghost in the Machine." It is the double notion that mind is in polar opposition to matter and that it is transparent to itself in self-intellection. This notion is Cartesianism stripped of all motive and qualification. The brutal elegance of Ryle's endeavor is due to its focus on such contextless dogma. An important part of the dogma so presented is that the mental life of the mental ghost that works the bodily machine, while open to itself by introspection, is inaccessible to the other ghosts in their machines. Hence "mental-conduct verbs," such as knowing, believing, remembering, and also imagining, are incorrigible by anyone other than the one who claims to be engaging in these activities at the moment.

The phrase "mental-conduct verb" intimates that imagining will be treated as a sort of inner behavior, though Ryle would really like to circumvent internality altogether. For example, in order to give an account of the visual recall of an object, it will be enough if people produce creditable drawings; one will not, he says, desire additional information about the qualities of their visual images. Now for the totally quiescent kind of event that imagining mainly is, this kind of account is usually unavailable. Therefore, since Ryle is not a crude behaviorist of the "there is only external behavior" sort, he can compromise his position a little for the case of the imagination, to allow for some sort of mental event.

Ryle's account is given in the chapter slyly called "Imagination" (VII)—slyly, since "there is no special Faculty of Imagination." There are only various ways of imagining. If the general attack is on Descartes, the particular butt in this chapter is Hume's complex of notions that ideas are in the mind, that they have inherent qualities like degrees of vivacity, and that they are shadow-sensations, weak sensation-images.

Since Ryle's account represents the extreme rationalistic opposite to the view of the imagination defended in this book, I shall accompany my review with my own parenthetical counter-arguments. The published debate will be reported following this review.

Ryle's opening question might indeed be thought to be the proper preoccupation of anyone who ever comes to think about mental images:

Where do things and happenings exist which people imagine existing?

This question is declared spurious. (I take it up, however, in Parts Two, Three, and Six, decomposed, as it has to be to become approachable, into two questions: "What kind of presence do images have in the mind?" and "What are the mental images, especially imaginary ones, images of?")

What is to be done instead is to describe what people "see in their mind's eye" or "hear in their head." For Ryle admits that they do such things even though he does not concede the existence of entities like visual or auditory images.

But why do people talk as if there were such images? Why do they insist on drawing an analogy between seeing and "seeing" in the mind's eye?

Ryle answers that it is an unfortunate consequence of the preeminence of sight that our imagination-language is largely drawn from vision. Since there are real simulacra, real pictures, portraits, and photographs in the visual world, people are induced to speak of visual mental images; since there are no dummy smells or tastes, smell-images are not at issue. (First, I ask, is it true that there are no image-tunes or smell and taste simulacra? Wittgenstein himself allows that something can taste like sugar and not be sugar, *Zettel* 657. Imitation vanilla and aspartame are intended as scent and taste simulacra; an electronic synthesizer produces real synthetic but false orchestral music. Nevertheless, we might just wish to deny that all the senses are equally capable of engendering imagination and to think of vision as a special but paramount case. We might even suspect that vision is preeminent just because it alone generates internal simulacra—Introduction B.)

Furthermore, Ryle says, real picture-seeing, such as looking at photographs, often stimulates inverted-comma seeing, but that does not mean that "seeing" belongs to the same genus as picture-seeing. For "to see is one thing; to visualize another," and "there *is* nothing akin to sensation." (In Part Two I shall cite much experimental evidence that bears on this assertion. It tends to show that in part the same perceptual apparatus is involved in imaging as in seeing. It will appear that percept and mental image are in fact sometimes non-pathologically confused. Furthermore, mental images will be shown to have specific pictorial features, including a medium. The conclusion will be that there is real validity in the ordinary usage of "seeing" for "imagining.")

"Seeing" and "picturing," though useful concepts, are then not to be taken as entailing the contemplation of inner pictures.

> Roughly, imaging occurs, but images are not seen. . . . True, a person picturing his nursery is, in a certain way, like a person seeing his nursery, but the similarity does not consist in his really looking at a real likeness of his nursery, but in his really seeming to see his nursery itself, when he is not really seeing it. He is not being a spectator of a resemblance of his nursery, but he is resembling a spectator of his nursery.

(The problem in this central formulation is, I think, first, its misstatement of the image-case. For that claim is precisely that imagining is quasi-seeing of unreal, non-material, likenesses. Furthermore, *to whom* does the seeming seem? Who notices the resemblance? No onlooker, since Ryle admits that imagining is not overt. Then what is meant by saying that the imaginer seems to see his nursery except that he somehow—and this is the very thing at issue—sees it? And how is "seeming to see" like seeing to begin with, if it is not a kind of seeing?)

Suppose, Ryle argues, there were "special status pictures" inside the head. Then a child who sees her doll smiling would be seeing "a picture of a smile" but not seeing it where the doll is, which is absurd. (Of course, I would say, she isn't seeing a picture of a smile but she is seeing a picture of the doll smiling, which she projects onto the doll.)

How then do people seem to see their nurseries or have ghost tunes running through their heads? One answer is that if they were really seeing they wouldn't be "seeing." (But this double seeing is just what puts poetry into the world—Conclusion.) For Ryle, a better reply is that it is a question about the wires and pulleys the ghost uses to work the machine and requires no answer because no account of ulterior or occult processes is necessary. Ryle has no need of the hypothesis of mental images.

(His refusal to deal with inner processes shows why Ryle's attack and the imagist's inquiry actually bypass each other: Ryle is looking for that economical account of conduct in which mental images are an unnecessary hypothesis; the imagist is interested in an inquiry into internal phenomenon in which images are a given experience.)

Ryle's positive answer starts from the claim that "seeing" images is only one of many widely divergent meanings of imagining. There is no nuclear operation called by that name. (This multiplicity of uses has been observed throughout the tradition, as I have shown in Part One. It may as easily serve as an incitement to develop an original and main meaning. But more to the point, isn't it just the claim of a loose concatenation of meanings that prevents anything following concerning any particular use of a term? If "imagining" may sometimes mean "conjecturing," why not then, at some other time, "having mental pictures"?)

The meaning pertinent to "seeing" is pretending, make-believe. (The germ of this notion occurs, I observe, in the *Philosophical Investigations*, no. 391, where Wittgenstein had suggested that imagining, say, another's pain, is, as it were, playing a role, pretending that the other is hurting.) Thus the child that plays bear pretends to be a bear by growling and stomping. It engages in a mock-performance. Such part-playing has an interestingly dual description: The child is intelligently being a brute, it is being bright and brutal simultaneously. But this playing does not involve pictures or shadow-sensations. (I dispute this. When as a child I was, for several years, the Scarlet Pimpernel, I was copying a vivid inner vision—still undimmed—of gallantry incognito.) In imagining, the pretending includes a refraining from overt conduct. Silent pretenders do not show anything to themselves or watch themselves seeing anything. One reason is that seeing is in any case not a doing or a performance. It is rather an achievement. (First, I reply, there are image-studies that show that some imagining does include seeing oneself watching the image. Second, perceptual studies show that seeing is very much a productive process or activity, and that one can indeed monitor one's own image-seeing.)

What people do, Ryle claims, is to engage in a kind of rehearsal that does not involve ghost pictures or tunes but does involve "fancying" oneself hearing or seeing—listening for a tune that one has "learned and not forgotten," "knowing and thinking how the tune goes." Therefore such fancyings do not materially aid cognition, since they are themselves willful uses of knowledge. (Ryle's emphasis on the necessity of knowledge in imaginative pretending pretty well excludes, it seems to me, dreams and semi-voluntary imagination, and, above all, eidetic imagery—Lawrie 1970. Thus it narrows the field to a certain inner role-playing. But if we consider imagining in the larger sense, his emphatic claim that we do not sometimes have vivid images whose identity puzzles us is just false. Our image-presences are often enigmatic. In Ryle's description, the correlative of the activity and the objects of the verb "to imagine" are simply tacitly suppressed. What, one might ask, is being listened to? Who is pretending what to whom? Moreover, how can "refraining" leave so vivid a psychic remainder? Visualizing, Ryle says, is like a silent soliloquy which is "a flow of pregnant non-sayings." What does this description signify besides the resolve to look at mentation strictly negatively and from the outside?)

Finally, Ryle assesses the value of visual memory and re-visualization. They are mere knacks, which we expect of most people and in "high degree of children, dress-designers, policemen, and cartoonists." In any case, it comes into evidence only in faithful description. (Here the cat is out of the bag: Ryle is in the tradition that has a low opinion of visualization—Part Six, Ch. I A. Concomitantly he tends—though only tends—toward propositionalism, as cognitive scientists will call the reduction of all mental activity to thinking.)

It should be said that Ryle himself, though reaffirming the thesis that imagining a tune is thinking how it goes in its absence, later confessed a "conceptual uneasiness" about pretending, especially in view of the evident vividness of some imagining (in Cowley 1968, 206).

Debate. Without hope of being able to do justice to the many close trains of argument raised by Ryle's thesis, I want to report some main positions.

Shorter (1952) hones the question concerning mental imagery to this sharp edge: What are the specifically non-representational properties of mental images, if any? For example, since we must sometimes say that these images are blurred, we must admit, at the risk of paradox, that in a way it makes sense to speak of mental images. (I observe that this "blur" argument becomes an issue in the literature: Agreed that one may distinctly visualize a blurry face, can one blurrily visualize a distinct face? Can one, instead of visualizing an unclear object, visualize unclearly, or fail to discern a mental image? What is at stake is the possibility of real inner seeing and independent inner objects of sight. It seems to me that according to introspection both are possible. One may visualize indolently and get a mere blur and one may imagine effortfully and get a near-blank. It is to the discovery of such features, the "privileged properties" of inner vision and its objects *per se*, that cognitive psychologists of the eighties have, fairly successfully, addressed themselves—Part Two, Ch. II B.)

Nevertheless, Shorter continues, some questions are addressed to imagery improperly, such as "Is that mental image you produced yesterday still in existence or have you rubbed it out?" (Such questions concerning the maintenance and fading of imagery are, nevertheless, asked in laboratories.) He contends, against Ryle, that visualization, which is only one particular kind of imagination, has a logic in the analytic sense, that is to say, has conceptual implications, more like depicting than like pretending. For visualizing is a performance in a way that seeing is not, as Shorter concedes to Ryle. In particular it is a performance which involves no image as direct object: To depict a mountain is to depict not a picture, but just a mountain. Thus the very analogy of active visualization to depicting speaks against mental images. Shorter concludes with a counsel of caution or despair: Ultimately the answer to the question what visualizing is, is that it can't be explained except to someone who has done it. Similarly, the answer to the question whether there are mental images is that it is sometimes convenient to talk about them, while being careful not to ask those questions about them that are sensibly asked only of real pictures.

Ishiguro (1967) agrees with Ryle's main distinction between seeing and imagining, which is also Wittgenstein's and Sartre's: It is not possible to have an image without knowing what it is an image of, though it is possible to see a picture without knowing what it represents. Since we do not have unidentified mental images, the object of our imaging is not a picture but must be the perceived thing itself. (Above I suggested that there are indeed inner images that are not immediately identifiable. Here, conversely, it must be pointed out that we can see without identifying what we see only in the most specific sense. To see is always to see something, so we do usually know what pictures represent on a generic level—about as often and accurately as we identify our inner images. Moreover, I must mention again the unintended effect that is produced by denying that imagining is having images. It is that imagining actually becomes harder to differentiate from seeing. For on the image-hypothesis, seeing, which has the thing seen as its immediate object, is clearly distinguished from imagining, which takes place at one remove from the perceptual original. But with the mediating image gone the differentia of seeing and imagining become utterly elusive, although Ryle wishes to emphasize the utter difference between them.) Ishuguru, while siding with Ryle against the sense-datum theorists—those Humeans who think that sensations are perceived in the mind—agrees with

Shorter that the term "depicting" comes nearer to describing most imagining than does the notion of merely entertaining a hypothetical description. A limited number of people do find mental images a necessary tool in certain kinds of exercises of the imagination, though most often images are mere accompaniments. (This "epiphenomenal" argument will play a role in the later imagist-propositionalist debate.) Ishiguro concedes that none of the authors had succeeded in saying what imagining actually is.

Hannay (1971) examines the logic of Ryle's inferences and shows that Ryle vitiates his point by making seeing and "seeing" so unlike as to render their likeness inexplicable. He also disagrees with Shorter's argument that because mental images can't be examined like ordinary pictures they do not share the picture-concept in some ways. Audi (1978) in turns shows that Hannay's arguments are inconclusive, especially his "simplest and best" defense of mental images. This defense is that, if in mental picturing "one is seeing something intentionally, it would seem wholly inexplicable that one saw nothing materially" (Hannay, 173). Audi admits, however, that Hannay's assertion does make anti-imagists confront the problem of convincingly establishing the similarities and differences between mental images and ordinary objects, with respect, for example, to their spatiality, dimensionality, and sensory content. This problem will be precisely the one to be next attacked (Part Two).

Here the specifically Rylean debate begins to turn in smaller and smaller logical or linguistic circles. One may, for example, show that the image issue is trivial simply by regarding the imagist position as following from a rule that doing something like seeing x implies doing something like seeing something like x. Or one may resolve it by a mere manner of description—for example, by construing the supposed object-accusative in "imagining x" not as a reference to an object, but as adverbial to the imagining itself, as descriptive of the properties of the imagining that is going on: "imagining x-ly". Or one may agree to talk of "seeing an image of x" instead of "visualizing x." Or one may consider imagining not as the having of images but as the instantiation of certain sensory properties (Matthews 1969, Rabb 1975a, Garry 1977, Audi 1978).

A more recent critique of Ryle's argument both in its eliminative and its positive aspect makes a fitting conclusion (Furlong 1982). Ryle attacks mental images exclusively as resemblance-representations. Furlong, however, discerns three degrees of representation: First are straight simulacra or copies, such as naturalistic portraits. Second are the cases of representation by a few selected features, such as cartoons. Third come non-representational representations (so to speak), which instantiate a more complex or higher entity, as an ambassador represents a country. Ryle, he argues, has failed to show proof against the existence of the last kind of mental image, which is however quite common. It occurs, for example, when the image is a vague or blurry presence standing for an intended object that is more fully endowed. Similarly the positive argument that shifts imagining into pretending fails. It fails because, again, there are three discernible types of imaging: There is thinking with images, or illustrated supposing; there is thinking through images, or interior dramatic rehearsal; and there is thinking in images, or being an internal spectator. This last case, which is the only one that requires images before the mind's eye, is just the one Ryle's attack ignores. The reason is that it simply falls outside the limits set by the dispositional theory of mind, namely the idea that the mind is nothing but a set of tendencies to act.

3. Developments. In the last forty years there has been a flood of works in the analytic vein. Most are characterized by a fine-meshed sifting and punctilious worrying of the issue allusively raised by Wittgenstein and abruptly disposed of by Ryle: how to speak of the ordinary accepted activities of the imagination without being drawn into positing internal image-objects. There has been a numerically inferior counter-rebellion, an insistence on the value of introspective experience (e.g., Danto 1958), or a defense of mental images by way of exposing the insufficiencies of the analytic arguments (Hannay 1971). By and large the debate has turned a deaf ear to Wittgenstein's injunctions to refrain from talking about internal objects and has become embroiled in a somewhat paradoxical hand-to-hand combat with these supposed ghosts. The intention has been sometimes to eliminate them outright, as does Dennett (1969), who reduces seeing images to giving descriptions, and sometimes just to say what they are if they aren't mental pictures, as does Scruton (1974). The debate up through the seventies is summed up by Russow (1978, with bibliography).

The next phase will be taken up in Part Two, under Psychology, particularly as a science of mind. For in the eighties the debate shifts to a new cognitive science. It involves old issues in fresh forms, three in particular: There is the issue of representationalism: whether the mind functions by having representations "before" it. There is the problem of materialism: whether and in what way imagery is reducible to brain phenomena. Most specifically there is the battle of imagism versus propositionalism: whether imagery is to be thought of as analog or digital, quasi-spatial or verbal. These questions are debated across the lines in philosophical and psychological journals. For example, Tye (1984) again argues on philosophical grounds that the experimental results whose interpretation is contested by imagists and propositionalists require neither hypothesis. The phenomena can be explained "adverbially," that is, in terms of a modification of the imagining person, without having recourse to mental representations at all. The representational issue, the most general context in which the nature of the imagination must be considered, will be taken up in the conclusion to Part One.

I shall turn to two particularly interesting and extensive discussions of the image-issue. Selection is indicated, since it is impossible to give a summary account of work whose essence is refined argumentation. But first I should mention a cluster of studies, done in the analytic spirit, but dealing with a special and intriguing use of the imagination. In these the imagination is considered as it is involved in questions concerning self, identity, and identification.

The starting point is Berkeley's defense of his main philosophical doctrine, that "to be is to be perceived" and that no corporeal sensible can exist otherwise than in the mind. It leads to the conclusion that an unperceived tree is unconceivable (*First Dialogue Between Hylas and Philonous* 1713). Since Berkeley anticipates Hume in asserting that it is only their constancy and vivacity that distinguish ideas of real things imprinted on the senses from ideas of the imagination (*Principles of Human Knowledge* 1710, para. 33), the mental mode of sense-ideas and image-ideas is the same. Therefore one may put pressure on Berkeley's argument by asking: Why is an unperceived tree unconceivable? Is it because the very attempt to unconceive a tree is in fact a visualization, an image-idea in the imaginer's mind? If that is the argument, it may be overcome by showing that one may imagine a tree without being present to "see" it. This solution, proposed by Williams (1966) broaches fascinating questions concerning the role of the self in imagining. He begins by distinguishing the vizualization from the imaginative project behind it. One may conceive of an imaginative project in which certain elements of the visualization are deliberately discarded, in this case the imaginer's looking at the imagined scene, that is, the presence of the self. Indeed, this possibility can be put more generally: It belongs to the very nature of visualization to discard the viewer's perspective. (This assertion will become an experimental issue.) A movie is a pertinent analogy, for viewers watch its scenes from the varying perspectives of the camera and only very extraneously from their own. So also the visualizers are not in the world they visualize unless they take the extra step of putting themselves in the picture. Consequently they normally have no perception-like fixed perspectival relation to it. The imagination, we might say, is a "contemplative" viewer, who is beyond all perspectives. Once the self is, as it were, out of it, one may indeed speak of imagining or seeing a tree that is unseen by the imaginer's self. This point brings out a peculiarly selfless aspect of the imagination. However, along with the advantage of self-lessness comes a disadvantage: The imagination can no longer be used to solve puzzles concerning personal identity. One such puzzle is the persistence of a self through all sorts of transformations, and one such use is the attempt to develop the paradoxical assumptions inherent in imagining oneself to be someone else in order to show that self-identity is the underlying condition of imagining (Brook 1975). On Williams's account this approach to the personal identity problem is blocked, for one may indeed imagine oneself as someone else without being involved *in propria persona*.

The phenomenon of identification, on the other hand—that is, the empathetic assimilation of or to another—seems to be very much an imagination-based phenomenon, as Wollheim (1970) shows. Imagining the being of, or simply being, someone else begins with a "repertoire" of his looks and ways, but it soon goes on involuntarily and passively. This suggests that it is cognate with feeling, with empathy. What guides such imaginative identification is, then, a peculiarly intimate, emotionally assimilated knowledge of another. Taken along psychoanalytic lines, such identification is controlled by an unconscious "master-thought," such as the intention of merging the self and the other so as to preserve within oneself, say, a lost love or, on the contrary, so as to obliterate the other. Wollheim distinguishes the latter intention as a kind of identification in which one imagines oneself to be someone else "to their detriment," that is, so as to deny the other independent existence. Again the oscillating position of the self in imagining is brought out, here from a psychological viewpoint: Imagining someone else is a harmless activity quite distinct from the potentially injurious activity of imagining oneself as someone else.

Scruton (1974) furnishes a theory of the imagination for aesthetic application. He employs Wittgenstein's terms, and sets aside the phenomenological approach as technically incomprehensible and "pleasantly uninformative." The project is to adumbrate Wittgenstein's connection of seeing-as with the imagination.

He chooses voluntariness as a first handy mark of imagination. It makes sense to be asked to imagine, in a way that being ordered to see does not. (This frequently repeated criterion seems to me, once more, very dubious; just as one can be bidden to see this figure as a mountain, one can be required to construe the perceptual world correctly. Anyone who has ever learned to stand a night watch on a boat will have been told by the skipper: "Learn to recognize ships' running lights!"—which really means: "See them! Pick them out!") Then imagination might at first blush be said to be a voluntary thought that is unasserted, not claimed as factual. Furthermore, imaginative thought goes beyond what is given and does so appropriately, namely with reasons. Hence imagining is thinking of x as y in a way that brings out something not immediately perceptible but that does make sense. The meaning of imagining analyzed here clearly distinguishes it from belief. So far images have been left out of account, because imagery is not a necessary part of such imagining.

Scruton addresses imagery next. A mental image is characterized as intentional; it is the thought of an object. It is, furthermore, incorrigible, voluntary, and attributable to the imager only from the description offered by him. (Thus, as usual in the analytic tradition, dreams are excluded.) So far images are thought-like, but they also have special characteristics. They can be more or less vivid, and they involve an irreducible analogy to sense-experience, an experience-like duration describable in terms of public, visual experience. (It is, I observe, a strange given of the analytic position that perceptual seeing is public—strange, because who knows what I see?) Scruton regards as a corroborating consequence of these marks the fact that under them images cannot be ascribed to a blind man. (But here I see a logical difficulty: If reporting in visual or in other sensory terms is truly a determining criterion of having mental images, and since totally and congenitally blind persons do often learn to talk in convincingly sensory terms of their "imagery," it seems to follow only that mental images need have no perceptual properties to be described in sensory terms, not that the blind have no imagery—Kielkopf 1968).

Now seeing-as has similar characteristics: It too is voluntary. It has a varying salience analogous to degrees of vividness. It can be more or less appropriate. It involves description. It seems to be a mixture of the thoughtful and the sensory, just like the mental image.

At this point Scruton can, therefore, bring together imagining, or rather imaginative thought with aspect-seeing or seeing-as: I see, say, a wedge in a picture but don't believe that it can be merely that. So I think of it as something else, say a mountain, which suddenly becomes embodied in the image. Thus an aspect dawns. Now we see, Scruton says, that the first concept of the imagination as just unasserted thought was too simple, for the imaginative thought complex was not really "thinking of x as y," but "thinking of y in x," that is, thinking of the mountain in the wedge-picture. Put this way, it becomes clear that the aspect leads the thought, or, better, that thought and seeing are indissoluble. So one might as well say that seeing-as is an unasserted visual experience. Inversely, thought asserted marks real experience, and imagination asserted marks involuntary experience, namely belief. For belief is, in strong contrast to unasserted thought, involuntary. Thus we return to the first mark of the imagination, the will.

(However, as I have said before, this continual assertion of willfulness as a special characteristic of imagination is a weak point in the analytic position. In particular, belief, too, is voluntary, if one includes a central form of it, which Scruton simply overlooks. It happens to be faith. In faith the command "*Crede!*" is not just a case of Scruton's special belief-imperatives, encouragements like "Trust me:" It really means "Believe!"—and it is not just nonsense.)

Imagination as unasserted visual experience can, now, be directly applied to aesthetic seeing. Seeing the sadness in a portrait face is like an unasserted visual perception, irreducibly analogous to seeing a real-life expression of sadness in a face. This analysis vindicates the old "affective theory" of aesthetics, the notion that aesthetic emotions are similar to real ones but somehow inactual. The force of such an emotion is not a function of its core-proposition, which asserts the cause for sadness, but rather of the degree of "imaginative involvement." In sum, Scruton thinks that aesthetic emotions are like real emotions minus their attendant beliefs, and nothing much more can be said about them. (Imagination and emotion will be again taken up in Part Six, Ch. III B.)

Finally, Furlong (1982) is the acute and lucid successor to Hannay in the defense of mental images. (His critiques of Sartre and Ryle are to be found under the relevant debates.) His own conclusions are derived in the spirit, but not bound by the letter, of Wittgenstein. They are, in sum, that there is no reason to banish the mental image, provided it is not made to enter into the concept of the imagination. The image may be allowed a purely phenomenal existence while the imagination is conceptualized as intentional. Or again, in Geach's terms (*Mental Acts* 1957), there may be a reference for the term (mental) image, but there is no sense. The term names something but tells nothing.

The argument is this: Like Scruton, Furlong recognizes intention as an element in seeing-as, but he distinguishes among the cluster of senses the one relevant here. Intention is not meant in the voluntaristic sense, as in "intending to see something," yet it is a matter of active thought, namely the direct relationship of the thought of x to x. This intention involves what Wittgenstein calls in the *Investigations* an "internal relation," internal insofar as the relation of the thought of x to the object x is immediate. (This non-voluntaristic meaning, close to phenomenological intention, is an interpretation, though a plausible one, of the Wittgensteinian text.)

Now in some of the literature the analogy between aspect-seeing and mental imaging is understood to lie precisely in this internal relation of the thought to the object. In aspect-seeing it is negotiated through a medium, namely the actual picture—the drawn wedge figure, say, that takes on the aspect of a mountain. In mental imaging there is the same internal relation, but the picture-medium drops out. The error in this analogy, Furlong argues, is that Wittgenstein is speaking not of internal processes or relations but strictly of linguistic concepts. In the analysis of the imaging concept the mental medium-analogue cannot well be said to drop out: It is irrelevant and simply does not figure.

Nonetheless, Wittgenstein is no crude behaviorist and, unlike Ryle, does not reject the existence of the image. Rather, since private meanings are disallowed, he assigns no sense to the term image. Hence the word, though without a sense, may nonetheless have a reference. It may be directed at something, though not something articulable.

It follows that mental images have no status as existent objects, for they are not visible and do not constitute meanings. But they might exist in another way, Furlong suggests, namely as states of consciousness of the "as if" variety. To image is to be in the same state one would be in if the object imaged were perceived. Thus seeing one's childhood home vividly before one's eyes involves an intention necessarily and an imaging experience non-necessarily. For it is not the image that marks the event of imagining. It is rather the intention. So at least the possibility of the image as an internal experience has been saved.

Now this solution is, for once, very satisfactory, since it does several desirable things. First, it shows clearly and cleanly what the Wittgensteinian project—the analysis of concepts from open and above-board evidence and in normal contexts—requires in respect to image-investigations. This explicitness enables those who cannot warm to the restrictive view of philosophizing which it implies to know exactly what they are doing when they transgress the Wittgensteinian limits. An important instance is the sense/reference distinction. Defenders of the articulable mental image must now acknowledge their implicit insistence that language that has a reference must also have a sense, which I indeed take here as a philosophical article of faith. Second, Furlong's thesis takes account of a prominent part of the imagination-experience, namely the pervasive sense of its doubleness. This sense is here accounted for insofar as imagining is at once the passive state of having images and an activity of intending. Third, the thesis tones down the overemphasis on the will in the imagination. Fourth, it brings together plausibly central elements from the two major schools, Phenomenology and Philosophy of Mind, that usually bypass each other. From the former it imports the Sartrean notion of imagining as "a consciousness"; from the latter it takes the Wittgensteinian denial that the term "image" has a sense. Finally, in tolerating images, as the hardened anti-imagist position will not, Furlong's solution leaves open the possibility, normally suppressed by that school, that such image-consciousness might have great, albeit extra-conceptual, human significance. This is something gained.

C. Neoromanticism: Imagination as the Humanizing Faculty

The antithesis of intellect and imagination—not only dividing the individual within but splitting humanity into opposing camps—as contrasted with the cognitive cooperation and affective reciprocity of these powers, is a chief tenet of romanticism. If there is any empirical argument for a doctrine so indolently willful it is the fact itself of the gulf between the Anglo-Saxon Analysts and their contemporaries, the French Neoromantics. For the former are as intent on the rational evaporation as the latter are on the rhapsodic elevation of the imagination. The French movement centers around Bachelard (1) and "bachelardism," though there are some writers who independently share in the spirit of image-fascination (2).

1. Bachelard: The Valorizing Imagination. Bachelard was a historian of science who turned to writing books distinctive in being academically unclassifiable. They concern imaginative life. They have strange and inviting titles: *The Psychoanalysis of Fire* (1938), *Water and Dreams: Essay on the Imagination of Matter* (1942), *Air and Musings: Essay on the Imagination of Movement* (1943), *Earth and Reveries of the Will: Essay on the Imagination of Forces* (1948), *Earth and Reveries of Rest: Essay on Images of Intimacy* (1948), *The Poetics of Reverie* (1960), and *The Poetics of Space* (1948), whose "topophilia" is considered in Part Six (Ch. III A).

Bachelard is both a romantic and a Romantic. He is a romantic insofar as he writes allusively, hyperbolically, and figuratively, rather than prosaically. He does not expound a theoretical thesis so much as he enthusiastically advocates the imaginative mode of being. He treats of imaginative dreaming through imaginative aperçus which have more resonance than center. Consequently the uncommitted reader finds it hard to judge whether the numerous startling juxtapositions are profound or fantastic, and whether the many contradictions, for which romantics characteristically have high tolerance, are deep or merely enthusiastic. Perhaps the reading of these books requires an effort that is difficult to make for lovers of the logos, the effort to relax one's critical attention to discrete articulations enough to allow oneself to be floated off on the continuous stream of insight.

He is a Romantic with a capital R in several specific ways. For one thing, he expresses his indebtedness (though mostly through secondary sources) to the Romantic poets, English and German—to Coleridge, Shelley, Jean Paul Richter, and, above all, Novalis. He is, moreover, a Neoromantic insofar as he both drives Romantic notions to extremes and makes untrammelled use of twentieth-century ideas from Psychoanalysis and Phenomenology. The following resumé of Bachelard's Romanticism is indebted to an article by Margaret Higonnet (1981). The relation of the older Romantics to the imagination is considered in Part Four, on literature (Ch. II B).

Above all, for Bachelard the imagination is preeminently the "humanizing" faculty (*hominisante*, in *Air and Musings*) in the same "ontological" sense as is found in William Blake, whom he cites (Part Four, Ch. II B). Bachelard is not consistent about the implied preference of imagination over perception as the source of reality, but he gives the imagination preeminence on many occasions: "There is no reality antecedent to the literary image" (*A.M.*); "*The imagined fact* is more important than the *real fact*" (*Water and Dreams*).

This "victory of the creative imagination over realism" (*W.D.*), here as with the older Romantics, betokens a conflation of knowing and making through the imagination: "The real world is absorbed by the imaginary world. Shelley supplies us with a veritable theorem of phenomenology when he says that imagination is capable 'of making us create what we see' " (*Poetics of Space*). Note that this is a bowdlerization. In the *Defense of Poetry* Shelley actually says something far more precise, namely that "all things exist as they are perceived," and that poetry "compels us to feel that which we perceive and to imagine that which we know. It creates anew the universe." Bachelard's Neoromanticism glosses over the careful older Romantic distinction between imaginative making and imaginary making-up, between productive and fantastic imagination.

Again, novelty is a Romantic obsession and Bachelard's interest:

People always want the imagination to be the faculty for *forming* images. But it is rather the faculty for *deforming* the images furnished by perception; it is above all the faculty for liberating us from primary images, for *changing* images. The basic word which corresponds to imagination is not *image* but *imaginary*. . . . Thanks to the *imaginary*, the imagination is essentially *open*, *escapist*; within the human psyche it is the experience of opening, the experience, even, of novelty." (*A.M.*)

(In this book, on the contrary, the "imaginary," so important in postmodern theory—Introduction A—is invidiously distinguished from the sounder "imaginative"—Part Six.)

Bachelard assigns an almost cultic importance to the images and metaphors of poetry. Particularly he regards them as expressions of what is primitive or primal in the human psyche, an idea he found in the writings of Novalis and Shelley and, of course, in Vico (Part Four, Ch. IV A). Similarly he is fascinated by alchemical analogies, the metamorphoses of nature, and the correspondences and transformations of life, in the vein of Novalis, Baudelaire, and Jung.

But the Romantic characteristic that most generally informs his writing is the penchant for juxtaposition and opposition. He opposes self to reality, poetry to science, and, above all, imagination to reason, with imagination, of course, triumphant. (The significance and the influence of Bachelard's pitting of concept against image are treated in a book by Roy—1977.)

How fairly, then, can Bachelard's work be said to contain a philosophy of the imagination? His earlier books on the imagination were "psychoanalyses" of fire, water, air, and earth. He uses the term to mean a recovery of the unconscious significances of these elements, through the four medieval types of psychic "temperament" which they dominated. The "psychoanalysis" is thus only allusively Freudian or Jungian. It actually proceeds as an essayistic musing on "subjective convictions." Later he comes to concentrate on the images of poetry and at the same time on the phenomenology of the imagination. By "phenomenology" he means the study of subjective consciousness by subjective means. He also speaks of studying the ontology and metaphysics of images and the imagination (*P.S.*).

In the course of trying to reach the being of images subjectively he eventually leaves aside the finished literary image to focus on the reverie, the conscious daydream. For it is the purest state of the imagination, sheer fluid, dynamic inwardness, in which the boundaries between subject and object are truly lost. The daydream is the seed-bed of the poetic image. To understand poetry the reader must become the perfect phenomenologist by putting himself into the state of inchoate poetry, into a reverie. Earlier in his literary studies, Bachelard had distinguished between the fixity of a fully formed image and the freshness of an image still close to elemental matter. A similar distinction with respect to reverie is now made in terms of mind and soul. Phenomenology is concerned with the image that "comes *before* thought; poetry, rather than being a phenomenology of the mind, is a phenomenology of the soul" (*P.S.*, Forsyth 1971). The imagination as vagrancy of mind is, of course, Rousseau's legacy (Fifth Walk, *Reveries of a Solitary Walker*, begun in 1776).

Of the several notions that arise in this enterprise, two are most characteristic and philosophically resonant. The first is that of "valorization." It is the subjective deformation of reality referred to above, one of the great "ontological" principles of the imagination: "*Valorization decides being*"

(*A.M.*). The imagination valorizes reality in two ways. It invests it with the passion that makes us see it, focus on it to begin with. Besides affectively informing the world, it transforms reality creatively, by subjectively re-making it.

The state of "ontological reciprocity" in which the daydreamer finds himself is closely connected to valorization. It is this state of isolated autonomy in which the imaginer merges with the world; he is diffused into it and it into him. The dialectic which defines his own being by an opposing non-being is relaxed: "Imagination does not know non-being" (*Poetics of Reverie*, Kaplan 1972).

If there is no articulable metaphysics in this, there is at least a call to a primal human mode. Opinions, it must be said, differ about both the primitiveness and the priority of imaginative existence. Some say that "early" inner life, be it of savages or of children, is sparse, dry, and prosaic. Some think that daydreaming is not the ground but the accompaniment of "real life." Bachelard provides no arguments, and so there is no contest; reasons have been obviated.

Hence the sum of this romantic rhapsody is hard to cast up, and its substance difficult to delineate. It represents the contemporary continuation of the "primeval battle" between philosophy and poetry (Ch. I, Intro.), except that its first protagonist, Plato, was converted from poetry to philosophy while its recent champion is a renegade from rationalism to reverie. But granted that the imagination is peculiarly in need of defense these days, the enemy is not reason *tout court* but reason in its unreasonable exclusivity. The imagination, moreover, like all tenaciously subtle spirits, thrives least under untethered praise and best under rational pressure. Like any elastic ether, it develops greatest force under confinement.

To put it another way: If, without prejudice to the possibility of an ultimately unitary intellectual root, the conscious life of the soul is indeed penultimately dual, such that thinking and imagining are two distinct powers (Conclusion), then the following is surely one of their greatest differences: Imagination is spontaneous exactly where thought is con-strained, namely in the development of consequences; while thought is free exactly where the imagination is contingent, namely in the dependence on sensory material. But in that case, for thought to yield to the imagination its place as the primary, or at least co-equal, "humanizing power" is a passionate futility. Thinking may indeed willfully surrender its virtue, which is to strive for clearly punctuated progress. But the pathos of this surrender is that the imagination cannot assume the abdicated power. It just becomes self-conscious and diffuse. The convert to romanticism becomes the imagination's most insidiously destructive friend.

2. Lefebve: The Fascinating Image. Lefebve's study (1965) bears a motto from Victor Hugo that will later stand as the epigraph to the Conclusion of this book: "The universe is an appearance corrected by a transparency." Lefebve's subject is the "mysterious empire" exercised by the "fascinating image" (*l'image fascinante*), and though he writes in the image-magnifying spirit of Bachelard, his thesis is distinctive and important, if not as philosophy, then for philosophy.

The images in question are natural and ordinary. They include not only shadows and reflections, but all appearances that may suddenly seem image-like: the moon pursuing a nocturnal stroller, the landscape rushing by the passenger on a train, a panorama suddenly revealed. "Fascinating" is used of such images not in the Sartrean sense, where the imager is will-lessly enthralled, but insofar as an image suddenly casts doubt on the reality of the visible object. In thus throwing the object into irreality, the image brings about a reaction of the spirit toward the menaced reality. This reaction reveals and projects to the viewer, by way of compensation, a new, true, and, as it were, absolute reality, a "surreality" (31).

In this vein Lefebve presents a "phenomenology," a description of the experience of dreams, of spatial as well as kinetic appearances, and of temporal images. A good example is the natural panorama. The viewer comes precipitately upon an enormous scene of great distances. For all its largeness, it can be obliterated by the palm of the hand. He experiences a sudden magic in which everything turns into a semblance of itself and into a metaphor. A solitary, still tree, startlingly and paradoxically discloses itself as being of the species poplar. A river in the valley suddenly has the aspect of a ribbon of unmoving water. The exuberance of nature is stilled. An immensity is under the domination of the eye. In solitary remoteness the viewer sees familiar nature under a new scale and aspect.

The "ontological value" of these aspectual images is that in stripping nature of its reality and substituting an imaginative "surreality," they lead the imaginer to a "metaphysics of the heart." It is a sporadic affective intimation of the great issues of philosophy: the appearance-nature of the visible reality and the knowable ground of things in a super-reality (268). These worldly images intimate to us our ambiguous spiritual position between a given, definite reality and its negation. Hence the experience of image-magic propaedeutically anticipates the fascination of metaphysics.

D. Philosophical Anthropology: The Human Significance of the Imagination

"Anthropology" is here used in the old sense: a systematic description of the specifically human aspects of images and imagining. It seems appropriate to end with three philosophical-psychological works of the European school. They were written during and after the Second World War but before cognitive psychology entered the picture. They are mildly under Phenomenological and Existential influence, but much less constrained by doctrine than by reflective observation.

First, there is Kunz's exhaustive treatise on the anthropological significance of the imagination (1946). Besides a thorough review of the work done on the imagination in German in the first half of the century, it contains multitudes of fine observations and distinctions set out in chapters on the imagination as involved with "drives," passions, cognition, time, wishing, love, perception, and action. For example, against Sartre's claim that intentional consciousness is constitutive of image-existence, Kunz makes a distinction which does seem to correspond better to introspective evidence, that between lived and experienced imagining (*er-lebt, ge-lebt*). The latter is indeed directed and intentional, but the former is a free-floating state, unanchored in any reference or intention, self-enclosed and concentrated on the phantasms themselves.

A chapter is devoted to the four-fold temporality of the imagination (a subject taken up in this study with respect to special "moments" in Part Six, Ch. II C). Kunz points out that the "timelessness" often attributed to extraordinary imaginative moments really better fits the intellect, and that the typical imaginative temporal state should rather be called "rapture" (*Entrückung*). The characteristic time of ordinary mundane imagination is, on the other hand, the present, as indeed comes out in Husserl's term "presentification" (A). Furthermore, as memory, imagination is past-affected and as projection it is future-laden.

Erwin Straus's reflection on images, in his essay on upright posture and human "beholding" (1963), begins with a reference to the underlying Heideggerian question of Kunz's book: What makes the human being a "being of distance"? Straus claims not so much that beholding of pictures is distance-preserving as, conversely, that it is the very experiencing of distance which makes image-seeing possible. He begins with the old phenomenological distinction between the picture's panel and its effigy, the material medium and the representation it bears. The spatiality of the effigy is totally diverse from that of the viewer, who cannot enter it to walk around in it. (That is, of course, what the anecdote of the Chinese landscape painter, told in the Introduction, contradicts; in his imaginative seeing the two spaces do indeed meld.) Not only is the space isolated but effigies are weightless and sizeless, "unencumbered." Here enters Straus's theme, the difference between seeing, which is practically involved in the world, and beholding, which is distantly contemplative. Effigy-seeing is a sort of paradigmatic beholding, in which the things contemplated are released from our grasping, manipulating, "incorporating" tendency (Part Five, Ch. III). In this looking, too, begins that philosophizing which attempts to discern the essential looks, the *eidos* or form, of things.

Finally, Jonas's companion piece (1966) to his essay on the nobility of sight, parallel to Straus's, albeit more substantial, connects the specifically human activity of image-making with freedom. Jonas begins with an epitome of the by now familiar complex of marks that any image bears: It is a recognizable likeness which is internally produced. It involves three elements, the image itself, the imaging medium, and the original reference. An image is necessarily incomplete insofar as it falls short of the original in some sense. This inherent incompleteness gives the maker latitude to make omissions and to heighten symbolic values. The chief object of representation is visual shape, which has the advantage of perspectival variety. The image-product, though it may represent motion, is ultimately static and permanent even in the case of moving pictures, since the completed image is divorced from its own productive genesis as well as from causal commerce with life.

Now the making of images so understood is peculiarly an expression of human freedom. Reality is an appearance which presents itself to the perceiver with a powerful affective thrust. Observant seeing abstracts from this causally affective present, and plays with different, visible aspects and their transformations into each other (much as in "eidetic variation"). Hence all seeing has in it something of image-seeing, and therefore something productive. Furthermore, human beings are temporarily enabled by image-memory to detach themselves entirely from reality. They can freely ponder whatever things in whatever aspect they wish. In imagining, human beings preserve something from the flux of things and entrust it to the flux of self. The externalization of this new inner shape in a picture is the occasion for exerting an additional power, the control of our bodily capacities. The resultant artificial image, the material, permanent, sharable, and cognitively valuable product of a beholding subject—the work of art—is therefore a testimonial to three freedoms which belong to us as imaginative beings. They are the freedom from the compulsions of the present, the freedom to control imaginative vision, and the freedom to show physical competence.

Bibliography

Aldrich, Vergil C. 1958. "Pictorial Meaning, Picture-Thinking, and Wittgenstein's Theory of Aspects." *Mind* 67:70–79.

————. 1962. "Image-Mongering and Image-Management." *Philosophy and Phenomenological Research* 23:51–61.

Altieri, Charles. 1971. "Jean-Paul Sartre: The Engaged Imagination." In *The Quest for Imagination: Essays in Twentieth Century Esthetic Criticism*, edited by O. B. Hardison. Cleveland: The Press of Case Western Reserve University.

Audi, Robert. 1978. "The Ontological Status of Mental Images." *Inquiry* 21:348–361.

Bachelard, Gaston [1884–1962]. 1938. *The Psychoanalysis of Fire*. Translated by Alan C. Ross. London: Routledge and Kegan Paul (1964).

————. 1958. *The Poetics of Space*. Translated by Maria Jolas. Boston: Beacon Press (1969).

Berkeley, George. 1713. *Three Dialogues Between Hylas and Philonous*.

Brook, J. A. 1975. "Imagination, Possibility, and Personal Identity." *American Philosophical Quarterly* 12:185–200.

Casey, Edward S. 1970. "Imagination: Imagining and the Image." *Philosophy and Phenomenological Research* 31:475–490.

————. 1976a. *Imagining: A Phenomenological Study*. Bloomington: Indiana University Press.

————. 1976b. "Imagination and Phenomenological Method." In *Husserl: Expositions and Appraisals*, edited by Frederick Elliston and Peter McCormick. Notre Dame: The University of Notre Dame Press (1977).

————. 1976c. "Comparative Phenomenology of Mental Activity: Memory, Hallucination, and Fantasy Contrasted with Imagination." *Research in Phenomenology* 6:1–25.

————. 1977. "Imagining and Remembering." *Review of Metaphysics* 31:187–209.

————. 1981. "Sartre on Imagination." In *The Philosophy of Jean-Paul Sartre*, edited by Paul A. Schilpp. La Salle, Ill.: Open Court.

Courtney, Richard. 1971. "Imagination and the Dramatic Act: Comments on Sartre, Ryle, and Furlong." *The Journal of Aesthetics and Art Criticism* 30:163–170.

Cowley, Frazer. 1968. *A Critique of British Empiricism*. New York: St. Martin's Press.

Danto, Arthur. 1958. "Conceiving Mental Pictures." *Journal of Philosophy* 55:12–20.

Dennett, D. C. 1969. "Mental Imagery." Chapter 6 in *Content and Consciousness*. London: Routledge and Kegan Paul.

Dilman, Ilham. 1967. "Imagination." In *The Aristotelian Society*, Supplementary Volume 41. London: Harrison and Sons.

————. 1968. "Imagination." *Analysis* 28:90–97.

Dufrenne, Mikel. 1953. *The Phenomenology of Aesthetic Experience*. Translated by Edward S. Casey. Evanston: Northwestern University Press (1973).

Flew, Annis. 1953. "Images, Supposing and Imagination." *Philosophy* 28:246–254.

Forsyth, Neil. 1971. "Gaston Bachelard's Theory of Poetic Imagination: Psychoanalysis to Phenomenology." In *The Quest for Imagination: Essays in Twentieth Century Esthetic Criticism*, edited by O. B. Hardison. Cleveland: The Press of Case Western Reserve University.

Furlong, John J. 1982. *The Ontological Status of Mental Images*. Dissertation, School of Philosophy of the Catholic University. Ann Arbor, Mich.: University Microfilm International.

Garry, Ann. 1977. "Mental Images." *Personalist* 58:28–38.

Gerhart, Mary. 1979. "Imagination and History in Ricoeur's Interpretation Theory." *Philosophy Today*, Spring, 51–66.

Gurwitsch, Aron. 1953. *The Field of Consciousness*. Pittsburgh: Duquesne University Press (1964).

Hallet, Garth. 1977. *A Companion to Wittgenstein's Philosophical Investigations*. Ithaca: Cornell University Press.

Hannay, Alastair. 1971. *Mental Images: A Defense*. New York: The Humanities Press.

Heidegger, Martin. 1925. *History of the Concept of Time: Prolegomena*. Translated by Theodore Kisiel. Bloomington: Indiana University Press (1985).

———. 1925–26. *Logik: Die Frage nach der Wahrheit*. Frankfurt am Main: Vittorio Klostermann (1976).

Hering, Jean. 1947. "Concerning Image, Idea and Dream." *Philosophy and Phenomenological Research* 8:188–205.

Higonnet, Margaret R. 1981. "Bachelard and the Romantic Imagination." *Comparative Literature* 33:18–37.

Husserl, Edmund [1859–1938]. 1900. *Logical Investigations* (Inv. I, paras. 17–18; II, Inv. V, paras. 39–40). Translated by J. N. Findlay. New Jersey: The Humanities Press (1982).

———. 1904–1910. *The Phenomenology of Internal Time-Consciousness* (Appendix II). Edited by Martin Heidegger, translated by James S. Churchill. Bloomington: Indiana University Press.

———. 1913. *Ideas: General Introduction to Pure Phenomenology* (paras. 4, 23, 42–43, 70, 90, 99–101, 109–114, 140). Translated by W.R.B. Gibson. New York: Collier Books (1962).

———. 1929. "Phenomenology." *Encyclopedia Britannica*, 14th ed.

———. 1937. *The Crisis of European Sciences and Transcendental Philosophy: An Introduction to Phenomenological Philosophy* (Part II, para. 9a). Edited by David Carr. Evanston: Northwestern University Press (1970).

———. 1930. [published posthumously]. *Experience and Judgment* (paras. 37–42, 87–88). Edited by Ludwig Landgrebe, translated by James S. Churchill and Karl Ameriks. Evanston: Northwestern University Press (1973).

Ishiguru, Hidé. 1966. "Imagination." In *British Analytical Philosophy*, edited by Bernard Williams and Alan Montefiore. New York: The Humanities Press.

———. 1967. "Imagination." In *The Aristotelian Society*, Supplementary Volume 41. London: Harrison and Sons.

Johnson, Mark. 1987. *The Body in the Mind: The Bodily Basis of Meaning, Imagination and Reason*. Chicago: The University of Chicago Press.

Jonas, Hans. 1966. "Image-making and the Freedom of Man." Seventh Essay in *The Phenomenon of Life: Towards a Philosophical Biology*. Chicago: The University of Chicago Press (1982).

Kaplan, Edward K. 1972. "Gaston Bachelard's Philosophy of Imagination: An Introduction." *Philosophy and Phenomenological Research* 33:1–24.

Kearney, Richard. 1988. *The Wake of Imagination: Toward a Postmodern Culture*. Minneapolis: University of Minnesota Press.

Kielkopf, Charles F. 1968. "The Pictures in the Head of a Man Born Blind." *Philosophy and Phenomenological Research* 28:501–513.

Kleiman, Lowell. 1971. "Imagining." *Journal of Value Inquiry* 5:267–275.

Kuehl, James. 1970. "Perceiving and Imagining." *Philosophy and Phenomenological Research* 31:212–224.

Kunz, Hans. 1946. *Die anthropologische Bedeutung der Phantasie*. Basel: Verlag für Recht und Gesellschaft.

Kuspit, Donald B. 1968. "Fiction and Phenomenology." *Philosophy and Phenomenological Research* 29:16–33.

Lakoff, George. 1988. "Cognitive Semantics." In *Meaning and Mental Representation*, edited by Umberto Eco et al. Bloomington: Indiana University Press.

Langer, Susanne K. 1942. *Philosophy in a New Key*. Cambridge: Harvard University Press (1978).

Lawrie, Reynold. 1970. "The Existence of Mental Images." *Philosophical Quarterly* 20:251–257.

Lefebve, Maurice-Jean. 1965. *L'Image fascinante et le surréel*. Paris: Plon.

Levinas, Emmanuel. 1963. *The Theory of Intuition in Husserl's Phenomenology*. Translated by André Orianne. Evanston: Northwestern University Press (1973).

Mallin, Samuel B. 1979. *Merleau-Ponty's Philosophy*. New Haven: Yale University Press.

Matthews, Gareth B. 1969. "Mental Copies." *The Philosophical Review* 78:53–73.

McCormick, Earl R. 1972. "Wittgenstein's Imagination." *Southern Journal of Philosophy* 10:453–461.

Merleau-Ponty, M. 1945. *Phenomenology of Perception*. Translated by Colin Smith. New York: The Humanities Press (1962).

————. 1961. "Eye and Mind." In *The Essential Writings of Merleau-Ponty*, edited by Alden L. Fisher. New York: Harcourt, Brace and World (1969).

Odegaard, Douglas. 1971. "Images." *Mind* 80:262–265.

Oosthuizen, D.C.S. 1968. "The Role of Imagination in Judgments of Fact." *Philosophy and Phenomenological Research* 29:34–58.

Rabb, J. Douglas. 1975a. "Imaging: An Adverbial Analysis." *Dialogue* 14:312–318.

————. 1975b. "Prolegomenon to a Phenomenology of the Imagination." *Philosophy and Phenomenological Research* 36:74–81.

Rankin, K. W. 1967. "The Role of the Imagination, Rule-Operations, and Atmosphere in Wittgenstein's Language-Games." *Inquiry* 10:279–291.

Ricoeur, Paul. 1974. "Sartre and Ryle on the Imagination." In *The Philosophy of Jean-Paul Sartre*, edited by Paul A. Schilpp. LaSalle, Ill.: Open Court.

————. 1976. "L'imagination dans le discours et dans l'action." In *Savoir, faire, espérer: les limites de la raison* I, Brussels.

Roy, Jean-Pierre. 1977. *Bachelard ou le concept contre l'image*. Montreal: Les Presses de l'Université de Montréal.

Russow, Lilly-Marlene. 1978. "Some Recent Work on Imagination." *American Philosophical Quarterly* 15:57–66.

Ryle, Gilbert [1900–1976]. 1949. "Imagination." Chapter 8 in *The Concept of Mind*. New York: Barnes and Noble Books.

Sacks, Oliver. 1987. *The Man Who Mistook His Wife for a Hat, and Other Clinical Tales*. New York: Harper and Row.

Sallis, John. 1975. "Image and Phenomenon." *Research in Phenomenology* 5:61–75.

Sartre, Jean-Paul [1905–1980]. 1936. *Imagination: A Psychological Critique*. Translated by Forrest Williams. Ann Arbor: University of Michigan Press (1962).

————. 1940. *The Psychology of the Imagination*. Translated by Bernard Frechtman. New York: The Citadel Press (1965). [French title: *L'imaginaire: psychologie phénoménologique de l'imagination*.]

Schuetz, Alfred. 1944. "On Multiple Realities." *Philosophy and Phenomenological Research* 5:533–575.

Scruton, Roger. 1974. "The Imagination I, II" and "Imagination and Aesthetic Experience." In *Art and Imagination: A Study in the Philosophy of Mind*. London: Routledge and Kegan Paul (1982).

Sherover, Charles M. 1971. *Heidegger, Kant and Time*. Bloomington: Indiana University Press.

Shorter, J. M. 1952. "Imagination." *Mind* 61:528–542.

Smythies, J. R. 1958. "On Some Properties and Relations of Images." *Philosophical Review* 67:389–394.

Snoeyenbos, M., and Sibley, E. 1978. "Sartre on Imagination." *Southern Journal of Philosophy* 16:373–388.

Sokolowski, Robert. 1974. *Husserlian Meditations: How Words Present Things.* Evanston: Northwestern University Press.

Straus, Erwin W. 1963. "Born to See, Bound to Behold: Reflections on the Function of the Upright Posture in the Esthetic Attitude." In *The Philosophy of the Body: Rejections of Cartesian Dualism,* edited by Stuart F. Spicker. Chicago: Quadrangle Books (1970).

Strawson, P. F. 1970. "Imagination and Perception." In *Experience and Theory,* edited by Lawrence Foster and J. W. Swanson. Amherst: University of Massachusetts Press.

Taylor, Paul. 1981. "Imagination and Information." *Philosophy and Phenomenological Research* 42:205–223.

Tye, Michael. 1984. "The Debate about Mental Imagery." *The Journal of Philosophy* 81:678–691.

Warnock, Mary. 1976. *Imagination.* Berkeley and Los Angeles: University of California Press (1978).

Williams, Bernard. 1966. "Imagination and the Self." *Proceedings of the British Academy,* Volume 52. London: Oxford University Press.

Wittgenstein, Ludwig [1889–1951]. 1933–1935. *The Blue Book: Preliminary Studies for the "Philosophical Investigations"* (pp. 32, 39, 53). New York: Harper Torchbooks (1965).

———. 1945–1948. *Zettel* (nos. 621-c. 646). Translated and edited G.E.M. Anscombe and G.H. von Wright. Oxford: Basil Blackwell.

———. 1947–1949. *Philosophical Investigations.* (Part II xi; pp. 193-c. 214, nos. 370, 388–400). Edited by G.E.M. Anscombe. New York: Macmillan Co. (1953).

Wollheim, Richard. 1970. "Imagination and Identification." Chapter 3 in *On Art and the Mind.* Cambridge: Harvard University Press (1974).

Chapter V

Conclusions: Why an Image-Forming Imagination Should, After All, Be Affirmed

The concluding thesis proposed in this chapter heading is not the outcome of the tradition detailed above. As I suggested at the outset, the sequence of treatments shows no progression toward a definitive result—not even, as some would have it, toward the final abandonment of the question informing this part: What is the nature of the imagination?

There is, to be sure, a current negative consensus which has been nearly a hundred years in the making: The imagination is not an isolable faculty; it does not function to form mentally immanent images; its images are not pictures. But a mainstream in full flood is ever the precursor of the turn of the tide, and the new century may well bring a reaffirmation—in new contexts and on new grounds. Indeed there are already signs. There are also, to be sure, vigorous voices to declare that the question is worn out or superseded. But the curious propensity of philosophers to proclaim the end of the philosophical project, be it by culmination, inanition, or self-destruction, is now two hundred years old. That fact encourages what seems to me the most vital philosophical faith there is: that the questions outlast the answers.

The concluding thesis offered here is, nonetheless, derived from and indebted to the theories set out above: they have provided insights and distinctions quite apart from their context in a system and their position in the tradition. These latter elements have, I hope, been given their due in the previous chapters.

My conclusion is just this: *There is a distinct psychic power, analogously described as a mind's eye, that "sees" representations immanent in an inner, psychic space. These are rightly called images. For, as memory-images, they actually copy*

193

their perceptual originals, and again, as imaginative images, they seem to image certain fictive archetypes. Consequently they have both the general feel and the defining features of pictures. In sum, it is the nature of the imagination to be a dual faculty that simultaneously forms and sees picture-like resemblances.

I hope this thesis is as explicit as it is unfashionable. Its motive is a version of the ancient astronomers' ambition to "save the [heavenly] appearances," to save them both *as* appearances and *for* reason, by undergirding them with a rational hypothesis. In this vein I would wish to save the inner appearances by proposing a hypothesis that is reasonable but not forcibly formal. For it seems to me that, whatever modern science must do, philosophy should underwrite rather than undermine such common opinion as we have left. Yet all the current critiques of the image-forming imagination are driven by motives other than the desire to account for it in terms that preserve rather than override the experience people persist in reporting. Even the Phenomenologists, who make the most earnest effort to take notice of how things actually appear to us, give their prior allegiance to the doctrine of the transparency of consciousness which eschews immanent mental objects, while the Analysts value above all the deliverance of philosophic speech from murky sense and elusive reference. And it must be admitted that such speech, called in a kinder vein "analogical," is unavoidable in all attempts to speak of the mind as inward. Most of all it is unavoidable in introspective reflection on the imagination. The prefix "quasi"—quasi-vision, quasi-picture, quasi-space—which signals a similitude, cannot help but abound in this book. For my working hypothesis is that as things present themselves, so they must be told. The philosophical account must respect the phenomenal description. "Quasi" is thus a quandary-prefix, dictated by the way things are with the imagination, namely double-edged. In this embarrassment it is almost a comfort that the other side achieves no unequivocal way of talking either. In fact, it offers no positive wisdom about inner images at all.

I make an issue of motive because it is clear to me from the preceding review of the tradition that all theories of the imagination, including the one affirmed here, have fatal flaws from some perspective. Which of these defects are then to be tolerated depends on the spirit in which philosophy is being pursued.

The way of introspection is proscribed by the Analysts because it trades on inner images by giving "privileged access" to them. In cognitive psychology, which is unquestionably a science, this issue, far from receding, will become even more acute, since all the imagery experiments designed to evade introspection in fact require introspective protocols at some point. So introspection is an inescapable problem. The charge of "privileged access" means that introspective assertions are valueless by reason of being hopelessly private and incorrigible, that is to say, not open to public view and critique. Yet without introspection the imagination is twice lost. For not only is any first-hand description of its effects proscribed, but its very activity, insofar as it is itself a type of introspection, is precluded. Privileged access must therefore be defended as part and parcel of the "internality" of images—it is, after all, one reason why we speak of "inner" images. (The other reason, explicated in Part Five, Ch. I B, is the essential immateriality of their spatial extension.)

Actually I cannot see why the special imaginative intimacy persons have with themselves should cause resentment. After all, in external life, where information can in principle be checked, it is in fact often and fatefully noncorrigible. We live with that incorrigibility, trusting in the verbal talents and the good faith of the informant who claims first-hand experience. But more to the point, people probe one another's introspective reports and encourage self-correction all the time, so that introspection is incorrigible only in a very narrow view of evidence. Moreover, "privacy" seems to be too privative a word to describe the status of experiences that often contain a powerful impulse toward externalization and communication. Such experiences do, after all, include the strenuous efforts, which cannot *always* be doomed, of painters and writers, to achieve pictorial verisimilitude and accuracy of description. In fact, the wonder is how well we can open our inner space to others, and how much empathy for its groping language people in fact have. They do continually try to "share" their inner life. Why then should reflective exchange in this realm be futile?

Mental images are, to be sure, originally invisible to all except one possessor and viewer. But that fact, once again, distinguishes them radically from perceptible views only if one takes a very cut-and-dried approach to the problems of perception and perspective. Otherwise, external vision is no more an obviously public event than imagining is a hopelessly private one. Indeed, shared seeing of the inner world is not so utterly different from common looking at the outer world. In each case one makes an effort in good faith to see what the other sees. In each case the verbal communication renders the visions only asymptotically and "sortally." That is to say, the visualization that is a re-translation from language is achieved in kind rather than in sensory particularity. (Such inter-modal translation is taken up in Part Four, Ch. I.) Nevertheless, a sensible effort can be made to assimilate the internal views of two people in more and more particulars, even in regard to perspectival properties. One might even claim, hyperbolically, that the world behind the eyes is more common than the world before them, because it is more suggestive.

There is another ulterior motive, already mentioned, for putting mental images under an inderdict. It is the phenomenological doctrine that nothing can be in or before consciousness that is opaque to it. It seems to me experientially dubious: There is much that is psychic but not fully transparent to consciousness—neither fully conscious nor fully penetrable by consciousness. I am speaking not of a Freudian unconscious, a place of primal passion, but simply of the background features of perfectly lucid mentation. Not only does consciousness sometimes fail to be transparent to itself, it is sometimes not even translucent. For it will become clear in the next part that certain aspects of psychic processes are hidden from self-consciousness, though they can be coaxed into observability. Some of these aspects can in fact be attributed to mental images.

Granted the possibility of introspection, and granted that there are opaque inserts into consciousness, such as images, it is time to make a first effort to say what, positively, the ingredients in the imaginative experience seem to me to be. All of them, I hasten again to say, have been previously suggested in the literature; all of them have in turn been specifically rejected somewhere by someone.

To begin with, the visual imagination produces a concatenation, almost a continuum, of image effects, from a vague atmospheric inner dawning to hard-edged eidetic projection, from deliberate daydreaming to hallucinatory possession, from the sensory seclusion of dreams to the open-eyed visions of imaginative seeing. Thus imaginative effects are spread out along the dimensions of the vague/precise, the active/passive, and the inner/outer. Images possessing combinations of these properties in any degree can usually be transformed into images in which the intensities are differently weighted. For example, a deep, vivid dream can be revisited as a vague, waking memory or projected as an atmosphere onto a landscape. The closed-eye imagination happens to yield images most obviously differentiated from percepts, but they are nevertheless just part of the continuum.

Next, through all its vicissitudes the imagination plays a dual role. It both envisions and looks at its visions. It looks within, introspectively, and itself presents the images, productively. The image-gazing, which, as was just said, may be done with eyes shut or open, can induce real ocular strain. Thus the effort to see seems on occasion to be indistinguishable from the production of inner sight, but often the image rises spontaneously from the depths or flashes in, unbidden, from memory. Occurrent and constructive seeing can be variously balanced. Consequently the imagination seems to be both a quasi-organ, a mind's eye, and a place of exhibition, an inner space.

The images of the imagination therefore have extensivity, spatiality, and visibility. One might say they have a patency or appearance-likeness analogous to perception. It is, however, not clear that the "internal" senses, those which deliver intensive rather than extensive qualities, like heat or pressure, can be imaginal. Indeed, it has been claimed that no philosopher has applied the term "appearing," which implies not only the display of sensory aspects but also the presence of something that can appear, to experiences other than those of "external" perception (Chisholm 1950). While that claim is not quite accurate, it reinforces my point that appearance is somehow bound to spatiality. That leads to the next element of the analysis.

Both memory- and imagination-images are experienced as being imaginal, namely as re-presenting something. They are likenesses of something, while conveying, in varying degrees, a sense of the non-presence of the original, its lack of thereness.

Nevertheless, images can have great presentness. The much-bandied term "vividness" is unfortunate because it implies a brilliance that is not a necessary quality of the strength of inner vision. Moreover, both strength and weakness of imagery are equally compatible with either lability or persistence, as these, in turn, are, strangely enough, compatible with each other: One may be persistently visited by an image that continually slips away.

Furthermore, inner images not only refer to originals but often embody meanings, verbally articulable thoughts, that are at once the source of the image and its message. It is that sense we have of image-meaning as separable from the mental sight itself, as at once causing it and conveyed by it, that reinforces the notion that images are not identical with thoughts—as does the experience of one thought-plot having many imaginal illustrations and one image having several meanings.

The last point leads to the consideration of what is now universally called the "creativity" of the imagination. The term is usually meant in two senses, both hyperbolic (Part Two, Ch. V A). One sense is that the imaginal profusion is somehow the imaginer's own production. That is a problematic observation if there ever was one in this realm. What is consciously and deliberately called for in imagining is summoned by the imaginer's thought in terms of sorts and kinds. The illustrative image, however, the one that actually occurs, seems to be quite adventitious, though subject to corrective modification. Hence to credit the imager with its "creation" is to credit the sub-intentional soul with creativity, which really says no more than that images somehow rise up. Whence they come in truth remains the question; the possibilities have been tabulated above (Ch. II A).

The second sense of the distinctness of thought and imagination comes from the freedom of the imagination from the veridical requirement applied to thought, namely that it must become adequate to the thing. Thus the imagination is regarded as unconstrained by conditions. I hasten to add that this freedom is not license: In actual human experience, imaginative adequacy plays a large role, for aside from relaxed, fleeting reverie, spontaneous images are attended by an aura of truthfulness, and effortful imagining is experienced as a labor toward adequacy.

The most difficult image-phenomena to articulate, finally, are those detailing the pictorial properties of inner images. These are hard to catch because introspection is subject to its own uncertainty principle: Images become elusive under reflective gazing. Nonetheless, like the antique gods, they can sometimes be glimpsed from behind, fading away. Let me present a number of these features, those that come up again and again.

Images feel framed; they are set within a peripheral inner space. Although movement is certainly an element of imagery, both insofar as images are often fluid (particularly "entoptic" imagery, Part Two, Ch. V C) and insofar as mobile objects are imaged, they are most characteristically static—still, timeless scenes, devoid of motion, though alive with emotion. This observation is a frequent theme of image-watchers. It is part of what gives imagination its kinship to the contemplative intellect. Images can be panoramic, and they can be detailed, but like paintings and unlike reality they do not lead the gaze through continuous acts of refocusing. Instead, passage from one to the other is by aspectual leaps. One or the other format suddenly takes shape, but it would require great effort to accomplish the transition by a steady approach or a continuous magnification.

The most tricky of all pictorial properties is imaginal depth. Inner imagery can be all-but-palpable, but true tangibility, reality, namely material thinghood, is what no one claims it possesses. If images in general are partially defined by a falling off from the substantial being enjoyed by their originals (Part Three, Ch. I), mental images, it is agreed, lack even the solidity and gravity a physical medium gives: They are all front, facade, and surface—appearance through and through. One might say that so is the external world. Wherever we confront it we see it and touch it as surface; it is by definition impossible for the senses to penetrate to the physical inside of things (Part Five, Ch. II A). Yet it is their very impenetrability which betokens material solidity. In physical terms, there are regular resistances and inertias at work. Both the shapes and the motions of internal appearances demonstrably lack such lawful forces. They undergo antic alterations and yield their walls to a whim. This fact is undoubtedly connected to the non-imaginal character of the sense of touch; if there were true touch-images, mental images might be almost indistinguishable from percepts. But the lack of tangible solidity does not mean absence of depth, no more in mental images than in paintings. The surfaces are indefinitely penetrable to sight, and each new image-transparency offers further views. No world is richer in promises of further prospects than the inner world, beckoning just as did the landscape painting of Wu Tao-tzu, when he walked off into its depths. This experience of image depth is corroborated in experiments. When asked to rotate in the imagination certain complex solids, people have an astounding ability mentally to depict depth effects correctly and to make perspectival transformations (Part Two, Ch. I B).

The description just given is explicitly at variance with one version of the common negative conclusion both anti-imagist schools reach: Whether the visual imagination is reduced to a kind of thinking (Analysts) or a kind of consciousness (Phenomenologists), it is said to be radically different from perception in having no object before it, not a quasi-sensory one, or, in fact, any at all. That way of putting the problem intimates that something wider than the image-forming propensity of the imagination is involved in the common critique, namely the representationality of the mind in general.

The mind is representational insofar as it is thought of as entertaining representational elements, symbolic or analogical, on which it operates according to more or less articulable rules. The most consequent representationalists were the English empiricists, Locke and Hume. The most influential philosophical opinion of this century is anti-representational, as set out above. The most active psychological investigations, on the other hand, are, as will be seen, of necessity representational. If they are to have anything to work with, they require the hypothesis of a symbol-manipulating mind. Since they often regard natural language as a reflection of that symbol-system (Field 1978, Harman 1978), it is clear that to opt for representationality is not to be committed to any sort of analogical or resembling representation. Moreover it has been argued that external presentations and internal representation may be experienced similarly without being similar; thus a representation experienced as, say, a real orange-colored orange, may not be orange (Block 1983). I am not sure how one grasps this possibility, which is logically undeniable. But its effect is clear. It is, again, to make sure that among mental representations none need be analogous or perception-like mental images. In other words, one may accept mental representation and deny mental imagery. These internal intricacies will be taken up in the next part, but it is clear that though the admission of representationalism does not *ipso facto* save mental images, its denial certainly precludes them.

There are, broadly, two current critiques of early modern representationalism. In Phenomenology, consciousness is taken to be essentially intentional, in the Husserlian sense. That is, the vexed question of feelings like pain aside, consciousness is always consciousness of something that is not itself in or before consciousness. In the Philosophy of Mind, the mind is taken to be a bundle of dispositions, tendencies towards overt behavior, rather than a "black box" with invisible gear. There is, of course, also the pre-representational Aristotelian theory of the intellect as the receptive capacity which, when actualized in knowing, becomes like its object. Without espousing any one of these three non-representational theories— the arguments would exceed the project of this book—I must say that their collective force against the representationality of thought, namely against the Lockean and Humean "idea," seems to me conclusive. The idea-theory produces a seething nest of intolerable difficulties, chief among them these: No one can satisfactorily specify the representational bond that connects an idea of the mind to its object in the world, or say whether the manipulations of ideas by the mind are yet further representational ideas or mere functions. The latter difficulty, particularly, will continue to haunt the representational theory of cognitive psychology.

Here I should forestall involvement with quite a different line of thought that runs athwart of the present discussion. In his radical critique of that representational tradition which sees the mind as man's "glassy essence," that is, as a looking glass, a Mirror of Nature, Rorty (1979) lumps together occurrent thoughts with mental images as phenomenal, intentional, and representational (24). In terms of the long-standing debate, the first and the third features are mutually exclusive. Furthermore, he considers the spatiality of the mind only in the Cartesian mind/body context, not in relation to the intra-mental space of the imagination. So on both counts Rorty's anti-representationalism is not directly relevant to the image debate.

One more preliminary: Thought is clearly distinguishable from imagination, at least as I have delineated it here. The images of this imagination are, I have argued, phenomenal, and as appearances they have a sort of spatiality, whose nature will be investigated in Part Five. Furthermore their production, their scanning, and their movements, take measurable time. Thought, on the other hand, is a-temporal and non-spatial. The thought in a judgment, for instance, does not come into being through the temporal order of the language expressing it, but is, at least arguably, there all at once (Geach 1957). Again, the logical relation rendered by a spatial diagram is located not in its spatiality *per se* but in the abstractable relation of its parts.

However, the argument for the non-spatiality of thought just reported, itself supposes that thought, or at least discursive thinking, is indeed imageable. Otherwise why would logic-diagrams be helpful or picturable myths form an evidently ineradicable part of philosophy? It is the Neoplatonists who first made an explicit point of the imagination's ability to receive intellectual influences in image-form. Not only does the intellect project the mythical images of its truths into the imaginative space, but discursive thought inscribes its geometric schemata into the inner medium. Indeed, the Neoplatonists are the direct forerunners of Kant with respect to the transcendental schematism. The discussion of the images of reason, such as logical and geometric diagrams, spatially disposed symbols, and pictures of mental models, will occupy much of Part Five.

Yet, once more, granted the possibility of representing reason in images that are by their nature analogues or resemblances, no one wants to say that, for example, a logic-diagram looks like the class relation it purports to depict, even if it does, just by being spatial, look remotely like the classes so related. There is no getting around the sense that such images are schematized exemplifications of a *mysterium tremendum*: that thought pertains to space. In sum, thoughts and images are as unbridgeably diverse as they are indissolubly coordinated.

Then why should we not say that, although thought does not consist of functions exercised over immanent elements and is not representational, the imagination has precisely those characteristics? The term "mind," with its rational overtones, ill accommodates this proposal; let me revive the old word "soul." By the soul I mean the complex of mental powers ranged in a hierarchy, where a hierarchy is a ranking that preserves the specific dignity of each element. For to recognize a strong distinction between thought and imagination is inevitably to be precipitated into the problem of their relation—which always turns out to be a question of subordination. Now, although I contend that the imagination is central both in the sense of being a mediating power in cognition and in the sense of having a crucial function in life, I also think, and will argue in the Conclusion to this book, that the imagination has this centrality by virtue of being subject and ancillary to thought. There might be, perhaps in animals, an a-rational imagination, mere memory and visualization in the service of reactive behavior. We do not know. In humans there is certainly an ir-rational imagination. That we do know. But irrationality is not pre- but post-rational; it is the willful setting-aside of reason, whose premier practitioners are the proudly paradoxical Romantics.

In fact, human imagination is always somehow under the aegis of thought. The more deliberate images of the imagination can be considered as a kind of incarnation of thought-intentions, while even its spontaneous reveries usually turn out to convey verbally expressible meanings. Indeed, although certain Romantic writers imply that the significance of imaginative images is to be found merely in further images—in an indeterminate web of image-references—I think that the ultimate meaning of an image, if it has one, is a thought. That bond between thought and imagination can indeed be suspended. Its preservation is, I think, a criterion of greatness in the works of the imagination, particularly in literature. In some Romantic poetry, for example, the images ramify *ad infinitum* into the subconscious vat of memory-resonances. Such reference-resonances are then said to exhaust the significance of the poem—to the detriment of its stature, surely. For great poems are not infinite allusions but determinate illuminations. Again, in some "philosophical novels," for instance, in Mann's *Magic Mountain*, cunningly drawn simulacra of intellectual life play a role, but only for the simulation of a spectacle, not for the truth of the argument. But in the great fictions the imagination is—tacitly—governed by what the reader is incited to pursue as the central thought and the formulable truth of the work.

It can even be argued (Sokolowski 1977) that the picture- or image-structure itself, whose chief function is the "presencing" of an object, meaning the re-presentation of an absent object, only becomes actual and appreciable for us through the thought-function of naming. For naming permits an object to be present and absent at once, absent in reality and present in name. This intellectual capability is then perhaps our condition of possibility for apprehending the analogous image-structure.

If the imagination is, so to speak, embodied intellect, intellect, in turn, seems in various ways to require the services of the imagination. This is what the old Aristotelian dictum, that there is no thought without its image, forcefully claims—of course within its particular noetic context. Tradition aside, however, the necessity of images for thought seems to be a matter of experiential fact. The old controversy in psychology about "imageless thought" was on balance resolved—insofar as such matters are resoluble—in favor of imagery. In any case, the contention of the anti-imagists was not so much that thinking is not accompanied by imagery as that the imagery is not relevant to the thought; and that too is experimentally questionable. The reciprocal relations of intellect and imagination will be further detailed in the Conclusion to this book.

Some version of the line started by Aristotle in *On the Soul* seems to me most plausible: *In the psychic hierarchy it is the function of the imagination to mediate between perception and thought.* Thinking is a seclusively concentrated activity. The imagination, by means of its "phantasms," brings to it the world's extended objects without the distracting pressure of their presence. It brings them released from the constraints of physicality and capable of playfully experimental variation. It brings them prepared for thought by abstraction from their material reality. In sum, the imagination is eminently *re*-presentational.

Such a view makes sense only if non-representationalism is affirmed not only at the upper end for thought but also at the lower end for perception. And indeed, perception most particularly is not representational. After all, the whole Humean trouble reported above starts at the lower end of the psychic spectrum, with the notion that the external world is always mediated to the mind by representational images that are essentially indistinguishable from memories—even from fantasies. There are plenty of philosophical arguments to the effect that the objects of external nature are present to us directly and immediately, not representationally. These arguments are reinforced by the psychological experiments on memory which reveal a distinction, almost in kind, between the perceptual "icon" and the stored memory-image. There is even one school of experimental psychology that regards perception as non-representational (Part Two, Ch. I C).

It is consequently a plausible conclusion that *if there is an image-forming imagination* (including memory) *it is our one and only representational capacity.* Re-presentation is the mediating mode of the imagination, and of the imagination alone. It is only as re-presenting things to thought that images play the role of go-between in cognition; by the same token, there is no good reason for the psychic extremes, perception and thinking, to function representationally.

Let me, finally, collect all the constituents of the claim that the imagination produces images of the sort that indeed live up to their name by being experienced as pictures: Images throw themselves, object-like, in the way of the inner eye. They have non-representational features, experimentally extractable, that are analogous to a picture-medium. They re-present by means of their resembling looks. Like pictures, they are commonly taken for images, and like pictures they are usually recognized as images of whatever they image at a glance, all at once. They are, furthermore, taken as resemblances, which look like the originals they are representing, rather than as symbols which do not represent by similarity. Like pictures, they are eminently capable of being enjoyed in their own right, despite and even because of the absence of the original. These last four criteria of pictures are given by Sokolowski (1977), who, however, denies that mental images meet them. His main reason is that there is a curious double function of the imaging self as image-haver and image-viewer, which seems so unlike the plain confrontation of picture-thing and picture-viewer. It has been pointed out, however, that in picture-drawing there is indeed a continual reciprocity between the nascent drawing and the viewing drawer. So one may, after all, assimilate the productive viewing of an external picture to the productive viewing of an inner image.

To complete this conclusion: The human significance of acknowledging an image-forming imagination seems to me very great, and the consequences of denying it very grave. This assertion seems to me to be true, even though I am chary of hyperbole. There are certain earnest assurances that often accompany philosophical attacks on image-imagining. They are to the effect that the possibility and quality of inner life will not be touched by these attacks. They all turn out to be untrustworthy. In the long run, whenever the philosophical inclination toward what might be termed "imaginational realism" is severely proscribed and its experiential counterpart is scarcely acknowledged, the imaginative activity itself is going to be damped, certainly in its philosophical employment. It is particularly inopportune that the human imagination should be in so tenuous a theoretical condition just when electronic image-mongering is in a period of hypertrophic growth. But laments make no case, need is no argument, and what really counts is the plausibility of the foregoing case for inner images.

The function of the imagination in inner life will be the subject of the Coda to this book. The object here has been and will be to mount a small revolt—unrabid and not unappreciative—against anti-imagistic rationalism, along with its inevitable complement, imagination-worshipping romanticism. The romanticism is perhaps the more dangerous to us all, insofar as it imputes to our whole philosophical tradition the arid and repulsive sin of "logo-centrism." This romantic imputation is self-destructive, for it defames the ground on which we all stand. It is also false. For close inspection has shown that, at least until recently, our tradition has not been logocentric but rather imago-centric: The logos may lead, but the imagination is always the crux.

Bibliography

Block, Ned. 1983. "Mental Pictures and Cognitive Science." *The Philosophical Review* 92:499–541.

Chisholm, Roderick M. 1950. "The Theory of Appearing." In *Perceiving, Sensing, and Knowing*, edited by Robert J. Swartz. Berkeley and Los Angeles: University of California Press (1965).

Field, Hartry H. 1978. "Mental Representation." In *Readings in Philosophy of Psychology*, Volume 2, Part One, *Mental Representation*, no. 5, edited by Ned Block. Cambridge: Harvard University Press (1981).

Geach, Peter. 1957. *Mental Acts*. In *Readings in Philosophy of Psychology*, Volume 2,

Part One, *Mental Representation*, no. 1, edited by Ned Block. Cambridge: Harvard University Press (1981).

Harman, Gilbert. 1978. "Is There Mental Representation?" In *Minnesota Studies in the Philosophy of Science*, Volume 9, *Perception and Cognition: Issues in the Foundations of Psychology*, edited by C. Wade Savage. Minneapolis: University of Minnesota Press.

Rorty, Richard. 1979. *Philosophy and the Mirror of Nature*. Princeton: Princeton University Press.

Sokolowski, Robert. 1977. "Picturing." *Review of Metaphysics* 31:3–28.

Part Two

Psychology: The Having of Imagery

Part Two

Psychology: The Having of Imagery

There ought to be something astonishing in the mere conception of an experimental science of the soul in general. It is all the more amazing that such a science has actually been developed, and that it has made the imagination one of its special fields. For a lay proprietor of a soul and an amateur of the imagination there might be an added element of aversion. Doctor Johnson, upon complaining of being annoyed by the virtuoso exhibition of an acrobat, was reminded by his companion that the feat was, after all, very difficult. "Difficult do you call it, Sir?" was his rejoinder; "I wish it were impossible." So too might someone absorbed in that most elusive, evanescent, and gauzy of inner activities recoil at the regimentation required to prepare the imagination for the laboratory, and shudder at the exposure in store for so private a power.

In vain. The science does exist and it is fascinating. The results themselves, ingeniously obtained and gratifyingly non-trivial though they may be, have not yet yielded, and perhaps never will yield, either a fully global or a completely corroborable theory. Theory, however, is in one way the least of it, since the preparations and preliminaries are themselves deeply interesting. For as always, when science comes to deal with the soul, methodology becomes absorbing.

The science of physical nature came about, according to Kant, when investigators began to force her to answer their questions, putting her to torture, so to speak. The inquisition into psychic nature has a prior task: to force her into the open to begin with, to make her merely show herself. The capture of the imagination as an observable piece of nature starts with devising ways to extract measurable evidence about imaginal structures and processes. It begins, in fact, even further back, with the tortuously difficult formulation of criteria for the existence of mental images, or, better, for having imagery.

This second part is therefore a review of the problems and findings concerning mental imagery of all kinds in all sorts of psychology. It is an outsider's overview, insofar as I persist throughout in finding strange what the trade finds familiar, in being doubtful of assumptions that are matters of faith to the profession, and in maintaining certain expectations that the science has renounced. In that spirit these six chapters are meant as a kind of reference and illumination for the rest of the book, for here is a rare case where science throws much immediate light on a pervasive human theme.

Chapter I

Cognitive Science: The Setting of Imagery-Investigations

The science in which the most telling imagery-investigations take place is Cognitive Psychology (Ch. II). Cognitive psychology in turn belongs to a group of new or renewed disciplines—including Artificial Intelligence, Communications Theory, and Linguistics—that make up a Cognitive Science. The unifying "cognitivist" view is that knowing is information processing—"cognition" here is not, as in philosophy, the apprehension of truth. This cognitivist attitude or method, leading to many theories, amounts to what historians of science currently call a paradigm—a paradigm being to scientists more or less what a world-view is to the intellectuals, namely the prevailing frame of hypothesizing. In the following discussion of imagery as it becomes a subject of science, the cognitivist paradigm will take the leading role, though the "humanist" psychologies, which approach imagery as a· human experience, will also require fairly long accounts (Chs. III-V).

Cognitive science, then, is the setting of cognitive psychology, which is indeed a specification of the former, at least with respect to imagery. In cognitive psychology the complex, embattled issues of cognitivism become simpler and sharper, whether as hopes or as hypotheses. A prime example of such issues is functionalism, the prevailing, though not unchallenged, cognitive position concerning the mind/body problem (Churchland 1984, Block 1978). Functionalism is a sort of neo-behaviorism, in that a mental state is understood as a disposition to act in certain ways, given certain sensory inputs. It differs from Behaviorism, old style, in allowing individual mental states to exist and to be themselves both the causes and the results of other mental states. Furthermore, the new behaviorism considers the mental functions as separable from their physical realizations. A human brain, a Martian brain, a computer, and a mere program all might "embody" the same functional economy, so that no type of mental state has one uniquely necessary embodiment. The point is that in cognitive psychology the hope is strong and the hypothesis general that to each particular mental state or event a corresponding brain state can be matched (Ch. VI). In the tendency to hope for a real embodiment of their theories cognitive scientists are true to the old pattern of the grander new sciences: Copernicus in his day bought trouble by claiming reality rather than mere hypothetical adequacy for his heliocentric orbits.

Information-processing is an approach to cognition which supports the functionalist obliteration of the distinction between human and a-human mental states and events. With respect to psychology the word "information" is not, however, to be taken very stringently. It does not here have the precise quantitative sense used in communication theory, nor yet the general formal meaning according to which information is whatever puts an organism or a system into a new state of readiness for response. The most immediately apt tenor of the term is broad: Information is anything that is representable (MacKay 1969), where the latter term refers not to the capability of an external element to be re-presented inside the system, but to any inside state or event which is there present to be processed (Dennett 1978). Thus "information" does not imply any matching of thought to thing. "Processing," the central cognitive term, then means any transformation of such representations, be it by elaboration or reduction, by storage or retrieval, applied in sequence or in parallel, from top down or bottom up.

These kinds, stages, and routes of the processing are the preoccupations of cognitive science. The chief tool in imagery-experiments will be the measurement of reaction times. The very fact that mental processes take measurable time suggests a physical underpinning. At the least, as the more reflective scientists point out, the assumption that reaction-times pertain to mental processes, implying that they have a temporal dimension, is no more to be taken for granted than that they might have mass, location, or magnitude. Except under some sort of brain/mind isomorphism, a one-to-one correspondence of physical and mental events is, in fact, far from being perspicuous. Moreover, time differences may turn out to differentiate not only the stages of a process but merely incidental properties, as they often do in computers. In spite of these theoretical caveats, the practical results are fairly compelling.

It follows that "cognitivism" has two related problems particularly relevant to imagery. The first is a tale here briefly told. It concerns the question of the place of consciousness in information-processing and of its imagery-aspect, the "mind's eye," in particular (A). The second is the problem of representation in general and of the representational type to which imagery in particular belongs (B). It should be said that the cognitivist theoreticians, who straddle the barbed wire fence between philosophy and science, get fascinatingly entangled in these matters. On the philosophical side there are old epistemological questions which seem to be experimentally intractable, while on the psychological side there are new experimental results which don't make much of a whole with human experience. A consequence is the odd indecision of the literature concerning the life-stage cognitive psychology has reached, especially with respect to imagery. Has it run its course to a conceptual stand-still, or are its quandaries the growing pains of lusty youth? It is a question for the future.

A. Consciousness

The question of consciousness, is, it seems, a lost cause for cognitive science. At least the theorists' dealings with it are mostly acrobatic—involved contortions and death-defying leaps. Consequently, for imagery the experiments are on the whole more illuminating without a theory of consciousness than with it.

The cognitive attempt is to catch consciousness within the concepts of information-processing, eschewing traditional terms such as soul, self, and subject (except in the experimental sense), and their associated insights. For example, the Kantian assumption that the possibility of self-consciousness must be a condition of consciousness is not at all an accepted axiom of cognitivism.

The difficulty cognitive science has with consciousness, and *a fortiori* with self-consciousness, is reciprocally related to the locus of its interest, which is below or behind consciousness. Most cognitive processes are in fact unconscious in the sense that they are not experienced by the knower. "Unconscious," however, though it is the current word, is not quite the right one, since the unconscious to which Freud accustomed the world, that pandemonium of asocial passions, is, whatever its ultimate biological basis may be, still conceived as of a piece with consciousness. Though it is an interdicted region of the soul, its libidinous contents can be forced up into self-knowledge by psychoanalysis. The cognitive unconscious, on the other hand, whose forerunner was the "imageless thought" of the Würzburg school, is not primarily passionate or emotional. In fact, the cognitive study of emotion has not gone very far. Furthermore, though aspects of the cognitive unconscious can on occasion become conscious—trains of thought having run underground for long stretches may slowly surface and imagery may make sudden epiphanies before the mind's eye—it is conceived not as in itself mental but as the explanatory mechanism of mental activity (Richardson 1980, 38). Since it is the reconstruction of cognitive processes which is the proper preoccupation of psychology and artificial intelligence, the question about consciousness is an extraneous worry forced on the practitioners of these sciences by a philosophical hope: They want, while working out the information-processing hypothesis, to shed light on the human being as well. But this valiant attempt to be Janus-faced, philosophical among philosophers and scientific among scientists, may be in the nature of the enterprise impossible. That too would be a lesson.

There is, to be sure, one area of unavoidable contact between philosophy and science in imagery-investigations. Such experiments begin with the informal assumption that people can form, have, and report a mental image. They therefore begin, willy-nilly, with an "autophenomenological" moment, a point at which subjects must give an introspective account of their own inner appearances. So the strait gate and the narrow way to mental processes is through self-conscious reports of conscious experience. Introspection, however, is obnoxious to science, because it is thought of as private: It is idiosyncratically "mine," imperfectly communicable, and incorrigible. Hence the faster it can be left behind, the better. A self-report of a mental representation is taken to imply reliably only that something is going on, but not what it is (Harman 1978).

So while experimenters do not gainsay the fact of an imagery-experience, they try to circumvent it for purposes of determining the efficacy and nature of imagery. It is relegated to being an epiphenomenon that rides in piggy-back on the causal unconscious processes. Conscious experience is an inessential by-product or, more sophisticatedly, an "emergent" phenomenon. Emergence is the most acrobatic or magical of all the notions absorbed by cognitive science. It is the modern inverse of a medieval "occult quality," for although patent enough, it applies to an experienced whole that is mysteriously other, and in some sense more, than the sum of its parts. The notion is useful because the elements of a scientific analysis never do quite synthesize into the object of common experience. For example, individual sensory stimuli often cannot account for the actual look of patterns, their "gestalt." This total impression is therefore termed an emergent property. "Emergence" can put Humpty Dumpty together again.

An alternative to such leaps to higher levels is to regard consciousness as a "control element" in a system in which it is characterized merely in terms of its special access. The following abridged schema of a cognitive theory of consciousness is Dennett's (1978): There are several functional areas in consciousness. For example, there is a perceptual component, which takes sensory input and stores percepts in the memory component. Functionally above these is the control component, which has access to them all. It directs the perceptual function through the focusing of attention, it sends commands to the speech components to perform speech acts, and it is in control of their execution. Above all, it directs inquiries and receives replies from memory. The control component can introspect, for introspection is said to be nothing more than the control sub-routine of addressing inquiries to and processing answers from memory.

Asking oneself questions may well be the prime index of human consciousness, but the preservation of this insight is precisely not the task for Dennett. His task is rather to make such intuitions go away (206) and to "construct a full-fledged 'I' out of subpersonal parts by exploiting the subpersonal notions of access . . ." He wants to show that a conscious being can be thought of as the complex of realizations of this flowchart headed by a control element, which, albeit "awfully fancy," is in concept as much a machine as the other components.

What view of consciousness makes this feasible? Dennett begins with Nagel's formulation: The essence of the belief that any being has subjectivity and experience is that one is willing to ask of it the question "What is it like to be an X?" (Nagel 1974). Note well that the "like" has no force here; the possibility of empathy is precisely not the test. What Nagel has in mind is whether we can conceive asking what it is to have just that perspective, not whether we can succeed in getting the answer. Dennett then asks: What would it be like to be such a machine as has been described and what grounds can you give for denying that it is in virtue of being a realization of this flowchart that there is something it feels like to be you? After all, the a-human realization will, by hypothesis, behave much as you do, and if its internal processes are obscure to it, so are your brain events to you.

The argument seems to me strange. First: It is admitted that no one has the faintest idea how to construct a fancy control component that contains an "executive homunculus" who can do what human consciousness does. So why does its barely possible existence outweigh for Dennett its actual nonexistence? Why does a fantasized subpersonal consciousness simulator even begin to demonstrate that consciousness can be so simulated? Second: But suppose such a machine exists. Is the Nagel question not doing curious work here? It is supposed to be an expression of the belief that a being is conscious, so that to ask it of the machine already amounts to an imputation of consciousness. Third: Why would agreement that the mind has organized functions advance the argument if one of those functions is precisely consciousness in all its mystery? If a component is capable of introspecting (in the sense of asking its fellow components questions, considering their answers, requiring the articulating of thought in speech, and directing attention to the world) who knows whether it doesn't have to be substantially different from the other subsystems—capable, for example, of becoming reflexive and thus self-conscious?

The reason for dwelling on a specifically cognitive theory of consciousness is that if attended to, it would effectively inhibit imagery-investigations. For there is "no room in the subpersonal explanation for images" (Dennett 1981a). Mental images, by their very nature, require to be "perceived" and recognized *as* images. If the mind's eye is nothing at all but a metaphor, every reason for holding on to the term imagery is gone. For it makes no sense to speak of an "unseen" or unconscious image, unless it would be in the sense of "unattended to." On the other hand, no verbal report can ever adequately represent a specific image, any more than words can render a spatial picture without remainder; words may do perfect justice to thoughts but never to sights. So the imaginal representations are actual nowhere if not before the subject's inner eye.

Such mental "seeing," however, would have to be an adjunct of consciousness. As the subject sees by means of the organic eye which is excited by stimuli, so it "sees" with a mind's eye which shares some of the perceptual processes of vision but works in the absence of external stimuli. Now not only do imagery-havers maintain that inner seeing is just what they *experience* but, weightier in this context, the experimental evidence can be reasonably interpreted as confirming their claim.

Here then, in sum, is the probably intractable perplexity: On the one hand, there is the experience of imagery, a particular kind of consciousness marked by sometimes vivid inner representations, which are peculiarly private in having no really adequate externalization such as thought has in linguistic utterance. There are, as will be shown, also experimental results strongly suggesting the presence of representations that have just the pictorial characteristics imagers say they do. On the other hand, the traditional understanding of consciousness as the agency for and through which mental states and events have their being is not easily assimilable into the information-processing framework of cognitive science. For that framework is essentially explicit, analytic, and inhospitable to categories of inwardness. In particular, the strongly representational consciousness before and to which picture-like mental states and events appear, the "mind's eye," is a standing embarrassment to this science.

Finally, I ought to note an ingenious cognitivist attempt to grapple with *self*-consciousness. It likens self-knowledge to a map of a land that has a map of itself traced on a plain within it. This is the "recursive embedding" model of self-awareness (Johnson-Laird 1983). Any automaton realizing such a program, it is claimed, must be said to behave with intentionality—a sure criterion of self-consciousness. It can, as it were, plan to have plans, and its intention will inform the plans it has. Such a machine achieves more than the mere self-imitation of those Turing machines that print out self-descriptions. It seems really to know itself. It even has such human cognitive features as being in ignorance of large parts of itself and being indefinitely recursive, that is, of knowing that it knows that it knows. Hence machine-realizable recursive embedding offers a model of self-awareness for cognitive science.

This resolution of the ancient mystery is beguiling, but it circumvents rather than confronts the traditional problem. For the notion of self-consciousness is rephrased so as to be realizable in automata, in rule-governed symbol-manipulating systems. Yet it seems that in matters of self-consciousness, if nowhere else, introspection, which is what the tradition looks to in its formulations, must be allowed the last word, and introspection supports a notion not of embedding but of reflexivity: In ultimate consciousness (for in actual human beings indefinite recursion is only a verbal possibility), so-called propositional attitudes such as "wishing that . . . ," "willing that . . . ," and above all "thinking that . . . ," are not so crisply separable from the propositions intended as they are in the map-model: *Noēsis noēseos*, thought not *about* but *of* thought itself, is the classical insight that cognitivists are forced to set aside.

B. Representation

It would seem on the face of it that mental imagery is the re-presentational experience *par excellence* (Part One, Ch. V). Its very name implies copying and correspondence. This representational character turns out, however, to be the second stumbling block of cognitive science. It seems to be agreed that this central notion of the science, representation, is terminologically muddled and conceptually perplexed in the extreme (J. Mandler 1983, Palmer 1978). In this section I will try to retail briefly how the issue develops.

With one important exception, set out in (C), cognitive scientists adhere to the representational view of mental states and events. This fact would seem to mean that the paradigmatic scientific tack bypasses the prevailing philosophical tendency as it sails headlong in the other direction. However, that philosophic flight is from representationalism understood as a "mirror of nature" theory of mind. In this tradition the ideas of the mind are copied from, and correspond to, the objects of the world, either faithfully or faultily. Cognitivist representation, on the other hand, does not necessarily include a "semantic" relation, that is, a reference to the world: "Fodor's picture of the mind as a system of inner representations has nothing to do with the image of the Mirror of Nature I have been criticizing" (Rorty 1979). Fodor has sharpened the cognitivist version of representation to which Rorty refers into a blunt admission of methodological solipsism (1980).

The thesis is that the processes open to treatment in cognitive psychology must be not only representational but representational in a particular sense. They are computational, by which is meant that they are both symbolic and formal. "Symbolic" is a word that has come far from its Greek use: a physical token fitting its mate to signify a contract. Here it means nothing more than that the processes operate on elements of some sort. "Formal" means that the processes work by explicit logical, syntactical rules, or by mathematical transformations. The latter are included expressly to take care of imagistic processes such as the mental rotations, which will play so central a role in imagery experiments. The burden of the formality-condition, however, is the absence of semantic properties. No truth, reference, or meaning is involved in computational processes so understood. Such a "rational" psychology is traced back to Descartes, who could offer no binding external criterion for distinguishing true from hallucinatory mental representations, depending instead on the inner coherence of the representational system. It is an alternative to the older "naturalistic psychology," whose aim it was precisely to study the semantic, causal, relations of stimulus to soul.

Such a rationalistic psychology does exist. An example is the impressive project of having a computer "live in," namely operate on, a simple world of block shapes. However, these blocks need not actually be there. The computer arranges its internal data and operates on them as if there were a real world. Its world is solipsistic. As for a naturalistic cognitive psychology, Fodor thinks the chances of regaining it are slim: "Computational psychology is the only one that we are going to get."

The supporting argument, vastly simplified here, begins by shifting attention to behavior, which is all that tells one what the subject actually "has in mind." Now the way to get from speech behavior to states of mind is typically by means of an "opaque" construal of the subject's utterances. Opaque construal means precisely that one sticks with the mental rather than the external pole of propositions. If a subject utters the belief that "the Morning Star rises in the East" and at the same time the belief that "the Evening Star rises in the East," these propositions are in the opaque mode taken as distinct mental events, even though in the world there is one planet, Venus, which is the single real-world object of both beliefs. A "transparent" reading, on the other hand, one which would insist on the objective identity of the two beliefs, makes more sense ontologically but is less useful psychologically, since it would stand in the way of discovering what the subject "has in mind." At this point it emerges that the formality condition of computational psychology and the opaque construal of mind-reading are closely related. Formality does not allow of distinguishing mental states by semantic properties, while transparency is at bottom a semantic construal of propositions. So if mental states are to be distinguished semantically, that is, by their meanings, then formality cannot be a condition. And inversely, when mental processes obey formal rules, they needn't refer to things in the world.

It should be noted, however, that the formality condition is not necessarily hostile to content taken in the sense of an "internal" meaning, namely the intentional or behavior-causing aspect of a representation. For the differences in such content may somehow show up in the formal distinctions.

It remains to say why the formality condition is all psychology has to work by, or why a naturalistic psychology, one in which the mind meets the world, and which is also scientific, is thought not to be in the cards. The blunt reason is that there is no semantic science in the required sense, no possibility of specifying the relations that hold between a particular mind and the world's object in a scientific, a law-instantiating, way. It is lacking not because people are too spontaneous for such a psychology to succeed, but because they do not yet possess a description of the objects that is complete, public, and scientific enough to make possible a lawful link between these objects and their mental representations. Such a descriptional link would relate the representation to the thing by virtue of what both truly are. Before that relation is worked out, Fodor obviously thinks, we'll all be gone. In the meantime, naturalist experimenters cannot know what their subjects have in mind when they receive instructions and make reports on the stimuli. It should be said that Fodor's extremist thesis, and argument, while very influential, also raised a storm of logical objections (Fodor 1980).

The point here, however, is the bearing of the thesis on the practice of imagery-investigation. Recall that Fodor's real example of a research strategy for psychology grounded in a solipsistic methodology is actually a simulation project in Artificial Intelligence. Imagery-experimenters, on the other hand, are normally as semantic as they can be. They always begin with some expectation of a correspondence between the stimulus picture and the mental representation. The experimenters cannot help but assume that they and the subject are looking at the same object, and that at the instruction "Form an image!" the subject intends to and does form an image that is somehow true to the picture shown. It is a fascinating situation. Productive experimental practice, once again, runs counter to central tendencies of current philosophy and, what is stranger yet, to the sincerest theory of its sponsoring science. It is not, it seems to me, a stand-off to be resolved by settling who tells whom what's what. It may well be that mental imagery is not reachable by a rational psychology or a philosophy that eschews imaginal representations in the strong sense—correspondence-representations.

Working psychologists consequently tend to employ the term representation with two groups of meanings. The first is the one whose implications are explicated above; here are meant the elements and structures of cognition with the processes that operate on them. By extension, the external representations of these internal ones are also included, with the proviso that they too are meaning-less: Cognition as knowledge of *something* is irrelevant to the enterprise. The elements are often called "symbols," because they do stand for, or represent something, namely other elements or structures of elements within the system. The second is the traditional meaning: "A representation is a spatial or temporal configuration of symbols which is conventionally regarded as standing in a certain relationship to something else. Mental images are representations in just this sense" (Richardson 1980). The "certain relationship" is elucidated by another definition belonging to the same group: One configuration represents a second when the former preserves some of the internal relations of the latter (Palmer 1978; compare Shepard's "second order isomorphism"—Ch. II D). "Conventionally" refers to the self-agreed intention of the imager. For since the configurational qualities of a mental image often do not define it determinately, just as the gender of a stick figure is indeterminate, how the image is taken depends on the description under which it was formed or by which it is interpreted (Fodor 1981).

While we do often form or interpret images from word descriptions, Fodor's phrase "images under descriptions" glosses over the representational problem as it arises *in medias res*, in ongoing imagery-investigations. Here the problem is not whether mental images correspond determinately to whatever they image but how they do so. The question with respect to mental images that agitates cognitive psychologists has to do not so much with the meaning as with the nature of images: What kind of representation is going on? (Ch. II C).

A last brief word about representation in general. The objects of the external world present themselves primarily under two aspects: as continuous and extended shapes and spaces, with their colors and other perceptible qualities, and as discrete, namable and countable items with their many kinds of relations. Pictures and diagrams fairly naturally represent the former, words and conventional symbols the latter. The most self-explanatory of representations is the picture or model, which preserves similarity, but there are many non-similar types of spatial representations, which preserve some features of the original. For example, the size of a rectangle may be represented by the length of a line, as Descartes suggests in the *Rules* (Palmer 1978). Words in sentences and symbols in formulas represent the world in terms of its elements and their syntax, which require certain conventions. (I am reporting two common views, not endorsing either a representational or a conventional view of language.) The two kinds of internal representations whose possibility is generally accepted in cognitive psychology follow this lead. There is an "imagistic" or pictorial and a "propositional" or verbal code (Ch. II C).

Along with representation, "code" and "encoding" are the key notions of cognitive science. Encoding refers to the way information is readied for internal processing. For example, it can undergo selection, as when only a part of the stimulus is admitted; or elaboration, as when words are remembered through the formation of imagery; or re-writing, as when the binary digits 11 are read as 3 (Bower 1972). But most generally, information is encoded in the sense of being transposed into either the imagistic or the propositional code. Within each code, there are, of course, specific representational devices for recognizing and placing incoming information, for example, prototypes and feature search (Ch. III A).

The great question arises: Is there an actual imagistic mental code and what is its nature? It is a question from which the propositional code is immune. From the point of view of evidence, human language is trusted to represent a corresponding mental encoding. From the point of view of its physical realization, the elements and the syntax of language are easily conceivable as mediated by the neural networks and firings of the brain. But above all, from the computational point of view, the artificial languages of computers offer excellent models for study. Consequently, there are numerous species of propositional or computational encodings. The question is only which are most adequate.

It is otherwise with the imagistic code. External evidence for imaging, as suggested in (A), is much less direct and trustworthy. There is at present no neural account of specific visual memories. Computers still have a hard time with complex perception-based pictures. Furthermore, propositionalists stand ready to account for the experience of depictive imagery as a mere epiphenomenon, coming on top of descriptional encoding, while they impugn the very possibility of imagist encodings. The ins and outs of the coding controversy are summarized in Chapter II.

The best hope of imagistic encoding is the fact that there is actually a computational model of mental imagery. The experimental evidence that it incorporates is also described in the next chapter. The arguments for it in principle are largely computational-convenience arguments, such as are exemplified in the common experience of answering, say, geometric questions. A propositional proof and its imagistic diagram are "informationally equivalent," since they say the same thing, but they are "computationally non-equivalent," for in simple cases, like the Euclidean theorem that the base angles of an isosceles triangle are equal, people can answer much faster by looking at the picture than by thinking through the proof (Palmer 1978).

It will be argued below that the imagistic computational theory has at bottom nothing much to do with imagistic, that is, picture-like, mental representation. Instead it turns out to be the claim that mental imagery encodings cannot be narrowly syntactic but must include mathematical structures like the arrays and matrices and their special transformations that describe spatial layouts.

The crux of the imagistic representation scandal is thus just the "inner picture" experience—the complement to the "mind's eye" perplexity of the previous section. Most people have the incorrigible sense of seeing internal likenesses, however behaviorally inaccessible and formalistically inarticulable they may be. These likenesses do not present themselves as mere proportions, mere identities of relation over two different realms. They are felt to be genuine space-like similarities, which preserve the essential extendedness that is lost in any verbal or numerical symbolization. Moreover, such imagery does carry information in the precise sense mentioned above: It puts the one who has it into a new state of readiness to know or to act.

The next chapter will illustrate in detail that cognitive science is baffled by experience in general and by space-like representations in particular. It will turn out to be no local difficulty but a perplexity of deep significance, reflecting equally on the nature of imagery, of our cognitive constitution, and of the science itself.

C. Direct Perception

There is a maverick theory opposing the representational theory of perception, that of James Gibson and his school. It does have its own imagery-theory, but its primary contributions in this context are the useful insights it sends up to philosophy rather than any directions it hands down to imagery-experimentation. For it is philosophically much bolder and more contemporary than the (self-styled) representational "establishment" (Fodor and Pylyshyn, 1981). It is eclectically contemporary in the very fact of eschewing representations; in its emphasis on intentionality; in its open recourse to phenomenological analysis; in its insistence on an interactive, ecological "being in the world"; and in its circumvention of the methodological solipsism of cognition by an unabashed realism.

1. Ecological Optics. Gibson's theory is worked out primarily for visual perception though it applies to the other modalities as well.

Whereas in the established information-processing paradigm a percept is the result of enhancement by inference (in the computational sense of intermediate transformations) and by memory, Gibson proposes a "direct pickup" of information. This information is contained by the ambient light, the light that impinges on the receiver from the whole environment, as opposed to the light that radiates from individual objects. It consists of certain invariances as well as of certain transformations that are correlated with the motions of the eyes, of the whole viewer, or of the environment itself. The information concerns the layout of the environment, for example, its "clutter," namely the increasing density of texture and the decreasing mobility that signal remoteness from the observer. This information is not transmitted through the passive senses, but it is available to the whole active perceptual system, consisting of a pair of eyes in a moving head on a mobile body.

This theory is realistic insofar as all the information is located in the external light. Of course, neither this nor any theory of perception is entitled to make claims about the relation of the information-carrying medium to the real objects from which it comes. For example, an experimenter watching a subject falling prey to a visual illusion is in no position to compare a misleading stimulus to the "real" object, but is rather distinguishing an abnormal stimulus situation from a normal one. But even this limited realism suffices to cut out both internal representations and their construals:

> The brain is relieved of the necessity of constructing such information by *any* process—innate rational power (theoretical nativism), the storehouse of memory (empiricism) or form-fields (Gestalt theory). [Gibson 1966, 267]

The epitome of a Gibsonian experiment is the visual cliff of Eleanor Gibson. It is a checkerboard surface with a steep right-angled drop, the whole covered by glass. Babies often shrink back from crossing the drop even as they put a hand on the glass beyond the edge and are encouraged to go across. This behavior indicates that the baby has, without previous experience, picked up the information of a sharp drop from the textural gradient itself, together with the "affordance" of this environmental feature. Affordance is Gibson's term for the opportunities an environmental feature offers, what it is good or bad for. It is part of the surrounding information, one way in which an environment reveals itself to perceivers in terms of their goals and intentions.

There is a toned-down version of Gibson's theory, offered in response to criticism, which admits some sort of mental processing, or representation in the widest sense of the term (Bickhard and Richie 1983). The authors argue that the precise target of Gibson's opposition is encoding, meaning here that kind of symbolization which represents elements and relations through correspondence. They modify Gibson's "direct" model of perception into an interactive model that permits the building up of a "situation image" by a goal-directed system as it goes about perceiving the environment. This image, however, is not a correspondence-representation but a structure of indicators, outcomes that set the system up for further interaction. Indicators are distinguished from encodings by their functions. Indicators are directly consulted by the system's "procedures." Encodings, which do occur under special, visually novel circumstances, must first be interpreted, in the sense that their representational stand-in relationships must be traced. The relevant point here is that even in the updated version the theory has no room for correspondence-imagery.

(Gibson 1966, 1979, Fodor and Pylyshyn 1981, Turvey et al. 1981, Ullman 1980.)

2. Illusions. On the way to the discussion of imagery in the Gibsonian theory, a word is necessary about illusions, which are the standard devices used by students of perception to distinguish between sensory stimuli and their perceptual elaboration. Naturally, a theory that opposes a purely sensory beginning to perception and eschews perceptual elaboration has little use for illusions. For these are eminently unecological, contrived, and without environmental context, and they require an unnaturally rigid position of observation. Nevertheless they must be accounted for. Because of their relevance to imagery-processes various attempts to explain the Müller-Lyer illusion in terms of perceptual processes are reported below; the Gibsonian approach to an explanation will be a convenient example.

The illusion is as follows: Two straight lines of equal measured length are shown side by side. One line is arrow-headed at both ends, while on the other the arrow's lines are bent out into a fork. The arrow-headed line will appear to be shorter. Gibsonian realism demands that the solution should be sought not in perception but in factors intrinsic to the figure as a whole, which can be picked up as information. For example, it might be possible to find a metric that is sensitive to overall structure. In sum, such figures are to be approached not as illusions but as appearing exactly as they ought to appear, once a basis of measurement common to the environment and the organism is discovered (Turvey et al. 1981, 280).

3. Imagery. In the next chapter, evidence will be detailed that strongly suggests some sort of imaginal correspondence-representation and processing for images. The experimental result implying that imagery can be mentally rotated is an example. Nothing in Gibsonian theory, it seems to me, prevents such explanations of imagery in principle, since the theory is specifically directed against perceptual encoding only. Images and their transformations may still be representational in the narrow sense even though percepts and their genesis are not, and there may be pictorial memory even though it plays no role in perception. All in all, it seems to be useful to the understanding of imagery at some point to separate it sharply from perception as being representational in a way perception is not (Part One, Ch. V).

In practice imagery regarded in the Gibsonian spirit of direct perception is imagery obviated. Gibsonians see the establishment view as taking images to be—abnormal—percepts: percepts formed from the inside, arising without a sensory trigger, and transversing the route taken by perceptual processing; when the processing reaches consciousness, the epiphenomenal results appear as if they were mentally transformable. As a first response to this view, Gibson sharply distinguishes the phenomenology of images from that of percepts. For example, imagery, he claims, is not subject to scanning, as are real perceived pictures (1979, 257).

The elaborated Gibsonian account of mental imagery is that it is perceptual "anticipation" (Neisser 1976). Visual perception is guided by "cognitive maps" of environments and "object schemata" of things; these are precisely the indicator structures mentioned before. Such maps or schemata are not understood as encodings, as representational elements in syntactic relations. They are instead dispositions of the nervous system to direct the interactive perceptual cycle, neural plans for accepting information, or "formats" in computerese. These hypothetical information-seeking and -accepting structures are not conceived as being organized in terms of successive levels or stages of processing, but they are explained as simultaneous embeddings of functions. Gibsonian perception is not a linear temporal process.

Now usually these schemata blend into the acts of locomotion by means of which the environment is explored in the activity of vision. But when they are somehow isolated from practice, they are imagery rather than visual perception: "Images are not pictures in the head but plans for obtaining information from potential environments" (131).

One occasion for schemata to stand alone occurs during locomotion. Since perceptual direction outraces muscular movement, there is a sustained anticipation of places and objects that are about to come into view. Imaginary images, then, are explained as contradictory and unrealizable—though not necessary useless—anticipations. For example, the venerable method of loci, of memory places (Ch. III B), is just an exploitation of the cognitive maps as a readiness to pick up information in a certain location. However, the desired memory-object is located in the environment as verbal information; no memory-pictures are involved in a Gibsonian schema.

This ingenious account of imagery is vulnerable to several objections. It does not do justice to the updated Perky effect, which shows that perception and imagery are under certain circumstances indistinguishable (Ch. VI A). It runs counter to the evidence that imagery does have depictive character-istics and can undergo real scanning, and it certainly does not take account of the experience of picture-like images. Yet as an account of perception, the Gibsonian theory, besides having some experimental backing, also has, as suggested above, the great advantage of preserving that presentational character of perception which in ordinary experience distinguishes it from the re-presentational constitution of mental imagery.

Bibliography

Bindra, Dalbir. 1970. "The Problem of Subjective Experience: Puzzlement on Reading R.W. Sperry's 'A Modified Concept of Consciousness'." *Psychology Review* 77:581–584.

Bickhard, Mark H., and Richie, D. Michael. 1983. *On the Nature of Representation: A Case Study of James Gibson's Theory of Perception.* New York: Praeger.

Block, Ned. 1978. "Troubles with Functionalism." In *Minnesota Studies in the Philosophy of Science,* Volume 9, edited by C. Wade Savage. Minneapolis: University of Minnesota Press.

———. 1983. "Mental Pictures and Cognitive Science." *The Philosophical Review* 92:499–541.

Bower, Gordon H. 1972. "Stimulus-sampling Theory of Encoding Variability." In *Coding Processes in Human Memory,* edited by A. W. Melton and E. Martin. Washington, D.C.: Winston.

Churchland, Paul M. 1984. *Matter and Consciousness: A Contemporary Introduction to Philosophy of Mind*. Cambridge: The MIT Press.

Dennett, Daniel C. 1978. "Toward a Cognitive Theory of Consciousness." In *Minnesota Studies in the Philosophy of Science*, Volume 9, edited by C. Wade Savage. Minneapolis: University of Minnesota Press.

———. 1981a. "The Nature of Images and the Introspective Trap." In *Imagery*, edited by Ned Block. Cambridge: The MIT Press.

———. 1981b. "Two Approaches to Mental Imagery." In *Imagery*, edited by Ned Block. Cambridge: The MIT Press.

Field, Hartry H. 1981. "Mental Representation." In *Readings in Philosophy of Psychology*, edited by Ned Block. Cambridge: Harvard University Press.

Flanagan, Owen J. 1984. *The Science of the Mind*. Cambridge: The MIT Press.

Fodor, Jerry A. 1980. "Methodological Solipsism Considered as a Research Strategy in Cognitive Psychology" [with commentary and response]. *The Behavioral and Brain Sciences* 3:63–109. [Also in Fodor (1981), without commentary.]

———. 1981. *Representations: Philosophical Essays on the Foundations of Cognitive Science*. Cambridge: The MIT Press.

Fodor, Jerry A., and Pylyshyn, Z. W. 1981. "How Direct is Visual Perception?: Some Reflections on Gibson's Ecological Approach." *Cognition* 9:139–196.

Gibson, James J. 1966. *The Senses Considered as Perceptual Systems*. Boston: Houghton Mifflin Co.

———. 1979. *The Ecological Approach to Visual Perception*. Boston: Houghton Mifflin Co.

Harman, Gilbert. 1978. "Is There Mental Representation?" In *Minnesota Studies in the Philosophy of Science*, Volume 9, edited by C. Wade Savage. Minneapolis: University of Minnesota Press.

Hills, David. 1981. "Introduction: Mental Representations and Languages of Thought." In *Readings in Philosophy of Psychology*, edited by Ned Block. Cambridge: Harvard University Press.

Johnson-Laird, P. N. 1983. *Mental Models: Towards a Cognitive Science of Language, Inference, and Consciousness*. Cambridge: Harvard University Press.

MacKay, Donald M. 1969. *Information, Mechanism and Meaning*. Cambridge: The MIT Press.

Malcolm, Norman. 1977. *Memory and Mind*. Ithaca: Cornell University Press.

Mandler, George. 1985. *Cognitive Psychology: An Essay in Cognitive Science*. Hillsdale, N.J.: Lawrence Erlbaum Associates.

Mandler, Jean M. 1983. "Representation." In *Handbook of Child Psychology*, 4th ed., Volume 3, *Cognitive Development*, edited by Paul H. Mussen. New York: John Wiley and Sons.

Nagel, Thomas. 1974. "What Is It Like to Be a Bat?" *The Philosophical Review* 83:434–450.

Neisser, Ulric. 1976. *Cognition and Reality: Principles and Implications of Cognitive Psychology*. San Francisco: W.H. Freeman and Co.

Norman, Donald A. 1981. "What is Cognitive Science?" In *Perspectives on Cognitive Science*, edited by Donald A. Norman. Hillsdale, N.J.: Lawrence Erlbaum Associates.

Palmer, Stephen E. 1978. "Fundamental Aspects of Cognitive Representation." In *Cognition and Categorization*, edited by Eleanor Rosch and Barbara Lloyd. Hillsdale, N.J.: Lawrence Erlbaum Associates.

Richardson, John T.E. 1980. *Mental Imagery and Human Memory*. New York: St. Martin's Press.

Rorty, Richard. 1979. *Philosophy and the Mirror of Nature*. Princeton: Princeton University Press.

Savage, C. Wade, ed. 1978. *Minnesota Studies in the Philosophy of Science*, Volume 9. Minneapolis: University of Minnesota Press.

Simon, Herbert A. 1978. "On the Forms of Mental Representation." In *Minnesota Studies in the Philosophy of Science*, Volume 9. Minneapolis: University of Minnesota Press.

Sperry, R. W. 1970. "An Objective Approach to Subjective Experience: Further Explanation of a Hypothesis." *The Psychological Review* 77:585–590.

Turvey, M. T., Shaw, R. E., Reed, E. S., and Mace, W. M. 1981. "Ecological Laws of Perceiving and Acting: In Reply to Fodor and Pylyshyn (1981)." *Cognition* 9:237–304.

Ullman, S. 1980. "Against Direct Perception." *The Behavioral and Brain Sciences* 3:373–415.

Chapter II

The Science of Mental Imagery: Cognitive Psychology

The imagination becomes the object of science by the strictest criteria under the succinctly revealing title of Mental Imagery. The collective noun "Imagery" signifies that what is at stake is the having of images in general, rather than their peculiar mode of being or their individual quality. "Mental" here signifies that imagery is to be investigated in terms of the cognitive structures and processes of a mind that is understood as a function of the brain rather than as a faculty of the soul. The heading naturally implies that the subject of mental imagery exists, though its chief proponents prudently abstain from defining it beforehand. Since the features of the mental image are about to be discovered, that would be premature. Imagery is thus treated as a name-like term, anchored in some phenomenal entity in the world, but not an immediately definable one. For one would hardly wish to commit its meaning to some set of properties which on further inquiry might prove mistaken (Kosslyn 1980, 469). The mere assumption of existence turns out to be one on which the tale to follow depends.

One more preliminary point: The science of mental imagery falls within Cognitive Psychology, which is in turn part of Cognitive Science. Here is a way to distinguish the psychology and the science: One chief aim of Cognitive Science is to mimic and even to outdo the capabilities of the human mind (as in Artificial Intelligence), but not necessarily by means of its actual specific structures and processes. In Cognitive Psychology, on the other hand, the factual functions of the human mind are to be discovered. If it proves ultimately impossible to attach these functions to specific brain events, Cognitive Psychology will fade out, as have other schools of experimental psychology. Not so Cognitive Science, for it has no life-or-death stake in there being an exact correspondence of neurophysiology with imagery.

A. Psychology as Science

1. The First Phase: Introspection and Immediate Experience. When, in the last quarter of the nineteenth century, psychology first tried to turn itself into an observational science, imagery was its chief preoccupation. That was quite understandable, since ever more refined introspection was its main technique of inquiry, and introspection by and large yields nothing in greater profusion than imagery. For it is probable that our mental life is almost continuously filled with images, noticed or unnoticed (where unnoticed does not necessarily mean unconscious, but merely unattended to). Moreover, the various kinds of mental activity shade into each other: percepts into imagery, imagery into dreams, dreams into hallucinations (Holt 1972). But not only the seamless and apparently universal experience of imagery itself was a spur to naturalistic observation. The investigation of thinking also pointed the new science toward imagery, since this enterprise was projected onto a philosophical background that was in general powerfully representationalist and in particular Humean. Hence thinking itself was regarded as the operation of the mind on ideas that are but "faint images" of sense impressions organized by laws of association. The "science of immediate experience," as one of its founders Wilhelm Wundt called psychology, was to analyze the elements of consciousness and to specify these laws. Of these enormous and acute descriptive and analytic efforts scarcely an echo remains except in the classificatory terms for imagery, such as visual, eidetic, hypnagogic, and hallucinatory.

But one of the earliest works on imagery, and certainly the work most frequently cited, already foreshadowed that drastic eclipse of imagery study, dubbed its "ostracism" from psychology (Holt 1964), which brought this first phase to a close. In 1883 Sir Francis Galton, who introduced statistics into psychology, conducted a study by means of a questionnaire sent out to one hundred men. He asked his subjects, about half of whom were distinguished scholars and scientists, to image mentally their breakfast table of that morning. Slightly over ten percent, among whom the men of distinction figured largely, were unable to respond, claiming never to have had any imagery. This result (which has not been found to be duplicable) raised a new possibility, that of "imageless thought."

In the first decade of this century, "imageless thought" became the doctrine of a school, the Würzburg school. It was observed that the introspective reports of conscious mental content during problem-solving did, to be sure, include images and vague sensations. But these were thought to be insufficient to account for the subjects' judgments or performances. Evidently the operations of thought were not fully conscious and the conscious imagery was often not functional. It followed that the significance of imagery was diminished, while the old method of introspection began to be discredited as being inadequate to the investigation of the unconscious. Counterarguments by Wundt and Tichener notwithstanding, imagery was about to disappear from psychology for half a century.

(Boring 1950, Holt 1964, Horowitz 1970, Kosslyn 1980.)

Disciplined introspection, careful protocols, data collection by questionnaires, and other psychometric techniques that treat imagery-features as measurable traits and are still used in memory-studies, were the methods of this first phase. Their application to imagery revived with the revival of the subject. The results of such imagery-studies are primarily an increasingly more precise classification and the descriptive differentiation of imagistic thinking from other kinds. An example of this type of differentiation is the distinction between "autistic" and "reality" thinking; imagistic mentation is assigned to the former, the unreality functions (McKellar 1972). Further results are rating-scales for the vividness of imagery in different individuals and for its spontaneous use in memory- and reasoning-tasks. These measurements of vividness and spontaneity go under the heading of "Individual Differences" (Ch. V D).

(Sheehan 1972.)

In its devotion to method and measurement this tack is at least science-flavored. But while it yields many interesting observations, it does not seem to lead to suggestive models. Consequently, it is conducive to that anxious frame of mind familiar to the trade as "physics envy." What would be the qualifying characteristic of a "real" science of psychology?

2. Three Fundamental Characteristics Required by Any Physics-like Science of Cognition. At this point it makes sense to try to articulate those most fundamental features the science of cognition must display in order to be as "real" a science as physics is (on the assumption that there is none more real), and, further, how cognitive psychology does display those features. Indeed, every new science seems to stay remarkably close to these requirements, first set out by Descartes.

From the point of view of the inquiring subject, science requires that immediate experience and its common sense conclusions be regarded as superable—that is to say, as capable not only of being thoroughly regimented but of being penetrated. In thermodynamics, for example, the scientist passes unheeding through the "subjective" feeling, the sensation of warmth, which is both very limited and highly relative to previous states, and uses it at most as a preliminary pointer toward the place where the measuring instrument should be applied. Then he reads some sort of thermometer, an instrument justified by a law of nature, which measures not felt warmth or chill but temperature, understood as a measure of the intensity of molecular motion in a body. Thus the sensory experience is merely a surface indication. It is not the phenomenon of science but an epiphenomenon only, somewhat like a colored buoy floating above a lobster pot: It shows that something is below to be hauled up, no more.

The example indicates that a science of subjectively conscious experience is a contradiction in terms. The real science of cognition must bypass self-consciousness and manipulate the reports of the experiencing subject. So the subject taken philosophically, which was a conscious self, becomes an "S," a "subject" taken psychologically, which is merely an informant. This subject reacts to instructions by speaking or by pressing buttons, but its introspective reports are not taken as the last word on the conditions and events of his mind.

From the point of view of the object of inquiry, too, it is of the scientific essence that this object must occur as availably public rather than as inaccessibly private. Thus it cannot be a constitutionally inward event but must have extension along some dimension. It must be understood as a phenomenon measurable in space and time. It must, further, present itself as an instance of a rule or a kind (rather than as a unique incident), capable of figuring in a general theory. Accordingly, in cognitive psychology, ways are found to externalize the mind, to force it to become a public phenomenon with measurable dimensions, and to frame research programs in terms of models that express general mental features concretely.

From the point of view of means and ends, since the single phenomenal dimension of the mind is time, the most powerful technique of cognitive psychology is chronometry, the measurement of reaction- or response-times. While in physics time is the prevalent independent variable, in cognitive science time is most often dependent on distance: Motions performed measure time. The end, however, is the same: the discovery of functions to incorporate in a model of the structures and processes of the mental system. The ultimate hypothetical expectation is that the temporal evidence can be given a spatial basis, that is to say, that it can eventually be fitted into a spatio-temporal physical neural system.

3. How These Features Appear in the Science of Mental Imagery. Cognitive Psychology is unlike physics in that subject and "subject," the observer and the observed, are identical in kind—conscious beings. So much the more is it necessary to the "objectivity" of the science that they should be distinct in number. In other words, a way has to be found around allowing the subject to share largely in, or to mediate, the observation of himself by self-reports. No more than people can safely be their own judges can they be their own cognitive psychologists. The subject in the philosophical sense, the person, has to undergo a division of labor into the task-setting psychologist and the responding "subject." The latter is a construct not coextensive with the human person.

The surface reason for cutting people's reports of their conscious experience out of the enterprise is simple, though perhaps surprising. People are demonstrably full of mistakes, illusions, and ignorances regarding the nature of their own mental events. The classic example is the Perky effect, according to which subjects think they are imagining what they were in fact perceiving (Ch. VI A). More generally, there is the surprise subjects often show when told the results of experiments in which they have participated: They didn't, as it were, know they had it in them.

The reason that lies deeper than the delusion or the lack of awareness that comes from gullibility or inattention is in fact the fundamental hypothesis of cognitive science and psychology. It is that one cannot in principle know one's mind, because it is a covert operation, ultimately a brain function, of which subjective experience is a kind of insubstantial effluvium or vaporous facade to be penetrated by the observer on the way to the scientific object. In cognitive science conscious experience stands to non-conscious mind much as sensory properties like warmth stand to physical properties like molecular motion in natural science. The non-conscious mind is the object to which the reports of the experimental "subject" give access.

Consequently, in imagery-studies this much but no more is initially presupposed about the subjects: They can, as indeed people claim they can, follow directions to "Image!" when it is explained to them that they are to picture things before their mind's eye (Kosslyn and Holyoak 1982). Furthermore they can, again as they claim they can, memorize a picture. These are large assumptions, for which the experiments are intended to tease out corroboration as they go. So, since there is no way to get altogether around the subjects' voluntary responsive utterance, the point is to compel facts beyond the subjects' awareness to emerge by rigorous control of the protocols of introspection.

Heraclitus's mysterious saying that "nature loves to hide" is thus exemplified with a vengeance by the science of the mind, for mental nature hides thrice. First, it hides insofar as it is veiled from visual inspection and is revealed only indirectly by the subject's reports or reactions. Second, it hides insofar as it is not open to unguided introspection either, since that has access only to the epiphenomena of consciousness and is ignorant of the mind beneath. And even on the third round mental nature remains well concealed, because the non-conscious mind is assumed by the science to be at bottom a function of the physical brain. Thus the final structure to which cognitive psychology means to penetrate—which is, strangely enough, again a portion of physical nature—remains well hidden too, because the actual functional relations of mind and brain remain largely unspecified (Ch. VI B).

Next it is necessary to find a way to draw out the object-contents of the mind, namely its representations. This is a particularly tricky proceeding for visual imagery. Quite aside from the assumption that its real structure is below consciousness, the surface itself is difficult of access, since it is private in several senses, even when the subjects wish to be informative. For although the representations are reported as having quasi-sensory character, they are not, as has been said, directly available for second-party inspection: There is no way, as yet, to get inside the head. Furthermore, there are special difficulties about getting imagery out. Words are in principle inadequate for describing pictures exhaustively, while drawings are practically insufficient because most images are fleeting and affect-laden, and because most people can't draw. Of course, the cognitive ideal would be to externalize images via the detection and projection of their patterns of cortical activity. Researchers dream about a device that would throw a person's imagery on the screen for all to see: a strange *déjà-vu* in which a subject might be fed back its very own imagery as a percept simultaneously with having it. But even a fantasy-"externalizer" has conceptual limits in the fact that most internal images are optically and affectively highly interpreted structures, like the famous ambiguous figures in visual illusions. What sort of machine could project that aspect? (Shepard 1980).

The solution in imagery-science is to regiment the mental image severely. The representations useful to the science are not the spontaneous, feeling-fraught shapes nor the delightful panoramic visions of the imaginative imagination, but memorized mundane pictures of isolated, usually uncolored, objects. In short, subjects are asked to memorize drawings not for pleasure but for business. It is thus that imagery is brought under control. Clearly, neither the quality of the imagery nor the subjects' ability to produce it are here the issue, though sometimes the question is raised whether the subjects use images spontaneously in problem-solving. Nor has the affective aspect drawn much cognitive attention so far (Ch. V B). Indeed, the imagery itself is only an interim object of interest; the real object is the underlying system of structures and processes. As was said above: cognitive science cares about the having of imagery, not the being of an image.

Finally, as far as the methods of imagery-study are concerned, "reaction-time" (Klatzky 1980) is the investigator's bread and butter. Subjects are asked to perform some precise mental task or to solve a well-defined problem in the hope that the measured reaction-times will reveal whether imagery was being used—that is, scanned, rotated, or otherwise transformed—and if so, what in particular its "privileged," that is, imagery-specific, features might be. These methods produce significant results precisely because subjects are often not conscious of time differences in their imagery processes—of the fact, for instance, that it takes longer to image a scene than an item (Kosslyn 1983, 100). A second method, used in the most successful imagery-study so far, is to work out a computational model. In it the computer plays a role analogous to that of the brain, while the program, playing the role of the mind, incorporates as computational structures and processes the features discovered through experiments (Kosslyn 1980).

4. The Picture-Metaphor. Hard though the scientists of mental imagery try, they cannot get around the fact that the representations they deal with are like pictures (Anderson 1978). The methods have to assume, and the experiments continually corroborate, that having imagery is somehow like perceptual seeing, and that it is somehow like seeing pictures. The very name of the subject, "mental *imagery*," implies such a hypothesis.

The minimal reason for this assumption is that people do naturally talk of seeing pictures before their mind's eye. The broadest reason is representationalism itself, the dominating hypothesis of cognitive science. The practical motives behind the picture-metaphor will emerge from the experiments described below.

The metaphor seems to cause constant confusion and put things at cross-purposes. Sometimes, for example, the theory that images are no more than recalled percepts is taken to be coextensive with the picture-hypothesis, though it is clearly only its most primitively photographic version. Because of such confusion it makes sense here to sketch out what is involved in conceiving a representation as being picture-like or as failing to be so. The sketch will draw on earlier descriptions and on the experimental results about to be set out. The point then is not to contrast the internal logic of pictures with that of propositions, or to distinguish different types of pictures (as will be done in Parts Three and Five respectively), but in the broadest possible strokes to outline the notion of a picture in general, and to see how it applies to mental imagery.

To begin with, a picture is physically seen. Later in this work evidence will be set out for the ways in which having images is akin to perceptual seeing; but two obvious points of similarity are revealed by introspection and corroborated by experiment. Imagery is "scanned" by the mind's eye just as the visual scene is scanned by the physical eye, and it is "seen" aspectually just as the visual object is perceived in terms of its various facades. On the other hand, having images is obviously unlike seeing in that is does not cease—in fact it often starts—when the eyes are closed and perception stops; indeed, it is known that even people blinded in childhood still imagine visually. But such differences between seeing and imagining will turn out to be, if anything, favorable to the picture-metaphor. Aside from their percept-like features, images, when taken as purely internal representations, have these pictorial features: They are apprehended as not being what they represent, or to put it another way, as being re-presentations and not the objects themselves; they are, in short, copies or replicas of an original existent—or even nonexistent—object. (Nonexistent originals are taken up in Part Three, Ch. III B.) They require, as will be shown, an appropriate field or medium upon which to appear, just as material pictures need a canvas. Such a medium will set a limit of resolution: Too tiny an area of mental image is no longer a significant part of the image, just as close-up details of a painting blur, whereas visible bodies remain almost indefinitely and continuously accessible to optically enhanced inspection. Mental images, like still pictures, lack their own principle of natural motion; such translations or transformations as they display they seem to undergo passively, and their motion is as much the act of the imager as of the image. As mentioned above, they often incorporate one or more points of view, like perspectival paintings; moreover, the aspectual properties of the image can be separated from the viewer's own perspective, as in picture viewing. Again like pictures, images are compositions, that is, parts are accentuated or omitted and shapes transformed; like paintings, they are intrinsically interpreted, significant.

There are, of course, also obvious ways in which mental imagery, though quasi-visual, is not picture-like: A picture has a material substrate, such as canvas, which is in turn itself in space, while the mental image is directly inscribed on the mental imaginal medium. Mental images, unlike pictures, are not, after all, entirely passive under scanning; they sometimes give the appearance of transforming according to intrinsic rules, that is, of having proper motions. Unlike most kinds of material pictures, they fade out quickly and are quickly regenerable.

At this point it has to be said that no cognitive scientist takes the picture analogy as anything but a metaphor. None thinks that the mind's eye is literally some sort of organ, viewing an internal exhibition. So the tricky question becomes just how to understand the analogy.

The picture problem is the more acute for the fact that current study of cognitive imagery is almost exclusively concerned with visual imagery.

When Galton did his early investigations he did ask his subjects to image in all sensory modalities, for example, "the beat of rain against the window panes," and "the taste of lemon." But it was not clear then, as it is not now, that all the senses do have their proper imagery. There is an experiment, done with blind subjects, analogous to the visual "mental rotation" about to be described, in which the original perceptual stimulus was tactile rather than visual (Kosslyn 1980, 324), and it became problematic whether there was any differentiated internal representation for touch at all. Even auditory imagery, which is certainly investigable (for example, Schwartz 1981), offers difficulties. Besides those set out in the Introduction to this book, there is a particular drawback for chronometric treatment in the fact that auditory imagery is itself a temporal process. (Recall that in visual imagery studies, the principal functions graph reaction-time against the image-space.) In short, visual imagery is the imagery of choice above all because of its pronounced representational character.

In the experiments about to be described, the material used is itself an implicit acknowledgment of the pictorial hypothesis insofar as the stimuli are nearly always themselves pictures. Pictures are used not only because in their rigidity they are practically the best way to regiment image-memory, but surely also because they seem to be themselves the most characteristic product of the imagination and are therefore the presentations most likely to elicit its peculiar properties.

B. Experimental Discoveries about Mental Imagery

Scientific psychology is nothing if it cannot be experimental. With respect to mental imagery, the trick would be to design experiments whose results could be interpreted as pertaining to the inner phenomenon—if such a phenomenon existed to begin with. The hope would then be that the actual results might show some significant regularity, which would simultaneously prove the existence and display some features of mental imagery. That project has proved to be possible.

The bulk of the work I am about to describe was done by Stephen Kosslyn (1980) and set out in a very accessible book called, most significantly, as we will see, *Ghosts in the Mind's Machine* (1983). The experiments recounted here are the most exemplary, namely the simplest and the most easily describable. They are mostly concerned with the "privileged" properties of mental images, meaning those that distinguish imagery from other forms of representation. It should be said right now that the results—for example, the functions discovered—seem to stand fast, but the interpretation continues to be the center of a storm of debates.

1. The Use of Imagery. Kosslyn guides certain lines of his experimentation by means of a "decision tree," a device that is particularly appropriate because the problem of imagery presents itself in terms of downward-branching yes or no issues. The top node is defined by the issue, introduced above, of "phenomenal *vs.* epiphenomenal" (Kosslyn 1980): Are images cognitively effective or just along for the ride?

This way of putting the issue begins by admitting the experience of imagery but asks if such an experience is useful. Roger Shepard, the inventor of the basic technique in imagery experimentation, had begun with the sense that a mental event so universally reported by humans, and so likely to be present in animals, must be an adaptive function. In a memorable moment he suddenly saw a way of testing whether imagery might involve a structure-preserving mental modeling of the world, and might therefore be employed in practical problem-solving rather than being mere idle and random mimicry (Shepard and Cooper 1982).

The way was this: Since rigid rotations form so large a part of the physical motions in our experience, it might be possible to make their mental counterparts disclose themselves through time-reactions. Subjects were shown pairs of perspective drawings of three-dimensional block shapes, arm-like figures with right-angled bends, built up of ten cubes stuck face to face (Fig. 1). A random half of the pairs were mirror images

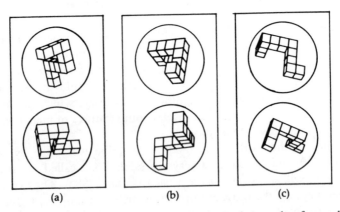

(a)   (b)   (c)

Figure 1. The stimuli used by Shepard and Metzler in their study of mental rotation. Reproduced from *Science*, vol. 171 (1971), p. 702 by permission of *Science* and Roger N. Shepard.

of each other; pair (c) is an example. This configuration meant that although the shapes were locally, that is, part by part, similar they could not be brought into congruence by any rigid rotation. The other pairs were identical. But for each pair the two members were drawn at different orientations, such that they might be brought into comparable or coincident positions by a rotation either in the picture plane (a) or in depth (b).

Subjects were to begin at a signal to inspect the drawings of the pairs and were to press a "same" or "different" switch to stop the reaction-timer as soon as they had reached a judgment.

Reaction-times, when graphed, displayed a beautifully clean linear function: The times taken to make the judgment were directly proportional to the angle of rotation (from 0 to 180 degrees) required to make the orientations the same or comparable. Different subjects had slightly different personal rates of rotation, but the rates were individually constant; whether the rotations were in the picture plane or in depth, the average rate of mental motion was 60 degrees a second.

The results were clearly interpretable as showing that a moving image, a mental model of the rotation, was used to solve the problem of comparing the figures. They were presumably first brought into like orientation and then either compared piece-meal or superimposed (Shepard and Cooper 1982, with Metzler, ch. 3).

Other experiments showed that the rotations were continuous through intermediate positions. Shepard's associate Cooper asked subjects to rotate mentally some well defined plane shapes which they had been asked to memorize. Other shapes were then presented for comparison at timed intervals. Judgments were fastest when the test shape was presented in the orientation calculated to have been reached by the mental image at various angles of rotation. Clearly the mental image was rotated as a whole over all positions.

The alternative possibility would have been to compare the pictures verbally feature by feature. This imageless procedure would have resulted in very different time functions. It was a strategy evidently not spontaneously preferred. Nevertheless, the interpretation of these results in terms of imagery use has been impugned on the grounds, applicable *mutatis mutandis* to most of the experiments, that subjects have enough tacit knowledge of physical motions like rotation to produce an internal word-like description. Such verbal renditions might mimic the stages of the transformation by discrete symbolic computations even up to consistency in the time needed to perform a real rotation. But this attack presents various difficulties. If discrete acts of understanding are involved, why isn't the 180-degree rotation the fastest rather than the slowest, since conceptually it is a simple flip? Why do we mentally rotate at a rate of 60 degrees per second, a rate certainly not determined by any law of external motion? But above all, the verbal explanation is not at all the most straightforward one, and it is clearly driven by considerations other than finding the most economical explanation of these results.

There exist profuse variations on these experiments leading to many detailed inferences concerning the having and the nature of images. For example, it seems to be the image-object itself that is mentally rotated and not its plane picture or its retinal image. This is indicated by the finding that the images of solids presented as plane drawings preserve proper perspective under mental rotation—a fact, incidentally, of central interest to the Cubist painters (Part Five, Ch. II A). Hence it is not the intrinsic conceptual structure of the object that is being immediately displayed but its apparent "visual" shape. Furthermore, images of objects variously arranged in three-dimensional space are mentally seen as in one picture plane, since the scanning times of these objects are proportional to the distances of their two-dimensional picture planes (Kosslyn 1983, 155). Evidently some imagery is indeed "seen" from a point of view, just as a picture, or, for that matter, a view, would be. It follows that the plane aspect of an image carries some three-dimensional information, for even without the opportunity to reach into actual space for further experience, novel imagery objects, especially those with simple geometric structures, can be internally rotated to reveal, for example, their backs. The fascinating but problematic implication of these discoveries is that while an image has pictorial characteristics, an imaged object has a status analogous to that of an actual object and may display itself, as it were, to our admiring gaze independently of prior perceptual knowledge.

A further problem arises over the "mental motion" implicit in these findings. The mental rotation appears to mimic not some natural motion but rather something like the deliberate turning of an object in one's hands. But then where does the specific uniform rate come from? And suppose the motions of mental objects did mimic, say, the acceleration of natural objects, should one say that tacit knowledge was at work or that some sort of imaginary mass was controlling the motion? The puzzles of image motions and the objects involved will be further discussed below.

An interesting development is imagery-testing on animals. The conjecture that animals imagine is as old as Aristotle (*De Anima* III 9). But only the technique of mental rotation made possible the experimentation on animals, an example of which is reported here in truncated form: Pigeons, pre-trained by food-reinforcement to peck at either a left or a right key according as a clock hand—which had first moved visibly at a constant velocity to the 90-degree position, and had then, moving invisibly, reappeared at fixed positions (135 and 180 degrees)—did so at the right or the wrong time for the established speed. The actual experiments followed the same procedure using new terminal positions (158 and 202 degrees). The pecking scores for these positions, to which the pigeons had not been trained, gave unequivocally positive readings. Evidently the birds represented movement to themselves in the absence of a moving perceptual stimulus, spontaneously and accurately. These results certainly accommodate the hypothesis of mental imagery. The special value of this discovery to imagery-studies is that learning patterns of animals are more amenable to neural and physiological experimentation than are those of humans. (Rilling and Neiworth 1987).

2. The Space-likeness of Visual Imagery. Shepard's first round of rotation-experiments had concentrated on cognitive effectiveness and merely broached the question concerning the privileged or constitutive properties of mental imagery and its motions. The series that deals with these systematically is by Kosslyn. Perhaps it would be more accurate to say that these experiments are largely designed to test whether the mental events elicited by instructions to image do have depictive character—whether they are indeed *images*. Consequently the first question was: Do they in fact have the kind of space-like dimension or extension that can in some sense be scanned?

In these experiments, in contrast to the Shepard series, subjects do not keep the stimulus-picture before them while doing the rotation; instead they memorize drawings. What is more, subjects are asked not to move the figures mentally but to scan them. This technique is carefully devised, first, to avoid the contamination of the imaging process by on-going perception, and, second, to get a handle on the agent of the mental motion.

Subjects memorized a fictive map of an island in which seven features, such as a hut, a tree, and a beach, were schematically depicted, each at a different distance from all the others (Fig. 2). Subjects were to focus on one designated location in the island. At the naming of a second feature they were to locate it by a glance, then to make a black speck move as fast as possible from the first to the second, and finally to press a button as soon as it had arrived. The results were that "scanning" times increased linearly with the distance from the original location. The subjects were evidently doing something analogous to visual scanning.

A double check was run. Since plus-or-minus-seven has long been known to be the number of items that can be stored in short-term memory, it was possible that subjects might simply be remembering the features as a list of

Figure 2. The fictional map that subjects imaged and then scanned across. The X's mark the exact locations of the objects. (Reproduced from *Ghosts in the Mind's Machine, Creating and Using Images in the Brain,* by Stephen Michael Kosslyn, by permission of W. W. Norton & Company, Inc. Copyright © 1983 by Stephen M. Kosslyn.)

names and checking the destination-feature against this list. In that case, it was predicted, reaction-times would no longer vary with distance. This time subjects were asked not to scan the map but just to respond as fast as possible without necessarily using imagery. The result was that no discernible function connected times and distances.

The conclusion is that mental imagery is scannable, hence somehow space-like or extensive.

(Kosslyn 1980, 43; 1983, 46.)

3. The Mental Imagery Medium. Pictures are seen on a medium like canvas or paper. If mental images are picture-like, they too might have a medium analogue. The notion of a mental medium is old. In the *Theaetetus* Plato uses the metaphor of a wax tablet capable of receiving impressions with different degrees of sharpness in different people. Guided by this figure, Kosslyn now devises experiments that will force the imagistic medium, if there is one, to reveal its features.

Pictures have a limit of resolution. The canvas, being grainy, will not take strokes below a certain size; the painted image itself is also grainy, since it is composed of brush strokes. Moreover, the eye is incapable of discerning parts that are too small. The image as a whole therefore has a limit of resolution on approaching in which details become increasingly harder to make out. In Kosslyn's experiment on mental images these three factors are not discriminated, but the whole effect is attributed to a mental medium. The aim is to see if this limit-effect is demonstrable.

Subjects were bidden to image a target animal, say a rabbit. They were to picture it at correct relative size, first as next to an elephant, and then as next to a fly (Fig. 3). The assumption was that the larger animal would crowd the smaller one into a tiny part of the imaginal space. The hypothesis of a mental "grain" predicts that tiny features are harder to "see" and therefore take longer to make out. And so it proved: Reaction-times for reading the features and answering questions about the comparatively small animals were longer. Now most people have more rabbit than fly information handy because they feel more affectionate toward the bunny than the insect. Lest results be influenced by this fact, subjects were also asked to image a huge fly next to a tiny target animal, with the same result: The small animal took longer to report. The results were interpreted to mean that the medium has, in some sense, a grain. Of course, this is being guided by the medium-metaphor with a vengeance. Introspection suggests that what takes time in "seeing" tiny images is the focusing of the mind's eye rather than the inspection of the grainy image. But as we will see, Kosslyn has motives for not making that interpretation.

This experiment was now extended to counter the claim, always lying in wait, that the chronometric results have an alternative non-imagistic expla-

Figure 3. A rabbit and an elephant versus a rabbit and a fly. (From Kosslyn, © 1983, by permission of W. W. Norton & Company, Inc.)

nation. Suppose subjects were expending the capacity of their short-term memory on storing the features of the larger animals, so that they had to dig into long-term memory for answering questions about small animals, such as "Does a fly have a mouth?" Suppose, moreover, it was not the largeness of the animal image that made for fast answers but the "associative strength" of features, namely how strongly one term calls up another, as "elephant" does "trunk."

These objections were tested by pitting associative strength against size. It can be ascertained that most people associate claws more closely with cats than they do heads. Thus when cats are mentioned they think of claws more immediately than of heads, although heads are much larger. Subjects were asked whether certain specific features belonged to certain animals. Without imaging instructions, the stronger association of features made for shorter response times. With imagery instructions the greater size of the features did. Evidently, when subjects were using imagery the medium's grainy characteristics came into play.

(Kosslyn 1983, 58.)

Material pictorial media have definite size and shape. The mental medium too is not unlimited, as the fact that a large animal crowds out a small one indicates. Can the size be more definitely determined?

The size of the medium, just like the perceptual field, is appropriately measured by the visual angle it subtends. Here is a simplified account of the main experiment determining that angle (Fig. 4). Subjects were asked to memorize line drawings of animals of different size. Larger animals were drawn larger but correct proportions among the animals were not preserved. There was, for example, a rabbit, a dog, a cow, an elephant. The participants were then asked to take a "mental walk" toward the images and to place a real tripod at that distance from a real wall at which they judged the imaged animal to be when it began to overflow the mental screen. The result was that the various distances at overflow were roughly proportional to the real-life sizes of the different animals. These distances, the dimensions of the animal, and a little trigonometry together gave the visual angle subtended by the medium as roughly 25 degrees.

The shape of the medium was also measured by a "mental walk," this time toward a foot-long ruler imaged once horizontally and then vertically. The image overflowed sooner in the vertical dimension, showing that the medium is roughly elliptical.

In these experiments it was found that imagery was fuzzy toward the edges of the medium, and, contrary to Kosslyn's intuition, that the area of greatest activity was small and roughly circular.

(Kosslyn 1980, 73, 84; 1983, 62.)

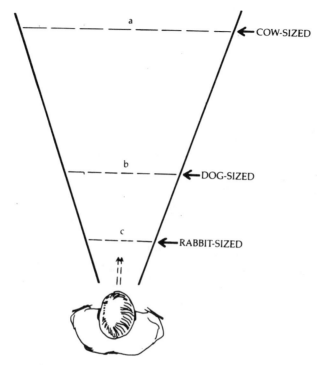

Figure 4. Measuring objects in terms of visual angle. A fixed angle implies that bigger things must be farther away. (From Kosslyn, © 1983, by permission of W. W. Norton & Company, Inc.)

Is the image-space thus discovered really a canvas-like medium or just a quasi-perceptual field? There is one obvious indicator of the difference between the mental medium and a material medium: It is impossible to tear a piece off an image as one may tear it off a photograph. A mental image cannot be mutilated through its medium, which is therefore, in effect, less, not more, concrete than the image it underlies. What this circumstance indicates is that the medium mimics the perceptual field. That field, too, is roughly a horizontal ellipse because of the horizontal setting of our eyes. It too subtends roughly the same visual angle, and it too has a similar area of acuity. But then, of course, the very conception of a mental walk presupposes that the mind's "eyes," as we might say in this context, have their quasi-visual field, just as the organic eyes look out on a delimited part of the world.

4. The Generation and Fading of Mental Imagery. Imagery is notoriously unstable. It is both fleeting and changing (Bugelski 1971). It fades continually and quickly, especially when fixated, as one can tell by mentally staring at the center of an image. This is the mental analogue to perceptual "adaptation," which occurs when neurons overused by staring at an object stop firing, so that the image fades. Eye movement is necessary to sight. An experiment featuring the memorized image of three concentric blobs showed that fixating an area adapted all of the medium within it, proving that it works as a whole: When the mental gaze was fixed on the largest blob, the middle blob was more adapted out than when it was first fixed on the innermost one (Kosslyn 1983, 67).

In the laboratory, imagery comes into being through time and in parts and is continuously transformed. It is not usually an on/off event, though there is a somewhat rarer "blink" transform, when an image is erased and reformed in a different position (Kosslyn 1980, 336). A deliberately formed image does not arise suddenly as a full-blown panorama. Imaging is less like the sudden epiphany granted to a seer and more like the compositional process engaged in by a painter.

The next experiment consequently deals with the temporal forming of imagery. Once it had been established that experienced imagery is indeed a quasi-pictorial representation, the next issue or node on the decision tree was: How is imagery stored when we are not experiencing it, and how is it retrieved from long-term memory, as a whole or in parts?

For the experiment to show that forming images takes time, subjects learned first to draw and then to image a series of color-coded squares (Fig. 5). Each square was six times the area of the preceding one. The largest just failed to overflow the mental medium. They were then asked to imagine various animals filling the different squares. In fact they were to imagine each animal in all the squares, in order to prevent variations in complexity from affecting response times. The results were straightforward: Larger animals took more time to image. Probably this means that images are retrieved section by section of the medium and not all at once as a unit; otherwise size would not matter. (For the matrix-hypotheses intended to account for this process, see 5, below.)

The amount of mental ink used, so to speak, for drawing an image does not, however, affect recall-time. For when subjects were asked to image on equilateral triangle inscribed in a larger one, they took less time to interpret the figure in the terms just described than when asked to see it as three triangles around a central one. Had the mere amount of drawn line mattered the times should have been identical. Like the pictorial medium, the imagery medium appears to bear shapes capable of Gestalt-shifts, since the same figure, when seen in terms of more parts, took larger to imagine. On the other hand, the medium seems to be activated in terms of differing units rather than of definite amounts of "ink"; unlike the pictorial medium, the imagery medium does not bear a fixed quantity of "paint," that is, of activated area.

(Kosslyn 1980, 95; 1983, 97.)

Figure 5. Relative sizes of imaged animals; each square was one-sixth the area of the square to its right. (From Kosslyn, © 1983, by permission of W. W. Norton & Company, Inc.)

Other experiments showed more ways in which images are generated in sections. Elements can be sequentially recovered from memory and overlaid or "glued" to make a whole. Parts are added not with reference to any coordinate system of the medium but directly to the image already present. They are, as it were, disposed not aesthetically in mental space, but contextually in relation to the figure. Furthermore, Shepard/Cooper had shown that larger angles of mental rotation take longer. Now it was shown also that larger images took longer to rotate (Schwartz in Kosslyn 1980, 290). Since, in addition, more complex images took longer to generate, while complexity failed to affect rotation times, the inference was that images are shifted as a whole rather than continually regenerated at new positions. Yet such incremental shifting also introduced incremental error. People reported that after rotating images through large angles the images grew deformed; presumably some realignment then occurred (Kosslyn 1980, ch. 8).

In general, transformations come in two classes, "field-general" and "region-bounded." The first means that the whole imagery-content of the field shifts, the second changes only the local contents. The transformations in each class have analogues in the other. Zooming is field-general; imaging the enlargement of an object is its region-bounded analogue (Kosslyn 1980, 341). This duality suggests once again that the mind's eye and the mental space are, somewhat mysteriously, obverses of each other: Either the mental medium or the mental eye may move.

The findings under this last heading, the generation and transformation of imagery, best support the computational model that is the crux of Kosslyn's work.

5. The Computational Model of Mental Imagery. The ambition of cognitive research is finally not to collect descriptive features of imagery but to provide a global theory. Moreover, it is in the nature of cognitive science to conceive of theories as essentially embodied in models. For models are incarnations of abstract principles that work and can be run as a program. Kosslyn was first brought to his computational theory by a crude but serviceable computer-mind analogy in which the physical computer served to suggest the elementary components of an imagery-theory. He called it the cathode-ray tube protomodel. It consisted of a television screen analogous to the mental-image space of our experience where the surface images appear; a central processing unit analogous to our long-term memory, which stores the deep representations that are called up onto the mental screen; and an interpretative processing device analogous to the mind's eye, which scans the surface images.

Kosslyn makes careful methodological discriminations, among them the distinction between those aspects of a model that embody the theory and those irrelevant areas that belong to the model insofar as it is a particular embodiment. The physical computer itself is such an irrelevancy, and in his full-fledged model Kosslyn comes to the point of abandoning the increasingly doubtful computer/brain analogy. The brain does not, in fact, effectively enter these studies at all, while it is only the functional aspect of the computer that models the mind. In sum, the model actually involves not a computer/brain analogy but a program/mind analogy.

Here is a sketch of the program model: It provides for two structures and for many processes. The first of the structures is an active-memory-matrix. This matrix is the imagery-medium which models the experienced imagery. A display screen for externalizing the imagery can be added, but is not integral to the model. The second structure is a long-term memory with storage facilities for information either of a potentially visual type, such as pairs of coordinates for points in the image space, or of a non-visual type, such as files listing features under category headings.

The actual memory is a matrix of cells with filled or unfilled locations from which an external picture can be generated on the screen. In computer terms, this storage device, intermediate between the central processing unit and the display screen, is a "visual buffer" (Kosslyn 1983, 96). This structure incorporates all the properties discovered: shape, size, fading, and limit of resolution. The last, for example, is gotten as a bonus from the fact that the number of cells is exceeded by the number of the dots that represent the "ink" of the image. This means that points sometimes overlap.

The propositional long-term memory stores lists with the most strongly associated features on top, so that when an item is called by category name, these come up fastest. Thus CAT PRP, which calls the propositional file on cat, will get up "claws" before "head."

Images are generated, inspected, and transformed by a variety of processes. For example, the IMAGE process is used to generate images. It first checks the propositional file for the name of a basic skeletal image, such as the body of a car, which is in turn used by the PICTURE process to activate the proper coordinates in the surface matrix at a requested size or location. Further processes fill in parts, such as tires.

The model generates ways to simulate the observed behavior and to predict the properties of images. But it is more than a mere device for predictions. It provides an account of underlying processes at work in the

having of imagery. Moreover, it embodies the basic theory that the mind
has cognitive structures and processes of a picture-like nature. The model
also helps to uncover indeterminacies and contradictions in the sub-models,
the devices for accounting for specific behavior, and it suggests further
inquiries.

No doubt it is marvelous to see a computer screen mimic, however
crudely, our own imaging. But what the theory behind the model does not
pretend to do is to give the deep reasons for our imagery capacities (Kosslyn
1980, 477). Nor can it claim that these structures and functions are those
actually and literally underlying imaging. One might say that it is more
similar to a Copernican hypothesis of epicycles than to a Keplerian theory
of real orbits. It is a possible, not a real, explanation.

C. The Interpretation of the Findings Concerning Mental Imagery

1. The Setting of the Imagery-Debate. The compound hypothesis required for imagery-study to get under way was that there are mental
representations, both structures and processes, and that some of these
behave like images. Both assumptions were regarded as anything from
unassailable to indefensible in the debate going on in philosophy and
cognitive science. This debate, passionate enough before, became rousingly
convoluted when an attempt was made to cash in on the promise, so often
made in those disciplines, to refer problems from the conceptual to the
experimental domain for final solution. For it then picked up additional
complexity from controversies and conditions internal to experimental
psychology itself.

Among these conditions was the so-called ostracism of the imagination
from experimental psychology (Holt 1964). The stage for this banishment
was set by the findings of the first phase described above (A 1). But it was
a second phase, Behaviorism, that would actually enforce the eclipse of the
imagination for half of the twentieth century, from its second through its
sixth decade. In reaction to the unverifiable method of introspection, the
Behaviorists rejected all internality. Not only was consciousness set aside,
but even unconscious mediation between the observable incoming stimulus
and the outgoing response, and imagery in particular, was declared nonexistent (Richardson 1980, Kosslyn 1980). Thus Watson, the main proponent
of this view, said of the vivid memory-images of childhood: "Touching, of
course, but sheer bunk." Behaviorists insisted that images were merely the
internal rehearsal of old verbal encodings. They were undeterred even by
such common experiences, inexplicable under the verbal hypothesis, as the

"tip of the tongue"—or "back of the head"—phenomenon, where the thought or shade is there but the word or picture won't come (Bugelski 1971). It is worth noting that Watson's psychological attack on imagery as an unverifiable figment of introspection was published in 1928, over twenty years before Ryle's philosophical assault. Between them they shaped the reaction to come.

Like the soft yin to Behaviorism's hard yang there was Psychoanalysis, the other prevailing school of the period. Brief mention should be made of its part in this history. Freud and Jung certainly cannot be accused of neglecting imagery. The symbolic interpretation of dreams and of archetypal images played, after all, an integral role in their respective theories, though around 1900 Freud decided against the psychoanalytic use of mental imagery. However, theirs was a preoccupation not with the nature and processes of imagery but with dream work and interpersonal, shared memory. It did not further the science of mental imagery.

By the sixties, mountains of quantified behaviorist data had led to no general results, while behaviorist method had grown gentle and sophisticated enough to admit appropriately defined mental phenomena. At that period, Behaviorism, having left its sting in psychology, not to speak of philosophy, lost its life.

Imagery came back. Besides the demise of crude Behaviorism, there were a number of positive reasons for "the return of the ostracized." First of all, it proved impossible to exorcise permanently all interest in so ubiquitous and engrossing a mental phenomenon, especially since some of the imagery-researchers, like Shepard, were themselves vivid imagers. Then there were the special circumstances of the sixties: "experimentation" with hallucinogenic drugs (Holt 1972, Richardson 1980), a new reaction to rationalism, an emphasis on spontaneity and "creativity," and a topical interest in pharmacological "brain-washing." But of most consequence was a whole range of new sciences, such as developmental psychology, which assigned to the imagination a special cognitive function in children (Ch. IV), brain science and psychology of perception (Ch. VI), information processing, and artificial intelligence.

From the last, too, comes the motivation for the invigorated new form of the old "imageless thought" attack on imagery, which has shaped much of the cognitive effort. The new claim is that all mental representations are propositional.

2. The Formulation of the Mental Imagery Issue. The propositionalist claim put the new science of mental imagery on the defensive from its inception, forcing it to stop before it had even started. Hence it begins not by trying to discover the properties of its objects but by trying to show that they in fact exist, that is to say, that we have mental images at all. The trick is to do this without depending on people's self-reports. Thus Galton's innocent old procedure of simply asking people is put out of commission. It may seem like a fatal first move, but such strong challenges to ordinary experience as are mounted by the successors of the Behaviorists have the force of a bear-hug; disengagement from it requires desperate measures.

To give the problem of existence some scientific bite, however, it is necessary to establish a conceptual criterion for distinguishing mental imagery from other representations. Space-likeness comes to mind. Yet to show that anything can be space-like without being spatial—no one wants mental images to be somatically spatial—is a subtle philosophical task. The same may be said for a more abstract criterion of imaginal representation, namely resemblance. Resemblance poses a great philosophical difficulty even for ordinary pictures (Part Five). So without clear conceptual marks for imagery the problem of its existence cannot be met head-on in cognitive psychology—though, as we have seen, it can scramble itself into very plausible conclusions.

If the issue of image-existence is not experimentally reachable, the question of image-use is not formally decidable in the science. The problem of imagery was indeed first broached via the investigation of the use of imagery in problem-solving. But it has been proved formally that for any apparently imagistic process, say rotation, an equivalent propositionalist explanation mimicking it can be constructed. As for processes, so for shapes: Any form can be encoded propositionally. For example, the letter R can be seen as a whole figure, but it can also be described algebraically, in terms of equations for points, straight and curved line segments, and angles (Anderson 1978). It turns out to be a matter of trade-offs. To get an imagistic interpretation one keeps the structures "holistic" and makes them bear much implicit information, thus keeping processes simple. To get propositionalist readings one makes the elements spare, symbolic, and explicit, with well-defined but complex transformations (Pylyshyn 1978). Seen from this angle, the whole problem is reduced to computational preferences—but that does not make imagery study futile (Johnson-Laird 1983, 151). After all, to show the impossibility of proof isn't to show that neither side is right. By the criteria of straightforwardness, closeness to common experience, and plausible accounting for the peculiarities of struc-tures and processes, the imagist side does better.

3. The Two Mental Codes. So far I have mentioned the battle without arraying the sides. Here, for a beginning, are the polar pairs that are pitted against each other, listed somewhat helter-skelter: propositionalist/imagist, description/depiction, category/continuum, symbolic/analogic, discrete/analogue, digital/analogue, word-like/space-like, what something looks like/how it looks (Bower 1972).

The following pairs refer to the representations involved in the two codes, distinguishing them with respect to their elements (proposition/image), their modes (description/depiction), their properties (discreteness/continuity), their external analogues (word/space), their computational counterparts (digital/analogue), and their memory types (what/how).

This set of polarities circumscribes the two mental codes pitted against each other in the debate. (For the meaning of a "cognitive code" in general, see Ch. I B.) I should say right away that if all mental systems of significance are "codes," then there may well be more than two. For example, there may be an affective code. Furthermore, the amodal unitary propositional code has multitudinous models and associated processes, such as feature search, symbol manipulation, verbal analysis, and categorization, which are not our business here. The imagist code is, on the other hand, really a set of codes, one for each of those sensory modalities that has associated representations. As was pointed out above, the other codes, excepting, perhaps, the auditory code, have not been studied much: Kosslyn's quasi-visual model is all there is at the moment. Furthermore, the question has been raised whether this code is not, more basically, a spatial rather than a quasi-visual code. Insofar as the Shepard rotation findings are duplicated for the blind, with touch substituted for sight, this wider description would seem appropriate. Finally, one may want to think of the two codes (if there are two) as ultimately rooted in one deep amodal code, a "mentalese," which is beyond experimental access. For present purposes, however, I will stick with the two codes, here referred to by their most concretely defined terms, namely the "propositional" and the "imagistic."

By mere combination these then yield the following possibilities: Cognition might be purely imagistic. This is an option entertained nowhere except in the most restricted experimental domains. Cognition might be purely propositional. This option is preferred by people interested in the computational mimicry of human intelligence. The chief proponent is Zenon Pylyshyn. Cognition might require a dual coding, a mixed model, with processes running either sequentially or in parallel. The present choice of imagists is the mixed model with parallel processing (Kosslyn et al. 1980). The originator was Allan Paivio in his memory-studies (Ch. III A).

To understand the difference between the imagist and propositionalist schools it is necessary to see how the term "proposition" is understood in the propositionalist code. A proposition is more abstract than a verbal sentence since it may be expressed in several linguistic versions. Consequently this code is not precisely verbal but word-like. Propositions are taken as having truth values; they are either true or false. They are made up of various kinds of discrete symbols and formed according to explicit rules of syntax, by which their well-formedness can be tested. They have something that can be read as a predicate/argument structure; thus they shouldn't be mere arrays or lists (Anderson 1978). This whole characterization has been criticized for lack of explicitness (Schwartz 1981), but it will do for the purpose. Some such characteristics are realized throughout the many differently conceived codes.

Images, on the other hand, are precisely *not* what propositions are: They are not abstract but concrete, since each image is a quasi-sensory particular. Neither are they unequivocal, since in contrast to a formal proposition an image can sometimes be "read" in various ways, as diverse conformations can be seen in a trick picture. They are not true or false, except in conjunction with a proposition. They are not discrete, but space-like and continuous, so that a part of an image is still an image, whereas a part of a proposition is no longer a proposition. For while the latter are formed according to general syntactic rules, images are governed, if by any rules at all, by Gestalt laws, laws of visual organization. Such laws organize the whole representation at once, "holistically," rather than sequentially or coordinately, as do syntactic rules. Moreover, images seem to be capable of an intrinsic fuzziness, while propositions (as distinct from actual human speech) are definite. On the other hand, images cannot be noncommittal, that is, simply blank, about the appurtenances of a visible feature, while propositional representations can be simply silent. For example, except in degenerate cases like stick figures (Block 1981a), a head in an image is either crowned by a hat or not; the sentence needn't say.

One characterization that does not seem to help is the likening of imagery to perception. Both sides agree that at some level the perceptual code matches its inner representations, and the question is precisely whether that level is imagistic or propositionalist (Anderson 1978).

The positive marks of imagery are precisely those collected in the experiments above: having a sized and shaped and grainy medium within which is inscribed a depictive structure activated part by part and subject to definite transformations.

These, then, are the two chief sets of terms of the debate, which begins with a propositional attack on the imagist position. Together with the imagist rejoinder it goes something like this:

The propositionalist attack is largely theoretical. There are not many clear experimental findings in favor of propositionalism, but here is an important one. It is the so-called "congruity effect." When subjects are asked which of two large items is the larger they respond measurably faster than when they are asked which of two large items is the smaller, that is, when the asking and the response categories are mismatched. This effect would seem to indicate that what matters is not the image but the categorization. Kosslyn, however, explains the effect in terms of the recalibration of the mental comparison mechanism for imagery, a process that might take just as long as category-rematching. He shows that both processes are at work in parallel, "racing" each other. Whichever gets there first, wins over the other. For example, when two memory-representations are in the same size category, it is fastest to compare the images directly without considering the categories (Kosslyn et al. 1980).

Some of the theoretical objections on the propositional side (here listed with the imagist rebuttals in parenthesis) go as follows: The imagery model still relies on self-report, which propositionalists eschew on principle. (However, some cooperative response on the subject's part seems unavoidable in either case.) The imagery code is computationally cumbersome to store, on account of the indefinitely large amount of information in an image and the indefinite number of unique one-time depictions. (However, the capacity of the brain for such storage is not known. Moreover, it is unclear why a description of a visual memory would be more parsimonious than a depiction. Imagine exhaustively describing a picture, especially in a symbolic code that was true enough to the particularity of an image to generate an individuated symbol for every item in it—Pylyshyn 1978.) Another theoretical argument is that if there are two codes they must be readily translatable into one another. For example, images can be described, descriptions can summon images, and sometimes people even forget whether the original source of information was visual or auditory. Such translatability seems to require a third, more abstract code as a common basis, and this "interlingual" code would be essentially propositional. (The objection to this argument is analogous to Aristotle's "third man" criticism of the Platonic forms: If two codes need a third to be related, then that third in turn needs yet another code to relate it to either one of the first two, and so on in infinite regression. Thus any coding becomes impossible.)

There is also a methodological argument against all imagery-experiments taken together. It is the claim that they are all contaminated by "task demands," which means that they reveal nothing about having imagery but only something about the expectations built into the task. For example, suppose it is the case that subjects cannot do mental rotations on very complex block figures unless they find a way to reduce the complexity of the task. Suppose they do so by discovering at a glance that large parts of the figures are the same and then comparing the rest piecemeal. One might conclude that Shepard's figures were simply of just the right complexity so that this process might mimic rotation times (Yuille 1983). (However, the imagist side in fact allows for such feature-by-feature comparison where that process is easiest. Moreover, it can parry the task demand objection by showing that in general subjects are kept in careful ignorance of the point of the experiment and cannot guess the results (Kosslyn 1980, 458; Pinker and Kosslyn 1983).

Finally, the deepest anti-imagist argument is the one based on "cognitive penetrability," which is Pylyshyn's phrase (1981). It signifies the fact that the influence of beliefs penetrates both perception and imagery. Neither percepts nor memory-images are strictly veridical, but they are vulnerable to transformations that depend on "tacit" knowledge. For example, people usually recall a panoramic scene not as an evenly distributed surface but hierarchically, in terms of a total initial impression whose detail can be recalled by using the whole as a cue. Or again, in an experiment reminiscent of those Piaget did on children, subjects were shown trick photographs of pitchers tilted at various angles, whose fluid levels were not horizontal. Over half the subjects failed to "see" anything wrong, although they correctly perceived that the levels were not parallel to some shelves in the pictorial background. In post-experimental interviews it emerged that those and only those subjects recognized the trick who could clearly articulate the principle of fluid-level invariance. Thus only those who tacitly knew the rule for the correct situation could recognize a wrong one. The others were blind to it, even though they must have seen often enough in real life that the fluid levels in tilted containers remain horizontal.

In short, what we know affects what we see and similarly what we imagine. Images do not represent percepts photographically; they do so in an interpretative transformation. Our propositional knowledge informs imagery. (The imagist rejoinder is that the imagery theory was never meant to be a crudely photographic one. It explicitly specified that efficient non-analogue functions have access to the imagery buffer. For example, images can, when it is convenient, be "categorized," that is to say, read propositionally, rather than scanned imagistically.)

All in all, then, the arguments against the parallel-processing dual-code theory, in which propositional and imagistic processes race or supplant each other, seem to be answerable, and the experimental evidence seems to favor the theory (Kosslyn 1980, 363; Kosslyn and Pomerantz 1981; Kosslyn 1983, 162). Here, to end with, are two very simple and telling experiments that support a dual coding in which both thinking and imaging processes figure. The first proves that thinking—here counting—influences the speed of image-production: Subjects take longer to complete the mental imaging of a three-by-six array of items when they are instructed to think of it as six columns of three items than when they are to think of it as three rows of six. The second experiment, which anyone may try, shows that we use whichever code is convenient: When first asked how many windows there are in their house, most people will take a mental walk and count as they conjure up the facade imagistically. When asked the same question later in the day they will have the answer handy propositionally, in terms of digits. Before long, however, the number is apt to be forgotten. Evidently picture-memory is, in some cases, not only more long-term than verbal memory but better for the purpose of active recall.

D. Conclusions and Consequences

1. The Remaining Perplexities and Obscurities. The mental imagery debate, carried on in terms of the question "How many codes?," tends to a conclusion favoring imagery. Yet there remain deep obscurities and perplex-ities, which become even more interesting once the cognitive effectiveness, and by implication the existence, of mental imagery is accepted. The outstanding questions are: Exactly how is mental imagery a bearer of knowledge? Just what is the literal meaning of the "mind's eye" metaphor? What actually is the object which the mind's eye sees, and what is the nature of that seeing? What is it that moves in mental motion and by what laws does it move?

One might demand that, once the fact of imagery is granted, all the metaphors should yield a literal interpretation. But then the difficulties detailed above start all over again, although now with a positive sign.

First, then, how do we know or learn by means of mental images? Just what do they contribute? Insofar as they are merely recalled percepts, their function, if not its explanation, is simple. They can act in two ways (Pylyshyn 1981): They can serve as a kind of mental photo album which simply brings back visual memories (fact retrieval), or, more actively, they can help to solve problems that have a spatial aspect (mental models—Part Five, Ch. II B). I am hewing the cognitive line here in taking cognition as information-processing. Of course, the imagination might also be the source of revelations for which the word "information" would be some-thing of a misnomer. That sort of visionary imagination is taken up in other parts.

Insofar as an image is straightforwardly a restored percept, a memory, as indeed it normally is in the laboratory, it is a perceptual stand-in and used as perception is used. In this case, having a mental image is cognitive only insofar as perception is having knowledge, namely insofar as some purposeful focusing, transforming, analyzing, categorizing, or feature reading is occurring (Kosslyn and Pomerantz 1981). Good examples for images as perceptual stand-ins come from elementary geometry. The famous old problem of "doubling the square"—put to such cognitively suggestive use in Plato's *Meno*—can be intuitively solved by imagining the corners of a square which has been circumscribed about another square to be folded in so as to cover the internal square, just as one might do with a piece of paper.

But images are not normally percept-photos for most people. They are, on the contrary, very much "cognitively penetrable," that is, they already arrive shot through with tacit knowledge and non-conscious intentions. Here arises the continually perplexing question: Does imagery give even marginally more than it gets? In other words, are images also to some degree cognitively *im*penetrable? Are they at all autonomous bearers of knowledge? Even though imagery often renders no small service by incorporating and bringing out unnoticed detail, hidden designs, and unspoken cognitions, yet the imagist would aim at a higher ideal. That ideal would be realized if images, quite independently of the subject's fund of propositional knowledge, transformed, anticipated, or accented perceptions in such a way as to reveal something genuinely new, as dreams were once thought to reveal not the subconscious of the dreamer but the nature of things.

Imagists often do cite anecdotes in favor of this power of imagery, especially anecdotes about scientific discovery (e.g., Shepard and Cooper 1982, Kosslyn 1983). Einstein himself, in a famous letter to Hadamard, has insisted that the "combinatory play" of the imagination "seems to be the essential feature in productive thought." One of those "thought"—or rather "imagination"—experiments, whose paradoxical implication first preoccupied Einstein at sixteen, is the mental image of a physicist riding a beam of light with a mirror held at arm's length before him. In our context, the question concerning this ingenious image would be: Does the rider learn that the mirror is blank by inspecting his own imagery, or does he imagine it that way because he already knows that the reflection can't outrun him? (Einstein 1949; Ch. V C).

Mental imagery, moreover, plays a vital role in linguistic expression. Langacker, in furnishing the theoretical foundations of a cognitive grammar (1987, 110), distinguishes "autonomous" cognitive events from those that are "peripherally connected," that is, directly dependent on perception. The autonomous events are predominantly, though not necessarily, visual; they are, in fact, mental images. They are employed to structure the situations that are then verbally expressed. The image, or "scene," is embodied in the linguistic expression and therefore constitutes a crucial fact of its meaning" (117). Such images vary with respect to a number of analyzable parameters. One example is the perspective taken on the scene. For instance, the verbal expression embodies a viewpoint, an imagined perspective, that determines the meaning of its spatial-relation terms such as "upright," "upside-down," "above," "below," "in front of," and "behind."

So, granting imagery various ancillary or even central cognitive uses, these deepest matters remain unresolved: Can we have veridical images of circumstances previously unperceived or in principle unperceivable? For example, having never come across a square while its corners were being folded in, could we image the process, not in the sense of constructing it rationally by thinking, but of finding it in the image-medium by looking? Or can we at least read perceptual memories more discriminatingly than we apprehended the original percept itself? To take a physical instance, could we "see" in visual memory that the trajectory of a ball was parabolic although this fact had escaped us in visual tracking? Or, at the very least and vaguest, does our mere having of images itself perhaps tell us something informative about the world as containing imageable natures? These cognitive questions shade into philosophical perplexities, which is to say that they may be in principle unamenable to empirical resolution. They certainly are nowhere near resolution now.

Next, how is "the mind's eye" metaphor rendered harmless so that it can be deployed in imagery-research? Mental imagery invites talk of "seeing" more spontaneously and properly than does any other kind of conscious awareness, and such imagery is more seriously involved in the snags associated with vision. We do have the experiences of internal seeing and of correlated objects of sight; but no cognitive scientist wants to admit that we have an organ of internal sight or to distinguish the process (the imaging) from the product (the image).

In a way, the "mind's eye" debate is beside the point. The mind's eye is a pseudo-organ that "sees"; the physical eye, however, although a real enough organ, doesn't see, since it is merely a transducer of stimuli. So the "organ" question is a diversion. The mind's eye is only a sub-problem of the problem of consciousness. At issue should be not the "mind's eye" but the "mind's I" (to borrow an obvious pun from Hofstadter, *The Mind's I*).

Image-investigators nevertheless feel obliged to show that imagery-representation is possible without the absurdity of an internal agent of sight. In fact, Kosslyn's second book on imagery is entitled *Ghosts in the Mind's Machine*. This was Ryle's phrase for any inner agent of awareness, including the mind's eye (Part One, Ch. IV B). One aim of Kosslyn's book is to reassert mental, especially imagistic, representation against Ryle while taking the teeth—or the eyes—out of that offensive homunculus, that little watcher within, and sending him packing: "Goodbye, Homunculus" is one of his chapter titles.

But there are obscurities hidden in this curt dismissal, though the difficulties are subtle. The easy criticism is that the display screen, where the images actually appear in the computational model, is not, after all, internal to the model; it is not the computer that sees the screen but the external viewer (Yuille 1983). The criticism is off the mark. Only in Kosslyn's proto-model was the screen an analogue of the image-space; later the screen acts merely as an image "externalizer," like a device for drawing one's mental images.

In the cognitive computer model the "mind's eye" is thought of as being the interpretative function that reads the imagery-space (the cell matrix). It determines, for example, whether this space contains points meeting the rule for the image of a straight line, and computes similarities or searches for identifying features (Pylyshyn 1978). The trouble is that this work is not what the mind's eye of common parlance does. That eye sees. It genuinely gazes. So whatever ghost is being exorcized, it is not the mind's eye of experience.

Furthermore, the computational model itself, or at least its explication, incorporates some strange exchanges of functions. One such is the somewhat unnatural assignment of the resolving power, as well as of size limitation and of shape, to the medium. After all, acuity, visual angle, and field of vision would normally be said to belong to the organ of sight itself rather than to its visual object. Similarly the scanning operation is assigned to the image itself. It is an imaginal translation-transformation. The image itself moves across the buffer (Kosslyn 1980, 329; 1983, 128)—which certainly contradicts our ordinary experience of imaging. To be sure, the model does embody features that replicate the feel of internal image-viewing. For example, it identifies seeing and summoning an image, which do merge in the common experience of visualization. Oddly enough, Kosslyn was surprised at the experimental finding that inspection was part of the generating process (1983, 103). But with respect to the forcible reassignment of functions from mind's eye to medium, one might say that the ocular ghost had been not so much exorcized as sacked.

The question "Exactly what is the image-object?" is thus the obverse or complement of the "mind's eye" problem. Image and inner eye stand and fall together. Once the—admittedly troubling—notion of internal perception-like seeing is proscribed, the image itself can no longer display itself as a quasi-spatial inner appearance inscribed into a medium possessing a quasi-physical extension.

Then what is there left for the image to be? Recall that the "visual buffer," the medium function, is modeled as a matrix of cells for storing active memory points. Now this matrix is actually in no way spatial. It is in fact only a list of coordinates that are under certain constraints. These are interpretable as locations yielding, when activated, image configurations that when displayed have the very properties that have been experimentally discovered. It is these coordinates that are inspected by the computational analogue to the mind's eye. The matrix is thus not propositional, since it has no syntactic rules, no predicate argument form and no truth values. Yet neither is it truly spatial, since it is digital, that is, a discretely numerical list rather than a resemblance-preserving continuum. It is a non-propositional digital structure which shares certain formal properties with space.

In fact, the medium matrix is really intended to be a *quasi*-quasi-space: It only functions as if it were the sort of image space that is in turn experienced as if it were a perceptual space. As Kosslyn puts it: "Something does not have to *be* a picture to *function* as one" (1983, 22). An image is "emergent," meaning that it is a whole different from its constitutive parts (Ch. I A). For the list of activated coordinate points does not at all resemble the image emerging from them.

But this argument leaps lightly over a philosophical abyss. One might insist that the image has not really emerged until it has been traced as an appearance in an extensional space. One might urge that the coordinate "points" are not yet the graphic dots from which an image can emerge, precisely because they are just number pairs and not actually spatial loca-tions or loci. From that non-metaphorical angle the term "visual buffer" is a kind of double-speak, glossing over a question as old as the Pythagorean inquiry into the relation of arithmetic to geometry: Doesn't the full notion of space have to include, besides its formal structure, a (non-physical) material element, namely its very extension? Couldn't one say that nothing can satisfyingly represent a spatial structure except another spatial structure? (Part Five, Ch. I).

If one answers yes to this question, the computational model will not ultimately seem to be about image-spaces and the depictions therein at all. On the other hand, if one opts for the negative, as Kosslyn does, the argument for the cognitive convenience of processing "holistic" represen-tations, on the ground that their information is on patent display and directly available to inspection, is much weakened. The patency, belonging as it does to the material side of space, is now gone, and who knows whether the full-blown matrix structures are very convenient or quicker to process than a propositional model would be? What is also gone is any bond of similarity between external and internal representations. This is a loss cognitive science isn't quite up to mourning.

Shepard, the originator of these imagery experiments, faces exactly this question: "In just what way are images spatial objects?" and he proposes to answer it by means of the notion of a "second-order isomorphism" (Shepard and Chipman 1970). A first-order isomorphism is one that preserves shape. Old-fashioned portraits are isomorphic with their sitter. Shephard cites philosophers like Wittgenstein as discrediting the possibility of access to such mental imagery. But since his experiments show that there *is* something isomorphic about imagery, he introduces a "functional" or second-order isomorphism. It is not the relation of figural similarity that obtains between an original and its image; it is a relation between two sets of relations, those that obtain among external objects on the one hand and among their mental images on the other. Such a relation of relations is like an old-fashioned proportion. For example, square A has to square B the same relation as number *a* to number *b,* and this sameness of relation holds even though numbers are not shaped like squares, indeed not shaped at all. Shepard calls the internal set of relational events, which might be no more than a specific activation of neurons, a functional relation. And now the problem is even more acute than it was for the medium–matrix. For although this hypothesis does avoid all talk of mental images being squarish, the price is that it also avoids determining them at all. Now the answer to the original question, in what the space-like, similarity-preserving nature of mental images consists, is that the experienced images themselves are not at issue at all, but only their interrelations. It is not a perfectly satisfying answer.

The last question—"Just what is mental motion the motion of, and what are its laws?"—is, of course, intertwined with the problem of the image-object. The propositionalists see an epistemological pitfall in imagery-studies, namely the tendency to yield to an "objective pull." This Quinean phrase means that mental motions tend to be taken as the movements of the objects represented rather than as the motions of their representations (Pylyshyn 1978). In their view the imagistic approach has no explanatory power because it derives the mental event from the properties of the natural object. For example, it might attribute an image-motion to the inertia of the body represented rather than to the cognitive mechanism. This attribution they consider mistaken, for that mechanism "has no access to properties of the represented domain *except insofar as they are encoded in the form of the representation itself"* (Pylyshyn 1981). Here is a succinct and extreme expression of what one might call, tit-for-tat, the "solipsistic pull" of cognitive science, namely the tendency to cut off the mental representation from any objective influence.

There is a large class of experiments by both sides (Pylyshyn 1978; Kosslyn 1980; Yuille 1983) showing that the mental motion rate is fairly constant, bearing out a guess ventured by Locke long ago about the limited temporal variation of mental processes (*Essay* II 14). Mental rotations done in the presence of the perceptual stimuli are slower than those done from memory. The mental rate decreases appreciably from the 60 degrees per second mentioned above as the conceptual complexity of an imaged solid increases. Such results might seem at first to be interpretable as being anti-holistic, that is, anti-imagistic. For a conceptually complex structure requires more propositional material to be processed, which takes time. However, so do the corresponding image-reading operations. A "holistic" reading, though done in no syntactic sequence, is yet not necessarily done all at once.

Oddly enough, in spite of the cognitive solipsism of some of its proponents, it is an implication of the propositionalists' view that imagery does in fact often stay close to external nature, since for them the "image" is just a simulation in propositions of the way they believe things are. Kosslyn tested this hypothesis, that experience informs such simulations, by having subjects handle two stimuli, a heavy lead–filled soft-drink bottle and a very long, light dowel. They were then asked to rotate them mentally in two ways, first by picturing the objects as physically turning and then by mentally rotating their imaginal representations. Both objects were to be thought of as pinned through their center to an imagined dial, and a button was to be pressed as they passed each 45 degree mark. According to Pylyshyn's view, the two imaged motions should come to the same thing— a simulation of the natural motion. In each case the bottle should show some inertial effects at the beginning and end of its rotation, and the dowel none. But Kosslyn predicted that in the second, the "turn the image" run, the dowel should take longer than the bottle. He expected this result because, as has been shown, rotation is a "region-bounded" transformation, namely the sort in which not the whole image field but only the image is transformed. In such transformations large areas take longer to process. And that is what happened: The image underwent a mental motion, not a simulated natural one (Kosslyn 1983, 149).

Note that Kosslyn insists that in his theory, too, it is the image-object and not the dynamic object which is moved—naturally, for that is what even the most unrefined notion of having an image implies, namely not having the dynamically real objects within: "Yet did I not swallow them into me by seeing, whenas with my eyes I beheld them" (Augustine,

Confessions X 8). Nevertheless, Kosslyn's theory takes account of some of the many subtle variations we may observe in the subject's relation to the image-motion: Sometimes we do recall it, icon-like, as a memory-replica of a real free motion. Sometimes we see ourselves moving it with a motion controlled by our own hand. We also watch it reveal itself freely to our wondering gaze. We constrain it to move with a merely mental motion. We scan the inert image. We take a mental walk around it. Sometimes the whole field undergoes translation; sometimes it teems with localized motions; sometimes the motion is localized.

Yet the best imagery-theory to date cannot be said to have unraveled the mysteries of mental motion and re-knit the strands into a coherent psychophysical theory. However, since such a theory would in any case have to begin with a phenomenology of internal motions, something has been gained from the mere descriptive analysis.

2. The Profits of the Study of Mental Imagery. To the question: "What is to be learned about the imagination from the science of mental imagery?" a curt answer might be: "Nothing—at least nothing very new or very firm or very relevant to the common experience." But there is more to it than that.

It might seem that imagery-study, like so many psychological studies, merely succeeds at what older Russians used to call "discovering America." It confirms belatedly and laboriously what had long been known to ordinary people: that we have a certain kind of mental picture which we use for doing tasks, for solving problems, and for entertaining ourselves. The science confirms common belief, however, not only by parrying the objections of non-believers but also by specifying and filling out the notion of mental imagery. To do the latter, the enterprise employs a method of "convergent operations." That means that it goes after its object from all sides by means of *ad hoc* experiments designed to establish progressively and in tandem both the definition of the concept and the properties of the object. The outcome is valuable because, with certain revealing exceptions, it provides a controlled corroboration of ordinary intuition.

What this method cannot do is to prove rigorously the existence of its assumed object. But it can delineate one kind of imaging capacity so vigorously as to make its existence highly plausible. The imagery of cognitive psychology is of the instrumental variety, yet it surely throws some light even on unregimented common reverie—the sort of imagination dismissed by cognitivists as "warm and fuzzy." Although this experimental project cannot convince the purists who have propositionalist agendas, the imagist side seems to have the edge with the profession, and for the general reader the results are impressive. Even if the imagination revealed is only skeletal, functional, mundane, and memorized—in sum, laboratory-bred—still it is one with indefeasible features. Moreover, some of the discoveries concerning the size, shape, motion, generation, and fading of images are surely not accessible to mere introspection.

Aside from positive results, the imagery debate, including even its deadlock, is itself revealing. Perhaps the argument has run itself into the ground; perhaps that constitutes a "crisis" that demands a shift in terms, even a shift away from the cognitive approach (Yuille 1983). But any new terms are likely to run into the same trouble. For they will continue to reflect the intractable cognitive question—cognitive in the larger, philosophical sense: What and how many are the roots of human consciousness? However, while cognitive science forces explicitness and precision about the issue, the issue in turn forces the science to display its defining limits.

One of the limiting assumptions is the materialism universal in cognitive science. Kosslyn's popular book (1983) bears the subtitle "Creating Images *in the Brain*" (my italics). There is little about the brain in the book except its picture. Neurons are referred to with respect to the image-matrix, but finding a precise connection between the computational model and brain functions is nothing more than an ardent hope—ardent because the model's theory will explain nothing until its structures and processes can be fitted to the brain as its neural functions. In the context of imagery this lack of explanatory power applies particularly to the "visual buffer" and to the mental motions of imaging, which may reasonably be expected to have some relation to the rates of neural processes. The expectation of succeeding in this liaison is the fundamental assumption of the science: In modern cognitive psychology

> we describe these neural patterns [those excited in perception] . . . in a vocabulary more abstract than actual neural firings, namely, in the vocabulary of mental representations and the computational processes that act on them. We then identify mental entities, such as percepts or images, with particular representations (factoring out of the problem the nature of the qualia, or subjective experiences, associated with visual processes, since they are as intractable as a scientific problem can be). [Pinker and Kosslyn 1983, 57]

The practical possibilty of this project is, as has been said, so far mostly conjectural (ibid., Anderson 1978). It follows that the future will tell, and what it will tell is of extreme interest. It will tell whether the structures and processes reached by going through consciousness can also be observed from the material end—whether mind is in observable detail a set of functions of the brain. It is hard to see how this inquiry could proceed, unless it had first been established what those functions are, and, in particular, whether they include a space-like component. The science of mental imagery seems to have provided such determinations.

As for consciousness itself, it remains untrapped either way. Claiming that the brain imagines is like saying that the mouth eats—a suggestive metonymical figure but not a sufficient account.

Bibliography

Anderson, John R. 1978. "Arguments Concerning Representations for Mental Imagery." *Psychological Review* 85:249–279.

Bleasdale, Fraser. 1983. "Paivio's Dual-Coding Model of Meaning Revisited." In *Imagery, Memory and Cognition: Essays in Honor of Allan Paivio*, edited by John C. Yuille. Hillsdale, N.J.: Lawrence Erlbaum Associates.

Block, Ned, ed. 1981. *Imagery*. Cambridge: The MIT Press.

———. 1981a. "Introduction: What is the Issue?" In *Imagery*, edited by Ned Block. Cambridge: The MIT Press.

———, ed. 1981b. *Readings in Philosophy of Psychology*, Volume 2. Cambridge: Harvard University Press.

Boring, Edwin G. 1950. *A History of Experimental Psychology*, 2d ed. New York: Appleton-Century-Crofts.

Bower, G. H. 1972. "Mental Imagery and Associative Learning." In *Cognition in Learning and Memory*, edited by L.W. Gregg. New York: John Wiley and Sons.

Bugelski, Richard. 1971. "The Definition of the Image." In *Imagery: Current Cognitive Approaches*, edited by Sydney J. Segal. New York: Academic Press.

———. 1983. "Imagery and Thought Processes." In *Imagery: Current Theory, Research, and Application*, edited by Anees A. Sheikh.

Einstein, Albert. 1949. *Albert Einstein: Philosopher-Scientist*, Volume 1, edited by Paul A. Schilpp. La Salle, Ill.: Open Court (1969).

Eysenck, Michael. 1984. "Imagery and Visual Memory." Chapter 7 in *A Handbook of Cognitive Psychology*. Hillsdale, N.J.: Lawrence Erlbaum Associates.

Gregg, L. W., ed. 1972. *Cognition in Learning and Memory*. New York: John Wiley and Sons.

Haber, Ralph N. 1971. "Where are the Visions in Visual Perception?" In *Imagery: Current Cognitive Approaches*, edited by Sydney J. Segal. New York: Academic Press.

Holt, Robert R. 1964. "Imagery: The Return of the Ostracised." *American Psychologist* 19:254–264.

————. 1972. "On the Nature and Generality of Mental Imagery." In *The Function and Nature of Imagery*, edited by Peter W. Sheehan. New York: Academic Press.

Horowitz, Mardi J. 1970. *Image Formation and Cognition*. New York: Appleton-Century-Crofts.

————. 1972. "Image Formation: Clinical Observations and a Cognitive Model." In *The Function and Nature of Imagery*, edited by Peter W. Sheehan. New York: Academic Press.

Johnson-Laird, P. N. 1983. *Mental Models: Towards a Cognitive Science of Language, Inference, and Consciousness*. Cambridge: Harvard University Press.

Klatzky, Roberta L. 1980. *Human Memory: Structures and Processes*, 2d ed. San Francisco: W.H. Freeman and Co.

Kosslyn, Stephen M. 1980. *Image and Mind*. Cambridge: Harvard University Press.

————. 1983. *Ghosts in the Mind's Machine: Creating and Using Images in the Brain*. New York: W.W. Norton and Company.

Kosslyn, Stephen M., and Holyoak, Keith J. 1982. "Imagery." In *Handbook of Research Methods in Human Memory and Cognition*, edited by C. Richard Puff. New York: Academic Press.

Kosslyn, Stephen M., Murphy, G. L., Bemesderfer, M. E., and Feinstein, K. J. 1980. "Category and Continuum in Mental Comparisons." In *Human Memory: Contemporary Readings*, edited by John G. Seamon. Oxford: Oxford University Press.

————. 1981. "The Medium and the Message in Mental Imagery." In *Imagery*, edited by Ned Block. Cambridge: The MIT Press.

Kosslyn, Stephen M., Pinker, Steven, Smith, George E., and Schwartz, Steven P. 1981. "On the Demythification of Mental Imagery." In *Imagery*, edited by Ned Block. Cambridge: The MIT Press.

Kosslyn, Stephen M., and Pomerantz, James R. 1981. "Imagery, Propositions, and the Form of Internal Representations." In *Readings in Philosophy of Psychology*, Volume 2. Cambridge: Harvard University Press.

Langacker, Ronald W. 1987. *Foundations of Cognitive Grammar I: Theoretical Prerequisites*. Stanford: Stanford University Press.

Lindauer, Martin S. 1972. "The Sensory Attributes and Functions of Imagery and Imagery Evoking Stimuli." In *The Function and Nature of Imagery*, edited by Peter W. Sheehan. New York: Academic Press.

McKellar, Peter. 1972. "Imagery from the Standpoint of Introspection." In *The Function and Nature of Imagery*, edited by Peter W. Sheehan. New York: Academic Press.

Paivio, Allan. 1983. "The Empirical Case for Dual Coding." In *Imagery, Memory and Cognition: Essays in Honor of Allan Paivio*, edited by John C. Yuille. Hillsdale, N.J.: Lawrence Erlbaum Associates.

Pinker, Steven, and Kosslyn, Stephen M. 1983. "Theories of Mental Imagery." In *Imagery: Current Theory, Research, and Application*, edited by Anees A. Sheikh. New York: John Wiley and Sons.

Puff, C. Richard, ed. 1982. *Handbook of Research Methods in Human Memory and Cognition.* New York: Academic Press.

Pylyshyn, Zenon. 1978. "Imagery and Artificial Intelligence." In *Minnesota Studies in the Philosophy of Science*, Volume 9, edited by C. Wade Savage. Minneapolis: University of Minnesota Press. [Also in Block (1981b).]

———. 1981. "The Imagery Debate: Analog Media versus Tacit Knowledge." In *Imagery*, edited by Ned Block. Cambridge: The MIT Press.

Richardson, John T. E. 1980. *Mental Imagery and Human Memory.* New York: St. Martin's Press.

Rilling, Mark E., and Neiworth, Julie J. 1987. "Theoretical and Methodological Considerations for the Study of Imagery in Animals." *Learning and Motivation* 18:57–59.

Schwartz, Robert. 1981. "Imagery—There's More to It than Meets the Eye." In *Imagery*, edited by Ned Block. Cambridge: The MIT Press.

Seamon, John G., ed. 1980. *Human Memory: Contemporary Readings.* Oxford: Oxford University Press.

Segal, Sydney J., ed. 1971. *Imagery: Current Cognitive Approaches.* New York: Academic Press.

Sheehan, Peter W., ed. 1972. *The Function and Nature of Imagery.* New York: Academic Press.

Sheehan, Peter W., Ashton, R., and White, K. 1983. "Assessment of Mental Imagery." In *Imagery: Current Theory, Research, and Application*, edited by Anees A. Sheikh. New York: John Wiley and Sons.

Sheikh, Anees A., ed. 1983. *Imagery: Current Theory, Research, and Application.* New York: John Wiley and Sons.

Shepard, Roger N. 1980. "The Mental Image." In *Human Memory: Contemporary Readings*, edited by John G. Seamon. Oxford: Oxford University Press.

Shepard, Roger N., and Chipman, Susan. 1970. "Second-Order Isomorphism in Internal Representations: Shapes of States." *Cognitive Psychology* 1:1–17.

Shepard, Roger N., and Cooper, Lynn A. 1982. *Mental Images and Their Transformation.* Cambridge: The MIT Press.

Yuille, John C. 1983. "The Crisis in Theories of Mental Imagery." In *Imagery, Memory and Cognition: Essays in Honor of Allan Paivio*, edited by John C. Yuille. Hillsdale, N.J.: Lawrence Erlbaum Associates.

Chapter III

The Science of Memory: Storage and Retrieval of Visual Imagery

All mental imagery is re-presentation and all representation is memorial: *In animo sit quidquid est in memoria*—"Whatever be in the mind is in memory," says Augustine (*Confessions* X 17). Imagery is part of memory in the wide sense in which memory is the mind's capacity to hold and yield up what is in it. Thus the study of memory is almost coextensive with the study of all cognitive contents. It investigates them insofar as they are contents, that is contained: held, stored, and restored.

It follows that memory in the wider sense does not necessarily have the sign of the past on it. What I am at present conscious of is in memory whether it has been recalled or, whether, as we shall see, it has just been perceived. Moreover, it turns out that not all that is recalled is restored from the temporal past. In the study of memory a distinction is made between "episodic" memory, which is temporarily indexed autobiographical memory, and "semantic" memory, which is not time-bound. Suppose a subject, in the laboratory on April 1st, memorizes a list of words including, say, the word "memory." The learning-event has a temporal marker, but the meaning of "memory," which is held deep in memory, does not. This holds for all meanings and truths, as Augustine, the greatest of all memorialists, observes (X 9–12). There remains the deep question how datable instances of learning are related to knowing, and how temporally indexed images are related to archetypal visions.

Memory is an inferred entity, as are all cognitive structures. There is a postulate undergirding classical physics which says that "In nature there are no gaps" (Kant, *CPR* B 281). Its analogue in the study of human nature demands that contents that come into consciousness sporadically should be considered as stored somewhere in the meanwhile. Thus the founder of the science of memory says at the beginning of his work: "Memory is revealed with a certainty like that with which we infer the existence of stars below the horizon" (Ebbinghaus 1885). A storage hypothesis is therefore the beginning of memory-science. Of course, just as in the case of the representational hypothesis for imagery, there are philosophical demurrers to this assumption.

If all imagery is somehow memorial, not by any means is all memory imagistic. (It is necessary to say "somehow memorial" because there may be aspects of productive memory to which the terms of information storage are not quite equal. I mean imagery—if such there be—that did not get in by the certified channels, for example, mythical archetypes.) Non-imagistic memory is for present purposes termed "verbal." The meaning of "verbal," however, should not be confined to "propositional"; it must include anything discretely symbolic, since memory investigators, beginning with Ebbinghaus, often make use of nonsense syllables or letter sequences.

Just as in imagery-studies, the visual memory is taken as imagistic memory *par excellence*. This priority goes back to the ancient tradition in which all memory is treated as primarily visual-spatial, as, for example, in Plato's figure of the mind as an aviary (*Theaetetus* 197) and in Augustine's reference to the "fields and spacious palaces" of memory (*Confessions* X 8). This "roomy treasury," as Augustine calls it, contains the images of things once seen and then stored, to use a contemporary figure, like slides in a carousel. Visual memory storage is a good candidate to represent all memory. First it seems to be the case that sensory memory is stored as such and does not undergo the radical transformations applied to verbal memories, which are stored semantically rather than verbatim. Second, the capacity of ordinary visual-recognition memory extends far beyond that of verbal capacity and is simply fabulous. In an often cited test, subjects were shown 2560 slides, each for ten seconds. They were then asked to do various kinds of "forced choice recognition" requiring them to decide which of two slides they had seen before. They could do so with about ninety percent accuracy (Standing et al. in Eysenck 1984). Visual memory is also wonderfully long-range. Subjects who had looked at 612 colored slides could do such recognition with fifty-seven percent accuracy four months later (Spoehr and Lehmkuhle 1982). (Examples of extraordinarily spacious long-range auditory memory are rarer; Mozart is a famous example.)

The metaphor of a storage bin has its difficulties, however. They arise when the requirements of retrieval are considered. Unless items were stored according to some conceptual map, trying to recall would be like trying to pull slides out of a carousel that had been loaded randomly. One could spend ages finding the picture that was wanted. Yet the conception of such a map shows it to be enormously complex: Imagine a "conceptual coordi-nate space" of two axes in which, say, animals and their activities are to be placed. Let the vertical axis stand for rising degrees of fierceness, and the horizontal axis for increasing size. A bird like a goshawk would have coordinates way up and out in the upper right quadrant, while a shrew-mouse would be in the lower left. But where would the picture of the goshawk pouncing on the shrewmouse be plotted on this conceptual map? The trouble is that a picture can be categorized in multiple ways. Therefore it requires a huge, cross-referenced, mental address index, even supposing that not all the infinite detail of any picture needed to be descriptively accessed. Clearly it is very difficult to produce a model that accounts for the quick searches through visually stored memories we seem in fact to conduct.

The other difficulty is that the sensory, visual memory is not just an accessible storage facility for perceptual traces, but also a workshop. Not only are perceptions transformed and even transfigured there, but also episodic, or dated, memory of particular moments and instances is turned into semantic, or atemporal, memory of general facts and universal cate-gories. Aristotle describes the transformation figuratively: One individual percept after the other is held until the universal is established, just as, during a retreat in battle, when one man halts so does another, until the original formation is restored (*Posterior Analytics* II 19). So memory is a field for re-formation. But the perceptual rout is turned back under cover of darkness, as it were; it takes place below consciousness. The memory-theories of psychology are attempts to reconstruct what must be happening.

A. The Codes and Kinds of Memory

The accounts that have so far found widespread acceptance in cognitive psychology refer to two codes or representational systems, the verbal and the imagistic, and to three kinds or levels of memory, the "iconic," the short-term and the long-term. The two codes are linked in a "dual code" system, and the three levels compose an interactive multi-level storage system. Naturally, these two aspects of memory are interrelated.

The imagery that emerges from Kosslyn's theory, discussed in the previous chapter, is a modification of the "dual code" system originally proposed for purposes of memory study by Paivio. The chief differences between Kosslyn and Paivio appear to be these two: First, Kosslyn is forced by his computational approach to deal more explicitly with the shape of imagery—or the absence of shape—at the deepest level, with somewhat ambiguous results. Paivio's version posits imagery almost all the way down, without specifying the nature either of imagery or of memory. For both investigators the possibility of an ultimate common code, neither word-like nor picture-like, is left open, though it may be beyond experimental determination. The second difference is that Kosslyn's linking of the codes is parallel, in the sense that the alternatively coded operations race each other, whereas Paivio's are more interactive. Kosslyn allows for images to be generated from long-term memory rather than merely retrieved from it. That is to say, the memorial units have the form of image-elements rather than of whole images. Both theories share the fundamental notion of unconscious processes, and the uneasy metaphor of the mind's eye (Yuille and Marschark 1983).

1. The Two Codes: Visual and Verbal. This is the place to point out that the dual code has a long line of descent. It is exemplified in the ancient distinction between imagination and intellect, and more particularly in the antique memorist categories of "things and words." Similarly, the two associationist categories of a synchronous and a successive sensory and mental order (e.g., James Mill 1829) prefigure the "holistic" imagist code and the sequential verbal code, the one being essentially spatial, the other temporal.

In contemporary psychology dual coding was supported particularly by an early series of experiments by Paivio suggesting that imaging aided memory. In one experiment subjects were given lists of paired nouns. Later they were given one member as a stimulus and asked to respond with its "paired associate." Subjects consistently recalled best when both nouns were concrete, least well when both were abstract (Spoehr and Lehmkuhle 1982). The implication is that mental imagery was used to help recall.

The two codes can be distinguished by three sets of criteria:

First, images tend toward concreteness, words toward abstractness. (The tendency to abstractness is understood in two ways, as a reduction in the specificity with which the object is defined, and as a widening of the field of reference.)

Second, Paivio cites William James's description of thought, its "alternation of flights and perchings." (Actually Locke had already observed this intermingling of idea-instants and intervening durations—*Essay* II 14.) The proper function of imagery in this punctuated flux is a matter of debate: Does it do better in activating the transforming interstices or in depicting the resultant resting places? Is it best for developing or for surveying representations? (For the static aspect see "momentariness" in the Index.) Paivio supposes that both codes can perform both functions, especially when they interact. A static visual situation may be transformed by the right verbal label, while imagery may animate the description of a state of affairs. Which of these occurs depends on whether the representation is concrete or abstract and whether it is dynamic or static. There are concrete nouns and detailed pictorial still-lives; there are motion verbs and their action images; there are abstract nouns and associated schematic images. In short, as Paivio points out, the two codes are really not very crisply distinguished along this functional dimension of static and dynamic moments. Yet generally images seem to be by preference still, while discursive speech runs on.

Third, a sharper distinguishing criterion is the sort of processing proper to each code. Words are mainly processed sequentially and discretely. Meaning usually depends on position. For example, compare the effect of saying "the goshawk pounced on the shrewmouse" to claiming that "the shrewmouse pounced on the goshawk." Visual imagery, on the other hand, undergoes parallel processing in two ways. From an operational point of view an image need not be scanned in any fixed sequence but may be viewed as starting from a number of origins. As Kant puts it: The apprehension of spatial representations has only a subjective, not an objective order. From a spatial point of view an image is processed holistically over a whole area, just as are visual percepts on the retina. Multidimensionality, in other words, is one distinction between spatial vision and temporal thinking.

Consequently, the two codes are differently positioned along the sequential/parallel continuum. Though an image is usually read all at once, that is, in parallel, it may occasionally require being taken up in a given sequence. It can even be inspected with a view to passing almost immediately through its spatiality to its descriptive properties. Words, in contrast, though they normally require being read sequentially, especially when they occur in descriptions, can sometimes be processed in parallel. For example, abstract ejaculations like "Liberty, Equality, Fraternity" are approvingly taken in as a whole by people who might be appalled by the meaning of the parts separately.

According to Paivio each of the two codes has three modes of activity. First, they can be brought into play representationally, by direct arousal. In this mode the verbal representations are the perceptual motor traces of words, and the images are the representations of visually apprehended objects. Second, they can come into play referentially, through the activation of each code by the other. In this mode a word arouses an image or an image calls for its name. Third, they can be activated associatively, by the formation of associative complexes within each code. In this way one gets verbal chains, such as the counting numbers and the trains of associated imagery.

From the hypothesis of these interactions within and between the codes follows a fundamental prediction: The concrete presentation of information, in the form either of the objects themselves or pictures or concrete words, should lead to better memorization. For objects and pictures simultaneously activate both codes, the imagery code very strongly and the verbal code at least fairly strongly. Concrete words cause some lesser degree of imagistic representation and involve the verbal system heavily. Abstract words have strong verbal coding only. The assumption predicts that the net memorial advantage will lie with the information that is both doubly and more strongly encoded. In sum, these factors favor the most concrete information. As was mentioned, Paivio's prediction was throughly corroborated. For example, subjects were tested with pictures, concrete words and abstract words. After five minutes they recalled the more concrete stimuli more successfully. After a week, although half of all the stimuli had been forgotten, they yet recalled twice as many pictures as concrete words and twice as many concrete words as abstract words.

It goes without saying that Paivio's experiments come under the same kind of criticism as the other imagist theories. However, the evidence for a superior, not to say spectacular, visual memory is even harder to account for with a single code theory. As it is, visual memory remains a deep mystery.

(Paivio 1971, 1984, Klatzky 1980, Arbinger 1984, Yuille 1983.)

2. The Three Kinds of Memory: Levels of Depth. If the mind regarded as a container is memory, how can this store be articulated except according to the marked features of the imagery it contains? One such ancient mark is apparent location. Most memory-imagery appears to the imager as internal, but some, like eidetic, hallucinatory, and, on occasion, dream-imagery, is experienced as external to the mind. The modern science of memory, however, does not attach central significance to this classification. Instead it classifies memories by the depth of their internal level: from nearly perceptual surface images, through thoroughly reworked reminiscences, to irretrievably forgotten events, in effect, unmemories.

There is a distinction along these lines going back to William James—the distinction between primary and secondary memory. The corresponding contemporary terms are short-term memory and long-term memory. These name two levels of storage "space." In addition, there is a third kind of memory, a sort of memorial reception-room called the sensory register. These three kinds of memory differ in various ways: in length of possible storage time, in storage capacity, in the mode of representation, and in the mode of retrieval. Possibly they also differ in the type of their contents. It should be said right now that things are of course far more complex than they seem in this schematic presentation. It should also be said that there are alternative theories, not so generally accepted or so significantly concerned with visual imagery, which articulate memory not in terms of levels of storage but in terms of levels of processing (Baddeley 1976). As usual, it is the visual mode that has received most attention.

The topmost level of memory is, then, a very short-term sensory store. A familiar example is the fiery letters one can trace by waving a glowing cigarette in the dark or the disk described by the revolving blades of a propeller. The representations within the sensory register are transient, modality-specific, and pre-categorical, meaning that they are briefly lingering perceptions which have not yet been conceptually analyzed. Only two specific modes are distinguished by name: the visual icon and the auditory echo. However, the other senses also have some sort of specific memory. Experiments have suggested that the icon is not just an after-effect in the transducing eye, but a genuine re-presentation (Eysenck 1984, 84).

The classical evidence for such a capability comes from a test by Sperling, here much simplified. It appears that people often have a sense of having seen much more than they recall, of having had a brief but comprehensive visual memory. In an attempt to capture such a memory, subjects were asked to view an array of three rows of three letters each, presented for one twentieth of a second by means of a tachistoscope (an instrument for displaying brief, timed stimuli, indispensable for reaction-time studies). They could report, on an average, only five of the nine letters. Next, high, middle, and low tones, designating respectively the top, middle, or bottom rows, were randomly sounded very shortly after stimulus offset. It was found that when thus cued, subjects could easily recall any row. Evidently they had all nine letters in iconic memory. After one second, however, the number had declined to less than five. The conclusion was that there is a very short-term iconic memory with a capacity of less than five items after one second.

This memory corresponds very nearly to Husserl's "retention" (1904) and to the traditional "spurious present." It serves to retain visual information long enough for recognition and comparison to take place, that is, for perceptions to come to consciousness, or perhaps to be processed for immediate passage to deep memory.

Short-term memory, the next level, is the conscious, active, working memory. It is the place where the living memory shows itself to consciousness. Hence it is to the imagination what the "window of appearance," where the Pharaoh showed himself to the populace, was to Egyptian palaces: In working memory imagery, not yet or no longer stored away, is on the scene, present, on display. It is more or less coextensive with the conscious experience of having memories. It is fed from the outside by means of perceptions, which are internalized by passing through the iconic stage, as the turn-off configurations on a highway map just consulted are held in mind. But this memory is also supplied from the inside, by means of purposeful recollection or of spontaneous remembrance (if there is such a thing, and if not all remembering is triggered associatively). Thus the short-term memory is in fact a place of re-membrance rather than of memory. It is also the level where ongoing activities, like mental rotations and transformations, take place.

This short-term memory, or at least its imagistic component, is of course the surface display (the visual buffer or medium matrix) familiar from the previous chapter. Recall that Kosslyn showed that visual imagery is held in a short-term memory store, which is responsible for its privileged or constitutional properties.

There is evidence for distinguishing the momentary iconic from the short-term imagistic memory. Subjects were asked, for example, to compare visual letter stimuli presented twice within a short interval of time. The interval was sometimes filled with a masking field of random patterns, such as would presumably erase an icon. But the interference did not affect comparison times. Evidently the icon does not play a role in such tasks.

The classical evidence that there is an abrupt discontinuity in the capacities of iconic and imagistic memory, evidence instrumental in establishing the latter as a distinct kind, comes from verbal tests. They showed that "the magical number seven, plus or minus two" is the limit of units or "chunks" this store can retain (Miller 1956; "chunking" refers to the interesting fact that the capacity is for units of meaning rather than for individual items: 40 x 1 bits of information are beyond capacity, but, properly chunked into 4 x 10 meaningful complexes, they can be retained). The time limit, as opposed to the item capacity, of short-term memory seems to vary individually.

What is held in this active memory must nonetheless be retrieved, in the sense of being inspected, scanned, or searched, that is, attended to in some order. This internal process, not specific to visual memory, can be made to reveal itself in experiments too complex to detail here. However, they show that when asked whether a given item is on a list held in short-term memory, subjects go through the whole list, performing an "exhaustive serial search" before making their decision.

In addition to searching, "rehearsal" is a work of short-term memory.

"Re-hearsal" refers specifically to the auditory reiteration of information, as when we say a phone number over and over between book and dial. But of course there is also a re-envisioning.

Moreover, two types of rehearsal are distinguishable. One is "maintenance," that internal re-saying of words or regenerating of imagery already mentioned, a process singularly vulnerable to distraction. The other is "elaboration," rehearsal that associates the item to be remembered with more memorable complexes. Mnemonics is the technique concerned with elaboration (B).

Short-term visual memory has characteristics comparable to those discovered for the verbal counterpart. Limited verbal capacity is matched by the limited visual angle of the buffer. Exhaustive list-search is matched by holistic field-scanning. Verbal maintenance-rehearsal is matched by the constant regeneration needed in imagery. Elaborative rehearsal is matched by mnemonic devices. One visual mnemonic device is the arrangement of imagery items into "scene schemata." These are generalized schematic settings which incorporate our notion of "a school room" or "a street scene." The items in such settings are better remembered than those in random heaps (Mandler 1983).

These latter memory-schemata suggest a yet deeper level of memory, long-term memory. So does the most familiar memory activity of all, the bringing up of memories from deep down. "LTM" is the complex of memorial activities ordinarily termed recall, remembrance, reminiscence, recollection. Even when such operations start consciously, they always end in the dark depths of memory proper. Memory proper is the place not of the remembered but of the forgotten event.

So much the more is empirical evidence concerning the specific constitution of deep memory important. The classical experiment here was again verbal. It used "free recall," a technique in which a list of words is presented for the subjects to recall in random order. A "primacy" and a "recency" effect were found. Subjects remembered the first and the last members better than those in the middle. If subjects were asked to count backwards by threes for half a minute after presentation, that interference drastically reduced the recency effect only. The conclusion was that the more recent final words were in short-term memory and were thus more vulnerable to interference, while the earlier words were already in long-term storage (Glanzer and Cunitz in Eysenck 1984).

The storage capacity of long-term memory and particularly of visual memory is enormously large compared to the meager five-to-seven-item capacity of short-term memory. This capaciousness is revealed especially if passive recognition rather than active recall is demanded. The slide experiments mentioned above attest to it. There are even more spectacular experiments in the recognition of names and faces (using members of the subjects' high-school class). They showed steady facial recognition of around ninety percent accuracy over a period of up to thirty-five years; faces were recalled slightly longer than names. This fact was the more amazing since a face carries far more features and therefore would seem to require much more storage than does a name. Toward the end, age-related memory-loss seemed to occur. The recognition of faces seems to be altogether a very special case. It actually improves up to a minute and a half after presentation if attention is aroused, and it seems to be particularly closely bound to interpretability, since inverted faces are hard to recognize at all (Baddeley 1978).

One explanation for the possibility of our amazing visual memory is that the quantity of information in a visual presentation is in fact helpful—a picture has so many features that a fraction only need be stored to catch the single discriminating feature needed for recognition. The storage process is perhaps facilitated by verbal means. But this explanation is weakened by certain tests devised to require more extensive consideration of features and to make verbal description less useful. Even under these conditions visual memory is highly successful; so the capaciousness of visual storage remains a mystery.

Long-term memory is also distinguished from active memory by its far slower speed of retrieval. Retrieving a memory that has been the recent object of attention is usually faster than the sometimes arduous process of recollection.

Evidence for this distinction comes from brain-damaged subjects with hippocampal lesions. Such patients have normal short-term memory, but they altogether fail to store some kinds of new information in long-term memory. The reverse correlation is rarer.

The long-term memory, as has been said, shows itself only in its effects, so that its constitution is hypothetical. There are alternative hypotheses to attempt to explain a pervasive, primarily visual, operation that reflects specifically on the nature of the imagination, namely, the recognition of patterns. The effect of recognition, once again, is in conscious memory, but its processes involve all three levels. Here is a simplified account that begins with the sensory icon becoming a short-term memory image. This image is then compared with the contents of long-term memory and recognized, which means that an identifying decision is made. But how?

These two hypotheses have currency: The template hypothesis treats long-term memory as a kind of library of replicas of stimuli. The comparison is done within this store by a matching operation, which first brings the image into a standard orientation and then tries to achieve a kind of coincidence, a congruent overlay as it were. The trouble with this otherwise perspicuous process is that the images derived from perception come in endless variants; how will they ever match a limited number of memory-templates? A propositional variant of the template hypothesis is the feature hypothesis, according to which the image is not fitted onto the long-term template as a whole but is analyzed into feature complexes. These are matched against feature lists that act as verbal templates, until a recognition decision is made.

The second, the prototype hypothesis, involves the image-schemata mentioned above. It supposes a set of rules for producing a model, a prototype or schematic representation, and a list of possible variations. There is some evidence favoring this hypothesis. It comes from experiments featuring sets of dot patterns that are displaced from a prototype—which is not shown—in such a way that the average of all the displacements yields the prototype. Subjects responded to the prototype itself, once it was shown, so fast as to lead to the inference that they had in fact already abstracted it from the displaced dots.

The prototype hypothesis is a recognizable empirical descendant of the Kantian schema of the imagination, "a rule for the synthesis of the imagination in respect to pure figures in space" (*CPR* B 180). And of course both the template and the prototype hypotheses are akin to Plato's myth of recollection and its application to mathematical learning (*Meno* 81). That myth, if treated as a cognitive hypothesis, implies that all imagery includes a moment of recognition when the matter under active consideration is matched against a prototype recollected from deep—mythically speaking, prenatal—memory. It seems that memory research tends to reinforce old intuitions.

(Baddeley 1976, 1978, Klatzky 1980, Richardson 1980, Arbinger 1984, Eysenck 1984.)

3. Forgetting: The Loss That Is a Gain. The pre-condition of remembering is forgetting. Neither what was never present in memory nor what is still active memory can be said to be recalled, recognized, retrieved, or restored.

In memory-study, however, forgetting is understood simply as any loss of information from any store. Hence it can have two meanings.

First, it can mean a dead loss. It is not known whether any information vanishes from memory without a trace. It is, however, a faith of laymen and psychologists alike, although it is an unverifiable faith, that no experience, no matter how apparently inaccessible, is ever totally lost (Eysenck

1984, 138). Penfield's famous experiments in the sixties seemed to support the common opinion. While operating on epileptic patients, he stimulated their brains in order to identify the affected areas; he found that they were re-experiencing, as opposed to merely remembering, events from their past. He inferred that we have a complete and neurologically accessible record or "imprint" of our personal past. But Penfield's results are doubtful. The number of patients who actually had such re-lived episodes was small (less than eight percent), and there was no way to verify that the recalls were actually biographical; they might have been imagined.

Psychoanalysis also hypothesizes, if not total storage of childhood events, at least a motivated deep forgetting, called repression, which can be reversed. Such recalls are again usually unverifiable. Furthermore, hypnotic recollections often turn out to be erroneous and subject to distortion, sometimes because of misleading questions. In short, the experimental evidence that memory never vanishes is weak, though perhaps unfalsifiable. Nonetheless, the sense that one's personal past is a permanent possession, stored like a reel of film, is not only beguiling. It is also, possibly, necessary to the maintenance of one's personal identity. Often enough twice-forgotten memories, memories one had fogotten that one had forgotten, swim up, raised by fortituous sensory cues, especially fragrances. Such recoveries do reinforce the belief that no experience is lost.

Ordinarily, however, forgetting just means losing information to another level of memory, where it establishes a memory-trace. Now each level loses and gains by its own special means. The following brief review of the established theory of forgetting is concerned only with visual memory, with imagery.

The sensory store is fed by ever new perceptual sights, but its icons decay speedily. They are taken up into short-term memory by the act of attention. Since this store has limited capacity, items are continually displaced into long-term memory. The implication is that the contents of this level do not fade but are pushed out. An ideal, though impossible, experiment would hold subjects mentally inactive for half a minute or so, to see if in that case items stay longer in this store. Intricate experiments show that the cause of short-term forgetting is in fact primarily displacement and only secondarily fading. Items in short-term memory are prepared by rehearsal for retention into long-term memory. Though this latter store is long in duration and enormous in capacity, it declines steadily over the years, particularly for verbal memory, the reason, apparently, being "interference." Interference may work either "proactively," when previously learned information makes it difficult to keep more recent learning in mind, or retroactively, when later acquisitions drive out the older.

One last important aspect of forgetting is "meta-memory," when, as Augustine puts it (X 13), "I remember myself as having remembered." This is the curious, little understood, and by no means error-free ability we have to tell whether we have forgotten something, and whether there is any use trying to recollect it. The peculiar deficit of this power is the forgetting of forgetting, which makes some of our memory store so inaccessible to intentional remembering that it may be said to be twice-forgotten. (Klatzky 1980, Arbinger 1984, Eysenck 1984.)

Forgetting and remembering are the less amenable to controlled study for being so deeply tied to affective significance. Think especially of the imagery of reminiscence and nostalgia, which is a quintessential but unregimentable part of memory, such as the aroma of scenes of childhood or the aura of places of history. Moreover the study of memory leaves largely unanswered questions involving our capacity for floating up incidental imagery: whether, for example, purely spontaneous reverie is possible or whether an associative cue is always required. Nor does the study deal with those memories that are marked by a sense of archetypal aboriginality. Reports of such imagery raise this question of questions: Is William James right when in his *Psychology* he opens the chapter on the imagination with this confident declaration?

> No mental copy . . . can arise in the mind of any kind of sensation which has never been directly excited from without.

Is this adoption into experimental psychology of the Aristotelian/Lockean dictum that "nothing is in the memory which was not first in the senses" necessary or warranted? Is memory stocked only by the senses, and are its images all replicas or recombinations? In sum, is all imagination memory? (Part One, Ch. II A; Part Three, Ch. III C).

Although this most pertinent of questions is not absolutely banished from memory-investigations, it has not been pursued very directly either. Experiments do provide the necessary starting places: namely the components and operations of the memory store, and in particular the storage and retrieval routes of perception-engendered imagery.

B. The Mnemonic Method of Places and Images

The practical side of the study of memory has a long history, but its effectiveness has been limited. This study is called mnemonics, the technique of remembering. Mnemonics is considered here because it sheds light on the nature of the visual imagination. There are, of course, non-visual mnemonic devices, such as jingles and acronymics, but these are just tricks. The ancient and long-lived art of visualized "places and images" is something more.

Only its fanatic adherents think that it is a generally useful art. Cicero gives a chief account of the method in antiquity (*De Oratore* I 34, II 86). One of his characters praises it faintly, saying "he doesn't altogether dislike it, being used to it." Some people, he adds, are merely crushed by the weight of imagery it involves. Another character gives this summary appraisal: "This practice cannot be used to draw out memory if no memory has been given by nature, but it can undoubtedly summon it to come forth if it is in hiding" (II 88). In 1596 the technique was even taught to the Chinese, by the Jesuit Mattei Ricci (Spence 1984). He reported to the general of his order a comment made by the eldest son of the governor of the Jiangxi province, who had successfully prepared for his civil service examination: "Though the precepts are the true rules of memory, one has to have a remarkably fine memory to make use of them." The real interest of the memory-art, it turns out, is not its usefulness as a recording technique but the vast and mysterious potency that it assigns to the imagination.

The method about to be described has a gruesome beginning in antiquity, a mysterious flowering in the Renaissance, and a meager but persistent after-life in the present. There is a recent theory that would even push the origin of memorial imagery back into prehistoric times. According to this theory, Stone Age caves like Lascaux and Altamira are in fact memory-theaters, whose murals were used in ceremonies revivifying tribal remembrances essential to survival (Pfeiffer 1982, Part Five, Ch. III B).

1. Contemporary Visual Memory Technique. Paivio's studies have shown methodically that the use of imagery enhances recall, a fact that is quite commonly known and exploited. Imagery is useful when it is necessary to remember things that have been forgotten through inattention. People quite naturally find things they have misplaced by mentally walking over the routes they have taken that day. Imagery is also used when the verbal description is cumbrous or sluggish. When asked which part of a sailboat is most forward, people tend to image the bowsprit before they name it. Finally, images have a memorial advantage when the memory-store has been deliberately prepared for its use. This preparation is the "method of loci" (Kosslyn 1983).

Contemporary presentations of this method give the following rules. In order to facilitate recall of an ordered list of things, use familiar visual images. Place these in connected locations, which can be mentally walked through. Make the images engage in some arresting but preferably not too bizarre interactions with their situations. For well-ordered retrieval, place one item in each place and don't do any shifting or changing. A current example involves a shopping list. The hot dogs in buns are disposed across the driveway and tomatoes are plastered onto the front door. Sometimes the imagery is suspended from some peg-word jingles, like "One is a bun . . . four is a door," that are used to bring objects to mind through their proper locations. These mundane enterprises are a great come-down from the historical art of memory.

(Bower and Bugelski in Spoehr and Lehmkuhle 1982.)

2. The Ancient Method of Loci. In Cicero's text, the method is referred to "as that device of places and replicas (*loci et simulacra*) which is taught in the art of rhetoric" (I 34). Its ominous founding anecdote is told by the character Anthony. The Greek poet Simonides (whose fame Ricci is later to spread among the Chinese as Xi-mon-de) was at dinner with a Thessalian patron, Scopas. The poet had just sung a lyric poem he had composed in honor of his host, embellishing it, as was the poetic manner, with a long passage celebrating the heroes Castor and Pollux, the Heavenly Twins. Scopas had meanly withheld half the honorarium agreed upon, saying that for the other half the poet should apply to the heroes who had shared the encomium. Now a message came for Simonides, to the effect that there were two young men waiting to see him outside. He left the banquet hall but found no one about. At this moment the roof fell in, crushing everyone inside and mangling the corpses beyond recognition, to the distress of the relatives when they came to bury their own. Suddenly it dawned on Simonides, the sole survivor, that he could identify their bodies by envisioning the guests' locations on the dining-couches. He inferred, Cicero reports, that one might train the memory by mentally forming "effigies" and storing them in chosen "loci." (The term of the art is Latin *locus* rather than Greek *topos*, which was already preempted by rhetoric.) The "effigies" represent the facts while the loci preserve their order, for orderly arrangement best aids the "light of memory."

Anthony goes on to say that our most complete mental pictures belong to things conveyed and imprinted by the senses, of which sight is the keenest. Therefore even items received by hearing or by "cogitation" are most easily retained when they are also mediated by sight. A sort of figure, or visual image, is presented even by objects not immediately in the field of visual discernment. Such para-vision enables us to hold in awareness things that we scarcely embrace by thought. (This observation prefigures the barely conscious "cognitive maps" of modern psychology.) In addition, visualized objects need a setting: "But the forms and bodies, like all things which come into view, require a seat, since a body without place is unintelligible" (II 87). In other words, the art of memory requires that items be fitted into spatial context.

Memory for words, he goes on, is less necessary for a speaker than memory for things. Anthony is here tacitly adapting Cato's rule of rhetoric: "Cleave to things; the words will follow." This holds particularly because words too can be turned into images. Since not only nouns but verbs and conjunctions can be imaged, a great variety of images is needed. However, these will be not natural "similitudes" but conventional constructs.

Most of Cicero's account is, as we see, concerned with rhetorical applications. Nevertheless, the Simonides story is something more than merely a founding myth for a curious technique. The dark tale of the poet's reward intimates that the two half-gods have given him, besides his life, not so much a mnemonic technique—for what would an original poet want with that?—as the traumatic illumination, bought at brutal human expense, of his own inner world, a storehouse, even a charnel house, of indelible sights. The tale fits the man who first said that "painting is silent poetry, poetry is silent painting," a man obviously attentive to the internal transmutations of experience (Part Four, Ch. I B).

Simonides's discovery comes to its most significant fruition in Augustine's description of the "spacious halls and fields of memory" within which he disports himself, searching out all the remembered world. This memorial terrain is certainly a version of the connected loci (filled with imaged objects) that the rhetoricians describe. Yet his inner circumambulations are not for the sake of practical remembrance. Instead they have a spiritual aim: He is rejoicing in the glories of his inner world while searching for God. Behind the rather trivial technique of memory loci there stands the conscious discovery of the soul's imaginative space, the world of the imagination.

3. The Two Compared. Ancient and contemporary mnemonics invite comparison. The "sharp images," the "effigies," and the "simulacra" recommended for practical use in the Roman texts are just those hard-edged, precise copies called for in modern experiments. The ancient accounts bring out the primacy, even in verbal contexts, of visual over verbal memory—the primacy that is corroborated in Paivio's experiments. They also prefigure the contemporary interest in the spatial representations of rational operations (Part Five, Ch. II B).

The ancient rules of "artificial memory composed of places and images" are most explicitly set out in the memory section of the Pseudo-Ciceronian textbook on rhetoric *Ad Herrenium*, of the late first century B.C. Here the rules for loci call for the visualization of a large number of places such as houses or columned spaces, seriated so as to allow equally orderly forward or backward movement. Loci may be reused. It is best to use solitary places, since crowds of people interfere with impressions. The places should not be too brightly lit or set too widely apart, "since like the external eye the inner eye of thought is less powerful when you have moved the object of sight too near or too far away." (This observation prefigures one of Kosslyn's "privileged properties"—Ch. II B.) The loci should be remembered sites, though fictitious places will do.

The rules for the images of the objects and persons themselves, on the other hand, call for dramatic invention. These images are to be as striking, extraordinary, and active as possible, very beautiful or very ugly, ornamented with crowns and purple cloaks, stained with blood or smeared with red paint. In short, the sights are to be as novel, grand, even lurid as imagination can devise (Yates 1966).

The contemporary technique is similar in most points. The settings are to be ordered and ordinary, sparsely populated, moderately lit, and spaced. What is strikingly different is the choice of images. The imaginations of the ancients runs to the drama of blood-stained kings, that of the moderns to the triteness of spattered tomatoes. My guess is that the reason is not uninteresting. The grander, pre-modern art of memory had raised the mystery of the imaginative world only tacitly. The recognition of a specific imaginative consciousness is very much a modern achievement. As this inner world was taken increasingly seriously, practical mnemonics was finally and completely abandoned to banality.

4. The Mnemonic Mysteries of the Renaissance. In the Renaissance the art of memory achieved the high point of the grandeur just mentioned. I pass over medieval memory-methods except to point out a serendipitous misreading made by its most famous theorist, Thomas Aquinas himself. Thomas accidentally introduces a new notion: an affective element in memory. He gives it as a precept that one should "dwell with solicitude on, and cleave with affection to" the things one wishes to remember. Thomas, reading "solicitude" for "solitude," had misread the ancient rule that loci should be unpeopled (*Summa Theologica* Qu. XLIX). The error points up a curious deficit in previous memory treatises. The enormous affective power of memory-images is, notwithstanding the gore, usually ignored (except, of course, by Augustine). What facilitated Thomas's error was the Christianization of memory, the investment of its places and figures with "spiritual intentions" and devotional intensity.

In the Renaissance all things come together to lead to a last and greatest flowering of the art. The following account of the high points—like the account of Thomas's misreading—is borrowed from the learned and wonderful *Art of Memory* by Frances Yates (1966).

From the point of view of their imagery, the most remarkable characteristic of the great Renaissance memory-methods is the mystery and magnificence of their places. (Memory-places are given special consideration in Part Six.) Recall that in the ancient treatises and in modern methods the loci are, in contrast, by preference mundanely real and merely remembered. They are the commonplace settings for the object images, necessary because "a body without a place is unintelligible."

Johannes Romberch was a Dominican trained in the memory tradition of Thomas and familiar with the ancient treatises. In his *Compendium of Artificial Memory* (1520) remembered mundane places are of low importance. His first place-system is the cosmos itself: the heavenly paradise, the elements, the planets, the stars, the celestial spheres, the nine orders of angels in ascending order, and, descending into the depths, the earthly paradise, purgatory, and hell. The images to fill this world are of secondary interest.

Miss Yates suggests that the *Divine Comedy*, especially Purgatory and Hell, may indeed be a memory-system for concentrating the mind on sins and their punishment, "a summa of similitudes and exempla." Indeed Romberch's Italian translator takes Dante to have meant just that: The places of Hell are memory loci for the punishment of sins. (Recall that Simonides's prototypical mnemonic was already a map of retributions meted out for impiety.) If the setting of the *Divine Comedy* is indeed a memory place, it corroborates the notion that the practical art of memory, so narrow in its mundane function, has enormous possibilities as the free art of vivid and capacious imagining.

The Dominican tradition comes to a riotous climax with the eclectically mythical and magical works of Giordano Bruno, published in the ninth decade of the sixteenth century. Miss Yates is persuaded that the rampant occultism of the memory treatises has a hidden agenda, a hermetic secret, something having to do with the power of the imagination to bring the cosmos inside the soul in such a way that not its appearances but its significance takes hold. For Bruno transforms the meaning of Aristotle's dictum that there is no thought without its image. For him, thinking *is* imagining; there is no separate intellectual faculty (Yates, 257). Thus he drives Simonides's discovery of the convertibility of painting and poetry to an extreme: The *phantastica virtus* belongs to painters, poets, and philosophers alike; in some way each of these is all the others. To read Miss Yates's patient explication of Bruno's fanatically ramified symbols and images is to experience the dual sense of frisson and tedium that is felt in the presence of a crazy approach to a wondrous possibility. The Romantics will elaborate this dualism (Part Four, Ch. II).

To Bruno's system of places and images was opposed the rational mnemotechnic of Peter Ramus, a system eschewing visual imagery in favor of dialectic divisions. Its interest in this context is that it exemplifies for the Renaissance the propositionalist approach to imagery.

Here is the place to mention again the Jesuit Matteo Ricci, who carried the art of memory to far places. He was himself a remarkable memorialist. In the short memory-method he wrote for the Chinese in 1596 he proposes, in opposition to the ancients, place-constructions of enormous complexity. The loci are to consist of several hundred palaces, pavilions, and divans, real, fictive, or mixed. These he fills with numerous statues, which he groups by tens with a mental mark, as *Ad Herrenium* had advocated—as providence would have it, the Chinese ideograph for ten is the sign of the cross (Spence 1984).

The place of scenic visions *par excellence* is the theater. The once-famous memory-theatre of Giulio Camillo (early 16th cent.) is an imaginative conception, but one intended for external realization. It was the plan for a set on which the beholder was to see with his eyes all that is hidden in the human mind, expressed by corporeal signs. There actually was a famous wooden structure that realized a plan of this sort. In effect it re-externalized the world that had previously been collected in memory through the senses.

Robert Fludd was Camillo's counterpart in England, a hermeticist and a proponent of "the science of spiritual memorizing which is vulgarly called *Ars Memoriae.*" His account of the memory art is headed by a picture, the only one I have ever seen, of the notorious mind's eye which so dominates imagery-investigations. It is a wide-open *oculus imaginationis* located in the upper part of a bald man's temple (1619). Fludd's theater plans again incorporate the world. What gives them special poignancy is Miss Yates's demonstration that their features turn up in the Globe Theatre. Shakespeare's Globe as a corporeal memory world—the story ends as it had begun, with the poets.

Thereafter printing and science drive out the art of memory. But "if memory was the Mother of the Muses, she was also to be the Mother of Method" (Yates 306). The Franciscan Ramon Lull, Thomas Aquinas's contemporary, had invented an art not at all of loci and replicas, but of moving geometric diagrams and symbols. This combinatory art could be used—here was a new turn—not only for remembering but also for logical investigations. Bruno had been proud of having assimilated Lull's method.

Leibniz knew it well, and it seems to have played a role in the invention of his combinatory art and the "universal characteristic," that is, symbolic logic. Lull's logic, the forerunner of Leibniz's logic, is thus a science neither of images nor of words, but of symbols. Of the three great mnemonic representational systems, it is the symbolic one which proves to be most specifically adapted to the modern world.

Twenty-four hundred years ago, Plato had Socrates issue a warning against external memory. He attacks writing as "that drug of recall rather than recollection," a drug which leads to learning without understanding (*Phaedrus* 275). Now the ancient mnemonic technique is described as interior writing by both Cicero and the author of *Ad Herrenium*. In this metaphor the reusable loci are like wax tablets and the erasable images are the script. Consequently, the mnemonic method is subject to the same Socratic strictures as writing. Mnemonic memory is as much a surface record as scribblings on papyrus. Indeed, just as memory techniques become pretty nearly obsolete with the advent of that massive external memory, the printed book, so memory itself falls into disuse with the proliferation of recording devices. Our memory-slate can afford to be empty because our file cabinets are full.

Insofar, therefore, as the method of loci and replicas teaches tricks for remembering speeches and shopping lists, it is in our day a peripheral technique at best. But insofar as the art of places and images exercises the human capability for inner world-making, it is as fresh as ever, for it is simply the imagination doing its cardinal work.

Bibliography

Arbinger, Roland. 1984. *Gedächtnis*. Darmstadt: Wissenschaftliche Buchgesellschaft.

Augustine. [c. 397]. *Confessions* (X).

Baddeley, Alan D. 1976. *The Psychology of Memory*. New York: Basic Books.

———. 1978. "The Trouble with Levels: A Reexamination of Craik and Lockhart's Framework for Memory Research." *Psychological Review* 85:139–152.

Block, Ned, ed. 1981. *Imagery*. Cambridge: The MIT Press.

Brown, Roger and Herrnstein, Richard J. 1981. "Icons and Images." In *Imagery*, edited by Ned Block. Cambridge: The MIT Press.

Cicero, Marcus Tullius [55 BC]. *De Oratore* (I 34, II 86).

Ebbinghaus, Hermann. 1885. *Memory: A Contribution to Experimental Psychology*. New York: Dover Publications (1964).

Ellis, Henry C., and Hunt, R. Reed, eds. 1983. *Fundamentals of Human Memory and Cognition*, 3d ed. Dubuque: Wm. C. Brown Company.

Eysenck, Michael W. 1984. *A Handbook of Cognitive Psychology*. Hillsdale, N.J.: Lawrence Erlbaum Associates.

Flanagan, Owen J. 1984. *The Science of the Mind*. Cambridge: The MIT Press.

Galton, Sir Francis. 1883. *Inquiries into Human Faculty and Its Development*. New York: E. P. Dutton and Company (1928).

Gruneberg, Michael M., and Morris, Peter, eds. 1978. *Aspects of Memory*. London: Methuen.

Hering, Ewald. 1870. *Memory: Lectures on the Specific Energies of the Nervous System*. Chicago: Open Court (1913).

Hunter, Ian M. L. 1957. *Memory: Facts and Fallacies*. Baltimore: Penguin.

Husserl, Edmund. 1904–05. *Phenomenology of Internal Time-Consciousness* (paras. 11–13).

Klatzky, Roberta L. 1980. *Human Memory: Structures and Processes*. San Francisco: W.H. Freeman and Co.

Kosslyn, Stephen M. 1980. *Image and Mind*. Cambridge: Harvard University Press.

———. 1983. *Ghosts in the Mind's Machine*. New York: W.W. Norton and Company.

Kosslyn, Stephen M., and Holyoak, Keith J. 1982. "Imagery." In *Handbook of Research Methods in Human Memory and Cognition*, edited by Richard C. Puff. New York: Academic Press.

Mandler, Jean M. 1983. "Representation." In *Handbook of Child Psychology*, Volume 3, *Cognitive Development*, edited by Paul H. Mussen. New York: John Wiley and Sons.

McCarthy, Rosaleen A., and Warrington, E. K. 1988. "Evidence for Modality-Specific Meaning Systems in the Brain." *Nature* 334:428–430.

Mill, James. 1829. *Analysis of the Phenomena of the Human Mind*. London: Longmans (1869).

Miller, G. A. 1956. "The Magical Number Seven, Plus or Minus Two: Some Limits on Our Capacity for Processing Information." *Psychological Review* 63:81–97.

Paivio, Allan. 1971. *Imagery and Verbal Processes*. New York: Holt, Rinehart and Winston.

———. 1984. "The Empirical Case for Dual Coding." In *Imagery, Memory and Cognition: Essays in Honor of Allan Paivio*, edited by John C. Yuille. Hillsdale, N.J.: Lawrence Erlbaum Associates.

Pfeiffer, John E. 1982. *The Creative Explosion: An Inquiry into the Origins of Art and Religion*. Ithaca: Cornell University Press.

Puff, Richard C., ed. 1982. *Handbook of Research Methods in Human Memory and Cognition*. New York: Academic Press.

Richardson, John T. E. 1980. *Mental Imagery and Human Memory*. New York: St. Martin's Press.

Seamon, John G., ed. 1980. *Human Memory: Contemporary Readings*. Oxford: Oxford University Press.

Sheehan, Peter W., ed. 1972. *The Function and Nature of Imagery*. New York: Academic Press.

Sheikh, Anees A., ed. 1983. *Imagery: Current Theory, Research, and Application*. New York: John Wiley and Sons.

Spence, Jonathan D. 1984. *The Memory Palace of Matteo Ricci*. New York: Viking, Elisabeth Sifton Books.

Spoehr, Kathryn T., and Lehmkuhle, Stephen W. 1982. *Visual Information Processing*. San Francisco: W.H. Freeman and Co.

Straus, Erwin W. 1970. "Phenomenology of Memory." In *Phenomenology of Memory: Third Lexington Conference on Pure and Applied Phenomenology*, edited by Erwin Straus and Richard M. Griffith. Pittsburgh: Duquesne University Press.

Yates, Frances A. 1966. *The Art of Memory*. London: Routledge and Kegan Paul.

Yuille, John C., ed. 1983. *Imagery, Memory and Cognition: Essays in Honor of Allan Paivio*. Hillsdale, N.J.: Lawrence Erlbaum Associates.

————, and Marschark, Marc. 1983. "Imagery Effects on Memory: Theoretical Interpretations." In *Imagery: Current Theory, Research, and Application*. New York: John Wiley and Sons

Chapter IV

Children's Imagery

The is general agreement that, for better or worse, as a form of childlikeness or of childishness, the imagination is the domain of children. Critics berate rationality for stifling the youthfully spontaneous play of the spirit, while philosophers denigrate poetry as being the unreflective mode of the juvenile mind (Part Six, Ch. I A).

Children are thought to exhibit special imagination in three ways: There is a specific kind of imagery that occurs in children more often than in adults (A). There is a developmental stage of childhood in which the imagination is a preferred cognitive mode (B). Children are thought to be more imaginative in the sense that the quality, intensity, spontaneity, and quantity of their imagery exceed those of ordinary adults in degree (C).

A. By Kind: Eidetic, or External, Imagery

Some people, about one in twenty children but fewer adults, have the ability to project their internal visual impressions onto an external surface so that they can, as it were, inspect them there. This ability is akin to photographic memory in that the imagery is a precise copy of the percept, though such external projections are not as long-term or as accurate as are the inner "photographs."

These children are called *eidetikers*, a greco-teutonic term based on the Greek word for a lucidly visible form, *eidos*. It signifies that the eidetic image (*Anschauungsbild*) is seen externally rather than internally. Such imagery was much studied in the twenties and thirties, primarily by Jaensch. He hoped that eidetic imagery would elucidate the relation of perception to thought, since it was an event unifying sensation and memory. This first phase of the investigation got side-tracked into speculation about *eidetiker* types. After an eclipse of more than three decades there was another surge of research in the sixties, whose main results are reported here.

The trouble, however, is that psychologists cannot quite make up their minds whether or not the subject is interesting in its own right. The reason is that it is hard to say whether a genuinely special kind of imagery is involved and whether such images are really peculiar to children.

A ten-year-old boy is shown a picture of Alice in Wonderland looking up at the Cheshire cat sitting in a tree (before vanishing). He looks at it for half a minute. After it is removed he looks at a blank easel and is given a few seconds to project the image. The question is asked: How many stripes did the cat's tail have? He answers correctly, sixteen. Most people could not do that unless they had deliberately counted the stripes in the picture—a non-imagistic response.

The older eidetic studies suffered from the uncertainties of self-reporting and the fact that the subjects were children and hard to monitor. In the later studies a fairly fool-proof technique was introduced. Subjects were shown two pictures in succession, so constructed that when superimposed on each other they yielded an entirely unpredictable new figure or scene. Some children could superimpose their imagery in this demanding way, which required them first to take in, then to project both pictures in turn, and then to compound the two—often to their own surprise—into a new one. As it turns out, the most spectacular results were obtained with Julesz patterns, which are apparently-random dot configurations that, when superimposed, yield a discernible figure. These results, however, were achieved by an (evidently unique) adult woman.

Eidetic images have a number of distinguishing features. They differ from afterimages, the alternating phases of positive and negative imagery (or of complementary colors for colored stimuli) seen after short, sharp flashes of light. Afterimages are "burnt on" the retina and so move with the eye, while eidetic images can be scanned. Eidetic images, unlike afterimages, do not require a brief, high-contrast stimulus, and they last about two-thirds of a minute longer.

Further characteristics of eidetic images are these: Eidetikers talk about their images as being "out there," sharp and vivid. These images do not blur as a whole but fade away in parts. They subtend visual angles of less than three degrees, roughly the angle covered by the fovea, where acuity is greatest. If asked to shift the images across the projecting surface, subjects report that they "drop over the edge"; in other words, they are surface-bound. Once gone, they cannot be revived. Labeling, attending to, or rehearsing the objects in the picture interferes with the image. Eidetikers do not seem to be otherwise distinguishable as a group.

There is less and less certainty that eidetic imagery is a distinct kind. It may be simply a very vivid visual memory, the iconic phase greatly prolonged and projected. Nor is it so clear as it once seemed that such imagery is the special preserve of children. Evidently in technologically less advanced societies the incidence of adult eidetikers is somewhat higher than among us. It may be that a speech-oriented environment interferes with a semi-perceptual ability certain individuals happen to possess. (Haber 1969, Spoehr and Lehmkuhle 1982, Eysenck 1984.)

Eidetic imagery does not require, in fact hardly allows for, the use of the imagination in the ordinary sense, and so it seems to be the least significant of second sights. There exists, however, a recent, highly speculative, proposal to include within the term "eidetic" any experience, recognized by the imager as subjective, that has an element of external projection and for which no sensory stimulus is present. It would thus include everything from very vivid imagination-imagery to crystal gazing. Under such an expanded definition eidetic imagery is said to be a universal sub-phenomenon, a "massive underground" of representations hitherto undetected by psychologists, and of great clinical and even therapeutic value.

The profit in all this speculation appears to be that it raises old questions, still unanswered, about the element in imagery that makes it seem to be "out there" rather than inside. Is it merely its vividness or is it something about the content of the image itself? What internal feature distinguishes eidetic imagery from hallucinations, which are precisely defined by the fact that the imager does not recognize them as subjective? Finally, what is it about projected imagery that makes our civilization rather severely unreceptive to eidetic vision, and ought we to try to encourage it more? (Marks, McKellar, and commentators 1982.)

B. By Stage: Imagination as a Cognitive Mode

In watching children through any day, the question arises whether they are the unspoilt exemplars of all humanity or perhaps not quite yet members of the human race at all. Its cognitive version is this: Is children's cognition merely more limited than that of adults, or essentially different?

Developmental psychology takes up scientifically questions concerning both the moral and the theoretical knowledge of children. All the great works on education acknowledge the centrality of the imagination in children's learning, although in different ways: In Plato's *Republic* the children are raised on the carefully selected images of poetry. In Rousseau's *Émile* children are described as capable of receiving images as easily as sensations, while ideas are merely reflected off their unready minds like images off a mirror. Rousseau's recommendation of imagery for the training of children and his aversion to book learning assumes that children have a genuine cognitive incapacity for reasoning, while Plato's preference takes account of their attentional, affective, and moral readiness. It has been shown that attention is indeed from the very beginning a crucial factor in learning. Babies had been thought to lack the most fundamental of all cognitive capacities, namely "object constancy," the expectation that objects will persist. It turns out that their failure to search for an object that has been made to disappear is largely a function of inattention. When their attention is engaged infants try to find the missing target (Siegel and Brainerd 1978). In short, the chief problem concerning children's imagination is whether it ought to be regarded as an expression of a cognitive deficit. Does the juvenile imagination operate before and, as it were, in lieu of the intellect?

1. *The Stage Theory of Development: Piaget.* The leading developmental theory of cognition is that of Piaget (Scholnick 1983). He calls his inquiry the science of "genetic epistemology." He means that cognition comes into being not alone through the pre-existent characteristics belonging to the object, nor only through the congenital internal structures of the subject (Piaget 1970, 14). Instead structures develop in stages by means of "adaptation," which is a process with two aspects. One is assimilation, which adapts the external object to the existing stage. The other is accommodation, which modifies the internal structure to fit the object. The balanced coordination of these aspects is called equilibration. The development as a whole is fulfilled in a fully operational intelligence, by which Piaget means the ability not merely to use the operations of logic but to use them formally, to recognize the general invariances of nature. In short, the end is the scientific use of reason.

This development occurs in four major stages. The imaginal stage is wedged between the first stage and the third. Before briefly sketching the surrounding stages, a word needs to be said about the notion of stage itself.

A stage is formally marked by these criteria: It has to be qualitatively discontinuous with its adjoining stages, but there must be recognizable transitions. The structures that identify a stage should form something of a coherent ensemble. Though the actual age for any stage may vary within limits and though there can be some unevenness of development for different tasks within each stage (*décalage* or "unwedging"), the structures themselves must develop in invariant sequences. This last criterion is crucial. It means that the development is "autonomous," essentially unmodifiable by affective or attentional factors.

The first stage of infant cognition is representationless. Piaget uses the word representation in a wider and a narrower sense. The wider encompasses intelligent cognition itself, or any knowledge "based on a system of concepts or mental schemata." The narrower sense refers to "symbolic representation," by which Piaget means "the capacity to evoke by a sign or a symbolic image an absent object or action not yet carried out." (The word symbol has a double use too. Sometimes it refers to "motivated" signs that signify by resembling—1946, 68; sometimes it means just the opposite: signs that represent arbitrarily or by convention.) The play of babies is pure practice, self-pleasing repetition. It implies no symbolism. They do not, for example, move little white objects around and say "meow," or search for objects that have disappeared from their view, or engage in "deferred imitation," re-enacting later some behavior they have seen earlier. (In contrast, Freud conjectured that the origin of thought is linked to the infant's hallucination-like recall of the mother's absent breast—*Formulations on the Two Principles of Psychic Events* 1911. This postulate provided the basis for later Freudian phantasy studies—Isaacs 1952.) Piaget calls this collection of sub-stages the "sensorimotor" stage, because before development of representations, manifestations of intelligence appear in sensory perceptions and motor activities. The baby follows objects with its eyes and grasps at things, eventually with purposeful and experimental intentions. It knows how to do a great many things but it does not know that something is the case.

In the last of the several sub-stages making up this phase, between a year and a half to two years, the child shows signs of having symbolic representations, namely those listed above as having been absent before. One might say that the internal sight of objects succeeds the touch of them. This sub-stage ushers in the second, the "pre-operational" stage, which is the time of the image *par excellence*, from two to seven years.

At about school age the child evidences a number of cognitive advances. These pre-operational children are so centered on themselves that they scarcely take alternative opinions into account. Since their views are, according to Piaget, narrow and dominated by their own present perception, they can pay attention only to one aspect of a total situation. Consequently, they fail in "conservation." It is a key ability, the recognition that in physical transformations one factor may remain invariant. In Piaget's most famous experiment, children are shown two identical glasses with an equal amount of liquid. When they have agreed that both glasses hold the same amount of liquid, the contents of one of the glasses is poured into a taller and slimmer glass. Pre-operational children will fail to observe conservation, for they will claim either that there is more liquid in the new glass because it is higher, or in the old one because it is wider. This stage will be taken up again below (2).

Seven-year-olds begin to conserve. Children are now less centered on themselves. They are substituting thought for perception, and of course they are more adept users of language. Underlying all these advances is the development of logical operations, in particular those of common arithmetic. These are, however, still applied to concrete situations. Hence this third stage is called "concrete-operational." The operations of this stage make possible a new kind of imagery with a more sophisticated use.

The fourth stage, called "formal-operational," begins at eleven or twelve. It marks the full development of reflexive rationality, in the sense that formal operations are performed on the propositions that were the result of the concrete operations. Thus they are "second order" or abstract operations. This stage corresponds to the scientist's hypothetical-deductive reasoning.

I might mention here another, derivative set of developmental stages devised by Bruner (1964). It consists of three stages dominated in turn by action, imagery, and language. In the first, the cognitive mode is enactive representation. Past events are represented by an appropriate motor response, such as the unreflective tying of a knot. The next mode is termed iconic representation. Now past percepts are represented by a selective organization into images. Finally, the symbols of language represent objects and events conventionally without resembling them. These symbols can be combined far more flexibly than can images. Again, the imagery stage initiates representation proper.

What characterizes both theories is that the old philosophic apprehension of the imagination as standing between perception and intellect is, as it were, cast into time and turned into a developmental sequence.

2. Piagetan Imagery. While imagery was still in the limbo of ostracism in America, in Geneva Piaget was subjecting it to an extensive experimental and conceptual inquiry. His study of children's imagination was not merely incidental to the fact that he was a developmental psychologist. For the imagination, he thought, held a front and center position at only one stage in the cognitive life span, in early childhood.

Piaget's theory, together with its elaborations by many collaborators is diffusely set out over several narratives. It is summarized here under four headings: philosophical assumptions and definitions, classification, developmental staging, and image-cognition.

(Piaget 1946, and Inhelder 1963, 1966, 1968, Mandler 1983; for Piaget's work on geometric imagery, which preceded that on perceptual imagery, see Part Five, Ch. I C.)

The cognitive study of Chapter II above opened with a minimal assumption: Mental images have certain "privileged properties." These, together with converging experimental results, yield simultaneously a full description and an existence proof of imagery. Piaget, on the other hand, begins with one strong philosophical assumption. "Images are an instrument of knowledge and therefore depend on cognitive functions" (1963, 653).

Two further axioms guide his experimentation on imagery. One is that the imagination is not an aboriginal faculty, but that it is to be understood as a level of semiotic development. The other is that there is indeed a cognitive level of figurative thought where the image rules.

The two cognitive functions, or poles of cognition, on which images depend are the "figurative" and the "operational." Between them these functions comprise all cognition, representationless and representational. Their activity is in turn based on the "semiotic" or signifying function. The semiotic function of representations is their capacity for conveying meanings. (To make this function all-encompassing, it is forced to include, by courtesy, the lowest, non-representational level.) The meaning-function has a double aspect: signs or "signifiers" and objects signified or "significates." Neither signs nor objects exist absolutely but both emerge together, level by level, through the reciprocal interaction of subject and object. Thus "objectivity is the result of progressive conquest." The account of this conquest, abstracted from the temporal development, is precisely a genetic epistemology; it is vaguely reminiscent of Kant's progressive synthesis, which issues in the construction of the knowable object (Part One, Ch. III D).

The level of cognition is higher as its object is more comprehensive. On the lowest, perceptual, level the sign is not separated from the signified object. The blue sky, for example, is perceived as a mere mute index of the presence of light. One might say the sign has no cognitive distance from the object signified. The next level is the first that is properly semiotic. The object is symbolically represented by a digested, transformed, inner schematization, a memory-image, though only on a restricted scale. But the image of the blue sky as a sensory object is not yet adequate to either the telescopic or the microscopic investigation of light. Objects of so expanded a scale of comprehensiveness belong to the ultimate, though indefinitely progressive, level of cognition. It is that of physical science. Its representations are neither percepts nor images but conventional symbols representing the invariances of light on the most general scale.

Thus the ultimate signified object comes into being. This genesis may be recapitulated on the side of the sign: On the first level the sky and its brilliant blue, signified object and sign, are one. True symbolic representation arises on the next level. The blue expanse is reproduced internally as a memory-image or externally in play-enactments and drawings. Piaget here takes the image quite traditionally, as a sign that signifies an object in its absence through resemblance. And finally arise conventionally symbolic signs, together with the properly symbolic use of natural language. These signify generalized objects. Thus equations represent the properties not only of celestial blue but of all light anywhere (1966, 385; 1968, 10).

This account of the semiotic function is misleading with respect to our central concern, the image-sign. It makes it look as if the figural image always signified a figural object. Piaget maintains, however, that an image can also signify a concept, as in the visualization of geometric objects. Images, it turns out, are evocations not only of figural objects but of relations and classes. (Piaget here anticipates the figurative mental modeling of logical relations currently important in cognitive science—Part Five, Ch. II B). The image converts these latter into concrete "simili-sensible" form. Hence images signify and evoke not only by resemblance but in some other (mysterious) way: The function of the image "is to designate, not to interpret" (1966, 383). That is to say, the image does not need to get involved in the object or concept it signifies; it just represents them from afar. Where objects are to be represented the image simply renders their figural properties; but how a concept is designated Piaget does not say.

Once again it is misleading to say that the image simply renders the object. Instead it usually schematizes what it represents. Piaget does not conceive of this imaginal schematization as an interpretive operation on the object in its own representative mode. The schema does not take its cue from the object. Rather it "stylizes" the object. For that is what figural symbolizing is—a simplifying and regularizing operation. The cognitive profit is economy: there are far fewer image-schemata than there are percepts.

The two chief cognitive functions on which imagery depends, operational and figurative, can now be seen as being just those which describe the cognitive business done on the several semiotic levels. To the already familiar operational function belongs the activity of the highest level, where logical operations are expressed in conventional symbols to formulate general laws. Since this function actually transforms its objects, it is essentially dynamic.

To the figurative function belongs the work of the lower semiotic levels. It has three phases: First, perception is an activity that takes place in the presence of its object; in it sign and signified object are one. Second, imitation begins as an internal motor reproduction of an object or action subsequently re-manifested; here a distance is beginning to be put between sign and object. Third, images represent objects in their absence by resembling symbols; on this, the semiotic middle level, sign and signified object are well and truly driven apart and figurative symbolic representation is in full force.

As operations are dynamic so the images themselves are quintessentially static. Piaget insists on this imaginal property over and over again, on philosophical and experimental grounds. Images are debarred from movement by a "congenital sin." When they do show motion it is because they are under the control of the operational function (1966, 375). In this insistence, Piaget seems to join psychological observation and deference to the tradition that opposes the functioning intellect to its passive mental matter. More particularly, Piaget defers to the Kantian distinction between the receptive intuition and the spontaneously functioning understanding.

If Piaget here maintains a vague connection to Kant, he vigorously opposes Hume, for whom images arise from the first as simple copies of perception and connect themselves by their own mechanisms of association (Part One, Ch. III C). Piaget, as has been intimated, thinks that the genesis of imagery is in motor imitation, not in sensory perception. Thus images are never mere percept-traces. They may seem subjectively veracious, but they are objectively only approximations of perceptions. Piaget justifies images cognitively, however, by the argument that the distortions caused by perception are worse than imaginal distortions. For perception is influenced by chance encounters with external objects, while the imagistic schematization distorts internally and therefore purposefully. The observational argument against Hume cites the very late genesis of non-static imagery; since percepts are highly mobile, if they were the source of imagery, it too would be mobile at inception. Hume's associationism, which puts the burden of connection-making on the imagery itself, is directly opposed by Piaget's view that images are inert and thought alone operates actively.

Piaget also classifies images by class as opposed to developmental stages, so as to get better experimental control of them. Since children usually cannot give good verbal descriptions, and since he did not have chronometric techniques such as mental rotation, he mainly used drawings for classificatory evidence.

The major division yields "reproductive" and "anticipatory" images. Reproductive images recall objects or events already known from direct experience; they are memory-images. Anticipatory images prefigure what has not yet been perceived or learned.

From the point of view of schematic type, both classes of imagery can be static, kinetic (figuring changes of position), or transformational (figuring changes of form). However, Piaget's experiments show that for children under seven reproductive evocations of motion are absent, so that pre-operational reproductive imagery is in fact only static. Indeed, Piaget claims that even adults have some trouble reproducing the continuity of motion, that the movement-image keeps getting stuck and prolonging itself (1966, 363).

In fact, pre-operational children are said to lack the whole class of anticipatory imagery. Anticipatory imagery is, for Piaget's purposes, always kinetic or transformational. It is the projective tracing of a motion or an alteration so as to anticipate its outcome. It follows that there is no place for static anticipatory imagery in his classification. This is interesting, because it is exactly a type of imagination-image, namely the depiction of magic and fantasy, which is thereby excluded: Fantasy largely consists of tableaux never yet perceived (Part Four, Ch. IV B).

There is one more cross-classification. Reproductive images can be immediate or deferred. On the face of it, since all memory-images are deferred evocations, an immediate image, which is simultaneous with its object, might seem to be a contradiction in terms. As a matter of fact, such simultaneous visions do, I think, occur and can be peculiarly affect-laden. However, Piaget explains that his immediate reproductive image is a "fore-image," not so much a vision as an incipient gesture. Such internal gesturing effects the internalization of perception. It plays an important role in Piaget's theory that images arise through imitation (1966, 4).

Rousseau is Piaget's forerunner in positing a purely imaginal stage of cognitive development: "Before the age of reason," Rousseau says, "the child receives images but not ideas." As has been mentioned, Rousseau, like Piaget, considers it futile to try to teach a child anything too early. But, as a proto-Romantic child-admirer, he values the imaginative stage for lacking precisely that socialized rationality which is for Piaget the perfection of cognitive development. Between them, the two Genevans span the range of estimations that the imagination has undergone in our tradition.

When the abstract epistemological levels are cast into time, we ought to see the cognitive stages of actual developing children. The first, third, and fourth, the sensorimotor and the two operational stages, have been sketched out above. The pre-operational imagery stage, the one pertinent to this exposition, arises when at the end of the sensorimotor period children begin to engage in "deferred imitation." Whereas at first they imitated objects and actions only while these were present, they now begin to enact the imitations in the absence of the perception. They evoke the object when it is not present. As soon as that process becomes entirely internal, the imitation has metamorphosed into an image.

The imagery of this stage, which lasts from about two to seven, is, as was said, reproductive and static. It designates the states rather than the processes of reality. Static, too, is its structure. Its content may change, but the forms undergo no development. Since it has no cognitive rival function, the imagery rules mental life by itself.

With the onset of the stage of concrete operations a new image-form develops, the anticipatory image mentioned above. It is not that the image-structure itself develops by adaptation and equilibration, but that an outside factor is superimposed, namely the "operations." A seven- or eight-year-old is capable of certain logical transformations that mobilize the image. Images are developmentally inert; their development is emphatically not autonomous but depends on operational thinking.

At this stage anticipatory imagery prevails over merely reproductive imagery. But this mobile imagery does not lead children to understand more than they are operationally ready for. They may in their imagination anticipate particular results of which they have general experience—for example, the level to which a liquid will rise when poured from a shallow and broad into a high and thin container. But they will do so without in the least understanding the operational invariances involved, such as conservation of quantity and the corresponding compensation in the dimensions.

With the coming of operations, imagery is put in the service of reasoning. It may be used for remembering past perception or illustrating concepts. Children reach the high point in imaginal precision later in this stage with the advent of geometric intuition. Geometric diagrams, static or mobile, act as signifiers of geometric transformations. They represent such transformations symbolically in a privileged sort of way, insofar as figures are representing figures: Geometric diagrams depict spatial configurations by spatial likeness. This is the ultimate use for imagery.

In sum, then, the biography of imagery tells of its emergence from motor imitation, its domination of mental life, and finally its subservience to operational thought. In that last role, however, imagery continues to be necessary to cognition. Piaget explains why there is a life-long need for imagery through the social character of language, the chief symbolism of fully operational reasoning. Because language is social and common, it must be conventional and abstract. Since it is symbolically underprivileged, it cannot help but be too abstract to convey inner or outer experience adequately. Therefore personal imagery must concretize it. Piaget cites as examples the numerous private representations people have of the sequence of counting numbers: serried sticks, piled disks, rising stairs. Moreover, language is unable by its nature to signify either the particularities or the affective content of private perceptions and of the personal past. Hence imagery serves to consolidate and to make memories available to reason, for memories are its matter (1966, 380).

Finally, what are the special positive features of image-cognition? Images serve in two ways: as memories and as visualizations. Up to now I have scarcely mentioned the enormous experimental side of Piaget's theory of imagery. This is the place to cite his two famous experiments dealing with imaginal learning.

The most startling discovery of Piaget's study of memory is the fact that in children specific memories can increase in accuracy over a lapse of time. Children three to eight years old were shown ten sticks of different lengths arranged side by side in ascending size. After a week they were asked to draw what they had seen. After a half a year or more they were again asked first to draw the arrangement from memory and then to reproduce it with sticks.

The older the children were the more their drawings reproduced the sticks in the given order. This successful grading was correlated to their increasing ability to use verbal comparatives. The oldest children, who did perfect gradings, were capable not only of comparing "short, long, longer" but of reversing this comparison. This same reversing operation when suggested to the middle children confused their drawings. Evidently image-memory in general improves as operational thinking and speech develop. But what was truly unexpected was that the memory–images themselves appeared to have made progress: The drawings of most of the younger children and almost all the children from five to eight were more accurate after half a year than they had been after a week (Inhelder 1976).

The memory–images, Piaget concludes, are subject to transformation by the developing reason. This improvement is, he thinks, probably a continuous subconscious process and does not occur only at the moment of recall.

The conjecture is of crucial cognitive importance. The memory is the "figurative aspect of the conservation of schemata." A schema is an acquired knowledge-structure, any generalized system of habits and operations, learned in the past. Hence the "conservation of schemata" refers precisely to the human ability to store not raw information but real knowledge. That the memory is the figurative aspect of this conservation means that the chief route of access to our knowledge is through imagery. Consequently, under a developmental theory it would be a cognitive disaster if the imagery which, as Piaget repeatedly says, is the signifier of these schemata and concepts, did not develop under their control. For if imagery did not keep internal pace with reasoning we could never profit from our learning (1968, 395).

All visualizations are, of course, at bottom, memory-images. Piaget points out, for example, that an anticipatory image is a recombination of the images of reproductive memory in a novel way, though one in which simple recall is less prominent. That is to say, it is a means of projecting, by an unexplicit reference to past experience, how a motion will go.

The imagery of the pre-operational stage, where imagery carries the main cognitive burden, has one characteristic peculiarity that Piaget determined experimentally. It is "pseudo-conservation." Here is an account of the leading experiment.

Children were shown two cardboard squares, one lying congruently on top of the other. They were asked to anticipate the results of pushing the top square over to the right and to draw the result. Children from four to seven regularly refused in their drawings to push both sides of the upper square beyond the boundaries of the lower one. They might widen the movable square on the right so as to make it overhang on that side, or they might narrow it on the left, but they would not move it over and set it down separately (Inhelder 1976, 136). Piaget calls this mode of pre-operation "pseudo-conservation." False conservations occur when the child clings to certain apparently salient characteristics of an object, in this case a common boundary, to the detriment of deeper features, like the transformations of the whole figure. Thus for Piaget pseudo-conservation captures the essence of the pre-operational mode. It is as if the intelligence, unable to anticipate global shifts, stuck stubbornly to its initial insights.

Let me conclude this review with an observation. It is remarkable that one of the most extensive and detailed theories of imagery ever worked out should have been devised by someone so insistent on its limitations, its cognitive inertia, its "original sin." The explanation seems to be that Piaget's ideal is a certain view of scientific knowledge in which imagery plays a strictly subservient role. In the interest of that ideal he vigorously opposes a knowledge-as-copy view and defends a knowledge-as-assimilation theory in which the object emerges by stages as the intelligence operates on it. He traces the former view to Plato who, he says, in his devotion to the image, established his *eidos*, the ideal object of contemplation, as a "living figural form charged with conceptual significance." In general, the "astonishingly static" thought of the Greeks, who were unreflectively unaware of the operational dynamics of reason, is responsible for their overestimation of the image (1966, 383). Now I think that Plato must be shuddering in Hades to hear his "invisible sights" taken for the images he so vigorously condemned, and "the Greeks," who discovered dialectic and actuality, must be laughing in Elysium to hear that they ignored the vital energy of thought. And yet there is a lesson in Piaget's charge, though it is not that the ancients clung impractically to contemplation because they were static iconophiles. The lesson is the inverse: When operative reason is allowed to define human maturity the imagination is very apt to be devalued.

3. Critique of Piaget. Piaget's developmental account of cognition comes under criticism from two sides: from later findings in the science he himself founded and from the kind of cognitive science described in Chapter II. Since these critiques have some bearing on the role of imagery in cognition, I will briefly sketch them out.

Experiments by developmental psychologists are pushing further back into infancy the first appearance of various cognitive abilities, among them symbolic representation (Mandler 1983.) As has been mentioned, it often turns out that children can perform tasks before the developmental stage calls for such performance, if their attention is engaged and the experimenter's language is accommodated to them, if they get proper "retrieval cues." Piaget's tasks were unnecessarily difficult and his instructions sometimes misleading. What is more, children can be trained to perform certain tasks before their supposed time. They can, for example, be trained in the pre-operational stage to perform mental rotations on imagery, although more slowly than adults. This is a possibility absolutely at variance with the stage theory, which claims that the capability is simply not there. Hence Piaget is faulted for prematurely inferring competence from performance (Siegel and Brainerd 1978). The criticism is especially applicable to imagery experiments that must rely on children's drawing performance, although such skill lags notoriously behind their internal representational competence (Mandler 1983, 440).

Similarly the attitudinal immaturities supposedly characteristic of certain stages seem to be overcome sooner than Piaget thought. Pre-operational children, for example, are supposed to be "centered," incapable of seeing the world from another's point of view. They supposedly cannot transform their imagery so as to envision how a scene might look from a different perspective. Recent experiments with scenic models show that three- and four-year-olds do well in turning such models to show how they would appear to a doll looking on from a different angle. Evidently they can in fact imagine another's perspective.

(Vuyk 1981, Mandler 1983, Gelman 1983.)

A most interesting objection to the developmental line is the inverse of the above: Many adults, it seems, are incapable of the formal-operational thinking that is supposed to characterize full-blown cognition. For example, children do not know the principle of fluid-level invariance; when they draw a tilted test tube, they represent the liquid level at right angles to the sides rather than as remaining horizontal. But neither do many adults recognize this depiction as faulty. In short, not all adults are all-round hypothetical-deductive scientists. Many scientists probably aren't either. It almost seems that what Piaget discovered was not so much that children lack cognitive competence as that they are natural-born Aristotelian philosophers. He noticed that they think of movements as being governed by their goals; that they apprehend qualitative place rather than coordinate space; and that they recognize motion before they isolate time. All these views are to be found in Aristotle's *Physics*. In sum, their cognitive ontology seems to recapitulate the historical phylogeny of physics. They have a fresh ancient perspective, not a deficient modern rationality. Piaget himself in fact noticed one such case: Children make the Aristotelian distinction between natural and forced motion (1946, 253).

The critique of Piaget from the quarter of contemporary cognitive science is many-pronged and fundamental. There is, of course, the general objection from the propositionalist to any cognitive imagery-theory whatsoever (Ch. II). There is also a "nativist" argument to the effect that final outcomes must be preordained in the initial structures, a thesis inimical to Piaget's claim that structures can become more complex and powerful through mere developmental functioning.

But anteceding these positive objections, cognitive scientists have logical and conceptual queries. Fodor, for example, asks how it follows from the mere fact that children think about past perceptions that they think with images. What can be meant by imagistic thinking and how can images be the vehicle of thought, as Bruner and, *mutatis mutandis*, Piaget claim? For Bruner's "icons," like Piaget's images, are pictures that represent by resembling. Fodor's criticism of iconic thinking begins with the strange concession that words do resemble what they stand for. He means, presumably, that names pick out depictable objects in the world and so do what images do. But sentences, at any rate, do not function that way: "The goshawk pounced on the shrewmouse" is not imaginable by compounding pictures of a hawk, a pouncing, and a shrew. Nor conversely does a picture of a pouncing goshawk give a necessary or unique rendering of that sentence. It could for instance mean: "Hawks exterminate vermin: good!" Moreover, Fodor goes on, sentences are what pictures, independent of descriptions, cannot be: true or false. So, he concludes, imagistic thinking, whatever it is, does not have the syntactical and truth-functional features of adult propositional thinking. It is therefore, strictly speaking, unintelligible to adults.

The confusion is compounded by the fact that pre-operational children do, of course, speak. Piaget, quite consistently, suggests that there is a non-operational verbal mode, a symbolic, figurative, metaphorical language (1968, 13). It seems to me that the trouble is that even if pre-operational speech is figurative in content—though one may argue that a good metaphor evinces a deep rather than a deficient insight—there is still its syntactical form to be accounted for. Doesn't the metaphor-making child possess all the logic that underlies the forming of verbal propositions, of sentences?

This argument against imaginative thinking as a separable type was worth dwelling on here for two reasons. First, the Piagetan pre-operational child seems to present an extreme case of the logical problem of "radical translation." Though the child's behavior may be externally observed, there seems to be no way to enter its world, the more so since this world is primarily described in terms of what the child is not, or at least is not yet. Second, the language of "visual thinking" is rife in aesthetics and education, and is equally obscure there (Ch. V A).

There are more particular conceptual difficulties too. One such difficulty is with Piaget's term "deferred imitation." It designates the first evidence that a child has symbolic representations, and thus initiates the genetic unfolding of imagery. How does it work? The child interiorizes a perceived motion, say another child's temper tantrum, by engaging in a kind of inhibited incipient motor reproduction. A day later this inner copy may in turn be copied, re-enacted in a deferred externalization, when the child screams and stamps its foot. This second imitation is a symbolic evocation, since its model is no longer externally present. Here is the problem: If interiorized motion is the genetic antecedent of images, it must be initially maintained without their benefit. But how is a motion kept in consciousness without memory-images except by constant rehearsal, which is surely infeasible overnight! (Senchuck 1981). Moreover, if "deferred imitation" is difficult to understand, the rise of imagery by interiorized imitation is even more mysterious. How does a motor imitation, a muscular performance, turn either gradually or suddenly into a figurative representation? How, for that matter, are objects and events other than behaviors like tantrums imitated by motions?

Finally, the cognitive model of Chapter II reflects critically on the developmental view. For one thing, Piaget simply assumes the outcome cognitive psychologists work so hard to establish, that mental imagery is a mode of cognition, even if an exceedingly restricted one. For another, Piaget delineates the imagery stage largely in negative terms, in terms of operational immaturity, while in cognitive psychology mental imagery is shown to be a positive and powerful system working in tandem with verbal processes. To put it another way, Piaget bypasses the inquiry that interests cognitive psychologists, namely the search for the actual structures and processes of imagery and their relation to propositions. In particular, he escapes the full burden of this last problem by losing interest in all imagery (except geometric figures) at that stage in cognitive development when it belatedly becomes adjunct to logical operations.

In truth, the problem of Piaget's insufficient cognitive analysis is built into the notion of an imagery-stage. If imagery is at its inception radically independent of thought, how can it ever become subject to logical operations or "evoke" and "signify" concepts, as in geometric visualization? From the point of view of the cognitive model, it may indeed be that the speeds of children's information-processing are in general slower than those of adults, perhaps because their brains are immature. Moreover, the processes of their image retrieval may often outrace their verbal ones (Kosslyn 1980, 412). But what the integral, non-temporal, cognitive model accommodates with difficulty is a theory that demands the evolution of figurative and operational structures through the mere interactive, internal, functioning of the system. For in the mainstream theory the mind is modeled as a pre-ordained whole, so that intellect and imagination are coeval.

(Siegel and Brainerd 1978, Vuyk 1981, Kosslyn 1980, Gelman and Baillargeon 1983, Mandler 1983.)

What, then, is the profit of the Piagetan imagery-theory if its two main points, the idea of the genesis of imagery in imitation and the notion of pre-logical image-thinking, are thrown in doubt? It seems that Piaget's great accomplishment is not in these particular new theories but rather in his adaptation of old observations to a new and ingenious experimental frame. Among these is the philosopher's rule that the intellect needs and uses the imagination, the educator's apprehension that children are imagination-ridden, and above all, the poet's sense that imaginative vision is somehow ultimately picture-like, momentary, and still.

C. By Degree: Quality and Quantity of Fantasy

The imagination of children is commonly supposed to be more spontaneous, more vivid, and richer in specific forms, as well as more abundant and pervasive than that of adults. The power described in these terms is something more than the cognitive competence that alone attracted Piaget's interest (1966, xi). It is the productive power of fantasy. In this context "fantasy" has two senses. It means any voluntary or adventitious imagining that is not mere perception-memory, such as make-believe, imagining, daydreaming, dreaming, and all sorts of projecting, up to hallucinating.

More particularly it means the strange and grotesque, marvelous and magical aspect of such imagery.

Does the fantasy life of children differ from that of adults? The simple asking of that question runs into the hermeneutic difficulty mentioned above, one that happens to be a great preoccupation of current logic and anthropology. There may be, the argument goes, in principle no way to translate ourselves into alien cultures and past epochs, to think and feel ourselves into the minds of their people. In the absence of empathy, we are forced to take an indirect way, that of construing the symbol-systems of these cultures (e.g., Geertz 1983). What then of the early ages of life, when symbolic expression is incipient? If children have representational modes truly different from those of adults, they will be more inaccessible than the inhabitants of the Antipodes ever were, the more so since Piaget's pre-operational imagination is, as has been said, a default position. For rational thought is missing from it, and what way is there for thinking adults to think themselves back into thoughtlessness?

The symbolic imagination is the central form of representational cognition in the pre-operative stage. Piaget describes its two peculiar modes as he observed them in the sayings of his own child Jacqueline between the ages of two and five. One mode is "artificialism." The child differentiates between "being made" and "making oneself": The sky is made, the sun makes itself, just as babies are brought into the world ready-made by the mother, but then grow up by themselves. The child thinks that most things belong to the made sort. Thus Jacqueline thought that it was Daddy's student, her current favorite, "who made everything, the sky and the water and the light and everything." (Here, incidentally is another instance of juvenile Aristotelianism. Aristotle, too, distinguishes between being by art and being by nature, that is, being externally made and having the principle of growth within.)

The other mode, closely related, is "animism." Objects are thought of as alive. The child asks: "Is the cloud an animal?" or "You can hear the wind singing. How does it do it?" It is not till about six that the artificialistic and animistic imagination begins by stages to develop into operational thought, with its spatio-temporal mode of causal explanation (Piaget 1946, ch. IX).

Figurative representation expresses itself in "symbolic play." Again, such play is a middle stage; it is preceded by "mastery play," such as repetitious banging done for the sheer pleasure in the emerging motor competence. In the middle stage, symbolic play—pretending and make-believe—is usually carried on alone. Eventually it develops into socialized imitations of real life. Then finally, at about seven, during the concrete-operational stage, rule-governed group games emerge. By twelve, symbolic play has come to an end (1946, 287), and the imagination is now mostly in the service of logical operations on reality. Marginally it goes underground in the form of daydreaming.

Psychoanalytic observers, however, discover very different elements in children's fantasies. They interpret them not as cognitively significant pre-logical representations but as highly charged inner expressions of guilt or desire. They see in them much less poetry and much more sex. Contrary to Piaget, this school takes particular notice of infantile fantasies with such themes as bodily functions and parental relations; prosaic but potent objects like pencils abound. Children's fantasies are not only broadly, but also very determinately symbolic. They are metaphors open to precise psychoanalytic interpretation (Davidson and Fay 1952).

These adult views of children's fantasies are, of course, subject to criticism. The psychoanalytic theory seems to be prone to "demand-characteristics"—Freudians get Freudian protocols. As for the Piagetan theory, whereas the recent trend has been to drive logical operations further back, the imaginative stages have been thought to come further up. Motor mastery, for example, often forms part of symbolic play—think of swinging on a swing while being a space traveler—and symbolic playing is often intertwined with games. In fact, whether or when the forms of play fade out seems to depend on two factors: One is cultural circumstance; if children are required to perform real-life duties like animal herding there is less make-believe (though presumably more solo fantasy). The other is individual difference: from very early on different children prefer different kinds of play. All in all, there seems to be good reason to think that fantasy life is very much a continuum for human beings. It may change its objects through life and may peak at certain periods—at about five, for example, and again in later adolescence—but it never ceases entirely (Singer 1981). The fully adult imagination, it seems to me, is perfectly capable of little Jacqueline's "artificialism" and of her "animism." For rationalistic deprecation apart, these turn out to be modes of worship and poetry. Thus the Psalmist speaks of him "who made the heavens . . . who laid out the earth above the waters . . . who hath made great lights"; and Shelley speaks for a cloud:

With wings folded I rest, on mine aery nest,
As still as a brooding dove.

For those who like that kind of explanation, one may even adduce an evolutionary mechanism for the survival of youthful poetic modes into adulthood. It is "neoteny": Certain species do not come to a sclerotic maturity but are biologically able to maintain their appealing, playful, youthfully flexible traits throughout their lives. Human beings belong to the only neotenic species that has a choice about its mental life. They can, if they deem it revealing, carry on in the imaginative mode of the child through all their lives. It seems to me that there is much to be said against driving too deep a wedge between children's and adults' fantasy life.

Beside the quality of fantasy in general, three types of fantasy content have been studied specifically in children's fantasy. First in line are the imaginary companions some children envision in all degrees of vividness, conviction, and secretiveness. Parents used to feel obliged to curb this fantasy-product, but the recent sense is that it is both a sign of emotional health and conducive to it (Piaget 1946, 131; Somers and Yawkey 1984).

Second, there is the "paracosm," the imagined world that is elaborately and lengthily evolved, with great attention to coherence and consistency. The most detailed description of such a children's cosmos I know of is to be found in C.S. Lewis's literary autobiography, *Surprised by Joy*. A recent study (MacKeith 1982) concludes that paracosmic fantasies are not very common, though almost five dozen detailed replies from adult "exparacos-mists" were received. The creations occurred between the ages of three and eighteen, and the peak was at eight or nine, presumably when objective interest in real facts most felicitously merges with fantasy life.

Third come internal tales, particularly the fairy tales children not only demand to hear but tell themselves. Fairy tales have certain features that distinguish them from myths, their graver counterparts (Part Four, Ch. IV). They use magical means and they have happy endings. They are about "everyman," as signified by the fact that usually no proper names are used. Heroes of myth, on the other hand, have well-known personal names, the story often ends in tragedy, and it is fate, not magic, that is at work. They are also said to serve a different psychological function. In Freudian terms, fairy tales depict the satisfaction of "id" desires, while myths, in modeling the ideal personality, fulfill the demands of the "superego" (Bettelheim 1976).

Finally, children are prone to experiencing what Wordsworth, the most enthusiastic chronicler of these events, has called "spots of time" and Virginia Woolf "moments of being" (Part Six, Ch. II C). These moments, "which, with distinct pre-eminence, retain a vivifying virtue" (*Prelude* XI) are brief "transcendental" experiences often including a flash of imaginative vision. They have been studied by means of questionnaires in English schoolchildren and undergraduates, in whom they seem to be not uncommon (Paffard 1973).

These four imaginative employments, the loveliest of subjects, will be taken up later, outside the psychological context. Here it is fair to ask: Do only children, or even mainly children, have imagined companions, inner worlds, magical adventures, and transcendent moments? If the answer is no, it again remains questionable whether the content of children's fantasy has a special, distinguishable quality.

As for its quantity and intensity compared to that of adults, the evidence is hard to come by. There are suggestions that fantasy life is universal for all ages (Klinger 1971). The assertion is as difficult to document as its extreme opposite, that there is perfectly imageless thinking, the province of scientifically gifted men. There are claims by psychologists that television watching, while increasing the degree of anxiety of children's fantasies, decreases the quantity of their occurrences, but these claims are disputed. It is even hard to tell for quantitative purposes just when a child is being imaginative. Children are great crypto-pedants: What looks like a flight of fancy to an uninitiated adult, may in fact be the most literalistic logic. Moreover, they are quite as quick as adults to go underground with their fantasies when they sense an invasive interest.

Children are certainly well situated for extended fantasizing. They have more leisure and a much broader latitude for silence than adults, who are, at least when in society, expected to be politely or productively uttering at decent intervals. Furthermore, new sights tend to feed the fantasy, and in the nature of things children see far more new sights than do adults. At the same time, a year is a century to them, so that each return of a celebration and every holiday evokes a sense of ancient remembrance. Yet it is, after all, the adults who record and invent the sustained fantasizing that goes, for example, into children's books. Indeed, some of the greatest children's books were written by an adult in tandem with a particular child's imaginative life, among them *Winnie the Pooh*, *The Wind in the Willows*, and the *Alice* books. So it is in fact the adults who are the great fantasts, who spin out meticulous and sustained fantasy worlds (some of them, like *The Lord of the Rings*, as detailed, and about as fascinating, as a doctoral dissertation in the field of ethnography).

However, there does come from cognitive psychology hard evidence that in certain particular cognitive situations children use imagery more than do adults. Six-year-olds, when asked to answer questions about a cat's features, answered faster for larger and more weakly associated features, an indication that mental imagery was being used. Ten-year-olds, on the other hand, were faster for smaller, strongly associated features, an indication that a propositional process had taken over (Ch. II B). The suggested explanation of this evidence is this: Imagery tends to be used in novel situations. As we already know, adults tend to find the first answer to the question "How many windows does your house have?" by means of a mental walk, while for some time thereafter the word answer is more quickly to hand. The frequent use of imagery may thus be a function of the simple fact that children encounter so many novel situations (Kosslyn 1983).

In the much agitated question of "the Child's Imagination" there are, in sum, two rival strains, an older, rational, and a newer, romantic one. The rationalists, who need not be genetic epistemologists (though Piaget is their purest representative), think of a child, to paraphrase Aristotle, as an "animal about to have reason," an adult manqué (Part Six, Ch. I A). The romantics, descended from Rousseau through the Romantic school to the contemporary enthusiasts of spontaneity, think of the adult as a child ruined by reason. Whereas the rationalist considers that maturity means irreversibly putting away childish things and putting the imagination in the service of morality and reason, the romantics hold that the adult must look to childhood, learn from it, and even try to recover it. The poets tend to express the Romantic view of the child as the paradigm of humanity most unabashedly: Through its "tacitly creative life . . . the child is . . . a lively representation to us of us in the idea, not indeed as it is fulfilled, but as it is enjoined," says Schiller (*On Naive and Sentimental Poetry* 1795). Or, again, Wordsworth apostrophizes a six-year-old: "Thou best Philosopher, who yet dost keep Thy heritage . . ." ("Ode on Intimations of Immortality" 1807). Here is Emerson in a yet more exalted strain: "A man is a god in ruins. . . . Infancy is the perpetual Messiah which comes into the arms of fallen men, and pleads with them to return to paradise" ("Nature" 1844; Plotz 1979). One might say that the romantics are intoxicated with the neotenic idea.

Though the two schools of thought value the imagination altogether differently, they do agree that it is preeminently the child's domain. Happily rationalist and romantic are a long way from dividing the world between them. There are other perspectives on the power of inner vision, which preserve the continuum of the human life-span (see Coda).

Bibliography

Ahsen, Akhter. 1977. "Eidetics: An Overview." *Journal of Mental Imagery* 1:5–38.

Bettelheim, Bruno. 1976. *The Uses of Enchantment: The Meaning and Importance of Fairy Tales*. New York: Alfred A. Knopf.

Brown, Geoffrey, and Desforges, Charles. 1979. *Piaget's Theory: A Psychological Critique*. London: Routledge and Kegan Paul.

Bruner, Jerome S. 1964. "The Course of Cognitive Growth." *American Psychologist* 19:1–15.

Cobb, Edith. 1977. *The Ecology of Imagination in Childhood.* New York: Columbia University Press.

Davidson, Audrey, and Fay, Judith. 1952. *Phantasy in Childhood.* Westport, Conn.: Greenwood Press (1972).

Eysenck, Michael W. 1984. *A Handbook of Cognitive Psychology.* Hillsdale, N.J.: Lawrence Erlbaum Associates.

Flanagan, Owen J. 1984. *The Science of the Mind.* Cambridge: The MIT Press.

Fodor, Jerry A. 1981. "Imagistic Representation." In *Imagery*, edited by Ned Block. Cambridge: The MIT Press.

Geertz, Clifford. 1983. *Local Knowledge.* New York: Basic Books.

Gelman, Rochel, and Baillargeon, Renée. 1983. "A Review of Some Piagetian Concepts." In *Handbook of Child Psychology*, 4th ed., Volume 3, *Cognitive Development*, edited by Paul H. Mussen. New York: John Wiley and Sons.

Ginsberg, Herbert, and Opper, Sylvia. 1979. *Piaget's Theory of Intellectual Development.* Englewood Cliffs, N.J.: Prentice-Hall.

Haber, Ralph N. 1969. "Eidetic Images." In *Image, Object, and Illusion: Readings from Scientific American.* San Francisco: W. H. Freeman and Co. (1974).

Inhelder, Baerbel. 1976. "Operational Thought and Symbolic Imagery." In *Piaget and His School: A Reader in Developmental Psychology*, edited by B. Inhelder and H. Chipman. New York: Springer-Verlag.

Isaacs, Susan. 1952. "The Nature and Function of Fantasy." Chapter 3 in *Developments in Psycho-Analysis*, edited by Melanie Klein and Susan Isaacs. Jersey City: Da Capo (1982).

Klinger, Eric. 1971. *Structure and Functions of Fantasy.* New York: Wiley-Interscience.

Kluever, Heinrich. 1928. "Studies on the Eidetic Type and Eidetic Imagery." *The Psychological Bulletin* 25:69–104.

Kosslyn, Stephen M. 1980. *Image and Mind.* Cambridge: Harvard University Press.

———. 1983. *Ghosts in the Mind's Machine: Creating and Using Images in the Brain.* New York: W. W. Norton and Company.

MacKeith, Stephen A. 1982. "Paracosms and the Development of Fantasy in Childhood." *Imagination, Cognition and Personality* 2:261–267.

Mandler, Jean M. 1983. "Representation." In *Handbook of Child Psychology*, 4th ed., edited by Paul H. Mussen. New York: John Wiley and Sons.

Marks, David, McKellar, Peter, and commentators. 1982. "The Nature and Function of Eidetic Imagery." *Journal of Mental Imagery* 6:1–124.

Paffard, Michael. 1973. *Inglorious Wordsworths: A Study of Some Transcendental Experiences in Childhood and Adolescence.* London: Hodder and Stoughton.

Piaget, Jean. 1946. *Play, Dreams and Imitation in Childhood* [*La Formation du Symbole*]. Translated by C. Gattegno and F. H. Hodgson. New York: W. W. Norton and Company. (1962).

————. 1970. *The Principles of Genetic Epistemology*. Translated by Wolfe Mays. London: Routledge and Kegan Paul (1972).

Piaget, Jean, Inhelder, B., Oléron, P., and Gréco, P. 1963. "Mental Images." In *The Essential Piaget*, edited by H. Gruber and J. J. Vonèche. New York: Basic Books (1977).

Piaget, Jean, Inhelder, Bärbel, et al. 1966. *Mental Imagery in the Child: A Study of the Development of Imaginal Representation*. Translated by P. A. Chilton. New York: Basic Books (1971).

Piaget, Jean, Inhelder, Bärbel, et al. 1968. *Memory and Intelligence*. Translated by Arnold J. Pomerans. New York: Basic Books (1973).

Plotz, Judith C. 1979. "The Perpetual Messiah: Romanticism, Childhood, and the Paradoxes of Human Development." In *Regulated Children/Liberated Children*, edited by B. Finkelstein. New York: Psychohistory Press.

Pulaski, Mary Ann S. 1980. *Understanding Piaget: An Introduction to Children's Cognitive Development* (Revised). New York: Harper and Row.

Scholnick, Ellin K. 1983. *New Trends in Conceptual Representation: Challenges to Piaget's Theory?* Hillsdale, N.J.: Lawrence Erlbaum Associates.

Senchuck, Dennis M. (1981). "A Philosophical Critique of Piaget's View of Images as Interiorized Actions." In *Imagery: Concepts, Results, and Applications*, edited by Eric Klinger. Proceedings of the Second Annual Conference of the American Association for the Study of Mental Imagery. New York: Plenum Press.

Siegel, Linda S., and Brainerd, Charles J. 1978. *Alternatives to Piaget: Critical Essays on Theory*. New York: Academic Press.

Singer, Jerome L. 1981. "Imaginative Play as the Precursor of Adult Imagery and Fantasy." In *Imagery: Concepts, Results, and Applications*, edited by Eric Klinger. Proceedings of the Second Annual Conference of the American Association for the Study of Mental Imagery. New York: Plenum Press.

Somers, Jana U., and Yawkey, Thomas D. 1984. "Imaginary Play Companions: Contributions of Creative and Intellectual Abilities of Young Children." *Journal of Creative Behavior* 18:77–81.

Spoehr, Kathryn T., and Lehmkuhle, Stephen W. 1982. *Visual Information Processing*. San Francisco: W. H. Freeman and Co.

Vuyk, Rita. 1981. *Overview and Critique of Piaget's Genetic Epistemology, 1965–1980*. New York: Academic Press.

Chapter V

Various Imagery-Topics

Outside of the grand systematic studies, imagery is a protean subject. It is pursued in psychology under various aspects, through diverse types, and by different approaches. Actually that is an understatement. There is a flood of work, of wildly mixed quality, stemming particularly from the so-called "imagery movement." These para-academic efforts run alongside studies of a more established sort. This chapter will briefly take account of both strains.

A. Cognitive Uses of Imagery

1. "Creation, Creativity, Creating" is a huge subject, with well over a thousand entries tightly stuffing a catalogue drawer, beginning disarmingly with the title "Create Something. A Handbook for Beginners," and going through "Creating an Annotation, a Self, Art from Anything, Credit," to "Creative Computing, Divorce, Politics, Power, Procrastination, Old Age, and Zen."

In psychology, too, creativity is an enormous subject, though it appears that the effort invested in its canonization stands in inverse ratio to the headway made in its elucidation.

How did "creativity" achieve its present incantatory status? The full answer would surely be the biography of the Western spirit, and it would begin with the dominating case of the Creation in *Genesis*. Though interpretations differ unendingly, the major Jewish and Christian tradition holds that when "in the beginning God created the heaven and the earth, and the earth was without form," the Creator not only shaped the world but first made the *tohuwabohu*, the chaos that was its matter. The first creation was *ex nihilo*, out of nothing, the making of radically new being. (The Hebrew term, used in *Genesis* 1:27, is *bara*.) Thus the strong meaning of creation in our tradition is also the prime meaning, certainly in the middle ages, as in Thomas Aquinas. However, Thomas admits a secondary sense as well: the making of something out of something, as an artisan works on a material according to a given or imaginary model. (The Hebrew term, used in *Genesis* 2:7, is *yatsar*.) This is the kind of activity the Greeks called *poiēsis*, a word which simply means "making," making something not from nothing but out of a material. At the inception of modernity, as the artisan turns by degrees into the Artist, the distinction between creator and maker loses its sharpness. Renaissance poets are apt to speak of themselves as successfully emulating God's creation. As creatures made in the image of a creator-god, they are themselves creative. Sidney will serve as an example:

> Give right honor to the heavenly maker of that maker, who, having made man in his own likeness, set him beyond and over all the works of that second nature; which in nothing he showeth so much as in poetry, when with the force of a divine breath he bringeth things forth far surpassing her doings. ["The Defense of Poesie" 1583]

But it is left to the Romantic philosophers and poets to propound the radical creativity of the human imagination as much more than a simile.

A development along these lines, too significant really to be so briefly disposed of, stands behind the present ubiquity of the term in ordinary life as well as in psychology.

What then does "creativity" mean in the current psychological literature? Neither a leading article on the subject (Wallach 1970) nor the introduction to the first issue of the *Journal of Creative Behavior* (1967) evidence any sense of obligation to address the embarrassing questions. But a definition from philosophy seems to meet the case: It means novelty. "Creativity is the principle of novelty," says Whitehead in *Process and Reality*. In creativity studies, however, novelty tends to be trivialized. As in the "novelties" sold in department stores, it means "the unique and unusual"—any index of personal difference, however piddling, as long as it is somehow measurable.

In philosophy the imagination was associated with creation as a productive or world-making power distinct from reproductive memory. This creative imagination brings forth not novelty in the trivial sense, but newness, difference manifest in time—a deep and problematic matter. In psychology the creativity of the imagination is thus by and large a much tamer property. In his classic *Essay on the Creative Imagination* (1900), Ribot distinguishes between a passive, repetitive and a constructive, creative imagination. He too makes newness the mark of the latter. Yet for him the creative mechanism depends on nothing more spontaneous than one of

Hume's laws of association, that of resemblance, in particular the kind of imperfect resemblance called analogy. He gives the example of an Australian aborigine who calls the first book he sees a mussel because it opens and shuts around a spine. For Ribot analogical thinking accounts for all the products of the creative imagination: for imitative play and the fanciful inventions of childhood, for the animism of primitive mythmaking and the symbolism of mystics, for the rationalized myths of religion and metaphysics, even for the ingenuities of commercial wealth-making.

Modern creativity-studies employ an even more restricted notion of the imagination. Recent work in creativity has, very roughly, two phases, a hard one and a soft one, or an establishment phase and an ecstatic phase. These reflect the changing temper of the decades. The hard-line phase took off in the fifties when the burst of economic growth, combined with the fear of being overtaken by the Russians, put practical ingenuity at a premium. Creativity then chiefly meant problem-solving, as the title of a very popular self-help book shows: *Applied Imagination: Principles and Procedures of Creative Problem-Solving* (Osborn 1953). Although the book opens with the irresistible hypothesis that "imagination made America," it goes on to propound pure neo-babbitry. The problem-solving exercises call for solution to the downtown parking problem, along with imaginative devices for straightening out your "Communistically inclined" son.

But aside from the unabashed philistinism of this phase, there seems to be something wrong with the very terms of such enterprises. The phrase "creative behavior" itself seems to be a contradiction in terms. Of course people are free to use the word imagination for ingenuity in action, but we should not forget that in their central meanings imagination and problem-solving are constitutionally contradictory notions. One solves a problem, like the parking problem, in order to dissolve it, to be rid of it. Acts of the imagination proper, however, are seldom meant to dissolve their preoccupations in that way. It is no accident at all that the thinkers who, at the dawn of modernity, set us in the course of expecting to formulate all perplexities as soluble problems, were engaged in overcoming the imagination in favor of a non-figural, symbolic mode of thought (Brann 1968).

After the fifties, academic attempts to analyze creative and imagistic abilities into their factors and processes accumulate, undeterred by the early failures to find an identifying "group factor" for the imaginative faculty (Hargreaves 1927). The problem-solving imagination is, for example, defined as the testable ability to burst through the apparent configuration of a given problem. An instance is the parlor trick where six matches lying on a surface have to form four triangles; the imaginative solution is to leave the plane and construct a pyramid. Again, this imagination is analyzed into a collection of measurable factors, ranging from an I factor (induction or seeing logical patterns) through an E factor (the match stick ability above) to a K factor (richness and variety of response to Rorschach ink blots). Once more, imaginativeness is defined in terms of divergent, or loosely ranging, as opposed to convergent, or narrowly focused, thinking processes (Ghiselin 1952, Wallach 1970).

Further efforts to define the specific role of the imagination in creativity lead to such new versions of the old opposition between imagination and intellect as Bleuler's A(utistic) and R(eality) thinking. A-thinking is self-enclosed, interior, autonomous. It is the "unreality" function. R-thinking is directed toward evidence and logical relations. It maintains its relevance to reality. According to McKellar (1957), the complex relation between these two types is responsible for many socially useful products, such as works of art.

The most heart-felt book on the role of the imagination in creativity is by Rugg (1963). He locates the meeting of A- and R-thinking in that threshold state on the conscious/unconscious continuum which he calls the "transliminal mind." Here A-imagery lives in incessant kaleidoscope activity, occasionally interacting with R-imagery, which designates voluntary imaginative constructions and perceptual memory. The "creative flash" that is the special object of Rugg's investigation usually occurs when after a period of prolonged formal preparation and pertinently observant stocking of the unconscious, the person puts the problem aside. In a moment of relaxed concentration, the flux of imagery and the conceptual content merge in a flash of creation. These components follow the stages established in a much-cited analysis of the creative process: preparation, incubation, intimation of the coming flash, illumination, and verification (Wallas 1926).

In retrospect, the trouble with these various analyses is that, if asked whether they are all different or the same, one would have to say "both." The outcome was what it always is at dead ends: a general resort to an operational definition. The creative imagination ends up defined as performance on one of the many creativity tests.

The imagination is a litmus test of the times—in base eras it is cool blue and in acid days red hot. In the pre-sixties literature, interest is uneasily divided between the fascination with distant genius and the sanguine sense that, but for a little further research, we could all be creative. From the seventies, besides the continuing work on what one might call normally abnormal mental life, especially topics like vivid fantasy, articles crop up on such formerly disreputable "altered states of consciousness" as mystic, psychedelic, ghostly, and hypnotic visions, whether induced by drug-taking or by other practices. Attempts are made to seize and measure in terms more telling than the old factor-analysis of creativity the mental patterns that lie behind such heightened imagery. Imagination is described as renunciation of control and receptivity to the unconscious. Creativity is, equally, disintegration of forms, surrender, acceptance, openness, and the building of new perceptual orders. In every case, the creative imagination is placed at the top of an ascending scale of insight, coordinated with the rising powers of creativity. The literary inspiration for such attempts comes from Blake (Part Four, Ch. II B), while the techniques of investigation come from clinical psychology—an inspiration as exalted as the results are flat. Here, as a sample, is a definition of the creative imagination from a recent article: It is a "chemistry of mental processing where interactive intellectual and emotive forces participate in stimulating, energizing and propagating the creative act." Yet one must sympathize with these tireless attempts to discipline a mystery by analyzing it into elements whose sum is yet more vaporous than is the living whole itself.

In the studies just mentioned, the latent longing for strong and strange stuff is kept under control by the decent pedantries of professional writing. In the late seventies all sorts of interests (therapeutic, archetypal, mythical, mystical, Eastern) from all sorts of professions (psychological, psychiatric, literary, philosophical, artistic), come together in the "imagery movement," dedicated to a "new science and practice based on the magic of image creation." (Some of its official and allied activities are listed in the chapter bibliography under "Imagery Movement.") The rigor and responsibility of this work in behalf of the imagination naturally varies widely: Some of it is serious, much of it is *Schwärmerei*. But beginnings are that way; and it is not the enthusiasm of these efforts that induces reservations but the sense that, self-consciously directed to countering contemporary deficiencies as they are, they themselves spring from a strenuously academic rather than a particularly natural relation to the imaginative life.

2. Discovery. The polar opposite to visionary imagery, located along the same dimension and yet a world apart from it, is the visual imagery of discovery and invention. The operational criterion of their difference is that the discovery-image can be externalized into publicly verifiable products, such as diagrams or models, and elucidated by rigorous prose. The interest in such imagery goes hand in hand with the recent emphasis in the philosophy of science on the intuitive approach as opposed to the hypothetical-deductive model.

There exists a much-studied roster of discoveries for which their authors have given credit to such imagery. Of the two cited most often, the first is the Special Theory of Relativity, which was associated with the image of the person riding on a beam of light described above. Einstein's mental mode figures prominently in imagery research because in response to a set of questions by the mathematician Hadamard he made an effort to articulate it, and in doing so he appeared to support the defenders of cognitive imagery. It is a document worth quoting at length:

> The words or the language, as they are written or spoken, do not seem to play any role in my mechanism of thought. The psychical entities which seem to serve as elements in thought are certain signs and more or less clear images which can be "voluntarily" reproduced and combined.
>
> There is, of course, a certain connection between those elements and relevant logical concepts. It is also clear that the desire to arrive finally at logically connected concepts is the emotional basis of this rather vague play with the above mentioned elements. But taken from a psychological viewpoint, this combinatory play seems to be the essential feature in productive thought— before there is any connection with logical construction in words or other kinds of signs which can be communicated to others. [See Ch. II D 1]

The second discovery is Kekulé's benzene ring (the symmetrical closed chain arrangement of the six carbon atoms of the benzene molecule). He came to it through a dream in which a twisting snake bit its own tail. As it happens, Kekulé dreamt not only productively but also learnedly: The *ouroboros*, the "tail-devourer," is the alchemical symbol of circulation in a retort.

According to Shepard's study of distinguished imagers (1978), a number of them had certain features in common as children. They were rather isolated. They were late language learners, but were early on engrossed in figures, models, and mechanisms. Later they often had a hero who was himself an imager, as Einstein had Maxwell and Maxwell had Faraday.

Faraday's work, it should be said here, represents the ultimate scientific use of visual imagery. For him the image is not the means but the end of discovery. His electrical researches are all communicated in prose without equations. His project is to render his descriptive accounts of the actions of electric and magnetic powers visible to the eye so as to "illuminate" these powers. His hypothesis is that the deep forces of nature are as figuratively representable as its surface. Experimental hypotheses are therefore essentially visible similarities, visual images of nature: "When the natural truth and the conventional representation of it most closely agree, then we are most advanced in knowledge." By this agreement Faraday means visual similarity (*Experimental Researches in Electricity* 1831–55). The great, dominating image is the field configuration of lines of force, which can be "illuminated" by the iron filings that orient themselves around a bar magnet (Fisher 1979).

In his study of "the externalization of visual images and the act of creation," Shepard singles out an expression of visual imagery in words or in music where the mental imagery is not rendered pictorially but is transformed into other modes. He is particularly interested in cases where an image not merely serves as a generally suggestive stimulus, but is quite precisely translated into a verbal or tonal sequence. His chief example here comes from a letter attributed to Mozart:

> Provided I am not disturbed, my subject enlarges itself, becomes methodized and defined, and the whole, though it be long, stands almost complete and finished in my mind, so that I can survey it, like a fine picture or a beautiful statue, at a glance. Nor do I hear in my imagination the parts *successively*, but I hear them, as it were, all at once [*gleich alles zusammen*]. What delight this is I cannot tell! All this inventing, this producing, takes place in a pleasing lively dream. Still the actual hearing of the *tout ensemble* is after all the best.

What is remarkable is that the first intimation of the temporal art presents itself pictorially, as if the famous saying that poetry is like a picture had been extended to music. One propositionalist has objected to taking Mozart's account seriously, on the plea that meaning cannot be attached to seeing a long piece of music at a glance, any more than to hearing it as a simultaneity—which would inevitably be cacophonic. Yet it is hard to set aside such testimony. Evidently in some way the temporal work has an atemporal shape that is most naturally conveyed by a spatial simile. Such a vision of sound, though a stumbling block to the scientist, must indeed be an intimation of paradise to the subject.

There is a distinction at least as important as that between mental images that are expressed as pictures and those that are translated into words or music and cutting across it. This second distinction is that between images of discovery and the so-called "creative" imagery, the imagination-imagery which underlies many works of the arts. Both types, the discovery- and the creation-images, are, in the language of the trade, "consensually validated," meaning that they each have their willing public. Arthur Koestler's formulation of the difference between them is this: "Artists treat facts as stimuli for imagination, whereas the scientists use imagination to coordinate facts." Aside from the complicating circumstance that even the brutest of facts is already to some extent dependent upon the imagination, that does seem a good summary of the distinction between the imagination in the sciences and in the arts.

3. Problem-Solving. This section is as brief as the subject is vast. Laymen and professionals agree that as imagery seems to play a role in making grand discoveries, so it is useful in solving problems both practical and theoretical—ordinary everyday problems, not only special laboratory tasks.

In the earlier problem-solving studies, mentioned above, mental imagery was not isolated as a specific factor. But since then there have been many investigations of its role. For example, skillful chess players are known to have and to use an amazing visual memory for board positions. This ability, however, extends only to patterns possible in the game, not to randomly arranged pieces, as if there were a kind of mental file of possible boards. More ordinary spatial problems, too, often call for imagery: Furniture arranging, tracing lost articles, and solving mechanical problems are all amenable to the use of imagery.

A number of practical imagery-devices have been hypothesized, among them "cognitive maps." These are internal representations of the environment which extend beyond the immediate perceptual surroundings. Their rationalized externalization is the geographic map that mixes analogue with symbolic features—the topographical outlines of the layout are similarities, usually schematized, while individual features, like a house or a city, may be marked by a symbol like a star or a circle. Such cognitive layouts are used to solve the most common of life's problems—how to get to a place that is out of immediate sight.

Another device is the analogy-making of the imagination that was emphasized by Ribot. Immediate visual analogies are often at work in quick solutions to practical problems. Mountain climbers, for example, advance by pushing pegs into crevices. Similarly, as one researcher suggests, a person wanting to get at the ceiling without a ladder might insert a screwdriver into a keyhole—an analogy, to be sure, though very likely a catastrophic one.

Finally, the most interesting of all imagistic problem-solving devices are logical diagrams, such as Venn circles for visualizing the calculus of classes, or step diagrams for comparisons. Spatialized logic models are currently much studied—happily so, for they provide the most clear-cut examples of reason represented through the imagination. The topic will be taken up in Part Five (Ch. II B).

(Kaufman 1979, 1984, Morris and Hampson 1983.)

4. Learning. Children, it is universally agreed, are image-prone: They imagine a great deal and are very accessible to imagery (Ch. IV). Through millennia, writers on education have drawn the consequences of this propensity. Plato in the *Republic* recommends gymnastics for the bodies of the children in his city, but "music" for the soul, that is to say, songs and stories. Rousseau keeps his boy Émile away from reasonings because a child's mind properly receives images, which are of objects, rather than ideas, which render relations. Dewey in his *Pedagogic Creed* (1897) writes:

> I believe that the image is the great instrument of instruction. What a child gets out of any subject presented to him is simply the images which he himself forms with regard to it . . . .
> I believe that much of the time and attention now given to the preparation and presentation of lessons might be more wisely and profitably expended in training the child's power of imagery and in seeing to it that he was continually forming definite, vivid, and growing images of the various subjects with which he comes in contact in his experience.

However, precisely insofar as imagery is a childish stage, the "rationalists" among the educators regard it as a representational mode that has to be taken into account mostly in order to be overcome. Bruner's "iconic" stage, for example, begins when the image, the "summarizer of action" for the infant, becomes autonomous. It is a time when the child is "distractible" by perceived and imaged particulars. Even if the child can solve conservation problems correctly in the absence of such particulars, as soon as permitted it immediately returns to the false answers suggested by the mere looks of things (1966). A natural consequence of this view is the narrowness of interest in image-learning generally displayed by the stage-developmentalists (Sheikh 1984). An important exception, however, is Bruner's own study in "enactive" iconic learning of mathematics, the kind of learning that proceeds by handling and looking at physical models (1966).

Meanwhile, the interest in imagery-aided learning for adult students has increased enormously, the quicker for the burgeoning of computer graphics. Memorization has, of course, been associated with imagery for ages (Chapter III). But it has also been shown that instructions to visualize or the presence of visual illustrations help the understanding and the interpretation of material (Haber 1981). Information presented in visual forms, such as flow charts or color coding, is more immediately grasped. History textbooks that are written in concretely pictorial language are shown psychometrically to be more accessible even if the words themselves are harder. The examples are legion. Furthermore, visualizations often work better the more analogous they are—which is why, for example, oceans on maps should be blue. Illustrative imagery can be ranged along a dimension whose poles are "simulation" and "notation." This means that imagery can be profitably more or less like what it represents, depending on whether it is intended to aid in understanding the visible aspects of the imaged objects or other, say logical, features (Kosslyn 1980).

Finally, a highly specific use of imagery is in "mental practice," particularly of sports. The idea is to envision the ideal form and then to rehearse it internally, either going through the movements in sequence or getting a feel for the shape of the whole event. During such static rehearsal there is evidence of both brain and motor activity (Suinn 1983). This method of neuromuscular training through modeling or patterning shows limited but definite results. Hence training videotapes are successful commercially. What makes the effect interesting is that it shows clearly how immediately important imagery is to overt action. In early imagery-study there were theories of the sensorimotor origin of imagery, such as Piaget's and Washburn's even earlier general hypothesis (1916). Here seems to be a practical demonstration of the reverse process: In adults, at least, imagery profitably precedes activity.

Once more, a sign of the times is the reciprocal interest: learning to use the imagination rather than using the imagination to learn. There is a lot of emphasis on the "education of the perceptual-imaginal capacities" (Bruner 1966), and on "visual thinking" (Arnheim 1979), even for adults. There are even courses in dis-inhibiting visual imagery so as to break away from the manipulative mind-set of our age—in short, antics for credit (Stewart 1985).

Along the same lines, guided imagery techniques borrowed from therapy (Richardson 1982) have been recommended as learning devices. Cognitive, affective, life-styling, values-clarifying, decision-making, and psychomotor role-playing scenarios are recommended to teachers for use in the classroom. The topics proposed for visualization and for other sensory imagery vary from exceedingly sensitive to utterly trivial: "Stages of Dying," "Venereal Disease Choices," "Angel Dust," "Saying No," "Parking."

What, to conclude, makes imagery good for much ordinary problem-solving and learning? It seems to be just what makes it good for more august uses. Imagery is neither constrained by the assertive determinacy of propositions nor subject to the loss of detail that language entails. Imagery is similar to the scene or object to be mastered, although it is more readily manipulable than the object; and, last but not least, it is more affectively engaging.

B. Other Uses and Aspects

1. Therapy. It has been long and well known that tedium, melancholy, and lonely longing can be assuaged by deliberate imagining—and also that excessive imagining can be deleterious. Such exercises of the imagination, whether for good or ill, have usually been very private amateur perform-ances. There is, however, an ancient and apparently potent practice in which revelatory and therapeutic imagery is induced under the guidance of a hermetic or shamanic wisdom. In fact, some of the contemporary profes-sionals who engage in imagery-therapy pride themselves (with how much faithfulness to the spirit of the thing, I am not competent to tell) on being in the line of such mystic practices, so producing a somewhat uneasy amalgam of old magic and modern technique.

In this country interest in imagery as a psychological technique began to flourish with the founding of the imagery movement in the late seventies. It was preceded by European techniques, such as "guided affective im-agery," and "oneirodrama," that is, waking-dream therapy (Watkins 1976). It should be said right off that results are somewhat soft, since the patients who are taught to use the technique on themselves are selected for their receptivity. Furthermore, though there are some statistics for particular projects, much of the evidence has the weakness of all anecdotal reporting— the null results do not show up. There is, however, statistical evidence that imaging does produce some low-level motor responses and behavior changes. Also many participants report that the "guided affective imagery" and "group psycho-imagination" methods reviewed below have signifi-cantly illuminating effects. By and large, however, guided imagery has among psychologists something like the standing that the art of memory once had among the rhetoricians; both are techniques for inducing imagery, techniques in which some enthusiasts but fewer mainstream professionals have great faith.

In image-therapy images are actively and deliberately induced. It there-fore differs widely from those mainly verbal interpretational and diagnostic techniques of psychoanalysis which are applied to such spontaneous im-agery as dreams or ink-blot visions. In fact, at the turn of the century Freud expressed just the opposite attitude to imagery, saying that therapy consists "in wiping away these pictures" (Sheikh 1983, 398). Indeed, imagery-therapy is partly intended to obviate Freudian analysis. However, imagery-therapy does owe much to Jung's "active imagination." This is a kind of meditative imagining that allows the images to develop a life of their own as symbolic events (1935). The Jungian analyst may ask the patient to capture the resultant image in a drawing— more, however, for the purpose of self-interpretation than of self-manipulation.

The basic assumption of imagery-therapy is that not only psychological but even physiological, supposedly autonomic, processes can be affected by altering states of consciousness. In other words, most illnesses are partly psychosomatic. An everyday example of such an induced effect is said to be salivation. If one intends to make one's mouth water it is easier to do so by envisioning slicing and biting a lemon. Such salivation effects correlate with standard vividness tests for imagery (Sheikh and Kunzendorf 1984).

There is a multitude of visualization techniques. Only a few are named here (Korn 1983). The induced imagery can in general be said to come in two types: "End-state" imagery is said to go back to a hermetic practice of envisioning an ideal type, say of perfect health, in order to achieve it. In "process" imagery, it is the mechanism for attaining success that is imaged. It is said to be of secondary usefulness.

Process-imagery has, for example, been used in attempting to control headaches. One image is supposedly borrowed from the shamans of the central Philippines: The headache is envisaged as a colored liquid in a certain location; it is mentally poured into a container of the right size and discarded. At that moment the pain should cease. Visualizing techniques are also used in treating sexual dysfunction, in physical rehabilitation, and even in the care of cancer patients.

The *pièce de résistance* of shamanistic healing practice is the gaining of direct access, unmediated by electronic feedback, to the immune system. In a study involving eight men and eight women, the subjects were instructed through five training sessions in the function of the immune system. The instruction included slides of neutrophils, the white blood cells chiefly responsible for fighting infections. The participants were also trained in imagery-techniques. At a final session they were asked to imagine the neutrophils as garbage collectors picking up trash at points inside the body and dumping it outside. Blood samples taken at the beginning and end of this session were reported to show a drop of the white cell count in all subjects, averaging sixty percent (at Michigan State, reported by Achterberg 1985, 200). I do not know if these results have been verified.

Such widely disparate conditions as jet-lag, bed-wetting, and grieving are also treated by means of imagery. For phobias there is a special desensitization procedure in which the patient makes a graded list of anxiety-producing situations and then, in a state of deep relaxation, imagines living through them, starting from the least worrisome and always switching the imagery off at the first hint of anxiety. There are a number of other techniques such as systematic imaging of "safe places" and "shields," and the semi-spontaneous summoning of an "inner adviser"—who is reminiscent of the imaginary companion of childhood mentioned before.

There is also a great deal of psycho-imaginative group therapy. The general purpose is that of "changing one's life" and of bringing out the participants' distortions of attitudes and feelings, without appeal to conscious thought. In a protective setting they are cued with an "imaginary situation," a theme upon which to fantasize for self-interpretative purposes; this procedure derives from the "guided affective imagery" technique of Leuner (Watkins 1976). For example, participants will be encouraged by the leader to imagine two animals each of which they characterize with a loaded adjective, and to set them talking to each other in a kind of surrogate argument (Shorr 1980, 192).

Even as a limited, alleviating technique suggested to patients by objective health professionals, imagery-therapy appears to be effective only for especially receptive subjects. Committed imagery-groupers seem to be willing to combine contrivance with spontaneity, and, of course, the very ill may be driven by desperation to open their imaginations to therapeutic management. However, besides being a controllable method, imagery-therapy is also a part of a proselytizing movement dealing in "altered states of consciousness" and including a mixed bag of rational and transrational practices, such as meditation, hypnosis, biofeedback, deep relaxation, psychedelic visions, ecstasies, and extrasensory perception. Some of these methods share in the intellectual insouciance affected in these realms. The phenomenon of this enthusiastic affirmation of the imaginative power is nevertheless worth attending to, for it is a prime example of a widespread longing, endemic in modern life, to escape the constraints of technical reason while remaining under the aegis of its efficacy and its prestige. (Klinger 1971, Shorr 1980, Korn 1983.)

2. Affectivity. Imagery is cognitively and therapeutically effective largely because it is affective. The poetic manifestation of the affective imagination is taken up in Part Six (Ch. III B). The present concern is psychological.

It has been shown that physiological patterns during self-reported episodes of imagery match those established for affective states like happiness, sadness, and anger. The indices used are heart rate, respiration, electroencephalogram readings, skin temperature, blood pressure, salivation, and numerous others (Qualls 1982). It seems also to be the case that imaginative children, such as those who have imaginary playmates, are at once in better control of their emotions, being less fearful, angry, and bored, and more emotionally concentrated, happy and prone to higher moods (Tower 1983).

Yet, what is most interesting about studies of feeling and imagery is their meagerness. The right terms are not available yet and perhaps never can be. The passions do receive enormous psychological and philosophical attention, but the precise intersection of emotion and imagery seems to escape psychological inquiry. There has been practical recognition enough: After all, psychoanalysis is based on the hypothesis that images are invested with passion. There has also been observation enough, though it does not add much to common knowledge or produce many unequivocal insights. For example, while imagery is repressed during the onslaught of sensory stimulation and the emotion that goes with it, yet much affectivity is initiated by images. It often accompanies great arousal, yet it also goes with deep relaxation. Psychic illness seems to be indicated when imagery is divorced from the emotion evidently proper to it, yet too powerful an investment of imagery with feeling can be both cognitively and emotionally detrimental. It should be said that the last condition, which used to be the great bane of educators, is considered only in passing nowadays. Where earlier books on education taught that "confusions of fact and fancy," "insistent reveries," and "indecent imagery" should be dealt with perhaps kindly and indirectly, but certainly firmly (Klapper 1918), present-day misgivings center more about the dangers of too little imaginative activity. Evidently when the lid is off, the juice dries up.

There is a recent suggestion to study emotion as a "third code" interacting with the imagistic and the propositional codes of Chapter II (Kosslyn 1983). For affective studies seem least to turn in circles when they can deal with mental representations such as codes. But it is an unsolved problem whether emotions are representational, whether they are mental objects. Hence for psychology as a science the great questions largely hang in the air: How can an image be invested with feeling? Are emotions the causes or the effects of imaginative activity? Or is the circle perhaps unbreakable, as a psychologist suggested almost four centuries ago?:

> The passion increaseth the imagination . . . and the stronger imagination rendreth the passion more vehement, so that oftentimes they enter but with an inch, and encrease an ell. [Thomas Wright, *The Passions of the Minde in Generall* 1604]

C. Kinds of Imagery

Imagery can be distinguished by the state of mind in which it occurs (waking, sleeping, hypnotized or drugged), the location of its appearance (psychic, entoptic or external), and its volitional character (autonomous or intentional). Psychologists try to establish the kinds of imagery that arise from various combinations of these factors. Often the mere attempt to classify imagery is already illuminating.

1. Daydreams. Open-eyed fantasies, reveries, seem to be not so much the sharp spice of life as its diffuse flavoring. They can be concurrent with any waking business, since they require only a semi-withdrawal from the perceptual world, though really devout daydreaming is associated with decreased motor activity, particularly with suppressed ocular motility. Suppressed eye movement is one observable way in which daydreaming differs from dreaming, which is peculiarly associated with rapid eye movements (below, *3*). Waking motions and imaginative mobility thus seem sometimes to be reciprocals: This observation is in line with the finding that subjects required to freeze in place while viewing ink blots tend to see them in terms of human motion, and subjects that stay still tend to give kinetic interpretations of imagery.

In its pervasiveness, weak daydreaming, such as wool-gathering, seems to be a "base-line" process, a default state, as it were, which shows up when nothing in particular is going on. William James discovered the "wonderful stream of our consciousness" that, "like a bird's life, seems to be an alteration of flights and perchings," in which the perchings correspond to "sensorial images." Often one of these initiates a flux segment that is not any more disciplined but a lot more willful than the ordinary stream. Daydreaming is not generally regarded as encompassing the various inner efforts to keep a sequence of thought logical, to work out a structured fiction, to plan a daily route, or to solve a problem, even though all these labors involve the imagination. As a fall-back position from physical mobility and directed mentation, such fantasizing has been dubbed a "diversive" as opposed to a specific activity. It is "response rather than stimulus oriented," "respondent" rather than "operant"; it shows "high response variability," tends to be "intrinsically motivated," and is "low in the motivational hierarchy." In English: Daydreaming, though it may be triggered from the outside, is not an effortful try at practical activity, though it is certainly in a way productive: "My eyes make pictures when they're shut" says Coleridge in "A Day Dream."

Thus daydreaming is often preoccupied with current concerns, though not with immediate interventions; it doesn't get the dishes done. Its resolutions, not being corrected by feed-back or regimented by the test of reality, go off in all directions; there is no such thing as an incorrect daydream. Daydreaming arises from wishing rather than from wanting; it is not focused on attainable goals. In sum, it is "autotelic"—done for its own sake. It is worth noting that these delineations are mainly negative. The human condition, it is assumed, is such that its base-line is not its norm, that the condition into which we "lapse" is not the one in which we are meant to be: Effortful activity is our natural but not our ordinary state.

There may be no goal in daydreaming, but there is often plenty of purpose. For one thing, since low-grade daydreaming can, as was mentioned, run side by side with mechanical activity, setting oneself on autopilot and starting a dream often serves the purpose of making labor less repellent. Daydreaming doesn't do the dishes, but the dishes may get done the sooner for such dreams. It is not, however, the instrumental but the intrinsic purpose that predominates. That purpose is free pleasure, pleasure untainted by the toil of mastering a recalcitrant world. If pride and desire are the specifically human preoccupations, or, in baser terms, success and sex, those are just the topics of purposeful daydreaming. In other words, daydreaming is eminently volitional, though in a peculiar mode: Here to want, to will, and to have are one. There is a classical division of human impulse into active will and willful passion; it is neither of these, but passive desire, that directs daydreaming.

Naturally it does so to its own advantage, which is aided by the secrecy of its proceedings. Freud combined this hoary knowledge, that daydreams are mostly wish-fulfillments, with a modern understanding of happiness as the total gratification of all desires. It was consequently his opinion that "happy people never make fantasies, only unsatisfied ones do." The implication was that daydreaming is an unsatisfying satisfaction. In particular, Freud offered a theory of fantasy-making as part of the "unvarying inventory" of neurosis. The chief daydreams are all "primal fantasies," a "phylogenetic possession," through which the individual reaches back in memory to the actual sexual experience of his primitive ancestors, to childhood seduction, to the observation of parental coitus, and even to ritual castration. Such fantasies are like nature preserves protected from the encroachings of the reality principle, in which a primeval condition is carefully saved from the inroads of civilization. When these memories become invested with frustrated libidinous energy they press for realization. Then neurotic conflict with the ego results. Wish-invested daydreams, Freud says, show "unmistakably the essence of imaginary happiness, the return of gratification to a condition in which it is independent of reality's sanction" (*General Introduction to Psychoanalysis* 1917, ch. 23). For Freud such open-eyed fantasies are sick simulacra of pleasure.

That appraisal of fantasy is no longer so clear to the profession. Daydreams can be truly pleasant, though they come, to be sure, in all degrees of pleasantness. Most have been found to be quite mundane and affectively fairly neutral. Current concerns flit across the mind: familiar faces, work settings, daily routes, and mild-toned elaborations of stories seen on television. Most daydreaming, it seems, is of routine rather than romance. Much daydreaming, too, is vaguely dysphoric. Guilt, anxiety, and obsession are recognized affects of daydreams, and its more miserable contents sink to sadomasochistic violence. Evidently the volitional compass of daydreams ranges from the happily intentional, through the welcome and the unbidden, down to the unwillingly compulsive. There seems to be, incidentally, no agreement on the great question whether daydreaming is more often an irritant or a cathartic, whether it incites or inhibits overt realizations.

The point is, however, that post-Freudian psychologists are ready to recognize both that euphoric daydreaming is frequently itself pure pleasure and that it also assists in "real" gratification. Many an intimacy owes its moments of sexual success to the presence of secret sharers.

An interesting relation has been observed between the pleasantness of daydreams and their "code." Self-pity, shame, defensiveness, and anger tend to be expressed verbally, in silent monologic diatribes, as if the mind's eye were averting itself from the unedifying sight. Euphorically contemplative reveries, on the other hand, tend to be imaginal, made up of songs and sights. The imagination has a bias toward bliss.

Visual imagery is in fact as characteristic of daydreaming as it is of fantasy. Indeed a daydream *is* a sort of fantasy, so that one study (Klinger 1971) prefers that term for the phenomenon. The trouble is that "fantasy" is already used for visionary, weird, and magical productions in painting and literature (Part Four, Ch. IV B). The compositional character of daydreams corresponds in its loose unstructured sequences not so much to fantasy in that sense as to the fantasia of music.

It is that lability of structure which makes the wakeful, usually open-eyed dreams of the day appear to be cousins to the dreams of the night. It turns out that daydreams can stand in for nocturnal dreams in psychic life. It has been shown that if sleepers have their dream episodes curtailed by being aroused during periods of rapid eye movement, they make up for it with increased daydreaming.

However, not all reveries are loose-structured. Aside from pathologically compulsive repetitions, some fantasies are rigidly and repetitively rehearsed simply because they are satisfying, very much as children demand the same story in the same words over and over again, and adults find episodes in novels that give utter satisfaction on the umpteenth rereading: Recall the chapter in *Pride and Prejudice* where Elizabeth Bennett faces down Lady Catherine de Bourgh.

As with the sequences so with the shapes. Some figures and scenes float vaguely by or swim up as auras rather than as definite shapes; yet others are so intensely modeled out of the imaginal murk that it seems as if only the most minimal of miracles were needed for them to materialize. These latter fabrications pose the danger that the dreamer may feel let down on emerging, or worse, may get lost in a private world. Incidentally, such palpable fantasies come in two sorts. Some are simply purposefully self-delusive, while others are, so to speak, reality-compossible. They go over smoothly into real life.

As daydreams are related internally to dreams, so are they related externally to play. There is a claim that for the first three years of life fantasy and play all but coincide.

Now all we know of adult daydreaming comes from introspective verbal reporting. Such protocols are tricky, both because describing imagery, especially imagery in flux, is an art, and because the content is apt to be embarrassing. What is difficult for adults should be impossible for very young children, except for the happy fact that they have as yet no inhibitions about their fantasies. Their inability to introspect deliberately is compensated for by what they give away as they act out their fantasies. As Piaget considered imagery to be interiorized play, so play may be considered to be externalized fantasy.

At about six, fantasy goes underground, daydreaming separates from play, and play turns into games. Internal fantasy now shows a strong surge, especially in gifted children. There is some evidence, however, that the peak period for daydreaming is late adolescence. It comes from imagery tests that correlate well with the counted daydreams of adolescents. Now the type of the imaginary companion of childhood re-emerges as an imaginary friend and lover, and such fantasies are strengthened by all the previous cognitive acquisitions, including a more extensively stocked memory. In adulthood variations in fantasy life are largely individual and possibly related to ethnic background. For example, there is some evidence (which will have some heads nodding wisely) that White Protestant Americans do less daydreaming, though one may wonder if it is not their reporting that is more inhibited. Male and female fantasy patterns may also tend to differ. There are observations reporting that men are more concerned with pride, women with caring. In old age, people who preserve themselves from senility seem to revert to more daydreaming, mostly to reminiscent reveries. This increase is a function of free time and of regressive memory.

(Singer 1966, Klinger 1971, Singer and Antrobus 1972, May 1980, Gold and Henderson 1984.)

Contemporary accounts of daydreaming tend to end with a call for stimulation, as they once used to end with demands for control. It seems to be a doubtful appeal because nothing is more recalcitrant to reformist intervention than this most fugitive and recreational activity. The proper tending of daydreams is the work not of the psychologists but of the Muses.

Here mention should be made of "waking dreams," sharply distinguished by its proponents (Watkins 1976) from daydreams. The waking dream is the product of a dream-discipline—it would be a distortion to call it a technique—which owes much to Jung's "active imagination." Whereas the daydreamer is immersed in fantasies, caught in a kind of inattentive absorption, the waking dreamer watches the imagery that rises up with attentive awareness. Such fully self-conscious yet entirely receptive attention requires the theorist to give up the mainstream view of daydreams, which is that they are interpretable signals and symbols of unconscious activity. The discipline of waking dreams eschews analysis in favor of a receptive awareness, a kind of imaginal contemplation, meant to leave the image its own life. Its motto is an alchemical dictum quoted by Jung: "Our work ought to be done through the true imagination and not the fantastic one." The true imagination here is the deep, spontaneous one, unmodified by antic fancies, Coleridge's "primary" imagination (Part Four, Ch. II B). The central idea is that to return to one's imagery is itself the cure for psychic disorientation. The trouble with these attractive notions is, as so often, that they are advanced in a spirit less sober and more sectarian than they deserve.

2. Hypnagogic Imagery is of all the imagery experiences the most definitely delineable. It was named by Alfred Maury in 1848 after that state in which it occurs, the transition "between asleep and awake." But it had been recognized long before. In his *Commentary on Scipio's Dream* Macrobius (c. 400 A.D.) classifies dreams under imaginations and divides them into true and false. Of the false there are again two kinds. One includes wish-fulfillments and nightmares (*insomnia*), and the other the fantastic dreams that appear between waking and sleep (*visa*). As the modern name says, hypnagogic dreams "lead into sleep." Here is a classical description by Edgar Allan Poe:

> There is a class of fancies, of exquisite delicacy, which are not thoughts; they seem to be rather psychal than intellectual. They arise in the soul (alas, how rarely!) only at its epochs of most intense tranquility—and at those mere points in time where the confines of the waking world blend with those of the world of dreams. I am aware of these "fancies" only when I am on the brink of sleep, with the consciousness that I am so.
>
> I so regard them, through a conviction that this ecstasy, in itself, is of a character supernal to the Human Nature—it is a glimpse of the spirit's outer world; and I arrive at this conclusion by a perception that the delight experienced has, as its element, but *the absoluteness of novelty*.
>
> At times I have believed it impossible to embody in words even the evanescence of fancies as I have attempted to describe. ["Marginalia," *Graham's Monthly Magazine* 1846]

Poe's delight in the experience in general accounts for his frequent literary use of the—preponderantly terrifying—scenes that swim up in hypnagogic dreams. In fact, there are a number of horror classics that were supposedly so inspired, such as Walpole's Gothic tale *The Castle of Otranto*, Mary Shelley's *Frankenstein*, and Stevenson's *Strange Case of Dr. Jekyll and Mr. Hyde*. There are, however, also bright hypnagogic dreams, such as Kekulé's famous benzene-ring dream, which came to him as he was drowsing off on a bus.

There is a complement to this nocturnal vision in the morning dream, which is called "hynopompic," meaning "ushering sleep out." About three quarters of the subjects interviewed in one study had experienced hypnagogic dreams, but the hypnopompic sort was far less common. A poignant example is the auditory hynopompic dream of one of Tolstoy's most lovable figures, the boy Petya Rostov. He has run away to war and on the morning of his first—and last—engagement he dreams this characteristic psycho-pompic dream in the musical mode:

> Rain-drops dripped from the trees. There was a low hum of talk. The horses neighed and jostled one another. Someone snored.
>
> *Ozhik-zhik, ozhik-zhik* . . . hissed the sabre on the whetstone. And all at once Petya heard a melodious orchestra playing some unknown, sweet, solemn hymn. Petya was as musical as Natasha, and more so than Nikolai, but he had never learnt music or thought about it and so the harmonies that suddenly filled his ears were to him absolutely new and intoxicating. The music swelled louder and louder. The air was developed and passed from one instrument to another. And what was played was a fugue—though Petya had not the slightest idea what a fugue was. Each instrument—now the violin, now the horn, but better and purer than violin and horn—played its own part, and before it had played to the end of the *motif* melted in with another, beginning almost the same air, and then with a third and a fourth; and then they all blended into one, and again became separate and again blended, now into solemn church music, now into some brilliant and triumphant song of victory.
>
> "Oh yes, of course, I must be dreaming," Petya said to himself as he lurched forward. "It's only in my ears. Perhaps, though, it's music of my own. Well, go on, my music! Now! . . ." [*War and Peace* IV]

These are the chief characteristics of the hypnagogic dream: It is a kind of sleeping hallucination, distinguished from the waking hallucination mainly by the fact that the dreamer is in no condition to assert the reality of the dream. But the immediate remembrance of the dream—in my experience, corroborated in the literature, one is startled back into wakefulness before going off to normal sleep—is as of a bodily presence. The visions, voices, or touches are inexpressibly vivid, they are *there* as sensed beings rarely are. The dream is "autonomous"; it comes totally unbidden and totally unexpected. The presences in all modalities are ineffably strange. They are uncanny faces, ominous voices, garish shapes, exotic animals—tinselled elephants and bug-eyed fish—as if alien civilizations had let loose the contents of their bestiaries. Sometimes the visions are episodic, sometimes they unroll in long sequences with archetypal auras.

Some strong internal activation of the senses seems to be involved, but otherwise the physiological indices are similar to those of early sleep. Yet the phenomenon is distinguished from dreaming in definite ways. The hypnagogic dreamer is very much the spectator of an apparition, whereas the normal dreamer is often a participant. That feature is the complement to the sense of bodily presence in the hypnagogic dream, a sense absent or weak in normal dreaming. But above all, whereas dreams usually play in a familiar world, the hypnagogic vision is quintessentially alien, an invasion. It has, in Poe's words, the "absoluteness of novelty." If creation were really quintessential novelty these visions would be its epitome.

Finally, a variant type is distinguishable, called the "perseverative" dream. It tends to occur after a day of strenuous visual focusing, and uses the day's visual material. The state seems to be closer to waking than to sleeping. The location is often clearly entoptic, which means it is felt to be within the eye. The imagery is extremely labile and yet persistent. It is as if one were viewing a movie while making it. One has the sense that the same optical effort required to hold the vision makes it stream away. I remember lying in a tent filled with green moonlight after a day of driving through the canyons of New Mexico and seeing behind my eyelids an incessant coming of arroyos suddenly streaming with water, latticed stems of dead chollas growing into stands of aspen, hogans metamorphosing into adobe cathedrals, red mesas shifting against blue mountains—as if the land itself had become mobile around a wearily stationary driver.

(McKellar 1979, Oliver, Breger and Zanger 1980, Mavromatis and Richardson 1984, Morris and Hampson 1983.)

3. Dreams are of all representational events the most imaginal in two senses: They are imagistic insofar as they consist largely of mental imagery, and they are imaginative insofar as they contain the most abandoned fancies.

Dreaming is also, to tell the long and the short of it, a mystery. In the Western literary tradition dreaming has been a preoccupation from the beginning, in Homer and also in the Old Testament, in which forty-three dreams have been counted (Le Goff 1985; the best known of ancient dreamers is probably Joseph, who dreamed in his own behalf and was also the interpreter of royal dreams.) Out of the pre-modern dream-tradition, rich in examples and short in theory, I mention only the tripartite typology based on origin, which was shared by Pagans and Christians: Dreams come either from the gods (or God), or from demons (or the Devil), or from the memories of the individual soul (Le Goff 1985). This typology supplements for dreams the tabulation made of the possible sources of the imagination in Part One (Ch. II A).

These days, there is an ever accelerating flood of dream-books. There are laboratory-studies and dream-therapies. There are "how to" manuals for do-it-yourself dreamers and dream-dictionaries for amateur interpreters. Yet so far the advances are more terminological than substantive and more conjectural than cumulative. These facts themselves indicate the recalcitrance in the subject; if by a mystery is meant a phenomenon that conceals itself in the very act of revealing itself, dreams may be called mysteries. And yet we spend on the average four and a half years of our life in dreaming (Coxhead and Hiller 1976, 4).

The following brief survey of the *terrae cognitae* and *incognitae* of dreams falls under these six headings: (a) the chief characteristics of dreams; (b) the relation between the two worlds of dreaming and wakefulness; (c) the internal and external evidence for dreaming that becomes available during dreaming: "lucid" dreams and rapid eye movements; (d) the reporting of dreams; (e) the interpretation of dreams; and (f) feeling and dream-imagery. Under this last heading I shall propose an understanding of dreaming as an imaginative activity in a very specific sense.

a. Certain observations about dreams are currently established. The Aristotelian explanation of dreams as illusions caused by persistent perceptual traces (*On Dreams* 460), and all similar theories treating dreams as some sort of confused or delusive perception, seem to be inadequate. One strong reason for thinking so is that there are amodal dreams. An example is the case of a young woman with a specific cognitive disability, the total absence of kinetic mental imagery, which is characteristic of Turner's Syndrome, a consequence of a chromosomal abnormality. She reported very vivid and dramatic dreams in which neither visual nor compensatory auditory imagery played a role. The dreams consisted simply of feelings, awarenesses— "just knowing." Blind dreamers report similar experiences (Kerr and Foulkes 1978).

That is not, of course, to say that the dream-state cannot be influenced by perceptual stimuli. Names whispered to sleepers can sometimes induce dreams of the persons named. The removal of covers can bring on dreams of icy wastes: "Lying cold breedeth dreams of fear" (Hobbes, *Leviathan* I

2). There is, moreover, a kind of general "vigilance"-state of sleep which makes the dreamer sensitive to specific onsets or cessations of stimuli. Thus sleeping mothers notice changes in babies' breathing.

By and large, however, withdrawal from the realm of perception and unresponsiveness to stimuli are the overt characteristics of sleep, and hence of dreams. In addition there are less obvious indices, such as the characteristic wave patterns recorded on electroencephalograms.

Dream-representations are independent not only of immediate perception but also of waking reason. Dreams are generally agreed to be "symbolic acts" or even "thought processes," since they are digested, processed representations. But the mode is not that of waking rationality. Freud specifies some differences between dream thought and waking logic: Dreams are devoid of certain logical operations, such as the alternative "either-or" and the relation of implication or, in Freud's terms, "cause and effect." These are, so to speak, positively missing. That is to say, their absence appears in dreams in terms of conflations and transformations. For example, the disjunction "either-or" goes into the conjunction "and." Above all, the negative is missing. " 'No' seems not to exist as far as dreams are concerned" (1900, 353, though this absolute is qualified and corrected, 361, 372). Therefore dream thoughts cannot be self-contradictory, for they do not simultaneously signify a thought and its negation in the manner of waking reason. Instead some one part of the dream is turned into the opposite of another (Freud 1901, 65).

It ought to be said here that Freud's discovery of a dream-logic is really the discovery that dreams are essentially pictorial. For in the logic of pictures these are the very features that are prominent. There is, for example, no pictorial negation (Part Three, Ch. I B). In dreams, it appears, the imagination is well and truly on its own and does things in its own characteristic way. That suggests the following distinction between having a dream and looking at the world: Waking appearances are obtrusively given, for aside from altering or stopping our senses we cannot escape them, while our waking reason is what philosophers call spontaneous, an expression of our controlling will. In dreams it is the reverse; the appearances are spontaneous and reason is under their spell. In the waking world the vistas presented are arguably neutral, while meaning is the subject's responsibility. In dreams meaningfulness is irresistibly given, while the visions that clothe it are the dreamer's free inventions. One might say that while the real world may be objectively interesting the dream world must be subjectively significant.

Dreams share their symbolic and their imagistic character with daydreams. In fact, the two must be closely connected because, as was mentioned, aborted dreaming results in increased daydreaming (Klinger 1971, 56). Dreams differ in showing an absence of volitional direction. Indeed, to Bergson (1920) this was the very nature of dreaming: the relaxation of the will, with consequent loss of precise adjustment among perception, memory, and reason—an essential whimsicality. There are some rare reports of intentionally summoned dreaming, but the usual experience is that the more ardently a dream-apparition is wished for the more recalcitrant it becomes. Malsuccess in summoning of a daydream, on the other hand, is rare. This volitional difference shows itself in the formal character of each fantasy. Daydreams may consist of fugitively labile sequences, but the persons and objects in them tend to persist; in dreams, on the other hand, both characters and settings are eminently unstable and transformable.

Dreams are distinguished from hypnagogic imagery by the absence of the hallucinatory element, which requires a sense of perceptuality. Sleeping dreams lack the sense of perceptual intrusion. They are, so to speak, hermetically sealed in their own worlds. The dreamer is—usually—so completely absorbed in these dream-worlds that dream presences are no more and no less marvelous than the existence of objects in the real world. I am speaking here not of the contents of the dream, which may well amaze the dreamer, but of their mode of existence.

The "real world"—the expression raises the paramount question about dreams. The having and the telling of dreams occurs in two different realms, in two different states of consciousness: How does one of these achieve the honorific "real"?

b. The *locus classicus*, the boldest statement of this old perplexity, is in Descartes's *Meditations*. His assumption that the mind is a substance obliged him to say that it is in all its states conscious, since consciousness is its substantial essence. At the same time his search for certainty drove him to make an issue of the question: Which set of representations, dream or wake, were in fact the illusions? The problem was confounded by his observation that there is clarity and distinctness—vividness and sharpness—to be found in dreams, while waking representations abound in uncertainty. His resolution does not have the compelling force of rational demonstration but it has the viability of a reasonable decision. The waking state is to have primacy most generally because it is the position from which the question is raised. More specifically, it has preference because it is characteristically coherent, whereas dreams are disjointed (*Med.* VI).

It seems perfectly correct to call the coherent realm the real world. "Real" means thing-like, and the waking world has the coherence of things and their categories, such as reciprocal interactions in space, cause and effect in time, extended shape, number, and degree of quality. Though by this test the dream world is in fact consigned to being unreal, in the sense of being more illusory than the real world, why should it submit to the positive criteria of reality? It is rather non-real, not the contradictory but the contrary of the waking world. But the contrary of reality is appearance. Thus the dream world is a realm of kaleidoscopic visibility (or audibility) in which not the universal laws of reality but the pervasive ways of appearances obtain—ways, not laws. For though dreams lack unbreachable regularities, they do have a characteristic mode. For instance, the first material of real-world cognition comes through sensation, while the stuff of dreams comes from memory—whence dreams do share with sensations the bare fact of spatiality and temporality though not their rules. Again, the waking material is at some level "cognitively impenetrable," which means that it opposes some solidity to the grasp of thought; dream-appearance, is, on the other hand, at least in the rationalist view, shaped through and through by the dreamer; it gets what renitency it may have from its inner meaning. That is why, as was said above, the real world is essentially interesting, and the dream world is essentially significant.

The residual question is still which realm embraces which, and which world is our home and our base. Is life, as Calderón claims, a dream with sober episodes, or does the coherent world enfold dreams as continents encompass unexplored places and lost cities? The Cartesian answer is a version of the attitude universally adopted in the enlightened West, though recently with—wilfully—bad conscience: The culture of cultures, it seems to me, is one whose nature it is to give critical and coherent accounts of itself and of all the others. So the world of worlds is the one in which dreams are studied. It seems to be reasonable for us to let the matter rest there, bearing in mind that the archipelago of dream-worlds need not lose but might rather gain significance by being willingly received into the waking *orbis intellectualis*.

But the reasonable solution, it must now be said, is not the end of it for everyone. In his book *Dreaming* (1959) Malcolm, a student of Wittgenstein, attacked the fundamental Cartesian assumption that dreams are a form of consciousness. He begins with Wittgenstein's postulate that "An 'inner process' stands in need of outward criteria," and he elaborates: "The concept of dreaming is derived not from dreaming but from descriptions of dreams." In other words, the description itself is the required criterion. Malcolm evidently assumes with Descartes that the possibility of making judgments, and particularly self-conscious judgments like "I am dreaming," is a necessary mark of consciousness. He also supposes, however, that the criterion-description of an inner process must be simultaneous with it, and so the utterance "I was dreaming" is not the binding evidence that "I am dreaming" would be. Having required the latter sentence as evidence of dreaming, Malcolm then undertakes to show its absurdity by a mere analysis of its use: It would imply the judgment "I am asleep," which is fatally inhomogeneous with the normal use of the observation "He is asleep." In other words, saying that one remembers dreaming is not evidence that there was a dream, while asserting one's dream state while dreaming is contrary to the concept of sleeping. Therefore the Cartesian question "How can I tell whether I am awake or dreaming?" is senseless, and any principle of coherence drawn in to support this judgment is irrelevant to it (110).

Now it happens both that self-conscious dreaming is currently a much-studied phenomenon, and that in the fifties overt signs simultaneous with dreaming were discovered. The evidence of neither of these phenomena can break in on Malcolm's argument, since for him "the senselessness, in the sense of impossibility of verification, of the notion of a dream as an occurrence 'in its own right' is logically independent of the waking impression." This reasoning is too tightly wound into its circle to be empirically accessible. But both phenomena together may bolster one's inclination to break through the severities of a merely linguistic analysis, of which, truth to tell, psychologists have not felt they need take much account (Fodor 1981).

c. The two pertinent dream topics are the so-called "lucid dreams" and rapid eye movement sleep.

There is a fairly rare but very impressive sort of dreaming that includes lucidity or an awareness that one is dreaming. The phenomenon had already been described by Aristotle in his little essay *On Dreams* (II): "For often something in the soul tells a sleeper that the appearance is a dream." Recent findings are that in such dreaming the dream-sequence itself is distinctive, insofar as the lucid dream tends to follow upon a particularly bizarre dream-episode. Whereas the majority of ordinary dreams are judged to be unpleasant, lucid dreams tend to be accompanied by euphoric affects, such as blissful relief, gratitude, a sense of control, and cognitive detachment from the dream content. During such dreams, dreamers may even be able to signal their awareness through eye movements (Gackenbach and Schillig 1983). Of course, one may argue that the lucid dreaming is simply a different state from that of unreflective dreaming. But the state seems to be similar enough to permit a suggestive analogy: Lucid dreaming is to dreaming as self-consciousness is to consciousness. Thus lucid dreamers, insofar as they straddle the states of dream-absorption and reflection, present something like proof that dreaming is indeed one of the states of consciousness.

The other piece of evidence, the one major physiological discovery about dreaming so far, is this: Periodically during the night a sleeper shows rapid eye movement. The episodes increase in length to over half an hour as the night wears on. About a quarter of the night is spent in REM sleep. The REM periods are linked with the cycles shown by brain-wave patterns during sleep. The cycles begin with active sleep, when the waves are fast and small, and go through stages to the deepest·sleep, when the patterns are slow and large. The rapid eye movements take place during all but the initial phase of active sleep. The great discovery was that subjects awakened during REM sleep regularly reported dreams and usually "fluid" dreams— dreams that had a spun-out narrative structure. Further, they remembered much more dream-activity than subjects allowed to sleep through the night. It was later found that subjects awakened during non-REM sleep had often also dreamed, but the dreams tended to be brief static bursts of imagery rather than narratives.

Some of the early hopes for dream-study were disappointed. At first it seemed as if the eye movements might be tracking-motions, so that a lateral direction might indicate, for example, train-dreams and an up and down direction waterfall-dreams. But that hypothesis was weakened when it turned out that not only dreamers who report no visual imagery have REM dreams, but that even the blind have them. Investigators concluded that organismic indices in general were poorly coordinated with dream-content. Furthermore, it was first thought that REM experiments proved that dreams had a strong function of some sort, since subjects deprived of REM sleep made up for the loss the next night and seemed to undergo some psychological disturbances, even psychotic episodes. But the connection between REM deprivation and psychological health has since turned out to be vague and variable (Evans 1985, 131). Dreams may in fact be epiphenomenal on some psychological function of which REM is a part. To confuse the matter further, it turns out that there is a kind of deeply relaxed "waking dream" during which there is both a loss of control and dramatic imagery, just as in sleeping dreams, but which lack the physiological signs cf sleep, including REM (Foulkes 1985). To top it all, many animals have REM dreams, including opossums, whose imagery-formation may be somewhat restricted.

What the REM discovery does seem to show is that dreams are not, as had sometimes been claimed, a flash phenomenon but an extended temporal event. The length of the dream-narrative tends to fit with the preceding

REM period, so that real dream-time and internal dream-time are at least comparable.

Malcolm's defense against the REM evidence is that it is an error to take the locution that dreams occur "in" sleep so literally as to suppose they must take time because sleep itself does. The post-REM reports, he points out, are not verifiably connected to dream 'events, and making rapid eye movement an index of dreaming is a definition rather than a discovery. At this point, it seems to me, the analytic distancing from straightforward experience borders on the jejune.

d. The reporting of dreams remains a perplexity. If in the study of mental imagery privacy was the problem, in dreams the issue is privacy raised to the second power, because of the altered state of sleeping consciousness. The problem of remembering is similarly compounded. It becomes a necessary exercise to sketch out the difficulties, distortions, and dubieties of dream-telling before going on to dream-interpretation.

First and last is the insuperable fact that dreams are dreamed and told in different worlds, whence dream-reports are infected with the hermeneutic difficulties analogous to those that anthropological accounts have with alien cultures. The waking report may, after all, simply miss the inwardness of the dream-event, though the possibility should not, it seems, so much inhibit dream-study as keep it healthily circumspect.

Second, dreams are based largely on memories. Some of these are "day residues," passing incidents that are not very deeply stored and are correspondingly fugitive. Moreover, apart from particular contents, dreams as a whole tend to be labile, easily overlain and obliterated by more recent events. Of course (for no assertion about dreams is without its contradictory) there are unforgettable "big" dreams and deep-level recurrent dreams. As the big dreams are important in certain tribal rituals, the recurrent dreams play a role in literature. A moving example is Mark Twain's "My Platonic Sweetheart," an account of a dream of love recurring over five decades. The reappearances are of that special kind in which the event is unmistakably identical while the appearances are totally diverse: It is always the same love, the same loss, well remembered through all the luminous transformations.

The memory that does persist is twice remote from the perceptual original. A plausible cognitive tracing of the dream-process suggests that the materials recalled in dreams are memories already processed, so that the telling of a dream is the recollection of a memory of a memory (Foulkes 1985). Naturally the waking account is shaky about separating perceived facts, old memories, and dream-transformations.

Third, dreams consist largely of imagery, and it is notoriously the case that depictions are not finitely convertible into words (Part Four, Ch. I). Not every picture is worth a thousand words, but every picture would take an infinity of words to render its complete description. In this sense dreams are not entirely articulable.

Fourth and most serious, dreams have an aspect that is in principle ineffable. Most dream accounts are concerned with the fluidly narrative aspects of REM dreams. But those dreams are heavily atmospheric, and even more so are the brief apparitions of non-REM dreams. The seat of significance seems to be not so much the tale itself as its aura, a complex circumambience for which the Freudian term "feeling-tone" is not quite adequate. The interpretative theories all invite verbal reconstruction and with it rational rectification. Dreams are always groomed to be tellable at the expense of their original, often chafingly mysterious, atmosphere. Furthermore, the people who are told dreams, or even the tellers themselves, tend to interfere with the dream-memory by suggesting neat constructions that are beguiling but fudge the dream's true outlines. The practically unavoidable dishonesty of dream-telling also, incidentally, accounts for the bored suspicion often induced by other people's dreams: The aura has been dissipated because the tale has been tinkered with.

e. In spite of these impediments, the only grand theory of dreams is an interpretational one. Freud works with two related claims. The first is that dreams have a definite function. They guard sleep by fulfilling wishes, mostly of an erotic sort, which would otherwise disturb the sleeper's rest once the sleeping ego relaxed its suppressive hold on them.

The second claim, of more interest here, is simply that dreams are interpretable—that both the dream-figures and the dream-sequences are symbolic. Children's dreams are candid; they dream of eating what they crave. Adult dreams, however, are cagey; they confuse the issue by introducing an intermediate symbolism as a front for the suppressed contents of the unconscious. (Recall that the Freudian unconscious is not the conscious mind in a state of sub-awareness but an independent agency operating with its own mechanism beyond conscious control.)

This "latent" content must be inferred through analysis from the "manifest" or remembered dream. It is, in fact, the interpretation of the dream. The unraveling of the manifest dream, the recovery of the latent meaning, is possible because there is much method in the madness with which the unconscious scrambles its meanings. Its dream-work, by which the latent dream is transformed into the manifest dream, employs four distinct operations.

Freud names the first of these "condensation." Each element of the dream conflates many memories and meanings; it is vastly overdetermined by the dream-material. Consequently an analysis of a motif, particularly one amenable to punning verbalization, such as the occurrence of a cock-chafer, may take up pages of print (Freud 1900).

The second operation is "displacement." This is the relocation of psychical intensity from one element to another, particularly from thoughts to vivid imagery. Displacement accounts for the strangely skewed affective bunching of dreams. In undoing displacement analytically, it is found that dreams are invariably instigated by the "day residues" of the preceding day. The discovery of these, no matter how apparently unimportant or trivial, makes it possible to identify the wish worked up in the dream.

The next operation is that of "symbolization" itself. Here the dream-work is guided by "considerations of representability." That is to say, it produces a kind of poetry by inventing pictorial similitudes for unconscious thoughts and desires.

Finally, like a pencil sketch that is rubbed to blur its outline, the dream undergoes a "secondary elaboration." This operation obscures its motives and leaves it apparently unintelligible to the dreamer.

These operations are mechanisms. The dream-work is assigned no creative power by Freud. It neither invents spontaneous fantasies nor makes independent judgments but follows the rules of psychic natural science. This fact makes the interpretation of dreams a science, which analyzes the form of dreams in terms of the established dream-operations, and their matter in terms of the wish-fulfillment function.

(Freud 1900, 1901.)

Freud's theory is open to the criticism of being at once too narrow and too unconstrained. It is narrow in restricting dreams essentially to one subject-matter, that appropriate to wish-fulfillment instigated by day residues. The trouble is that in at least one careful four-year record of dreams such wish-instigating day residues showed up in not much more than half the dreams (Foulkes 1985, 24). The lack of constraining rigor on interpretations comes not only from the notorious suggestibility of dreamers in analysis but also from the "free-association" encouraged in dream-reporting, which, by attaching significance to waking improvisations relaxes the effort to remember and report the dream faithfully. It is also inherent in the dream-work itself. For it is part of the logic of dreams to reverse positive and negative signs freely, and finally to cap this obscurantism by means of the secondary elaboration.

The broadest kind of critique, however, and the most pertinent here, concerns both the function and the idea of the dream-symbolism, as opposed to the processes. It was broached by Piaget in the form of the following questions, which really impugn the very notion of an anti-rational unconscious: How can symbolization, which is the human cognitive mode *par excellence*, be understood as functioning to dupe consciousness? How can cognitive activity result in the suppression of knowledge? (1946, 191). A more recent criticism, as radical as it is sensible, resists the very notion of dreams as symbolic acts requiring interpretation. Dreams may, after all, be imaginal without being metaphors whose tenor is hidden in the unconscious. Dreams may simply be dreams, and have their meaning not in an unconscious reference but in themselves. Dreams may be patent to the dreamer (Watkins 1976). Of that more at the end of this section.

The Freudian theory of dreams gains plausibility as it is increasingly diluted by Freud's followers with modifications and inclusions. Jung adds to Freudian causality the idea of "finality." He means that dreams not only function as wish-fulfillments but also reveal the dreamer's plans and projections; they bear practically on the future. Whereas Freud looks only for the universal cause behind the dream, Jung includes the idea of a purpose as well. The effect a dream is meant by the dreamer to have may even be ethical; it may induce moral soul-searching. Hence dreams can have diverse meanings, highly specific to the dreamer's particular context. Hence the symbolism, too, is no longer a fixed, usually sexual, vocabulary of images but varies with the individual. A further Jungian widening of dream symbolism, though in an opposite direction, are the "mythologems," themes that rise up from the dreamer's collective unconscious: helpful animals and a wise old man, hidden treasures and a walled garden, a great snake guarding a golden bowl in an underground vault. Sometimes there occurs what in primitive tribes is called a "big dream," an unforgettable dream of superpersonal significance. Indeed, all the dreams arising from the deepest unconscious have not merely personal but widely human meaning. Whatever one may make of the collective unconscious, it has proved liberating to relearn that not all dreams need be centered on the Freudian point of points (Jung 1909).

The theory of Fromm is even more plausible in proportion as it is even more general. Succinctly put, it is that a dream is an experience during non-activity, a kind of imaginal contemplation, that is not subject to the categories of practical action and the logic of reality, such as the law of identity. In waking fantasies unreal logic works in an "as if" mode; in dreams that caution is thrown to the winds. Insofar as reality imposes, through nature or civilization, restrictions that are on the whole beneficial, there is some truth in the idea that dreams are escapist regressions. But insofar as our reality is negative, dream-life may be better and wiser. Thus sleep has an ambiguous function, and to tell whether a dream expresses irrational passion or sober reason one must know the dreamer's circumstances (Fromm 1951).

f. Finally I come to feeling and dream imagery. It is, oddly enough, simply unproven that dreaming has either a psychological or a cognitive function, at least if the notion of a function is taken narrowly, as the filling of a definite need, as a specific work that must be performed for survival. There are plenty of theoretical candidates for such functions. There is the Freudian hypothesis that dreams guard sleep. There is the idea, inspired by a computer analogy that dreaming is off-line time for memory-consolidation and program-updating (Fishbein 1981, Evans 1985). Yet another theory sees in dreams a kind of cognitive rehearsal or practice play (Foulkes 1985). None of these is so far more than a conjecture.

But to be without assignable function is not to be without purpose. Isn't there an argument that the best things in life are un-functional—necessary not for living but for living in plenitude? So it might be with dreams.

Dreams, I want to propose, are *essentially feeling-informed* imagery. It is the lay opinion that the arts express emotion and that artists make art at once to expel, express and enhance their feelings (Part Six, Ch. III B). Professionals and critics of the arts have often enough ridiculed this notion as the amateur's view of artistic genesis. Yet it persists. What is behind it? I think the experience of our dreams is behind it. Dreams, to be sure, are not properly expressive because they are not on display to the outside, but they *are* the inward epiphanies of passion. Dreams are a kind of anti-art, an amateur's art, the obverse of professional production. In the waking world the typical work of the imagination is thoroughly cognitive. Here the imagination wisely recognizes and takes advantage of sensory material supplied by nature. It works to standards of public intelligibility and employs passion to some ulterior purpose. In the dream realm, on the other hand, the imagination uses memory materials already in the soul; it gives internal appearance to the affects of the soul. It does really body forth feelings—not just the describable motions and passions of the soul, but the nameless senses and feels of scenes and people. Dreams are visual or musical precipitations of feeling, the shaped appearances of passion. They need be nothing more than the soul's representation of its affective life to itself.

The dreams of the blind and of people with imagery deficits, made up as they are of feelings and apprehensions, seem to underwrite this notion. Such dreams are like an unfinished sculpture cut out of living rock: They show more of the affective raw material than of its imaginal formation. They demonstrate that although dreams tend toward imaginal expression, they can be imageless if the memorial forms are lacking.

The "egotism" of dreams, the fact that in almost all REM dreams the self is somehow present (Foulkes 1985), also fits this expressional hypothesis. For the self, as the subjective pole of any representation, is the source of those lines of force that turn the imaginal space into a field of feeling and give images their affective distinction. Similarly, the "hypermnesia" Freud found in dreams (1900), the obverse of the post-dream amnesia psychologists work hard to explain (Foulkes 1985), points to dreams as the shapes of affects. In hypermnesia small forgotten incidents, if they had been, in dreams, once attended by a feeling, return to waking memory at affectively charged moments of a like sort. The unaccountability of dreams and their recalcitrance to rational suggestion also fits. For the logic of dreams combines the contradictoriness characteristic of the passions with the incapacity for negation that is a constitutional part of depictions. As the heart has its reasons, which the reason cannot reach, so images have their logic, which words cannot render.

The main counter-evidence to dreaming as affect-in-appearance is the claim that subjects awakened during REM sleep frequently give mundane, colorless reports. Yet however dull the account, it is hard to believe that the dream itself was emotionally quite so neutral. A dream that feels insignificant is a contradiction in terms. Still another difficulty is posed by an observation, going back to Freud and reinforced in later studies (Foulkes 1985, 183), to the effect that dream-imagery sometimes shows a striking disconnection from what might seem to be its appropriate emotion. But then, why should skewed feeling not be one of the expressible affects? After all, in waking life feeling drained of feeling is among the strong emotional experiences.

If there is something in what I have said, dreams are indeed meaningful, but they do not have separable meanings and hence do not require interpretation. They are manifestations but not symbols, and so want not deciphering but appreciative attention. (It is at least interesting in this connection that besides the word "dream," whose sense is related to the German word *Trug*, deception, there was once a homonym—it is not known whether etymologically identical or not—which meant "joy, music" and, which, in Old English, drove out the "illusion" meaning.) Similarly, dreams have no psychomechanical function but they do serve the soul's purpose. They are "world-analogues," but of the world seen from its psychic center outward. They reveal not the dreamer's psyche directly but the world as invested by the dreamer's feelings. They display in images that the subjective sense of things which is usually held at arm's length by the objective busyness of the day. The affectivity of the waking imagination will be taken up in the last chapter of this book.

Of course, neither this, nor any psychological theory so far, accounts for the main mystery of dreaming: How do we come to spend one part of our life amongst scenes and with persons so strange-familiar to the other? How is it, moreover, that among these dream-beings there are some that come in such a questionable shape that our certain sense of their identity is in itself an enigma? Above all, how is it that these dream figures, never-before-seen though they often may be in their particularity, are still perfectly familiar generically—are clearly namable by kinds? (Part One, Ch. III D). There is a classic case of the eclipse of visual memory, studied by Charcot in the later nineteenth century, in which the patient was unable to recognize either the streets and houses of his native town or the members of his own family. Yet he was perfectly aware that he was seeing streets and people. Analogously, in the dream state the visual imagination seems to produce new perceptions that are absolutely strange as sensible singulars but perfectly recognizable as generic shapes. So perhaps the most remarkable psychological aspect of dreams is that they alone, of all psychic events, vividly underwrite the perceptual theory that vision is somehow sortal: What we see we know in kind even when the sight is alien in its particulars.

4. Hypnotic Imagery and Hallucinations. It appears that, by and large, no types of imagers emerge. No set of traits has been found to be regularly correlated with tests for high imaging ability or preference. People who are susceptible to hypnosis tend to be "fantasy-prone," but since the converse is not shown, no imager-type emerges here either.

Hypnosis is a trance-like altered state of consciousness, usually not self-induced, in which the subjects become peculiarly suggestible to the instructions of the hypnotist. During the hypnotic state, which is one of withdrawal from the perceptual influences of the world, the subject is frequently asked to imagine a situation. Such imagining is understandably freer and more intense. It is, of course, that fact which suggests that hypnosis might be diagnostically and therapeutically useful. Clients can be asked to call up suppressed memory-images of past traumas and to project pictures of future healing.

A large portion of those responding well to hypnosis seem to have particularly pervasive fantasy lives, to judge not only impressionistically but by performance on standard tests. In general they are susceptible to imaginative experiences and welcome them. As children they engaged in extensive make-believe and they still sometimes do so as adults. They are very alive to sensory experience, but they can also vividly imagine with eyes not only closed but open—even to the point of self-induced hallucinating.

These findings suggest that hallucination is not necessarily a pathological state, since people occasionally hallucinate who are sane by other criteria. Indeed, Freud hypothesized—untestably, of course—that hallucination is the origin of mental representation: When the infant feels the pangs of hunger it comforts itself by hallucinating the absent breast. In any case, there seems to be a continuum from innocuous wool-gathering to full-scale hallucinating. The sparsest list of intermediate stations would include, besides highly absorbing daydreams, vivid visualizations of remembered and imagined events, "unbidden images" such as intrusively irrepressible revisualizations of traumatic scenes, post-hallucinogenic flashbacks, mirages and phantasmagorias, and hypnagogic dreams, as well as their auditory or tactile counterparts.

Hallucination, literally "mind-wandering," is the altered state of consciousness *par excellence*. To be hallucinatory in a strict sense, imagery has to meet these criteria: It has to be waking imagery, so that the imager can make present claims about its reality. The claim has to be that, as distinct from the eidetic case, the apparition is externally present. The representation has to seem autonomous and independent of the imager's volition, just like the real world. Finally, it has to be scannable. That is, the eye must be able to run over it; it must not be burnt on the retina of the organic eye, as are afterimages, which move with the eye. It should be said that positive hallucinations have a negative counterpart. Some hallucinations involve the un-seeing of persons and objects that are really there.

Besides the hallucinations that appear spontaneously to mainly sane persons, there are, of course, also the psychotic visions and those induced by hallucinogens. The content of the psychotic hallucinations is usually extremely idiosyncratic, obsessively repetitive, and disjointed. The hallucinogenic visions, however, have a somewhat generic content.

By and large, the attempt to arrange imagery by content is love's labor lost. The categories are more than coextensive with the world, for they must cover all that is and is not within it. Diagnostically elicited imagery does, to be sure, seem to cluster into situations, because the deep troubles they signal so often stem from the limited repertoire of childhood memories. Furthermore, although analysts who work under the expectation of certain kinds of contents do seem to obtain them, be they Freudian sexual symbolism or Jungian archetypes, investigators who work outside these theories get imagery that, although interpretable, is not really classifiable.

Drug-induced hallucinations, however, seem to be distinguished by highly type-specific contents. These effects are apparently due to physiological effects on the optical system. In LSD-induced hallucinations, for example, these phosphemes occur: rainbow fringes; double, triple, and multiple visions; an alternately infinitesimal or immense scale of views; and, above all, recurrent shapes like funnels, cones, tunnels, spirals, lattices and honey-combs. Thus the once popular term "psychedelic," that is, "soul-manifesting," is a misnomer. What appears is probably largely the internal structure of the eye. Perhaps it is in any case unlikely that the soul of a tripper would choose to show itself as a geometer. Furthermore, in contrast to spontaneous hallucinating which usually inserts extra presences into the normal world, open-eyed drug-induced hallucinating transforms everything it lights on in the environment: Objects glow, pulsate, and distort themselves (whence, to be sure, such experiences are not hallucinations in the strictest sense).

The rapturous high priest and recorder of mescaline dreams is Aldous Huxley, who gave the psychedelic cult its bible with his book *The Doors of Perception* (1954). What he repeatedly attempts to convey is the overwhelming significance with which objects are invested during a drug episode, as if in each a *mysterium tremendum* had been made manifest. (Huxley 1954, Horowitz 1970, McKellar 1972, Wilson and Barber 1983.)

The psychologist's working definition of hallucination is that it is a perceptual response in the absence of an external stimulus. It is essentially an observer's definition, since it presupposes that to be real is to be observably perceptible. Without this prime axiom of all objectivity, one might suggest that here at the extremes, where the imagination pays back with usurer's interest the perceptual loan taken out from the world, this definition is not quite sufficient. On the physical side the desideratum would be to find specific neurophysiological signs for distinguishing imaginal from perceptual events, even, perhaps, to find physical indices for the sense of externality that attaches to some imagined representations, such as hypnagogic dreams and hallucinations. On the psychic side what is wanted is a way to acknowledge the significance of even these extreme works of the imagination without surrendering the sober standards of unaltered states of mind.

5. *"Near-Death Experiences."* A last—indeed ultimate—state of consciousness, which has been methodically investigated in the last two decades, is the visionary experience of persons on the point of death. The phrase "altered state of consciousness," which has been used several times in this chapter, evades definition. It simply refers to an experience that is felt by the subject or by an observer to be out of the normal. Near-death experiences are both out of the normal and highly distinctive.

"Near-death" is defined as a condition of extreme physiological catastrophe, such as cardiac arrest or severe traumatic injury, warranting the "Code

Blue" emergency call in hospitals. The phenomenon investigated is narrowly circumscribed, experiences under anesthesia being excluded. There remains a remarkable group of strongly typical and statistically significant reports.

One recurrent feature reported is "autoscopy," that is, seeing oneself. Patients report themselves as leaving their bodies and watching the emergency-room procedures being performed from the outside. The reports of autoscopists evidently contain more details specific to their medical case and more accurate descriptions of the hospital setting than can be easily accounted for by prior knowledge of the procedures or by clues subconsciously absorbed from a supine position in the emergency room. This "separated self" condition, recognizable from present-day protocols, seems to be depicted in Blake's drawing, "Soul Hovering Over the Body Reluctantly Parting with Life" (1805). It is evidently an old experience, though obviously the success of current resuscitation procedures increases the opportunity for reports.

The second typical feature, which is sometimes mixed in with autoscopy, is the "transcendental" vision. This is a vision of scenes and presences felt to be from beyond. Often there is a dark, tunnel-like space to be traversed toward a brilliant source of light at the end. Sometimes there are kindly presences, beckoning or averting, familiar or unknown. Very often there are ravishing panoramic visions, pastoral or heavenly places never before seen. There is a suffusing sense of ineffability, of timelessness, of overwhelming actuality, and, always, of serenity. Each vision ends with a return, a strong sense of being turned back or of choosing not yet to enter into a realm clearly recognized as death.

(Sabom 1982.)

The question whether such experiences are properly assigned to the imagination further forces a half-dormant issue. To begin with, autoscopic visions are, if they are imagery at all, a very peculiar kind—a sort of extra-corporeal perception. The "transcendental" panoramas are, furthermore, reported not as memories or dreams or fantasies but as genuine glimpses of the approaches and pastures of the other world. It would be overriding too cavalierly the subjects' abiding sense of the "reality" attaching to their experiences simply to classify them as imaginary. On the other hand, any inner vision might be in some sense claimed for the imagination. These considerations force the following question: Does the imagination have material sources other than memories of normal perception? It is a question wisely left unsettled by the physician-investigators of this phenomenon (Part Three, Ch. III C).

There is, however, a very recent historical and thematic treatment of near-death experiences, Carol Zaleski's *Otherworld Journeys* (1987), in which, on the basis of near-death evidence like that presented above, the eschatological imagination is investigated in categories beyond the medical and psychological.

What makes *Otherworld Journeys* especially pertinent to the present study is the author's attempt to steer a middle course between rationalistic reductionism and naive acceptance of these accounts as proof of an after-life. Zaleski's gallant intention entails directly facing certain crucial but, as it were, questionable questions about the eschatological imagination. They are the questions about the truth of its intimations—the very questions that are also the ultimate preoccupation of this book. In sum, the courage of her attempt flinches, as I will argue, before two complementary modern conventions: the litany of social conditioning and the dogma of subjective experience.

Let me begin by distinguishing three aspects under which the problem of the revelatory imagination seems to me to present itself. First is the telling of the experience, the narrative. Then there is the experience itself, the actual vision. The third consideration is the world of which it is the experience, its source. Zaleski is constrained by the above-mentioned dogmas to collapse these elements, treating narrative, experience, and source as essentially one. Consequently her book is not only an illuminating study of near-death experiences but it also displays, incidentally, the contra-dictions in which a modern approach to the imagination—it turns out to be Pragmatist—for all its admirable sincerity, is apt to become enmeshed.

The contemporary sympathizers of near-death experiences, Zaleski points out, tend to dismiss their specific "mythical" form. That is to say, they play down the particular figures and topographies that constitute the visual specificity of each vision—precisely because myths are nowadays commonly regarded as mere fictions. They insist instead on the thematic recurrences (detailed above), which appear to them to point to a common root-experience. Zaleski, on the other hand, proposes to focus on the differences in the near-death narratives, especially those distinguishing the accounts of medieval and modern afterworld pilgrims. In medieval reports, for example, there is often a "two-deaths" element. The dying are con-fronted with the possibility of two exits. The sinner must go in agony to hell, the saint is blessedly wafted to heaven. In modern cases, on the other hand, the near-death experience is almost exclusively hopeful of bliss. Again, in medieval experiences the dying meet tests and torments on the way. In the modern counterparts these trials have been softened into a learning-process. On his return, the medieval visionary has a clear commis-sion to promote particular penitential institutions. The modern missionary feels a much vaguer testimonial mandate. In other words, the modern experiences are altogether less fierce and more comforting than those reported in medieval times.

From these and other differences the author draws the conclusion that behind these experiences, when taken over time, there is no single visionary eschatology, no unitary picture of the extreme border. Consequently they contain no testimony suggesting a universal truth. It is rather the case that each experience is, while deeply subjective and almost ineffably private, also culturally conditioned, shaped by the religious training and the inherited imagery of each individual. Not only is its telling culturally structured, but the experience itself is already a work of the culturally conditioned symbolic imagination. The experience is, in fact, a cultural narrative. That is to say, the vision is not the memory of otherwordly things revealed to inward sight and hearing, but a construction based on individual experience and the cultural environment.

The theory of the eschatological vision as a type of symbolic imaginative product is intended to preserve the visionary significance while denying neither the cultural relativity nor the scientific incorrigibility of the vision. That is its great virtue. The symbolic function is understood to be that by which the religious imagination gives pictorial, vitally vivid existence to the individual's own ideas. Attention to such corporeal imagery, Zaleski hopes, can free theology from its dry and dead intellectuality and turn it into a living therapeutic discipline. Such a living theology would concern itself with the health of our symbols, validating those that heal both the will and the intellect (192).

Zaleski's assumptions and solutions appear to me to run into the following difficulties. First, she overlooks the fact—which is the more strange in a book explicitly devoted to bringing out hidden presuppositions—that, for all its opposition to mere intellectualism, the hypothesis behind the symbolic theory is that for humans intellectuality is ultimate. For if the imagination is understood as always functioning to give visible form to the subject's ideas, then it essentially represents or symbolizes thought. Thus it has neither independent access to transcendent truth, if such there be, nor, what is more, any original visions of its own.

Second, the claim concerning the cultural conditioning of near-death experiences is in equal parts true by definition and not quite convincing. It is unconvincing insofar as there does seem to be a kind of unchanging hieratic vernacular for these experiences: the luminousness, the pastoral setting, the white-garbed guides. This fairly uniform visual vocabulary is the more surprising since it is certainly part of contemporary cultural conditioning to make free with forms and costumes from a great variety of religions and times. On the other hand, the claim is true by definition insofar as the near-death vision is *ex hypothesi* treated as "an Experience," in the strong sense, that is to say, as a subjectively significant event, which testifies to its objective, common cause even less certainly than does ordinary experience. For one has "an Experience" in a uniquely personal mode. To put the question without the preconceived category of the Experience would be to ask whether there is discernible in these events across the ages, diversely conditioned by individual experience though they may be, not so much a universal root-experience as a common cause, a unitary manifestation of truth, an actual intimation of a transcendent topography. In short, it would be to ask whether what shows itself near death could in fact be a paradise, perhaps one containing many provinces—Elysian Fields, Edenic gardens, celestial pastures. This questionable question is what the treatment of the near-death vision as an experience evades in principle. To face it is, of course, the business not of history and psychology but of theology.

Zaleski, however, understands theology as the merely therapeutic art of detecting and serving the changing needs of imaginative symbol-systems (194). The symbolic religious imagination is to be respected because it communicates meanings through created forms and expresses in images individual conceptions. It is "the power that makes our ideas and ideals come to life and act on us." This view does not, of course, honor so much as override the central element of near-death experiences, which is the sense that transcendental truth is being visibly, if personally, revealed. The trouble—an old one—is that in the realm of faith the pragmatist dogmas self-destruct: The suggestion that a vision is true only because it aids life taints its credibility and vitiates its force.

The great question concerning the revelatory power of the imagination, so powerfully raised and so problematically put aside in the context of near-death experiences, will be taken up more than once again in this book (e.g., Part Three, Ch. III C; Part Six, Ch. II C).

D. "Individual Differences"

It will surprise nobody that the gift of producing and reproducing images is unequally distributed among human beings. That is precisely why studies of "individual differences" in imagery, statistically tabulatable variations, are the old psychometric standbys of experimental psychology. The results, however, do not seem to be very cumulative or coherent. Often studies correlate badly or even contradict one another. Certainly no clearly outlined types of human imagery have emerged in a hundred years of study. That result was already augured at the beginning. The most famous result of Sir Francis Galton's *Inquiries into Human Faculty and its Development* (1883), one of the founding works of both "psychometry" (his term) and imagery-study, was that "scientific men, as a class, have feeble powers of visual representation." Galton was amazed by this finding but had no doubt of the fact. He accounted for it by surmising that "an over-ready perception of sharp mental pictures is antagonistic to the acquirement of habits of highly-generalized abstract thought." No one can account for Galton's finding anymore; the fact seems to be just the opposite, as the examples of previous sections indicate. According to recent estimates, only three percent of all subjects are totally incapable of getting visual imagery (Kosslyn). One possibility is that some respondents, as abstract-thinking scientists, system-atically failed to attend to such imagery as they did have; according to Galton's own observation, it is only the "women and intelligent children" who take special pleasure in introspective reporting.

The *Inquiries* is nevertheless a wonderful work, full of scientific anticipation and stylistic felicities. The section on mental imagery is well worth a brief summary, into which I shall intersperse a few notes on subsequent developments.

Galton composed and sent a questionnaire to a hundred men, mostly distinguished scientists. It began by asking them to think of that morning's breakfast table and "to consider carefully the picture that rises before your mind's eye." They were to report on the brightness, definition, and coloring of the imagery. They were further to consider its visual angle (whether wider than that of perceptual sight), its possibly holographic character (whether more than three faces of, say, a sugar-cube could be imaged at once), its location (whether imagery appeared in the head, the eyeball, out front), its projectibility (whether it had what was later called eidetic character), and its stability (how much effort was needed to maintain it). They were further to comment on visualizing familiar faces, on turning descriptions into pictorializations, on using imagery in doing mathematics or playing chess, and on employing the imagery of all the other sense-modalities. In sum, Galton anticipated most of the topics still preoccupying imagery-study and, along with standard imagery features and abilities, discovered some that were strange.

As for individual differences, he was amazed to find that among the men of science, many of whom were his friends, the great majority "protested that mental imagery was unknown to them." Some demurred at the very term "mind's eye" and "image." For the others, there were great individual differences in vividness.

What makes these findings interesting is, as I have said, that they anticipated an epoch in imagery-study. At the beginning of this century a group of researchers working at Würzburg discovered in their subjects not only "imageless thought" but something beyond—what might be called "thoughtless thought," or unconscious thought (Kaufman 1979). The first finding contradicted the old notion that imagery is necessary to thought. The second anticipated the principal axiom of cognitive psychology, that consciousness is epiphenomenal on non-conscious processes. The introspective techniques used in the "imageless thought" school were, however, impugned on the grounds that subjects had been required to be conscious of their own mental contents while attending to difficult tasks. To this day it is an open question whether there really are individuals who are imageless in every modality for which they have the sensory capacity.

Galton next turned to the general population and found that here a larger proportion of people "declared that they habitually saw mental imagery." Women and children were found to have a greater power of visualizing than men. Galton extended his inquiries to the Continent. The French, he determined, are high visualizers, as indicated by their love of spectacle. Recent judgments are that Bushmen of South Africa and the Eskimos are also, judged by their drawings, great imagers; but no group surpasses prehistoric cave dwellers (Part Five, Ch. III B).

The point is that Galton is extending the study of individual differences to age, ethnic origin, and sex. One delightful finding along the lines of age, recently supported, is that vividness of imagery increases as people get older (Morris and Hampson 1983). On the other hand, Galton's conclusion that imagery is "primitive," in the sense of being developmentally early not only in individuals but also in cultures, has also had some recent scattered anthropological support. Members of various pre-literate cultures seem to have very vivid imagery, a greater incidence of eidetic images and very powerful dreams (Doob 1972), while Anglo-Saxon Americans as a group do less daydreaming than other groups. But all these findings are inconclusive.

Even more uncertainty reigns in the current study of sexual differences, which has gotten entangled in the problems of hemispheric lateralization. The simpler popular version, that males tend to be right-brain dominant and visual-spatial, and females left-brain superior and verbal, is far from taking into account the increasing complexity of the situation, part of which is that individual differences may run askew of gender differences. How popular schematizations by-pass each other is actually more interesting than the experimental results so far. Galton's findings fit in with the older notion that females are more immediate, sensory, practical, emotional, and imaginative, while males are distant, abstractive, theoretical, and rationally verbal. The recent wisdom, on the other hand, sees men as the inarticulate makers of visual-spatial constructions, while women are the talkative mistresses of the word. Take your pick.

I should add that there are a number of not very coherent, rather weak recent findings about sexual differences. Women evidently have more hypnagogic but not more hypnopompic imagery than men. Men and women are equally aroused by pornography, but the affect of the imagery is less pleasant for women than for men. Female adolescents daydream slightly more than males. The sum total seems to be that gender differences in imagery are negligible (Sheehan et al. 1983).

After his study of memory images, Galton looked at the imagination-imagery of "visionaries," by which he meant vivid imaginers. A fascinating kind of low-level imagery exhaustively studied by him are the "number-forms," the various idiosyncratic shapes people use to picture the counting numbers, a form of imagery rediscovered by Piaget. Galton thought such fantasies were hereditary in families. (This is the place to mention incidentally that the *Inquiries* were written with the purpose of furthering the "hereditary improvement" of the race, since Galton was one of the founders of the not-so-innocent Darwinian Eugenics movement.) Galton also found that his visionaries had fixed image-vocabularies. They attached persistent images even to connectives. One subject, for example, pictured the interrogative "what" as a fat man cracking a whip—some sort of auditory association. Stronger types of visionary imagery Galton distinguished were "phantasmagorias," crowds of internal phantoms vivid to the point of hallucination. Galton's explanation of religious visions precisely anticipates Jaynes's hypothesis of the "bicameral mind," which is one consciousness divided in function between god and man (1976). As Galton puts it: "Dividuality replaces individuality, and one portion of the mind communicates with another portion as with a different person" (148). For all his interest in imagery, however, Galton ultimately sides with his men of science. Visionaries tend to be "ecstatics, seers of visions, and devout fasting girls who eat on the sly." Here is imagery dismissed in anapests.

Galton tested his subjects for vividness, manipulative control, sensory modality, and, above all, what is now called "cognitive preference"—whether words or images are the representations of choice. These are still the chief factors looked for in imagery tests. Such tests are of two types: subjective self-reports like Galton's questionnaires and objective behavioral tests. Unfortunately, results obtained subjectively and those attained objectively do not correlate very well on the whole. But one example of a positive correlation is that of decreased eye movements to high vividness ratings in the 1973 Marks Vividness of Visual Imagery Questionnaire. These movements are regarded as an independent imagery-index because during visualization competing perceptual input is presumably reduced.

Such correlations are of great importance for two purposes: first, to see if some sort of imaging personality can be described, and second—a great preoccupation of psychologists—to test the tests, to see if they really get hold of any imagery-dimension, preferably the intended one. This verification is quite a task in view of the fact that there are well over two dozen such tests (Tower 1983), and more coming. One suspect non-correlation found in earlier testing was that between vividness of imagery and performance of cognitive tasks. The recent experiments in cognitive psychology, which tend to show that imagery is indeed cognitively useful, have not mainly addressed themselves to individual differences, or have attended not so much to variations in vividness of imagery as to preference for its use in the first place. The consensus seems to be that individual differences in the use of imagery come out most strikingly in novel situations, precisely those that are defined as demanding "creativity" (A above).

In spite of his finding that vivid imagery hinders rather than helps thought, Galton also concluded that "the highest minds are probably those in which it is not lost, but subordinated, and is ready for use on suitable occasions." Thus Galton in fact concluded that individuals cannot be typed in terms of the ability to think or image. Indeed, Kosslyn (1983), on the basis of the processes distinguished in his model, has suggested that imagery is not a unitary ability at all. The findings, beginning with Galton, support him. People's abilities to make imagery move, to do very speedy rotation, or to maintain imagery well may all vary independently.

(Galton 1883, Kaufman 1979, Morris and Hampson 1983, Sheehan, Ashton and White 1983.)

"Individual Differences" comprises the longest and least conclusive of imagery studies. There are, to be sure, some recent statistics about imagery differences among people. For example, for the three percent who are evidently imageless, there are an equal number who are superb imagers. About four-fifths of all images are in color and two-fifths move. Some people can image over several sensory modalities—and so on (Kosslyn in *New York Times*, Science Section, Aug. 12, 1986). However, as has been said, there is not yet an established working typology for imagers. Indeed, it is not even clear what is meant by the type most often distinguished, the "high imager." Is being a high imager a result of a skill, a state, a preference, a way of presenting oneself? (Katz 1983). It seems that the imagination is not very amenable to study in the range of features subject to statistical variation, but becomes more accessible at the two extremes of universality and uniqueness. There the constitutional properties of imagery in general and the qualitative nature of imaginative life in particular are respectively taken up. The former has been the chief subject of this part; the latter will come to the fore later in the book.

Bibliography

Achterberg, Jeanne. 1985. *Imagery in Healing: Shamanism and Modern Medicine.* Boston: New Science Library, Shambala Publications.

Ainsworth-Land, Vaune. 1982. "Imagery and Creativity: An Integrating Perspective." *Journal of Creative Behavior* 12:5–28.

Arnheim, Rudolf. 1979. "Visual Thinking in Education." In *The Potential of Fantasy and Imagination*, edited by Anees A. Sheikh and John T. Shaffer. New York: Brandon House.

Barber, Theodore X. 1971. "Imagery and 'Hallucinations': Effects of LSD Contrasted with the Effects of 'Hypnotic' Suggestion." In *Imagery: Current Cognitive Approaches*, edited by Sidney J. Segal. New York: Academic Press.

Bergson, Henri. 1920. "Dreaming." In *Mind-Energy: Lectures and Essays*. New York: Holt and Company.

Brann, Eva. 1968. "The Student's Problem." *Liberal Education*, October, 369–384.

Bruner, Jerome S. 1966. *Toward a Theory of Instruction.* New York: W.W. Norton and Company (1968).

Bugelski, R. R. 1982. "Learning and Imagery." *Journal of Mental Imagery* 6:1–22.

Coxhead, David, and Hiller, Susan. 1976. *Dreams: Visions of the Night.* London: Thames and Hudson.

Doob, Leonard W. 1972. "The Ubiquitous Appearance of Images." In *The Function and Nature of Imagery*, edited by Peter W. Sheehan. New York: Academic Press.

Evans, Christopher. 1985. *Landscapes of the Night.* New York: Washington Square Press.

Eysenck, Michael W. 1984. *A Handbook of Cognitive Psychology.* Hillsdale, N.J.: Lawrence Erlbaum Associates.

Fishbein, William, ed. 1981. *Sleep, Dreams and Memory.* New York: Scientific Books.

Fisher, Howard. 1979. "The Great Electrical Philosopher." *The College* [St. John's College] 31:1–13.

Florisha, Barbara L. 1983. "Relationship Between Creativity and Mental Imagery: A Question of Cognitive Styles?" In *Imagery: Current Theory, Research, and Application*, edited by Anees A. Sheikh. New York: John Wiley and Sons.

Fodor, Jerry A. 1981. "Operationalism and Ordinary Language." In *Representations.* Cambridge: The MIT Press (1983).

Foulkes, David. 1985. *Dreaming: A Cognitive-Psychological Analysis.* Hillsdale, N.J.: Lawrence Erlbaum Associates.

Freud, Sigmund. 1900. *The Interpretation of Dreams.* Translated by James Strachey. New York: Avon Books (1965).

———. 1901. *On Dreams,* Translated by James Strachey. New York: W.W. Norton and Company (1952).

Fromm, Eric. 1951. *The Forgotten Language: An Introduction to the Understanding of Dreams, Fairy Tales, and Myths.* New York: Holt, Rinehart and Winston (1976).

Gackenbach, Jayne, and Schillig, Barbara. 1983. "Lucid Dreams: The Content and Conscious Awareness of Dreaming During the Dream." *Journal of Mental Imagery* 7:1–14.

Galton, Sir Francis. 1883. *Inquiries into Human Faculty and its Development.* New York: E.P. Dutton and Company.

Gerard, R. W. 1952. "The Biological Basis of Imagination." In *The Creative Process,* edited by Brewster Ghiselin. New York: New American Library.

Ghiselin, Brewster, ed. 1952. *The Creative Process.* New York: New American Library.

Gold, Steven R., and Henderson, Bruce B. 1984. "Adolescent Daydreaming." In *International Review of Mental Imagery,* Volume 1, edited by Anees A. Sheikh. New York: Human Sciences Press.

Gowan, J. C. 1978. "Incubation, Imagery, and Creativity." *Journal of Mental Imagery* 2:23–31.

Guilford, J. P. 1950. "Creativity." *The American Psychologist* 5:444–454.

Haber, Ralph N. 1981. "The Power of Visual Perceiving." *Journal of Mental Imagery* 5:1–40.

Hargreaves, H. L. 1927. *An Enquiry Concerning the Existence of a General 'Faculty', or Group Factor, of Imagination. The 'Faculty' of Imagination: The British Journal of Psychology.* Monograph Supplement X. London: Cambridge University Press.

Hilgard, Ernest R. 1981. "Imagery and Imagination in American Psychology." *Journal of Mental Imagery* 5:5–66.

Hillman, James. 1964. *Emotion: A Comprehensive Phenomenology of Theories and Their Meanings for Therapy,* 2d ed. Evanston: Northwestern University Press.

———. 1975. *Re-Visioning Psychology.* New York: Harper and Row.

Horowitz, Mardi J. 1970. "Therapeutic Uses of Imagery Formation." In *Image Formation and Cognition,* Part IV. New York: Appleton-Century-Crofts.

Huxley, Aldous. 1931–63. *Moksha: Writings on Psychedelics and the Visionary Experience,* edited by Michael Horowitz and Cynthia Palmer. New York: Stonehill Publishing Co. (1977).

Imagery Movement [1976 on]:
  a. *Imagination, Cognition and Personality* 1 (1981–   ).
  b. *Imagery Today, Newsletter of the I.I.A.*
  c. International Imagery Association [runs annual national and international imagery conferences].
  d. *International Review of Mental Imagery*, Series I (1984–   ).
  e. *Journal of Mental Imagery* 1 (1976–   ) [quarterly of the *International Imagery Association*].

Jaynes, Julian. 1976. *The Origins of Consciousness in the Breakdown of the Bicameral Mind.* Boston: Houghton Mifflin Co.

Jung, C. G. 1909-. *Dreams.* Translated by R.F.C. Hull. Bollingen Series. Princeton: Princeton University Press (1974).

————. 1935. *Analytical Psychology: Its Theory and Practice.* (The Tavistock Lectures.) London: Routledge and Kegan Paul (1968).

Katz, Albert N. 1983. "What Does it Mean to be a High Imager?" In *Imagery, Memory and Cognition: Essays in Honor of Allan Paivio.* Hillsdale, N.J.: Lawrence Erlbaum Associates.

Kaufman, Geir. 1979. *Visual Imagery and Its Relation to Problem Solving: A Theoretical and Experimental Inquiry.* Bergen, Norway: Universitetsforlaget.

————. 1984. "Mental Imagery and Problem Solving." In *International Review of Mental Imagery*, Volume 1, edited by Anees A. Sheikh. New York: Human Sciences Press.

Kerr, Nancy, and Foulkes, David. 1978. "Absence of Visual Dream Imagery in a Normally Sighted Subject with Turner's Syndrome." *Journal of Mental Imagery* 2:247–264.

Khatena, Joe. 1978. "Identification and Stimulation of Creative Imagination Imagery." *Journal of Creative Behavior* 12:30–38.

Klapper, Paul. 1918. *Principles of Educational Practice.* New York: Appleton-Century-Crofts.

Kleitman, Nathaniel. 1960. "Patterns of Dreaming." In *Altered States of Awareness: Readings from Scientific American.* San Francisco: W.H. Freeman and Company (1972).

Klinger, Eric. 1971. *Structure and Functions of Fantasy.* New York: Wiley-Interscience.

Korn, Errol R., and Johnson, Karen. 1983. *Visualization: The Uses of Imagery in the Health Professions.* Homewood, Ill.: Dow Jones-Irwin.

Kosslyn, Stephen M. 1980. *Image and Mind.* Cambridge: Harvard University Press.

————. 1983. *Ghosts in the Mind's Machine: Creating and Using Images in the Brain.* New York: W.W. Norton and Company.

Le Goff, Jacques. 1985. "Dreams." In *The Medieval Imagination*, Part Five, translated by Arthur Goldhammer. Chicago: The University of Chicago Press (1988).

MacKeith, Stephen A. 1982–83. "Paracosms and the Development of Fantasy in Childhood." *Imagination, Cognition, Personality* 2–3:261–267.

Malcolm, Norman. 1959. *Dreaming*. London: Routledge and Kegan Paul (1976).

Mavromatis, Andreas, and Richardson, John T. E. 1984. "Hypnotic Imagery." In *International Review of Mental Imagery*, Volume 1, edited by Anees A. Sheikh. New York: Human Sciences Press.

May, Robert. 1980. *Sex and Fantasy: Patterns of Male and Female Development*. New York: W.W. Norton Company.

McGuiness, Diane, and MacLaughlin, Lorraine. 1982. "An Investigation of Sex Differences in Visual Recognition and Recall." *Journal of Mental Imagery* 6:201–212.

McKellar, Peter. 1957. *Imagination and Thinking*. Basic Books: New York.

———. 1972. "Imagery from the Standpoint of Introspection." In *The Function and Nature of Imagery*, edited by Peter W. Sheehan. New York: Academic Press.

———. 1979. "Between Wakefulness and Sleep: Hypnagogic Fantasy." In *The Potential of Fantasy and Imagination*, edited by Anees A. Sheikh and John T. Shaffer. New York: Brandon House.

Morris, Peter E., and Hampson, Peter J. 1983. *Imagery and Consciousness*. New York: Academic Press.

Oliver, George W., Breger, Louis, and Zanger, Robert. 1980. "Symbolic Aspects of Hypnagogic Imagery Associated with Theta EEG Feedback." In *Imagery: Its Many Dimensions and Applications*, edited by Joseph E. Shorr et al. New York: Plenum Press.

Osborn, Alex F. 1963. *Applied Imagination: Principles and Procedures of Creative Problem-Solving*, 3d ed., revised (1st ed. 1953, 2d ed. 1957). New York: Charles Scribner's Sons.

Paivio, Allan. 1971. *Imagery and Verbal Processes*. New York: Holt, Rinehart and Winston.

Piaget, Jean. 1946. *Play, Dreams and Imitation in Childhood*. New York: W.W. Norton and Company (1962).

Qualls, Penelope J. 1982. "The Physiological Measurement of Imagery: an Overview." *Imagination, Cognition and Personality* 2:89–101.

Ribot, Th. 1900. *Essay on the Creative Imagination*. Translated by A. H. Baron. Chicago: Open Court (1906).

Richardson, Glenn E. 1982. *Educational Imagery: Strategies to Personalize Classroom Instruction*. Springfield, Ill.: Charles C. Thomas.

Rogers, T. B. 1983. "Emotion, Imagery, and Verbal Codes: A Closer Look at an Increasingly Complex Interaction." In *Imagery, Memory and Cognition: Essays in Honor of Allan Paivio*, edited by John C. Yuille. Hillsdale, N.J.: Lawrence Erlbaum Associates.

Rugg, Harold. 1963. *Imagination*. New York: Harper and Row.

Sabom, Michael B. 1982. *Recollections of Death: A Medical Investigation*. New York: Harper and Row.

Samuels, Mike, and Samuels, Nancy. 1976. *Seeing with the Mind's Eye: The History, Techniques and Uses of Visualization*. New York: Random House.

Sheehan, Peter W., ed. 1972. *The Function and Nature of Imagery*. New York: Academic Press.

Sheehan, Peter W., Ashton, R., and White, K. 1983. "Assessment of Mental Imagery." In *Imagery: Current Theory, Research, and Application*, edited by Anees A. Sheikh. New York: John Wiley and Sons.

Sheikh, Anees A., ed. 1983. *Imagery: Current Theory, Research, and Application*. New York: John Wiley and Sons.

———. 1984. "Imagery and Children's Learning: An Issue of Declining Developmental Interest?" In *International Review of Mental Imagery*, Volume 1, edited by Anees A. Sheikh. New York: Human Sciences Press.

Sheikh, Anees A., and Kunzendorf, Robert G. 1984. "Imagery, Physiology and Psychosomatic Illness." In *Imagery: Current Theory, Research and Application*, edited by Anees A. Sheikh. New York: John Wiley and Sons.

Sheikh, Anees A., and Shaffer, John T., eds. 1979. *The Potential of Fantasy and Imagination* (chapters 7–8). New York: Brandon House.

Shepard, Roger N. 1978. "Externalization of Mental Images and the Act of Creation." In *Visual Learning, Thinking and Communication*, edited by Bikkar S. Randhawa and William E. Coffman. New York: Academic Press.

Shorr, Joseph E., Sobel, Gail E., Robin, Penee, and Connella, Jack A., eds. 1980. *Imagery: Its Many Dimensions and Applications* (Parts II-IV). New York: Plenum Press.

Singer, Jerome. 1966. *Daydreaming: An Introduction to the Experimental Study of Inner Experience*. New York: Random House.

———. 1979. "Imagery and Affect in Psychotherapy: Elaborating Private Scripts and Generating Contexts." In *The Potential of Fantasy and Imagination*, edited by Anees A. Sheikh and John T. Shaffer. New York: Brandon House.

Singer, Jerome, and Antrobus, John S. 1972. "Daydreaming, Imaginal Processes, and Personality: A Normative Study." In *The Function and Nature of Imagery*, edited by Peter W. Sheehan. New York: Academic Press.

Spoehr, Kathryn T. and Lehmkuhle, Stephen W. 1982. *Visual Information Processing*. San Francisco: W.H. Freeman & Co.

Stewart, Doug. 1985. "Teachers Aim at Turning Loose the Mind's Eyes." *Smithsonian*, August, 44–45.

Suinn, Richard M. 1983. "Imagery and Sports." In *Imagery: Current Theory, Research, and Application*, edited by Anees A. Sheikh. New York: John Wiley and Sons.

Taylor, Gordon R. 1979. *The Natural History of the Mind*. New York: E.P. Dutton.

Tower, Roni B. 1983. "Imagery: Its Role in Development." In *Imagery: Current Theory, Research, and Application*, edited by Anees A. Sheikh. New York: John Wiley and Sons.

Wallach, Michael A. 1970. "Creativity," in Mussen, Paul H., ed., *Manual of Child Psychology*, Volume 1, 3d ed. New York: John Wiley and Sons.

Wallas, Graham. 1926. *The Art of Thought*. New York: Harcourt, Brace and Co.

Washburn, Margaret F. 1916. *Movement and Mental Imagery: Outlines of a Motor Theory of the Complexer Mental Processes*. New York: Classics in Psychology, Arno Press (1973).

Watkins, Mary. 1976. *Waking Dreams*, 3d ed. Dallas: Spring Publications, Inc. (1984).

Wilson, Sheryl L., and Barber, Theodore X. 1983. "The Fantasy-Prone Personality: Implications for Understanding Imagery, Hypnosis, and Parapsychological Phenomena." In *Imagery: Current Theory, Research, and Application*, edited by Anees A. Sheikh. New York: John Wiley and Sons.

Yuille, John C., ed. 1983. *Imagery, Memory and Cognition: Essays in Honor of Allan Paivio*. Hillsdale, N.J.: Lawrence Erlbaum Associates.

Zaleski, Carol. 1987. *Otherworld Journeys: Accounts of Near-Death Experience in Medieval and Modern Times*. New York: Oxford University Press.

Chapter VI

The Organs of the Imagination: Eye and Brain

This final chapter on the science of imagery must make brief reference to the two organs between which visual imagery arises, the organs that are its somatic condition. The congenitally blind, who have no stored visual memory, are generally agreed to have no visual imagery, however expertly they may use the language of sight. Patients who have the relevant brain lesions similarly lack imagery-functions. Of course, the same is true, *mutatis mutandis*, for other modal imagery. But the eye alone is considered here because sight is the paramount sense, in control of both touch and hearing. In a classic experiment, for example, J. Gibson shows that subjects wearing distorting lenses feel that a straight edge they are touching is curved, at least until they close their eyes. Similarly, sound is, after a brief period of adaptation, heard as emanating from its visual source—from the movie screen, for instance, rather than the loud-speakers (Murch 1973).

The eye is only the receptor and transducer of sensory information which the brain processes. Yet the optical system and its function, vision, are an inseparable part of imagery-study. The reason goes beyond the fact that memory-imagery is the heir of sight, of afferent messages brought to the proper locus in the brain and later returned efferently to whatever part of the optical system functions as the mind's eye. The eye is part of imagery-study because there is evidence of an imaginal element already present in the early stages of the visual process. Visual perception is part of imagery-study because it certainly includes an imaginal factor: As in mental imagery the imagination acts to represent objects in their physical absence, so in visual perception, it helps to shape objects in their perceptual presence. In the first part of this chapter various imaginal aspects of perception will be sketched out (A). The second part is a brief review of the difficulties of finding the neurophysiological agencies of imagery-functions (B).

365

A. The Imagination in Visual Perception

1. Stages: Sensation to Perception. The eye proper figures only at the very first sensory stage of perception. Here the world is imaged for the first and last time in any near-literal sense. The lens focuses an inverted image on the light-sensitive retina, a part of the surface of the brain that has budded out and is thus the true interface of brain and world. The retinal image is, to be sure, not an image in the most literal sense, a recognizable replica of the object (Gibson 1966), but it has, at least in some respects, a kind of spatial correspondence to the object. Further along in the perceptual process all simple similarity disappears. The image is transmuted, so to speak, into as yet obscure neural isomorphisms. Indeed, the perplexed relations of the extended image to vision are already evident at the retinal stage of perception. It is possible, by presenting the elements that constitute a form successively, to isolate the phenomenal from the retinal location of a set of points and to show that there may be perception of an extended object where there never was an extended image on the retina. For example, subjects required to track very briefly, by following with the eyes, a luminous moving spot, so that there is no time for an extended line to be "painted" on the retina, see the shape of this path as accurately as those observing the spot while keeping the eye fixed (Rock and Halper 1969). Evidently the mind's eye does not need an extended "icon" in order to see shape. Perhaps some sort of schematic mental map binds the information together (Kaufman 1979).

Sensing and perceiving are distinguished differently in philosophy and in perceptual psychology. The philosophical argument for a separable stage of sensation is usually based on two kinds of experience: One is our occasional unfocused vision of a mere, unstructured sensory field. The other is our normal propensity to overlook the objective stimulus in favor of an interpreted percept—when, for example, a factually elliptical stimulus like a plate in perspective is seen as a round object because it is known to be round. In current psychology the distinction between sensing and perceiving is made not through the phenomena of experience but in terms of a process. That process begins with the sensory stage, the "proximal" stimulus in the peripheral organ (as opposed to the "distal" stimulus in the environment) and its interaction with the brain. It progresses by temporally and locally discernible stages to complete object-perception. It should be said that some psychologists consider the process more continuous and others, like J. Gibson, more disjunct than this description implies.

The major work in shaping vision done at the sensory stage is that of figure/ground segregation. In seeing, as in imagining, some shapes stand out boldly while others form a background that is merely potentially noticeable. This discrimination of vision is almost the first to be made. Subjects report seeing a black shape that has been flashed on a white ground for a few milliseconds as just a dark and light field. As the exposure-time is gradually lengthened they begin to see a black blob against the white field; contour recognition takes longer. Blind persons whose sight is restored tend to report first seeing unidentified figures against a ground. Recognition takes time, as does depth perception (Gregory 1978).

Perception proper may be said to begin with the transfer of the partially processed proximal stimulus to short-term storage. There the contouring and the specifying of the object are advanced. This again is shown by experiments in which duration and sometimes intensity of exposure are varied. In the final stage many processes, as well as experiences encoded in long-term memory, are at work in shaping an interpreted, invariant object. Object-constancy, the seeing of one object under many aspects, is apparently the crowning work of perception. (There are, however, information-processing models that progress along different lines—Marr 1982.) Object-constancy includes size- and shape-constancy. A familiar example of the latter, analogous to the one mentioned above, is the perceptual interpretation of different ellipses as a circle variously slanted. Such identifications improve with the normalcy of environmental cues, and, of course, with experience. But the perceptual capacity itself seems to be ready to go very early in life. Shape-constancy has been observed in two-month-old infants (E. Gibson 1969, Murch 1973).

Mental imagery, too, displays object-constancy. As in perception many aspects are attributed to one object, so in the mental rotation of one imaged object, a whole sequence of perspectivally correct aspects appears. Here first arises an issue that will persist through this chapter. Put as a philosophical question it is this: Does the perceived object inform the mental image through memory, or does the imagination play an originally constitutive role in perception? In cognitive psychology the issue takes the form of the hypothesis that percept and image are stations along a shared, two-way process that is experimentally articulable.

2. Optical Illusions. Just as error best reveals the nature of knowledge, so illusions are indispensible to the study of perception. One difficulty in the study of perception, so deep as to be practically hidden, is the fixing of the beginning, the external stimulus. That this distal stimulus is accessible is an assumption of the science. Yet it is without much warrant, since the observer who watches the subject perceive an object is usually himself also perceiving it. Whatever perceptual processing the stimulus undergoes in the subject, it undergoes in the observer as well. Illusions afford the opportunity to distinguish the sensory stimulus from the perceptual impression. Here, for once, the observer can know the stimulus more "objectively" than the subject does, and so the perceptual process stands out better as well. That is why these otherwise trivial effects are so important to psychology.

Perceptual illusions in general, and the scores of optical illusions in particular, can be defined narrowly or widely. In the narrow sense, an illusion is a mistake of vision. The most famous example is the Müller-Lyer illusion (Ch. I C) in which two lines of equal measured length are compared, one tipped at both ends with two lines bent inward arrow-fashion, the other with lines bent outward, fin-fashion. The second line appears to vision to be appreciably longer. There are a number of explanations which are unfortunately neither connected nor conclusive. One is that it is the outline enclosing each figure that is judged, the fin-figure being of course longer than the arrow-figure.

Another explanation is in terms of size-constancy: Each of the lines is seen as the edge of a solid in perspective, the arrow-headed line representing a corner toward the observer, the fin-tailed line a corner away from the observer. Now it is a remarkable fact of vision that although the measured image of an object is proportional to its distance, the object itself continues to look as if it retained nearly the same size at various distances (Fieandt 1977). Inspect your hands, for example, one held close to the face, the other at arm's length, and they will seem to you to be very much the same size, though if they are made to overlap, the great difference in their visual size will show up. The Müller-Lyer illusion is then explained as an inappropriate functioning of the visual mechanism for size-constancy due to the fact that the plane figures give false depth cues: the perspectival feature of the arrow-headed line gives cues for closeness that induce down-scaling, while the fin-tailed line is interpreted as farther away and therefore enlarged. In either case a misplaced effort to preserve size-constancy brings about the apparent difference in length (Gregory 1978, Kaufman 1979). Some support for this version comes from the fact that people from cultures lacking large rectangular structures are apparently less amenable to the Müller-Lyer illusion (Segall et al. 1968).

Illusions not quite in the narrowest sense, since they involve no measurable mistakes, are the several types of the "multistable" figures. We expect each single object in the world to furnish an indefinite number of different views, but it always comes as a small shock that one single view might in turn be constrained to represent two or more alternate views or even objects. The most famous example of such multiple reading is the perspective reversal of the Necker cube, a transparent solid whose closer and farther corners uncontrollably alternate places under fixation. The best-known examples of another type, the figure-ground reversal, are the Escher woodcuts like "Heaven and Hell" and Rubin's white goblet on a dark ground which reverses to show two confronting faces in silhouette.

But the most interesting peripeties are those of "rival scheme" and "ambiguity." One example is Jastrow's notorious duck-rabbit, the one cited by Wittgenstein, a figure whose duck bill may suddenly turn into a pair of rabbit ears. Another is Hill's "My Wife and My Mother-in-law," in which the hag's nose doubles as a beauty's chin.

Reversing figures are usually artificially designed to give ambiguous views and to lack all the cues that uniquely determine objects in nature. Since each visual "hypothesis" is an equally good perceptual resting place, the switches are probably involuntarily neural. There is some sort of flip-flopping in the visual or attentional systems. Thus the imagination is not needed to account specifically for the moment of reversal any more than it was needed for the illusions. It must, however, still be constitutively invoked in the original organization of the sensory signal given by the drawing. For example, the goblet-face figure has to be construed originally, indeed twice; in both aspects the areas of minimum and maximum curvature, such as the cusps of the open lips, which will turn into the flanges of the stem, are determinative (Hoffman 1983).

It is otherwise with the figures that show schema-ambiguity, such as the duck-rabbit and the hag-beauty. Here the switches are not obligatory and do not occur at neurally controlled rates. Each of the best-known figures has one slightly more obvious aspect, respectively the duck and the hag. Consequently, re-seeing is at least partly intentional, and one can hold each figure at will. This activity of semi-deliberate "seeing-as," which falls between straight perception of a simple sensory signal and unconstrained imagining (Shepard 1980), is surely the imagination's most significant work in the world. It was discussed at length in Part One (Ch. IV B).

3. Patterns: Gestalt-Seeing. The seeing of patterns more organized than the sensory stimulus seems to warrant is so ordinary a part of perception that it belongs among the illusions only in the widest sense. The chief laws of pattern-seeing, always cited, always criticized, are those of Gestalt theory, set out over a half-century ago (Koffka 1935). *Gestalt* is German for integral form. The Greek word *eidos*, the identifying look of a shape, would serve similarly.

It should be said right off that the imagination does not officially figure in these phenomena. Gestalt psychologists, writing as scientists, have attributed them to not yet identified cortical organizations. Nonetheless, Gestalt-effects invite reference to the imagination.

Gestalt-patterns, unlike reversing figures, are chosen to be uniquely stable, though their organization is equally spontaneous. For example, a square matrix of alternating rows of crosses and circles will always be seen in terms of these rows, while the same matrix with the column elements more closely spaced than the row elements will be perceived in terms of its columns. The Gestalt factors at work are those of "similarity" and "proximity." Furthermore, a narrow wavy swarm of dots will be seen as a snake band. Broken parts in a field, if they are construable as closed shapes, are seen as complete figures. Any assembly that moves together, such as a field of runners in a stadium full of spectators, will be perceived as a group. These tendencies are governed respectively by the factors of "good continuation" (continuity of contouring), "closure" (completeness of figure), and "common fate" (association by shared motion).

The law summing up these and other factors is named *Prägnanz*, "fraughtness," also called the law of "best figure." These terms designate the spontaneous tendency of perception to prefer a simple and stable figural organization of the visual field.

The law shows up not only in spontaneous organization but also in pattern preferences. Some of these may have a purely physiological basis. For example, the liking of rough approximations to the golden rectangle with its long dimension taken horizontally, which is evident in painting, architecture, and laboratory tests, may derive from the fact that it fits nicely into the visual—and imaginal—field. The dimensions of this field indeed already approximately embody the golden section, the ratio 1 to 1.6. But other tests seem to show Gestalt-governed preferences. In tests of preference for simple geometric figures, graduate students gave first place to the equilateral triangle (Murch 1973, 123). It would be a good bet that the youngsters who hung around the Platonic Academy would have picked the circle, which is simpler still, and more philosophically pregnant.

The difficulty of quantifying the Gestalt notion of goodness is one of the criticisms advanced against the theory. Another is that the "law" sometimes does not work over the complete field or even at all. On the whole, however, the essence of the principle of simplicity, that, all things being equal, those perceptual responses will occur which require least information, has found favor (Hochberg 1969).

Gestalt-theory, which distinguishes between the stimulus and the seen pattern, was worked out to combat the "constancy-hypothesis." This is the claim that proximal stimulus and perception are always in one-to-one correspondence. As a theory of spontaneous organization, Gestalt-theory is likewise opposed to the idea of an experiential genesis of perception. It introduces instead a factor of "objective set." Such a set allows the figure just inspected to influence the organization of a pattern. For example, after looking at a cube, or being instructed to look for one, an observer will be apt to perceive any line patterns that are presented as having depth. While it has been shown that prior learning and experience, as distinguished from objective set, do influence pattern seeing, some Gestalt effects appear not to be amenable to training (Murch 1973, 143).

Gestalt-theory is in turn opposed by Gibson's claim that the environment declares its own shapes, that the distal stimulus arrives already organized. In comparing the two theories, it seems to be important that Gestalt situations are not an environment: they are prepared drawings in which the investigative imagination of the observer plays to the perceptual propensities of the subjects. Real-life settings may often have neither a need nor an application for these indubitable but special Gestalt abilities. The aesthetic realm seems to be their particular bailiwick. They are a spontaneous form of a specific sort of picture-seeing: non-representational "seeing-as." It is an unsettled question whether imagination-functions are here reaching down to guide perception or perceptual mechanisms are informing the imagination. Either way the imagination is involved in Gestalt effects.

4. Equivalence of Percept and Image. In a classical experiment (1910) Cheves Perky asked subjects first to fixate a point on a screen, then to imagine a colored object, for instance a tomato or a banana, and finally to describe the object as it took shape. Meanwhile, without the subjects' knowledge, images of such objects, with fuzzed outlines and diffused colors, which could be gradually adjusted from subliminal to just visible, were being actually projected on the screen. (This was technically no mean task in 1910.) She showed the viewers, for example, a red tomato and a yellow banana—the same fruit they had been asked to project imaginatively. The subjects varied from children to graduate students, but the results were unambiguous: All were delighted by the vividness of their imaginations. In their reports they invented imaginary contexts. They described a can on which the tomato appeared as a label. They wondered at the fact that while they were thinking of the banana as lying flat they were imagining it as standing on end. They were mistaking projected transparencies for mental images.

The experiment was partially replicated in a series of the seventies (Segal 1971, 1972). Subjects were again asked to image objects, with the difference that the projected stimuli were either congruent or incongruent. Thus the imaged tomato might be accompanied either by a projected tomato or by a glass of beer. The results were not as positive as Perky's, partly because these students were more alert to the possibilities of slide projections. Yet they showed significant assimilation of the stimuli to the images, especially if the stimulus was brightened gradually. The form and color of the stimulus influenced the image more than did its content. The tomato imaged against a beer can looked brownish. In general, congruent pictures made the images more typical, and incongruent ones made them more idiosyncratic.

Perky-type effects raise a great question: To what degree are imagining and perceiving identical cognitive functions? Imagery is normally thought of as a representation that takes place in the absence of the external stimulus. Of course, remembered perceptions are a prerequisite for having imagery in general. Also, the immediate sensory triggers, which are vividly described by Proust (Part Six, Ch. III A), are often responsible for calling up an image in particular. Imagery is closely related to perceptual processes in other ways too. Subjects asked to "hallucinate" a red square onto a white surface often see a green afterimage on the sheet; there is, moreover, the McCollough effect (B, below). In eidetic imaging deliberate fusion of seen and imaged objects may take place.

However, the Perky results show something stronger: that under carefully controlled conditions perception can actually be assimilated to mental imagery. The stimulus has to be somewhat weak, since experimental imagery is usually described as dimmer than perception. (This Humean distinction seems, however, not to hold for spontaneous real-life imagery.) The effect is, as it were, a reverse hallucination; instead of judging that imaginary objects are real, the imager thinks that external stimuli are imaginary.

A way to approach the problem of distinguishing imagining and perceiving is through the cognitive notion of levels of processing. There is an old hierarchy of activities—perceiving, imagining, conceiving—that affords an acceptable beginning. The hope is that each of these levels has effects that distinguish it from the others, so that functional equivalences will emerge. For example, experiments show that people categorize objects conceptually in the same way whether they are perceived, imagined, or named. Hence on the highest or conceptual level perception and imagination function equivalently. But on the lowest or perceptual level subjects can, for example, by fixating an object, experience afterimages of a color complementary to that of the stimulus. Such afterimages are normally absent in mere imagining (excepting the special effect described above), and they have, of course, no conceptual analogue. Evidently perceiving, imagining and thinking, though ingredients of perception, are usually not equivalent on the perceptual level.

Similarly for the middle, the imaginative level. If perception and imagery were to prove functionally equivalent, that fact would not be considered attributable to the subject's conceptual knowledge of objects, but would be interpreted to mean that perceiving and imaging share processing mechanisms.

One such finding of equivalence comes from a study of magnitude-estimation of real as compared to imaged objects. The size of a perceived object tends to be underestimated according to a certain power-function, while the size of an imaged object is underestimated according to the square of the object-function. The inference is that image estimates are a double application of the perceptual process. The implication is that percept and image are equivalent for estimation purposes and share a scaling process.

There are more functional equivalences betokening common processing. One emerges in the Kosslyn finding that the imaginal field is shaped like the visual field and that there are variations of imaginal acuity similar to those of the visual field. Another shows up in the visual aftereffects of mental imagery seen in the McCollough effect (B, below). A particularly interesting set of experiments is based on the observation that subjects, when attempting to point at a target through displacing prisms, can correct themselves if allowed to see their errors. When the prisms are then removed, the subjects point erroneously to the opposite side. Now subjects who were asked simply to imagine making repeated prism-induced errors displayed similar aftereffects, smaller on the average, but proportional to their rating on the test for vividness of imagery. The special value of these findings is that they can hardly be set aside as resulting from a mere memory of the proper perceptual effect, which is unknown to most subjects: the imagination is here perception-like in its functioning.

(Finke 1980.)

Perceptual studies thus suggest this answer to the question raised above, how to distinguish between imagination and perception: by the same token by which strong equivalences between perception and imagining can be established these powers are also distinguishable. For if the subject cannot differentiate between them, the methodical observer can. Here is a case where observational science convincingly comes to the rescue in resolving experimental confusions about the relation of external seeing to internal imagining.

B. Imagery and the Brain

The brain is, oddly enough, the skeleton in the cognitive closet. The structures and processes discovered by cognitive psychologists are supposed to reveal it at work, and yet so far their physical realizations have eluded observation. Recent neurophysiological discoveries have been concerned mostly with the neural coding of sensory stimuli—with, for example, the suggestion that spatial information might be temporally encoded, and with the analysis on a somewhat higher level of sensory data by "feature detector" cells that would fire only for certain features, such as bars at different orientation (Hubel and Wiesel in Fieandt 1977).

The ideal would be the discovery of conformations and transformations of brain structures and neural events which are in some way exactly isomorphic with psychological faculties, states, and changes. Aside from the fact that even a very thoroughgoing isomorphism of mind and brain would not constitute a proof of their identity, this enterprise is beset with deep theoretical difficulties. First among them is that the introspective phenomenological approach, which cognitive psychologists study so hard to bypass, appears to be unavoidable. Without reference to the descriptive distinctions of inner experience, the interpretations of neurophysiological observations cannot even begin (Arnold 1984, viii; Shepard 1981, 281).

The most persistent project, ushered in by the second century A.D. with Galen's advocacy of the brain as the body's neural center, is to localize the mental powers established by philosophy. For example, a sketch of the head by the Carthusian monk Gregor Reisch (1504) shows the *sensus communis* located in the front of a forward ventricle, the hind parts of which are occupied by the separate powers of fantasy and imagination (Harth 1983). Contemporary localization of the imaginative function, as distinguished, for example, from memory, center on the amygdaloid complex, an almond-shaped region of several nuclei or fields in the anterior temporal lobe, which appears to serve as a particular relay station for imagination-circuits. Not only do all the relevant sensory, motor and memory systems project onto the amygdala, but besides these there are efferent relays especially to the areas identified for emotion and attention. Stimulation of the amygdala provokes complex hallucinations as well as fantasy-images that are more dreamlike and vague. Amygdalectomy in animals results in inappropriate behavior interpretable as lack of imagination, while lesions impair learning by interfering not with memory but with the ability to imagine possibilities.
(Arnold 1984.)

An even more desirable goal, especially in the pursuit of the mind/brain identity thesis, is the identification of particular events and occurrences in the brain with the introspectively discerned phenomena of experience. The philosophical pitfalls of this enterprise are many and deep (Fodor 1981). First among them is the difficulty of even discerning, classifying, and describing the elements of experience through which mental events can be picked out. Take a common case, the image of a scene: Normally the viewer's perspective shifts or the scene itself transforms. Even absolutely static sights, perfectly fixated, in which nothing but time marches on, could not be counted as experimental units, precisely because the subject himself still lives through discernibly different moments. Consequently, unless it is allowed that the kaleidoscope of scenery occasionally freezes around "platonistic elements" (Malcolm 1977), and, in addition, that these could be finitely indexed, the fitting of—particular—mental states to brain events becomes in principle impossible. This logical impossibility of picking out the elements of experience is one of the main arguments used by Malcolm against the very concept of a psychological isomorphism (230). In practice, however, things are more hopeful: We classify living scenes much as we do pictures: still-lifes, hunt scenes, land-, sea-, and city-scapes. And, of course, in the laboratory it is possible to work entirely with simple a-contextual imagery.

Nonetheless, the fitting of physiological and neural indices to introspective reports has been for imagery, as for dreams, a series of promises and disappointments. In the sixties, Penfield, operating on numerous epileptic patients, stimulated the surface of the brain with weak electric currents to find the affected site. A small percentage of his patients experienced very vivid imagery, which felt almost like the reliving of an event. His contention was that the stimulation activated specific remote-memory sites. However, some of the visions included the presence of the subjects themselves, and this fact spoke against these excitations being memory-imagery in the strict sense. Furthermore, the lack of success in ever restimulating the same hallucination reduced the explanatory usefulness of mnemonic "engrams" to account for the storage of memories in the brain (Horowitz 1970, Eysenck 1984, Marr 1982).

Eye movements provide slight and crude indices of imagery. Paivio studied pupillary dilation in the hope of detecting differences between internally generated verbal and imagistic experiences, with negative results (Paivio 1973). Voluntary visual imagery does seem to produce some retinal response (Sheikh and Kunzendorf 1984). Correlations of a very narrow sort between ocular tracking motions and image movement were found (Zikmund 1972), though, as observed above, by and large open- and closed-eye fantasizing seems, as opposed to dreaming, to involve reduced eye movement, a withdrawal from perception, as it were (Singer 1966).

One more use of the visual system which is relevant to the brain and important to imagery-research is to determine levels of processing, that is, to discover whether representations are shaped at the periphery (nearer the eyes) or centrally (in the cerebral cortex). The McCollough effect can be used to elicit information of this sort. This phenomenon, unexplained to date, is as follows: First, subjects look alternately for ten minutes at patterns of black and red vertical stripes and patterns of black and green horizontal stripes. When they are then presented with black and white vertical and horizontal test patterns, they report seeing green on the vertical and red on the horizontal white stripes. Now when they are asked instead merely to imagine the black stripes on the red and green patches, subjects report the same effect, but fainter in direct ratio to their rating on standard tests for imagery vividness. The image-effect persists for up to two weeks. It does not occur if subjects are then asked to imagine the color patches against real black and white stripes. These results, once again, suggest that perception and imagery share some processes. The fact of their persistence further indicates that these processes are cortical rather than peripheral. Furthermore, color imagery, such as occurs in dreaming, appears to be processed in a different part of the brain from that mediating the McCollough effect. (Finke 1980, Block 1981, Kosslyn 1983.)

A finding relating brain activity more directly to the having of imagery goes back to the discovery in 1943 that subjects who had been identified as "visual thinkers" showed electroencephalographic readings of suppressed alpha rhythms while engaging in visual imagery tasks. (Alpha rhythms are brain-wave patterns with eight to twelve peaks per second.) However, the suppression may be a feature of arousal in general, since it occurs more often during difficult tasks requiring both visual and non-visual effort than during easy visualizing. The arousal results themselves may, in turn, be the effect of averaging more localized effects (Zikmund 1972, Sheikh and Kunzendorf 1984).

Cerebral laterality seems to hold the most specific promise. Up to the seventies the right hemisphere of the brain, which had been identified in the nineteenth century as "the chief seat of the revival of images," was neglected in favor of the supposedly dominant left hemisphere and its cognitively superior linguistic functions. Scientific and popular interest in the right hemisphere coincided with the return to psychology of the ostracized image. It was further propagated by the imagery movement as supporting its project of "re-visioning" mental life, that is, returning it to imaginative modes. Moreover, the two main schools of neurology were composing their differences. One of these schools consisted of the "localizers," who pursued the pin-pointing of brain/behavior correspondences; the other was made up of the "holists" who, by means such as Pribram's holographic model, drew consequences from Lashley's discovery in 1929 that impaired performance in the image learning of rats was a function of the size rather than the locus of ablation. They were driven to compromise by many studies showing, on the one hand, that the hemispheres were asymmetrically organized for different functions, and, on the other, that memory was markedly resistant to destruction by local lesions.

Lateralization tests for perceptual stimuli have been done by presenting material to the subjects in the right or left visual field. This material is then projected to the opposite hemisphere for processing. However, for the investigation of imaginal stimuli, reliance has been on alpha blocking. Briefly stated, the right hemisphere seems to mediate spatio-visual (as opposed to linguistic) abilities. These appear to include imagery-components, such as the ability to rotate objects mentally and to recognize the same object in various orientations. The conjecture that this half mediates imagery-processes is therefore reasonable. There is in fact much evidence that lesions to the right hemisphere both impair imagery-abilities and impoverish dreams.

(Springer and Deutsch 1981, Ley 1983.)

However, after recent studies of people with brain impairments, the lateralization issue has become more complex. For example, *both* hemispheres seem to mediate the arranging of shapes in mental imagery, but they respond to different sorts of information. The right brain works better when relevant information is spatial, and formulable in terms of coordinates, but the left brain comes into its own when the information is language-like and categorical (Kosslyn 1988).

On the other hand, there is now evidence of a more deep-lying split between the visual and the verbal codes than had been contemplated in the "imagery debate." A subject with impairment of the left brain has recently been studied, who displayed almost normal visual knowledge but was gravely deficient in verbal knowledge of living things—but not of objects! This fact leads to the speculation that the brain has "dissociable modality-specific meaning systems" (McCarthy and Worrington 1988), that is to say, the distinction between the two codes is neurologically deep.

Lateralization findings thus broadly but suggestively connect two sets of distinctions: First, imagists interpret these findings as underwriting the verbal-imagistic dual-code thesis. Second, the often cited opposition between "primary" and "secondary process," that is, between imaginal dream-thinking and inhibiting reason, early on set out by Freud in his *Interpretation of Dreams* (ch. 7 E), seems to be realized physically in the right and left hemispheres of the brain.

The ancient Pythagoreans had a Table of Opposites, headed "Right" and "Left" or "Sinister"—form opposed to anomaly. The "double brain" discoveries have been worked up into a cult with a similar table of adjectives, though with a romantic reversal. Nowadays the evil L-mode features verbal, analytic, symbolic, abstract, temporal, rational, digital, logical, and linear approaches (Edwards 1979). The humane R-mode, however, yields a type that is non-verbal (directly aware), synthetic (puts things together), concrete (relates to things as they are at the moment), analogic (understands metaphoric relations), non-temporal (lives without time sense), non-rational (is willing to suspend judgment), spatial (sees things in relation), intuitive (has leaps of insight), and holistic (sees wholes and tolerates diversity). Here is a veritable dictionary of the imagery movement. The double-pronged question is whether these neoromantic oppositions delineate actually realizable human complexes, and if they do, whether a systematic sanctioning of the Right actually enhances the whole of human existence or even merely the imaginative mode. The negative answer to both parts is defended throughout this book (Part One, Ch. IV C; Part Four, Ch. II B, D; Conclusion).

For all these studies, the basic question remains in one sense practically unbroached: in cognitive psychology it is an axiom that the brain is the basis of imagistic representation, while in some philosophical quarters any psychophysical isomorphism is taken to be an impossibility. It seems fitting to end this section with a reference to a brave and rare speculation by Roger Shepard, entitled "Psychophysical Complementarity" (1981).

"Psychophysical" does not here mean the relation of psychic experience to either perception or the brain. Though he believes that cognitive inquiry cannot help beginning with a phenomenology of experience, Shepard nevertheless sets the mystery of experience aside so as to forestall collegial impatience. Instead, he investigates the relation of external as well as non-external imaginal stimuli to quasi-sensory internal responses. The problem, then, is this: There is a three-dimensional Euclidean external world. There is a similarly constituted brain. Between them there is a two-dimensional interface. How has this brain come to represent this world adequately? (Shepard presupposes an evolutionary adaptive genesis for the match.)

Two answers are set aside as not very satisfactory. First, moment-by-moment plotting of billions of neural events cannot be expected to add up to an account of the brain's mirroring of the world. Second, a strictly logical, propositional model of the brain's functioning is too general, too devoid of world-analogous constraints, to have a hope of explaining our faculty for dealing with external space and its objects. Moreover, this model suggests no mechanisms for converting spatial sensations (be they real or, as in pitch, metaphorical) into the cognitive brain-code.

Shepard, who is, recall, the discoverer of mental rotation, of course favors an analogue model, which will exploit the fact that natural and imagined motion both share the physical dimension of time. Concrete "first-order isomorphisms" in the brain, such as the actual visual appearance of a squarish structure upon perceptual presentation of a square, seem to be out of the question. "Complementarity" is Shepard's speculative suggestion for the relation that might obtain between world and brain. The word refers to an epistemological principle first enunciated by the physicist Bohr. It is to the effect that a certain state of affairs may have to be described in terms that are at once mutually exclusive and complementary, in the sense that the state in question is seen under two different aspects and the descriptions are made within two different contexts. So the world and the brain, the outside and the inside, being separated by an unbreachable bounding surface, may have to be described in essentially incompatible terms which must yet mesh precisely and efficiently.

"Complementarity" is, of course, in this context more the name of an enigma than of a solution. But here are a couple of examples of the kind of inquiry that it promotes: In the working world objects tend to remain rigid under translation and rotation through time. So, the Shepard-Cooper experiments show, do their mental images. In particular, successive momentary displays of real objects tend to be perceived as continuous, in such a way that at each moment an object is identified with that one in the preceding display which has the greatest metrical or metaphorical (that is, qualitative) proximity. The brain action complementary to external rigidity and continuity is conjectured to be one in which the firing of a neural structure always primes a host of other closely related structures so as to trigger a wave of excitation. Likewise, in the world objects tend to be determinate. When stimuli are ambiguous or paths equivalent the internal system tends to favor one alternative to the exclusion of the other. The complementary brain action may be some sort of lateral inhibition, a mechanism by means of which local stimulations inhibit adjacent reactions. Two other such obligatory perceptual principles of "impletion," which by inviting neural construals bespeak complementarity between world and brain, are Gestalt-like: One is "least path," according to which partially perceived paths are filled out as Euclidian geodesics (shortest distance). The other is "induction," by which paths are completed so as to be coherent with those already perceived in neighboring space.

This speculative effort to conceive what it might mean for the spatial world of perception to be mirrored in the brain can be read as one attempt to save cognitive science from methodological solipsism—from the principled renunciation of all semantic reference for the representations it investigates. For it stands to reason that if the mind is a function of the brain, it cannot represent external objects to us unless the brain somehow meshes with the world. There are two assumptions intertwined here. One is that the mind is physically present in the brain, and the other is that the mind is complementary to the physical world. Ultimately trying to adhere to both at the same time may prove as feasible as making two bodies occupy the same space simultaneously. But in any case, it is the second assumption that is of more consequence. It is important not only for imagery-investigation in particular—since the findings of this science are not interpretable imagistically unless the mind is allowed to have some sort of room for the spatial world—but for cognitive science in general: Mind/world complementarity expresses the faith that in some sense knowing preserves the shape of the world.

This part, which was devoted to the science of imagery, ends with the brain, for that is the arena of the wished-for consummation. The faith of the science is that imagery is nothing but a brain-event, though so far it is hard to find a place where neurophysiology puts any constructive constraint on imagery-investigation. When asked by Napoleon what role there was for a deity in his mechanistic system, Laplace dismissed the mathematical God of Newton's theological physics with the words: "I have no need of that hypothesis." Does the science of imagery need that diametrically opposed hypothesis, the imagining brain? Does it further cognitive psychology to be physiological? That is one of those rare imagery-questions that may indeed find an answer in the future.

★ ★ ★

The preoccupation of imagistic science has been with the having of images: whether, how, what sort, to what effect. It is high time to inquire into their being.

Bibliography

Anderson, John R. 1978. "Arguments Concerning Representations for Mental Imagery." *Psychological Review* 4:244–279.

Arnold, Magda B. 1984. *Memory and the Brain*. Hillsdale, N.J.: Lawrence Erlbaum Associates.

Attneave, Fred. 1971. "Multistability in Perception." In *Image, Object, and Illusion: Readings from Scientific American*. San Francisco: W.H. Freeman and Company (1974).

Baddeley, Alan D. 1976. *The Psychology of Memory*. New York: Basic Books.

Block, Ned. 1981. "Introduction: What is the Issue?" In *Imagery*, edited by Ned Block. Cambridge: The MIT Press.

Bower, T.G.R. 1966. "The Visual World of Infants." *Scientific American*. December, 80–82.

Brown, Roger, and Herrnstein, Richard J. 1981. "Icons and Images." In *Imagery*, edited by Ned Block. Cambridge: The MIT Press.

Eccles, John C. 1958. "The Physiology of the Imagination." In *Altered States of Awareness: Readings from Scientific American*. San Francisco: W.H. Freeman and Company (1972).

Edwards, Betty. 1979. *Drawing on the Right Side of the Brain*. Los Angeles: J. P. Tarcher.

Eysenck, Michael W. 1984. *A Handbook of Cognitive Psychology*. Hillsdale, N.J.: Lawrence Erlbaum Associates.

Fieandt, K. von, and Moustgaard, I. K. 1977. *The Perceptual World*. New York: Academic Press.

Finke, Ronald A. 1980. "Levels of Equivalence in Imagery and Perception." *Psychological Review* 87:113–132.

Fodor, Jerry A., and Block, Ned. 1981. "What Psychological States Are Not." In *Representations*, edited by Jerry A. Fodor. Cambridge: The MIT Press.

Gibson, Eleanor J. 1969. *Principles of Perceptual Development*. Englewood Cliffs, N.J.: Prentice-Hall.

Gibson, James J. 1960. "Pictures, Perspective, and Perception." *Daedalus* 89:216–227.

———. 1966. *The Senses Considered as Perceptual Systems*. Boston: Houghton Mifflin Co.

Gregory, R. L. 1978. *Eye and Brain: The Psychology of Seeing*, 3d ed. New York: McGraw-Hill.

Harth, Erich. 1983. *Windows on the Mind: Reflections on the Physical Basis of Consciousness*. New York: Quill.

Hochberg, Julian E. 1969. "Effects of the Gestalt Revolution: The Cornell Symposium on Perception." In *Perception: Selected Readings in Science and Phenomenology*, edited by Paul Tibbetts. Chicago: Quadrangle Books.

Hoffman, Donald D. 1983. "The Interpretation of Visual Illusions." *Scientific American*, December, 154–162.

Holt, Robert R. 1964. "Imagery: The Return of the Ostracized." *American Psychologist* 19:254–264.

Horowitz, Mardi J. 1970. *Image Formation and Cognition*. New York: Appleton-Century-Crofts.

Kaufman, Lloyd. 1979. *Perception: The World Transformed*. New York: Oxford University Press.

Koffka, Kurt. 1935. *Principles of Gestalt Psychology*. New York: Harcourt, Brace and World (1963).

Kosslyn, Stephen M. 1980. *Image and Mind.* Harvard University Press: Cambridge.

———. 1983. *Ghosts in the Mind's Machine: Creating and Using Images in the Brain.* New York: W.W. Norton and Company.

———. 1988. "Aspects of a Cognitive Neuroscience of Mental Imagery." *Science* 240:1621–1626.

Kosslyn, Stephen M., and Pinker, Steven. 1983. "Theories of Mental Imagery." In *Imagery: Current Theory, Research, and Application,* edited by Anees A. Sheikh. New York: John Wiley and Sons.

Ley, Robert G. 1983. "Cerebral Laterality and Imagery." In *Imagery: Current Theory, Research and Application,* edited by Anees A. Sheikh. New York: John Wiley and Sons.

McCarthy, Rosaleen A., and Warrington, E. K. 1988. "Evidence for modality-specific meaning systems in the brain." *Nature* 344:428–430.

Malcolm, Norman. 1977. *Memory and Mind.* Ithaca: Cornell University Press.

Marr, David. 1982. *Vision.* New York: W.H. Freeman and Company.

Murch, Gerald M. 1973. *Visual and Auditory Perception.* Indianapolis: Bobbs-Merrill Educational Publishing.

Paivio, Allan. 1973. "Psychophysiological Correlates of Imagery." In *The Psychophysiology of Thinking: Studies in Covert Processes,* edited by F. J. McGuigan and R. A. Schoonover. New York: Academic Press.

Perky, Cheves W. 1910. "An Experimental Study of Imagination." In *Readings in Perception,* edited by David C. Beardslee and Michael Wertheimer. Princeton: D. Van Nostrand Company (1958).

Rock, Irvin, and Halper, Fred. 1969. "Form Perception without a Retinal Image." *The American Journal of Psychology* 82:425–440.

Segal, Sydney J. 1971. "Processing of the Stimulus in Imagery and Perception." In *Imagery: Current Cognitive Approaches,* edited by Sydney J. Segal. New York: Academic Press.

———. 1972. "Assimilation of a Stimulus in the Construction of an Image: The Perky Effect Revisited." In *The Function and Nature of Imagery,* edited by Peter W. Sheehan. New York: Academic Press.

Segall, Marshall H., Campbell, Donald T., and Herskovits, Melville J. 1968. "Cultural Differences in Perception of Geometric Illusions." In *Contemporary Research in Visual Perception,* edited by Ralph N. Haber. New York: Holt, Rinehart and Winston.

Sheikh, Anees A., and Kunzendorf, Robert G. 1984. "Imagery, Physiology, and Psychosomatic Illness." In *International Review of Mental Imagery,* Volume 1, edited by Anees A. Sheikh. New York: Human Sciences Press.

Shepard, Roger N. 1980. "The Mental Image." In *Human Memory: Contemporary Readings,* edited by John G. Seamon. New York: Oxford University Press.

———. 1981. "Psychophysical Complementarity." In *Perceptual Organization*, edited by Michael Kubovy and James R. Pomerantz. Hillsdale, N.J.: Lawrence Erlbaum Associates.

Singer, Jerome L. 1966. *Daydreaming: An Introduction to the Experimental Study of Inner Experience*. New York: Random House.

Spoehr, Kathryn T., and Lehmkuhle, Stephen W. 1982. *Visual Information Processing*. San Francisco: W.H. Freeman and Company.

Springer, Sally P., and Deutsch, Georg. 1981. *Left Brain, Right Brain*. New York: W.H. Freeman and Company.

Taylor, Gordon R. 1979. *The Natural History of the Mind*. New York: E.P. Dutton.

Zikmund, Vladislav. 1972. "Physiological Correlates of Visual Imagery." In *The Function and Nature of Imagery*, edited by Peter W. Sheehan. New York: Academic Press.

Part Three

Logic: The Being of Images

Part Three

Logic: The Being of Images

Here, *in medias res*, is the place to ask the question: "What is an image?" In Parts One and Two I have been concerned with the philosophical inquiry into the imagination as a principle of human nature and with the psychological research into the structures and processes by which we in fact have imagery. In Parts Four and Five I shall deal with verbal and visual images—the imagining that is done in words and the imaging that is done in space.

In passing from the imaging activity to its products, the images presented in this third part, I must point out two facts: First, the imagination differs from the other cognitive capacities, such as perception and reason, in being named after its object or product. Second, there are four kinds of images: memorial and imaginary *mental* images, and natural and artificial *real* images. Clearly an analysis of the term image and its four kinds must be the pivot-point in the study of the imagination.

The approach in this part will be logical in the ancient as well as the modern sense: It includes the discovery of the essential being of any image and the analysis of the propositions and inferences attached to the concept—and both inquiries are to proceed through thought and language only.

The words "real" and "unreal" appear in all the chapter headings. Reality, existence, and being are terms often muddled. But since all are needed to talk about so strange a mode of being as is image-nature, I shall distinguish them according to one fairly approved philosophical practice. "Reality" I use in its literal meaning, namely "thinghood," and material thinghood at that; it has no particular dignity here, nor, since the unreal may be highly actual, is "unreal" derogatory. "Existence" means being in time and space, here and now or then and there. "Being" will be circumscribed below.

Images range through degrees of association with reality: We are confronted by countless real images, by which I mean images in or on real media, ranging from natural reflecting planes like water to highly prepared artificial surfaces such as paper. Most of these real images have—in some

387

sense at least—real originals which they copy or imitate (Chapter I). We have, secondly, mental images, which are unreal in the sense that the inner medium, whatever it may be, is not a material surface. Many of these internal images reproduce real objects as memories (Chapter II). Finally, we have imaginary images, perhaps better, imaginative images, "unreal" inner representations of unreal, that is non-remembered objects (Chapter III). Of course, just as memory brings the real world into the mind, so the mind's imaginations can be brought out into the world as real fictive images, in, for example, the fictions of literature and of paintings.

Since concepts are few whereas facts are many, this logical part will be much briefer than the previous, psychological, part.

Chapter I

Real Images: Real Depictions of Real Objects

What does it mean anywhere and everywhere to be an image? There is no treatment of this question that is equal in scope and depth to the first one, which occurs in Plato's dialogue *The Sophist*. It will therefore be the guiding text for the inquiry into the nature of images in general (A). The second section will be concerned with the logical analysis of a particular but prime example of an image, the visual picture, primarily real but also mental (B).

A. The Being of Any Image: Plato's *Sophist*

To be an image means to be a curious conflation of being and non-being. An image taken *as* an image is another, a second presentation of the original it images. We say: "That's him, alright," identifying a mug shot of a burglar. Or, in a nicer vein, we bring absent friends back by gazing at their pictures. Or still more significantly, we hang pictures or place busts of the founders of our country to show that they are still present in spirit. Of course it is not the paper or canvas or bronze that constitutes this second presence, but the image on or in it: With that proviso the image *is* what it images.

But then again, life among images can be notoriously unsatisfying. If the original has absconded, or is absent or dead, the image is an unfulfilling substitute: The image *is not* the original.

This not-being-the-original has two aspects. First, an image is not what the original is in the deprecating sense in which we say "It's only a copy." It has a secondary, a derivative, and therefore a diminished sort of existence. It might be reduced in dimension, as a pictorial scene has lost real depth, or it might lack the life of the thing it images and be thinner in properties.

Above all, it is generally bereft of the powers, functions, and dignities the real being possesses. Take the most obscure sitter for the most valuable of portraits, like one of Rembrandt's Dutch burghers. The painting has, when all is said and done, a price, but the person was, in his day, priceless. In sum: an image is a lesser being than its original.

Secondly, an image is also not-the-original insofar as it is different from or other than it. Being-different-from-the-original implies a certain imaginal independence: An image has special features that belong to it by reason of its being something else than the thing itself. These features are of two sorts. There are those that belong to an image insofar as it is a special kind of production with its own materials and processes, natural or artful. And there are powers specific to an image insofar as it is able to elevate the passing moment into a lasting revelation and a mere appearance into an epiphany.

This language of being a non- or not-being, which captures something both very fundamental and very formal about images, comes from *The Sophist*, Plato's most metaphysical work, to apply to it an anachronistic term. The discussion of images is embedded in the dialogue in two ways. It forms part of the dramatic hunt for the sophist as a human type, and it is presented as the paradigmatic application of a grand metaphysical discovery. To convey something of the breadth of significance that this dialogue assigns to images, the briefest summary of the purpose and the course of its conversation, as well as of its crucial reinterpretation of common terms, is unavoidable.

1. The Setting: The Hunting of the Sophist. The chief speaker in the conversation is a nameless guest from Italy, a "truly philosophical man," one of the companions gathered about Parmenides, the discoverer of the notion of Being. Socrates raises the question whether in Italy people regard the statesman, the sophist, and the philosopher as three different kinds. He himself thinks that true philosophers sometimes present themselves in the illusionistic image (216 d) of statesmen and sophists. Now in the common understanding sophists are merely traveling professors who lecture for a fee on subjects apparently conducive to success in life, such as developing a powerful character and a persuasive rhetorical style. But for Socrates, as we know from other dialogues, sophists are what their name literally means, wisdom-mongers, and therefore charlatans. Thus Socrates' admission is exceedingly unsettling, yet having made it, he must become a mute listener. After all, anything he might now say would open up abysses of possible duplicity: Would he be speaking as true or false philosopher or as false or true sophist? So, having handed over to Theaetetus the role of responding to the Stranger, he falls silent. We know from the preceding dialogue, named after Theaetetus, that the young mathematician is said to be in looks the spitting *image* of Socrates.

So much for the suggestive and complex setting of the search for the sophist, which the Stranger now undertakes. (The statesman is to be pursued later, in the dialogue of that name.) He has a method that he applies again and again, six times, with illuminating but not definitive results. The rock-bottom nature of the sophist always escapes. The method is to survey the field in order to propose a large genus of activities in which the sophist might be found, then by a logical insight to subdivide it until an ultimate species is reached, and finally to gather all the terms of the division into a definition. What we call classification is being given an early workout here. When the sophist's activity has been traced to six different fields, the suspicion arises that he is in fact in the business of making and doing and being anything and everything, by the simple expedient of universal imitation. Insofar as wisdom involves a certain universality, the sophist (*sophistes*) is an imitation of a wise man (*sophos*, 268 c).

Therefore the seventh and last classification begins with the large genus Image-Making or Imitation. It culminates, as does the dialogue, with the comical cumulative definition of the true sophist (268 c). He belongs "by descent and blood" to

> the imitative [*miming*] part of the dissembling [*ironic*] part of the art of seeming, belonging to the art of contradiction-making of the illusionistic [*phantastic*] genus which has been defined as a section of that poetry not divine but human, which produces wonders [magic tricks] in words and belongs under the image-making [*idolopoeic*] art.

Socrates ought to be satisfied with the tinselly sophistical fraud as well as with the veritable lexicon of image-analysis that the Stranger's method of division has produced. But the point here is that he presents the art of image-making as a disreputable kind of poetry, playing on the fact that the Greek word for making or production is *poēsis*. Consequently, there are not only picture-images but also word-images. The analysis of such images of speech forms the high point, and involves the great discovery, of the dialogue.

2. The Center: The Being of Images. The true sophist bewitches the young by purveying "spoken images" (234 c). The word used for image is *eidolon* (whence the word "idol"). It is a diminutive of the Platonic term *eidos*, meaning aspect, look, and, above all, form or idea, the intelligible nature and being that gives existent things their characteristic appearance. An *eidolon* is a little or a diminished being with a borrowed aspect, and an *eidolon*-maker, like the sophist, makes make-believe beings. He deceptively imitates beings in words, as do painters in pictures. But there are two seriously different kinds of images, exemplified by two intentions in painting. One intention endeavors to produce an image that is in itself the truest, the most measurably accurate, and the most correctly colored possible; the Stranger calls it the likeness-art (*eikonikē*). The other aims at the most beautiful and persuasive appearance possible, even changing proportions and colors at the expense of truth; it is called the appearance-art (*phantastikē*, 336 c). This division holds for word-images as well. The Stranger very likely thinks that the sophist's image-mongering is of the illusionistic, phantastic sort, but instead of saying so, he stops portentously to remark that this is a very hard inquiry.

One might interject here that the propensity for "phantastic" rather than "iconic" imaging probably best distinguishes the true sophist from the true philosopher. They have various features in common: Both try to bewitch the young men with argumentative and paradoxical talk. Both dissemble— recall Socrates' notorious "irony," literally "dissembling," the very term used of the sophist. But above all both make word-images. Here their difference shows up, for Socrates' famous myths are, and moreover are called, "iconic" images, images in the service of truth. The sophists, on the other hand, speaking for appearance's sake, give false or "phantastic" pictures of the way things are.

To return to the argument: The Stranger hesitates because he sees the sophist, wily beast that he is, once again eluding the hunt. Whenever he is accused of being a speaker of falseness, he can lose himself in the elusiveness of such speech. For to speak means to enunciate one or more determinate thoughts or beings of thought, and a person who is saying what is not (the case) is saying nothing, uttering a no-thing, non-being. But how can one think or say what is nakedly nothing? (Recall that the honest Houyhnhnms in *Gulliver's Travels*, too, have this problem with lying. Those virtuous horses find lying unintelligible because it means "saying the thing which is not.") To make false speech intelligible one would have to admit that in some sense non-being is, that is to say, is one among the other beings. The sophist is laughing up his sleeve, because that admission is particularly hard for a follower of Parmenides, who is known to have claimed that the affirmation of non-being is unviable. The sophist's particular kind of intentional falseness, namely deceit, seems to be sheltered by the non-articulableness of falseness in general.

"Father" Parmenides had made at its very origin what turns out to be the most consequence-laden discovery in Western philosophy. A shrunken version of his blazing insight is as follows: The most characteristic human utterances include the copula "is." Moreover, a sentence conveys a full thought even when it stops right after the copula: The sophist is; the philosopher is; anything that is anything is—has being. Being is what unifies and makes the sphere of things one. Being is what our thought and speech above all get hold of. But in his enthusiasm for the "way of truth" Parmenides goes too far. He forbids any attempt to think of non-being or no-thing, because, he says, it leads along the "way of seeming." It follows that a Parmenidean cannot think about a thing insofar as it is different from another, for that means that it is *not* that other. Even less can such a philosopher acknowledge speech insofar as it says what is not so. The sophist's trick of hiding in the unexplored place of non-being has confronted the Stranger with the limitations of his mentor's great dogma: his strict insistence on being as alone thinkable and speakable.

Indeed, the sophist—quite tacitly—teases the Stranger with the fact that it is not just "phantastic" word-images that the Stranger can't speak about, but any images whatsoever. He can speak about neither god-made natural reflections, nor painters' pictures, nor yet the philosophers' true word images, nor even about the visible world itself. For all existent things, here and now, are but images of intelligible beings. And all speech (*logos*) about images, the very "logic" of images, requires reference to what they are not.

Theaetetus tries the easy and obvious way out: An image is made to resemble the genuine article and to be "another such thing." What one can positively say of any image is that it is really and truly a likeness. The Stranger easily shows him that the "absurd entanglement of being with non-being" reappears in explaining what resemblance or likeness is: "Another such thing" is either a second original and no image (cf. *Cratylus* 432), or it is a copy and *not* the original. Simple talk of likeness or resemblance or similarity is not enough to resolve the perplexity.

The Stranger then offers a grand and elegant solution which was indeed implicit in the Parmenidean way of speaking. Non-being can be a second great unifying principle besides Being, but it must be Non-being understood as Not-being. Every being is, to be sure, what it is, but it is also *not* all the many other natures, for they are what *they* are. This Non-being is the principle of difference or "Otherness" (258 b). It permeates all Being and splits it into the many diverse beings or ideas, each with its own "form" or look. It then goes on in the same way to duplicate that look in the ordinary appearances of the world, the things that are thereupon, somewhat falsely, called by the name of the idea they copy. Thus Non-being can function as a principle of mere difference insofar as beings of equal dignity are each simply not what the other is. However, in its doubling—one might say, its duplicitous—capacity, it also imparts something of Parmenides's unmentionable Non-being: It can effect a loss of genuineness—as Otherness splinters Being into beings, so it separates mere Appearance from genuine Being. I must add that the Stranger also introduces, in passing, a complementary principle, namely "Sameness," to account for the steadfast self-sameness, the persistence in their own self-identical suchness, of these beings that are distinguished from each other by otherness. Unlike its opposite, Otherness, which coincides with Non-being, Sameness is not identified with Being but is deliberately distinguished from it (255 b). One might say that Otherness is responsible for the external differences among all the beings, while Sameness accounts for the internal distinctiveness, the suchness at work within each being.

The Stranger's Otherness then accounts for falseness. To say what is not, is not to say nothing but to say something other than the truth. The sophist's kind of word-imaging has been made intelligible; he is caught. But of course the point at issue for Plato is not to nail down any particular human profession of image-makers—nor should it be for us, though its practitioners are vastly more powerful and sophisticated in our time than was Plato's poor sophist in his. The point is to get at a logic of images.

Here the principle of Otherness has real explanatory value. It turns out to be at bottom a principle of relationality. Things are different or other only in relation to one another. That is what being different or other means (255 d); it is the *vice versa* relation *par excellence*. One thing differs from another in just the reciprocal way that the other in turn differs from it: A triangle differs from a quadrangle in having three angles rather than four and a quadrangle differs from a triangle in having four angles rather than three. So much is in the dialogue. What follows is, I think, implicit.

(Benardete 1984, Cornford 1934, Klein 1977, Owen 1971, Rosen 1983.)

Images are a specific and yet a centrally significant case of Otherness or Not-being at work. Otherness itself is a central feature of a complex of logical properties, elements with their relations, that are necessary to any fundamental way of speaking about images in general. Here is a summary recapitulation:

First, any image is affected by Otherness in the sense that it is irrefragibly bonded by that not-being to an original. The image is-not the original; it is related by difference to its original. Moreover, that not-being is not mere difference but also a loss of status. That loss enters the image as an element of non-being; an image does not exist as fully or truly as its original. Every image necessarily displays this double relation of being other and being less.

That way of putting it, however, while a necessary beginning, does not sufficiently specify what it means to be an image. After all, not all beings that merely differ from others in kind and status should be called images. The special unbreakable bond between an original and its image is not brought forward enough in the negative account of image-being as not-being. To do justice to this bond requires an analysis of the positive features of imaginal being—the similarity or likeness that makes an image "another such" being: One must explain why the word "verisimilitude" is not just a contradiction in terms. This analysis is avoided in the *Sophist*.

What similarity seems to be is this—a limited sharing of suchness. Therefore, second, besides being other and less, an image must have a relation of limited sameness to an original. (Sameness, similarity, and resemblance, incidentally, are all etymologically cognate.) Again, however, not all things that are similar are related as image and original. For example, there is geometric similarity, a particularly determinate case of limited sameness. Similar, say rectilinear, figures have angles that are respectively equal (they have the same sizes though distinct positions) and sides that are in respectively the same ratio (they have the same relations but different lengths). Yet a figure that is geometrically similar to another is not really its image. In particular it lacks the first condition of "lesser being" that makes for an asymmetrical relation of image and original. Similar geometric figures are not distinguishable as original and image.

In sum, an image displays two aspects: Taken in its own nature it is and is not; one might say it is a pretend-being. But it also is and is not something, for taken together with its original it is in a limited way the same as the original, another such; one might say it is a representation.

It seems to me that this way of speaking of images is illuminating—because it is in fact unavoidable. Even if we leave aside the capitals and abstract nouns with which Plato's concrete speech about the ideas has to be rendered in English, even if we say "is the same as" rather than "shares in Sameness," the analysis survives a conversion from metaphysics back to ordinary logical thinking and speaking. For no matter what idiom we use it will include some reference to the mixed nature of images.

At some point, though, some metaphysics, by which I mean here an affirmation or denial of some kind of being, will have to enter. In the present case, the assumption that conditioned the whole account was that there are such beings as images, meaning that some things, natural and artificial, display the look of other things without being as fully what those others are. What testifies best to the potency of this assumption is the vigor with which it can be attacked from two sides. On one side there are the defenders of the representational arts, particularly painting. They say that images have truer and deeper meaning than their originals: No one now alive much cares about one Jan Six, burgher of Amsterdam, who sat for Rembrandt in 1654, but many are deeply interested in the painting that bears his image. With these the Stranger could have a congenial but complex dialogue, consisting of discovering how an image may be more than a mere image.

On the other side, there is a school of aesthetic logicians, considered in Part Five (Ch. III), who positively deny the possibility of anything proclaiming itself as an image by reason of its own similar looks. Nothing, they say, resembles anything except by a prior convention. It goes without saying that in this book this view is opposed. However, truth to tell, at crucial junctures both sides take refuge in their favorite respective obscurities, so that to resolve the question the scale of formal argument must be tipped by a motive—here the wish to acknowledge and account for the common human experience of recognizing images.

B. The Logic of Pictures

This section is about pictures proper and what can be said of them in general. By pictures proper I mean physical surfaces on which there are marks recognizable as images. By what can be said of them in general I mean what pertains to their logic, to the formal elements and relations that make pictures be and function as pictures.

Although images in the prime sense are picture-images, the Stranger, as has been pointed out, also mentions "spoken images," by means of which the sophists manage "to bewitch the young through the ears with words when the former are yet at a distance from the truth of affairs" (234 c).

Who would disagree that speakers and writers can convey images of the way things are, perhaps charmingly deceptive, perhaps grimly honest, and that they produce imagery, mimicry, metaphor, and depiction? Now to do these things at all effectively is, by and large, to do them well. Hence, verbal imaging is an art, belonging to literature; to this art Part Four will be devoted. Such literary images appear to work largely through an enigmatic sort of imaginal evocation. Somehow words call up pictures without being like them.

But there is also the possibility that the words or sentences of speech in general, that is to say, of perfectly artless and mundane speech, function as images on their own, without the benefit of literary effort and, what is more, without benefit of visualization. Insofar as a word or a sentence can thus constitutionally be an image, one might expect it to feature some sort of resemblance. Somehow words must be like the objects they image.

Yet there must be a world of difference between such pictures and visible pictures, a difference so great that one wonders how, if the latter are the typical resemblances, the former can be called likenesses at all. Except for minor examples like pictographic symbols and onomatopoetic vocables, words and sentences are in no sensible way similar to what they name or say. Indeed, one and the same word, quite aside from the many forms it has in different languages, can be audible in speech, visible in writing, and even tangible in deaf-and-blind hand-signing. This multiplicity of sensory shape shows what everyone indeed knows, that the appearance of the word is an indifferent and evidently to some extent an arbitrary matter. If the image-form is variable, the perplexity becomes even more serious at the other pole, that of the original: What is the putative speech-image an image *of*? Does its original reside in the world of real things, in the context of language itself, in the realm of human thought or in a sphere of trans-personal intelligible beings? Each of these would require a different sort of isomorphism, each with its own deep difficulties.

To make a long story short, the idea that language is imaginal has no successful version that I know of. (It is, incidentally, different from the common claim, no more plausible, that language is symbolic, meaning that it is representational without likeness. That, however, is fortunately outside our business.) In the Platonic dialogues the doctrine that words signify "by nature"—that they are indeed natural images of things—which was evidently seriously held by the Pythagoreans and Atomists, is taken up by Socrates, only to be driven to absurdity: If words are only images they are useless for learning anything about things, for why not look at the originals directly? (*Cratylus*, 439 a). Nonetheless, the notion is perennial in various versions. To pick a particularly striking example, there is Lavoisier's linguistic theory of chemistry. In the preface to his *Elementary Treatise*, every branch of physical science is said to consist of three things, related "like the three impressions of the same seal": the series of facts, the ideas that picture them, and the words that express the ideas. For Lavoisier it follows from the picture-theory that a reformation of the nomenclature, instituting a better versimilitude of the word-pictures, will lead to an improvement in the science. Therefore his chemical revolution begins with a new vocabulary. The picture-theory is a vivid spur to the notion that language reform expressed in neologisms is essential to progress.

1. Proposition-Pictures: Wittgenstein. There is one picture-theory of language that must be included here, although it was eventually repudiated by its author: Wittgenstein's proposition-as-picture theory of the *Tractatus* (1921, 2.1 ff.). It is not only the neatest paradigm of any such theory, but is also rich in incidental observations on the logic of pictures.

It sounds simple and bold: A proposition, the physical expression of a thought (3.1), is like a picture, because it represents a state of affairs in the world and because it does so by having the same elements and relations as that state. The fact that the elements of the proposition are related in a certain way makes it say what it does. It shows its sense—or at least the possibility of its sense—in its arrangement, just as a picture displays its sense in its surface arrangements. Pictorial shapes are recognizable in themselves and also as representations of the world by the likeness of their looks, though, to be sure, this cannot be said of the physical expression of propositions, which consists of conventional symbols. Propositions nevertheless picture worldly states: what is the same for both is the "logical form" or "logical space."

The representational relation between propositions and the world is not purely conventional because, although it is we who psychologically make those correlations to the world which give the proposition its actual sense, we are logically bound by rules in doing so. Whatever the particular physical form of the proposition may be, to be a proper proposition it must have logical form. In itself the form is simply the possibility of any proposition having the structure that it has. Only through such a form do the elements, the names in the proposition, begin to have meaning. This structure is, furthermore, what the proposition shares with reality. Wittgenstein used a geometric term to describe the representational rule by which propositions and states of affairs are correlated: the law of projection. The existent state of affairs to be talked about consists of ultimately simple atomic objects fitted, in ways determined by their nature, into a particular logical multiplicity. Objects thus regarded are facts in their logical space. The space is, again, simply the possibility of their being what they are and so fitting together as they do. For example, a color can combine with a shape but not with a pitch. The projection therefore correlates the logical space of the world and its object-distribution with the logical form of the proposition. Or rather we correlate the two when we use the sensibly perceptible signs as a projection of a possible state of affairs.

What Wittgenstein himself chiefly repudiated in this account was the idea that a logic of reality underlies and is reflected in the logic of propositions. In his later work the rules of logic are found *in*, not behind, language. The element that seems to me suspect in the picture-proposition theory is not the location of the rules, but the nature of the logical isomorphism between the world of fact and propositions. In this theory a proposition describing a state of affairs seems really not to be distinguishable from the logical fact, the state of affairs as Wittgenstein conceives it, except by the asymmetry of the picturing relation, by the circumstance that we correlate the parts of the proposition with the parts of the world and not *vice versa* (Anscombe 1959, 67).

Yet even while they suffer from indiscernibility, the logical space of a state of affairs and the space of its propositional representation seem, genetically considered, to be inverses of each other: Since there are no "natural names," the names in a proposition get their sense entirely from the propositional context. On the other hand, the arrangement of the logical space derives entirely from the nature of the objects and is not antecedent to them: The fact that spatial objects have color but not pitch, for example, is not a matter of context but of the nature of the object (Mounce 1981, 19). This curious inversion shows how difficult is the notion of the pictorial projection by which the parts of the proposition are correlated to the parts of the world as the elements of a picture are to its original: Why should the natural enchainment of the ultimate, simple objects of an ordinary experience (simples which, incidentally, Wittgenstein could never produce) have the same logical form as its—quite diversely derived—description? (Malcolm 1958).

Nevertheless, Wittgenstein's own picture-theory, though set out only in aid of this theory of logical language, is a central contribution to the logic of pictures. Here is a summary, with comments:

All pictures in general, including proposition-pictures, have in common, as was said, a logical form of representation; but some pictures, those that are visible and real, also have a specific spatial-logical form (Ramsey 1923). Therein, it seems to me, lies the root of the difficulty just broached: How do we know that where logic gets enmeshed with appearance, especially with pictorial space, it retains its own form? What if the real-space medium were somehow to reshape the logical space? To tap Wittgenstein's own repertoire of examples, there is the notorious duck-rabbit, a figure which spontaneously assumes different aspects—now a duck and now a rabbit (Part Two, Ch. IV B). Logically, one would think that the laws of projection require that a billed figure be correlated with a duck, period. But applied to visible space the projection is "multistable": Turn the figure through a quadrant and the open bill can also represent two rabbit ears. So the picture-object exists as an indeterminate nature while the conceptual duck-rabbit exists as a monster or not at all.

The most interesting implication of Wittgenstein's theory concerns pictorial negation. A proposition has two facets (4.022): "A proposition *shows* how things are *if* it is true. And it *says* that they are so." The showing-how is its picture facet, the being-so is its proposing—affirming or denying—facet. So a picture, it is implied, does not say or deny that anything is the case until it is correlated with an existing state of affairs, or with the thought of a possible but nonexisting state, and is held up with the words: "This is so," or "This is not so." This non-assertiveness of pictures apart from words will be, I think, their most puzzling and magical property.

The profit in considering speech as imaginal thus turns out to be in emphasizing the inherently spatial nature of images properly so called.

2. Pictures Proper. Real images, pictures in particular, are analyzable in two respects. First, they hang together internally, as picture-structures; they have a peculiar pictorial logic (a). Second, they connect externally with the object they picture; they have a representational logic (b).

a. The Pictorial Structure. Finding the notion of logical pictures and proposition-pictures problematic is the best beginning to thinking about the logic of real pictures of real objects, because it is by contrast with the logic of speech that the logic of pictures stands out.

Here is a list of properties belonging to the very concept of an image. It is much modified from Kosslyn (1980, 1983):

First. Since Aristotle (*Metaphysics* 1027 b), truth has been considered a characteristic of thinking and specifically a value of speech—its correspondence to the facts. Thus only propositions have truth-value. However, in ordinary speech truth is also attributed to objects insofar as they are genuine and faithful to some standard. Therefore pictures can be said to be true in two ways. One, a very deep and strange way, applies insofar as pictures reveal the true or genuine being of what they depict; this kind of truth-in-appearance is discussed in Part Five (Ch. III B). In the other way of speaking, pictures can be true insofar as they are more or less correct resemblances corresponding to the visual facts. This possibility depends, of course, on pictorial representation being understood as a resemblance-function; that understanding nowadays requires a defense such as is, again, mounted in Part Five (III A). In these senses then, pictures can reasonably be said to have truth-values. But unlike propositions, which already are assertions, a picture needs to be asserted, as it were, in addition to being shown. As has been said, it needs to be held up with a brief description of the state of affairs intended and with something like the pronouncement "This is the case"—a title will do. At that point the picture attains a truth-value. Some pictures, like the multistable figures, are ambiguous in a way that is analogous to equivocal propositions (Anscombe 1959).

The occasional claim that pictures have no truth-value (Kosslyn 1980, 32) is best met by listing the ways in which they can be intentionally false and misleading (Roskill and Carrier 1983). Visual lying, the making of false images, is an art in which resemblance and dissemblance are cunningly confused. Sometimes the whole picture is a plausible semblance of a fictive state of affairs, as in an invented map of a piece of non-existent real estate. More often the picture is a doctored version, a retouched, cropped, composite image of a real state of affairs. Sometimes the facts themselves are staged for pictorial purposes, as when a celebrity poses with a certain product in an advertisement so that the image will imply a closer connection between the two than holds in fact. The deceptions of the eye, as in *trompe l'oeil* or in visual illusions like the Escher woodcuts, are self-revealing and therefore not properly lies; they invite perceptual suspicion (Roskill and Carrier 1983). The imaginary images of painters, too, deceive, though only in a deep and delicate sense; as they are not vulgar lies, they may in fact be higher truth or higher illusion.

Pictures, then, differ from propositions not in having simply no truth-value, but in requiring an act of assertion beyond just being made and shown. Though painters often talk of "making a statement" with their canvas, they can do that only within a context of public showings; statements are made in galleries.

Second. The straight propositions of mere logic are asserted simply, without respect to source; they are not logically perspectival. Pictures, on the other hand, even when they leave the hand of the maker, have a built-in point of view, a perspective, though it may be a bird's-eye view or a composite of several aspects. They are more like the declaratory statements of actually spoken human speech, which always carry within them a background of "I think that . . . ," and are, as it were, psychologically perspectival.

Third. Propositions are formed according to explicit syntactical rules: "well-formedness" requires obedience to these. There are, however, no articulable rules of pictorial syntax for pictures in general. Whatever mark-making is physically possible and can gain acceptance is allowed. Even for representational pictures there are no formalizable necessary and universal rules. The laws of perspective, for example, are formal representational rules, but though they may be exemplary, they are by no means obligatory or even usual in depictions. Pictures may contain incomplete or perturbed or indefinite or physically unrealizable or perceptually impossible shapes without being any the less well-formed. Indeed the notion has no precise criterion in depictions. One may argue that "picture" is a genus encompassing several species, each defined by its own syntax. Some pictures are direct or rule-constructed projections. Some are "anamorphoses," recoverable projective distortions. Some are a composition of cognitively preferred aspects, some are schemata, some collages, and so on. But even then the specific syntactic rule rarely constrains the painter completely: the very requirement of resemblance and truthfulness may call for breaching the laws of perspective. In sum, a picture cannot be proved to be garbled except under ad-hoc conventions.

Fourth. Propositions are composed of subject-terms and predicates. Or better, propositional functions take discrete arguments, and the functions themselves denote distinct properties or relations: "The cat is on the mat" picks out a cat as subject and a "being-on-the-mat" as its relational predicate.

Pictures do not contain a discrete, unequivocally countable number of subjects. The reason is that while pictures are as continuous as the continuous real space to which they belong, they do not neccessarily allow for the insights and operations that make objects in real space appear discrete and discriminable. In the real world there are naturally discernible individuals and separately manipulable objects, but on a pictorial surface it is not always obvious what the element of meaning is. Try for instance to discern the number of "arguments" of—that is, the objects in—a Cubist painting.

Although pictures have no unequivocally given elements, they do often have bounded regions one can separately point to as representing this or that object. What one cannot point to separately are the relations among these objects. In a proposition, such as "the cat is on the mat," the proposition "on" can be picked out as articulating the relation of being on top of. In a picture, as in the real world, that relation has no symbolic appearance separable from the fact that the cat occludes part of the mat. Hence pictured relations are often ambivalent; there are representational systems in which the cat so pictured could be read as being in front of, above, or in the mat. Wittgenstein made the often-cited observation that the picture of an old man leaning into a mountain-side as he climbs up a steep path is indistinguishable from that of a man sliding down it backwards. In real life, of course, time will tell. In a picture, only context and the viewer's "pictorial competence" can.

Fifth. The general names occurring in propositions are "abstract," here meaning that (their sensory symbols aside) they do not look like anything at all and are therefore fitted to intend abstractions and classes—which do not look like anything at all either. The isolable figures in a picture, however, always do look like something and are therefore concrete or determinate. Just how determinate they are has been a matter of debate ever since Berkeley cast doubt on the possibility of framing an abstract and yet pictorial idea, or of drawing a schematic diagram, representing, for example, a triangle-in-general (*Treatise Concerning the Principles of Human Knowledge* 1710, Intro.; he doesn't, of course, mean that one cannot show one's lack of interest in specific triangles by the sketchiness of the drawing).

Thus one side claims that a propositional tiger may just have stripes, but a pictorial tiger always has a determinate number of stripes; or a described person's clothes may be left unmentioned but a depicted person either has or hasn't got clothes on. This difference between descriptions and depictions holds, moreover, no matter how great the plenitude of properties that occur in the proposition. The other side calls this the "photographic fallacy" (Block 1981, 1983) and shows that certain depicting techniques may well make stripe-counting and sartorial discernment impossible. For example, a pointillistic drawing can be indefinite about the exact number of stripes, and a stick figure can be noncommital about the wearing of clothes. Furthermore, there are indeed schematic drawings that depict a class, namely by abstracting from individual differences and averaging the class-specific features.

The even balance in this debate suggests that the notion of pictorial specificity has to be better articulated. One way a picture is more specific than language is that it cannot usually show simply this sentence: "Here is a mountain," full stop. It has to show some mountain features, such as peaks, slope, color, and relative size. Even a stick figure shows legs and is therefore usually interpreted as wearing pants rather than a skirt. Thus, where language can remain so utterly silent as not even to raise a question, even a sparsely-detailed sketch gives indices to the imagination for "projection," the quasi-visual fulfillment of images (Part Five, Ch. III B). This kind of specificity does have exceptions: a mountain range too vanishingly small on the horizon to have articulated features, or a very schematic drawing.

There is, however, a kind of specificity or concreteness that is never at all absent. All pictures represent a picture space in which the objects represented are located. So even a vanishingly small pictorial mountain has what a propositional mountain gets by without, namely, a pictorial location, while any object occupying a sizable expanse either already has more internal detail than any proposition conveys or, as was said, invites the inscription of such detail (Howell 1976).

In sum, all pictorial representations are specifically somewhere in the picture-space and most are dense with determinate detail. No picture can do what a word can, which is to refer to something as merely one example of a kind. But then a thousand words can't do what a picture can, which is to represent objects in the indefinitely multitudinous detail of their appearance.

Sixth. Propositions are "digital" and pictures "analog." This is only a way of saying what has already been mentioned, that language is discrete while pictorial representations, being spread on a spatial medium, can be regarded as continuous. It follows that there is a countable infinity of possible sentences in English, but a far greater number, a nondenumerable infinity, as it were, of possible pictures. For each representable object has continuously transformable proper aspects, projections, magnifications, and spatial relations to other objects (Sober 1976). And so, again, there are not enough sentences to match all pictures. This multitude of possibilities, incidentally, also brings home how great a winnowing-out takes place when a painter chooses the subject, aspect, and size of a representation.

Seventh. Just as in the third paragraph the syntax internal to a picture was contrasted with propositional syntax, so there is a pictorial calculus to be distinguished from the propositional calculus. One may ask what the logical operations on pictures, regarded as representational units, might be. For example, propositions are related by an operation called conjunction, effected by putting "and" between any two of them. What is the pictorial analogue, and what can be said of the result? (Sober 1976). The answer would seem to be the concatenation—two pictures stuck together. But the result of pictorial concatenation can be exceedingly different from the conjunction of sentences. Logical conjunction does nothing to the sentences conjoined, but when two pictures are pasted together, it may happen that the interpretation of the parts changes in the light of the whole, and that the whole itself has an unexpected interpretation. The bizarre possibilities are left to the reader's imagination. Consequently, pictorial conjunction must be said to operate indeterminately. Furthermore, in logical conjunction the order of propositions makes no difference, but in concatenating pictures the order can obviously make all sorts of difference.

The reason for the inapplicability of logical conjunction to pictures might be put like this: All propositions live in the same logical space, so to speak, but each picture has its unique picture-space (Howell 1976), a space usually not immediately compatible with another such space. Hence the integrity of both collapses when two are brought physically together.

Disjunction, the either/or operation of propositional logic, seems to have even less applicability to pictures. The interpretation that suggests itself is to treat disjunction as a kind of superposition or oscillation of aspects, as in the pictures of the duck-rabbit. But such a picture is not a representation of either a duck or a rabbit; it represents now a duck and then a rabbit.

Eighth. No logical properties of pictures are, as was said above, more intriguing than those that are positively absent: Negation and Contradiction. There is nothing one can do to a picture to turn it into its own contradiction, and nothing one can do within a picture to make it self-contradictory. It is this latter feature that makes the imagination so indispensable to reconstructions of fact (Oosthuizen 1968). For example, a judge who hears all sorts of spoken testimony about a spatial event the contradictions in which are not evident, can visualize the scene so as to make these contradictions reveal themselves. They glide smoothly by in words but they emerge in the unsuccessful attempt to image them. However, the same pictorial property that eases the work of the judge complicates the life of the geometer: the diagrams that accompany negative proofs, proofs that proceed by eliciting a geometric absurdity from a contrary-to-fact proposition, either fail to depict the false assumption made about the object or fail to depict the object at all. Try, for example, to draw the falsehood, so easily expressible in words, that a straight line has more than two points in common with a circle. Beginning students tend to be baffled by the resulting disparity between word and picture.

There are, to be sure, pictures that show physically impossible objects, such as those seen in the Escher woodcuts, which work in large part by deceptively concatenating pictures of perfectly possible objects. In fact, even actual objects can be made to give impossible-looking projections (Gregory 1970). One cannot say that these pictures are self-contradictory; they merely look impossible. No space negates another. Whatever exists in a picture space, as indeed in real space, can co-exist—geometrically if not dynamically—with anything else. And that is what contradictory propositions cannot do without the collapse of logical truth.

I cannot keep from mentioning one poetic picture, at the pinnacle of our tradition, which tries indeed to depict self-contradiction, Dante's mystic vision at the end of the *Divine Comedy*. He sees three coinciding yet non-coincident circles of light whose surface is filled by the human figure. It is a sight whose nature is beyond words to tell and reason to resolve, indeed beyond the imagination itself to hold except as a sudden glory: "For this high image, force now failed." The imagination cannot encompass a coincidence of opposites.

Above all, a picture cannot contain a negation. One can speak of what is not, but one cannot depict it. Whatever is shown is positive; there is no "not" in a picture—though one might have a negative belief about it. A proposition denied, as Russell puts it, is a changed content similarly believed; a negated picture, on the other hand, is the same content differently believed (1919, Part Four, Ch. 1)—that is to say, the picture negated looks the same as that picture affirmed. People have argued that pictures do contain negation: in depicting a certain state of affairs a picture also contains the non-existence of its appropriate alternative. Thus if a photograph shows a dictator it contains the denial of his assassination. But it only implies the negative fact, it does not show it. Some even argue thus: The formalization of the observation that a picture shows two plainly distinguishable trees in a meadow is $(\exists x)$ $(\exists y)$ (x and y are trees in a meadow and $x \neq y$)—and this formula includes the negation, "x does not equal y." But again, all this analysis really shows is that the logical articulation seizes hold of the visible world in a way unbridgeably different from a depiction. Only speech and thought have truck with negativity. This positivity of spatial representation will turn out to be of tremendous importance to the human function of the imagination, which is, after all, a kind of picture-space (Part Six, Chs. II, III). One example of a psychological consequence, already mentioned, is the fact that, as Freud observed, negatives are all but absent from dreams.

Picture-logic has been presented here in terms of its difference from word-logic—inevitably, since word-logic, as logic proper, is both better established and really prior insofar as it encompasses picture-logic: If logic is concerned with the forms of speech in general, the logic of pictures is a special segment of logic concerned with formal speech about pictures in particular. But that does not mean that thinking about pictures should always be subservient to logic. Although in logical investigations pictures are analyzed sententially, that procedure may be precisely the way to miss their essential properties—if there should be some that are well and truly non-verbal. These essentials of picture-nature may, however, elude logic without being therefore inaccessible to reflection. In Part Five I shall attempt such a reflection on the quintessentially spatial nature of the imagination.

b. The Representational Relation. Besides the logic of pictures in themselves as depicting-structures, there is also the logic of pictures as having a representational relation to an original. Representation can be analyzed from two points of view: One is the warrant for interpreting a picture as representing this particular object, and the other is the nature of the representational relation itself.

As for the *object* of representation, there seem to be at least four theories. The first is the "causal" theory, in which the representational relation is considered to be warranted by the history of production. Here the object represented must have played the main causal role in the making of the picture, as when a person sits for a portrait, or a camera is focused on a scene. In spite of its apparent practicality, for instance in deciding which of two identical twins is represented in a photograph, this theory quickly shows its limitations. What if a Sunday painter sets up an easel in front of Fujiyama and produces a miserable molehill? Must he be said to have painted that lovely volcano? What about the fact that representational attributions are often confidently made in total ignorance of the specific physical original? For example, one can recognize a portrait bust in a painting as blind Homer without knowing him or even supposing that he sat for the painter. What, finally, about the representational character of fictions that have no causes of this sort to begin with?

Second, there is the "authorial" theory: A picture represents an object if the maker intended that it should (Wittgenstein, *Blue Book* 1933, 32). This runs into difficulties similar to those of the causal theory. The maker may not be there to testify or he may have failed to realize his intention. The failure may have several causes, like lack of acquaintance with the looks of the thing intended, or lack of skill (Carrier 1973).

Third is the "inferential" theory, which throws the burden of representation and identification on the "pictorial competence" of the viewer (Sober 1976). "Pictorial competence" is the ability to "read" the marks on the picture plane, to use these physical stimuli as clues. This inferential ability does not prepare one to say "That mountain is Fujiyama," but it does permit one to identify it as an instance of a kind: quiescent volcano, conical, snowy-sloped. What the competence consists of is the application of conventional or perceptual rules of seeing, such as the Gestalt-laws. For example, the flat projection of a cube is a complicated system of numerous overlapping trapezoids, but a competent picture-seer will choose the economical inference that it is one solid that is depicted. Such pictorial competence is included in perceptual competence. To see objects and to see representations of objects requires a similar process of inference. Therein, however, lies the weakness of the theory. Since it is so general it is not very illuminating for picture-seeing specifically.

Fourth and last is the "projective" theory. A representation is related to the original by a rule of projection. A simple example of such a rule is a "central projection," where straight lines issuing from a single center throw the points of one plane onto another. If an object is thus projected onto a picture-plane one is entitled to say that the object is represented in the picture. The projection may range from a central projection so dense in points and faithful in color as to produce a picture that is a visual substitute for the original (as in *trompe l'oeil*) to one that is deforming and perturbing to the nth degree. Several projections may even be combined, as in those composite vistas that lack a unitary perspective, or superimposed, as in those Cubist paintings where the figure is the resultant of numerous geometric forms. This theory suffers from some of the same insufficiencies

as do those above. In particular, for many sophisticated paintings that are, according to their title, representations, the rule of projection would be so difficult to articulate that the attempt to verify the representational relation by recovering the projection would be lost labor. Indeed, one would conclude that the painting deliberately avoided the discernment of any projective rule.
(Black 1972, Howell 1976, Sober 1976.)

It seems to me that these four theories—really four criteria for saying whether or not something is a pictorial representation—are far from being mutually exclusive. They are, in fact, complementary. Combinations of them are indeed often proposed (Howell 1974). Their respective weight in judging representationality depends on the situation. Perhaps one ought to say that the four happening together suffices for something to be deemed an ideally representational representation (quite different, of course, from an idealized representation). Such an ideal representation would have these four properties: It would exist in a world in which the causal history of the copying is preserved. It would be exactly what the maker intended it to be. It would appeal to just such visual competence as is suitable to the recovery of objects in a pictorial plane. And it would be related to the original by a fairly perspicuous projection.

The logical nature of the *representational relation* is expressible in three theories: the "make-believe" theory, and the two major rival theories of "denotation" and "resemblance."

Before I set these out, a word is necessary about a sort of null-theory, the extreme notion that representation plays no role in pictures at all. Gibson, for example, extends to pictures his perceptual theory of direct information pickup, which requires no internal representation (Part Two, Ch. I C). There is no such thing as true re-presentation because the optical array, which carried the original information, never can be reduplicated; at most a pictorial representation may preserve some optical invariants (Gibson 1979). Of course, one might object, these invariants are what make certain arrays readable as images.

There is also philosophical opposition to representational terms in general, particularly from Wittgenstein and Sartre. Take for example a portrait. One may see it simply as an oil-on-canvas object, or one may recognize it as a portrait of someone (Ishiguro 1967). In the first case, it is claimed, there is no question of representation, and in the second what one sees is not a representation of the sitter but just the sitter himself in the picture. Such theories are economical—too economical, in fact, since they cut out the vivid human experience of mental picturing (Part One, Ch. IV).

The "make-believe" theory regards pictures as props in a society-wide game, played according to internalized rules that circumscribe a non-literal way of talking about depiction. Speaking within the game, one may, while looking at a picture, say truly: "Here is a mountain." It is not at all necessary for the figure in the picture to resemble a mountain, though such resemblance facilitates the game (Walton 1973). This theory is really more about what people learn to say and do in front of pictures than it is about the nature of pictorial representation. In other words, representation is explained as a relation between the viewing society and the picture rather than between the picture and its original.

The "denotation"-theory claims that pictures refer to their originals in the same way as words refer to things. The representational relation is a symbolic, "stand-for" relation, which is defined only within a conventional symbol-system and in no way depends on resemblance. The objections to this influential theory, chief of which are that the treatment of imaginary subjects in particular is unsatisfying and that the denotative, stand-for relation in general is opaque, are detailed in Part Five (Ch. III A). But here one point is in order. One might argue that a stand-for relation really cannot be given even a conventional meaning (short of issuing a universal symbolic dictionary) except as something is in practice used to stand for something else. For example, under this theory a picture of a mountain cannot really be said to stand for a mountain until it is actually used that way (Novitz 1975). That reasonable stipulation drives the denotation-theory into a kind of representational operationalism: the denotation of a depiction is given by its use-context. This is, to say the least, a peculiar position for a supposedly aesthetic theory to be in.

The "resemblance"-theory backs a spectrum of techniques, from straight copying to the most cunning illusionism. Behind all of them stands the notion that the essence of pictorial representation is visual similarity, likeness of looks, however indirectly achieved.

Here we have the most naively straightforward and, of course, the most commonly held theory. Such theories are always preferable, as long as they save the main appearances. The resemblance-representation theory as applied to painting specifically will be defended in Part Five (Ch. III).

Meanwhile there are in it plenty of linguistic and logical difficulties to deal with. First of all, the words "resembling" and "looking like" seem to have a whole cluster of uses (Black 1972), some of them not very helpful to the present context, such as "It looks like rain," or "These theories have points of resemblance." What really should resemblance mean in the context of pictorial representation?

Certainly pictorial resemblance must in principle be testable for spatial similarity, either by some sort of projection such as was described above, or through a side-by-side comparison. But that does not mean that the resemblance-character of a picture requires an actual physical comparison. The original might be unavailable by reason of being dead, elsewhere or imaginary, and yet the picture is seen as an image. For the resemblance-theory is simply the image-theory of depiction, where an image is understood as a lesser likeness. One might say that in the cases just mentioned instead of seen re-semblance there is sensed semblance. The physical picture displays semblances of scenes and figures. This display leads to more than the game of make-believe, described above, played by the viewer with the picture as a prop. For the picture is seen as re-presenting on its surface the look of things without presenting the things themselves. The representation is sensed *as* an image, though the original is forever out of reach.

Although proof of an actual projection is not required in the resemblance-theory, still the spatial similarity to an original that is always felt to be, and often is, actually involved poses difficulties. They are most economically stated by Wittgenstein in the *Blue Book* (1933, 32).

He poses the now-famous question, "What makes a portrait the portrait of so-and-so?" The same question can be asked of any depiction "from life." Take a painting of Fujiyama. The resemblance-answer, which Wittgenstein eschews, seems to me to have two phases: What makes a picture of Fujiyama a picture of that mountain is just what makes a prospect of this snowy-sloped quiescent volcano a view of that mountain, namely its particular aspect or looks. And what makes a picture of the mountain a picture simply is that it contains various pictorial indices, such as the reduction of the cone to two dimensions and the liberation of its bulk from the laws of physics. These turn Fujiyama into a picture-mountain.

But, says Wittgenstein, a portrait, be it of a man or a mountain, can be good or bad, and the similarity-theory doesn't seem to be able to account for this fact. Certainly the most correctly similar copy isn't always the most revealing picture. Wittgenstein's stricture brings out the fact that presenting the essentially same looks is not necessarily identical with being similar in configuration and color. A likeness is often the more revealing of the original for involving deformation of shape, blurring or sharpening of edges, revisions in color, omissions of detail, emphases of features, and many other almost ineffably subtle liberties. The problem of representational painting centers on the noble cunning of illusionism, on telling truth through deception, on Plato's "phantastic" art. The painters of such pictures commonly agree that when the intention is to capture the most revealing looks of the sitter or the scene, some rough sort of literal similarity to a real or possible object is always present, though it may be discernible only by the eye capable of seeing the significant aspects.

In addition, all sorts of fairly marginal objections are mounted for the resemblance-theory (Walton 1973, 315 n.). One, already mentioned, is the "twin problem": The same photograph is a likeness of both twins, though it is a picture of only one of them. Hence resembling something is not sufficient for being a picture of it. This case shows that the resemblance-theory has to be coupled with the causal theory in certain cases, especially where replicas, natural or artificial, are imaged. Alternately one could argue that where two originals have the same look, the picture is *ipso facto* a picture of both.

Another difficulty is posed by the case of Lot's wife. A picture shows a pillar of salt and bears the title "Lot's Wife." The title denotes a human being while the picture resembles a spur of sodium chloride. Hence, one might conclude, resembling something is not necessary for being a picture of it. But, it seems to me, the pillar of salt does resemble Lot's wife in one of her appearances. Hence the difficulty is not with the resemblance-theory but with the miracles of the Lord.

A third, specifically logical, difficulty is serious. The reading of pictures is articulated in forms analogous to those of ordinary intentional speech, in which characteristically an intended proposition or object is put forth together with an indication of the intentional mode, such as believing or imagining, in which it is uttered. For example one may say "I imagine that Fujiyama has snowy slopes," intending a proposition about the mountain, or "I imagine snowy-sloped Fujiyama," intending the mountain as a direct object. The picture-reading analogues to such utterances are: "This picture shows that Fujiyama has snowy slopes," and "This picture shows snowy-sloped Fujiyama." Now it is usually not held permissible in logic to quantify existentially over propositions in intentional contexts: The fact that I believe something is the case doesn't make it in fact the case; and the fact that I imagine something can't make it in fact exist. So too with pictures—the mere fact that they show a state of affairs or an object does not tell us the nature, or guarantee the existence, of an original. Therefore picture-reading appears to supply us with no representational relation. Yet the case for the existence of Fujiyama does not seem to me so desparate. We do not even have to go to see it for ourselves, since we can see it in a photograph, and the production-history of an image on film is so much built into its very concept as to exempt it from the intentional rule. Hence at least "This photograph shows Fujiyama" is normally—barring fraud or miracle—taken as proof of the mountain's existence and state.

But it is otherwise in the case of many of the most delightful and desirable representational subjects, those not taken from the real world. The pictorial showing by which they appear so persuasively as images of something imaginary rebuffs our quest for their originals. It offers no warrant at all for any originating existences in any real world. Yet while the seeing of semblances evidently does not require an original to be physically available for comparison, the very concept of resemblance—as well as the feel of the depiction—seems to drive the viewer willy-nilly into positing an original in some realm: without such a reference the pictorial image is not truly an image and a representation, and is stripped of its standing and its savor. I will enter this twilight zone of image-logic, the imaginer's faith, in Chapter III.

Bibliography

Anscombe, G.E.M. 1959. *An Introduction to Wittgenstein's* Tractatus. London: Hutchinson University Library.

Benardete, Seth. 1984. *The Being of the Beautiful: Plato's* Theaetetus, Sophist, *and* Statesman [translated with commentary]. Chicago: The University of Chicago Press.

Black, Max. 1972. "How Do Pictures Represent?" In *Art, Perception, and Reality*. Baltimore: The Johns Hopkins University Press.

Block, Ned. 1981. "Introduction: What Is the Issue?" In *Imagery*. Cambridge: The MIT Press.

———. 1983. "The Photographic Fallacy in the Debate about Mental Imagery." *Nous* 17:651–661.

Carney, James D. 1981. "Wittgenstein's Theory of Picture Representation." *Journal of Aesthetics and Art Criticism* 40:179–186.

Carrier, David. 1973. "Three Kinds of Imagination." *The Journal of Philosophy* 70:819–831.

Cornford, Francis M. 1934. *Plato's Theory of Knowledge: The* Theaetetus *and the* Sophist [translated with running commentary]. New York: The Liberal Arts Press (1957).

Gibson, James J. 1979. *The Ecological Approach to Visual Perception*. Boston: Houghton Mifflin Co.

Gregory, R. L. 1970. *The Intelligent Eye*. New York: McGraw-Hill.

Howell, Robert. 1974. "The Logical Structure of Pictorial Representation." *Theoria* 40:76–109.

———. 1976. "Ordinary Pictures, Mental Representations, and Logical Forms." *Synthese* 33:149–174. [Review of Sober 1976.]

Ishiguro, Hidé. 1967. "Symposium: Imagination." In *The Aristotelian Society*, Supplementary Volume 41. London: Harrison and Sons.

Klein, Jacob. 1977. *Plato's Trilogy:* Theaetetus, *the* Sophist, *and the* Statesman. Chicago: The University of Chicago Press.

Kosslyn, Stephen M. 1980. *Image and Mind.* Cambridge: Harvard University Press.

———. 1983. *Ghosts in the Mind's Machine: Creating and Using Images in the Brain.* New York: W.W. Norton Company.

Malcolm, Norman. 1958. *Ludwig Wittgenstein: A Memoir.* London: Oxford University Press.

Mounce, H. O. 1981. *Wittgenstein's* Tractatus: *An Introduction.* Chicago: The University of Chicago Press.

Novitz, David. 1975. "Picturing." *The Journal of Aesthetics and Art Criticism* 34:145–155.

Oosthuizen, D.C.S. 1968. "The Role of Imagination in Judgments of Fact." *Philosophy and Phenomenological Research* 39:34–58.

Owen, G.E.L. 1971. "Plato on Not-Being." In *Plato: A Collection of Critical Essays,* Volume 1, edited by Gregory Vlastos. Garden City, N.J.: Doubleday and Co.

Plato [second quarter, 4th cent. BC]. *The Sophist.*

Ramsey, Frank P. 1923. "Critical Notice, *Tractatus Logico-Philosophicus* by Ludwig Wittgenstein." In *The Foundations of Mathematics.* London: Routledge and Kegan Paul (1954).

Rosen, Stanley. 1983. *Plato's Sophist, the Drama of Original and Image.* New Haven: Yale University Press.

Roskill, Mark, and Carrier, David. 1983. *Truth and Falsehood in Visual Images.* Amherst: The University of Massachusetts Press.

Sober, Elliot. 1976. "Mental Representations." *Synthese* 33:101–148.

Walton, Kendall L. 1973. "Pictures and Make-Believe." *The Philosophical Review* 82:283–319.

Wittgenstein, Ludwig. 1921. *Tractatus Logico-Philosophicus* [with German text]. Introduction by Bertrand Russell. Translated by D. F. Pears and B. F. McGuiness. London: Routledge and Kegan Paul (1961).

———. 1933–34. *The Blue and Brown Books.* New York: Harper and Row (1965).

Chapter II

Mental Images: Unreal Pictures of Real Objects

If it were granted that mental images are non-material pictures, as the title above avers, the work of this chapter would have been largely done in the previous one. It would only remain to modify the logic of material pictures so as take account of the unreality of mental pictures. But mental images are not to be had for free; they require the pomp and circumstance of a prior inquiry into their existence.

There is, as we know, a group of purists who deny that mental images exist in any way at all and who claim that imagining is the same as descriptive thinking (Dilman 1967). People at large, however, agree that we do visualize things, especially when we remember past perceptions. For them the question is more apt to be whether images are some kind of object, entities with discernible features.

In the psychological investigations of Part Two, the question of existence was favorably resolved on empirical grounds, in tandem with the progressive confirmation of certain "privileged properties," several of which were picture-like. Mental images were thus established as objects of some sort, in fact, quasi-pictures.

But when one considers the logic of mental images, namely their necessary and articulable structure, it is not the empirical fact but the possibility of their existence as objects that might seem to be the first problem: How can mental images be objects of some sort to begin with? ("Object" is taken here in the primitively literal sense: any entity, not necessarily physical, that "throws" itself in the way of our apprehension by means of its properties and confronts our cognition. "Thing" and "real" are reserved for physical objects.)

Now how can one get hold of this prickly problem without getting stung? If we begin by analyzing the nature of mental images we might find

ourselves talking about the conceptually impossible—that is, talking nonsense. If we begin by proving the possibility of their existence, we will
soon find ourselves having to reach into their nature for help, and thus
arguing in circles. I propose to break through these difficulties by assuming
the existence of mental images, favored as it is by the agreement of common
opinion, the certainty of introspection, and the evidence of experiment,
leaving the possibility of such images to fend for itself. I shall, however,
give the briefest summary of the inconclusive "object"-controversy, which
is the form the existence question takes in logic (A). Then, proceeding by
way of yet another empirically justified assumption—that if mental images
are objects, they a picture-like objects—I shall set out the logical features by
which mental pictures are distinguished from real pictures (B).

A. Mental Images as Objects

Here is the disavowal of mental objects as put by its chief proponent Ryle:
We speak of singing a song and of dancing a dance, and might likewise
speak of imagining an image. Song, dance, and image are "internal accusa-
tives," a grammatical form in which the performance meant by the verb is
treated as if it were its object or product. But it is a misleading way of
speaking: none of the three, song, dance or image, are anything but doings,
kinds of conduct or behavior, and an image is not something imagined. On
the contrary, to understand the word "image" we need to understand the
verb "imagine," and then we notice that imagining is at least partly a
"factual disclaimer" concept: To imagine a mountain is not to see a
mountain of peculiar kind, but it is rather *not* to see a mountain (1949).
Notice, by the way, that Ryle's explication is the contrary of the Platonic
Stranger's solution, which was that to imagine means to see a non-
mountain.

Again, Ryle admits, we speak of seeing a scene "before the mind's eye,"
and since we do not mean that the landscape itself is in the head, we suppose
that it is a picture we are seeing. For pictures seem to be like visualizations
in being voluntary productions that more or less vividly or accurately make
visible what is not really there. But this assimilation is excessive. We do not
need pictures in the head in order to imagine something. There is a genus
"seeming to see," which includes both seeing something when looking at
photographs and seeing something when there is no physical object (1949).

Besides these broad Rylean objections there are a number of specific
points made against image-objects by various authors. (Recall here that I
distinguish between the "image-object," which is a particular conception of

a mental image, and the "imaged object" which is the thing represented in any image.) One argument by Shorter (1952), begins with the utility of the concept. If having an image of a mountain is "something like seeing" a mountain, then the object must be conceived as taking its nature from the manner of its apprehension. So the mountain thus quasi-seen is also a quasi-mountain, something merely like a mountain. But this concept of a mental image is gaining its image-object character by mere transfer from its mode of apprehension: It is an object only by the empty courtesy of a manner of speaking.

A second argument arises out of Sartre's understanding of consciousness (1940). Imagining anything is being conscious of *it* itself and not of its image. If, in imagining, the image were the object of consciousness, the image as object would rival and replace the object in the image; we would see the picture-object and miss the pictured object. In fact we are aware of the imaged object, not the image. Moreover, an image could not be "in" consciousness, because consciousness is always transparent to itself; it is through and through conscious. It cannot harbor an opaque, alien, unassimilable object such as a mental picture would be. So one cannot speak of a mental image as something in itself. There is not in consciousness any image-thing that images some other thing.

A third set of arguments consists of all that cannot be said of or done with mental images that could be said or done with objects. One cannot ask whether an image that once existed exists any longer or whether it has been "rubbed out" (Shorter 1952). One cannot attend to it rather than to the object it images, for it will immediately fade. Although what one visualizes is often vague or indeterminate, one cannot say of the image that it is blurred, as one might of a photograph. For that matter, one cannot say that it is anything—colored or torn or blotted.

The general reasons for finding these attacks on the image-object unpersuasive have been given in Part One (Chs. IV, V). Briefly recapitulated they are these: Ryle's objections are such as to make it in principle impossible to give any positive account of the almost universally acknowledged phenomenon of seeing in the mind's eye. Instead of respecting a perplexity his approach issues an interdiction. Sartre's claims that consciousness is wholly transparent and cannot include opaque items, and that it is impossible to attend to image-object and object-image at once, are highly arguable. Shorter's observation concerning linguistic transfer fails to consider the possibility that, far from trivializing the concept of a picture-object, the analogy might direct us to take it seriously, to grapple with quasi-objects as entities, albeit unreal ones. Finally, the collection of ways one can speak about objects but not about images is altogether dubious. Each of these ways of speaking could indeed also be used of images if they had the so-called "privileged properties" mentioned above—observable characteristics belonging to the image as image rather than to its content, what it images. And that does appear to be empirically the case. At any rate, there is nothing particularly logical about these prohibitions; they are—probably faulty—empirical observations.

The most persuasive positive argument for mental images as objects is couched by Hannay (1971) in these common-sensical terms: "If in picturing, hallucinating and dreaming one is seeing something intentionally, it would seem wholly inexplicable that one saw nothing materially." Here "seeing intentionally" means the viewer's belief, right or wrong, that he is in fact seeing some object. "Seeing materially" means that the seeing has an actual object answering to the viewer's description. In other words, whenever one thinks one is seeing something there must be something one is seeing. It might be an object directly, or it might be a mental picture with the object in it; there is, however, a necessary and natural transition from the first to the second, insofar as mental figures must sit in a mental medium. For all its simplicity, Hannay's point is so plausible that it is deniable only at the peril of becoming arbitrary. One should concede that the question whether mental images are entities of some sort is not resolvable by logical or linguistic analysis, and believe what makes sense of experience.

B. Mental Images as Pictures

Once the object-character of the mental image is accepted, what could it be but a picture of a sort? It is an image insofar as it represents something that is not actually there; here is the object *in* the image. It is a picture precisely insofar as it has an independent medium-like existence; here is the image *as* an object. And, of course, insofar as it is mental, the image-picture has, as was indicated, an existence of a special sort; it is an unreal object.

Though mental images will be shown to coincide conceptually with pictures in important ways, they do also display some non-pictorial features, which belong to them precisely insofar as they maintain a certain identity with perception. While pictures, whether painted from a unitary or a composite perspective, can be indirectly inspected from various, even inappropriate, points of view, mental images, insofar as experiment and introspection can tell, are usually seen directly, like perceived vistas, from the point of view that establishes the perspective to begin with. Furthermore, while pictures are enframed within a space that is itself set within physical space as a whole, the inner space where the imagined figures and scenes occur is like the visual field of perceptual space in being a close-up window opening on the appearances; its frame is, as in perception, the periphery of the visual field. That circumstance is, after all, what makes the discernment of mental images as pictures somewhat tricky: They are not surrounded by a non-imaginal space, as are real pictures.

Before the—suitably modified—picture character of mental images is sketched out, a word on the psychological topic of "individual differences" is in order. As has been shown (Part Two, Ch. V D), there are great divergences in the vividness of color, outline, and detail of mental imagery, and in the accuracy of visual memory, ranging from the all-but-perception of eidetikers to nothing-but-description of the imaginally blind. Very likely the normal imagery-faculty, as established from introspection and laboratory evidence, has many individual nuances. To some, Sartre evidently among them, it delivers its presentations *in toto* with no hidden facets. To others an image evidently presents more than they consciously know of. Some see integrated scenes, others isolated figures. Some must think before they envision, others see spontaneously and reflect later. In the analysis that follows, I am assuming the imagery of the imager *moyen imaginatif*, such as is described by those who can follow all sorts of imaging instructions and who report an ordinary range of imagery experience.

Here, then, are the pictorial properties that should enter into the concept of "mental image," particularly as distinguished from a real picture.

The first set of properties concerns the medium that confronts the mind's eye and the vision that corresponds to it. The most obvious distinction between a painting and a mental image is the absence in the latter of a physical medium, such as a canvas and the marks upon it. It is the material substrate that makes a picture an obviously material object, a "real" picture. The material medium can be perceptually attended to quite separately from the image-viewing. There is, equally, something legitimately called a mental medium, for a mental image has underlying properties that belong to it not by reason of its particular image-subject or image-syntax, but as an image *tout court*. The difference between real pictures and mental images is in the accessibility of these properties. In mental images they are not so readily observed by the imager. Some just escape attention; others are even constitutionally subconscious. The former yield to a phenomenological analysis: under careful inspection mental images show degrees of clarity, from evanescently dim to blazingly bright. (Clarity is a purely pictorial characteristic, distinguishable from the "vividness," the sense of realness, that was Hume's criterion for distinguishing perception from imagination.) They also have texturality—different kinds of surface quality, roughness, smoothness, hard-edged or soft contours—whatever the imaged subject may suggest. And they show degrees of directness; the image context may present itself well up front or be skulking in a murky background (Casey 1976). These features, which were detailed in Part Two, have to be tricked into the open by chronometric experiments. We must admit that it remains obscure about some of them whether they are ultimately to be assigned to the image-medium or to the image-seeing—to the image-producer or the image-process—and, indeed, whether these two aspects are always experimentally or introspectively distinguishable.

In fact, the distinction between seeing of real pictures and the "seeing" of mental images is a crux of the debate about mental images (Hannay 1971). Even though looking at real pictures includes an element of construction, it nevertheless possesses an indubitably public occasion and cause in the picture-object. Inner seeing, on the other hand, though it is similar to real seeing insofar as it utilizes the channels of perception, differs in its conceptual structure insofar as the status of the stimulus-object is ambiguous: Is the image a given object confronting mental sight, or is it a product resulting from the process of visualization? The reports of introspection go both ways. Sometimes images confront the mental eye, apparently arising before it spontaneously as do percepts before the real eye. Sometimes the strained concentration of inner seeing betokens the simultaneous production of the image, particularly of its detail. Here, where image-seeing melds with image-production, imaging distinguishes itself from seeing but parallels depicting: In drawing, for instance, making and inspecting are so closely intertwined as to be one unitary process. So, too, the activity of attending to detail brings out the fact that mental scanning is closer to pictorial inspection than to perceptual observation. A physical object invites close scanning by offering the promise of an indefinite sequence of ever finer detail. Both a picture and a mental image, on the other hand, have limits of resolution and of significance beyond which inspection cannot profitably go. In sum, although internal "seeing" is probably in some respects an insuperably equivocal term, it is also in certain respects more like looking at pictures than like looking at the objects they depict.

A second set of properties concerns the author-viewer's relation to his own mental picture. Real pictures, at least those that are depictions, are separable from their authors, their originators, whose authority they leave behind when they enter the public realm, for example, when they are sold. (In this country paintings once alienated are even legally protected from the interference of the painter.) Moreover, they have viewers who may look at the painting from whatever perspective they please and interpret it as they like. While mental pictures, too, have authors who summon them with more or less natural talent and more or less practiced skill, they differ in a number of other ways: The mental picture never, except apparently in madness, passes beyond the originator's authority. It can be continually revised or continually reiterated, as the possessor pleases. In short, the triad of maker, work, viewer is collapsed into one. Hence it makes no sense to speak of taking the wrong point of view *vis-à-vis* one's image. Nor is the meaning of an image normally as opaque to the imaginer as pictures often are to viewer, though it certainly happens, especially in dreams, that images arise whose meaning and even identification is a nagging mystery—hence the pseudo-science of dream interpretation. Both picture-viewer and imager can abrogate the sight by deliberately or inadvertently ceasing to pay attention, and in both cases staring too intensely dissipates the image. But only for mental pictures is it a problem where the picture is located when it is unattended. This problem, investigated in the cognitive and physiological science of memory-storage and -retrieval, is so far unsolved. The conceptual aspect of the problem is reduced to this: Is it logically legitimate to speak of a subconscious mental image? If not, the contents of image-consciousness are consigned to a randomly discrete life of occultations and apparitions. Consequently the notion of being somehow held or stored over separate appearances, like a painting in a studio, seems to have to belong to a mental image (Part Two, Ch. III A).

As mental pictures differ in some ways from real ones with respect to the place they occupy *vis-à-vis* their author, they also differ with respect to their time. A photograph, for example, is the representation of an arrested moment in the existence of the object represented. Hence that object is strictly speaking always in the past with respect to the present picture. However, that fact need not be evident in the picture unless it is dated or contains internal indices of its time. It is otherwise with memory-images, which carry with them constitutionally a sense of pastness, as Aristotle observes in his treatise *On Memory*: "Always when someone is engaging in the act of memory, . . . whatever he saw or heard or knows, he has in addition the sense that it was before. But before and after are in time" (450 a). Some imagination, however, has upon it a feel of things to come, of futurity, and yet another, choice, sort has about it a sense of positive timelessness.

In sum, whereas a real picture is spatially and temporally separable from its maker and is eventually, even if sometimes reluctantly, released into the world by its author, the mental picture never leaves the intimacy and authority of the imager. It is, even in extreme cases like hallucinations, insuperably one's own.

Third and last, there is a difference between real and mental pictures with respect to intentionality. Intentionality in this context is a term for the central logical fact about pictures: They are meant, intended to be, pictures *of* something. (For present purposes non-representational pictures are an anomalous case.) The hypothesis defended later in the book is that the representational intention of real pictures is usually self-revealing, meaning that pictures represent by resembling what they intend. But there are certainly cases of failed or obscured resemblance, and in that case the picture-maker's avowed intention is authoritative; sometimes it is expressed in the title written under a picture. To the viewer these two, picture and title, present themselves quite separately, not to say divergently. Usually, the verbal description is regarded as the secondary text, a commentary to be consulted after the picture is allowed to speak for itself (though some museum-goers are hopelessly title-bound).

Not so in most mental pictures. Here the imager and the viewer are identical and the consciousness of the intention is usually part of the consciousness of the image. Memory-images of real objects take their looks from previous experience (Cousin 1970), but they are—usually—summoned by the imager's intention. This fact puts each of them "under a description" that defines the imaged object (Richardson 1980). However, this descriptive or defining thought works from behind or from within, as if the mental image were a title-in-appearance, a kind of epiphany of intention. So that antic disparity between picture and title sometimes perpetrated by painters is in principle impossible in fully conscious mental imaging—though not in dreaming, which is a kind of limit case in this respect: in dreams it does sometimes happen that aspect and intention are curiously diverse, that persons and places do not look like what they are known to be.

In this chapter the imaged object, insofar as it has entered at all, has been taken in the most pedestrian sense as a memory: something once experienced and later recalled, once real and then retrieved. But of course the power of the imagination is more than memorial; it depicts many objects which never were or could be percepts.

Bibliography

Audi, Robert. 1978. "The Ontological Status of Mental Images." *Analysis* 21:348–361.

Casey, Edward S. 1976. *Imagining: A Phenomenological Study.* Bloomington: Indiana University Press.

Cousin, D. R. 1970. "On the Ownership of Images." *Analysis* 30:206–208.

Dilman, Ilham. 1967. "Symposium: Imagination." In *The Aristotelian Society,* Supplementary Volume 41. London: Harrison and Sons.

Hannay, Alastair. 1971. *Mental Images: A Defense.* New York: Humanities Press.

Ortega y Gasset, José. 1914. "An Essay in Esthetics by Way of a Preface." In *Phenomenology and Art.* New York: W.W. Norton Company (1975).

Richardson, John T. E. 1980. *Mental Imagery and Human Memory.* New York: St. Martin's Press.

Ryle, Gilbert. 1949. *The Concept of Mind.* New York: Barnes and Noble.

Sartre, Jean-Paul. 1940. *The Psychology of the Imagination.* New York: The Citadel Press (1965).

Shorter, J. M. 1952. "Imagination." In *Ryle: A Collection of Critical Essays,* edited by Oscar P. Wood and George Pitcher. Garden City, N.J.: Doubleday (1970).

Warnock, Mary. 1976. *Imagination.* Berkeley and Los Angeles: University of California Press.

Chapter III

Imaginary Images: Unreal Pictures of Unreal Objects

The most intimate capacity of the imagination is for the twice unreal. It is once unreal in respect to its images, which, though objects, are not real but mental. And it is again unreal insofar as the most characteristic objects depicted in its images are "imaginary," meaning that the originals of mental images are not, and perhaps cannot be, found in the real world. I shall call such images of imaginary objects for short "imaginary images" or, as the psychologists say, "imagination-images." In the previous chapter it was argued that the word "object" could be properly used of the mental images; in this chapter it will be suggested that even behind the imaginary image must stand some sort of original (somewhat confusingly but unavoidably called its object as well).

The special propensity of our imagination for the imaginary is only to be expected. Mental images have, after all, escaped some of the constraints of reality and are therefore particularly suitable for picturing beings and states of affairs that are partially absolved from the laws of matter and motion. I phrase this observation tamely, hoping to suppress the facile leap to the most pervasive and least examined supposition about imagination-images. It is that these objects are nothing but the creatures and consequences of our imaginative constitution, being entirely produced *by* and thus in no sense presented *to* the imagination.

But if the logical passage from a real picture to its real original proved to be fraught with difficulties, so much the harder is the way from the imagination to its originals, its source-objects. Candor seems to me to require the assumption that where there is an image being entertained there is something of which it is an image; it requires arguing that imaging something means that there is something that is being imaged. Moreover if it is true, as I shall try to show in Parts Four and Five, that pictures and

425

stories are images of mental images of imaginary objects, then these external products of the imagination will in fact image, at second remove, just these arcane imaginary originals. If, however, there are no such originals, works of art may well be "about nothing at all and the names they contain denote neither possible nor actual objects" (Plantinga 1974).

"So what?" one might say, and consign the subject to that academic suburb where "deviant logic" tries to subject the demimonde of nothings, non-entities, and nonesuches to a reconditely formal discipline. But it proves to be humanly impossible to treat these nothings either as logical refuse or as utterly formal problems. "Unactual" objects, at least for many of us, behave with a potent effectiveness that on occasion precedes, over-rules, and outdoes that of the world's "realest," "most actual" existences—to heap up the chief terms of real-world prestige. I will leave the detailing of the particular ways in which the imagination works in the world to Part Six, but the fact itself is a platitude, a truth told so often as to be nearly inaudible: Fictions have force. But even when these human aspects are kept well in the background, there is still the fascination exerted by the formal problem of nonexistence. The haunting question "What is 'behind' the imagination?" is indeed avoidable enough and is in fact usually avoided, but it is not permanently suppressible.

I shall sketch out two main treatments of that problem in its purest terms—logical terms—in the first section (A) under the heading Entities, namely of Nonexistent "Homeless Objects" (1) and Possible Worlds (2). The next section (B) I shall devote to the application of these logical terms to the fictional objects depicted in visual images and described in verbal accounts. In fact, "fiction," although etymologically related to the "feigning" or fashioning of anything from a plastic material, is primarily used of verbal feigning, and most of the contemporary treatments deal with the figures found in literature. This section will therefore serve me as a transition and introduction to Part Four, which I devote specifically to verbal imagining. Finally, in the last section (C) of the present part I shall consider the being and the realm of imaginary scenes and figures (1) and their function as the originals of visual or verbal fictions (2).

A. Nonexistent Entities: The Mode of Unreality

The first question pertinent to the imagination is, then, whether there must not be things and states of affairs that do not exist. To exist here means to be in time and space. Must not some sort of alternative standing be assigned to the "forms of things unknown," "the airy nothings" which the poet's pen shapes and gives "a local habitation and a name"?

A parade of candidates for being, but not being here and now or there and then, presents itself: There are possible but unactual objects like golden mountains. There are special or composite natures like angels, ghosts, unicorns, and centaurs. There are intuitively impossible objects like round squares (Grossman 1974, 34), logically impossible objects like five-sided hexagons, dynamically impossible states like a mathematical point exerting gravitational force, and physically unconstruable things like the objects depicted in Escher wood-cuts. There are exceedingly improbable facts like a monkey typing out *The Descent of Man*. There are absent beings such as persons no longer or not yet in existence, the long dead and the yet unborn. There are ideal beings like numbers, Platonic forms and Being itself. And then there are all the entities not only nonexistent but also so far unthought of.

Some of these are not amenable to the practices of logic and others are not relevant to our subject. Chief among the latter are the nonexistences best established within philosophy: ideal objects. To them pertains a kind of being distinct from existence, which is traditionally called subsistence; it is a being outside the spatio-temporal context by reason of its own nature. The logical standing of another set of non- or quasi-existents like angels or ghosts would seem to follow on prior theological commitments. Again, the pastness and futurity of existence, though fraught with much human pathos, has not been considered by the logicians of nonexistent entities who, for simplicity, consider existence as an untensed, once-and-for-all, either-or state (Parsons 1980, Pears 1963). The nonexistent beings of immediate interest make up a remaining class: such possible and unactual entities, both objects and states of affairs, as have been the objects of someone's imagination, together with occasional inspired impossibilia. The beings under consideration are those that people stories, paintings, and the landscapes before the mind's eye.

1. "Homeless Objects": **Con and Pro.** This forlorn phrase, introduced by Alexius Meinong, can be used to cover just about the group so established: entities that are neither concrete existent individuals nor "abstract" objects (Chisholm 1982). The question is what recognition to accord to them and where to place them: Do fictions have being?

a. *Con:* Brentano and Russell. Brentano, who first occupied himself with what later came to be called intentionality, spoke early on of "intentional inexistence." He may then have meant that when we intend—direct—our thoughts, to objects that do not exist, they do have some sort of "not-existence" (Chisholm 1960). It is certain, however, that he later offered a brusque solution: Nothing is but what exists, nothing exists but what is a concrete individual; these alone are "genuine." The rest are fictions, not in the sense that they are fictional objects but in the sense that it is a sometimes useful fiction to say that they are objects.

Another way to put this is that one may properly affirm or deny much about a thing or state, but not its existence or nonexistence, for these are not properties of the thing. A centaur is not a being that besides having the property of being half horse, half man also has a property of nonexistence. There are several old arguments against existence as a property like any other, which apply *a fortiori* to its negative. For example, though one can say "This mountain is snow-covered," one cannot say, "This mountain is nonexistent" without falling into a contradiction in reference through pointing at what is not there (Pears 1963). Brentano concludes that the carefully determined object of logic is really much narrower than the loosely taken concept of a—possibly fictional—thing (1911).

Russell pursues this course to its conclusion by approaching the existence problem in terms of logic—in terms of formal propositions about things and states of affairs. How are sentences to be formalized? In Russell's solution, called the "Theory of Descriptions," a sentence is formalized in such a way as not to hide the fact that a centaur, for example, is not at all a proper name denoting something but only shorthand for a "definite de-scription." One can then say "There is no centaur" without risking refer-ence to nonexistence, by means of the logical locution "Something is such that it is a centaur, and nothing else is a centaur and it is a mythical monster and it is half horse, half man." The existence or nonexistence is now attached to the "something" by means of an existential quantifier: "There is an x," or "It is not the case that there is an x." By means of this device one can talk about centaurs without being committed to their existence by the very sentence meant to deny it. The translation of this new, negated version, fleshed out for x and abbreviated for the centaur is: "No animal is a centaur."

Now, to go beyond logic into poetic rhetoric for a moment, that is probably not what the original centaur-sentence was meant to say. For "No animal is a centaur" means: "Corral all the animals and note that there is not a centaur among them." Naturally not, for a centaur begotten (accord-ing to Pindar) by man upon mare, could not be caught in such an enclosure. In fact if it were found among the true animals it would not be what is meant by a mythical centaur: a hybrid, eminently describable and visualizable, that is at once beastly and humane and is, for all its vehement pathos, oddly enough not around.

Moreover, Russell's version also offers logical difficulties—as it happens, at the other extreme (Chisholm 1982, 38). The centaur, wherever it isn't, is certainly in the imagination. Thus the true sentence "The centaur I am imagining has a monster's pathos" goes into "There exists an x, such that x is a centaur I am imagining and x is monster-pathetic, and . . ." But now the Russellian form seems to say that being imagined is one among the many features of this (or any) existent object. That, however, is something stranger than even a strong believer in the real-life powers of the imagination might be willing to assert.

However, Russell's motive for overcoming the being of nonexistents is more relevant to the present inquiry than his means. That motive is best appreciated by going through the theory he made the chief target of his attack, that of Meinong.

b. *Pro:* Meinong and Parsons. That motive, grown if anything more dominant in the philosophical taste of this century, is what Meinong calls "the prejudice in favor or the actual." (Whereas I shall be using the term "actual" to mean "having the vitality of a being" quite aside from being here and now, he means by the actual simply the existent—1904, 79). The project of opposing this mundane tendency in favor of the here and now, a project until recently not very successful, is summed up by Meinong thus: "Those who like paradoxical modes of expression could very well say: There are objects of which it is true to say that there are no such objects." What makes this paradox plausible? Exactly what drove us into this inquiry: It is possible to have objects in mind, to think of or imagine things, that are rich in characteristics or properties but are not real. Furthermore, even in order to deny them their existence it is necessary to get a handle on them, so that they must *somehow* be.

This mode of possessing properties Meinong calls "such-being" (*Sosein*). Now Meinong affirms a basic principle: the independence of such-being from being. The object's possession of the properties it has is in no way affected by its being or non-being, here meaning its existence or nonexistence. So there are objects that have such-being but are not in any other sense. Indeed, anything one considers has to be given with some characteristics before its being or non-being is determined. (Some objects, like the round square, have, to be sure, the sort of such-being which nips existence in the bud: contradictory being.) The mode of being-given, which any object whatsoever has prior to being or non-being, is called "beyond-being" (*Aussersein*). It is peculiar insofar as it is at yet one further remove from existence than is the subsistence of ideal or imaginary beings. Unlike respectable existence, beyond-being has no opposite; it might, Meinong says, be called "pseudo-existence," except that the term would leave a false impression.

It is in this beyond-being that the homeless objects are sheltered. They do have a kind of being, but, critics complain, there is no way of specifying it that does not cause confusion and embarrassment (Quine 1953). Here is a fair evaluation:

> *Aussersein* is a strange sort of desert in which no mental progress is possible, but the desert has many oases, as no one who has read a fine novel can possibly doubt. [Findlay 1963]

It is because of the desert that Russell attacked the theory, and it is because of the oases that the Meinongian enterprise has recently been revived by Parsons (1980). The point of his work is to provide a formal development for the denial of the philosophically popular notion that everything that is a thing exists and that only existents are entities. Parsons's central assumption is therefore this: To every concrete individual object is correlated one unique set of properties—on the understanding that all objects differ from each other in *some* way. These properties are the sort real objects have, like {snowiness, mountainhood}; they pertain to the existent objects. Now if one goes on forming further sets of such properties, like {goldenness, mountainhood}, and correlates objects to these sets, they won't be existent objects, but they will, nonetheless, be objects. The properties such real or unreal objects can have are called "nuclear" properties. Existence is not among them, for if it were to be included with {goldenness, mountainhood} it would, magically, produce an existent golden mountain. Existence, mythicalness, imaginariness are, however, "extranuclear" properties. It is not urgent to decide about their standing, since the nuclear properties do all the important work of object-discerning for us. Parsons then shows formally that admitting these objects does not lead to the "slum of possibilities . . . , a breeding ground for disorderly elements" which Quine (1953) foresaw. But the most pertinent application of Parsons's theory comes in regard to fictions (B).

(Chisholm 1960, 1982, Findlay 1963, Grossman 1974, Lambert 1983.)

2. Possible Worlds: Plantinga. Any realm delineated by the imagination such as has a certain closure, an embracing shape, or a pervasive atmosphere, can be called a "world." The realms of the imagination tend to be worlds in this informal sense: Part Six will, in fact, be devoted to the proposition that the imagination is the preeminent world-making power. Hence the notion of a "possible world" is on the face of it enticing to someone inquiring into the works of the imagination. What is attractive is the possibility of rigor in this dreamy field, since in logic a "possible world" is a precise notion: It is a state of affairs that is (a) possible in the sense that it is real or could be; and is (b) "maximal" or complete. The possibility is of a broad logical sort, wider than causal or natural possibility—whatever is not repugnant to reason. The completeness can best be understood as mirrored in the set of propositions "entailed" by a world. This description of the world is called the "book" on it, or the "complete novel" about it (Hintikka 1969). The "book" contains all the true and consistent statements about the world and is maximal or complete in the sense that any additional sentence would make it inconsistent; it has all the sentences it can absorb, just as its world contains all the states of affairs that can go together. Applied to literary works, this definition means, of course, that any actual novel is much smaller than the associated world and its book, which would contain everything that "goes without saying." Thus the logical notion of a "book" on a possible world illuminates the relation of a novel to its fictional world: a novel, one might say, is a fairly minimal "book."

In the logic of possible worlds Plantinga attends especially to a question close to an issue considered below (C): the interrelation of fictional worlds. His question is whether one individual can inhabit several worlds (1973). Is there "transworld identity" or is each individual "worldbound"? He answers that individuals must be able to exist in different worlds and to preserve their identity even when the states of affairs pertaining to them are quite different. To say otherwise is to imply that individuals have no contingent properties undetermined by their context and that everything about them is necessary—an unacceptable idea. It seems that Plantinga's affirmation of transworld identity legitimates logically one of the chief works of the imagination: transporting people from one world to another.

Yet it must be said that Plantinga does not intend the modal logic of possibly real worlds as a logic of fictions, which are sometimes beyond realization. In any case, the imagination would get little help from him on the main issue here, the existence of fictional objects. Objects in possible worlds do exist, but they exist precisely *within* their worlds, inactually. This means only that if those worlds would have been actual, then the objects would have (really) existed. Such iffish existence is even less of a comfort to imaginary beings than honest nonexistence.

3. Conclusion: Homeless Still. But even the defenders of existenceless being for the orphans don't really have much to offer by way of a place for them. Meinong's beyond-being is perfectly elusive in its flitting between the poles of being and non-being. Parsons's extranuclear properties are finally only a fascinating formalism. This outcome was, of course, foreseeable. The secondariness of imaginary objects was assumed on all sides to begin with: They are, whatever else they may be, "nonexistent," "not genuine," "unactual." Their logic is called "deviant" (Woods), and discourse concerning them "non-serious" in the sense that authors are not committed to the literal truth of their assertions about them (Searle 1975).

So, as things stand, if the objects of the imagination are thought of as constituting an irreplaceable treasure, then the account-books of that hoard have, to be sure, been unscrambled but now the coins have to be catalogued as counterfeits. Let me at this moments merely mention that an opposite beginning is possible: One might shun what Russell called a "robust sense of reality," and start out instead with an energetic indifference to the real, and a suspicion that existence is far from exhausting actuality.

B. Fictional Objects: The Logic of Imaginative Literature

The logic of fictions is doubly motivated: by the desire to account for what authors write and for what readers say (*1*). It comes, roughly speaking, in two schools: Those who say fictional literature is about nothing (*2*), and those who say it is about something (*3*).

1. The Motivation for a Logic of Fictions. Odysseus is a man, underslung but impressive of stature, in character bloody, cruel, and exquisitely courteous, ingenious, deceitful and utterly truthful, luxurious and tough, rapacious and impulsive, a leader among men and a solitary survivor, winning with women and tenaciously mindful of his wife, his son, and his rocky island-realm. But above all he is a man full of poetry.

This remarkable hero makes his appearance in many accounts over three millennia: in Homer's *Iliad* and Odysseus's own *Odyssey*, in Sophocles's *Philoctetes*, in Dante's *Divine Comedy* (*Inferno*, Canto XXVI), in Kazantzakis's modern sequel to the *Odyssey* by the same name, in Tennyson's and Stevens's "Ulysses" poems, and under the name of Bloom in Joyce's *Ulysses*—to give but a sampling.

Here is a theory about his voyages. Twice in Homer's epic Odysseus tells fairy-tale-like stories of his wanderings, stories spiked with subtle indications that neither Homer nor his clear-eyed hero takes these tales for fact. Odysseus also tells certain tricky tales of another sort, accounts that intimate that he has in fact seen, and has been seen in, the most mundane

Mediterranean ports of call, engaged in the mixture of trading and brigand-
age historically ascribed to the roving sea-people of his time. The twelve
adventures that comprise Odysseus's odyssey proper distill from the episodes of these dangerous, dreary, sordid, and eye-opening itineraries their
essential experience, the vivid vision behind the mere fact. Thus in sober
fact his crews, reconnoitering an island, come upon a fancy bordello
presided over by an accomplished harlot. They make metaphorical pigs of
themselves and are imprisoned in their lusts. In Odysseus's poem the party
of sailors finds the house of the sweet-voiced, divine sorceress Circe, who
turns the passive lot, as she has so many before them, into bristly swine
whose "minds remained stuck were they had been before." Odysseus
comes to rescue them. Warned by Hermes, he alone retains his manhood
before the goddess. He masters her by running at her aggressively with his
sword; then he sleeps with her safely. Similarly with the other adventures:
Within the fictional world of the *Odyssey* it is in mere fact false, though in
human actuality true, that they occurred (Brann 1974).

The case of Odysseus-Ulysses, properties, accounts, theories, and all, is
an exemplary motivation for working out a logic of fiction. After all, the
poet himself, by putting his liar-poet-hero irrepressibly to work within the
poem, brings forward questions of fictionality.

In the sentence "Odysseus is a man," what is the force of the copula and
its tense? Was he ever a man and is he one now? In what way does he possess
those of his properties explicitly mentioned in the text and how do we
come to ascribe to him traits of character and other predicates not so
mentioned? Is the color of his hair determinable? Is it one and the same
Odysseus who appears in all the texts? Can Dante be said to be mistaken in
sending Ulysses straight from Circe beyond the Pillars of Hercules into the
Atlantic without letting him come home to his wife Penelope first? Does he
have a right to do it? In what sense is Leopold Bloom's day in Dublin a
reprise of Odysseus's decade on the sea?

Among the delights of literacy is the access it gives to fictional "worlds"
in which to disport oneself, spinning out theories, conjectures, elaborations.
What is the nature of those worlds and the status of those theories about
them? In what sense can one say that an episode in an epic did or did not in
fact occur in the world of the poem? What does it mean to pass into the
text of the *Odyssey* as into a world?

This is a sampling of the swarm of questions raised by fictional texts and
the talk that goes on about them. They invite rigorous formal analysis, and
the logic of fiction is the response. But in all candor, and to forestall
disappointment: Logic can pose austerely phrased problems and propose
soberly conceived attitudes to their solution; but it is powerless to allay the

confusion of the spirit before great works of the imagination—to formalize the actual dominion fictional beings can exercise over the heart or to rationalize the sense that, but for some small deficiency in them or in us, they might appear incarnate in our world.

The logic of fiction quite unavoidably begins with the "literal" understanding of fiction as some sort of feigning of an activity in and about which the terms "existence" and "truth" are used deviantly. Thus the formal theories of language about imaginary objects are worked out by adapting the logical operators appropriate to standard reality. Consequently some of the formalization perforce consists of double-talk, rewordings by means of which states of being that are embarrassing to logical taste are paraphrased away. Russell's "Theory of Descriptions," mentioned in (1), is, of course, the grandfather of all such exercises. Nonetheless, it is just at these junctures that the discipline is most illuminating.

Before presenting examples of such theories, I should mention the relation that the logic of pictures (and mental images) has to the logic of literary fictions (and internally told tales). They share some problematic features and explanatory categories. Both visual and literary fictions are, for example, hospitable to "immigrant objects" (Parsons 1980), intrusions from the real world or from other fictional worlds. Thus a painting on a Greek vase depicts an "immigrant" scene from the *Odyssey*, Odysseus shooting his wife's suitors; the composition, the costumes, and the furniture, however, are the "native" inventions and conventions of a painter living in the fifth century B.C., some seven centuries after the "fact." Similarly, Ulysses wanders from his own epic into the *Divine Comedy* for a brief appearance. Furthermore, in both pictures and poetry there are nonexistent, impossible, and incomplete objects. Both arts require some acquaintance with the representational tradition for their subtler interpretation. Moreover, both pictures and literary fictions have an arguably analogous compositional logic: Just as figures in a painting are identifiable because they are some sort of projection of real-world (or imaginary) originals onto a picture-space, so characters in novels are individuated not so much by lists of properties, as by an analogous verbal projection: Each imaginary being might be said to occupy a certain "attention-coordinate" in the author's imaginative field. What sets up a character to be just this recognizable individual is the articulation in language of this epic or novelistic space in which each figure has its place and its attendant situation (Howell 1979).

Despite the parallelisms, literary logic is a richer subject than picture-logic. The obvious reason is that the truth is more clearly defined for language than for visual representation and therefore beomes more sharply problematic. All the colorful perplexities of imaginariness, when submitted to the logic of fiction, can be trimmed down to this problem: What sort of truth attaches to propositions to whose literal factuality their author is not committed?

2. Texts About Nothing. One answer, straight and decisive, is, No sort of truth. The reasoning runs roughly like this: Literary texts precede the fictional objects they circumscribe. Nothing pre-exists for them to be truthful about. Their authors offer them only as pretend-assertions. Here not the fictionality of the subject but the unassertedness of the sentences is the issue.

One version of the negative answer is that all intra-textual propositions about fictions are false because they are about nothing. This is not meant as an interesting reflection on the nature of non-being or on the lying of poets. Fiction-speech is vacuously false, just empty.

The other version, that such propositions are neither true nor false, has more bite. It was set out early in the debate by Ryle. The claim is that "being imaginary" is, like existence, not an attribute of being. The name of a purported imaginary being, like "Odysseus," is a pseudo-designation, and the properties attributed to him by the author, or the theories about his doings evolved by the reader, are only pretended assertions of truth, derived from the hypothesis that if there were someone real with the complex of characteristics fictionally attributed to Odysseus, he would act that way. Nor is Odysseus the linguistic articulation of a mental image: imagining is not visualizing a direct object, such as a manly Odysseus, but always thinking a statement, such as "that Odysseus is manly." In sum, Odysseus is a perfect candidate for Russellian description by way of a collection of predicates, such as "is manly," and "is prevaricating," and "is truth-knowing," around an x that need not, and in this case does not, exist.

This unhedged denial of truth-value to fictional statements runs into trouble with Mrs. Pringle (Blocker 1974). Mrs. Pringle teaches the *Odyssey* to her English class and, unfortunately, believes in true-or-false tests. In one of these she includes the statement "An hour after Odysseus returned home from Troy he was murdered by his wife in his bath." Her students lose points for answering "True," since this statement is True of Agamemnon, King of Mycenae, but False of Odysseus, King of Ithaca. Mrs. Pringle won't budge on this. Her naive—and normal—view is that it is possible to be correctly informed or ignorant about these veterans of the Trojan war. Though she will agree that they are fictional people, she will not admit that they are nothing.

To accommodate her, there are less brusque treatments. One can quietly neutralize all questions of being without disallowing truth and falsity in fiction, by saying that fictional sentences are true if they are literally found in the text or can be derived from other statements in the text (Woods 1974). This apparently sensible proposal runs into grave trouble with the notion of derived truths. Most of the true statements one thinks of as derivable from the text and thus true are not *logically* implied in it—consider, for example, "Odysseus was at least forty-five when he returned to Ithaca." So according to what rules is the deriving done? They are surely extra-textual.

This type of treatment takes fictional truth as pertaining not to whether a thing is so (*de re* construal) but to what has been said about it (*de dicto* construal). The latter construal of the truth-claim of a fictional sentence leads straight to the author's intention and thus to the question: What does it mean to intend or to take sentences "fictionally"? If Homer says (fictionally) that Odysseus is "a man of many devices" then it is right and legitimate to mark the statement "Odysseus was an ingenious man" on Mrs. Pringle's test "T." But that still leaves the question: What manner of speech is poetic speech?

Certainly fictional intending is set apart from the other "propositional attitudes," such as believing and fearing (Walton 1978). If one believes or fears that a person is about to commit a crime, it makes sense to try to forestall its commission. On the other hand, if one watches the Odysseus in Sophocles's *Philoctetes* intending wretchedly to betray a friend, and is in a properly fictional frame of mind, it makes no sense to leap onto the stage to warn the victim. For the world of belief and the world of fiction are, it is said, totally isolated from one another. One can stop the performance, but one can't stop Odysseus. Even if Sophocles himself, summoned from Hades by popular outrage, were to write a change of heart into the text, he would not be affecting the fictional Odysseus but only producing a new one.

The reason for this divergence of fictional from ordinary intending is said to be this (Walton 1978): The making (and reading and watching) of fiction differs from believing and fearing in being in its very nature a kind of pretending to assert something. To interfere with a fiction from the outside is to evaporate its status as a pretended assertion (while to omit the fictional intention-operator—to suppress its pretending character—is rather to enhance that status: a tacit fictionality is most potent).

This understanding of fictionality as make-believe seems to me not quite up to the intricate seriousness of fictional intention. For example, at the inception of fictional composition, doesn't the author somehow exercise real control over his characters? And don't they, reciprocally, take hold of him? Don't fictions have actual psychological potency and doesn't a fictional fate somehow lie with its reader? Above all, can the isolationist theory account for the uncanny way authors can irrupt into their fictions? In 1897 Samuel Butler published a book called *The Authoress of the Odyssey*, in which he argued that the epic was really composed by Nausikaa, the youngest and last and most charming of the women in the *Odyssey* to be captivated by its hero—and the one by far most gently let off. The thesis may be silly but it is not impossible in principle. Were it true, the sixth book of the epic would be fiction and confession at once, and "pretending to assert" would hardly cover the strange iridescence of this fictionality.

3. Texts About Something. The logical theories above may satisfy Mrs. Pringle, but they aren't quite adequate to that most companionable of activities, when friends talk, even gossip, about the characters in a book, mining the text for clues to their nature. (I use the example of friendly talk rather than the purposeful theorizing of critics, since their profession requires commitments extraneous to the amateur's delight in conjuring up literary beings, such as making points in terms of a preestablished universe of critical discourse.)

So there is a second set of approaches to the problem of fictional truth: Here the objects of fiction are assumed to antecede their texts, which refer to them and tell, or fail to tell, the truth about them. Readers are invited by the text to pass through it to these same objects. The question then becomes: How do these objects antecede their texts? The logic of fiction seems to permit two kinds of antecedent being, the two set out in (A) above: There are nonexistent entities individuated by their sets of properties and nonactual entities defined by their possible world settings.

Take the latter first. A "possible world," recall, was defined in terms of a "book" or "novel" on it that was complete in containing determinate answers to all questions one could ask about it and consistent in containing no mutually contradictory statements. As I pointed out, this logical structure seems, at least at first sight, to fit novels or epics, which are often thought of as being books describing a whole world. The trouble is that such works often seem contradictory and are, as was said, inevitably incomplete. I say "seem contradictory" because often contradiction is a matter of interpretation. I can cite a celebrated case from the *Iliad*, where Achilles, the best runner at Troy, is called "swift-footed" while sulking stationary in his tent. One may call that a mechanical, contradictory use of the epithet or an inspired subtlety; it is a matter of imagination. However, insofar as the contradictions cannot be interpreted away, the peculiar "fictional world" that is logically (and physically) impossible—a fantasy, for example—must be distinguished from the "possible world" that is conceived as being metaphysically possible, meaning that it might exist. It then becomes an interesting question for the latter what *is* included in such a fictional world besides what the author indicates explicitly. Is it everything that would naturally occur if some part of this possible world became actual, or is it only what the author expects his intended audience to believe would occur under such circumstances? (Wolterstorff 1976). For the former, the fantasy world, all bets are off—that is really what distinguishes fantasy (Part Four, Ch. IV B).

As for the incompleteness, that merely means, as I said, that as the "novel" on life is infinite compared to any account, so the "book" on the epic is immensely larger than the epic itself. It is in knowing how to consult the book behind the book that the arts of reading come into their own and the pleasures of the imagination are at their subtlest. Thus to the question, unanswerable from the epic itself, "What was the color of Odysseus's hair?" the book behind the book gives the answer to those who will but consult it: When he was first washed up in Ithaca, it was dull iron-grey, but when he finally draws his bow in his own hall it is gleaming silver. The practical trouble with "the book" is that so much of it is composed by personal experience.

The other treatment is by way of the Meinongian nonexistent objects, distinguished by the set of their nuclear properties sketched above. Such objects are assigned their properties *according* to the story: It is not quite right to say, as one would in a possible-world-book account, that they are *in* the story. The reader of the text does not, as in the theories set out above, establish the object, but he amasses information about it. Objects "native" to the story, those that lead their lives completely within the fiction, have only those properties given to them in the story. This theory requires a special case to be made of the above-mentioned "immigrant objects," whose nuclear properties are at least partly imported from real existence or from other works of fiction. All the native objects have the extranuclear property of fictional existence, which the theory is not required to worry about (Parsons 1980).

The Meinongian approach is, however, fascinatingly vulnerable. For example, Odysseus left Troy with twelve ships, each manned by an unknown number of mostly anonymous men who all perish in various ways as the voyage progresses. Is each of them an individuated object? The theory has difficulty with this puzzle. The incompleteness of objects also gives trouble. Some fictional objects are "merely" incomplete in the sense that the *Odyssey* says nothing about the color of Odysseus's hair one way or the other. Others are "radically" incomplete in the sense that the nymph Calypso, to whom Odysseus is enslaved during the last seven of the ten years between Troy and home, is neither a mortal woman nor an immortal goddess. She is a radically impossible being whose attentions drive Odysseus into a prolonged, weeping depression. Neither the indeterminates nor the impossibles of fiction are quite satisfactorily covered by the Meinongian account. Furthermore, the "native/immigrant" distinction can become very murky: There is a never-ending impulse to prove that the Homeric epics are historical. But if Troy was real and the Greek expedition against her was a fact, why should not reports concerning the captains of the fleets admiralled by Agamemnon have come down to Homer? So the *Odyssean* Odysseus may be part immigrant—but then, which part and to what degree?

Finally, here is the broadest and most obvious supra-logical question raised against the Meinongian theory of fiction—actually the same as against his general theory: What metaphysical meaning attaches to the extranuclear predicate of being a nonexistent object, a predicate that belongs to all native fictional objects? When all is said and done, do we understand what sort of being they have? Unfortunately we do not: the going accounts of nonexistence are tied up in a knot with embarrassment at having to give their subtly devised logical notions some metaphysical standing.

(Blocker 1974, Devine 1974, Howell 1979, Lewis 1978, Parsons 1980.)

So it seems that the logical consideration of imaginary objects cannot be the end of the matter, and in the next section (C) I will try to go further. In the meantime, the approach that puts the fictional object antecedent to the text seems both to capture more of our life with fiction and to lead to the more captivating difficulties. As for its alternative versions, the "possible world" and the "nonexistent object," it seems unnecessary to have a preference, for they can be understood as two complementary ways of approaching both reality and fiction: either in terms of the common context that defines the individual objects enmeshed in it, or in terms of the individuals that establish a community through their relational properties.

C. Imaginary Originals: The Object Behind the Image

Here are two questions, inwardly actual to the point of preoccupation, though publicly next to disreputable, questions that philosophy and logic shun in embarrassed silence, though poets and painters may muse about them: Keats, for example, devotes a letter to dealing with a friend's sudden confusion, his "momentary start about the authenticity of the Imagination" (Nov. 22, 1817).

First. External depictions and descriptive literature, the main works of representational art, immediately speak to the imagination of the viewer and reader and raise in it a sort of answering image; then what are the originals behind such works? What are such real-world images images of? (*1*).

Second. If the most intimate virtue of the imagination is the internal representation of pictures and descriptions not taken from the real world, then what are the originals behind the imagination's image? Whence and what is their being? (*2*).

Nowhere is an inquiry more on its own than in approaching these wonderful perplexities. There is plenty of fluent talk about them, but it is fluent precisely because it is so riskless and mannerly. It does not trouble itself to mean what it says. One speaks of "living in the world of the imagination" and escapes meaning anything vital by taking "world" either in a vapidly vague or a desiccatedly rigorous sense. One observes that reports of a real disaster on television elicit but a passing pang, while a fictional tragedy in a novel evokes reverberating emotions, allowing that "the figures of the imagination can become very real," and escapes the enigma of their reality by not meaning anything determinate. Here, at the center of this effort not only to gather the sum but also to approach the substance of the imagination, is the moment to face the implications of these apparently unavoidable ways of speaking. I must confess at once that the results will not be binding; they will not even be positive. Their main force will be in specifying the plea and the litany of this book: to recognize the imagination for the uncanny place it ultimately is.

1. What Is Imaged in Works of the Imagination? I begin with this question because it is simpler than the second perplexity, which concerns the originals behind the mental images in the imagination. My reply, consistent with the representational thesis of this book (Part One, Ch. V), is the so-called "naive" answer of current aesthetics. It is, however, the one to which those who themselves produce works of the imagination even now commonly subscribe: Such works are, insofar as they are representations and not mere aesthetic configurations (if such there be), copies of the maker's mental images, memorial and imaginary (Part Five, Ch. III B). It would be foolhardy to present this answer as obvious, since in the contemporary intellectual climate such "folk" solutions are normally regarded as highly problematic. What follows is simply a list of reasons for believing that the images of art are essentially copied from inner images. These reasons pertain both to the visual arts and to literature, where the role of visual imaging, though less direct, is equally vital (Part Four, Ch. I).

First. The imagination is inherently momentous and momentary, in the sense that it appears in significant epiphanies and at high moments; its rhythms seem to be natively in contrast to the unpunctuated continua and eventless longueurs of mundane times and spaces. Wallace Stevens bears witness to this feature of the imagination in his essay on "The Relations between Poetry and Painting" (1951) when he speaks of the "momentous world of poetry" and its "instantaneities." Probably no property of the imagination is more often referred to in literature than its propensity for luminous tableaux. The depictions and descriptions of art are never indifferent slices of undifferentiated flows of life (though certain novelistic theories require an artful pretense that a perceptual rather than an imaginative time and space are presented—Part Four, Ch. II C). Most often the depictive or descriptive attention is directed to choice subjects to begin with: choice scenes, choice events, choice figures. But even—or especially—when the imagination is trained on the dimly unattractive, flatly ordinary, or depressingly banal, the resultant works themselves are not, at least insofar as they are works of art, dim, flat and depressing. One might call this selective mode, shared by the imagination and art, "distilled discreteness," the propensity for compressing ordinary affairs into segments of significant appearance.

The partial complement of this compression might then be called the mode of "integral import," the tendency to signify as a whole. The real world—and not only the man-made part—is given to sprawl: intellectual, urban, continental, and astronomical sprawl, our *Lumpenwelt,* as Stevens calls it. It gains distinction only as its parts happen to be useful or as the wholes are put under a law. Thus the commercial outskirts of a town become intensely interesting if you're running out of gas, and the celestial wasteland becomes fascinating if you're studying astrophysics. But it is not the business of the imagination to discriminate among the parts or aspects of an indifferent agglomeration, as does the focused will or the inquiring reason. When it takes up a scene, its wholeness and significance appear to be coeval. Thus through the imagination the dreary infinitude of the ocean is taken integrally, and so taken, as aestheticians of the eighteenth century were fond of observing, it has an impact of sublimity (Part Six, Ch. III A). Works of art in general and painting in particular work analogously. A painted cityscape expressing amorphous ennui is anything but "unsightly." Think of Edward Hopper's vibrantly desolate roof and street scenes.

The remaining complement to the momentousness and the integrality of the imagination is its peculiar unbrokenness. Whatever part of the imaginative field the mind's eye might be trained on immediately offers something to its view. This mode, which might be called the "replete field," holds eminently of paintings: No part of a canvas, not even if unmarked, is representationally empty. Indeed there are some styles that emphasize this principle of the imagination by introducing a deliberate near-parity of interest for figure and ground, such as occurs in the magical, detailed landscapes behind Renaissance portraits.

These three complementary modes in fact characterize the imagination and its products as world-making, if not in the rigorous sense described above (A 2), then in a vigorous sense that is more germane to this quintessential imaginative function. It will be considered at the end of this book.

Second. Imagination and depiction also share what might be called "empowering privations." One might say that the imagination teaches not only painting, the premier art of two-dimensional image-making, but all arts depicting in a plane, that their deficiencies are their opportunities. Later on the dimensionally defective character of mental and real depictions will be considered (Part Five, Ch. II A). Here I am referring to a different sort of defect: The imagination's imaginative pictures are notoriously incomplete in the sense of being indeterminate intimations, rather than hard-edged, fully detailed displays of explicit visual information. A like indeterminacy holds for depictions in general and paintings in particular. Not only do styles that work with low definition of outline and spatial detail appear peculiarly "painterly," but the whole enterprise of making depictions is predicated on the picture-viewing eye's ability to act as the mind's image-viewing eye does: It must read full meanings into a sketchy indication. This competence goes under the name of "projection" (Part Five, Ch. III B). Moreover, the viewing eye must refrain from playing the precise detective and inspecting the pictorial surface below its "limit of resolution"; a real mountain searched by telescope reveals ever more mountain-features, but a picture mountain viewed through a magnifying glass disintegrates into paint on canvas.

Third. Yet another similarity favoring the notion that mental images are the originals of paintings is found in their respective functions. Both images and paintings are effectively memorial and, for lack of a more handsome word, concretizing.

The battle against the effacement from memory of the significant visible aspects of bygone things—faces, events, scenes—is among the most ardent, if intermittent, labors of the human spirit, one in which the memorial imagination, the art of depiction, and various recording techniques co-operate. Human beings try to keep vivid the memories of their high moments internally, and, so far as they are able, to transcribe them into an external record. That is why, contrary to current opinion, we so often recognize the claim to significance of depictions whose symbolic vocabulary is alien to us: We may not be able to decipher them, but we apprehend them precisely as projected human memory, as an alien content produced under a familiar impetus.

Moreover, imagination and works of art also concur in giving concrete shape to things never experienced. It is not in a midsummer night's dream alone that the "imagination bodies forth the forms of things unknown." Such forms differ from those of reality in being non-unique. In the real world, if two things are discernibly different in shape they occupy different places or times and are insuperably diverse. Only in the realm of inner or outer images can two shapes image the same subject. For instance, Odysseus, the hard-worked hero of this chapter, is depicted in continually different guises, from the pottery of the eighth century B.C. to the movies of our time. There can be ever-new pictorial treatments of the same matter precisely because the imagination, though memory-fed, is not memory-bound.

For those who find banal or dubious the points made so far in behalf of the proposition that the visual imagination furnishes the originals of the arts, there is the practical argument from picture-making.

I pass over the persistent testimony of painters that they work to realize an inner vision, in order to attend to an analysis of representational drawing (Wollheim 1964, Carrier 1973). It was induced by Wittgenstein's remark in the *Philosophical Investigations* (p. 198) that the criterion of visual experience is the representation of "what is seen." He means that often the answer to the question "What did you see?" is given by a pictorial representation. What is behind this claim is the rule that every inner process stands in need of an outer criterion. This maxim implies that it is putting the cart before the horse to explain, as I have been doing, the external representation by the internal one. Moreover, the criterion-rule fits one aspect of our experience with the visual arts, namely that they cause us to see, that they reveal the visual world to us. Following the current theory of the social construction of consciousness, one might even go as far as to say that it is ultimately not private inner visions that are imaged in the painting, but the external representations that feed and shape inner visions. For example the mystical visions of Catherine of Siena show evidence of having been modeled on contemporary religious paintings (Carrier 1978). This particular extension of the outside-in view, however, emphasizing as it does the close relation of pictures to mental images, appears incidentally to grant the existence of such images, and that is an admission out of keeping with the Wittgensteinian strain. Thus Wollheim rejects it out of hand:

But the fact that the visual experience can be in this way operative after it has passed should not lead us into the view that it somehow persists in the form of a lingering image, which we then try to reproduce when we set ourselves to represent what we have seen. For there is no reason either in logic or in experience to believe in the existence of such an image. We do not need it in order to explain the facts of the case, nor do we have any independent evidence for its existence in our actual consciousness. It seems a pure invention conjured into being to bridge the gap between one event—our seeing as we do—and another event, when what we have seen asserts its efficacy. [1964]

Here's the rub: Wollheim regards it as indubitable that a drawing is made and corrected on the basis of something. Now the actual visual experience is often over and done with by the time the drawing comes to be made and, it must be added, a drawing is often based on no particular visual perception to begin with. Hence, if one eschews mental images, the gap remains unbridged: at least no bridge has been proposed which the mind can pass over. In view of the fact that there is actually plenty of reason in the logic of fiction, in introspective experience, and in controlled experiments, to believe in images, and on the supposition that a bridging hypostasis is better than a willful hiatus, I revert to the oldest, the aboriginal idea. It is that, aside from the depictions that are direct replications from life and the modifications that arise from happy accidents of execution, the contributions of the medium, and conceptual tampering, the images of visual art reproduce the images of the imagination.

2. What Is Imaged in the Imagination? Even the approaches to this question are clogged, because there is no longer any unaffected, heartfelt language about the work of the imagination. The obligatory laudatory rattle attributes to it creativity but this term is almost empty of meaning (Part Two, Ch. V A). It vaguely signifies something ultimately subjective, uninhibitedly spontaneous, and splendidly unfaithful to models, though much less is necessary for the word to be applied. Insofar as it is taken seriously it must imply that the answer to the question in the heading is a resounding "Nothing." For the imagination, insofar as it is to be regarded as radically innovative, must create its images and their meaning out of nothing and according to nothing. At the other extreme is the notion that the imagination is a physiologically based mechanism. Yet dramatically opposed as this version of the imaginative process is to creation, its effect is oddly identical: the imaginative process, though it may involve symbolic elements, certainly intends no extra-mental objects. Somewhere between these extremes is the Hume-inspired theory, no longer much favored, that the imagination works by associating, spontaneously or inventively, the image-blocks stored in perception-memory. Again, none of these views of the imaginative process considers it as imaging an imaginary original—where by an "imaginary" or an "imaginative" original I mean one that does not enter the imagination through the front doors of perception (Part One, Ch. II A).

There is another, much older, group of understandings that does presuppose such imaginary originals: The imagination is taken to be stimulated by a source other than perception or perceptual memory, by "inspiration." Here poets and painters are accorded a hermeneutic function, mediating between the spirit-world and the real world, bringing to earth the stories of the gods and the visions of paradise. The doctrine of inspiration comes down from both branches of antiquity, from Christian religion and from classical poetry. "All scripture is God-inspired," it says in 2 Timothy, while the *Odyssey* begins with the words: "Tell to me the man, O Muse. . . . " In his *Ion* Plato makes fun of the chain effect implied in the naive notion of divine inspiration: The goddess inspires the bard Homer and Homer inspires the rhapsode Ion and Ion inspires his fans; they are like rings hanging in series from a lodestone. Of course, literal inspiration begins to fade as the gods recede. And yet the "furor poeticus," poetic possession by a supra-subjective source, remains an experience of poets and novelists in our times; they claim that their figures come to them or rise in them from a region too deep merely to be called their own invention. Alice Walker's *The Color Purple*, for example, closes with a postscript in which the author, thanks her figures for coming to her, signing herself "A.W., author and medium." What holds for words also holds for visions, not to speak of external visions like those of the Apocalypse (1:12); my business here is only with imagery this side of miracle or madness.

In the multitudinous versions of the modern inspirational mode, imaginative visions are variously characterized. Sometimes they come as open-eyed transformations of the real world, sometimes as images of beings approaching out of psychic depths and temporal distances, and sometimes as beings present *in propria persona* in the space of the imagination. Although what might be called the metaphysics of imaginations implied in each of these is different, they are alike in requiring the imagination to be regarded as receptive rather than constructive. The going name for the source from which imaginative receptivity is fed is the "unconscious," which, all agree, is a latent reservoir of significances, though regarded in some schools as a private and in others as a collective store. Graham Greene writes:

> So much of a novelist's writing, as I have said, takes place in the unconscious; in those depths the last word is written before the first word appears on paper. We remember the details of our story, we do not invent them. [*The End of the Affair*]

Nonetheless, the unconscious is a term whose best service is to advertise a perplexity: Whence comes the memory of things never seen?

The long and the short of it is that what one might call the spiritual production-history of imaginary images—as opposed to the genesis of their cognitive process—is an enigma. For memory-images the cognitive account goes pretty far: There is a percept that is the original whose image is retrieved, recovered, recalled, remembered, and refreshed. The reiterated prefix "re," which suggests a return or reappearance, is taken into account in the working metaphor of a memory-store, with its experimentally verifiable processes of storage and retrieval, and its controlled comparisons between the perceptual original and the memory-image (Part Two, Ch. III).

But the imaginary image, as opposed to the memory-image, is amenable neither to this "causal" nor to an "authorial" theory of representation (Ch. I B), because the originating causal objects are not available and because the authorship of an imaginary image is not determinable. (I should repeat here that, although later on the term "imaginary" will be defined more specifically—Introduction to Part Six—here it describes what psychologists call the "imagination-image" as opposed to the image originating in perceptual memory.)

To settle whether the imagination functions inspirationally or creatively, or better, whether it is essentially receptive or constructive, one would have to produce in all seriousness a metaphysics of imaginary images, in the sense of saying what it is they image, what is behind them. Some logics of fiction, as we have just seen, do posit imaginary possible worlds or nonexistent objects antecedent to their fictional expression. But these are, as I said, logical formalisms, ways of speaking, which imply no degree of actuality, less even than logicians are inclined to assign to ideal or intellectual being. The very term Meinong chose for fictional being, "beyond-being," insists on this ontological poverty. (It is, as it were, a parody of the phrase "beyond being" that Plato used in the *Republic* of the Idea of the Good, his most potent source of both being and being-knowable—509 B.) In any case, whatever the source-being of imaginary apparitions is, it is surely not the same as the intelligible essence of the metaphysicians.

What propels one into these abstruse and anomalous meditations is the actuality, intimated earlier, of the imaginary realm. Not only does the imagination seem to be activated by beings from beyond: sometimes it seems in turn to be on the brink of actualizing its figures in the external world, perhaps behind our backs. There is a poem by Thomas Hardy that accurately expresses the intellectual unease before the uncanny possibility of mental imagery bodied forth. He goes out into the garden "by the Druid stone" and sees the rhythmically shifting shadows of a tree's branches upon it:

> And they shaped in my imagining
> To the shade that a well-known head and shoulders
> Threw there when she was gardening.

He wants, Orpheus-like, to turn and look but refrains:

> But I thought once more: 'Nay, I'll not unvision
> A shape which, somehow, there may be.'

So without turning he leaves her:

> As she were indeed an apparition—
> My head unturned lest my dreams should fade.

The "somehow" contains the great question at issue here.

It is an evasion to denominate the figures of the imagination simply the results of a "psychic" activity. The unquestionable power real and mental images possess to contain and reconstruct the world ceases the moment they are apprehended as merely mental: We cannot, I claim, sustain a feeling induced by an acknowledged construct of our own mind; it is tantamount to pulling ourselves up by our boot-straps. Such attempts, for instance to find comfort in a divinity that is nothing but the psychic answer to a psychic need, regularly self-destruct. For the same reason there is no help for construing what it means to entertain images to be found in Coleridge's solution, formulated in the famous phrase about "the willing suspension of disbelief." Tolkien rightly nailed it as a frame of mind that is apt to be "tired, shabby, or sentimental" (1947)—a simulacrum of self-delusion. (The sense of fictional truthfulness, as distinct from the logical topic of fictional truth-value here at issue, will be taken up in the next part, which is on literature—Ch. IV B.)

People are moved, I make bold to state, by imaginary images because they believe that they are images of something that is to be inwardly cherished and outwardly re-presented. I cite as one of a myriad of examples the most enduring, the most personally and politically potent of all "imaginary" images in the West, the City of God: Its numerous depictions and descriptions are surely meant not as phantasms, frothy appearances with nothing behind them, but as true images, responsible representations of something. But what?

At this point I must refer to a work in which these ticklish questions are given serious consideration: Ingarden's phenomenological study *The Literary Work of Art* (1930), subtitled "An Investigation on the Borderlines of Ontology, Logic and Theory of Literature." It is obviously an inquiry of the greatest relevance to this context, although it addresses itself to the deliberately shaped external work rather than to imagined spontaneities.

Two features in particular make Phenomenology relevant to the present preoccupation. The first is its devotion to a description of experience which overlooks and suppresses nothing, inconvenient though it might be. The second feature is the famous distinction, the first-fruit of such description, between the mental act and its intended object (Part One, Ch. IV A).

Applied to imagining, the distinction yields the "*purely* intentional object." This object is not autonomous or independent with respect to consciousness (as are perceived objects), for it is indeed merely imagined. Yet it too is "transcendent"—beyond the act of imagining itself; the intentional object is the aim, as it were, of the act. Such an object is apprehended in a double consciousness, once as being the object it is and again as being only imagined. Although it is truly transcendent, it is yet half-understood to be without independent substance:

> If one may put it this way, some of the elements assigned to the purely intentional object fool us . . . ; they seem to play a role which according to their essence they are truly not capable of playing. . . . [This object] draws its illusory existence from the projecting intention . . . of the intentional act. [122]

Ingarden is, however, concerned not so much with the mode of being of imagined objects as with the ontology of the work in which they play a role. He understands such a work as a stratified unity encompassing both material and ideal elements, a unity that is by both the author's and the reader's contribution. The first stratum consists of the sensuous sound of the words; the second consists of their meaning-units; the third consists of the objects intended in those meanings; and the last stratum consists of the "schematized aspects." The notion of "schematized aspects" is so useful to the next part (Four), which is on literary imagining, that I want to give the briefest account of it here.

Perceived objects show themselves in views or aspects that promise but do not themselves fulfill the promise of yet further views. An instance would be the steep mountain that, viewed from its base, gives promise of a magnificent view from the summit down the other side. In literary works such aspects and promises abound, but only schematically, in the sense that they are implied generally by the words rather than projected by an actual particular experience. (This schematic sparseness of words is the same descriptive deficiency that I shall be emphasizing in the next part, when discussing the relation of word to vision.) For the object to become vivid, it is by no means necessary that these promissory aspects be themselves well described. Indeed, if they are in fact described then they themselves become the intentional object. (There is, incidentally, a modern literary theory that tends toward displacing the nuclear object itself with an extended description of its aspects, as in the novels of Robbe-Grillet—Part Four, Ch. II C.) The aspects coordinated to the object, namely all its possible appearances, can be concretely and directly evoked in the work through various devices that require the reader to actualize these aspects then and there, or they can be merely prepared for possible actualization by the active reader, through the use of intimations, such as allusions and figures of speech (265).

To return to the fictionally represented object: Ingarden treats it from the point of view of its "space," just as I shall attempt to do later (Part Five, Ch. I). Literary representations live neither in the unitary physical space of the real world, nor in the homogenous ideal space of mathematics, nor yet—and this is the subtle point of interest—in an "imaginational space." It is easy to see that neither physical nor ideal space can encompass fictions: It is impossible to walk out of a novelistic room into a real city or into an ideal manifold. But imaginational space would seem to be the right receptacle for the literary fictons. Here is why it is not: "Imaginational space" is the phenomenological term (or near enough) for the imaginal medium, that inner space whose experimental and experiential features are set out in Parts Two and Five respectively. It is the space for visualization. Now this imaginational space differs from representational space, which for Ingarden actually *is* the space of literary fictions. Imaginational space is "immanent," while representational space is transcendent. The immanence of imaginational space here means that all the figures that are visualized there, all the "imaginational objects" that take shape within it, are seen as parts of the inner space—the activated space that in this book is thought of as the imagination proper. Representational spaces and their representational objects (the objects represented in works of literature), on the other hand, are what a "directed" act of imagining intends. These are transcendent and "imaged" as opposed to "imaginational." In sum, they are *intended* as external to the imaginer, as imaginations projected into the world.

Ingarden says, however, that "by means of a lively intuitive imagining" one can see "*directly* into the given represented space and can thus in a way bridge the gulf between these two separate spaces" (225). In other words, the representational object can be so powerfully visualized as to be all but *in* the imagination—pulled back into it, so to speak. The effect is evidently something like what people mean by "living in the imagination."

How far does the descriptive analysis go in solving the problem concerning the beings of the imagination? In pin-pointing the being of represented objects, Ingarden characterizes them as deporting themselves as real, without being independently rooted in the real world. The essential distinction between real and represented objects is that the real objects are in every respect unambiguously determined—or perhaps better, are expected to be so—while the represented objects have "spots of indeterminacy," the incompleteness noticed above (B):

> A peculiar modification of the character of reality takes place here, one which does not remove it, yet almost reduces it to a mere claim to reality. For it would obviously be a mistake to assert that represented objects possess no character of reality at all.

Nor can they be said to have ideal existence, like mathematical objects, or to be merely neutral with respect to existence—unasserted as existing. Their world is indeed relatively real enough itself to contain in turn dreams and imaginings. In sum, the being of imaginary represented objects is "something so unique that it can hardly be adequately described" (222).

This is fine corroboration of the urgent elusiveness of the subject. Moreover, it comes close to saying that, but for an added quantity of determinacy, but for an increase in repleteness, the imagined objects would go over into real objects. They seem to be kept from existing by a quantitative factor!

What makes the phenomenalist object of imagining and its space nonetheless not fully satisfying is the equivocality of this deficient being. Like Meinongian beyond-being, the imagined object is strictly neither here nor there, neither real nor ideal. It is in some sense behind the imaginational visualization as a cause. But in what sense? What, where, how is this object the self-same object that directs the act of imagining?

I can think of the following possible answers, passing fairly cursorily over a couple of dry and dreary theories that do not do justice to the power and depth of the phenomenon. The first of these thin theories is essentially the logician's solution and really fits best with an imagination understood to be imageless, as hypothesized by Ryle. It is the notion that imagining is a kind of propositional pretending or make-believe with nothing behind it: active suspension of disbelief. It has already been discussed (B). Another insufficient theory is that of simple memory-association, which understands fictions as collages of remembered percepts. Thus the unicorn is a horse plus a horn. What the associationist explanation of mental fictions cannot account for is their integral significance: What makes a unicorn elicit worship while a one-horned horse induces curiosity? Finally, it is possible, though not very satisfying, to think of fictive forms as symbols that stand for ideas. This ancient critical theory leads to extended allegorical interpretations of imaginative works. Homer tells how Odysseus, having finally been delivered home to Ithaca by a magical Phaeacian ship, was laid down sleeping on the beach near a cave sacred to certain nymphs. This and other rocky hollows are allegorized by the Neoplatonist Porphyry (third century A.D.) in a famous essay "On the Cave of the Nymphs in the *Odyssey*," the earliest surviving work of literary interpretation (Lamberton 1986). All grottoes "symbolize" (his term) the cosmic clearing in the primal matter— surely a critical approach of limited charm and less credibility.

Another kind of proposal, powerful but not, I think, credible either, is the psychoanalytic theory of primal phantasies. These can be either phylogenetic memories of primitive ancestral sexual behavior (Freud) or a collective store of significant, archetypal scenes (Jung). Although it is not unthinkable, it is not plausible that individual human beings have personal memories of facts they have never experienced or common visions of things they have never actually seen.

Now to the more adequate possibilities. To begin with, it is possible that the Meinongians may be wrong in distinguishing firmly between fictional being and ideal being. Works of art may in fact express or represent ideal being to the senses through fiction. Schopenhauer is the chief thematic expositor of the view, traceable to the Neoplatonists, that the arts accomplish a mimesis of transperceptual prototypes. In *The World as Will and Representation* (III), he identifies these prototypes with the Platonic ideas. The representational arts present to aesthetic contemplation not particulars but the eternal species or archetypes. There are two difficulties with the theory that ideal being is the object of aesthetic intuition and that images are particularized universals. The first is that, by annexing the imagination to the intellect, it abstracts from the strong affective elements in the imagination or at least takes inadequate account of them. The second is that is seems to throw the real and the aesthetic appearances too much together, since nature at its best does, after all, express the ideas in its species at least as well as high art does, and perhaps not very differently.

A second possibility is that what is behind the imagination-images is, so to speak, the same as what is in front of the eyes—the real world. There are "illuminated moments" when the world, transfigured, reveals itself in its significance; the imagination remembers or elicits the aspect the world wears when it comes into its own. This notion, that the imagination-images

are the world at the moments of its epiphanies, is attractive. The trouble is
that it does not account for images of imaginary objects.

One may try to explain away the difficulty thus:

> Fiction, then, whether written or painted or acted, applies truly neither to
> nothing nor to diaphanous possible worlds but, albeit metaphorically, to actual
> worlds. Somewhat as I have argued elsewhere that the merely possible —so far
> as admissible at all—lies within the actual, so we might say here again, in a
> different context, that the so-called possible worlds of fiction lie within actual
> worlds. Fiction operates in actual worlds in much the same way as nonfiction.
> [Goodman 1978]

This description of the relation between the real and imaginary world is
very fine, but it lightens the difficulty by loading part of it onto the adverb
"metaphorically." Metaphors are "a way we make our terms do multiple
moonlighting service"; thus the name and character of Odysseus applies
literally to none of us but metaphorically it applies to everyone who feels
like a storm-tossed home-seeker. The trouble with this metaphorical mixing of world and fiction is that we love and live with imaginary heroes not
only because of what we have in common with them, but also because they
increase the world by that many uniquely captivating individual human
beings.

So here is a third possibility: There is indeed a world of the imagination,
suspended between ideal and real, in which the figures and scenes imaged
in imaginary images have their being. This is a kind of "imaginary world"
theory, but it differs from the worlds of the logicians, possible and fictional,
in determinate ways: Different "possible worlds" cannot be logically conjoined because they are already logically complete. Different pictorial spaces
can indeed be amalgamated, but there is no logical closure for the operation;
that is to say, two picture-spaces put together usually do not yield a third
space which is the same as its component spaces and only larger in
extension. Instead, there often arises an incomparable new space (Ch. I B).
Different incomplete "fictional worlds" are similarly incapable, except by
an artificial stipulation, of the interrelations that real worlds naturally
maintain through real time and real space:

> How are the singularizations of temporal points, temporal durations, etc.,
> related to one another within different imaginary worlds? We can speak here
> of the likeness and similarity of the components of such worlds but never of
> *their identity,* which *would have absolutely no sense*; hence, no connections of
> incompatibility can occur, for these would indeed presuppose such identity. *It*
> *makes no sense, e.g., to ask whether the Gretel of one fairy tale and the Gretel of*

another are the same Gretel, whether what is imagined for the one and predicated of her agrees or does not agree with what is imagined for the other, or, again, whether they are related to each other, etc. *I can stipulate this*—and to accept it is already to stipulate it—but then both fairy tales refer to the same world. [Husserl, *Experience and Judgment* Part I, Ch. 3, cited in Dreyfuss 1982, italics there added]

Thus imaginary worlds are "quasi-worlds" precisely because they do not cohere in real objective time and certainly not in space. Since time and space are

> the necessary condition for any object to belong to the order of reality, *no world of imagination is a sub-order of reality.* Hence *every world of imagination* must be considered as an *order of existence in its own right.*
>
> Not only are different worlds of imagination divorced from reality, but they may also be disconnected from one another. [Gurwitsch 1957]

Any unification that may be achieved is perfectly extrinsic to the products of the imagination themselves and results entirely from the arbitrary imposition of the imaging subject's free fancy. Each individual imagined world may be self-consistent but

> no question concerning consistency or inconsistency between happenings in different worlds of imagination may be legitimately raised. There are then as many independent and autonomous orders of existence as there are separate worlds of imagination. This is exemplified by the multiplicity of novels, plays, and epic poems. [Gurwitsch 1957]

I quote Husserl and Gurwitsch at length because, though Phenomenologists, they state so clearly the logician's position on the relations of fictional worlds. Plantinga did opt for the identity of individuals across "possible worlds" (A), but the analogous position for fictional worlds does not seem to have found much favor. Generally individuals are thought to belong exclusively to one world and to have no conceivable relations to inhabitants of another. On the alternate hypothesis of nonexistent objects, too, one can argue that by reason of the inactuality of their "beyond-being" they are incapable of constituting a world:

> We speak of the *world* of *Aussersein*, but in reality the objects which have no being do not constitute a world. They are a chaos of incoherent fragments, and the only relations that subsist between them are those of similarity and diversity. Between actual existents we can always discover a large number of

intimate connexions; they people a single space-time and influence each other profoundly. Beyond the boundaries of being no such connexions subsist: there is no fixed distance between Valhalla and the islands of the blessed. [Findlay 1963]

And yet—when one considers these matters materially from within the imaginative ambiance rather than formally from without it, it is equally evident that the multitudinous worlds of the imagination, including the real world, *are* one world. The land of the imagination is a continuous terrain in which the passage from Valhalla to Elysium can somehow be negotiated. The real world sends emissaries to "immigrate" into fictions, while the world of the imagination colonizes parts of real space and time and the beings of Faerie form a fraternity (Part Four, Ch. IV B). It is a oneness sensed by children and articulated by poets: Hugo von Hofmannsthal tells of a little girl who finds a finely-wrought golden fruit. With every glimpse

> an immense dream which never waned through all the years fell about the soul of the little one with the cloud of its inconceivable fragrance: This golden apple was of a kind with the most wonderful things in fairy-tales, its life somehow connected with the speaking bird, the dancing water and the singing tree through subterranean passages which ran here and there in dark vaults among the swaying dwellings of the sea-queen. ["The Golden Apple"]

Moreover, some fictional beings have lives beyond the constraining bonds of their texts: We hear of Jane Austen telling her nephews and nieces "many little particulars about the subsequent career of some of her people." For example, her concerned readers will be relieved to hear that Mr. Woodhouse died about two years after Emma's marriage to Mr. Knightly, allowing the couple to take up residence at Donwell (told in Austen-Leigh's *Memoir* of 1870).

Having now pushed beyond the logic of images I stop. The inquiry is hung upon the horns of a dilemma. This third and last possibility, that all the worlds of the imagination form a coherent realm with its own actuality, is attractive and perilous in equal parts. It has a concomitant notion: that imaginary scenes and figures must image some sort of original, since they can never be accounted for without remainder either as concoctions brewed exclusively from perceptual ingredients or as creations conjured up *ex nihilo*. To embrace it is to stand as a self-admitted phantast. However, to reject the notion is to fall continually into frivolous, unmeant manners of speaking. The worst solution is the one most often proposed: to consign the imagination to the dark sanctuary of irrationality. The norms of logic may be inadequate to the sense of actuality and self-presentation that adheres to fictions, but that fact itself could be the spring-board for further thought. The more recalcitrant the imagination is as a problem for formal reason the more thought-provoking it can become as a mystery for philosophical reflection; the Conclusion of this book will enlarge upon this point, that it is better to maintain the mystery than to dispel it. The theory—and surely the practice—of the imagination is, in sum, best served by a candid and unwearied recognition of its prime question: What does the imagination image? For a living question offers prospects of answers that a fixed theory could not dare to entertain.

O immaginativa,

chi move te, se il senso non ti porge?
Moveti lume, che nel ciel s'informa
per sè, o per voler che giù lo scorge.

[Dante, *Purgatorio*, Canto XVII]

Bibliography

Blocker, H. Gene. 1974. "The Truth about Fictional Entities." *The Philosophical Quarterly* 24:27–36.

Brann, Eva. 1974. "The Poet of the Odyssey." *St. John's Review* 25:5–12.

Brentano, Franz. 1911. "Genuine and Ficticious Objects." In *Realism and the Background of Phenomenology*, edited by Roderick M. Chisholm. Atascadero, Calif.: Ridgeview Publishing Co. (1960).

Carrier, David. 1973. "Three Kinds of Imagination." *The Journal of Philosophy* 22:819–831.

———. 1978. "Imagination and Our Image of the Mind: A Note." *The Philosophical Forum* 9:393–399.

———. 1982. *Brentano and Meinong Studies*. Atlantic Highlands, N.J.: Humanities Press.

Chisholm, Roderick M. 1960. "Editor's Introduction." In *Realism and the Background of Phenomenology*, edited by Roderick M. Chisholm. Atascadero, Calif.: Ridgeview Publishing Co.

Devine, Philip E. 1974. "The Logic of Fiction." *Philosophical Studies* 26:389–399.

Donnellan, Keith S. 1974. "Speaking of Nothing." In *Naming, Necessity, and Natural Kinds*, edited by Stephen P. Schwartz. Ithaca: Cornell University Press (1977).

Dreyfus, Herbert L., with Hall, Harrison, eds. 1982. *Husserl, Intentionality, and Cognitive Science*. Cambridge: The MIT Press (1984).

Findlay, J. N. 1963. *Meinong's Theory of Objects and Values*, 2d ed. Oxford: Clarendon Press.

Goodman, Nelson. 1961. "About." *Mind* 70:1–24.

———. 1978. *Ways of Worldmaking*. Indianapolis: Hackett Publishing Co.

Grossman, Reinhardt. 1974. *Meinong*. London: Routledge and Kegan Paul.

Gurwitsch, Aron. 1957. *The Field of Consciousness*. Pittsburgh: Duquesne University Press (1964).

Hintikka, Jaakko. 1969. *Models for Modalities: Selected Essays*. Boston: D. Reidel Publishing Co.

Howell, Robert. 1979. "Fictional Objects: How They Are and How They Aren't." *Poetics* 8:129–177.

Ingarden, Roman. 1930. *The Literary Work of Art: An Investigation on the Borderlines of Ontology, Logic, and Theory of Literature*. Edited by George Grabowicz. Evanston: Northwestern University Press (1973).

Lambert, Karel. 1983. *Meinong and the Principle of Independence: Its Place in Meinong's Theory of Objects and Its Significance in Contemporary Philosophical Logic*. Cambridge: Cambridge University Press.

Lamberton, Robert. 1986. *Homer the Theologian*. Berkeley and Los Angeles: University of California Press.

Lewis, David. 1978. "Truth in Fiction." *American Philosophical Quarterly* 15:37–46.

Margolis, Joseph. 1977. "The Ontological Peculiarity of Works of Art." In *Philosophy Looks at the Arts: Contemporary Readings in Aesthetics*, edited by Joseph Margolis. Philadelphia: Temple University Press (1978).

Meinong, Alexis. 1904. "The Theory of Objects." In *Realism and the Background of Phenomenology*, edited by Roderick M. Chisholm. Atascadero, Calif.: Ridgeview Publishing Co.

Mohanty, J. N. 1982. "Intentionality and Possible Worlds: Husserl and Hintikka." In *Husserl, Intentionality, and Cognitive Science*, edited by Herbert L. Dreyfus and Harrison Hall. Cambridge: The MIT Press.

Parsons, Terence. 1980. *Nonexistent Objects*. New Haven: Yale University Press.

Pears, D. F., and Thomson, James. 1963. "Is Existence a Predicate?" In *Philosophical Logic*, edited by P. F. Strawson. Oxford: Oxford University Press (1967).

Plantinga, Alvin. 1973. "Transworld Identity or Worldbound Individuals?" In *Naming, Necessity, and Natural Kinds*, edited by Stephen P. Schwartz. Ithaca: Cornell University Press.

———. 1974. "Possible But Unactual Objects: On What There Isn't." Chapter 8 in *The Nature of Necessity*. Oxford: Clarendon Press.

Quine, Willard V. O. 1953. "On What There Is." In *From a Logical Point of View*. Cambridge: Harvard University Press (1980).

Ryle, Gilbert, Braithwaite, R. B., and Moore, G. E. 1933. "Imaginary Objects." In *Creativity, Politics and the A Priori*. In *The Aristotelian Society*, Supplementary Volume 12. London: Harrison and Sons.

Searle, John R. 1975. "The Logical Status of Fictional Discourse." *New Literary History* 6:319–332.

Tolkien, J.R.R. 1947. "On Fairy-Stories." In *Essays Presented to Charles Williams*, edited by C. S. Lewis. London: Oxford University Press.

van Inwagen, Peter. 1977. "Creatures of Fiction." *American Philosophical Quarterly* 14:299–308.

Walton, Kendall, L. 1978. "How Remote are Fictional Worlds from the Real World?" *The Journal of Aesthetics and Art Criticism* 37:11–23.

Wollheim, Richard. 1964. "On Drawing an Object." In *Philosophy Looks at the Arts: Contemporary Readings in Aesthetics*, edited by Joseph Margolis. Philadelphia: Temple University Press.

Wolterstorff, Nicholas. 1976. "Worlds of Works of Art." *Journal of Aesthetics and Art Criticism* 35:121–132.

Woods, John. 1974. *The Logic of Fiction: A Philosophical Sounding of Deviant Logic*. The Hague: Mouton.

Part Four

Literature: The Translation of Imagining

Part Four

Literature: The Translation of Imagining

It is the mundane miracle of our human existence that we can catch the visible world and communicate our perceptions of it through speech. So it is only a subsidiary wonder that we can do the same for imagined worlds. This lesser marvel, largely documented in that artful use of written language called literature, is the concern of this part. It is not, however, my intention here to deal with the underlying issues of speech, such as meaning, sense, reference, denotation, and connotation (though brief considerations of these in their relation to the act of imagining will be necessary—Ch. I C); but I want to consider how inner imaginings are turned into words and words back into inner visions. By "imagining" I mean, for present purposes, the deliberate activity of producing or entertaining imagination-images. Again, and with the same rationale as in the previous parts, I shall emphasize the traditional sister activities of speaking and depicting, but this time with respect to their mutual translation.

In Part One, I dwelt on the fact that in philosophy the imagination as a faculty is not so much a neglected as a repressed subject. Nothing of the sort can be said of the activity of imagining and its verbal versions and expressions. It is the subject of exuberant comment, comment that at its best often is distinctly antagonistic to the philosophers' reason and ready to subvert their opinions. This opposition reveals two facets of the imagination as subject: It is intellectually forbidding and humanly fascinating. On the other hand, a topic that was dominant in the last two parts, the rivalry of word and image in psychology and logic, is in literature brought quietly to a practical resolution, insofar as sights and words there coexist comfortably as versions of each other. This mutuality will be traced out in several forms, devices, and genres of literature.

So in Chapter I, I take up, first, the linguistic description of the world, both perceived and imagined (A), and then the correspondences of painting and poetry (B). Next, in Chapter II, I discuss two chief literary forms and distinctive theories concerning the activity of imagining pertinent to these forms (A). The first form is poetry, and in this context the Romantic imagination, which often passes for the imagination *par excellence*, is of prime interest (B). The second form is the novel, especially its descriptive prose, and here the assimilation of this prose to the spatiality of vision is the focus of attention (C). I devote Chapter III to the chief devices of the literary imagination, simile and metaphor. In Chapter IV, finally, I deal with two genres of literary imagining in which the imagination best shows its peculiar powers. One is fantasy, in which the imagining activity lightly casts loose from the common world and where the question of literary truthfulness is correspondingly acute (B). But higher than fantasy is myth, which is the graver imagining of timelessly archetypal events (A).

Chapter I

Visions into Words and Words into Visions

The same Simonides who in the sixth century B.C. discovered memory-images as devices for verbal recall (Part Two, Ch. III B) is reported by Plutarch to have observed that

> painting is poetry keeping silent: poetry is a talking picture. [*On the Glory of the Athenians* III 346]

What can this copiously quoted dictum effectively mean but that pictures invite verbal description and poems elicit visual imagining? These translations are the topic of this chapter.

Of course, not every use of language is image-fraught. First of all, as was observed in the discussion of the logic of pictures in the previous part, things can be said that cannot be seen: There are the so-called syncategorematic terms, such as conjunctions and prepositions; there are negative propositions and abstract words; there are the invisible visions of first philosophy. To descend steeply, there is all the business-like speech that gets blindly on with some purpose, such as commands, polite jabber, and ideological rhetoric. I do not include logical speech, because it turns out to be closely bound to its own imagery (Part Five, Ch. II B). Moreover, in general, any language that gives the soul even a little scope for internal activity is attended by a multitude of imaged shades: *Phanopoeia*, "throwing the object (fixed or moving) onto the visual imagination" is, in one poet's judgment, the first of the communicative means that speech possesses (Ezra Pound 1934).

A. Descriptions and Sights: Asymmetrical Versions

One of the great functions of literature is to turn things seen and things imagined into language. In neither case are the sights so conveyed or induced true recoveries of the originals. Word and vision are forever divorced. Yet this divorce, which in the case of prose description appears as a kind of fatality urging the writer into longer and more accurate expression, is exploited in poetry so that it becomes a spring of activity for the reader. This difference stems from the two diverse modes of description at work: I term them "extensive" and "intensive."

The intensive mode centers on individual beings and their relations, bringing them to the foreground and capturing them by means of adjectival specification. Such description differs from scientific classification in beginning, as it were, below the limit of the latter, which is usually the species. It starts instead with the inner nature of a unique yet paradigmatic individual. This intensive description seeks not so much to induce a determinate visual representation as to activate an imaginative frame for each reader's own, free, diverse depictions (2). Prose is, of course, often intensive, but lyric poetry is paradigmatically so—for such poetry concerns the motions of the soul.

By extensive description, or description simply, I mean the language that establishes the visual backgrounds and details the characteristic appearances of narratives—for such prose conveys the appearances of space. Its description may be rich in sensory and subjective modifiers or it may proceed by a flat, unadorned, objective detailing of the lie of the land and the look of its figures. It provides all necessary visual clues to the attentive reader and may even lay traps for the wool-gatherer. (This is, for example, Robbe-Grillet's novelistic practice—Ch. II C.) In any case, it calls for precise accompanying visualization (1). In fact, cognitive research establishes that when verbal descriptions reach sufficient fullness, determinate visualization does take place, while an unspecific, sparse text is retained verbally without images (Johnson-Laird 1983, 160). Here surely is one of the reasons why lyric poems are short and historical narrations, true or imaginary, are long: Poetry evokes free images, descriptive prose induces constrained visualizations.

One test of good novelistic writing is the success of its extensive prose. Thus in a review Henry James asks the novelist:

> You construct your description from a chosen object; can you, conversely, from your description construct that object? [Edel 1953, 213]

Similarly a test of good novel reading is the effort devoted to re-translation, to visualization: Nabokov, in telling what a good novel-reader is, assigns a central place to the "impersonal imagination," the effort "to get clear the specific world the author places at his disposal." So in his own lectures, for instance the one on Jane Austen's *Mansfield Park*, the lion's share of obsessive attention goes into drawings of the lay-outs of Mansfield Park itself and of other places that play a role in the novel (1940). Reading a novel without topographical visualization is, one might say, like driving through a lovely countryside while intent on a personal conversation—it misses the object of the exercise.

Novelists are, then, the great modern practitioners of the extensive mode, but the historians preceded them.

1. The Eyewitness: Herodotus. I want to begin with the utility and pleasure of turning the visible world into words. Before the perfection of naturalistic painting and photographic replication, language bore the major share of fixing and communicating sights. To make oneself alive to the pristine force and pleasure of the descriptive word, one cannot do better than to read Herodotus. For he is the father not only of the "inquiry"—the Greek word is *historia*, whence our "history"—that proceeds by hearing tales and seeing sights, but also of extended prose as a literary form, a fresh new form combining an inimitably artful naiveté with great visual vividness. This prose is as good for bringing human tableaux, strange sights and grand geographies before the reader's inner eye, as for conveying a deep, subtle, and sometimes wickedly funny anthropology.

Herodotus was apparently the first writer to have made a meticulous distinction between what he had seen for himself as eyewitness (*autoptēs*) and what he knew through verbal description. Thus he is the first to have reflected self-consciously on the relation of the retelling word to the presented sight. One effect seems to have been that he made a special effort to write descriptive prose as "sightly," or, to use the word in an older sense, as "plastic," as possible: As *autopsy*, "seeing for oneself," is the chief authorial warrant of truth, so visuality, the reader's seeing, is the greatest persuasive device (Hartog 1988, 251). The multiple culmination of his history is the trio of great battles in which the Greeks repelled the invading Barbarians (for some of whose customs Herodotus has, incidentally, a great respect; it earned him the epithet "barbarian-lover"). Athenian Marathon, Spartan Thermopylae, and Salamis where the Greeks were united—these were battles whose outcome determined the shape of our West. Each of them is presented as a kind of verbal vision, a word-painting *à la* Simonides. But it is in the Athenian battle that sight plays the greatest role (VI). Not only are several visual prodigies reported: The god Pan briefly and momentously appears to the runner Philippides (the man who later made the first Marathon-run) as he is racing to Sparta for help; an Athenian, as he will later tell Herodotus, sees a gigantic bearded warrior pass over him to kill the man next in the line, and is himself struck blind for life. But also the psychological crux of the battle itself lies in the fact that for the first time in history Greeks and Persians really *saw* each other. The Persians were stunned by the novel sight of men in full armor running in good order over a great distance, while the Athenians "were likewise the first who dared to look upon the Median garb." As for the Athenian phalanx, Herodotus leaves the looks of that swiftly advancing, gleaming engine of battle to the informed imagination of his Greek readers (I 76). He will, however, later on describe in detail the Median dress which, as he had earlier told his readers, the Persians had adopted. Here is the apparition the reader must retrospectively reconstitute and that the Athenians had actually seen climbing ashore on the beach of Marathon: hordes of creatures whose heads were covered with the felt caps called "tiaras," whose chests were protected by wicker shields, who were wearing fishscale armor over multicolored shirts, and whose lower bodies were oddly bifurcated by barbarian trousers (VII 61). The visualizing reader of this encounter, which determined the fate of Europe, will apprehend the sense of participating in a prodigy, of being called to join in battle with monsters, that must have been induced by the sight of this invasion of mermen.

Marathon took place in 490 B.C. Herodotus published the *Persian Wars* after the mid-century. In between, the battle had been depicted, on the basis of a somewhat divergent account, by the painter Polygnotus in the Painted Colonnade at Athens. The painting, now lost (which Herodotus would have come to see, just as he heard eyewitnesses), was described some six hundred years later by the traveler Pausanias in his *Description of Greece* (I 15). Thus the chain of translations and retranslations, from eyewitness descriptions to depictions to redescriptions and redepictions goes on. Are they—description and depiction—exactly inverse operations?

Of course not. Operations are inverses of each other if when applied successively they get one back to the starting point. But a visual percept cannot be recovered from a description. Think of the wild graphic surmises attending even a meticulous account of an unfamiliar sight. The distorting link is apt to be the verbal one, since a description passing through a fairly faithful intermediary depiction is more likely to emerge quite recognizable than a depiction that is repictured from a description. For even very accurate language puts far fewer constraints on the pictorial visualization than a careful picture puts on a verbal description.

The fact is that no writer can do what Leonardo proposes—perhaps injuriously—the poet do: to become the painter's equal, to represent definite objects of nature so as to "satisfy the eye with words as the painter does with brush and color." That is precisely what is impossible. A myriad of well-chosen words cannot delineate a visual shape determinately—though *not* because there aren't words enough, informationally precise and atmospherically nuanced, to describe sights seen so as to produce a click of satisfaction. There are plenty of verbal means, specifyingly pedantic and resonantly poetic even for rendering color, that most irreducibly visual aspect of vision: Think, for example, just of that small corner of the palette where browns are mixed: raw sienna, burnt sienna, raw umber, burnt umber; or reddish brown, yellowish brown, brownish yellow, brownish purple; or auburn, russet, tawny, puce. Yet the aptest of words does not *show* the color.

The impossibility of turning even precise descriptions into determinate depictions—the literary reflection of the old philosophical teaching that individuality is unknowable by the intellect and inexpressible in words—betokens a non-translatability far more radical, more incurable, than that between two languages. With words enough and time one is entitled at some point to say: This is how that sentence is to be rendered in my language; this is where the meanings coincide. But depictions and descriptions are forever asymptotic. It is a preoccupation of prose writers who meditate on their métier:

> How many literati before me have moaned over the unfitness of language for achieving visibility, for bringing forth a truly exact picture of anything individual! The word was made for laud and praise. To it has been given the power to admire and bless and characterize appearance through the feeling that it arouses, but not to invoke or reproduce it. [Thomas Mann, *Doctor Faustus*]

Of course, neither laud nor obloquy nor feeling is the first office of language but the declaration of subjects and predicates. That is why collectors and cataloguers of the world's sights can, after all, dispense with pictures rather than do without words. Consider that the chief product of Darwin's momentous travels was words: The natural historian *par excellence* came home with two thousand pages of verbal observation besides the six-hundred-page diary that became *The Voyage of the Beagle*. In archaeological excavations the sentences in the excavation notebooks heavily outnumber the photographs or drawings. For if words cannot achieve the informational density of depictions, these in turn, precisely because they represent their wordless perceptual originals as analogues, are mutely unable to explain themselves and can talk only through their captions (Sontag 1977).

There are evidently two ways, distinguishable though never quite distinct, in which language can translate real sights or their visual documentation: It can range over them descriptively, and it can penetrate them interpretatively. It is in the latter office that language outdoes in potency both the visual scene itself and its picture. This interpretative power of language is of course the virtue that redeems the vices of verbal incompleteness and indeterminacy that were discussed in Part Three. Language is celebrated for the ability of its words to distinguish particular things by general names, of its sentences to relate the terms in judgments, and of its paragraphs to connect the judgments into arguments. In sum, what language lacks in density, it makes up in depth: An infinity of words cannot become a picture, but one word can tell what a picture means.

Wonder at the ability of words to capture the visible world thus leads, as has already been intimated, straight to high philosophy. The business at hand, however, is the recovery or solicitation of vision from verbal descriptions—not so much that private labor of love devoted to tethering down a prized perception by means of language, as the literary art of eliciting momentary (or moving) tableaux in the reader's imagination.

2. The Blind Seer: Homer. The very defect of historical description, the fact that it is not visually univocal and cannot convey uniquely its originating perception, is the glory of imagined description. For in the freedom of fiction, each attentive reader has the right to furnish a different, yet textually defensible, visual version.

I am assuming here something that is by no means universally granted: that imaginative literature is meant to be seen. The Athenian orator Isocrates, for one, ignores the visual element of poetry. When Homer, he says, "did his tale-telling" (*emythologēsen*) of the heroes' contests and wars he meant it to be merely heard; it was left to the dramatists to let us see these events as well (*To Nicocles* 374 B.C.). Modern critics too have denigrated visualization. Thus I.A. Richards derides Lord Kames for having insisted that reading requires forming accurate mental imagery from metaphors (1936). Herbert Read pointedly says that "in the degree that they are poetic . . . words are automatic associations of an aural rather than a visual nature."

Those who emphasize the timbre of language and its various other auditory qualities tend also to think that poetry and even prose is well-nigh untranslatable into another language. Croce cites the translator's dilemma as "faithful ugliness or faithless beauty" (*Aesthetic* 1901), and Santayana asks "What could be better than Homer or worse than almost any translation of him?" (*The Sense of Beauty* 1896). Since besides the action it is the scene and the spectacle that best survive translation, the denial that any translation can be worthwhile implies the rejection of the visual element.

But there is also respectable testimony on the other side:

The poet's eye, in a fine frenzy rolling,
Doth glance from heaven to earth, from earth to heaven;
And, as imagination bodies forth
The forms of things unknown, the poet's pen
Turns them to shapes, and gives to airy nothings
A local habitation and a name. [*Midsummer Night's
Dream* V 1]

James Russell Lowell takes this poetic bodying-forth in a very grand way: It
is to be understood as *verbum caro factum,* "the word made flesh" (1855).
When he makes his imaginings appear the poet performs a kind of literary
incarnation—visualization is near-realization.

The "visionary" view had in fact, *pace* Isocrates, been the standard theory
of antiquity. The poet envisions, the listener re-envisions and is moved. In
his book on the education of an orator, Quintilian says:

> What the Greeks call *phantasiai* we call visions, through which images of things
> absent are so represented in the mind that we seem to see them as present
> before the eyes. He who understands them well, will have most power over the
> feelings. [VI 2]

People who can envision especially well, he continues, are called "imaginative" (*euphantasiōtos*), but inasmuch as everyone daydreams, all can learn to
use their visual imagination. Cicero further characterizes the contribution
of such images to literary composition: They add "brightness" (*enargeia*),
which in turn gives brilliance (*illustratio*, the word eventually used for textual
pictures) and visual vividness (*evidentia*).

But better than citing the testimony is showing the practice. So let me
demonstrate what vividly beautiful sights are to be gotten out of the
supposedly untranslatable Homer in any fairly faithful version, beautiful or
not. I shall cite one such visual episode from the *Iliad* and one from the
Odyssey, each crucial to the understanding of the poem.

At the high point of the *Iliad* occurs the dream-like episode in which
Achilles, the swiftest of runners, is suspended in a timeless chase around
the walls of Troy in pursuit of the heavy-set Hector (XXII). Finally, by the
guile of the gods, Hector is made to face about and to confront Achilles. It
is not going too far to say that the whole meaning of the poem hangs on
seeing what Achilles sees at that moment: He sees a warrior wearing a suit
of armor—Achilles's own. It is the armor Hector had stripped from
Achilles's friend Patroclus, the friend for whose death they are jointly
responsible. As time stands still before Troy, Achilles is facing three beings

in one familiar and menacing figure: himself in his former aspect, his best friend as he last looked when Achilles let him go to his stand-in death, and his worthiest enemy among the Trojans. The whole pathos of this poem about a young hero's fateful wrath is concentrated in this vision. But Homer does not say a word. One must *see* it for oneself.

The quiet denouement of the *Odyssey*, which casts its sheen over Odysseus's bloody repossession of the palace, is similarly a matter of visual inference. Odysseus has come home incognito (XIX), and Penelope interviews the traveller. A teasing, allusive colloquy ensues. During it Odysseus weaves into the conversation more than one moaning allusion to his own name (which means the Sorrower and sounds like a doleful sigh) as he tells her more about Odysseus's farflung itinerary and imminent return than it is credible for anyone but that hero himself to know. She in turn says with significance: "Neither *will* Odysseus come nor will *you* get a send-off from here . . . Never *again* will I receive him home." There is much more of this kind of play for the ear.

Next the wife orders his old nurse to do the ritual foot-washing. The nurse immediately recognizes an old hunting scar on Odysseus's foot. Time stops while the story of his wounding gets a leisurely telling in a long interlude. This interlude has seemed to call for critical justification (Auerbach 1946), but it makes perfect human sense—a moment of recognition always bears in itself the whole history of its mark. At the end of the poet's reminiscence the old nurse drops the foot into the basin with a clatter. Odysseus hisses at her to keep silent, while Penelope wisely allows herself to be distracted by Athena. The wife ascends to their chamber while the husband sleeps downstairs. Towards dawn he hears her weeping and "it seemed to him in his heart that she already knew him and was standing by his head."

Of course those two have known each other from the first. From his first hidden appearance till his public self-disclosure the air is tense with the scheme of teasing and trusting played out between them, a scheme in which Athena, Odysseus's own subtle goddess, finds that his wife is his equal in canny self-possession. Of course in that extended moment before the clatter they have been giving each other a long, long look. Of course toward dawn she steals downstairs to look at him, longingly and warily. Of course they refrain from conjugal intimacy until the whole bloody business of clearing out her suitors is done—conjugal conspirators that they are. The point is that here too the pathos of the scene comes not so much from what is explicitly said (recall the "schematized aspects" of the previous chapter), but from the undercurrent of hints for the visualization of several revealing tableaux such as will partly countermand the tale as told (Brann 1974).

Here I cannot keep from commenting on a famous and pertinent work, Schiller's essay "On Naive and Sentimental Poetry" (1800). A sentimental poet reflects his objects through his impressions and ideas, while the naive poet, for whom Homer is the paradigm, sees the world directly in its shapely actuality. Schiller tells how at first he felt rebuffed by the spare matter-of-factness Homer displays at poignant moments and by the poet's failure to anticipate with exclamations of sentiment the reader's readiness to be moved. Finally he realized that this simple unemotional directness is as much the glory as the limitation of the naive poet. This reading of Homer seems to me to miss something: Homeric scenes are so charged with significance and feeling and complexity that what keeps the poet out of them is surely not naive immediacy but artful tact. The poet's discretion draws the listener into a participation that doubles the pleasures of the imagination: While the ear attends, the eye is at work. We enjoy at once Homer's work and the exercise of our own imaginations (Feagin 1984).

No wonder Aristotle observed that "just as Homer excels in other respects, so also in this, it seems: in seeing finely, be it by art or nature" (*Poetics* 1451, Else 1957). The blindness of the first and dominant poet of the West seems to be the emblem for a characteristic use of language: to instigate visual imagining. Homer's epic mode is in the unexalted sense visionary—that is, intended for visualization. As it happens, the practice of meticulous and intense visualization is known to be of special significance to the once-sighted blind (Carroll 1961).

In dwelling on the crisp indicative mode of Homeric visualization I do not want to slight another sort: the evocative mode, which is the one commonly thought of as preeminently poetic. Evocation exploits another asymmetry of articulated speech and visual imagery. It is a fact that from the first word on, any sentence increasingly constrains the reader's understanding of itself, whereas the images evoked come in flitting throngs, spontaneously generated from first to last. Because evocative words can release burgeoning visions, evocative language is the mode in which love and poetry most often meet. Here the poet's subject is wreathed about with associated sights and saturated with the aura of attendant visions:

> What is your substance, whereof are you made,
> That millions of strange shadows on you tend?
> [Shakespeare, Sonnet 53]

The pseudo-explanatory word for such clusterings of the inner vision is "association." Its laws, in spite of valiant tries such as Ribot's, have eluded formulation. Nevertheless, the sense that imaginative associations have a rightness that is more than random is unsuppressible. Imagery is the chief means of such evocation (Ch. III).

So far I have been concerned with the description of perceived sights and the instigation of imagined ones. What if the activity of visual imagining results in external pictures, in paintings? Then vision, before freely variable against a fixed text, becomes itself determinate and unique—unique and determinate enough now to make the written text in turn seem Protean. For a material painting is the one and only member of its class, while a text can not only appear in many copies but may indeed survive the destruction of them all (Carrier 1973). Word and vision cease to be asymmetrical. They achieve a certain parity.

B. Poetry and Painting: Non-Mutual Sisters

If there is parity of the arts it is not in the respect they command. It scarcely needs documenting that literature has always stood above painting. After all, a literary text speaks its mind throughout the world as it circulates in a multitude of copies, while an original painting is mute, unique, and rooted to its place. The inequality is already evident in the first book on the arts, Aristotle's *Poetics*. Here poetry is the paradigm while painting is dispatched with the refrain "So also do the painters" (e.g., 1448 a 5). Traditionally literature has provided texts for the honorable liberal arts, while painting is ranged among the lesser mechanical arts (Curtius 1948). Consequently, painters have often felt constrained to take their themes from canonical lists furnished by literature (Ahsen 1982), while poets have felt free to take or leave suggestions from the visual arts.

A rare but passionate defender of the view that painting is paramount is Leonardo da Vinci. Earlier I enumerated the realms into which the imagination might reach for its originals (Part One, Ch. II A). One of these was the visible world itself. Leonardo is the unflagging defender of this view: nature herself is the source of all beauty, variety, and wonder. Therefore the power of sight, the *virtù visiva*, of the painter is a finer sense than the obscure inward eye of the poet. Painting stands to poetry as a body to its shadow, for "poetry puts down her subjects in imaginary written characters while painting puts down the identical reflection that the eye receives as if it were real." Leonardo is here introducing the opposition between the natural signs of painting and the artificial signs of poetry, which was later elaborated into a defense of painting over poetry by the Abbé du Bos (Lee 1940). Moreover, Leonardo holds—anticipating Lessing—that while poetry describes its subject piecemeal through time, painting has a panoramic simultaneity that alone can do justice to the significant coexistences of nature. It is the property that corresponds to the characteristic of the imagination I have called "momentousness" (Part Three, Ch. III C). Thus for Leonardo, world and imagination coincide, and painting is their common mirror: Mirroring is his great preoccupation.

Leonardo's view is echoed two hundred years later by Addison: "Description runs yet further from the things it represents than painting; for a picture bears a real resemblance to its original which letters and syllables are wholly void of." Here he speaks as a fair-minded and visually appreciative man of letters, though he adds that "words well chosen, have so great a force in them, that a description often gives us more lively ideas than the sight of things themselves" (*Spectator* no. 416, 1712). By and large, though, such defenses of the analogue art notwithstanding, the great majority who use the word prefer the word. The word alone can reach the inward, invisible nature of human beings, can render the development of their actions in time, and can reveal the significance of both. Thus poetry rather than painting, and of poetry, tragedy rather than epic, is the art of choice, the deep art.

There are really two issues here; the subordinate one has already been broached: Can language be adequate to the visible world? Schopenhauer—one of the philosophers who puts tragedy at the pinnacle of the representational arts—demonstrates how language can and does achieve a sort of visibility, by using these lines from the *Iliad*:

Into the ocean fell the radiant light of the sun
Drawing black night over the grain-giving land.

Three nouns are modified by adjectives, and that is how intuitive concreteness is achieved—by the multiple intersections of enough abstract concepts (*World as Will and Representation* III 51). Schopenhauer is here banking on the magical philosophical doctrine that, with enough specification, visibility supervenes at some point. It is a wonderful and dubious idea even for indefinitely extensive prose, one which cannot, at any rate, help poetry, where the required specification never goes far enough. Language, I argued above, has the power, sufficiently remarkable, to circumscribe a class of visualizations or to instigate free visions, but it can never achieve fully determined visibility.

The second, deeper, issue is the age-old rivalry between sight and word: Is significance ultimately located in the visible surfaces, real and imagined, that present themselves to the eye, corporeal and mental, or does it reside in the invisible depths that can only be penetrated by speech? Or can the

differences perhaps be composed so that surface and center become complementary? While that question is the preoccupation behind this entire book
(see the Conclusion), the particular issue for this chapter is a lesser derivative: How can poetry be said to paint?

1. *"Ut Pictura Poesis."* "Poetry is like a picture" is a phrase from
Horace's *Art of Poetry* (361). The phrase is, for all the meaning eventually
loaded onto it, innocuous in its original context: some pictures, Horace
says, bear looking at often and close up; others do not—and "as in painting
so in poetry." It was, however, the fate of the phrase to be taken up and
reinterpreted as the watchword of a powerful tradition that coagulated
about the issues just raised.

Note that the famous "sister arts," as Dryden called them in "A Parallel
of Poetry and Painting," have a not-quite-mutual relation: poetry usurps
the virtue of painting without granting her sister her own. In accordance
with her preeminence, poetry is the art primarily illuminated by the
Simonidean saying that painting is poetry keeping silent and poetry is a
speaking picture. Not only was it the second clause that was to gain
currency, but Simonides's dictum had skewed the relation of the sister arts
ab initio by making speech and its absence the common reference. He could,
after all, have said: "Painting is visible poetry; poetry is invisible painting."
Indeed, the defense of painting often makes the most of its muteness,
emphasizing its abstention from speech as Simonides himself does. It is in
this vein that Ortega y Gasset writes:

> All the marvelousness of painting rests on its dual condition: its will to express
> and its resolve to stay silent . . . like a spring it depresses itself in its muteness
> in order to be able to bounce back with the suggestion of ineffable things.
> [1946]

There is, nevertheless, a classical, if lesser, tradition of painting as visible
poetry, also ranged by scholars (with slight inaccuracy) under the banner
of *ut pictura poesis*. When characterized as visible—rather than as silent—
poetry, painting needs to make no appeal to ineffability. Ineffability is,
after all, a dangerous compliment to pay an art, for it removes it from the
realm of reflective discourse. If there is in the visual realm something
wonderful that is also unreachable by speech, it must be more than merely
unsayable. In the Renaissance, when the analogizing of painting and poetry
was at its high point, painters thought of themselves as humanists and of
their craft as informed with all the liberal learning needed to represent the
world revealingly—learning that had always appeared to be the poets'

prerogative. Then for a while painting and poetry were truly sister arts. On that footing painters proudly gave their own versions of themes found in poetry, classical and contemporary (Lee 1940, Praz 1970).

a. The Doctrine of "Speaking Pictures." As I have been at pains to point out, the Simonidean doctrine is primarily literary. It is the teaching that the glory of literature is verbal depiction, painting in words. It concerns a technique somewhat blunter than the subtle imaginal counterpoint I attributed to Homer, though obviously germane to it. It governs a long and varied tradition, which, it will come as no surprise, regards Homer as its avatar. Thus Cicero speaks of Homer's ability to produce vivid painting, whatever his subject (*Tusculan Disputations* V 39), a judgment echoed some fourteen-hundred years later by Petrarch, who calls him "the first painter of ancient memory" (Lee 1940, 197). This is the moment to mention, regretfully only in passing, that the doctrine of speaking pictures—and of visible poetry—has a strong and wonderful life in Chinese painting.

The doctrine has many facets (Hagstrum 1958, Steiner 1982). One is that from the first it is intrinsically related to the mimetic theory of representation. When Plato says that poets are like painters, he means precisely that both are imitators. Since in poetry imitation is not by direct analogue-resemblance, its assimilation to painting is primarily the metaphorical expression of an ideal, and one strong element of that ideal is what the ancient rhetoricians called *enargeia*, "pictorial vividness." This was regarded as a virtue of descriptive prose as well as of poetry: Plutarch, for example, praises Thucydides—a historian, *nota bene*—for displaying it in an account of a military expedition (*Moralia* 17).

This desideratum for "speaking pictures" survives into the eighteenth century, kept urgent by the ill-assorted pair of facts that while poetry is considered the most serious of arts, vision is praised as the grandest of the senses. Its definitive statement is found in Addison's seminal "Pleasures of the Imagination" series in the *Spectator* (1712). The imagination in general, Addison says, is stimulated primarily by the direct perception of nature and secondarily by reminders from paintings and descriptions. But the art of poetry in particular, though lacking the natural signs of painting, must nonetheless endeavor to learn from the visual arts how to get as close as possible to nature. Vividness is achieved by the accurate representation of particular visible nature. However—and here Addison diverges from Leonardo and originates a new aesthetic—this vividness is not a function of mirroring nature directly but of seeing her *through the imagination*.

The mirror-theory of imitation is old and long-lived. Aristotle already reports—disapprovingly—that people hyperbolically call the *Odyssey* "a beautiful mirror of life" (*Rhetoric* III 3); they mean, presumably, that it possesses great pictorial vividness. But for Addisonians pictorialism is no longer mirror-like. Addison's friend, Hugh Blair, saw in depictive description "the highest exertion of genius"; he thought it possible that a poet might render nature with such life that a painter could copy him. Such a transmission from the poet's depiction would not, however, be to the painter's eye, but to his imagination: What the imagination in turn imparts and apprehends is the selection and intensification of circumstances that heighten the vividness of nature herself (Hagstrum 1958).

The lesson relevant to the interest of this book is that the doctrine of literature as word-painting explicitly calls on the mediation of the visual imagination in particular and on the intervention of literary imagination in general. No wonder, then, that it was under the aegis of the *ut pictura poesis* tradition that the proto-Romantic notion of art as an affair essentially in and for the imagination should first have been broached.

b. "Iconic" Poetry: Homer, Longus, Dante, Keats. The Simonidean tradition has a sub-strain that is fascinatingly to my point: so-called "iconic" poetry. If poetry is to produce visible pictures, then, by a natural transition, it might as well sometimes be *about* the visual arts. A Greek writer, Philostratus the Elder (second century A.D.), was one of several to write "Images," *Eikones*. These were descriptions, produced with the utmost pictorial vividness, of real or imaginary works of graphic art. He was, so to speak, returning the compliment of the painters who had, of course, been painting literary themes all along: The *Odyssey*, for example, had been illustrated on pottery as early as the eighth century B.C. and was still the subject of wall paintings in Roman times. In writing "Images" he was hoping to reinforce in readers the sense of the sisterly bond between poetry and painting: "*Whosoever* loves not *Pictures* is injurious to Truth and all the wisdom of Poetry" (Ben Jonson's translation in Hagstrum 1958). This contrived way of demonstrating that poetry is like a picture by using it to imitate a picture, real or imaginary, may be a small strain in the tradition, but it has at least four great instances. One, coeval with poetry itself, is once again to be found in Homer: One of Homer's rare descriptive passages depicts the Shield made by Hephaestus. It was intended to replace the shield of Achilles mentioned above, the one that was stripped from Patroclus and worn by Hector on his last day. This work of a god, which Achilles carries before him as he circles Troy on that same day, is quite simply the world— the heavens, the encircling sea, and the land, in war and in peace. But even aside from the role this portable cosmos of chased metal and precious inlay plays in Achilles's epiphany, it is the blind poet's master-stroke. For through it he lays down the tacit claim that the epic poet (who plies the preeminent art of the word—*epos*) is able not only to image within his poem the whole visible world, but also to teach the metal-worker how to do depictions.

A second ancient case is the one and only full-length pastoral novel of antiquity, *Daphnis and Chloe* (of uncertain date, perhaps third century A.D.). Longus claims to have written it after he had seen in a grove of the Nymphs "a most beautiful sight, a painted image." He so admired it that he was seized by a desire to write in response to the painting (*antigrapsai tēi grammēi*; the Greek words for a writing and a painting are conveniently the same—both are "graphic"). So, having searched out an interpreter, he wrote his four books of woodland romance, turning a tableau into a narrative.

A third, grander, case of iconic poetry is Dante's description of the three bas-reliefs in Purgatory showing scenes of humility (X); he calls them "visible speech" (95). Aside from their meaning-fraught iconography, the fact that iconic poetry is present exclusively in Purgatory is itself significant: Purgatory is a place of suspension, lacking present life, where all is past or future, burdensome memory or remote hope, and this is appropriately expressed in the description of static, stony images (De Sanctis in Hagstrum 1958).

Finally, there is a more modern poem, Keats's "Ode on a Grecian Urn" (1819, Vendler 1983), which is as canonical and yet as original an example of the iconic genre as one might hope to find. The urn combines elements from real marble vases, particularly the vase of Sosibios in the Louvre (which Keats had seen in drawings by Piranese), with the front-and-back pictorial composition of Attic pottery (Bowra 1950). The ode is an "*eikon*" in the Philostratan tradition. As if to reinforce his iconic intention, Keats adds an epigram: The urn, "a friend of man," at last utters five oracular words: "Beauty is truth, truth beauty" (Hagstrum 1958). An epigram is a metric inscription affixed to pictures, statues, or grave-monuments by way of breaking through their muteness, to make them effectively "speaking pictures." The epigrammatic tradition goes back to the Archaic period in Greece. Keats carries it on faithfully (Spitzer 1962), but he also adds a wonderful complication. In the outer stanzas of the ode, the whole urn, the whole *memento mori*, is addressed:

Thou still unravish'd bride of quietness [first stanza]
. . .
O Attic shape! Fair attitude! [last stanza]

until it finally responds in *propria persona* through its epigram. In the three inside stanzas, on the other hand, the urn itself recedes, to become the mere silent bearer of mute pictures that implacably rebuff the poet's wildly passionate questioning.

But although the reticent antique urn, that "Sylvan historian," depicts its silent scenes with classical clarity—the *enargeia* so valued in Thucydides— the poet himself reads into their bright stasis types of Romantic meaning. In the sprightly love-chase of the obverse he sees "forever" and "not yet" coalesce in the endless prolongation of ever-unconsummated love that furnishes the Romantics with so much dolorous bliss:

Bold lover, never, never canst thou kiss.

In the sacrifice of the reverse—the poet has been circling around the vase— he sees an invitation to breach the boundaries between art and life—the art of the vase and the life it is drawn from. He wanders, musing, off the picture into an invisible, ghostly little city with its forever-vacant acropolis. It is the city that the revellers and celebrants had left behind one morning several millennia ago for the chase and the altar in the woods, there to be caught in a static enchantment forever. Any romantic wanderer about an antique site, where the presences are palpable but the people very long gone, will recognize Keats's intimation: it wants but an infinitesimal extra effort of the imagination and the place will come back to life! Evidently the ancient ritual scene of the classical vase is also read Romantically: with a mournful pleasure in the enchantments of absence, and an artful insouciance about breaching the boundaries separating different imaginative domains.

Thus the *ut pictura poesis* tradition (with which Keats had opportunity to be acquainted—Vendler 1983, 305) has a complex Romantic culmination in this "iconic" ode. Here is a poem depicting the work of a stonecutter, which, in turn, displays scenes that, in their turn, refer the imagination to the world they image. The artifact is addressed by the poet and responds delphically, but not, as some think, vapidly (though, to be sure, not originally either; the association of truth and beauty could have come to Keats from Shaftesbury *via* Akenside's "Pleasures of the Imagination").

The urn's epigram is, in fact, one poet's answer to two questions raised above somewhat hesitantly and irresolutely (Part Three, Ch. III C), and so it at least confirms the validity of a preoccupation with them. Two years before the writing of the ode, on November 22, 1817, Keats had responded to Benjamin Bailey, intending to "end all your troubles as to that of your momentary start [that is, discomfiture] about the authenticity of the imag- ination" (Forman 1952). "What the imagination seizes as Beauty must be truth," he writes, "whether it existed before or not," for all the passions are "creative of essential Beauty." "The Imagination may be compared to

Adam's dream—he awoke and found it truth." The reference is to *Paradise Lost* where Adam imagines Eve:

Mine eyes he closed, but open left the cell
Of fancy, my internal sight; by which,
Abstract as in a trance, methought I saw,
Though sleeping, where I lay, and saw the Shape
Still glorious before whom awake I stood. . . . [VIII
460]

Thus the first proposition of the epigram, "Beauty is Truth," encapsulates Keats's long speculations on the question raised by me above in a logical context: What existence is associated with the images of the imagination? The answer is that passionate imagining itself bestows existence on its imaginations. Yet his answer is not quite consistent with another passage in the same letter where he intimates that the envisionings of the imagination must have prototypes, their "empyreal reflection." In this context a reasonable reading of the first member of the aphorism is nevertheless: "What is strongly enough before the imagination thereby exists."

The converse proposition, "Truth is beauty," is Keats's answer to another question raised above: Is meaning in visions or in thoughts? In the same letter, in the context of his "favorite speculation," Keats raises another version of this question, which was indeed his lifelong preoccupation (Vendler 1983): whether truth can possibly be reached by "consequitive reasoning." Is the way to truth through thought and philosophy or is it, as the poet is inclined to think, through the sensory imagination? The urn's dictum that truth is beauty states a concise answer that fits its iconic source: Here and beyond, truth is essentially in the immediacies of vision, not in words.

Thus the urn, consenting finally to break its silence and to seize the iconic occasion, answers pertinently the poet's storm of questions. The convertibility of beauty and truth, far from being mere phrase-making, forms a resting point in a passion of poetic speculation. The objects that the imagination "seizes" are thereby actual: moreover, what is ultimately actual is apprehended in visions. For the moment, comments the poet through his speaking vase, "that is all ye know on earth, and all ye need to know." The crown of Romantic artfulness is that this reflection emanates from the urn not in the form of a properly engraved, clear-speaking Greek distich, there for everyone to read in letters, but as an unspoken truth, not communicated by speech but conveyed by the urn's mere aspect—a truth nonetheless heard by us in epigrammatic English. What device could better render these

Romantic complexities than the iconic recursion—the poet's imaging of the urn's depiction of the stonecutter's vision?

★ ★ ★

Ut pictura poesis as accepted doctrine comes to an end when its enabling doctrine, the mimetic theory, ceases to drive either poetry or painting. Lessing's forceful early attack, not on mimesis itself but on the confusion of mimetic modes, is set out in (c). From the Romantic period onward a non-imitative theory of the imagination progressively takes over. For that painting should say something and poetry depict something—that is the condition of their mutuality as well as the crux of the representational mode. Now the sisters part; music comes forward as the preferred sibling of literature. The iconic literature of our century thus runs to music, as in the elaborate imagined compositions in Proust and Mann. What painters now peculiarly value in their painting is no longer its humanistic communicativeness, its silent poetry, but its silence, simply. Delacroix, for example confesses his "predeliction for the silent arts. . . . Words are indiscreet; they break in on your tranquility, solicit your attention, arouse discussion" (Abel 1980). Poets share this appreciation of the muteness of painting. Nemerov says: "Where the poet was lucky his poem will speak the silence of the painting; it too will say nothing more than: It is so, it is as it is" (1980). Language and visual imagining have deliberately drawn apart.

When Wallace Stevens tries to rediscover their connection in his essay "The Relations of Poetry and Painting" (1951), what comes to his mind is the imagination conceived in the widest sense as an agency that "always makes use of the familiar to produce the unfamiliar." It is a sensibility specific to artists across the arts, allied to a thoroughgoing humanism:

> Modern reality is a reality of decreation, in which our revelations are not the revelations of belief, but the precious portents of our own powers. The greatest truth we could hope to discover, in whatever field we discovered it, is that man's truth is the final resolution of everything. Poets and painters alike today make that assumption and this is what gives them the validity and serious dignity that become them as among those that seek wisdom, seek understanding.

Here the arts have ceased to be sisters, but now the artists are brothers.

Insofar then as modern art still has room for iconic writing, it is no longer intended to display the miraculous convertibility of words and vision, but designed artfully to confuse the representational frame (Steiner 1982). A prime example is the long meticulous description of a framed nineteenth-century tavern scene in Robbe-Grillet's novelette *In the Labyrinth*. A character writing in a hermetically sealed room invents an outside that he presents to himself as a kind of moving picture, and from which the picture described is one excerpted frame. In this description the framing story and the framed picture are so deliberately entangled, so rulelessly recursive, as to disorient the reader completely. This is not the romantic frisson Keats finds in wandering off the vase but a premeditated game of representational confusion intended to display the artist's "decreative" power: the power to obliterate the distinction between the object and its representation. But it must be observed that all this artful confusion is still ultimately parasitic since it depends on the stolidly natural representational cleavage between original and image.

c. Lessing's Criticism. Lessing's full-scale attack on *ut pictura poesis* is set out in the *Laocoon* (1766):

> The first man who compared poetry and painting was a man of refined feeling who sensed that a similar effect was exerted on himself by both arts. *Both*, he felt, *represent to us absent things as present, illusion as actual*, both deceive, and the deception of both is pleasing. . . . The brilliant antithesis that *painting is mute poetry and poetry speaking painting* was . . . a bright idea . . . whose true part is so evident that one feels obliged to overlook the indefinite and the false which it carries along.

For Lessing the falsity of the Simonidean antithesis taken as doctrine is that it confines poetry within the narrow limits of painting, and forces painting to fill the wide sphere of poetry. It induces in painting a rage for description and in poetry a mania for allegory. Properly practiced the two arts differ in their objects and in the manner of imitation. Both ought to be governed by the relation to time appropriate to each art. Painting represents the moment. It ought accordingly to choose for representation a situation that is pregnant but not transitory. Poetry is concerned with development. It must therefore choose to imitate that single sensual aspect of an object through which its functioning best appears.

Lessing argues that Homer—and by Homer his theory is to stand or fall—imitates only progressive action, and things only insofar as they have a role in it. His descriptive vocabulary is narrow, and each utensil is described only as its parts come to hand, as equipment. Be it chariot or armor, each is translated into a temporal sequence of uses.

What Lessing is proving in this brilliant analysis of Homer as the first existentialist (I am thinking of Heidegger's existential analysis, in which objects make their first appearance as "equipment") is that the poet hardly

ever *describes* the visible world because poetry is unsuited to such surveys.
Linear language is simply incapable of keeping pace with the instantaneous
eye, and its piecemeal operations cannot add up into a vision; in Lessing's
words: "*The coexistence of bodies* comes into collision with the *consecutiveness
of speech*" (*Laocoon*). Temporal sequence is the proper realm of the poet,
space that of the painter.

Yet I think Petrarch is right, and Homer remains the "first painter." For
Lessing it was probably a mistake, though a bold one, to choose an epic
poet as an example of his new doctrine. Lyric poetry sounds in the ear
before it turns into figures, oratory captures the spirit with large invisibili-
ties, tragedy can move the mind with the darkness of fate—but Homeric
epic is first and last for the eye. I have tried to show how: not by description,
which is the attempt to make language render the spatial continuum
through temporal accumulation, but through discreetly seeded indications
designed to provide the verbal poem with a counterpoint of visualization—
not mere accompanying illustrations but realizations of the text. The poet
speaks, the reader sees.

One might say: That applies to Homer—but to whom else? I answer that
this "verbal-indication" version of *ut pictura poesis* can be taken not only as
doctrine for the working poet but also as advice for the receptive reader.
Such advice, as I shall later argue, serves well wherever metaphor is at work
(Part Four, Ch. III). And where in literature is it not?

2. *"Spatial" Prose*. Lessing's doctrine has in turn met strong specific
opposition in this century. His sharp distinction between the arts of time
and space was in general not apt to be convincing once the moving and
then the talking picture had come on the scene. It is much harder now to
cite stasis and silence as the distinguishing mark of the visual arts. Moreover, popularization of the physical theory of relativity has propagated a
sort of science-flavored sense of the interdependence of space and time. It is
expressed, for example, in the prefatory note to *Balthazar*, the second book
of Lawrence Durrell's *Alexandria Quartet*:

> Modern literature offers us no Unities, so I have turned to science and am
> trying to complete a four-decker novel whose form is based on the relativity
> proposition.
> Three sides of space and one of time constitute the soup-mix recipe of a
> continuum. The four novels follow this pattern.

Durrell then goes on to say, however, that the first three parts are
developed only spatially, that they "interlap, interweave, in a purely spatial

relation." He is placing himself in a novelistic practice that rebuts more specifically Lessing's thesis that literature is essentially temporal.

The literary theory of "spatiality" was originally formulated by Frank (1945) as an account of the temporal—or atemporal—mode of modernist literature such as the poetry of Pound and Eliot (Brooker and Bentley 1990) and particularly certain novels, above all *Ulysses* and *Remembrance of Things Past*. The narration in these novels is not linear. It cuts back and forth between different times and places. In Joyce's novel, whose sequences are, Frank says, so perturbed that it can "only be reread," this technique serves to build up a simultaneous layout of the lines of daily life in Dublin. In Proust's novel the notion of spatiality is meant to accommodate the timeless revelatory moments that punctuate the narrative (Part Six, Ch. III A).

By means of techniques like the "fragmentation" of the action, the "juxtaposition" of events without temporal transition, and the "reflexive reference" back and forth within the text, a "secondary illusion" of "spatiality" is derived from the primary linguistic text: The reader is invited to build up a space from temporally discrete references (Gullón 1975). Frank's theory of spatiality in literature, which has proven applicable far beyond the "modernist" school, is not intended as a revival of the *ut pictura poesis* doctrine, for it includes no notion of a simultaneous verbal and visual imitation of nature. The literature he particularly analyzes is not so much "representational" of a given order as "generative" of its own, which develops in the course of the work. Consequently, as these insights were elaborated into a grand theory of modern literature, this question came to the fore: If the "spatiality" of the novel is not representationally depictive, is it to be taken literally or metaphorically? (Mitchell 1980).

There is, of course, a real, physically spatial element common to all literature, the written or printed text. A work has as many physical existences as there are copies. Because our alphabet is now conventional and its ideographic roots have been forgotten, we commonly read right through the visible, typographic presentation (Richards 1924), whereas texts written in pictographic, ideographic, or hieroglyphic, that is, in more or less natural signs, are really *seen* first. Here the lettering itself greets the eye with meaning and ushers the reader into the text. Such writing tends to be physically beautiful. For example, on Lafcadio Hearn's first day in Japan in 1890, he was simply enchanted by a cityscape festooned with calligraphic visible speech (*Glimpses of Unfamiliar Japan* 1894). Our unconsciousness of visible print is, of course, largely responsible for the fact that to us literature comes disembodied, as it were, comes neither through ear nor eye. The monastic scriptoria once defended themselves against printing partly on the grounds that the letters of scripture should be beautifully illuminated

(N. Brann 1979). I must mention here that fringe phenomenon of literal spatialization, the "concrete" or pattern poem, laid out in the shape, say of a snake, like the Mouse's long, sad tail-tale in *Alice in Wonderland*.

Whether its effect is for better or for worse, the importance of the literally spatial text is not to be overestimated (Frank 1977). On the one hand its physical existence corrupts memory: who now could match Homer's feat of oral composition in carrying cues, lines of action, and references over a hundred thousand lines? On the other hand, the physical spatiality of the text permits prodigies of novelistic complexity, such as require of the reader continual reprise, back-reference, and reconstruction. In sum, the imaginal web of the immense modern novel is unthinkable without attachment to a physical location in a text. Is it not the case that the great scenes of a novel are somehow also set for us in a region of the physical book?

But not only signs and indices in texts are spatially disposed. The whole event-structure of a literary work, not for nothing denominated by a surveyor's term, "plot," often makes a concretely spatial appearance. Consequently the plotting of treatises, poems, and novels is often amenable to geometrical representation. It is, in fact, a staple of literary criticism. For example, the plot of that most symmetrically structured of books, Plato's *Republic*, is representable by the diameter through a set of concentric circles: At the measured center stands Socrates's strange assertion that a just city will never come to be until philosophers become kings; around it, as waves moving to the periphery, are the symmetrical accounts of the coming to be and the passing away of the just city, with balancing disquisitions on the dangers of the mimetic arts and encircling myths about the rewards of justice (Brann 1967). A not unusual example of lyrical plotting is the Keats ode discussed above. One can find its Romantic crux in the geometric center by applying a ruler:

More happy love! more happy, happy love!
For ever warm and still to be enjoy'd . . .

But above all, physical plot structure is found in novels. Sometimes it may even take architectural form. For example, Kestner (1978) shows that the six books of *Jude the Obscure* act as a quasi-spatial re-creation of the sexpartite structuring of early Gothic cathedrals, inspired by the fact that the Classicists of Hardy's time called Gothicizing architects "obscurantist." Jude himself is, of course, enmeshed in Gothic affinities.

The non-physical spatiality of large works of prose, however, naturally raises deeper questions about more facets (Mitchell 1980). One of these, the descriptive inducing of visualization in epic poetry, was discussed above.

But of course the fulfillment of the text through visualization is equally required by novels; thus Conrad says that it is his aim "to make you *see.*" In fact novelistic envisioning can be used for purposes similar to those of the epic. It is part of the visualizable tension in the Ithacan scenes of the *Odyssey* before his return that Odysseus has dropped out of sight, that he has been invisible for ten years. So also a visibly invisible figure informs the atmosphere of the best English novel of the middle of our century, Paul Scott's *Raj Quartet*: The instigator of the action, the anglified Indian Hari Kumar, disappears from sight early in the story to reappear only once under the strong light of an interrogation-room in prison, as seen by a hidden observer. By the end he is a ghost, a boundlessly nostalgic, nameless voice, writing poignant essays for the *Rampur Gazette* signed "Philoctetes," the shunned hero with the malodorously incurable wound. In both the epic and the novel it is the invisible shade that puts in relief the events of the visible scene, be it Ithaca or Rampur (Brann 1989).

Another interesting facet of literary visualization is that there are perspectival possibilities similar to those in painting (Stanzel 1984). The description may be all-seeing, as in pictures with composite perspective, or it may be done from a point of view, that of a first-person observer or of a participant in the action. Yet novelistic description also permits a sort of a–perspectival viewing hard to achieve in a picture. For it follows from the indeterminacy of language that people and objects need not be definitely scaled (or located), a fact which gives their images a dreamlike elusiveness. An example is the narrating heroine, Miss M., of De la Mare's *Memoirs of a Midget*, a person of large pathos and small stature whose actual size may approximate anything from Thumbelina to child; like a discreetly hidden defect, the most prying perusal of her self-revelation does not disclose it. And to pass from pathos to drollery, I defy anyone to fix the absolute size of the animals of *Wind in the Willows*. Such conditions are visually realizable because imaginative space, too, has a certain inherent scalelessness, about which more will be said later (Part Five, Ch. II A).

A last facet of literary spatiality distinguished by critics is the "meaning of the whole," a whole that, though apprehended through vision and plot, is somehow separable from them. It is as hard to deny as it is to understand: we experience even essentially temporal works through a kind of insight that is both visually panoramic and temporally telescoped. Mozart wrote of seeing his compositions in this way (Part Two, Ch. V A).

Yet a caveat is in order, for it is surely not the case that whatever casts loose from time is therefore spatial, or that just by scrambling time-sequences one can effect spatiality. So while techniques of visualization and of structured plotting have some real or virtual relation to space, much of what is called "spatialization" in literary criticism (Smitten 1981) has very little to do with space and a lot with confounding time. In terms borrowed from Saussurian linguistics, such literature is synchronic rather than diachronic.

But synchronicity is always a somewhat eccentric mode for novels. The three usual modes of novelistic report are all diachronic, though in different ways: Narration reports occurrences in a reading-time which may be considerably less than the time of the real event would be. Dialogue is read in a time somewhat closer to that of real speech. Description usually requires more time to take in than does the scanning of a real scene (Rabkin 1977). These observations, implying that spatiality in the critical sense is a forced novelistic mode since all reading is temporal, lead to a critical battle.

It turns out that the "spatial" current of criticism, *pro* and *con*, has a fierce political undertow. Although its analyses have some bearing on literature of all periods, it is, as has been said, particularly concerned with works of the Modernist school, Proust, Pound, Joyce, Eliot. These writers were rebelling against the time-ridden notions of physical determinism, biological evolution, and social progress in favor of timeless, mythical, ahistorical modes. Consequently their spatializing techniques invited attack: they were accused of being antihistorical to the point of obscurantism and they were unmasked as being conservative to the point of reaction (Curtis 1981, Frank 1977).

While evading the question insofar as it involves actual politics, I think it only candid to admit that a temperamental leaning toward the spatial aspects of literature, toward a panoramic visual contemplation in preference to an essentially temporal narrative development, does betoken a sort of pre-political conservatism, conservatism in the literal sense, a liking for the timeless looks of things. This involvement of an imaginative mode with a specific political perspective is a small exemplification of the concluding claim of this book, that the imaginative life *per se* has not only a strong intrinsic nature but also definite consequences in the world of action.

C. Speaking and Imagining: Unobvious Obverses

So far in this chapter I have been concerned with literary imagining as it has specifically to do with envisioning, be it of the figures or the structure of a text. The objection will be raised that the "literary imagination" has other, more peculiarly literary functions, particularly the narration of events and the development of the inner characteristics of people, places, and objects. I readily grant that all these are the business of the imagination in the wide sense. My project in this book is, however, to attend to the imagination in its root-sense, as visual imitation. That is why the power of verbal imagining to imitate, within its limits, the visual world, real or imaginary, is here the center of attention.

That there is such a power, that words are closely and fittingly associated with real and fictive visions, seems to be a belief unquenchable in most human breasts. Yet it is ultimately unprovable, a mere belief, full of difficulties. Here finally must be broached a question, ticklish and deep, that goes somewhat beyond literary criticism: What explanatory grounding is there for this mutual translatability of words and visions?

I must first mention the approach taken in the extensive debate carried on in cognitive psychology about the ultimate reducibility of images to words (Part Two, Ch. II). The fact that the most successful imagery-theories are computational suggests that just as in computer programs the encoding of imagery takes the form of lists of propositions like "in square 1, put a dot" (or functions that are summaries of such lists), so human mental images are ultimately manipulated and stored in a word-like mode (Kosslyn 1980). Now no one is claiming that people can consciously generate extensive analogue representations by filling in a mental matrix from verbal instructions. One could study the coordinate description of all the data making up a newspaper picture forever without having the faintest notion what it depicted. If such translations do take place, they occur at a level far below consciousness, a level about which little is known; the study of the brain functions mediating the relation of verbal and imaginal abilities has few fixed findings. In any case, what is meant by "description" in the cognitive imagery-context is called verbal only by courtesy. It is really an arithmetization of space rather than the verbalization of vision, a mathematical, not a literary description.

Second is the oldest and most naive solution: Names are copies (*mimē-mata*) of things. Certain words can instigate mental images because they themselves are images, natural signs quite like portraits. This theory, set out in Plato's dialogue *Cratylos*, is there expounded only to be driven into absurdity: There are only two ways words can be literally images: either as sound portraits, by a sort of universal onomatopoeia (434), or figuratively, by mirroring in their etymologies the nature of things (437). Of course, neither theory is long tenable (Part Three, Ch. I B).

Third, Russell once held a very pointed version of the Lockean theory that the meanings of words are ideas: The meaning of a word is its associated mental image, and the meaning of a proposition is a complex of images. This is a theory spanning logic and psychology, for meaning, according to Russell, is a psychological problem. His essay "On Propositions: What

They are and How They Mean" (1919) was written in opposition to Watsonian behaviorism, which denies that there is any mental intermediary between speech and response (Part Two, Ch. II C). He points out that words function in the absence of objects and bring us in touch with what is remote in time and place precisely through calling up memory-images or by creating imagination-images that often affect us like the objects themselves. Thus words are counters which "mean" images, and images in turn mean objects. These meant objects are either specific individuals or they are universals, taken as the collection of all the individuals resembling the image. Further, just as propositions are complexes of words, so their meant counterparts are complexes of images.

The notion that the meaning of a word is an image is vulnerable to several objections, all of which are answerable. At the outset it must be granted that the notion is stated too inclusively: Not all words have associated images to begin with. For example, in the *Foundations of Arithmetic*, which Russell knew, Frege had argued that names of numbers are essentially unimageable. Nor are the imagistic intermediaries always in play when words are efficiently used, as experiments and introspection amply show. Next is the argument that this theory in fact makes meanings "psychological"—private and untrustworthy; Frege had made this point also. Russell replies that "private" can only mean "not localizable" in real space. There are, he argues, many things of great importance to us, such as feelings and sensations, that are in various degrees unlocalizable and that we do not and should not therefore mistrust. Yet another objection is raised by Ayer (List 1981): The theory induces an infinite regress insofar as the meaning of the word-symbol is fixed by the interpretation of the image-symbol and for the symbol in turn by a word-interpretation, and so on. This objection is answered by Russell's view of images as natural signs: They are not symbols themselves in need of interpretation, but they have meaning straight off and self-evidently, a possibility I shall defend in the next part. So far it seems to me that if meaning is understood as the psychological correlate to speech, then mental images fill part of the bill, because they are, in fact, aroused by words.

There remains a much-debated question which is particularly fascinating in a literary setting: How is the match possible? How can a word exercise the captivating power of semi-specificity, of pointing to a kind while conjuring up an individual? How does a word elect its image and how does an image attract its word? "How," in this context, requests not the nature of their interaction—if that is the right term; it does not ask for the mechanism by which they call each other up, and indeed, such causal relations are as yet a near-total mystery to us. It asks instead for the conditions and circumstances of their bonding.

The standard difficulty in explaining these circumstances is that nouns other than proper names are generic while images are particulars: How can any mountain-image render the generic meaning "mountain?" The response is, first, that images too can be to a degree generic, "universal particulars," schemata that take advantage of an apparent weakness possessed by cursory and schematic images, their pictorial indeterminacy, to incorporate in a non-particular way the specific features of a class. Or one might argue that the psychological, as opposed to logical, meaning induces a sort of instantiating or illustrating intention best realized in pictures. Second, one might counter the generic/particular objection by the argument that it is *too* powerful, since along with the word/image connection it does away with the word/object relation. Real objects are, after all, even more thoroughgoingly particular than images—and yet one names them with generic words (Paivio 1971, 62).

While the objection to the word/image bond may be answerable, the objection to the notion of image-propositions is not. Aristotle, in the very passage broaching the traditional idea that thought requires images understood as matterless sensation, insists that there is an irreducible difference between images and propositions: Images, unlike thoughts, do not assert or deny (*On the Soul* 432). It is for this Aristotelian reason that there can be no "Iconic English": Even if "words resemble what they refer to, . . . sentences don't resemble what makes them true" (Fodor 1981). Put another way, facts and states of affairs as such do not look like anything and cannot be imaged. Hence images make determinable assertions only insofar as they are "under description." A disarming example is to be found on the first page of *The Little Prince*. Saint Exupéry shows a drawing he had made as a little boy. It was construed by ever-obtuse grown-ups as a sideways view of a fedora, though far from being a view of a man's hat with a brim, it was, as a matter of fact, the image of a boa constrictor digesting an elephant. In any case, the deep logical divide between words compounded into intending propositional assertions and figures composed in extended pictorial displays has already been treated in the preceding part (Part Three, Ch. I B).

Fourth, spanning logic and aesthetics, Goodman (1976) proposes a "semantic" theory for bringing words and pictures together. It assimilates depiction to descriptions (or vice versa) by making them both denotational symbols—labels—of objects, whose meaning is contextual and conventional. The residual difference between these meanings is merely this: Descriptions are discrete and pictures are continuous. This understanding makes possible a simple parallelism between the language of words and the all-but-language of pictures. But there is a price to be paid: the "iconoclastic" reduction of pictures to symbol-systems. In the next part I attempt to show that this reduction does not do justice to pictorial experience (Ch. III).

If these explanations do not exhaust the enigmatic power of word and image to invoke each other, it is because they are only subtheories of the vast inquiry concerning the mutual engagement of language and perception. The present particular problem has a false air of solubility because words and images, as distinct from externally extended objects, are equally mental. However, it has been the thesis of this exposition that mental images must also be regarded as quasi-sensory and quasi-spatial. Therefore the common suspension of both words and images in the mental medium solves nothing at all. The relation of the image-obverse of the poetic coin to its word-reverse remains unobvious: we simply have not found the one blank on which both faces can be struck—the concrete relation holding word and image together.

Bibliography

Abel, Elizabeth. 1980. "Redefining the Sister Arts: Baudelaire's Response to the Art of Delacroix." In *The Language of Images*, edited by W.J.T. Mitchell. Chicago: The University of Chicago Press.

Ahsen, Akhter. 1982. "Principles of Imagery in Art and Literature." *Journal of Mental Imagery* 6:213–250.

Arnheim, Rudolf. 1970. "Words in Their Place." *Journal of Typographic Research* 4:199–212.

Auerbach, Erich. 1946. "Odysseus' Scar." Chapter 1 in *Mimesis: The Representation of Reality in Western Literature*. Garden City, N.Y.: Doubleday (1957).

Bowra, C. M. 1950. *The Romantic Imagination*. Oxford: Oxford University Press (1980).

Brann, Eva. 1967. "The Music of the Republic." *AGON: Journal of Classical Studies* 1:1–117. [Reprinted in *The St. John's Review* (1989–90) 39: 1–104.]

———. 1974. "The Poet of the Odyssey." *The St. John's Review* 25:5–12.

———. 1989. "The English *War and Peace*: Paul Scott's *Raj Quartet*." *The St. John's Review* 38:75–87.

Brann, Noel L. 1979. "A Monastic Dilemma Posed by the Invention of Printing." *Visible Language* 13:150–167.

Brooker, Jewel Spears, and Bentley, Joseph. 1990. "A Wilderness of Mirrors: Perspectives on the Twentieth Century." Chapter 1 in *Reading the Waste Land:*

Modernism and the Limits of Interpretation. Amherst: The University of Massachusetts Press.

Carrier, David. 1973. "Three Kinds of Imagination." *The Journal of Philosophy* 70:819–831.

Carroll, Thomas J. 1961. *Blindness: What It Is, What It Does, and How to Live with It.* Boston: Little, Brown and Co.

Croce, Benedetto. 1901. *Aesthetic: A Science of Expression and General Linguistic.* Translated by Douglas Ainslie. New York: The Noonday Press (1958).

Curtis, James M. 1981. "Spatial Form in the Context of Modernist Aesthetics." In *Spatial Form in Narrative*, edited by Jeffrey Smitten. Ithaca: Cornell University Press.

Curtius, Ernst Robert. 1948. *Europäische Literatur und lateinisches Mittelalter.* Bern: Francke Verlag.

Derrida, Jacques. 1981. *Dissemination.* Translated by Barbara Johnson. Chicago: The University of Chicago Press.

Edel, Leon. 1953. *Henry James: The Untried Years 1843–1870.* Philadelphia: Lippincott.

Else, Gerald F. 1957. *Aristotle's Poetics: The Argument.* Cambridge: Harvard University Press.

Feagin, Susan L. 1984. "Some Pleasures of the Imagination." *The Journal of Aesthetics and Art Criticism* 43:41–55.

Fodor, Jerry A. 1981. "Imagistic Representation." In *Imagery*, edited by Ned Block. Cambridge: The MIT Press.

Forman, Maurice B. 1952. *The Letters of John Keats.* London: Oxford University Press.

Frank, Joseph. 1945. "Spatial Form in Modern Literature." In *The Widening Gyre: Crisis and Mastery in Modern Literature.* New Brunswick: Rutgers University Press (1963).

———. 1977. "Spatial Form: Thirty Years After." In *Spatial Form in Narrative*, edited by Jeffrey Smitten. Ithaca: Cornell University Press.

Frege, Gottlob. 1884. *The Foundations of Arithmetic* (paras. 59–60). Translated by J. L. Austin. Oxford: Basil Blackwell (1953).

Gadamer, Hans-Georg. 1965. *Truth and Method*, 2d. ed. Translated by Garrett Barden and John Cumming. New York: Seabury (1976).

Gardner, Howard. 1985. *Frames of Mind: The Theory of Multiple Intelligences.* New York: Basic Books.

Goodman, Nelson. 1976. *Languages of Art: An Approach to a Theory of Symbols.* Indianapolis: Hackett Publishing Co.

Gullón, Ricardo. 1975. "On Space in the Novel." *Critical Inquiry* 2:11–28.

Hagstrum, Jean H. 1958. *The Sister Arts: The Tradition of Literary Pictorialism and English Poetry from Dryden to Gray*. Chicago: The University of Chicago Press.

Hartog, François. 1988. *The Mirror of Herodotus: Representation of the Other in the Writing of History*. Berkeley: The University of California Press.

Horace [late first century BC]. *Art of Poetry*.

Johnson-Laird, P. N. 1983. *Mental Models*. Cambridge: Harvard University Press.

Kestner, Joseph A. 1978. *The Spatiality of the Novel*. Detroit: Wayne State University Press.

Kosslyn, Stephen M. 1980. *Image and Mind*. Cambridge: Harvard University Press.

Langer, Susanne K. 1942. *Philosophy in a New Key: A Study in the Symbolism of Reason, Rite, and Art*. Cambridge: Harvard University Press (1978).

Lee, Rensselaer W. 1940. "Ut Pictura Poesis: The Humanistic Theory of Painting." *The Art Bulletin* 22:197–269.

Lessing, Gotthold Ephraim. 1766. *Laocoon, or the Limits of Painting and Poetry*.

List, Charles J. 1981. "Images, Propositions, and Natural Signs." In *Imagery: Concepts, Results, and Applications*, edited by Eric Klinger. New York: Plenum Press.

Lonergan, Bernard J. F. 1958. *Insight: A Study in Human Understanding*. New York: Harper and Row (1978).

Lowell, James Russell. 1855. "The Imagination." In *The Function of the Poet and Other Essays*, edited by Albert Mordell. New York: Houghton Mifflin Co. (1920).

Massey, Irving. 1980. "Words and Images: Harmony and Dissonance." *Georgia Review* 34:375 ff.

Mitchell, W.J.T. 1980. "Spatial Form in Literature: Toward a General Theory." In *The Language of Images*, edited by W.J.T. Mitchell. Chicago: The University of Chicago Press (1980).

Nabokov, Vladimir [c. 1940]. *Lectures on Literature*, edited by Fredson Bowers. New York: Harcourt Brace Jovanovich (1980).

Nemerov, Howard. 1980. "On Poetry and Painting, With a Thought of Music." In *The Language of Images*, edited by W.J.T. Mitchell. Chicago: The University of Chicago Press (1980).

Ortega y Gasset, José. 1946. "Reviving the Paintings." In *Phenomenology and Art*. New York: W.W. Norton (1975).

Paivio, Allan. 1971. *Imagery and Verbal Processes*. New York: Holt, Rinehart and Winston.

Panofsky, Erwin. 1937. "Style and Medium in the Moving Pictures." *Transition* 26:121–133.

Pound, Ezra. 1934. *The ABC of Reading* (chapter 8). London: Faber and Faber (1961).

Praz, Mario. 1970. *Mnemosyne: The Parallel Between Literature and the Visual Arts.* Bollingen Series XXXV, 16. Princeton: Princeton University Press (1974).

Rabkin, Eric S. 1977. "Spatial Form and Plot." In *Spatial Form in Narrative*, edited by Jeffrey Smitten. Ithaca: Cornell University Press.

Richards, I. A. 1924. *Principles of Literary Criticism.* London: Routledge and Kegan Paul (1963).

―――. 1936. *The Philosophy of Rhetoric.* New York: Oxford University Press (1965).

Russell, Bertrand. 1919. "On Propositions: What They Are and How They Mean." In *Logic and Knowledge*, edited by Robert C. Marsh. London: George Allen and Unwin (1956).

Santayana, George. 1896. *The Sense of Beauty, Being the Outline of Aesthetic Theory.* New York: Dover (1955).

Schopenhauer, Arthur. 1819. *The World as Will and Representation.*

Smitten, Jeffrey, ed. 1981. *Spatial Form in Narrative.* Ithaca: Cornell University Press.

Sontag, Susan. 1977. *On Photography.* New York: Farrar, Straus and Giroux.

Spitzer, Leo. 1962. "The 'Ode on a Grecian Urn,' or Content vs. Metagrammar." Chapter 5 in *Essays on English and American Literature.* Princeton: Princeton University Press.

Stanzel, F. K. 1984. *A Theory of Narrative.* Translated by Charlotte Goedsche. Cambridge: Cambridge University Press.

Steiner, Wendy. 1982. *The Colors of Rhetoric: Problems in the Relations of Modern Literature and Painting.* Chicago: The University of Chicago Press.

Trimpi, Wesley. 1983. *Muses of One Mind: The Literary Analysis of Experience and Its Continuity.* Princeton: Princeton University Press.

Vendler, Helen. 1983. *The Odes of John Keats.* Cambridge: Harvard University Press.

Chapter II

Literary Creation: Imagining Apotheosized

Whereas in the last chapter the preoccupation was with an old and comprehensive enigma, the mutuality of verbal and visual imagining, now a more modern and more pointedly literary problem is to be taken up: the arrogation to the poetic imagination of the power of quasi-divine creation. This potentiation of the imagination is the work particularly of the Romantic poets. In his great Romantic manifesto, "A Defense of Poetry" (1821), Shelley says: "Poetry, in a general sense, may be defined to be 'the experience of the imagination.' " To us this coupling of poetry with the imagining power comes so fluently that it seems aboriginal, as does, in turn, the linkage of the imagination with the Romantics. To our ears the phrase "Romantic Imagination" is almost a redundancy.

It is certainly the case that the imagination, the *vis abscondita* of philosophy, comes into its own in this association, which, far from being hoary, is in fact modern. The first task of this chapter will therefore be to trace briefly how imagination and poetry came to be conjoined at all (A). Then the center and the extremes of Romantic theory concerning the poetic imagination will be sketched (B). There follows a consideration of the Romantic aftermath in the theory of the novel (C). And finally, a cursory critique of Romanticism will be set out, a brief expression of the misgivings which cannot help but inform this chapter (D): T.S. Eliot diagnosed the main disease of Romanticism as the disrelation of subject and object. The Romantic imagination is, of course, the particular locus of this disorder.

A. The Slow Conjoining of Poetry and Imagination

To show that the poetic activity and the imaginative faculty were by no means conjoined *ab ovo* but that their coupling is in fact significantly

495

modern, I shall summarize the testimony briefly—more briefly than it deserves.

In Aristotle's *Poetics* (c. 330 B.C.), which lurks somewhere behind all theory of poetry in pre-Romantic times, the well-conditioned poet is actually contrasted with those melancholy-mad people who tend to see strong visual imagery, *phantasmata* (*Poetics* 55 a, *On Memory* 453 a), a separation the modern interpreter finds hard to accept (Else 1957, 499). In Longinus's *On the Sublime* (c. 80 A.D.), the chief critical work of antiquity, the ability to make imaginative images (*phantasiai*) or image-poetry (*eidolo-poiia*) is still only one of five equal "fountains" of fine style. Longinus comments: "Imagination in the prevailing meaning is when in your enthu-siasm and feeling you seem to see what you speak of and put it before the sight of your listeners" (15); it is a poetic talent, but one of several.

In the middle ages, the imagination continues to be thought of as primarily a cognitive power for forming images. Although from a distance it looks as if "no medieval author mentions either phantasy or imagination as a characteristic of poets" (Lewis 1964), closer study shows that the *vis imaginativa* does play a role (Kelly 1978), especially in courtly poetry. The role is, however, fairly technical and it is under the influence of rhetoric: The courtly "trouvère" clearly "found" and did not create poetry. Chaucer, bred in this tradition, uses the vocabulary of rhetorical inventive skill in speaking of his powers of persuasive imagery:

Now harken well, because I will
Tell you of the proper skill
And a worthy demonstration
In my imagination. [*House of Fame* 725]

More generally, in medieval theory the imagination continues to occupy its ancient place between sense and intellect, and the process of poetry is geared to this scheme: "In the exercise of the poetic faculty, the image of the perception precedes, then follows the thinking out of the words and . . . the organization of the treatment ensues" (Matthew of Vendôme, in Kelly 1978). But the process may work in reverse, going from concept to percept. The grandest function of images is to make the invisible visible in an activity analogous to God's creation. The reason conceives a form; there ensues imagination "wherein the aforesaid form is impressed and por-trayed"; the execution follows (*Commentary on the Echecs amoureux*, in Kelly 1978). Through such *imagines* human beings come to know truths not accessible either to the sense or to mere reason, ideal prototypes and things of the spirit: "And so it is sweet to hold in memory by imagining what the intellect is not yet able to apprehend by reasoning" (Richard of St. Victor, *Benjamin Minor*). As long as the soul is united to the body, human understanding must be through images, according to the old philosophical tradition. As Thomas Aquinas says: "Incorporeal things of which there are not mental images [*phantasmata*] are known to us by comparison with sensible bodies of which there are mental images." The imagination here has no more and no less than the workaday dignity of being the necessary mediator in perceptual as well as spiritual cognition.

Traditional medieval school exercises provided training in "invention" and particularly in "description," namely "discourse which gathers together and presents to the eyes what it demonstrates" (Priscian, *Praeexercitamina*). The object of the training is the old *enargeia*, visual brilliance: "*Enargeia* is imagination which submits an action to the incorporeal eye and does it in three modes: person, place, time" (ibid.). It is an effect identical with that central to the last chapter.

This mediating function of the poetic imaging faculty by no means exalts poetry. When Langland makes "Ymaginatif," the *vis imaginativa*, appear in the shape of a man to the Dreamer in *Piers Plowman*, the dream shape tells him much worth knowing of "kynde and his konnygne"—of nature and its wisdom (Passus XIII 15). But he also warns the dreamer against meddling with "makynges"—with poetry—rather than saying his psalter (Passus XII 11, Minnis 1981).

In the Renaissance, the preoccupation shifts from mediating image to truthful imitation. Under the pretense of recovering Aristotle, there arise theories of a specifically poetic imagination. Boccaccio, in his book on poetry (1360s), says that poetry "proceeds from the bosom of God," that "it brings forth strange and unheard-of creations," and that it "veils the truth in a fair and fitting garment of fiction." Clearly, he regards the poet as a maker of new and revealing worlds. And later Sidney, though he still defines poetry as *mimēsis*, "a representing, counterfeiting, or figuring forth—to speak metaphorically, a speaking picture . . . ," places great emphasis on the Aristotelian notion that poetry improves on nature. He proudly assigns to the poet the office of giving

> right honour to the heavenly maker of that maker, who, having made man to his own likeness, set him beyond and over all the works of that second nature; which in nothing he showeth so much as in poetry, when with the force of a divine breath he bringeth things forth far surpassing her doings. [*The Defense of Poesie* 1583]

In tune with this spirit, that learned poet-critic of Plato, Torquato Tasso, shows that the poet is not an imitator of Plato's "phantastic" type, one who produces images of imaginary things, but rather an "eikastic" imitator of what is, was, and will be (Part Three, Ch. I A). For this is "the matter fit for poetry according to this requirement of verisimilitude." As an eikastic faculty in this sense the poetic imagination reveals intelligible being and is on a level with philosophy and theology (*Discourse on the Heroic Poem* 1592, Gilbert 1940).

Latent in these fair examples of Renaissance writing on poetry are two closely related issues that will inform, bedevil and finally explode the Romantic imagination: the creator function of the poet and the double aspect of poetic mimesis.

It is a humble Christian notion that "Our way is to become like God" (Augustine, *City of God* IX xvii), and that the being that was made in the image of a creator is appointed to make things in its turn. But that the poet in particular is the imitator of God to the point that his second creation might even surpass God's first—these are new notions, which march uneasily not only with Christian humility but with the mimetic understanding of poetry. The Renaissance poets and painters appear to be generally oblivious to this difficulty. (Even in the middle of the nineteenth century it is still more or less latent. In *Modern Painters* Ruskin wavers in a typical fashion between two mimetic possibilities: painting as copying "honestly and without alteration from nature" and painting as penetrating nature, "ignoring all shackles and fetters of mere external fact"—Sprinker 1979).

In his "Description of the Intellectual Globe" (c. 1612), originally designed to become part of the *Great Instauration*, Bacon divides all human and divine learning according to the three faculties of the mind, assigning history to memory, poesy to the imagination, and philosophy to reason. Since history is concerned with individual facts, the "first and most ancient guests of the human mind" and the primary material of knowledge, poesy "is feigned history." While in philosophy the mind compounds and divides actual things according to their true parts by finding similarities and differences, in poesy it arbitrarily transposes, joins, and separates individuals into imaginary beings; poetry is the "sport" of the mind. This decided identification of poetry with the imagination at the beginning of modern times reaches influentially into the Enlightenment: In d'Alembert's "Preliminary Discourse" (1751) to Diderot's great *Encyclopedia* it is specifically incorporated into the organizational principle of that work.

To lay the complete foundation for the Romantic take-over of the imagination by poetry one more condition is needed: a new assignment of function to the imagination in philosophy. Shelley announces it:

Reason is the enumeration of quantities already known; imagination is the perception of the value of those quantities both separately and as a whole.

Reason respects the differences, and imagination the similitudes of things. Reason is to the imagination as the instrument to the agent, as the body to the spirit, as the shadow to the substance. ["A Defense of Poetry" 1821]

What has made it possible for the poetic imagination, so long defensive in the face of reason, to turn triumphant aggressor?

Locke's new theory of knowledge made the beginning, since in it ideas are nothing but images; the presentations of an image-entertaining mind have displaced the ideal forms of the intellect. Since the mind's only material comes from sense experience, there is no need of a faculty for bringing supersensibles before the mind's eye. The operations of reason are narrowly instrumental. There is little room in this imaging reason for a non-utilitarian function, whether it be spiritual edification or pleasurable play (Part One, Ch. III B).

The momentous consequence is a dissociation of the sensibility or aesthetic imagination from Lockean reason. Its agent was Addison, in his "Pleasures of the Imagination," published in the *Spectator* during June and July 1712 (Addison 1712). These six essays, written in the exemplary "demure" style, slide by all too easily in their apparent innocuousness. In fact they are revolutionary. Under the guise of formulating common opinions they turn them upside down.

Addison's title announces a new idea: It introduces a pleasure that is neither merely sensual nor in the service of reason and truth—what we now call an "aesthetic" pleasure. It is a pleasure "not so gross as those of sense, nor so refined as those of the understanding," yet fully as "transporting" as those: "A description in Homer has charmed more readers than a chapter in Aristotle." Yet, like philosophy, it is a contemplative pleasure:

> A man of polite imagination is let into a great many pleasures, that the vulgar are not capable of receiving. He can converse with a picture, and find an agreeable companion in a statue. He meets with a secret refreshment in a description [to which June 30 is devoted], and often feels a greater satisfaction in the prospect of fields and meadows, than another does in their possession. [June 12]

The imaginative pleasures themselves are differentiated into two kinds. The primary ones proceed from contemplating objects directly before our eyes. The secondary pleasures flow from the ideas of visible objects when those objects themselves are absent but are called up in memory and formed into "agreeable visions." The primary/secondary distinction will play a major role in the Romantic theory of the imagination.

The pleasures of vision proceed from the sight of what is great, novel, and beautiful. One might say of these three Addisonian terms that they encompass the temporal succession of esthetic interests: Beauty is the preoccupation of antiquity, novelty is going to be the obsession of modernity, but in Addison's own day sublimity in nature, the "rude magnificence" of its "stupendous works," had captured the imagination. The sublime marked out a new worship, in which the pleasurable amazement of the imagination in the face of natural grandeur takes the place both of spiritual absorption in God and of rational speculation on eternity; religious feeling, no longer intent on overcoming time, now invests space. The essay entitled "Divine Philosophy" (June 2) says nothing at all about God, but engages in a cheerful English version of a Pascalian meditation on the human spatial sensibility in the face of telescopic expansion and microscopic diminution: To a certain extent, these extremes please, but the human imagination has strict limits—which Addison, remarkably, already connects with its physiological basis. Beyond these limits it ceases to function (Part Six, Ch. III A).

(Tuveson 1960.)

A generation later Mark Akenside (1744) wrote a versified "Pleasures of the Imagination," borrowing largely from Addison. Akenside, like Addison, uses the terms fancy and imagination interchangeably, but he tries harder to define their nature and function. The imagination is now a collection of powers located not, as in the tradition, between sense and reason, but between veridical sense and "moral perception." It has this particular intermediary position because of the place Akenside, echoing Shaftesbury and prefiguring Kant, gives its province, beauty:

> . . . Truth conspicuous with sister-twins,
> The undivided partners of her sway
> With Good and Beauty reigns. . .[I 415]

Fancy clothes Virtue, arising unadorned out of Truth, in charm and makes human hearts responsive to it. The imaginative powers themselves are analogous to those at work when the world was created from chaos; for them the heavens

> Disclose their splendour, and the dark abyss
> Pours out her birth unknown . . .[III 389]

They compare, blend, divide, enlarge, extenuate, oppose, and infinitely vary the "rising phantoms." These imaginative powers are "plastic powers"

(III 381), world-shaping powers. As beauty is their province, poetry is their chief representative.

Addison and Akenside set the stage for the Romantic imagination. The imagination is now independent of reason; it has its own "abysmal"— unconscious—source, its own separate, aesthetic feeling, to which novelty is a necessary stimulant. Nature is spiritualized, while the imagination itself engages in creation, especially as it expresses itself in poetry.

In the course of the eighteenth century, the endemic activity of the Enlightenment, namely "criticism," resulted in numerous critical or analytical treatments of the imaginative faculty. Dr. Johnson emphasizes the appetitive element, the "hunger of the imagination" (*Rasselas* 1759), which makes it more concerned with what is "before or behind us" than with what is present. Hume initiates the analysis of the imagination in associationist terms, which are applied not only to the psychological workings of the imagination but also to the interpretation of clusters of imagery in poetry. The notion of genius as the offspring of an imagination that now encompasses both judgment and passion comes clearly on the scene in Gerard's *Essay on Genius* (1774). Sympathy, including what we call empathy, is here brought forward as a characteristic of imagination that serves to heighten sensibility. It supplies the condition for a new mimesis, the imitation of the inner character of human beings, of their natural passions, and even of the spirit of inanimate nature. Hazlitt sums up: "Imagination is another name for our interest in things out of ourselves" (1805).
(Engell 1981.)

B. The Romantic Imagination: Poetry

Romanticism is the most peculiarly fascinating mode of the Western tradition, both as an ever-present possibility and as a historical movement, as a universal human mode and as a particular reaction to the shadeless rationality of the Enlightenment. The features of Romanticism, insofar as they bear on the imagination and indeed circumscribe it as the Romantic faculty *par excellence*, have just been delineated. To occupy these Romantic faculties, there are, of course, also specifically Romantic topics. One such topic is nostalgia (Part Six, Ch. II C), which is expressed in a preference for the medieval past over a timeless classicism. Another topic is the association of love and death. But on the vast subject of the Romantic rubrics it is not necessary to enter here (Ch. I B). The issue now is the peculiar role of the Romantic imagination in poetry, its most articulate realization.

The center in English theorizing about the Romantic imagination is held by the poet-friends Wordsworth and Coleridge (*1*). The extreme exaltation of the imagination will be represented by Blake and Stevens (*2*).

1. The Center: Wordsworth and Coleridge. William Wordsworth and Samuel Taylor Coleridge are the chief proponents of the Romantic poetic imagination, certainly in England. Wordsworth is central in the sense that in the intellectually self-conscious vision that informs his poetry, the endemic confusions of Romanticism—the paradoxes of subjectivity and the perturbed ordering of the mental faculties—are, for once, resolved. Coleridge is central in the sense that he propounds the most noticed Romantic theory of the imagination while composing unmistakably Romantic poetry which in some points directly contradicts it.

a. Wordsworth's understanding of the imagination is to be found in his poetry, which is, in fact, one long commentary on the poetic imagination. *The Prelude* (1805) is, so to speak, a biography of the imaginative faculty as exemplified in the autobiography of a poet:

> This faculty has been the feeding source
> Of our long labour . . . [XIV 193]

The elements of this faculty are briefly sketched out below.

Of the poet's particular imaginative nature Wordsworth speaks most succinctly in the "Preface to the Lyrical Ballads:"

> What is a Poet? . . . He is a man speaking to men: a man, it is true, endowed with more lively sensibility, more enthusiasm and tenderness, who has a greater knowledge of human nature, and a more comprehensive soul, than are supposed to be common among mankind; a man pleased with his own passions, and volitions, and who rejoices more than other men in the spirit of life that is in him; delighting to contemplate similar volitions and passions as manifested in the goings-on of the Universe, and habitually impelled to create them where he does not find them. To these qualities he has added a disposition to be affected more than any other men by absent things as if they were present; an ability of conjuring up in himself passions, which are indeed far from being the same as those produced by real events. . . . [1802 version, in Halsted 1969]

This view of a poet's imagination as being intensely his own, an individual gift, is, I think, the chief legacy of Romantic to modern poets and it peculiarly marks literary modernity as a Romantic aftermath. Stephen Spender, for example, in *The Struggle of the Modern* (1963), repeats an observation Wordsworth makes later on in the "Preface." Spender pits the poet's "personal and individual" knowledge against the scientist's impersonal universality. He only adds that in a time when "there is no such thing as a public imagination," no common faith or tradition, when poetry has no longer the faintest hope of legislating to mankind—as Shelley had proposed—"imagination means individuation." "Imagination is Personal": The occasion is modern but the response remains Romantic.

This personal poetic sensibility also has a special imaginative temporality, Wordsworth's much-cited "spots of time":

> There are in our existence spots of time,
> That with distinct pre-eminence retain
> A renovating virtue. [*The Prelude* XII 208]

Wordsworth recounts and analyzes epiphanic moments: "Such moments are / Scattered everywhere, taking their date from our first childhood" (223). They are instants when a scene is powerfully "invested" with feeling. In Wordsworth's experience the originating feeling is one of overwhelming "visionary dreariness." What gives it its delight is the revival; its glow is afterglow. It is an effect similar to the "tranquil restoration" of a landscape in a lonely room of which "Tintern Abbey" speaks, except that in the *Prelude* the poet returns to the place in body and in a happier mood:

> And think ye not with radiance more sublime
> For these remembrances and for the power
> They left behind? So feeling comes in aid
> Of feeling.

The poet in fact longs to "enshrine" the spirit of the past for future restoration,

> Those recollected hours that have the charms
> Of visionary things . . .

to which the song always returns. In sum, the filtering of moments through memory, creative nostalgia, is of the essence of this imaginative mode.

Ancient poetry, sculpture, and painting are full of visionary vignettes, which show that the poet, sculptor, and painter has had a sudden high moment. But these Romantic "spots" are different. Here the feeling-imbued moment itself has become the artist's theme. As Wordsworth observes, these instantaneities of the imagination belong particularly to childhood. Indeed there is a book about this genre of childhood experience with the apt title *Inglorious Wordsworths* (Part Two, Ch. IV C). In the twentieth century such special moments become a great preoccupation of novelists: Proust, Mann, Woolf, C.S. Lewis (Part Six, Ch. II C). In other words, the momentary imagination is no longer the peculiarity of poets, or for that matter of artists at all. It is a possibility of the imaginative life open to any mere, muse-less imaginer, a poignant human possibility. This lay mode will be considered in the Conclusion of this book.

Next, the Wordsworthian imagination has specific operations that must be taken up. This imagination is, to begin with, a power of mental imagery, of being affected by and of volitionally shaping "absent things as if they were present." While the ordinary experience with mental images is that they tend to fade when subjected to attention, the poet has had from childhood on the "precious gift" of receiving impressions

> with portraiture
> And colour so distinct that on his mind
> They lay like substances, and almost seemed
> To haunt the bodily sense.

This gift matures into "An *active* power to fasten images / Upon his brain," over whose "pictured lines" the poet can "Intensely brood even till they acquired / The liveliness of dreams." ["The Pedlar," 1798 version.] The haunting afterimage—Coleridge will call it the "distinct recollection, or . . . after-consciousness" (*Biographia Literaria*)—will play a major role in the modern Romantic tradition, and especially in Wallace Stevens's poetry (Bloom 1976).

The strength of the imagery stems from the depth of feeling with which it is imbued. (Of course, the absence of this affectivity is just what distinguishes laboratory imagery from poetic depiction.) Such emotional heightening causes the scenes and situations of life to be tinctured with "a certain coloring of the imagination, whereby ordinary things should be presented to the mind in an unusual aspect." This estrangement of the ordinary, the transformation of the familiar into the unfamiliar, an estrangement in which are combined the Romantic virtues of novelty and intensity, is reiterated as a central property of the poetic imagination by Shelley and later by Stevens.

To the subjectivity of the vision, the temporality of the moment, the vividness of the visualization, the affective alienation of the ordinary, must now be joined the alembic power of the imagination: "The imagination also shapes and *creates*; and how?" Wordsworth asks. For him this creative imagination is the conscious, willful "plastic power" through which the soul's imagery can follow its "promptings to put on / A visible shape" and "knowingly conform itself" to literary expression. The creative power works by a controlled distillation, intensification, and concentration, in sum, by a transformation of scenes and objects. Thus it is, strictly speaking, a "poietic" rather than a creative power, for it does not imagine out of nothing but makes its works out of given material.

These views are the coping stone of Wordsworth's imaginative constitution, and give his poetics stability. Romantic writers, as poets before them (A), tend, often unknowingly, to be caught up in a contradiction mentioned above, now called the "Romantic paradox." Concisely put, they imply at once that the poets see into nature, penetrating her familiar surface to gain insight into reality, and that they create a nature, onto which they project their own feelings (Brooks 1956). In other Romantics these doctrines are often incongruously combined, but Wordsworth has a theory—of course not argumentatively grounded, but nonetheless consistent—that obviates the paradox: Individual Mind is fitted exquisitely to external World, and the converse: "With blended might" they accomplish a creation. The ground for this fit is found in the philosophical idealism of which there are indications in Wordsworth's poetry. While the mature "plastic power" is "for the most / Subservient to external things / With which it communed" (II 366), these things have themselves been informed by the poet's feeling: "I gave them moral life, I saw them feel." What holds for the adult poet was already true of the child, who is an active inmate of this active universe by reason of his power of feeling, a power

> That through the growing faculties of sense
> Doth like an agent of the one great Mind
> Create, creator and receiver both,
> Working but in alliance with the works
> Which it beholds. [II 256]

It may well be that Wordsworth, through Coleridge, had been excited by the notion of a Kantian transcendental imagination that works underground and beforehand to shape nature (Warnock 1976). It is certain that as for Kant the imagination is not separate or opposed to reason but is reason in its sensuous employment, so it is for Wordsworth identified with reason as the intuitive power: Imagination

> Is but another name for absolute power
> And clearest insight, amplitude of mind
> And Reason in her most exalted mood. [XIV 190]

This absence of antagonism between imagination and reason is what distinguishes Wordsworth's reasonable Romanticism from that of the extremists—who were finally more influential.

b. Coleridge puts the seal of a much-quoted formulation on a long tradition distinguishing between the creative imagination and the lesser faculty of fancy:

> FANCY, on the contrary, has no other counters to play with, but fixities and definites. The Fancy is indeed no other than a mode of Memory emancipated from the order of time and space; while it is blended with, and modified by that empirical phenomenon of the will, which we express by the word *choice*. But equally with the ordinary memory, the Fancy must receive all its materials ready made from the law of association.

Fancy so defined seems to be the perfect instrument of an associationist poetics, of the sort that had been in fashion since the 1770s (Engell 1981). Coleridge means to distance himself from an associationist system he embraced as a student at Cambridge, and also to express a distinction between himself and Wordsworth, who attributes to the imagination operations similar to those Coleridge assigns to fancy. In fact, though, Coleridge's poetic practice seems to bear his friend out, for it is, according to Coleridge's own terms, fanciful rather than imaginative.

"Kubla Khan," for example, represents the type of a Romantic poem to the point of caricature: Magical and unmeaning, it imposes an impression of bottomless significance and escapes all efforts to discover any literal intelligibility.

Yet it is also inexhaustively interpretable, through associationist reference. Coleridge read widely, and, what is more, often pursued the references in his reading. The mysterious allusions and echoes in this poem—as in "The Rime of the Ancient Mariner"—are all traceable to remembered passages that have been connected and transformed by the "spontaneous chemistry of the mind," as one of the associationists, Thomas Brown, put it. Lowes (1927), in an enormous labor of literary detection, has recovered these associations by tracing Coleridge's reading. Here is the beginning of the poem:

In Xanadu did Kubla Khan
A stately pleasure-dome decree:
Where Alph, the sacred river, ran
Through caverns measureless to man
    Down to a sunless sea.

Coleridge himself published an account of its genesis with the poem. He was reading *Purchas His Pilgrimage* at the passage: "In Xamadu did Cublai Can build a stately Palace." The palace was set in an enclosure within which were "delightfull Streames . . . and in the middest thereof a sumptuous house of pleasure." While reading he fell into a deep sleep of three hours. During these hours, he reports, "he could not have composed less than from two to three hundred lines; if that indeed can be called composition in which all the images rose up before him as *things*, with a parallel production of the corresponding expressions, without any sensation or consciousness of effort" (in Lowes 1927, 356). On being awoken he was detained on business for an hour and found that all but ten or so lines had gone, though he retained the vague purport of the vision. The poem had to be deliberately reconstructed from bits of memory—exactly as the description of the operation of the fancy requires.

Lowes succeeds in recovering from Coleridge's reading not only the sources of the mysterious figures but of the exotic names of the poem: the Alph, usually taken as the specific Romantic symbol of the unconscious, is traced to an ancient account of the underground river Alpheus; the "Abyssinian maid," similarly allusive to the abysmal fount of the imagination, together with the "Mount Abora" of which she sings, goes back to multiple sources, including *Paradise Lost* (I 375).

Strangely enough, this pedantic exposure of the poem's "magical synthesis" adds to rather than detracts from its enchantment, because it thickens the reader's own reservoir of associations. Yet there is no getting around the fact that it may also bring with it a certain disenchantment with the practice of poets who are, as Coleridge called himself in his notebook, "reverie-ish and streamy," who marshal associations from "the twilight realms of consciousness"—whose meaning consists of allusion, and whose *significance is exhausted in reference*. This beguiling cul-de-sac of fancy has lively later reverberations (Ch. IV B).

The paragraph on fancy quoted above is the second of two that form the most famous statement on the Romantic Imagination; it comes from Coleridge's *Biographia Literaria* (chps. XII–XIII, 1817). Here is the first:

The IMAGINATION then, I consider either as primary or secondary. The primary IMAGINATION I hold to be the living Power and prime Agent of all human Perception, and as a repetition in the finite mind of the eternal act of creation in the infinite I AM. The secondary Imagination I consider as an echo of the former, co-existing with the conscious will, yet still as identical with the primary in the *kind* of its agency, and differing only in *degree*, and in the *mode* of its operation. It dissolves, diffuses, dissipates, in order to recreate; or where this process is rendered impossible, yet still at all events it struggles to idealize and to unify. It is essentially *vital*, even as all objects (*as* objects) are essentially fixed and dead. [XIII]

This passage is far from self-explanatory; Coleridge actually planned to write a long treatise on the imagination (XIII). To determine its meaning, it would be useful, however difficult it may prove to be, to decide whether it is intended as an adumbration of Addison's primary and secondary pleasures, of Schelling's theory of the imagination, or of Coleridge's own original views.

It is in fact possible to schematize these remarks so ingeniously as to make them fit with systems known to have been studied by Coleridge, notably those of Schelling and Kant (Park 1968, Hume 1970). But this procedure is never quite to Coleridge's advantage, for the results are neither persuasive metaphysics nor illuminating poetics. Part of the difficulty is that Coleridge does not maintain primary/secondary distinctions in those places where he is not speaking of the poetic imagination in particular but is expounding, in a philosophical vein, the general imagination. There he employs a muddled Kantian scheme in which the imagination in the higher reaches mediates between reason and understanding (Warnock 1976) and fancy at the lower end mediates between understanding and sense (Jackson 1969).

At any rate, the notion of the Primary Imagination hovers between Kant's and Schelling's conceptions. Like Kant's, it is a function constitutive of perceived appearance; like Schelling's, it is a creative faculty (Part Six, Ch. I B). Coleridge's own contribution is the identification of Schelling's subjectivity (which seems to be what the "infinite I AM" refers to) with the creative act of God, which is mirrored in the human imagination. (Of course this God does not quite fit into an idealist system.) Coleridge's hybrid faculty is evidently meant to represent the unconscious—transcendental—aspect of the human imagination, analogous in Schelling's system to the productive faculty by which the "absolute I" creates nature.

The Secondary Imagination, then, is, as in Schelling's system (and as foreshadowed in Addison), the specifically poetic faculty. It has a bundle of shaping functions, but above all it is "esemplastic." This Greek-derived term, referring to the ability "to fashion into one," was coined by Coleridge. Perhaps he was following Schelling's creative etymology, intended to suggest, incorrectly, that the prefix of the German word for imagination, *Einbildung*, has something to do with a unifying function. (*Ein* means "one" as well as "in" or "into.") That function is indeed continually brought forward by Coleridge, though it is not the unifying organization of material that he attributes to the esemplastic power, but the melding of the psychic powers themselves. Accordingly the poet

diffuses a tone and spirit of unity that blends and (as it were) fuses each [faculty] into each, by that synthetic and magical power to which we have exclusively appropriated the name of imagination. [XIV]

The imagination, albeit "first put in action by the will and understanding," reconciles sameness with difference, idea with image, judgment with feeling. In short, the poetic imagination now does all that the intellect once did.

(Shawcross in Coleridge 1817, Richards 1960, Abrams 1971, Warnock 1976, Engell 1981.)

2. The Extremes: Blake and Stevens. Two great poets go to the limit in divinizing the imagination.

a. William Blake is described by Yeats as a "too literal realist of the imagination" because he believed that "the figures seen by the mind's eye, when exalted by inspiration, were 'eternal existences.' " Yeats is too mild: Blake is an extremist of the imagination, which is for him much more than a force to turn mental images into ideal existences.

The imagination is "the Divine Humanity":

Oh Human Imagination, O Divine Body I have Crucified, I have turned my back upon thee in the Wastes of Moral Law.

And, conversely, "Man is all Imagination":

The Eternal Body of Man is the Imagination, that is God himself
        Jeshua, Jesus: we are his Members.
The Divine Body
    It manifests itself in his Works of Art (In Eternity
All is Vision).

The imagination is also a place, Eden, Heaven:

The world of Imagination is the world of Infinite and Eternal. . . . There Exist in that Eternal World the Permanent Realities of Every thing which we see reflected in this Vegetable place of Nature.

And again, the imagination is opposed to reason:

> Abstract Philosophy warring in enmity against Imagination
> (Which is the Divine Body of the Lord Jesus, blessed for ever).

These sayings, culled from various places, add up to a theology of the imagination in which original elements are mingled with those taken from Christian and classical imagination-mysticism (Part One, Ch. I F, G). In particular Blake modifies Neoplatonism to his purpose by replacing the intellect with the imagination as the faculty for contemplating the divine ideas. Coleridge aptly called him an "anacalyptic" poet, one who "recovers" the old prophetic function, at once restoring and obscuring it through his intensely personal symbolism.

Yet the doctrinal outlines of this divinization of the imagination emerge quite sharply: It is the Logos, the Word, Christ, who is transformed into the Imagination. He is the God-man, the Universal Man, Divine Humanity Itself, with whom individual man is called to dwell. In the mind of the universal person is created, not newly but in an "eternal Birth," the world of true existences, the World of Images, to which the human spectator has access through his imagination, and into which he enters as into his divine body.

To summarize this doctrine is, of course, in no way to understand it—if understanding be what it requires. This much, however, follows fairly plainly: Whenever ultimate existence is regarded as being sensuously visible and passionately sensual, and at the same time "Mental things are alone Real," then it is the imagination and its "Divine Arts" that must of necessity be the salient human faculty. For to be mental and sensuous at once is the proper nature of the imagination. Here is the culmination of its exaltation at the expense of reason, with its "Abstract Philosophy" and its rational "Wastes of Moral Law." Yet the human imagination is itself only a derivative of the Creative Imagination, whose space of appearance is Heaven and whose moving power is God himself.

(Raine 1968.)

b. Wallace Stevens likewise conjoins God and the imagination:

> We say that God and the imagination are one. . . .

And although this coupling is Romantic on the face of it, Stevens resists Romanticism. In the essay "Imagination as Value" (1948) he sets out to "cleanse" the imagination of three flaws: positivism, psychoanalysis, and above all the taint of the romantic. "The romantic . . . is to the imagination what sentimentality is to feeling," that is to say, it is a corruption of feeling. The imagination, contrary to Blake, is "intrepid and eager and the extreme of its achievement lies in abstraction," while the romantic person achieves only "minor wish-fulfillments, and is incapable of abstraction." Moreover, insofar as the imagination is vital, "one must deal with it as metaphysics."

Stevens's proscription of this defective romanticism does not quite reach the great Romanticism. Indeed, in describing the imagination, Stevens remembers or rediscovers Shelley's formulation in the "Defense of Poetry": "The imagination makes familiar objects be as if they were not familiar." It is, says Stevens on his part, "the typical function of the imagination [that it] always makes use of the familiar to produce the unfamiliar" (Stevens 1951). But although the defamiliarization of the world is thus common to both poets, the mode is different. Shelley's poetry "lifts the veil from the hidden beauty of the world," while Stevens's imagination "makes its own constructions out of experience; . . . what it really does is to use it as material with which it does whatever it wills"; Stevens's poetry derives more from the constructive imagination than from the revelations of perception. For Stevens an image is the modern descendant of the Coleridgean "after-consciousness"—"a haunting, part percept and part concept" in Bloom's words (1976, 170). Indeed Stevens describes it as "Part of the *res* and not itself about it"—not a likeness of, but an addition to, the world. This too is Romanticism (Kermode 1957), though of a new sort; perhaps it is even hyper-Romanticism.

Stevens reiterates often that poetry, the "Supreme Fiction," "must be abstract." In the "Notes Toward a Supreme Fiction," his poetic metaphysics, he reveals that for him an "abstraction" is in fact an eminently philosophical notion. It is the atemporal species, the fixed, generic, invisible looks of things:

The major abstraction is the idea of man
. . .
More fecund as principle than as particle,
. . .
The major abstraction is the commonal,
The inanimate, difficult visage. . . .

Yet according to the Romantic legacy this metaphysical power

to confect
The final elegance, not to console
Nor sanctify, but plainly to propound [X]

is most effectively exercised not by the philosopher but by the poet. For the poet is able "to abstract reality . . . by placing it in his imagination" (Stevens 1948). For Stevens, as for Blake, the works of the poetic imagination far exceed the episodic revisioning of the world and the literal making of poems. When in her poem "Poetry" Marianne Moore significantly inserts a self-quotation from a prose piece in which she modestly defines poetry as "imaginary gardens with real toads in them," she is speaking of the prosaic center of stark reality secreted in the made-up paradise of this or that particular poem. When Stevens inversely argues that "if the imagination is the faculty by which we impart the unreal into the real, its value is the value of the way of thinking by which we project the idea of God into the idea of man," he is, like Blake, assigning to the imagination a hugely universal function. So far he might, again, be called an arch-Romantic.

But then again, that function is exercised in a new, a godless world, and upon this de-divinization follows a great difference in tone. While Blake exalts the imagination in a theophantic strain, Stevens strives to define it soberly: his poetry is itself a theory of the human imagination taken to the limits of self-sufficiency.

The death of the gods, one and all, and consequently of their poetry-generating myths, has brought with it another demise, another loss for poetry. In the "Marriage of Heaven and Hell" Blake had revealed that "a true poet . . . [is] . . . of the Devil's party." In this spirit Stevens writes:

> The death of Satan was a tragedy
> For the imagination. . . .

for it meant the destruction of "many blue phenomena," the loss of the sheer saliency of a world that holds a devil within.

Along with the Romantic vision of vivid spiritual evil the worlds of dreamy significances are de-created. Stevens announces with ridicule the end of the figure who stands for streamy Romantic meaning, Kubla Khan: he proclaims "the twilight of the mythy goober khan." Nor do the more modern myths, the secular myths of progressive perfection, escape this decreation: finally the poet must overcome as well the rationalist's anti-romantic view of the "politic man" who "ordained Imagination as the fateful sin ("Academic Discourse at Havana"). Dark Satan and bright Progress, both must go to make way for the ultimate imagination.

What emerges for a new start is the god within, the poetic imagination. Its proper work is, first, preventive: to keep the consciousness of brute reality from usurping the place of the imagination: "The poetry of a work of the imagination constantly illustrates the fundamental and endless struggle with fact" ("Prose Statement on the Poetry of War"). And then its work is constructive: to rebuild the world's significance.

The ultimate poem of the human imagination is "The Final Soliloquy of the Interior Paramour," which contains the line at the head of this section: "We say that God and the imagination are one. . . ." The title designates the poem as the self-communing of a lover of the recreated world. It is an inner discourse in the sense that it is held by one who is housed indistinguishably within his soul and within the world. The austerely abstract poem of last words, the poet's eschatology, tells how little, and yet how sufficient, is our cause for thinking that the world imagined is the ultimate good. That thought is the lover's "intensest rendezvous," in which we humans come to ourselves, "collect ourselves, / Out of all the indifferences, into one thing." Wrapt within the warm shawl of the imagination's light, the world becomes for us a significant space, a lighted "room / In which we rest," "a dwelling in the evening air," at once, indifferently, outside and inside. There, "Within its vital boundary, in the mind" we feel obscurely, "an order, a whole, / A knowledge" that is responsible for this communion. Then

We say God and the Imagination are one. . . .

Here the Imagination is what God once was, the creator of all such world as there may be.

But again, to extract the poet's thought is one thing, to see its truth another. The difficulty in understanding Stevens has much in common with that of following Blake. In both cases it stems from the level at which their thought is pitched. If Blake's fails to afford a clear conceptual grasp because it is over-exalted, Stevens's is too under-entailed for a metaphysics. Granted that the human imagination must replace God, how do we know of His death? Does it follow from a lapse of His metaphysical substance or of our human faith? Why should one assent to these proclamations? The unwillingness of the Romantic devotees of the imagination to follow to its conclusion the path of "consequitive" reason (as Keats calls it—Ch. I B) turns out to be the most telling characteristic of Romanticism: its technical name is irony, as I shall show at the end of this chapter.

C. The Factual Fiction: Novels

As a small but telling coda to the large subject of the Romantic Imagination, I want to consider briefly the novelistic theory of Alain Robbe-Grillet.

This choice serves two purposes: The theory most revealingly carries some central Romantic tenets to an antithetical extreme, and it delineates in exaggerated form certain features that distinguish prose fiction from poetry.

1. The Novelistic Mode: The Extensive Imagination. The two major genres of literature, poetry and the novel, make very distinct, almost opposing demands on the imaginative attention. Where poetry seizes the sensibility in taut episodes, novels are savored in long sessions of relaxed absorption. Poetry is properly spoken, while novels are read; whereas the verbal auditory element of poetry is of the essence, the language of novels is a means through which the reader passes to their matter. (Epic, the most inexhaustible genre, combines both these imaginative modes.)

In sum, the poetic mode is intensive, the novelistic mode extensive (Ch. I A). Examples are easy to supply. The European proto-novel, *Don Quixote*, is a vast story-studded expanse. Some of the earliest English novels, like Richardson's epistolary *Clarissa* are very bulky. And in the novelistic tradition since, hugeness has generally been a necessary (though of course not a sufficient) condition for greatness: *Moby Dick, War and Peace, Remembrance of Things Past, Ulysses, The Magic Mountain, The Raj Quartet* (Burgess 1967). There are, of course, exceedingly fine small prose fictions: short novels, novelettes, short stories. But these are a different genre, at least in the way the imagination works in them and they in turn work on the imagination. Novels *par excellence* take time to read. For weeks a daily portion of life must be given over to the solitary activity of spinning a cocoon, an imaginary, containing cosmos, from which the reader finally issues with no small sense of bereavement and as a slightly different being. The investment of what is nowadays called "real time," clock time, in perusing the textual structures that induce the imaginary time, and the solitude of the activity—both belong to the essence of novelistic extensivity. Spending time gives a certain factuality to the prime effect of novel-reading, the sense of living in the imagined world; being alone leaves the reader at liberty to turn freely back and forth, to engage in that cross-referencing by which novelistic space is built up (Ch. I B).

As individual novels tend to be large, so the genre as a whole is amorphously enormous. The bulk of the modern literary imagination is invested in prose-fiction. Moreover, before the time that visual imagery became narrative through the movies and was brought into the home through television, it was certainly the chief stimulant of the imagination—a fact recognized in all those nineteenth-century preachings against the evils of novel reading (Part Six, Ch. I A). There are many reasons for the overwhelming quantity of surviving novelistic prose, of which one is surely our wider tolerance for awkward narration than for bad poetry: many readers for whom mediocre poetry is positively repellent to ear and heart, find that even a bad novel half-attended to can stimulate the imagination. The chief reason, however, seems to be that human life furnishes a vast array of situations that sprawl by nature, so that justice can be done to them only *in extenso*, and that it offers very few concentrated and concise "spots" requiring the intensities of poetry.

The quasi-factual mode described belonged to novel-writing from its inception, as the English name tells: *novella* means "news" (while the continental term, *roman*, recalls the remote roots of the novel in the ancient prose romances, of which *Daphnis and Chloe* is an example (Ch. I B). What was distinctive about the new English genre was its relation to journalism. It grew by differentiation out of the serial news-books that began to be printed in the 1720s (Davies 1983). This origin is preserved in the curious and close relation the novel bears to the mode of factuality—and, significantly, to the subject of criminality. Novels are aboriginally fake-reportage, pretend-documentaries, and their subjects are gossip, scandal, accidents, affairs: They are extended "in depth" treatments of news-worthy events, written in prose, the language of the mundane. If the universal truths of poetry are a seductive snare, the particular facts of novels are a deliberate delusion: the pretense of factuality is a constitutional element of novelistic fiction; it feigns that its figures are time- and place-bound individuals and pretends that its stories are histories. Thus the opposition made in ordinary English between poetry and fiction, meaning novels, makes perfect sense. Novels feign more strenuously than poetry, and that is how their fictions manage to invade the space, take up the time, and cohabit with the people of real life.

Consequently, although it is hopeless to summarize the imaginative styles or contents of the novelistic form, it is possible to treat the imagining activity required in reading them. There are, of course, many books devoted to "The Imagination" of this or that period, its social setting, stock situations, moral constraints, prevailing mood, narrative tempi, or structural techniques—in short, all the factors that go into the delineation of the Eighteenth-Century, the Victorian, the Modernist Novel or the Classical, the Romantic, the Naturalist Imagination. But that broad sense of the term is not at issue here.

Because novel writing has a history—a beginning and successive periods—there arises the notion that "the Novel" is an organic entity and that its development has a destination. This thesis has as corollary a characteristically Romantic tenet (with roots in Vico's theory of history—Ch. IV A).

It is that the artist "must be of his time," and, moreover, is elected to anticipate and define each epoch in its novelty.
(Boas 1950.)

2. Robbe-Grillet: The Objective Imagination. Robbe-Grillet carries out the mandate, that the novelist must anticipate his era, in his novels and his theorizing. He sees the old novel as finished, and a new one in the offing. For this new novel, his theory is intended to be prescriptive while his novels are exemplary.

Robbe-Grillet presents his theory as a reaction against the Romantics. Yet in one crucial point it is an extreme of Romanticism—in the power he attributes to the writer of inventing freely and radically, of being "a creator in the proper sense." Such a writer overcomes the metaphysical dependency of the Romantic artist, who might still regard himself as a "mediator between the common herd, and some obscure power . . . , a god," and who acknowledges the limitations imposed by working from a model—a dependency that is the traditional mark of the craftsman as opposed to the creator.

What does Robbe-Grillet's radically free imagination choose to create? Oddly enough it begins by regimenting itself severely: It sets itself the task of bringing out the specifically prosaic capability of fictional prose, the precisely observational and dryly objective properties of novelistic language.

I have made much above of the descriptive power of prose, its power to register observational vision (Ch. I A). The factual fiction of novels represents, of course, the consummate use of this power. It is, for example, no accident that men of observational science tend to fare well as characters in the novels of the last century or at least to fascinate the novelists: Think of George Eliot's Lydgate and Mrs. Gaskell's Robert Hamly. The scientists themselves return the compliment in their passion for novel-reading. A telling *cri de coeur* from Darwin's *Autobiography* laments his inability to read poetry:

> [My] mind seems to have become a kind of machine for grinding general laws out of large collections of facts. . . . On the other hand, novels, which are works of the imagination, though not of a very high order, have been for years a wonderful relief and pleasure to me, and I often bless the novelists.

He goes on to say that he likes all novels, if they are moderately good and don't end unhappily. He seems to regard novels as a kind of science-sans-responsibility.

In twentieth-century novels the factually descriptive mode often figures obsessively. The case is caricatured in Borges's *Chronicles of Bustos Domey*, written in collaboration with Bioy-Casares (1967). Here a mad novelist writes a huge book describing the arrangement of his desk top. In Nabokov's *Invitation to a Beheading* (1935) there occurs—by reference only, praise the Lord—a three thousand page novel, *Quercus*, devoted to the scientific description and history of an oak tree. This conception is "considered to be the acme of modern thought," though it is said to affect its reader with a distress in part dull, in part nostalgic. What lover of Russian novels could fail to start musing here on the contrast with the two brief but poignant visions of that oak of oaks in *War and Peace*, which in winter, gloomy and gnarled, speaks to Andrei of death, but later, miraculously transfigured by a canopy of luminous green, releases in him a flood of joy at the vernal revival of life.

This latter-day obsession with description has an eminently "creative" impetus. If it was the ambition—never to be achieved—of earlier writers that they might bring the word to visibility, here the inordinate urge is to bring things into veritable being, to create over, to replace nature by sheer creation (Albright 1981).

The force of this creation arises from certain abnegations that guarantee the artist's freedom, in particular the rejection of depth. The cultivation of dimensionality, of incursions into the depths of character and penetrations behind the social facade, was a particular virtue of the old voluminous novel. Robbe-Grillet now intends to abrogate all depths, heights, and unseen presences, to prevent what he calls "speleology," the delving into psychological and metaphysical profundities. The design is to cut objects from their imagined roots, to separate them from their fake secrets and mysteries and to bring them out as flat presences in their own right, as *visible* surfaces to be meticulously described. "By his exclusive and tyrannical appeal to the sense of sight, Robbe-Grillet undoubtedly intends the assassination of the object, at least as literature has traditionally represented it" (Barthes 1958). The deliberate superficiality is intended to cut out "the romantic heart of things," to deprive them of the responsive soul with which Wordsworth imbued them. Robbe-Grillet wants programmatically to negate the Romantic sense that nature reciprocates human attention by wearing an aspect of significance, a sense pointedly expressed in Baudelaire's poem "Correspondences:"

Nature is a temple from whose living columns
Commingling voices emerge at times;
Here man wanders through forests of symbols
Which seem to observe him with familiar eyes.

Robbe-Grillet, on the other hand, says: "Man looks at the world, but the world does not look back at him."

Consequently, all subjectivity is expunged from nature so as to reduce it to mere objects, a proceeding called *chosisme*, "thingism." Yet these objects are kept from acquiring any substantiality. They neither collect themselves into a world nor coagulate into a solid thinghood; they remain fragmented into aspects and perspectives. Thus in the novel *Jealousy*, careful attention to the meticulous description enables the reader to draw a detailed plan of the house where the events unwind, but not to come away with any resulting sense of environment. The language is tailored to achieve the same effect. There is a stringent avoidance of the concretizing adjectives Schopenhauer admired in Homer and an almost total absence of the figurative speech that brings out the unifying correspondences of the world. (Morrissette 1963, Robbe-Grillet 1963, 1965, Wicker 1975.)

It is a kaleidoscopic show mounted in an anechoic chamber, at once a limit-case of the Romantic imagination and a reaction to it. The radically self-sufficient imagination is utterly without resonance: "The artist who strives for unthinkable concreteness finds his art growing abstract, disembodied" (Albright 1981). This attempt (and this failure) to revise imaginative modes would not be so significant if they were isolated. In fact, a sense that the literary tradition—or rather the whole representational tradition—has corrupted the imagination is widespread in the literary reflections of this century. With it come repeated efforts to cauterize or to kill both the tradition and the imagination. That is the theme of Samuel Beckett's fictional fragment "Imagination Dead Imagine," which verbally refracts—"describes" would be the wrong word—a world where the activity of imagining incomprehensibly goes on in the absence of images. It is a world bleached white and frozen in the attitudes of rigor mortis, an abstract "phantasmagoria" which bespeaks "the entropic decline of the imagination into emptiness" (Kearney 1988). But however the killing cure is framed, the crux is to divorce the image from its controlling original, to cut it loose from its representational anchor: it is an effort that flies willfully, even zestfully, in the face of the fact that an image that represents nothing is, like a shadow without its body, an uncanny contradiction in terms (Introduction A).

Needless to say, life takes no notice of these literary end-games. In 1964, for example, a decade after Robbe-Grillet's "new novel" was launched, the great novel of the mid-century, the *Raj Quartet*, that English *War and Peace*, was begun and executed with traditional, or only the most reticently innovative, means. Paul Scott thinks of a novel as "a series of *images*, conveyed from me to you, in such a manner that my view of life is also conveyed" (1975). Accordingly the first book of the *Quartet, The Jewel in the Crown*, begins and ends with an explicit demand on the reader to visualize the landscape that contains and adumbrates the story. This appeal to the visual imagination carries through the quartet of novels, as if to demonstrate the indefeasibly imaginal nature of prose fiction (Brann 1989).

D. Romantic Irony: Reason Superseded

Romantic irony is a mode of impassioned sophistication in which the imagination is discharged from the responsibility of reason. It is a conception of the German Romantic philosopher-poets and plays no comparable role among English writers. Yet, since it is a dialectic formulation of the peculiar frame of mind implicit in any romanticism, it is a touchstone for identifying the Romantic period and its aftermath.

In the ancient Greek meaning, irony is dissembling discourse; Socrates, who made the term famous, is presented as dissembling for a benignly pedagogic purpose: he hides his own knowledge and opinions to provoke an inquiry. In the ordinary current usage, "heavy irony" is sarcasm, a way of insinuating superiority and distance by telling the slow-witted world the opposite of what one means, while "gentle irony" is friendly playing on tacit understandings. Sometimes irony just means discrepancy. In the Romantic sense of irony all these elements appear in modulated form: There is no particular element of ridicule, but there is superiority and distance and insouciance and play—superiority to the naive and lumpish business of coming to moral or theoretical conclusions, distance from the sticky imbroglios of reasoning, insouciance in the face of paradox, and play with philosophical positions, carried on in the airy realms of artfulness.

The mode of aesthetic irony, formulated originally by Friedrich Schlegel, was taken up by K.W.F. Solger, criticized by Hegel and, more wittily, by Heine in his *Romantic School* (1835), chosen as a dissertation subject by Kierkegaard, and revived as a major theme by Thomas Mann (Prang 1972). Solger, in his *Lectures on Aesthetics* (1819), which were admired by Hegel and ridiculed by Kierkegaard, couples irony with imaginative inspiration: "No work of art can arise without irony which, together with inspiration (*Begeisterung*), constitutes the center of artistic activity" (II 3). For through the inspired imagination actuality is first created; through the imagination the spirit enters reality. The creating artist is possessed by "enthusiasm," which means in Greek "having a god within."

But the artist must be aware that when the idea of his inspired imagination comes to be realized in literature it loses its ideal character and becomes a concrete symbol, falling far short of the divine inspiration. This awareness is irony: the artist knows that his figures are not naively true and that, for all his enthusiasm, his highest and grandest creations are willful play, make-believe. Solger cites Homer's "innocent irony" about his gods, his artistry, which, unembarrassed by belief or unbelief, invests them with their magic charm. (It seems to me necessary here to save Homer from the imputation of Romantic Irony. It may be true that he played with his Olympians from a sort of smiling distance, but never with his Trojans or his Greeks. Whatever unresolved ambiguities attend men stem from the seriousness of their being, not from the levity of art.) The complementary imaginative modes of enthusiasm and irony are thus an inspired soaring and a willful hovering, a passionate exaltation and an intellectual levitation. The creative genius floats above flat-footed obligations and commitments. The Romantic ironist is, as Hegel sees it in his *Lectures on Aesthetics* (1835), constitutionally unserious; in the less uncompromising mood of a later time, Thomas Mann describes him as one who draws from the reader "an intellectual smile" (1953).

Irony is thus the mental mode in which the imagination denatures thought by refusing to face the question of the being or non-being of its own creatures. It is the Romantics' escape from the burden of their own claim to creativity. A Romantic who is not an ironist but, like Blake, a "literalist of the imagination" falls into intoxicated eccentricity. An ironist escapes that charge by refusing to have the courage of his creation.

The imagination soars while the reason traipses. But that great emblem of the liberated imagination, Icarus, soared toward the sun only to fall into the sea. For his father, Daedalus, the ancestor of all artists, had fashioned his wings of wax. The imagination that flies on artful wings of liquescent wax, unstiffened by judgmental thought, is bound toward self-extinction. The trouble with romanticism and the primacy—or better, the apotheosis—of the imagination is that they imperil, as Hegel says, the declarative seriousness of speech, of yea being yea and nay, nay (Conclusion). In its impassioned irresponsibility the imagination makes meanings hover and leaves them finally unmeant. When man is god and god imagination, all those distinctions between subject and object, substance and appearance, nature and art, so laboriously discovered and maintained by our thought, are confounded with an easy sort of exaltation. Hence no study reveals the power and the limitation of the imagination more vividly than that of its fateful attempt at self-sufficiency, which goes under the name of Romanticism.

Bibliography

Abrams, M. H. 1971. *Natural Supernaturalism: Tradition and Revolution in Romantic Literature*. New York: W.W. Norton and Co.

Addison, Joseph. 1712. *Essays*, edited by J. G. Frazer. London: Macmillan (1915).

Akenside, Mark. 1744. *The Poetical Works*, edited by George Gilfillan. Edinburgh: James Nicol (1857).

Albright, Daniel. 1981. *Representation and the Imagination: Beckett, Kafka, Nabokov and Schoenberg*. Chicago: The University of Chicago Press.

Barthes, Roland. 1958. "Objective Literature: Alain Robbe-Grillet." In *Two Novels: Jealousy* and *In the Labyrinth*, by Alain Robbe-Grillet. New York: Grove Press (1965).

Blake, William. Between 1790 and 1820. *The Poems*. Edited by W. H. Stevenson. London: Longman (1971).

Bloom, Harold. 1976. *Wallace Stevens: The Poems of Our Climate*. Ithaca: Cornell University Press.

Boas, George. 1950. *Wingless Pegasus: A Handbook for Critics*. Baltimore: Johns Hopkins University Press.

Boccaccio, Giovanni. Late 1360s. *Genealogy of the Gentile Gods*, Book XIV, vii. In *Boccaccio on Poetry*, translated by Charles G. Osgood. New York: The Liberal Arts Press (1956).

Bowra, C. M. 1950. *The Romantic Imagination*. Oxford: Oxford University Press.

Brann, Eva. 1989. "The English *War and Peace*: Paul Scott's *Raj Quartet*." *The St. John's Review* 38:75–87.

Brooks, Cleanth. 1956. *The Well Wrought Urn: Studies in the Structure of Poetry*. New York: Harcourt, Brace and World.

Burgess, Anthony. 1967. *The Novel Now: A Guide to Contemporary Fiction*. New York: Pegasus (1970).

Coleridge, Samuel Taylor. 1817. *Biographia Literaria*, edited by John Shawcross. London: Oxford University Press (1907).

Davies, Leonard J. 1983. *Factual Fictions: The Origins of the English Novel*. New York: Columbia University Press.

Else, Gerald F. 1957. *Aristotle's Poetics: The Argument*. Cambridge: Harvard University Press.

Engell, James. 1981. *The Creative Imagination: Enlightenment to Romanticism*. Cambridge: Harvard University Press.

Enright, D. J. 1986. *The Alluring Problem: An Essay in Irony*. Oxford: Oxford University Press.

Gilbert, Allan H., ed. 1940. *Literary Criticism.* Detroit: Wayne State University Press (1962).

Halsted, John B., ed. 1969. *Romanticism,* New York: Harper and Row.

Hines, Thomas J. 1976. *The Later Poetry of Wallace Stevens: Phenomenological Parallels with Husserl and Heidegger.* Lewisburg: Bucknell University Press.

Hipple, Walter J. 1957. *The Beautiful, The Sublime and The Picturesque in Eighteenth-Century British Aesthetic Theory.* Carbondale: The Southern Illinois University Press.

Hume, Robert D. 1970. "Kant and Coleridge on Imagination." *Journal of Aesthetics and Art Criticism* 28:485–496.

Jackson, J. R. 1969. *Method and Imagination in Coleridge's Criticism.* Cambridge: Harvard University Press.

Kearney, Richard. 1988. *The Wake of Imagination: Toward a Postmodern Culture.* Minneapolis: The University of Minnesota Press.

Kelly, Douglas. 1978. *Medieval Imagination: Rhetoric and the Poetry of Courtly Love.* Madison: The University of Wisconsin Press.

Kermode, Frank. 1957. " 'Disassociation of Sensibility.' " Chapter 8 in *The Romantic Image.* New York: Ark Paperbacks (1986).

Langland, William. c. 1377. *The Vision of Piers Plowman.* Translated by Henry W. Wills. London: Sheed and Ward (1959).

Lewis, C. S. 1964. *The Discarded Image: An Introduction to Medieval and Renaissance Literature.* Cambridge: Cambridge University Press.

Lodge, David. 1971. *The Novelist at the Crossroads.* New York: Ark Paperbacks.

Lowes, John Livingston 1927. *The Road to Xanadu: A Study in the Ways of the Imagination.* Boston: Houghton Mifflin Co.

Mann, Thomas. 1953. "Humor and Irony." In *Thomas Mann,* edited by Henry Hatfield. Englewood Cliffs, N.J.: Prentice-Hall.

Minnis, Alastair J. 1981. "Langland's Ymaginatif and Late-Medieval Theories of Imagination." *Comparative Criticism* 3: 71–103.

Morrissette, Bruce. 1963. *The Novels of Robbe-Grillet.* Ithaca: Cornell University Press (1975).

Park, Roy. 1968. "Coleridge and Kant: Poetic Imagination and Practical Reason." *British Journal of Aesthetics* 8:335–346.

Prang, Helmut. 1972. *Die romantische Ironie.* Darmstadt: Wissenschaftliche Buchgesellschaft (1980).

Prescott, Frederick C. 1922. "The Imagination: External and Internal Elements." Chapter 9 in *The Poetic Mind.* New York: The Macmillan Co.

Raine, Kathleen. 1968. "Jesus the Imagination." Chapter 24 in *Blake and Tradition,* Bollingen Series XXXV 11. Princeton: Princeton University Press.

Richards, I. A. 1960. *Coleridge on Imagination*. Bloomington: Indiana University Press.

Robbe-Grillet, Alain. 1963. *Pour un nouveau roman*. Paris: Les Editions de Minuit.

————. 1965. *Two Novels: Jealousy* [1957] and *In the Labyrinth* [1959]. New York: Grove Press.

Scott, Paul. 1975. *On Writing and the Novel*, edited by Shelley C. Reece. New York: William Morrow and Co. (1987).

Shelley, Percy Bysshe. 1821. " A Defense of Poetry." In *Literary Criticism*, edited by Allan H. Gilbert. Detroit: Wayne State University Press (1940).

Sherwood, Margaret. 1937. *Coleridge's Imaginative Conception of the Imagination*. Wellesley: Wellesley Press.

Sidney, Sir Philip. 1583. "The Defense of Poesie." In *Literary Criticism*, edited by Allan H. Gilbert. Detroit: Wayne State University Press (1940).

Solger, K.W.F. 1819. *Vorlesungen über Ästhetik*, edited by Karl W. Heyse. Darmstadt: Wissenschaftliche Buchgesellschaft (1969).

Spender, Stephen. 1963. *The Struggle of the Modern*. Berkeley and Los Angeles: University of California Press.

Sprinker, Michael. 1979. "Ruskin on the Imagination." *Studies in Romanticism* 18:115–139.

Stevens, Wallace. 1915–1955. *The Palm at the End of the Mind: Selected Poems and a Play*, edited by Holly Stevens. New York: Vintage Books (1972).

————. 1942–1951. *The Necessary Angel*. New York: Vintage Books. [Includes "The Imagination as Value" (1948) and "The Relation Between Poetry and Painting" (1951).]

Tasso, Torquato. 1594. *Discourses on the Heroic Poem*. In *Literary Criticism*, edited by Allan H. Gilbert. Detroit: Wayne State University Press (1940).

Tuveson, Ernest L. 1960. *The Imagination as a Means of Grace: Locke and the Aesthetics of Romanticism*. Berkeley and Los Angeles: University of California Press.

Warnock, Mary. 1976. *Imagination*. Berkeley and Los Angeles: University of California Press.

Wicker, Brian. 1975. *The Story-Shaped World, Fiction and Metaphysics: Some Variations on a Theme*. Notre Dame: University of Notre Dame Press.

Wordsworth, William. 1805. The Prelude: *A Parallel Text*, edited by J. C. Maxwell. New York: Penguin Books (1971).

Chapter III

Literary Language:
Two Figures of Speech

In the last chapter I inquired into the modes of imagination appropriate to the two chief forms of verbal art. Now the question is how the imagination functions in the two chief figures of literary speech.

Among the abilities specific to our power of visual imagining, there is one which is better educed by verbal than by pictorial means. It might be called "double exposure," as in photography, where however it is either an inadvertency or a technical trick. But the particular kind of diction that is called figurative speech or literary imagery induces superimposed visual transparencies with purpose and high art. Such double exposures are the peculiar delight and bear the specific wisdom of our imaginative life as I shall claim in the Conclusion of this book. Here I shall try to show how the production of visual simultaneities is a leading function of the leading figures of speech: simile and metaphor, the preeminent literary images.

The distinctions and definitions of the art of rhetoric as fixed from late antiquity on, though depressing in their rigid profusion, turn out to be helpful for my purpose. I am treating of "diction," the manner of verbal expression, whose two chief divisions are "schemata," meaning figures of speech, and "tropes," meaning "turns" or "twists" of speech. Chief among the figures of speech is the "simile," *similitudo* in Latin. Most rhetorical terms are originally Greek; the word for simile is *eikon* or, simply, image. It is generally defined as the comparison of a picture and a counter-picture— of a first basic representation with a usually more impressive second figure. This second figure is comparable with the first in some aspect, called the *tertium comparationis*, "the third element of the comparison." The purpose is said to be heightened vividness of speech.

Chief among tropes is the "metaphor." The Greek term is itself metaphorical, for it means a "carrying over" and its Latin rendering is *translatio*.

This intra-linguistic translation consists of putting a non-literal or "improper" expression for the proper word. The impropriety, its "semantic impertinence" in Jean Cohen's phrase (Ricoeur 1936), is often mitigated, if not vitiated, by the fact that in the classical and medieval literary tradition metaphors tend to fall into established categories (e.g., Curtius 1948). (Arbusow 1948.)

In the following section I shall exploit not only these codified terms and definitions of the trade but also a suggestive early alternative found in the two basic texts on metaphorics, Aristotle's *Poetics* (21, 22) and his *Rhetoric* (III). Aristotle expressly plays down the difference between metaphor and simile by ranging the latter under the former and by classifying both together as tropes—a significant mistake, I want to argue.

Discussions of metaphor almost always begin with accounts or criticisms of Aristotle. Although he considers metaphor to be of special importance to prose (which has a smaller repertory of rhetorical resources than poetry) this device comes to be considered the special prerogative of poetic diction. Metaphor belongs to poetry because in general the poetic import of a message can be more decidedly opposed to its referential or descriptive function than is appropriate to prosaic discourse (Jakobson in Sacks 1978). Furthermore, poetry is regarded as peculiarly geared to the senses—as being, in Baumgarten's famous formulation (1735), "sensate discourse," in which the sensuous heightening traditionally attributed to figurative diction is especially at home.

I shall begin with Aristotle on metaphor in order later to deal with simile as the eminently poetic image (A).

Since the middle of this century there has been a burgeoning industry of metaphor-study (Nieraad 1977). Whereas the older field of metaphor had been strictly rhetorical and its study correspondingly narrow and tradition-bound, in the new study metaphor is given the widest possible function: scientific, political, theological, philosophical. Literary critics and philosophers enjoy issuing death certificates with the cause of death usually filled in as "our time": so at the very moment when in some quarters the metaphor has been elevated to the universal mode of human understanding, it has been declared debilitated or dead in others. And as happens so often in matters of the imagination, while the traditional understanding is being subverted by certain humanists for the sake of a refined rigor, a band of experimental scientists is merrily confirming it in the laboratory. These matters, metaphor as a philosophical issue and imagination as a cognitive affair, are the subject of (B).

A. Simile: The Poetic Image

In Aristotle's treatment of tropes, the following pronouncements are most important to future discussions of metaphor: In the *Poetics* (21) metaphor (*metaphora*) is defined as the importation (*epiphora*) of an "alien" term from genus to species or the reverse, or across species. This kind of part-for-whole function is later called "metonymy" and acquires some importance in current treatments. Aristotle also establishes a second kind of metaphor, analogy. It takes place when in the *analogia* or proportion B:A::D:C, the terms D and B are alternated: For example, since a cup is to Dionysus, the god of wine, as a shield is to Ares, the god of war (both being concave attributes), one may speak of Dionysus's shield or Ares's cup, and, deriving the simile from the metaphor, say that a drinking bowl is like a shield.

Aristotle says that metaphor is the greatest poetic device by far, and he repeats that it alone cannot be learned from others but is a gift of nature. For to "transfer well" is to "intuit likeness" (*theōrein to homoion*, *Poetics* 22, *Rhetoric* III 2). Consequently, since metaphors pose a kind of puzzle, they result, when apprehended, in a sort of learning. The soul seems to say "How true, I had missed it." (*Rhetoric* III 11). The cognitive value of metaphor will become a great modern issue.

Metaphor bestows perspicuity, pleasure, and piquancy. The last of these is what the trope or "twist" in its metonymous form is peculiarly designed to effect. For all its beauty, Aristotle requires also that it administer a shock, that it have "semantic impertinence," or in Aristotle's term, "strangeness" (*Rhetoric* III 2).

Analogical metaphors, in contrast to metonymy, are "civilized" (*asteia*). Their wit goes down easy; they work by "putting things before the eyes." Aristotle stops to explicate this important phrase (*Rhetoric* III 11). It signifies "making things actual." Actuality is, of course, a weighty Aristotelian term. His examples show what he means: Analogical metaphor is life-giving, animating, vivifying. To call a good man "four-square" is correct but dead metaphorical diction. But to call stones ruthless, arrows eager, spears rapacious (*Odyssey* XI 598, *Iliad* IV 126, XI 574)—that is to vivify objects: "Because they are animate, they appear actual"; they live and breathe like individual substances. Thus the vivifying and the visualizing functions of metaphor are clearly connected.

The visual character of metaphor will be emphasized throughout the rhetorical tradition; Cicero, for example, says: "Every metaphor is directed to the senses, but chiefly to the eye" (*Orator* II). The rhetorical code-word for metaphoric visibility, "vivacity," becomes a standard rhetorical virtue, alongside of perspicuity and elegance. Thus Campbell's textbook of rhetoric (1776), on which the American post-Revolutionary literati were brought up, places its discussion of metaphor under vivacity. Incidentally, it takes the dimmest view of unperspicuous metaphor-making. The requirement of visual lucidity is nowadays, for various reasons given below, no longer enforced.

As for simile, Aristotle says: "The simile is also metaphor, for there is little difference" (*Rhetoric* III 3). Whether the poet says of Achilles that "he rushed on like a lion" (simile) or "a lion, he rushed on" (metaphor), it comes to the same thing.

As it happens, Homer actually prefers the first, the simile. To my feeling, the most memorable Homeric imagery is couched as simile. This fact shows, I think, that Aristotle is wrong here: metaphor and simile are very different, and later pedants are in the right. When the terms of the overt comparison that express the explicit analogy of simile are conflated and the *tertium comparationis*, formerly manifest, is now compressed into concisely covert metaphorical meaning, the results are transforming. Metaphors differ from similes both in their cognitive status and in their effect on the sensibility. From the cognitive point of view metaphors are always literally false while similes are always vacantly true. Metaphors are false because they cavalierly effect a transfer of properties—though it must be allowed that under special circumstances metaphors can also be literally true, as in the Circe metaphor "Men are animals" (Goodman 1984). Hence metaphors are in general more cognitively piquant than similes, for similies are inevitably somewhat true simply because all things are somehow alike (Davidson 1978).

Let me illustrate the different sensibilities attaching to these tropes from a Homeric simile used only once in passing, but to me especially beautiful. One Gorgythion, a most obscure child of one of Priam's concubines—we may imagine him very young and a little weedy—is fatally hit in the chest by an arrow meant for Hector:

> Like a poppy he hung his head to one side,
>> a poppy which grows in a garden
> Freighted with fruit and with showers of spring;
> Thus he bowed to one side his head heavy with helmet. [XXIV 495]

Poppies are wild flowers in Greece, whose thin, blowy, crepe-like petals, borne on slender stems, glow red in the sun. This one is in a garden and flourishing, perhaps cultivated for the sleep-inducing powers of its unripe pods. For a moment it overlies our vision of a thin boy who is still on his feet, with his bloody head fallen forward as in sleep.

What does this simile do? It reproduces an experience characteristic of the first awareness of irreversible catastrophe: the sudden desperate flitting and fleeing of the soul to visions of beauty, a swerve of anticipatory nostalgia. This dreamy remote vision ("Like a poppy") which is the *eikon* or image proper, is superimposed on the harsh present sight ("thus he bowed"). Together they produce the poignancy of this brief interlude in the general slaughter.

The effect of the words "Like . . . thus," the words omitted in metaphor, is to give a contemplative distance and a ruminative tempo to the diction. Mental imagery, it has been proved, takes time to visualize; the words give time for both images to arise, to overlay each other, and to come alternately to the fore. By metaphor, on the other hand, the sensibility is seized suddenly. Metaphor is often adjectival, a curt attribution of a surprising property. Sometimes it is, as Aristotle observes, the imputation of soul to things, such as Donne's "faithful" or "unruly" sun. Sometimes it is the ascription of characteristics discordant with fact, such as Homer's "swift-footed Achilles" when the hero is tent-bound. This compactness is the soul of metaphor: Wordsworth, in his "Preface" of 1815, points out specially how "the full strength of the imagination is involved" in just one metaphorical word, with the poet's whole daring behind it.

Similarity, in contrast, asks for a slowly savoring sensibility. Similes are extended and give us time to consider. Thus metaphoric diction can, as it flashes by, get away with more than can simile. Speaking metaphorically, the poet may be allowed to aver that:

> There is a garden in her face
> Where roses and white lilies grow. [Thomas Campion]

for the attributions go by too fast to leave anything but a rosy and white visual blur. But give the imaging a little time and the poet grows more cautious:

> Her body is not so white as
> anemone petals nor so smooth. [William Carlos Williams]

Now let there be the leisure of an extended simile, a full comparison, and lovingly open-eyed truth prevails:

My mistress' eyes are nothing like the sun;
. . .
I have seen roses damasked, red and white,
But no such roses see I in her cheeks. [Shakespeare,
Sonnet 130]

I do not mean to overdo the distinction between metaphor and simile, for they do have a common purpose:

The motive for metaphor, shrinking from
The weight of primary noon,
The ABC of being. [Wallace Stevens, "The Motive for
Metaphor"]

The shared aim, as Stevens spells it out, is what one might call the "ensignification" of the literal, flatly-lit world. Only the imaginative tempi are diverse.

Simile and metaphor also have in common the simultaneity of a complex of representations. But I want to claim that the representational complex of similes tends to be simple and imaginal: the image of this held for comparison against the image of that. C. Day Lewis (1947) says that "an image is a picture made out of words"; I say that it is *two* pictures made out of words. Metaphors, on the other hand, involve strata that are explicitly affective and intellectual as well as visual. What will distinguish post-Aristotelian metaphorics is the conflation of these strata. Consider Ezra Pound's definition: "An Image is that which presents an intellectual and emotional complex in an instant of time." Or Herbert Read: "Metaphor is the synthesis of several units of observation into one commanding image: it is the expression of a complex idea . . . by the sudden perception of an objective relation." Even Ortega y Gasset (1914), who begins the exposition of his seminally modern proto-theory of metaphor with a lovely description of imaginal transparency and superposition, veers off into the description of an emergent new unified complex. Indeed, his view of metaphor, as a fused whole, is fraught with modern issues and is a good introduction to the theories of this century.

B. Metaphor: The Philosophical Issue

Metaphor, says Ortega (1914) is like glass: It can be looked at or through. To explicate this understanding he uses a metaphor of the Valencian poet,

López Picó, likening a cypress to "the ghost of a dead flame." There is the cypress-silhouette and the flame and their visual resemblance, "and because of this it was thought that the metaphor was essentially . . . an assimilative juxtaposition of very distant things. This is an error." The visual coincidence is a mutely meaningless "geometric" fact. The true process ends in the constitution of a new and specifically "aesthetic" object, in opposition to the image of the real cypress. This metaphorical object, to be called "the beautiful cypress," has the "double condition of being transparent and of having what is seen through it be itself, not something else." The beginning of the constitutive process is that the real and the metaphorical image "annihilate" each other and resist fusion until they crack each other's "hard carapaces" and become fluid. The second metaphorical operation then is an act of the subject's consciousness: The metaphor continues stubbornly to suggest an identity, and this pushes consciousness into another, an aesthetic, world, where such identifications are possible. Here the image of something, the cypress, is also an image of *mine*, my state; within me the cypress is gradually transformed into an internal activity. Thus we are to see the image of a cypress through the image of a flame, to see it *as* a flame and vice versa. Though each real image is opaque to the other, in reading the verse we discover their fusion. A transparency occurs in the emotional space common to both: "Cypress-feeling and flame-feeling is identical. Why? Ah! That we do not know. It is the ever-irrational fact of art, the absolute empiricism of poetry."

What is new and characteristically modern in Ortega's understanding is, first, his rejection of similarity as the crux of such imagery, aided by his collapse of simile into metaphor. In the cypress-flame simile it is the difference rather than the likeness that is felt to be in operation. Closely related is, secondly, his emphasis on the subjective construction of one novel aesthetic object out of the differences: metaphor induces an identification of abruptly presented differences. He explains the metaphoric consciousness philosophically in terms of the phenomenological distinction between the intentional act of consciousness and its object, between the "mineness" of the act of "seeing-as" and the aesthetic construct that is its resultant object (Part One, Ch. IV A). Evidently he anticipates the notion of "seeing-as" later to be worked out by Wittgenstein (Part One, Ch. IV B). And finally, he does not shun the unavoidable consequence of this approach: the irreducible idiosyncrasy or irrationality of metaphorical invention.

Such themes will continue to inform the study of metaphor. C. Day Lewis, for example, says that "we find poetic truth struck out by the collision rather than the collusion of images." With the rejection of metaphor as abbreviated simile, and of simile as based on similarity, on an observed, natural sameness of relation, the cognitive function of poetic metaphor declines. Homer's similes and metaphors could be understood as having a proto-philosophical force: They uncover the bond of shared ensoulment between human beings and their world (Riezler 1936). The Romantic Shelley could still proclaim the poetic imagination as a power for knowing "the similitudes of things," as reason knows their differences ("A Defense of Poetry" 1821). In this century, however, it is claimed that "metaphor no longer has its telos in reality." Instead it is used as a weapon to break the referential hold of language on reality by shocking the ordinary sensibility, which has no access to the poet's private and arbitrary *tertium comparationis* (Harries 1978). For the "motive for metaphor" is not the discovery of the similitudes of nature but the making of an artifact: "Literature belongs to the world man constructs, not to the world he sees" (Frye 1964). It follows that knowledge is not gained from metaphor so much as invested in it: It takes a world of experience to unpack a trope (Lakoff 1981). One particularly telling example of this truth is the strange governing metaphor of Flannery O'Connor's story "Parker's Back." Here the metaphorical tenor is actually a visual image, the Christ-figure tattooed on Parker's back. To complete the metaphoric meaning the reader must bring to this vision the memory of the martyr Saint Christopher, who bore Christ on his back. The martyr is the vehicle through which is conveyed the burdensome, dyed-in-the-wool spirituality that brands the brutish Parker.

Let me give substance to this survey of opinions with brief reviews of three contemporary approaches to metaphor. The first proscribes it, the second universalizes it, and the third redefines it.

First, then, a long-lived rationalist strain of hostility to figurative uses of words is to be noticed: Such words merely "move the passions, and thereby mislead the judgement" (Locke, *Essay* III 10). If a message is important "why are we not given it straight in the first place?" asks Quine three centuries later (Sacks 1978). His hostile answer is that metaphor is used in the absence of literally communicable scientific content: "The neatly worked inner stretches of science are an open space in the tropical jungle, created by clearing tropes away" (though some scientists would add: "and planting new ones"). This linguistic enlightenment is, of course, particularly applicable to religious language, and consists of showing that what is a mystery to the believer is merely a metaphor to the critic.

Not an absence but a superfluity of meaning is the cause of the sophisticated proscription of metaphor from fiction required by Robbe-Grillet. For every metaphor carries with it a powerful though intrusive metaphysical implication: that nature and humanity are mutually responsive (Ch. II C). Robbe-Grillet's attack is in fact a radicalization of Ruskin's protest against that morbid and false attribution of sentiment to nature which he termed, in *Modern Painters*, "the Pathetic Fallacy" (1856, III iv).

(Nieraad 1977.)

Second, the austere and yet unsatisfiable passion for literal speech is overbalanced by the urge to expand the metaphoric function, be it analogic or metonymous, beyond all bounds, to promote it from being merely a category of diction to being the universal root-device not only of language but of science, psychology, metaphysics, theology. The rule of metaphor in these disciplines is now the subject of vast inquiries which throw much less light on the specific power of literary imagining than on the possibly analogical and constructive character of insight and reason. The use of the term metaphor in these contexts, being itself often metaphorical, is not always notably perspicuous.

(Höffding 1924, Turbayne 1970, MacCormac 1976, McFague 1975, Nieraad 1977, Shibles 1972, Wicker 1975. Turbayne does introduce a fruitful precision into the notion that scientific models are extended metaphors.)

The claim that language itself might be metaphorical, not as a matter of dictional discretion but radically and unavoidably, is more to the present point. The concrete evidence is the large quantity of "dead metaphor," of diction that has lost its imagery, in our daily speech. Sometimes such metaphoric debris is practically unavoidable. Fowler gives the example of "sifting" evidence; to substitute "examining" would only mean passing from a dormant to a dead metaphor, since *examen* is Latin for the tongue of a balance. Dead metaphor is, he says, sometimes "liable to galvanic stirrings indistinguishable from life." It is a wickedly delightful employment of the imagination (and a bonus for knowing some Greek and Latin) to bring routine utterance to a grinding halt by "taking" a "moment" to "revive" all the "dead" "tropes" "deposited" "in" the "language." This midden heap, or treasure trove, of dead metaphor and metonymy is testimony not only to the fact that, as Barfield puts it, "somebody at some time had the wit to say one thing and mean another" (1947), but also, in the more misty terms of the metaphoric theory of speech, that the language itself has some sort of primal wisdom.

In that latter understanding dead metaphors are thought to be the fossils of an aboriginal metaphoric function identical with early language itself. Primeval metaphor in this context is usually taken to be metonymy, the part-for-whole, individual-for-species function that brings the metaphor close to the symbol in Coleridge's sense:

A symbol . . . is characterized by a translucence of the special in the individual, or of the general in the special, or the universal in the general; above all by the translucence of the eternal through the temporal. [*Statesman's Manual* 1816]

Aboriginal speakers do not observe similarities so much as they apprehend original unities, unities of feeling and nature, of individual and kind, and express them in concrete images. These speculations are at least not implausible.

(Cassirer 1940, Langer 1942, Herder 1772.)

Third, the starkly opposed claims concerning the value and breadth of metaphor are balanced by a lively current reconsideration and redefinition of metaphor, largely in terms of diverse critiques of the Aristotelian similarity theory.

The leading literary revisionist is I.A. Richards (1936). A metaphor, he argues, is very inaccurately called one image. It is in fact a verbal complex, a double unit, of which one part, the subject, may be called the "tenor," while the other, which carries the attributed comparison, is the "vehicle." Thus in Yeats's lines

An aged man is but a paltry thing,
A tattered coat upon a stick . . .

the old man is the tenor, and the scarecrow is the vehicle. The object of this terminology is to overcome the notion that the metaphoric effect is bound to visual imagery present in the mind's eye (98). On the contrary, the metaphoric meaning is the result of an interaction between tenor and vehicle, in which their relative contribution may vary, and in which "the peculiar modification of the tenor which the vehicle brings about" is "even more the work of unlikeness than of likeness." Such mutual modification of words, such shifts in sense due to context, characterize language in general; in that sober, intra-linguistic sense language is fundamentally metaphorical.

In Black's almost equally influential philosophical treatment (1954), metaphor is understood as a semantic phenomenon, a production of meanings that includes not only verbal terms but the intention and situation of the speaker. His objection to what he calls the "substitution" theory (the similarity theory) in which an expected ordinary expression is replaced by an analogous, more or less unusual one, is that the notion of likeness is imprecise or vacant. What the subsidiary subject (the vehicle) in metaphor does is to organize a "system of associated commonplaces" through which the view of the principal subject (the tenor) is filtered. Here we have a completely conceptual non-imaginal understanding of verbal imagery.

In another semantic theory (Goodman 1976) metaphor is understood as a transfer of word-labels, or rather label-complexes, called schemata, from one extensional range or realm or part thereof to another. Since labels as symbols are here doing double duty, Goodman coins the figurative quip that "in metaphor, symbols moonlight" (1984). Again the visual imagination is not involved.

(Empson 1951, Nieraad 1977, Polanyi and Prosck 1969.)

Finally, there is a major theory that is presented explicitly as conceptual, though in fact its virtue is that it brings together conceptual and visual elements (Lakoff and Johnson, *Metaphors We Live By* 1980, 159); the following review has benefited from correspondence with the co-author.

Since it is presented as a radical new departure, its background claims must be briefly considered. What is rejected is, first, a central assumption "taken for granted" in the Western tradition, the possibility of objective or absolute truth. But, it seems to me, the notion that knowledge is relative or perspectival is coeval with the beginning of philosophy, with Heraclitus and Protagoras. What is new is the kind of analysis, an analysis in terms of underlying conventional metaphors. Secondly, the tendency from a devotion to literal truth to push metaphor to the periphery of philosophy is to be reversed. Again I must object that the analogical way has perennially been and currently is a lively theme of philosophical theology; also myth and metaphor are principal modes of the philosophies of being. However, Lakoff and Johnson are thinking primarily of empirical and positivist practice.

A third, related, point of departure is that metaphor is culture-bound and culture-constituting; it both expresses and shapes our "concept-system," a somewhat underdefended and dubious notion, I think. *Metaphors We Live By* consequently contains a fascinating listing of culturally potent metaphor-types. I see, however, certain difficulties: The authors do not give much weight to counter-examples that impugn the idea of a systematic nature shared by common and even conventional metaphors; for example, to the type "Time is a resource," one can oppose metaphors that treat time as the reverse: unexchangeable, unhordable. Time metaphors are eminently inconsistent (Brann 1983). The time chapter of Merleau-Ponty's *Phenomenology of Perception* in fact anticipates some of the authors' own observations of variant conceptions of time and makes them philosophically plausible. Perhaps our eclectic, cosmopolitan civilization is simply capable of any thought and every perspective; perhaps a person familiar with its heritage has, rather than a conventional concept-*system*, every conceivable sort of metaphorical resource.

A second difficulty I see is with the very identification of a metaphor.

One interesting type is the "ontological metaphor," and one of its primary examples is: "Mind is an entity." The specific examples given belong to the subspecies of mind as a material machine or container, which is indeed, except for primitive materialists, a metaphor. Yet the species itself, the mental "entity," is not so obviously metaphorical. The mind might in fact be a non-material *thing*. There happens to be a passionate current debate about the fateful Cartesian understanding of *mens* as *res*, whose issue is inopportunely short-circuited by demoting "Mind as an entity" to metaphor, and a vacuous metaphor at that (27).

Yet a third, similar, difficulty arises in *The Body in the Mind* by Johnson (1987). This work, discussed in Part One (Ch. IV A), is devoted to showing how the body works its way into our rationality through metaphor. It (tacitly) adapts certain phenomenological ideas to the analytic mode, in particular Merleau-Ponty's thesis that space and time have a structure radiating from the body-subject as focus. Now one of Johnson's exemplary metaphor-structures in the "geography of human experience" is that "physical appearance is a physical force." But how does one identify the metaphoricity of such speech as an ordinary, a "folk" assumption? When Aristotle speaks of the unmoved mover, when Dante speaks of the love that moves the sun and the other stars, when Shakespeare speaks of those who moving others are themselves unmoved, and above all, when people speak of the power of love, how, I would ask, is it determined that they do not sometimes speak literally? After all, beauty does exercise its compulsion to physical effect. People who say that a beauty is "stunning" may be speaking exaggeratedly rather than metaphorically: beauty can make one literally swoon. How it does so is an unsolved problem of tremendous complexity. At any rate, it might turn out, under very skillful questioning, that the "folk" often take the metaphor the other way around: Three hundred years of physics notwithstanding, people tend, I think, to regard expressions of forces that act at a distance, like attraction, repulsion, and vibrations, as literally psychic and only metaphorically physical. Again, to identify locutions as metaphors and to determine which is the "source domain" and which the "target domain" (analogous to tenor and vehicle) would seem to me to require settling the literal, objective fact. But that possibility is explicitly denied.

To return to *Metaphors We Live By*, the main issue here is the theory of metaphorical truth and understanding. Truth is taken as pragmatic and experiential, as relative to the conceptual system defined largely by conventional metaphors. Metaphorical truth and understanding are connected through the figure of "viewing" or "projection." To understand a metaphor is to understand one thing in terms of another. For example, in the sentence

"Inflation is up," one has to begin by "viewing" inflation as a substance, a thing. Then one "projects" onto the situation an orientational system, in this case given, of course, not so much by culture as by the upright human posture. This projection yields the direction of increase as "up." "Up" is in turn viewed as "more." Next the sentence itself is understood in terms of these metaphors. We are then ready to "fit" the sentence so understood into our understanding of the situation, and this fit, achieved partly by active structuring, partly by receptive observation, is metaphorical truth. The procedure, as I have rendered it, involves two metaphorical re-visionings (inflation as a thing and increase as up) joined in a proposition and matched to a situation. The pertinent critical point I want to make is that this attractive analysis remains indefinite as a process in the absence of any commitment concerning visualization. Is the hypothesis of projection itself just a figure of speech? Do we have here a metaphorical theory of metaphor? A solution of philosophical interest is given in Johnson's later work on bodily metaphors (1987) where an image-schema is introduced to ground the notion of metaphor-projection (Part One, Ch. IV A).

There is a profusion of additional theories out of which I want to pick some relevant points. One, made by Wheelright (1972), concerns the connection between metaphor and symbol: Symbol is metaphor stabilized, and the stabilization may come about in two ways. First, the original metaphoric shock imparted by the aberration of meaning may be so blunted that the metaphor becomes a block or counter with a fixed literal meaning; an example is our blindness to the visual figure in the speech-symbol "skyscraper." The second stabilization retains the tension. The Symbolist poets especially work with such tensive symbols, fixed yet living metaphor. Their imagery is meant to be a kind of set vocabulary that expresses intensely private inner experiences while yet functioning as a public code. The consequence is, as Edmund Wilson puts it in his famous study of Symbolism (1931), that these metaphors are "detached from their subject"; their mysterious life comes from the fact that the vehicle is a fixed code whose tenor, the reference, is inaccessible to the reader.

Another theory (Wicker 1975) represents a special effort to show under what conditions metaphors can have cognitive and revelatory value, how they can illuminate the world. Aristotle had distinguished two kinds of metaphor: analogical and metonymic. Wicker opposes metaphor to metonymy. Metonymy, as set out by Thomas Aquinas (*Summa Theologica* I 13 5), is a way of knowing the whole through the part. Analogy functions by intimating similarities that are grounded in the actual analogical constitution of the world.

Finally, there is an anti-semantic theory, one that eschews the notion of an emergent, specifically metaphoric meaning. It seems to me the most acute of all (Davidson 1978, reply by Black in Sacks 1978, also Goodman 1984). Metaphors communicate no special meaning aside from the literal meanings of both parts. This denial is not meant to be in the tradition of denigrating the cognitive value of metaphoric language, for while metaphors mean nothing special they can be used to work wonders.

The objection to "metaphoric meaning" is that it has no plausible sense. The usual explanation, that the vehicle takes on an extended or multiple or ambiguous meaning, is unsatisfactory because in that case to "get" a metaphor would mean primarily to get hold of a new verbal meaning, not a new insight into the world. Thus we would understand a metaphor, for example "mouth" as applied to rivers and bottles, by learning that the meaning of "mouth" extends to all sorts of apertures. But there is in that verbal learning no specifically metaphoric illumination, which consists of being brought to notice a likeness.

And indeed, according to Davidson, metaphor has no hidden, paraphrasable message. It does not, as Black argues, organize a complex of meanings, or, as Barfield claims, say what it does not mean. It has no special cognitive content different from literal language. What *is* special in the use to which such diction is put is this: It is like a lie, except that instead of blinding us it helps us to notice similarities. Davidson does not specify the manner of the noticing, but visualization is not for him its salient feature.

This special function of metaphor is most easily identified with the literal meaning of the corresponding simile when spelled out. Davidson makes a subtle distinction between his identification theory and the Aristotelian understanding (which he attributes to various moderns) that metaphor is elliptical simile: like his own, the classical theory gives no ground on which to look for a separate figurative content. However, he says the trouble is that it denies access to the literal meaning of the metaphor as well. But, I would ask, why should it be said to do that? The terms that occur in metaphor are the same as those that occur in simile: "a lion, he rushed on"—"like a lion he rushed on." Why should the literal meaning of a metaphor not be the same too, drawing the same insight to the reader's notice?

The crux seems to me to be that Davidson's theory is really the same as Aristotle's. Both are use-theories; metaphor is seen as a tool for learning. But the ancient theorist says how: by seeing similarities.

Here I must say that the modern theories, both semantic and anti-semantic, seem not so much to be candid accounts of the time-honored name and the common experience of poetic imagery, as they are tailorings of the term metaphor to certain logico-linguistic tastes. But of the two sets, the anti-semantic accounts seem to me better precisely because they leave room for the imagination as a faculty of similitude. The semantic "special meaning" notion, of which Ortega's "aesthetic object" is a first version, implies that by means of metaphor a novel complex of meaning is constructed. It is hard to see how such innovative speech can communicate that sense of illuminated recognition, that sense of seeing familiar figures in a raking light, which belongs to the imaginative realization of figurative speech.

However, this preference stated, just how is the revelatory imagination engaged by verbal imagery? How is imagistic seeing in fact done, and does it produce primarily the satisfaction of a fit or the shock of a discordance? Ricoeur intends to resolve these questions, to connect verbal meaning with imaginative vision, through what he calls the "semantic role of the imagination" (1936).

The metaphoric process consists, he intimates, of a semantic clash from which emerges a new predication—new, that is, to the reader; literal incongruence turns into metaphoric congruence. But how? There is an insight, not unlike Aristotle's intellectual vision, that is at once a thinking and a seeing, a "predicative assimilation." Ricoeur ascribes the work of rapprochement to this semantic, meaning-making imagination, whose operation is comparable to the Kantian schematism of the imagination (Part One, Ch. III D). I think he means that, as in the schematism the fixed differentiations of concepts are made fluid in time, so in metaphor the imagination makes the semantic difference fluid. It at once preserves and fuses these differences in the seeing of similarity.

How does the second, the pictorial aspect of the imagination enter? "Imaging or imagining . . . is not to have a mental image of something but to display relations in a depictive mode." Ricoeur, anxious not to be associated with "obsolete theories" of visualization, seems to mean that the mental picture is not the mere iconic ghost of a sensory impression but has built-in possibilities of interpretation. In fact, he refers to "seeing-as," the ubiquitous Wittgensteinian notion of aspect-seeing (Part One, Ch. IV B), anticipated and put in the service of metaphor by Ortega y Gasset.

Ricoeur's intimations do not show whether or how aspect-seeing can actually be applied to "getting" metaphors. I think it might be done as follows: Wittgenstein himself says of that famous picture which can be alternately seen as a duck and a rabbit: "It is as if an *image* came into contact, and for a time remained in contact, with the visual impression" (*Philosophical Investigations* 207). For metaphor-seeing the process of "seeing-as" is reversed: Whereas in the duck-rabbit one shape-percept is actually given and is to be seen as two diverse objects, in a metaphor two objects are first separately imaged and are then to be seen together; where in the ambiguous picture the imagination sees two aspects of one sketch, the metaphorical imagination sees the oneness of two images. If one sets aside the "as if" by which Wittgenstein introduces ·the term "image," one might indeed say that aspect-seeing and metaphor-imagining are related imaginative accomplishments (Hester 1966). At any rate, metaphor-imagining functions by seeing similarity in a "concrete milieu," which is to say, by *seeing* similarity.

Ricoeur's theory has a third element: The imagination imparts a moment of "suspension" into the metaphorical process. What is suspended in poetic language is the straightforward, single-minded reference to reality that is attached to description: metaphoric reference is split between the world that is and the world that is not—between the real world and a world that, although fictive, reveals the deeper structures of reality.

These are welcome, albeit fancy acknowledgments of the three problematic elements of metaphoric imagining: discernment of similarity in disparity, imaginal double sight, and disclosure of what might be called truthful unreality. Can there be metaphor entirely without the middle factor, the imaginal element?

It seems to me impossible. For example: "The brain is a computer" is a metaphor in which the soft brain and the hard computer are images disparate enough to keep tenor and vehicle from collapsing (while the *tertium comparationis* is vague enough to rank this trope among the walking dead). On the other hand, its careful non-imaginal counterpart, "The human reason is a Universal Turing Machine," is no metaphor but a straight identity (a proposition that is very much alive). In other words, as the sensory shape drops away, the metaphor, or rather its simile-expansion, first yields an intellectual analogy, and the analogy in turn yields, upon further abstraction, an identity of relations. Unenvisionable metaphors often turn out to be statements proposing unexpected identifications.

Of course, since many metaphors have a non-sensory subject or tenor, imaginal superimposition is obviously not always present because there is only one image. Indeed the semi-imaginal figures and tropes furnish both the grandest and the most vulgar of their kind, such as "the eye of the intellect" and "the packaging of ideas." No doubt such examples, together with the general linguistic bent of contemporary thinking, are the reason why imagistic interpretations of metaphor are unfashionable.

In a recent, full-scale treatment, Kittay (1987) joins Richards and Black in dismissing the visual-image theory and announces a "perspectival" theory. It is meant as a corrective elaboration of their "interaction" theory, which explains the metaphoric effect in terms of two simultaneously operative concepts. The relevant gist of Kittay's version is this: The meaning of a metaphor is the result of a "perspectival juxtaposing" of two ideas. These are not, however, to be taken as isolated concepts but are to be considered as seated in their respective systems. The systems involved are as follows. There is a "content domain," something like an as-yet-unarticulated area of experience. As an element of this domain there is the "topic," the literal subject (corresponding to Richards's "tenor"). There is, secondly, a semantic field, a set of words applied to, or articulating, the content. As an element of this field there is the vehicle (as in Richards). These two systems function as the "simultaneous perspectives" under which an entity is to be viewed. That is to say, in a metaphor the relations obtaining within one system, that of the vehicle, are transferred to the other, that of the topic. The cognitive gain is in the consequent reconceptualization of the information involved. Clearly "juxtaposition" is here the conceptual analogue of what I call visual "superposition." Similarly "reconceptualization" is the linguistic counterpart of the imaginative revisioning that occurs in double-seeing. Note that the linguistic theory of metaphor seems to be itself naturally proposed in terms of visual metaphor.

So I conclude by reiterating the claim that figurative speech is, characteristically, literal "imagery," and, in the most captivating cases, superposition of images. I won't scruple, finally, to call to aid the findings of experimental psychology. They are so much the more valuable for the well-known fact that they often confirm the obvious—for the reinstatement of the obvious is part of my purpose. It turns out that in general an aptitude for comprehending metaphor is correlated to capacity for visualization (Kaufmann 1979). In particular, it is confirmable by tests that the understanding of metaphors begins with the visualization of the vehicle (Paivio and Begg 1981).

The best corroboration of all is the outcome of the following experiment in "homospatial" thinking (Rothenberg 1979, Rothenberg and Sobel 1980). "Homospatial thinking" describes a type of visualization that "consists of actively conceiving two or more discrete entities occupying the same space. . . ." It is a kind of inner double vision, the double exposure mentioned at the beginning, a projection of image-transparencies upon each other; their conflation produces a new spatial whole containing piquantly disparate presences.

In the relevant experiment two groups of subjects were shown the same set of pairs of slides, displayed side by side for one group and superimposed for the other. They were then asked to invent metaphors to go with them. The metaphors stimulated by the superimposed pairs were judged by literary experts to be appreciably more novel and significant. I am in no position to claim that metaphor is made by such mental superposition of images, but I think it is often apprehended that way: First arises the double vision, then supervenes the semantic thought—metaphorical apprehension is an exercise of our powers of compound visualization for the sake of discerning essences.

But, of course, such double seeing already contains an implicit cognition, a sudden, immediate insight. This human—perhaps exclusively human—power of discerningly compounding worlds, of casting significant and fitting second surfaces over the worldly scene or recognizing beneath it archetypal, illuminating, figures, has been the object of endless fascination (see Conclusion). The Roman poets and writers, those moderns among the ancients, had already captured the enigma of this talent by a word, namely *ingenium*. By it they meant an inborn power both of nature and of human beings: It could be the *ingenium loci*, the informing spirit, of a place in general or the design-forming growth of a tree in particular. But it could also be the human power for envisioning the hidden shape of things (Grassi 1979). This volatile word continued to acquire meanings—and made-up etymologies—in medieval and humanistic texts, until, as "genius," it burst into flame among the Enlightenment aestheticians and was consumed in a blaze of glory at the time of the Romantic poets. As a result we really no longer have a respectable term for the power that bridges intellect and imagination; intelligent imagination or imaginative reason no longer have a name. We would be the better for missing it more.

Bibliography

Arbusow, Leonard. 1948. *Colores Rhetorici*. [A selection of rhetorical figures and commonplaces.] 2d ed. Edited by Helmut Peter. Göttingen: Vandenhoeck and Ruprecht (1963).

Aristotle [4th cent. BC]. *Poetics* (21–22), *Rhetoric* (III).

Barfield, A. O. 1947. "Poetic Diction and Legal Fiction." In *Essays Presented to Charles Williams*. Grand Rapids: William B. Eerdmans Publishing Co. (1968).

Baumgarten, Alexander Gottlieb. 1735. *Reflections on Poetry*. Translated by Karl Aschenbrenner and William B. Holther. Berkeley and Los Angeles: University of California Press (1954).

Black, Max. 1954. "Metaphor." *Proceedings of the Aristotelian Society* 55:273–294.

Brann, Eva. 1983. "Against Time." *The St. John's Review* 34:65–104.

———. 1989. "The English *War and Peace*: Paul Scott's *Raj Quartet*." *The St. John's Review* 38:75–87.

Campbell, George. 1776. *The Philosophy of Rhetoric*. Edited by Lloyd F. Bitzer. Carbondale: Southern Illinois University Press (1963).

Cassirer, Ernst. Pre-1940. "The Power of Metaphor." In *Language and Myth*, translated by Susanne K. Langer. New York: Dover Publications (1945).

Curtius, Ernst Robert. 1948. *Europäische Literatur und lateinisches Mittelalter*, 4th ed. Bern: Francke Verlag (1963).

Davidson, Donald. 1978. "What Metaphors Mean." In *On Metaphor*, edited by Sheldon Sacks. Chicago: The University of Chicago Press.

Empson, William. 1951. "Metaphor." Chapter 18 in *The Structure of Complex Words*. Norfolk, Conn.: New Directions Books.

Fowler, H. W. 1936. "Metaphor." In *A Dictionary of Modern English Usage*. Oxford: Clarendon Press (1954).

Frye, Northrop. 1964. "The Motive for Metaphor." Chapter 1 in *The Educated Imagination*. Bloomington: Indiana University Press.

Goodman, Nelson. 1976. "Modes of Metaphor." Chapter 2, 8 in *Languages of Art: An Approach to a Theory of Symbols*. Indianapolis: Hackett Publishing Co.

———. 1984. "Metaphor as Moonlighting." Part III, 2 in *Of Mind and Other Matters*. Cambridge: Harvard University Press.

Grassi, Ernesto. 1979. "Die Metapher." Part III, ii in *Macht des Bildes: Ohnmacht der rationalen Sprache*. Munich: Wilhelm Fink Verlag.

Harries, Karsten. 1978. "Metaphors and Transcendence." In *On Metaphor*, edited by Sheldon Sacks. Chicago: The University of Chicago Press.

Herder, Johann Gotfried. 1772. "Haben die Menschen, ihren Naturfähigkeiten überlassen, sich selbst Sprache erfinden können?" ["Were Human Beings, Left to Their Own Natural Capacities, Able to Discover Language for Themselves?"]. In *Sprachphilosophie: Selected Writings* (I 1), edited by Erich Heintel. Hamburg: Felix Meiner (1964).

Hester, Marcus B. 1966. "Metaphor and Aspect Seeing." In *Essays on Metaphor*, edited by Warren Shibles. Whitewater, Wisc.: The Language Press.

Höffding, Harold. 1924. *Der Begriff der Analogie*. Darmstadt: Wissenschaftliche Buchgesellschaft (1967).

Kaufmann, Geir. 1979. *Visual Imagery and Its Relation to Problem Solving: A Theoretical and Experimental Inquiry*. Bergen: Universitetsforlaget.

Kittay, Eva Feder. 1987. *Metaphor: Its Cognitive Force and Linguistic Structure*. Oxford: Clarendon Press.

Lakoff, George. 1981. "The Metaphorical Structure of the Human Conceptual System." In *Perspectives on Cognitive Science*, edited by Donald A. Norman. Hillsdale, N.J.: Lawrence Erlbaum Associates.

Lakoff, George, and Johnson, Mark. 1980. *Metaphors We Live By*. Chicago: The University of Chicago Press.

Langer, Susanne K. 1942. *Philosophy in a New Key: A Study in the Symbolism of Reason, Rite, and Art*. Cambridge: Harvard University Press (1978).

Lewis, C. Day. 1947. *The Poetic Image*. Los Angeles: Jeremy P. Tarcher (1984).

MacCormac, Earl R. 1976. *Metaphor and Myth in Science and Religion*. Durham, N.C.: Duke University Press.

Man, Paul de. 1960. "Intentional Structure of the Romantic Image." Chapter 1 in *The Rhetoric of Romanticism*. New York: Columbia University Press (1984).

McFague, Sally. 1975. *Speaking in Parables: A Study in Metaphor and Theology*. Philadelphia: Fortress Press.

Nieraad, Jürgen. 1977. "bildgesegnet und bildverflucht:" *Forschungen zur sprachlichen Metaphorik*. Darmstadt: Wissenschaftliche Buchgesellschaft.

Ortega y Gasset, José. 1914. "An Essay in Esthetics by Way of a Preface." In *Phenomenology and Art*. New York: W.W. Norton and Co. (1975).

Paivio, Allen, and Begg, Ian. 1981. "Figurative Language." Chapter 12 in *Psychology of Language*. Englewood Cliffs, N.J.: Prentice-Hall.

Polanyi, Michael, and Prosch, Harvey. 1969. "From Perception to Metaphor." Chapter 4 in *Meaning*. Chicago: University of Chicago Press (1975).

Richards, I. A. 1936. "Metaphor." Chapter 5 in *The Philosophy of Rhetoric*. New York: Oxford University Press (1965).

Ricoeur, Paul. 1936. "The Metaphorical Process." In *On Metaphor*, edited by Sheldon Sacks. Chicago: The University of Chicago Press (1978).

Riezler, Kurt. 1936. "Das homerische Gleichnis und der Anfang der Philosophie." In *Um die Begriffswelt der Vorsokratiker*, edited by Hans-Georg Gadamer. Darmstadt: Wissenschaftliche Buchgesellschaft (1968).

Rothenberg, Albert. 1979. *The Emerging Goddess: The Creative Process in Art, Science, and Other Fields*. Chicago: The University of Chicago Press.

Rothenberg, Albert, and Sobel, Robert S. 1980. "Creation of Literary Metaphors as Stimulated by Superimposed Versus Separated Visual Images." *Journal of Mental Imagery* 4:77–91.

Sacks, Sheldon, ed. 1978. *On Metaphor*. Chicago: The University of Chicago Press.

Shibles, Warren, ed. 1972. *Essays on Metaphor*. Whitewater, Wisc.: The Language Press.

Turbayne, Colin M. 1970. *The Myth of Metaphor*, revised ed. Columbia: University of South Carolina Press (1971).

Wicker, Brian. 1975. *The Story-shaped World, Fiction and Metaphysics: Some Variations on a Theme*. Notre Dame: The University of Notre Dame Press.

Wheelright, Philip. 1972. "Semantics and Ontology." In *Essays on Metaphor*, edited by Warren Shibles. Whitewater, Wisc.: The Language Press.

Wilson, Edmund. 1931. *Axel's Castle: A Study in the Imaginative Literature of 1870–1930*. London: The Fontana Library (1961).

Chapter IV

Literary Imagining:
Two Genres of Fiction

So far, I have considered literary imagining with respect to the forms and devices of verbal art. Now, finally, I must say something about two literary genres, one of which has the most serious and the other the most sportive relation to the imaginative act.

Mythology and fantasy are the accepted literary genres in question, the one somewhat out of style, the other very much in. Formerly a family library would include a well-worn copy of a mythology like Bulfinch's popular ancillary to the reading of "elegant literature," *The Age of Fable* (1855), or Frazer's classic of comparative religion, *The New Golden Bough* (1890). They were the staples of "cultural literacy." Nowadays university students are apt to have in their personal libraries volumes from several going fantasy series. These two genres merge in the territory of legend, fable, and even fairy-tale. But in their pure form they are distinguishable, for they are the products of different, even antithetical, modes of imagining.

So while poetry and novels are commonly distinguished as literary forms by their format (short verse and long prose), mythology and fantasy are most tellingly defined by a characteristic employment of the imagination. In the case of fantasy, the name says as much. "Fantasy," the original Greek word for imagination, comes by a long down-hill slide to stand, together with its contraction, "fancy," for the irresponsible imagination (Introduction C). It is because they are sensitive to the levity of the lawless imagination characteristic of the genre that certain fantasy writers seem so acutely interested in the problem of the truth of their fancies and so specially inclined to ground them in meticulous topographies of imaginary places (B).

Mythology is characterized by a double involvement of the imagination. As a written account it has an author, a known writer, who may elaborate old mythic content into grand drama, as in ancient tragedy, or reduce it to more or less charming mere fiction, as in mythological compendia, or even make altogether new myths—engage in *mythopoiia*, as do the philosophers, statesmen, and novelists here to be discussed. Behind this mythological genre of myth-forming and myth-making stands the mythic mode itself with its proper mythic matter, the primeval myths. These are traditional; they are handed down author-less, though *not* from time immemorial. On the contrary, most myths commemorate beginnings in time, the geneses of customs and cities, besides the origin of the cosmos itself. Genuine myths are not fictitious feignings of the imagination, but have the gravity of recollected fact.

Therefore the mythic mode of the imagination is not a special kind of fancy-free invention but is essentially a timeless repetition. The temporal formula for fairy tales, "Once upon a time," signifies a one-time event that occurred in an indeterminate and indifferent past. The peculiar temporality of myths is much stranger: They are non-unique events which yet occupy an actual and significant moment of the past. Theirs is the mode of the perennial return (A).

A. Myths and Their Time

The term "myth" encompasses several meanings. The most shrivelled one is also the most current: Myths are systemic public illusions, spontaneous or manipulated by the image-makers. The derogatory sense registers the decline in dignity that is often the fate of the grand terms of Western discourse. This comedown is the complement of the long process of "demythification" that is one aspect of our tradition. It goes back to antiquity, for example to Plato's subtle undermining of the Homeric gods as models for humans and to Euhemerus's bold exposure of the mythic gods as historical men. However, it is in modern times that the process has succeeded so well as to become a mark of the times.

There are light-hearted and heavy-hearted demythifiers. The former analyze myths away as error, most frequently as the naive collapse of a metaphor into literal assertion. Their assumption is that at all times there is one way things are: an unequivocably determinate phenomenal surface, and a discoverable understructure of rational explanation: In untutored ages people discover analogies which they express in metaphor or part-whole relations which they express in metonymy; then they proceed to take their figures literally. Myth thus analyzed is myth diminished. The nostalgic party, on the other hand, regards the mythic mode as a once-adequate way of truth-telling but acknowledges it as untenable in the face of the progress of reason and its product, science—doing so sadly and with a sense of loss. The poet Schiller's distich about the sun expresses the sentiment perfectly:

Where now, as our wise men say, a soulless fire-ball revolves,
There once in quiet majesty did Helios drive his fiery car.

In twentieth-century theology the issue of "demythologization," of the supposedly inevitable passing of the mythical frame of mind and the consequent lapsing of the divine story into myth in the latter-day sense, has become acute (Jaspers and Bultmann 1954, MacCormac 1976).

The point here is that the same literalizing process invoked in the speculations of rationalists (perhaps wrongly) against traditional myths is in fact working overtime on the contemporary secular scene. Accordingly, the processes of contemporary opinion-making evoke their own species of current debunking, just as once the fact of the then-recent apotheosis of Alexander incited Euhemerus to expose Greek anthropomorphism. For as it happens, many modern myths are indeed literalized metaphor lifted from science and technology; the brain-computer identity, mentioned in the previous chapter, is a prime example.

"Myth" in this reduced sense, be it tinged with regret or condescension, is, in sum, a critical term applicable to gullibly fancy thinking rather than to vivid imagining.

In a middle sense, myth is applied to certain literary artifacts. When in antiquity *mythos* begins to be opposed to *logos* as story to argument, myth is assigned to poetry and reasoning to philosophy (Part One, Ch. I A). There dawns the possibility of *mythopoiia*, of myth-making as opposed to myth-recounting, and hence of essentially literary myths: invented fictions or sophisticated fictionalizations of traditional myths. Thus starts a long literary tradition, one that simultaneously undermines and preserves the mythic mode.

In modern criticism an understanding that fairly thoroughly reduces myth to literature was effected by Frye (1957, 136), who presents myths as "an abstract or purely literary world of fictional and thematic design." On the spectrum of literary artifice such designs stand opposite to naturalism, for they imitate actions "at or near the conceivable limits of desire"—which is to say that they come close to fantasy.

In the high sense, finally, myths are not made up, not figments of authorial imagination. In societies where myths are alive they are true stories, often carefully distinguished from the fables or tales that are actually called "false stories." Myths narrate sacred history and are associated with ritual, or perhaps have their origins in it. Myths are sacred because they are about beings higher and more powerful than mere humans and their ordinary world; they are about gods and the heroes close to them. They are history-like insofar as they tell of the origin or beginning of the ways things are, referring cyclical occurrences to the primordial, prodigious time in which the significant event first took place. In the telling of the myth and the enacting of its ritual, that time is reactualized, repeated, reiterated. Human beings become contemporary with the deeds of the gods in aboriginal time (Eliade 1975). Myth may, to be sure, also be said to have its own qualitative space, in which a place and its content are inseparably intertwined (Cassirer 1925); but above all, myth has its own recoverable time, in which an event and its moment are so involved that to re-enact the event is to be back "in that time," *in illo tempore*. The participant in mythical ritual or the auditor of its ritual narration is each time again in the primordial present with the gods and heroes: the ever-present beginnings take place and shape here and now. This repeatable time, which does not pass away, is sacred and distinct from the irreversible profane time of datable secular history (Eliade 1975, 33).

These observations suffice to reveal the false position in which most of us find ourselves *vis-à-vis* the mythical mode—not now in theory but in actual experience. For we are trained to make a critical distinction, perfected over two and a half millennia, between the stark disclosures of thinking and the vivid fictions of imagining, and in all honesty to hold with the former. For us integrity lies in discrimination: thought is the conscience of the imagination, and we *cannot* believe visions that oppose the rules of reason or that we think we ourselves willed or wished into existence. In much of modern philosophy, to be sure, the synthetic imagination is assigned a constructive world-shaping power, but only insofar as it is non- or un- or sub- or pre-conscious. With us the imagination is no sooner patronized with permissiveness than it ceases forthwith to exercise real force in the world and withdraws into antic privacy. My very phrasing shows how hopeless it is to speak adequately of true myths. For to those who live with them and through them, they are evidently not projections of the imagination into the world but apprehensions of presences already within the world.

The modern study of myth is a vast field. There are dozens of theories concerning the origin of myths: etiological, allegorical, autonomous, historical, linguistic, metaphorical, ritual. They seem pretty nearly to cancel each other out, leaving a workable remainder: a pragmatic approach which eschews universal explanations in favor of particular observation both of myth-telling cultures and of the myths themselves. Whatever the satisfaction of the theoretical impulse may require, the pragmatic absorption in the particulars is bound to come closer to actual mythical experiences. For those who live by myths do so through their particular myths, their particular visions. Thus the comparative study of myth, illuminating as its parallelisms may be, must, for the most part, be a piece of "enlightened curiosity" in the service of a tolerant exposure of superstition—as a reading, for example, of Frazer's introduction to *The New Golden Bough* shows. Nothing more neatly denatures myth than the universalizing approach, Campbell's "comparative-mythological equations" (1986). With each critical abstraction of a universal theme or a general experience the recovery of living myth recedes further into impossibility. What the lay reader in search of help must soon notice is that our serious accounts of the imaginative mode of myths are in principle insidious. Anthropology, the melancholy profession of culture-spying, participates in order ultimately to expose; a myth exposed is, however, nothing but a superstition. Anthropologists belong, with reason, to the most self-aware of professions, but, turn themselves inside out with anxious empathy as they will, it seems they cannot give a plausible account of mythical life. Some seem to come near, especially those who are sure of their roots and engaged in practical business, like the famous Sir George Grey, Governor General of New Zealand, who first studied Polynesian mythology in order to understand what his subjects were saying to him (1855).

But in general we—all moderns—appear to be doubly debarred from entrance. First we are excluded by the discipline imposed on imaginative vision by the tradition referred to above. And next we are locked out by a complementary circumstance: Few of us have escaped infection by the paradoxical involvement of faith with reason in the Christian tradition that makes belief a rationally deliberate non-rational assent: *Credo quia absurdum* is a proposition of and for reason. So when native informants speak about their myths, the manner of their belief is peculiarly hard for us to gauge. The solution has often been to circumscribe a savage or aboriginal primitive or "mythic mind." For these myth-believers, places and things are invested with vivid visions and charged with powerful feelings—for us such visions issue from their minds, but for them they emanate from the world.

Consequently, the candid modern remains suspended between a deep-rooted reluctance to give up the notion that nothing human is ultimately alien and the honest admission that the grandest experiences of the imagination might no longer be accessible. There is a tale of a man who was promised a fortune if he would only refrain from thinking of a white elephant for an hour. To break through the bar of our endemic self-awareness would be to succeed where the man in the tale failed, to enter ingenuously into the realm of myth.

(Eliade 1960, 1975, Kerényi 1967, Raglan 1855.)

Yet this much is clear: Myth is the mode of the imagination acting as the power of significant vision. And the questions precipitated by reflection on this power are these: First, is this imaginative mode independent of, or perhaps even antecedent to, critical reason, so that the post-rational categories of reality and fiction fail? This question is treated seriously by Vico (1). The second question is: Can this peculiar visionary power be somehow regrafted upon a tradition that has lost its mythic innocence? That concern is addressed in the activity of the latter-day myth-makers, philosophical, political, and literary, as exemplified respectively by Plato, Lincoln, and Mann (2).

1. The Mythic Mode: Vico. Since Plato, philosophical mythology, the exploitation of myths in philosophy, has been a fairly usual practice. But mythological philosophy, the explanation of myth as being a kind of philosophy, is a rare undertaking. Its exceedingly original founder is Giambattista Vico in The New Science (1725). Vico himself refers to his "odd ideas" (Autobiography 1725); their exposition suffers from the obscurity, pedantic and eccentric in equal parts, that sometimes attaches to true, future-laden novelty.

To come circuitously to Vico's own answer to the first question asked above—the question concerning the independence of the mythical mode— it seems to have the following range of responses. They have been indicated by Lord Raglan:

> Those who regard myths as the products of the imagination have clearly not considered how the imagination works . . . The kind of imagination which the myth-maker is, according to some, supposed to have possessed is in fact something which nobody has ever possessed. When Grote, for example, says that the ancient Greek, instead of seeing the sun as we see it, "saw the great god Helios, mounting his chariot in the morning in the east, reaching at midday the height of the solid heaven, and arriving in the evening at the western horizon with horses fatigued and desirous of repose," he is postulating a type of mind which never existed. [1855]

So, of course, had Schiller. Raglan explains that the chariot of the sun was a ritual chariot and the god Helios was seen during the ritual in the form of a priest who drove the chariot. The ancient Greek believed that the sun was the god; "but what he saw was just the sun"—he saw what we see. As he *saw* the revolving sun and *believed* him to be a god, so the worshipper saw a priestly charioteer and took him for Helios. In addition, Raglan seems to agree with Malinowski's opposition to the widespread symbolic understanding of myth, the notion that mythical figures and actions stand for concepts of some sort. Instead, living myth is a "direct expression of its subject matter," a reanimation in story of an original actuality. But if it is not fancy-ridden perception, neither is it dressed-up conception.

These, in sum, are our possibilities when approaching myth: First, mythical beings may have been visible within the world, either because the world was once filled with such spirits or because the mythical mind was literally, materially, projective; this view can be held by a modern only in an access of poetic levitation. Second, myths are told and enacted merely symbolically or emblematically; this view is contradicted by the observations of living myths made by anthropologists. And third, the forces of nature, ritual enactments, and works of ritual art are somehow all invested with mythical character without the sacrifice of their factuality. Some such apprehension is expressed within different frames by any number of scholars: Cassirer characterizes a "mythic consciousness" that does not distinguish between existence and meaning, and knows no mere depiction or representation that is not also actual and patent (1925). And for Lévi-Strauss "the elements of mythical thought . . . lie half-way between percepts and concepts" (1962). Two hundred years earlier Vico had worked out his own version of this last imaginative mode of myths. His intention was to find an epistemological ground for claiming that myth conceived as an aboriginal coincidence of these unresolved opposites is one mode of truth-telling.

Vico expressed this coincidence of opposites in two phrases that are really oxymora, terming myths "imaginative universals" (*universali fantastici*) or "imaginative genera" (*generi fantastici*), frequently also "poetic types" (*caratteri poetici*). Imaginative universals are opposed to intelligible universals (*New Science* 1725, paras. 34, 204–10, 403, 809, 933–34). This imagination-theory of myth has recently been studied by Verene (1981), whose explication of a text that is scattered and obscure I largely follow.

The imaginative universal belongs to a constitutionally early mentality, the mentality of primitives of all kinds: savages, peasants, children. It is also the mentality of a historical time, the age of gods and the age of heroes, the age when men made the world intelligible to themselves through gods and then through heroes. Therefore "the first science to be learned should be mythology or the interpretation of fables" (51). For the science of human knowledge should begin where that knowledge begins. The science of mythology combines philosophy, which uncovers universal principles, and the study of ancient literary texts, which presents human particulars.

It is through myths, then, that the imaginative power of the human mind first gives shape to the world. Vico is evidently the originator of the currently most prevalent epistemological principle, that truth is "something made" and that what the mind makes is "something true": *Verum* and *factum* are reciprocal causes. The imaginative universal is the prime example of the *verum/factum* principle. Myth is both true and literally poetic, which means "made." How, then, does it work?

The intelligible universal, characteristic of the mentality of Vico's third age, the age of man, is a concept: the mind selects the common property of a multiplicity of particulars. The imaginative universal, on the other hand, which is to poetic thought what the concept is to rational thought, is a particular directly conceived as a universal. The poetic mind asserts identities, not similarities: A man and the hero he imitates or the god he represents are not alike but are *one*. "We cannot at all imagine and can understand only by great toil the poetic nature of these first men" (34). Their poetic mind can univocally predicate a poetic genus of a mere collection of particulars in a way that seems nonsensical to the logical mind.

Thus myth, the imaginative universal, is eminently metaphorical, and conversely, metaphor is a fable in brief (403), because a metaphor is a unity-in-difference. But note well: neither fable nor metaphor is at all analogical. Neither does the imaginative universal arise from a comparison of similarities nor is the myth-metaphor an elliptic simile. Myths are *true*: "The fables in their origin were true and severe narrations, whence *mythos*, fable, was defined as *vera narratio*" (814).

For the imaginative universal is the realm of the faculty called *fantasia*, which does not conceive by abstracting similars. Instead it makes identities by the formation of a metaphor that interrupts the temporal flux of successive, self-canceling sensations. In doing so it cuts out from the stream one perceptual cross-section which then becomes a permanent reference for all sensation. Here the *verum/factum* principle shows itself as the spring of the mythic imagination insofar as the imagination makes truth by seizing out of the flux of sensation what I might call a "made given," an "is," which has the stability to achieve meaning on its own and thus to accommodate the meaning of the whole of perception.

By this fixing of sensation in a point, this collecting of the whole flux in the single sensation, universality is achieved in the particular. So here is the epistemology of myth: A mythic hero—Vico chooses Odysseus (809)—is a poetic, a "made" individual, by whom a whole species is expressed in an "ideal portrait" (209). Conversely, all wary, dissimulating, clever men *are* Odysseus. And myth, the imaginative universal, is possible because of the primitive power that structures the world by carving out of the sensory flux, out of time, a place-like moment, and by collecting into it all other sensory moments of the same kind. (Such possession by the sheer compressed immediacy of a sensory impression is how Cassirer too will later characterize mythical thinking—1925.) This is the moment for speech, for a first articulation, when the metaphoric naming eventuates and the fable is first made. The power responsible for this arrest is the above-mentioned myth-making *fantasia*, or, more precisely, an imagination-triad called *memoria* (810). It includes, first, memory in the narrow sense, which occurs when the object-element cut out of the sensory flux is simply remembered. Second comes *fantasia* proper, which serves to take up the object subjectively, to re-present and re-feel it. Last supervenes *ingegno* (the *ingenium* mentioned at the end of the last chapter), the perceptive inventiveness by which the universal particular articulated as a name is fitted into a significant web, a true narration, with other such names. Accordingly, human beings are not primevally characterized by reason but by imagination.

Vico's theory seems to me not as plausible as it is valiant. To begin with, it is not clear in what sense of the term the imagination is peculiarly at work and how it performs unaided the identification of significant conformations usually assigned to the intellect. Consequently, the theory that the generic human mind has a necessary cognitive history in which imagination precedes intellect, Vico's great anticipation of Hegel, is thrown in doubt. It might, after all, be that the near-inaccessibility of primitive people's meanings is not at all constitutional but entirely circumstantial: Perhaps it is due to the diverse economy of our lives and the dissimilar drift of our thoughts and does not call for a theory of mental stages at all. Surely Vico is right in emphasizing that we have a difficulty in entering into the mythical mode, but that need not be because myth-makers had and have a differently constituted, more primitive "imaginative mind." Had we but world enough and time, the full meaning of some living myth might after all dawn on us.

Vico emphasizes the "made" origin of traditional myth, but he is speaking only with respect to the poets, the great imaginers. The "dull and stupid Greeks" *en masse* receive their myths as givens; it is myth that makes their world the given fact that it is for them. For us, their modern successors, I might add, such myths as still have any force or dignity tend, on the contrary, to be artfully made by authors we know or ought to know: we may be as obtuse as Vico's Greeks, but we cannot be as innocent. We know where myths come from, and therefore they no longer make our world. Yet they can still enhance its parts.

2. Made Myths: Plato, Lincoln, Mann. Philosophy, politics, literature— in all three has a use been found for some aspect of that peculiar temporality and spatiality in which lies the power of myths to illuminate their particular realm. The three authors about to be taken up furnish prime examples of intentional myth-making in each of these arenas in turn.

Plato makes his own myths in purposeful rivalry with the tradition and the poets. Though in his dialogues *mythos* is on occasion opposed to *logos*, "made-up myth" to "genuine account" (*Timaeus* 26 e), his Socrates actually does not care much for his contemporaries' rationalistic exposures of the old myths; he bids these clever irrelevancies farewell and attends to the knowledge of his own soul (*Phaedrus* 229 e). His way is rather to tell myths of the soul and its world, using, revising, correcting, and superseding the tradition. But he also has a specific new use for them.

Rational account and argument (*logos*) are always incomplete and often inexpedient, especially when Socrates wants his interlocutor to make a dialectical leap, to catch a preview of a truth that can be reached legitimately only by a long dialectical road. For that purpose, Socrates uses not myths but images, grand similes that acquaint the learner immediately with a remote intellectual truth, by letting him see an imaginative likeness. The prime example is the sun simile in the *Republic*, where the Idea of the Good as the principle both of Being and of its intelligibility is prefigured by the sun as the source both of growth and of light (508). Such similes occur appropriately in conversational mid-course. The longest argument and the best similes, however, cannot levitate reason beyond words so as to encompass the wholeness of things; nor can it show the soul itself in its cosmic setting. Myths supply such consummations by an imaginative vision and are therefore apt to come at the end, if not of the whole dialogue then of a distinct stretch.

These characteristic, vividly visualizable alternatives to argumentative speech that Plato inserts in the dialogues are, to be sure, not always called "myths"; nor, conversely, are all passages identified as myths of this sort. Often—though he does it subtly and ironically—he opposes false *mythos* to true *logos*. Nevertheless the brilliant non-dialogic episodes I mean are distinguishable as myths insofar as they share their traditional features. They are about the vault of the heavens, the surface of the earth, and the hollows of the underworld. They are about the gods, demons, and humans that inhabit this cosmos, the rites and sacred stories that are played out within it, the journeys and the trials of the soul to which it is home; they are, in short, about first and last things. Almost all the mythic episodes are accounts of the genesis of a human condition or of the world itself. All are set in a vivid place and a transcendent time. It is this power to depict timeless beginnings and to represent invisible transcendence that enables the mythic mode to provide the consummation of Socratic discourse. For that discourse drives toward the atemporal sources of sensory becoming, the intellectual visions called the ideas, the "invisible shapes." And finally, these myths, though they have cast loose from any public ritual occasion, are intended to draw the reader into an interior mystery, a high moment when the ends at which contentious, plodding, reason aims take a visible shape.

Whatever else may be said of this inexhaustible subject, Platonic myths are at once eminently poetic, artfully devised for their purpose, and specifically visual—full of spatial grandeur, colorful splendor and brilliant figures. Why it is permissible and how it is possible to put the imagination thus in the service of the intellect—these questions were taken up in Part One. The Platonic answer was that both Being and its knowledge involve imaging essentially, so that images fittingly represent the nature of things. It explains why the Platonic Socrates warns against "made-up myths" and thinks that the myth-making poets need supervision (*Republic* 377 b). For although he is tolerant toward minor local legends, he opposes the meddling of the poets with the grander myths as false and dangerous. His own are accordingly conceived as corrective counter-myths, myths of truth—set down by Plato but dictated by Being.

(Friedländer 1928, Brann 1967, Zaslavski 1981.)

As a coda, it should be said that though philosophical image-making has by no means ceased, its stature has changed. The contemporary inventions, whose authors are fearful of what Wittgenstein called "image-mongering," are mythlets, lean and mean, and meant not to consummate a dialogue with a vision but to start an argument by posing extreme cases. Such images often draw on the two nearly genuine mythologies now in vogue: space and robotics. They run to spying Martians, space flights, Antipodeans, counter-earths, brains-in-a-vat, artificial humans (one such is called "Art"), and various "magical procedures," and their end is to score logical points (Wollheim 1965, 269). They are good intellectual fun with a sharp edge, but there is no soul-elevating, color-resplendent vision in them. That is proscribed as impossible and is impossible because it is proscribed.

Next, Lincoln is, I think, to political what Plato is to philosophical mythmaking. He, too, employs splendid metaphors for conveying conclusions laboriously reached through study. The finest of these, as beautiful in its imagery as it is pregnant with theory, occurs in a fragment of c. 1860. It conveys the proper relation between our two founding texts:

The assertion [in the Declaration of Independence] of that *principle* ["liberty to all"], at *that time*, was *the* word, "fitly spoken" which has proved an "apple of gold" to us. The *Union*, and the *Constitution* are the *picture* of *silver*, subsequently framed around it . . . The picture was made *for* the apple—*not* the apple for the picture.

The metaphor relates the Declaration to the Constitution (and the Union) as the source of a cherished principle is related to the framework within which it is to be realized. The figure employed, that of the golden apple in the silver frame, is borrowed from *Proverbs* 25:11. It conveys a very pointed thesis: the Declaration is to be seen, as it were, within our governmental framework, the Constitution; its "Framers" designed the Constitution to embrace and preserve the great principle of liberty.

Lincoln's myth does not, of course, consist of the metaphor but of the vision it conveys: the vision of the Founding as the deduction of a particular government from a universal principle. When I call this vision a myth I do not mean to say that it is false, but that it is presented here *as* a vision rather than as an argument. (There is, of course, a counter-argument, for whose exposition this is obviously not the place. It is to the effect that our political system has two irreconcilable sources, one radically revolutionary, the other conservatively constitutional. I would not call this argument at all mythical but I do not thereby mean that it is true.)

As the example indicates, Lincoln's myth-making is usually about the beginning, the Revolution and the Founding. That is what identifies it as genuine. But it is assuredly not political myth-making in the usual contemporary sense of skillful fabrication by "image-makers." Since the original events are historical—set in profane time and carried on by specific mortals—Lincoln makes myths by telling true history while transmuting it into the mythic mode of reiteration and rebirth. Thus he projects the Revolution as a hallowed beginning upon the sacred time of the Bible, and the Civil War, in turn, as a second Founding, upon the venerable Revolution, as in the Gettysburg Address. This projection of current events upon recollected scenes, I will claim at the end of the book, is the premier mode of the imagination. Political myths of the Lincolnian kind are probably the only sort—outside the fantasies of entertainment—that still have a strong hold on us communally.

(Brann 1976, Thurow 1976.)

Thomas Mann, finally, is among the numerous modern writers who fictionalize myth. The use in novels of myths with their iterative temporality is an ingredient of the modernist "spatiality," discussed above (Ch. I B), a mode that "may be described as the transformation of the historical imagination into myth" (Frank 1945, 60). Mann, however, is the writer who uses myth most literally and most freely, most extensively and most self-consciously and, so to speak, in the best and the worst faith. His work therefore offers the most telling example of the purely literary use of myth in which it becomes an essentially aesthetic experience. Here it is released not only from the solemnity of public ritual but also from the seriousness of political purpose. I call this mode the fictionalization of myth because here free personal invention is cunningly superimposed on the received story.

Mann used myth in many, indeed most, of his major works: Greek myths in *Death in Venice*, Bible stories in *Joseph and His Brothers*, medieval legends in *Doctor Faustus*. The *Joseph* tetralogy is a retelling of *Genesis* 37–50, in which twenty pages turn into two thousand, designedly: "To tell the truth," says the authorial voice, "we are frightened before the abbreviating sparsity of a report which does as little justice to the bitter minutiosity of life as does our documentary base" (III 6). Myth is brief and leaves much to each imaginative reincarnation, while novels are long and engage in circumstantial description. However, Mann's "minutiosity" is not realized only in specific visualization. It consists above all in filling out the sparse original with episodes that are designed as vehicles of a subtly-spun psychology, in making the mythic figures into complex individuals in the modern sense: "Myth plus psychology"—that is his element, as he says in a letter to the anthropologist Kerényi (Gronicka 1956). He also speaks of the "humanization of myth" (*Letters*, March 8, 1942). The two other works are not retellings but modern-dress versions of their respective mythical or legendary motifs. As in the case of the Joseph books, Mann prepared for them extensively by a kind of absorptive grazing among scholarly and original sources. Of the three, *Death in Venice* (1911) is the best example for present purposes, since it is the most succinct and yet the richest instance of Mann's use of myth.

It is a characteristically Romantic work. Jacob Burckhardt wrote in his *History of Greek Culture* that "if Romanticism means something like continual back-reference of all things and views to a poetically shaped primordial time, then the Greeks in their myth had a colossal Romanticism as the all-governing spiritual presupposition" (c. 1885). What Burckhardt leaves out of consideration in this misapplication of a very acute apprehension is the eminently public ritual discipline through which Greek myths came and stayed alive. Romantic ritual, in contrast, whether celebrated with sacred fires on German mountain tops or with ceremonial smoking on the meadows of Woodstock, is an essentially private experience and, being unsupported by public purpose, ends when personal involvement peters out. But Burkhardt does indicate what element in myth makes it amenable to romantic literary exploitation. It is the element that Mann himself calls "back-reference" and "allusive play" (*Anspielung*). Accordingly, he says: "I love the word 'reference.' For me its concept coincides . . . with that of significance" (*Autobiographical Sketch* 1930).

Mann has two fondly derogatory terms that between them define the notion of romantic reference: "parody" with respect to style and "irony" with respect to matter. Parody is a linguistic illusionism, such as the Hellenic feel achieved by working dactylic meter and classicizing diction into the prose of *Death in Venice*. Irony is nothing less than the mode through which myth can become an aesthetic genre to begin with.

Vico had, opportunely, touched on the incompatibility of irony and primeval myth. Irony, he says, "is fashioned of falsehood by dint of a reflection which wears the mask of truth, . . . [while] the first fables could not feign anything false" (*New Science* 408). The immediacy of myth, which manifests, and the distance of irony, which feigns, would seem to be, like oil and water, immiscible. It is literary art that mixes them in a piquant suspension, and the essence of that art is romantic reference. *Death in Venice*, a novelette in format, is a compendium of the imaginative stock and the topical issues of European culture: reminiscences, allusions, symbols, citations, and quotations. All these recollections are mediated through music, art, and above all literature. Plato, Xenophon, Goethe, Nietzsche, Wagner, and the childhood mythology book make only a beginning. As the severely classical German writer-hero of the story advances in his psychic surrender to the Greek eros, he succumbs physically to the Indian cholera. Simultaneously his Apollonian vision, whose centerpiece is a beautiful aristocratic Polish boy, an animated Greek marble, is invaded by a Dionysian nightmare. This pandemonium mixed from elements of the Indian East and the German North is the mythic antipode and complement of the serene Hellenic pantheon. Yet the most significant fact in this mythico-literary love affair is that it is an utterly private and tacit experience: not one word ever passes between boy and man—no *logos*.

(Brann 1972, Gronicka 1956, Kaufmann 1957, Lehnert 1965, Mann 1936.)

The author at his desk, the novel-readers in their chairs, the boy who is only seen, the man who only gazes—all are caught up in an utterly private, subjective rite of recollection. Romantic reference evokes the diffuse aroma of myth and the mere sense of its significance; it is a matter of deliberate aesthetic enchantment. Consequently, the way the "mythically oriented story-teller looks at the phenomena . . . is an ironically superior way; for the mythic recognition is located in the beholder only, not also in the object beheld" (Mann 1936). Ironic myth-telling makes evocative reference its be-all and end-all. The significance of such compositions arises within the allusions of the literary sphere, not from reference to an extra-literary world. The purely ironic imagination engages in an unanchored play of meanings and overlays of images (Ch. II D).

Yet Mann endeavors to redeem the mythic mode from the levity of pure aestheticism, albeit in a most modern way. The quotation continues:

> But what if the mythic aspect became subjective, entered into the active ego itself, and awoke in it, so that it became with glad or somber pride conscious of its "return," its typicality, celebrated its role on earth, and found its dignity exclusively in the knowledge that it re-presented a prototype in the flesh?

That would be lived myth, life through myth, life as a consecrated repetition of a historic form of life. Mann effects a modern revival of the mythic mode as a kind of role-playing. His characters—Joseph above all—see themselves as achieving a supra-personal dignity through reference to a traditional persona; they view themselves in the light of an archetype and are projected by others against a mythic scene, but their individuality is always enhanced rather than washed out by the mythic illumination. The identification is, of course, neither so spontaneous nor so seamless as it evidently could be in antiquity, when Alexander *was* Achilles, or Cleopatra *was* Astarte-Aphrodite. But insofar as it is the function of myth to enhance mundane existence, Mann's recovered mode is, after all, not so unlike the ancient model: "The citation-shaped life, life through myth, is a sort of celebration: insofar as it is a re-presentation it becomes . . . a sacred action." Such an act is a "cancellation of time . . . , a festive action which runs its course according to a pre-formed original image."

What Mann has done is to adapt to the modern condition the distinction observed by anthropologists, such as Kerényi and Eliade, between the profane individual existence and the sacred time of communal rites. Initiation to sacred ritual is replaced by the cultivated recollection of the prototypical images of civilization. The great residual function of the riteless modern mythic imagination may well be—must be—to project timeless contours upon individual "self-images." That is the remythification most congruous with our spiritually scattered state.

B. Fantasy and Its Place

Fantasy is the imagination at play. The quality of play encompasses the absorbed seriousness of self-regulated freedom, the high spirits of spontaneous fun and games, and the treadmill-like distractions of arranged amusements. So, too, fantasy as a literary genre encompasses at once the fragrant walled garden of the imagination and its honky-tonk outskirts, places for children and locations marked "over sixteen only" (2).

How fantasy came to be distinguished and named as a lesser mode of the imagination was set out in the Introduction (C). The genre of fantasy, I want to suggest, is a product of the fantastic mode. This is not quite so bland a claim as it might at first seem. For the fantastic genre, which has received great attention of late, not least as a test case in the theory of literary genre-identification, turns out to be too protean and elusive to be captured in the available categories of literary genre: It does not belong to a particular period of history, nor does it have a peculiar logic, nor does it make definitely definable demands on the readers, nor, above all, does it have a limitable subject matter. Various ingenious attempts to fix the genre through these headings are promptly undermined by counter-instances. It is left, in the phrase of the textbooks, as "an exercise for the reader" to show that the three following current definitions are, though not false, too narrow: First, fantasy induces in the reader that discombobulation experienced by a person who has faith only in the laws of nature, when confronted by a supernatural event; the reader emerges from the interlude to find that in retrospect it appears uncanny or marvelous—uncanny if he decides that it is explicable in terms of the old laws of nature, marvelous if it seems to require new ones. So defined, the term fantasy is most properly applicable to the nineteenth-century Gothic novels, such as the works of E.T.A. Hoffmann or Poe (Todorov 1970). Second, fantasy is said to deal essentially with the impossible, with intellectually arbitrary constructs involving the supernatural; it is intellectual sport, therapeutic make-believe (Irwin in Manlove 1982). And third, more simply: Fantasy is stories about fairies, elves, and little people.

(Brooke-Rose 1981, Frye 1957, Jehmlich 1980, Wolfe 1982.)

An alternative to these definitions is the attempt to fix the fantastic genre through the mode of imagining called up in the reader and presumably employed by the writer; though it does not yield very sharp criteria, it will at least avoid rigid exclusions or antic inclusions. Therefore it is worth trying. But it requires saying what is meant by the "imagination at play."

A central property of all sorts of play seems to be its hermetic/parasitic quality. Play is hermetically sealed against the surrounding world by nothing more than the will of the participants, who can break the seal by simply refusing to play. It has its own rules, its own time-span, and above all, its own place (Huizinga 1938). Play, *ludus*, is essentially interlude, something set between the acts of real life. But by the same token it is parasitic on the real world: its time is parallel to real time, and its places are superimposed on real space—the jutting boulder becomes the prow of a boat, and a weedy lot becomes a big-league diamond. Transpose these features of external play point for point back into the imagination and you get its sportive mode, fantasy. Like playing, fantasizing in general seems to be a human necessity, though particular episodes can range from the voluntary to the willful, from the repose of enchanted reverie to the strain of conjured sex (Part Two, Ch. V C). However fancy-free fantasy may be, without self-imposed limits similar to the rules of play it becomes at once rank and wearisome. Again, like play, fantasizing usually has some real underpinning, however hermetically transmuted it may be—some actual experience upon which it is based, some remembered scene or event, some persistent terror or fleeting delight. What distinguishes fantasy from imagination is how each is related to the real and particularly the ordinary world. Whereas the imagination is eminently in contact with real and daily life, fantasy delights in casting loose from its moorings and entering unreal and extraordinary realms. Something more will be said about this distinction in (1), but let me here exemplify it.

War and Peace, the novel of novels, numbers about thirteen hundred pages of war and sixty pages of peace. The pages of peace are all in the first Epilogue, which shows the after-life of the people who have lived through the great crisis of Napoleon's invasion. In particular Natasha, that apotheosis of Russian girlhood, reappears now as a dowdy and demanding housewife. Some readers think this is a melancholy and flat ending to so grand an epic. I think it is a consummation. The fact that Tolstoy has found so wonderful an exit into ordinary life warrants the novel as a work of the imagination in the soundest sense: the intensities undergone by the land, the families, the individual souls, subside into a sort of gleeful mundaneness, a rapturous ordinariness; this cadence shows that the author cares for his characters beyond their high moments, as we do for our friends: for in its true employment the imagination keeps faith with mundane fact.

By way of contrast, take as exemplary a piece of fantasy literature as one may hope to find, George MacDonald's *Phantastes* (1858). The adventures of the hero Anodos—a Greek name meaning both "Up-way" and "Way-less"—are told as a hypnopompic or morning dream (Part Two, Ch. V C). The magical events are recognizably dream transformations. The final awakening comes with "a writhing as of death." Anodos takes up his daily duties "somewhat instructed, I hoped, by the adventures that had befallen me in Fairy-land. Could I translate the experience of my travels there into common life? . . . These questions I cannot yet answer. But I fear." Coming out of a deep fantasy is a culture-shock, as it were, a shift of realms that drains the color from the real world, a death that throws in doubt the efficacy of the fantasy lesson. It is a let-down similar in quality to the termination of any non-literary fantasy that is too fantastic and leaves the fantasizer sitting amidst insipid and unsatisfactory realities. And as the exit-feeling of fantasy literature is often disenchantment, so the entering senti-ment is nostalgia—the idle longing for lost lands and beings. The chief distinction between the serious imagination and its playful fantasy mode seems to be that the imagination effects the transition from fiction to fact smoothly while fantasy effects it abruptly.

I do not in the least want to convey a sense that fantasy is worthless. It is an enchanting, albeit a lesser mode of a great cognitive faculty, a mode which has its own way with truth, though a doubly problematic one (1).

1. Truth in Fancy. The following question, posed by E.M. Forster (1927), seizes the issue in the truth-in-fantasy problem: "Once in the realm of the fictitious, what difference is there between an apparition and a mortgage?" How is one to distinguish between the simple untruths of fiction and the compounded untruths of fantasy-fiction? This question is an extension of the unresolved logical problem concerning the actuality of fiction broached in Part Three (Ch. III A). It comes back at this point because conscientious fantasy writers—as opposed to the hacks—are peculiarly sensitive to the truth-status of their genre.

Let me try to say what is behind that acute interest. Fantasy is generically associated with the super- and the sub-natural: with beings that have no natural genesis or ordinary bodily existence, beings that possess extra-human powers and effect significant events without physical explanations; with places that are accessible only by a special dispensation and times not measurable by natural clocks; and finally with potent, positive evil. Now religion, too, is concerned with potent divinities, normally invisible but sometimes become incarnate; with non-natural births, miracles, eternity, and heaven; and finally with heaven's mighty Adversary.

The parallelism is an old story and has long been used to ridicule religion. The fourth part of Hobbes's *Leviathan*, for example, ends in a graphic, and wickedly funny, point-by-point comparison of the Roman clerical hierar-chy to the kingdom of the fairies. Item: "The fairies marry not; but there be amongst them *incubi*, that have copulation with flesh and blood. The *priests* also marry not." Full stop. One implication is that priestcraft turns fantasy into religion.

On the other hand, some of the finest writers of fantasy, as devout Christians, are anxious about the obverse danger—that of faith taking the form of a fairy-tale, namely that fantasy should become a substitute for religion.

C. S. Lewis, a master of religion-tinted fantasy, gives over large parts of his autobiography, *Surprised by Joy* (1955), to this quandary. His first austere judgment is that "the lower life of the imagination [he means fantasy in my sense] is not a beginning of, nor a step toward the higher life of the spirit, merely an image." This denigration is, however, mitigated. An image can at least reflect heavenly truth; therefore there may be a genuine, a more than incidental resemblance between the Christian and the merely imaginative experience. This view seems to have governed Lewis's writing even of children's fantasy, and it leads to a daring and doubtful conflation of the "lower imagination" with theology. *The Last Battle* (1956), the final book in the Narnia series, ends with a great rushing pseudo-Neoplatonic ascent from Narnia, the fantasy-land repeatedly entered by the children from this world through a wardrobe. The ascent leads through realms that at once encompass and penetrate the other world's inner being: "like an onion, except that as you continue to go in and in, each circle is larger than the last"—a characteristic assimilation of mysticism to magic. What is very unusual (though not absolutely unique) in a book supposedly for juveniles is that as they participate in this ascent the children discover that they are well and truly dead, having in real fact been killed in a railway crash; this time they will not, as they have in all the previous books, re-emerge through the closet into the real world. This fantasy is no interlude, which is to say it is no fantasy; in its last pages it stands revealed—or rather unmasked—as spiritual fiction, a risky fusion of genres.

For in fantasy the eventual re-emergence into the real world is mandatory. Tolkien (1947) does argue that fairy-stories, at least, "should be presented as 'true,' " and that they should therefore not be framed in a fiction explaining them as a dream or in some naturalistic way. For such rationalizations cheat one of "the primal desire at the heart of Faerie: the realization, independent of the conceiving mind, of imagined wonder." Other kinds of fantasy, he admits, above all the *Alice* stories, do have successful dream transitions—but that is why they are not fairy-stories in the strict sense.

But the emergence I am thinking of is in no way dependent on framing rationalizations. On the contrary, it validates Faerie as a realm founded on desire and its marvels as fantastic apart from devices. Such emergence has to do rather with the fact that when any fantasy story is over, when the full moon wanes, when magic tunnels debouch into ordinary backyards, especially when that hand-washing formula "and they lived happily ever after" is uttered, we return quickly and entirely to our earth. There may be a fragrance lingering about, but on the whole we find it much as we left it. The fantasy interlude was, after all, only a recreation.

So a resolution within the story of the reader's hesitation about the "reality" of the fantasy (Todorov 1970) seems to me of less account than the purity of the reader's absorption in the fantasy and the cleanness of the distinction between the modes. There is cause for squeamishness not only when fantasy issues in apocalypse, but also when it irrupts into imaginative fiction. I can think of two great novels that harbor such a disconcerting corruption: *Jane Eyre*, with the uncanny night-communication between Jane and Rochester over several shires, and *The Magic Mountain*, with the spiritual seance at which Hans Castorp assists at the ectoplastic materialization of his dead cousin, the young officer who appears uncannily in the uniform of the Great War to come. My point is that, unlike business and pleasure, fiction and fantasy really do not mix without weakening the profit in each. So much for the peculiar truthfulness, the clean distinctions, that fantasy seems to require in the telling. What about the truth it might convey?

Tolkien identifies as the highest function of the fairy-tale the "eucatastrophe" or happy ending, and the sudden turn to joy, which also figures in C.S. Lewis's autobiography as a "sudden and miraculous grace." Here again fantasy is described in the terms of faith. But what I wish to show is that fantasy, just because it is eucatastrophic, is, as it were, especially good at evil. In fact, of course, not all fairy-tales end well, or gracefully. For example, the unpretty Grimm version of the Frog Prince ends, unlike its supermarket bowdlerization, without any deliverance through kindness: When the frog reminds the princess of her promise to keep him as companion and attempts to crawl into her bed, she becomes enraged and smashes him against the wall. As he falls he turns into a beautiful prince and they marry—scarcely a morally edifying eucatastrophe. But the merry brutality of this fairy-tale is nothing to the morbid darkness of much fantasy.

The definition of literary myth which Frye gives, that it is the imitation of action at the conceivable limits of desire, is in fact much more applicable to fantasy. True myth is not willful or desirous, since it is not told or enacted as a private invention; but fantasy is, as Tolkien admits, driven by desire. It is, moreover, often a desire for extremes and extremities, for never-before-seen monstrosities and unheard-of suffering. This drive toward the excruciating is a feature literary fantasy shares with day-dreams, especially childhood fantasies. In the inconsequential arena of the fantastic interlude the soul can disport itself comfortably, confronting frightfully bizarre or uncannily shapeless evil. For as in theology, so in fantasy evil comes either as an amorphous privation of good, as in L'Engle's *Wrinkle in Time*, or, more often, as a positive, personal fiend—fantasts tend to be Manicheans—as in Cooper's *Grey King*. Something similar holds for other moral-theological themes; in fantasy they get a free work-out. Though to be just, children's fantasy, as exemplified in the two works just mentioned, tends to be more serious and more subtle than the adult genre; as "children's ethical fantasy" it is an acknowledged, earnest sub-genre (Molson 1982). But perhaps these moral dry runs do not so much represent the truth specific to fantasy, as they are a bonus incidental to the genre. Perhaps, unlike sacred myth and secular fiction, fantasy is, when all is said and done, not true in any but the most airy manner of speaking.

The obvious reason is that fantasy deals in impossibilities. Fantasy is much else besides impossible, not all fantasies are impossible; many impossibles are not fantastic. But impossibility does prominently figure in fantasy (Wolfe 1982). Human beings, children included, do not believe the impossible if they know it to be impossible, despite the hypocritical assurances of fantasts and students of fantasy. They may believe *because* it is absurd, or beyond the understanding, but they do not believe *although* it is impossible, where "impossible" means that ordinary and natural ways are being extensively contravened. The reader or listener plays along—with avidity and absorption, to be sure, but without belief. It is one of the pleasures of fantasy (which it shares with the horror story) that the hair may stand on end when the understanding is perfectly relaxed.

It has been argued that fantasy becomes a problem only in an age that is committed to universal rational explanation. It seems to me that the ingeniously playful use of the imagination, isolated for a moment from those of its uses grounded in reality, must always have seemed at once remarkable and questionable. Certainly it was so to those natives who distinguished serious myth from made-up false stories. H.V.G. Dyson once said about his friend Tolkien that "his was not a true imagination, you know: he made it all up" (Davenport 1981). Fantasy is more purely invented than fiction.

That is the reason why calls for the revival of fantasy, especially for its use in religion, such as abounded in the sixties, are so paradoxical. Take those issued by Cox (1969). It is not only that spontaneity, and, God forbid, "creative ecstasy," make themselves notoriously scarce in the face of avid mothering. There is also this consideration: Although Cox well describes contemporary ritual as driven to bankruptcy between the claims of ideology and those of idiosyncrasy, his cure is surely inconsistent with the very nature of ritual faith. He thinks that ritual should be restored "not as a content to which people must comply, but as a structure within which they can pulsate and pirouette in unprescribed ways." How can fantasy help to revive ritual and faith when the one is the disciplined imaginative reenactment of a prototypical event and the other is the affirmation of an eternal truth? Fantasy, which is the imagination in its antic and uncommitted mode, surely lacks the gravity for this high office.

Now insofar as fantasy is made up, it has certain additional generic features. Mere unreality is not enough. In the *Labyrinth*, for example, Robbe-Grillet does his deliberate best to de-realize his environment, to present the real as unreal (Brooke-Rose 1981). But one would not call the result fantasy, above all because he eschews what fantasy writers do best and most extensively, the building of spirit-invested worlds. Tolkien speaks of the "secondary world" or subcreation a fantasy writer aims to make, though he asks how this world can be internally consistent if its peculiar qualities are not "derived from Reality." Of course, the rejoinder would be that fantastic consistency depends on subcreating this secondary world in such a way that it is in its peculiar essentials dirempt from the real world and incomparable to it; usually only its unregarded features are borrowed from reality.

A thesis by Goodman (1984), that "there are no fictive worlds," contradicts my claim. To say that a work of fiction is about a fictive world "amounts to saying *that there is something such that there is no such thing*. Thus there are no pictures *of* unicorns or stories *about* ghosts but only unicorn-pictures and ghost-stories". Apart from the fact that unicorns have a well-documented natural history (Shepard 1956), this argument, the old one against Meinong's nonexistent objects (Part Three, Ch. III A), is inopportune here: If ever such objects were called for, if ever fictive worlds were needed, it is with respect to fantasy. For the fact that there is a psychic fantasy mode behind literary fantasies would suggest that written fantasies are indeed the creatures of psychic fantasizing. I mean that besides their bookish existence they have psychic actuality, while yet being about nothing believed to be real or to fit into reality. Again, the fact that these baseless beings somehow cohere speaks for their having a world, where by a world I mean a containing setting, a quasi-sensory place, which the text describes concretely and the devotee embellishes imaginatively.

The *Dictionary of Imaginary Places* (Manguel and Guadalupi 1980) contains more than fifteen-hundred such past or present evironments (by a wise policy omitting those of the future), often with maps, sometimes with pictures. It happens to exclude what is probably the most extensively chronicled, affectionately mapped land in literature, the Barsetshire described by Trollope in the last century and by Angela Thirkell in our time. Why? The reason must be that this English shire is precisely fiction and not fantasy; it does not hide beneath or hover above the terrain of southern England but sits *in* it, being of that world. Fantasy places, with their enchanted castles and haunted woods, magic rivers and forbidden mountains, are, one way or another, *out* of this world, in the sense of showing some abrupt discontinuity with it. Their function is to provide an extrawordly home for the motley fantastic crew and to give it local coherence. So these cities and landscapes are as weird and wonderful and invested with powers as strange as those possessed by the fantasy creatures themselves. Often, I imagine, the places are made up first and then colonized to suit. Their multitude, in sum, bears witness to three impulses: the wish for the untrammelled, godlike fun of making up environments, the need to contain the creatures of fantasy in a suitable world, and the desire to make the reader explore and take possession of the alien world as a concretely visible place.

As places figure pre-eminently in fantasy, so do their visual depictions. While in fine novelistic fiction illustrations are *de trop* and usually inane—as James and Flaubert complained (*Daedalus* 1985)—fantasy literature welcomes pictures. The fantasy writers who inveigh against illustrations, especially Tolkien, are, significantly, those who consider fantasy high literature. Fantastic forms, they say, should not be counterfeited. The word appeals more strongly to the fantastic imagination because it makes each reader give things his own personal embodiment (Holländer 1980). The usual practice, however, is the opposite because in fantasy the imagination is on holiday and takes it easy. That is why definition and detail are so welcome in fantasy illustration and why visual fantasy tends to be so accomplished. It does all the easier things—prefers kinds to individuals, costumes to physiognomies, the bizarre to the normal, and details to composition. (It is an experimental fact that detail facilitates visual memory, and so obviates original imagining. These observations do not, however, in the least apply to children's picture books, a genre in which narrative and illustration are often vitally and subtly integrated—Nodelman 1988.) Furthermore, as long as they are visible at all, even naturally impossible beings pose no difficulty to depiction since pictures are immune to self-contradiction (Part Three, Ch. I B). Thus illustration supplies a sort of eye-witness existence proof, like Conan Doyle's famous publication in 1920 of two photographs of fairies, taken in Yorkshire.

To sum up: Fantasy as an imaginative mode is what Coleridge said fancy was; it "has no other counters to play with but fixities and definites." It is memory emancipated from the order of time and space and from cause other than the will. As a genus it can be sincere, but scarcely true.

2. Adult Amusement and Children's Literature. The fantasy genre functions as differently for grown-ups and children as does their play: With respect to need and nourishment the one is to the other somewhat as black coffee is to chocolate milk.

Adult fantasy is a habit and is swallowed in continual, semi-satisfying draughts; it comes conveniently in series. It acts both as relaxant and stimulant, and it services certain spiritual needs. Before saying a word about its recent explosion, let me give a guide to listing its multitudinous sub-genres. To derive them, take every resultant to be gotten by adding vectors along the following dimensions: In time: take the dangerous or dreary present, the historic or mythical past, the dreadful or glamorous future, and the dateless indefinite. In place: take the world beneath, the interstices of earth, the heavens with their galaxies and their coexistent "alternative worlds." Among creatures: take persons or powers, super- and sub-human, visible or invisible, traditional and new-made. In scale: take the monstrous or the mite-like. For the operant device: take magic or science. For atmosphere: take the pastoral, uncanny, sinister, horrifying, or mystical. As means of access: take inadvertence, dream, or special election. Take these in any combination and there will be on the market a current fantasy series to match.

The nineteenth-century antecedents of both our light and dark fantasy are to be found in the works of Poe, MacDonald, William Morris, and Wilde. In our century, the genre languished during the sombre decades of the depressed thirties and the war-preoccupied forties of this century, though the most influential fantasy classics were then being conceived or written. The fathers of current fantasy are three Oxonians belonging to the literary group that called itself the "Inklings": Tolkien, C.S. Lewis, and Charles Williams. Williams is the least overtly Christian, but he is mystical; his "Powers" are uneasily at work in the humdrum English present. C.S. Lewis's *Narnia* series can be read as a re-imagination of Christianity in fantasy terms, with Aslan, the wild, beguiling, beautiful golden lion as Christ. The chief of Tolkien's middle-Earth stories, *The Lord of the Rings*, which is also a spiritual parable, was written over nearly two decades and was published in 1954–55. But it achieved its phenomenal popularity among the students, classified for present purposes as adults, of the sixties. Since then all sorts of fantasy have burgeoned and some of it revels in literary sophistication. For example, Gene Wolfe's *Soldier in the Mist* (1986), dedicated to Herodotus, is both linguistically learned and historically evocative. Fantasy is probably the most copiously read of any literary genre, particularly if science-fiction is, as it ought to be, included as a sub-genre. (Carpenter 1984, Searles et al. 1982.)

This growth industry is less in want of explanation than most literary phenomena. For one thing, the stuff is obviously fun to write. One gets to make worlds and their laws, to be bound by them or to blow and bend them at whim, to invent topographies and draw maps for them—charts of unknown lands along with Celtic names are practically *de rigeur*—and generally to disport oneself as both the writer of the rule-book and a player freely bound by it. The reader shares in this license; the imagination is, as was said, at once stimulated and relaxed; the need for both conditions together seems to be an index of modern maturity. Everything runs according to the generic and the individual formula, which includes plenty of verbal wit and plot-complexity. And the reader can take or leave all of this without penalty. Furthermore, fantasy by turns exploits the frisson that comes from giving palpable shape to the menacing future and feeds nostalgia with an exuberant glamorization of the past—certain fantasy buffs maintain a "Society for Creative Anachronism." Moreover, in fantasy great deeds are done, laboriously, but always without the grey, diffuse devices of modern efficiency, and—this appeals especially to students—without record-keeping bureaucracies; fantasy is entirely in glorious technicolor. But above all, fantasy preserves the spiritual tinge its founders imparted to it. It is a non-obligating excursion into higher realms. It is obvious that people have a spiritual need for all that; it is equally obvious that there is not much nourishment in it: adult fantasy is more an index of a desire than the source of its satisfaction. Aesthetically, the chief objection seems to me to be that it is all too hectic and garish to have much delicacy or fragrance.

One word about the large sub-genre known among aficionados as *sci-fi*. It ought, of course, to be called not science—but technology-fiction—the stodgiest paragraph from an elementary physics book usually has more interesting science than a whole sci-fi series. Yet real perplexities related to science are often introduced, though the entertainment character of sci-fi precludes them from being seriously pursued. Moreover, since these stories abound in the application of pseudo-theory—for example techniques for temporal perturbations, as in Isaac Asimov's *The End of Eternity*—they are often visually arid. Hence science fiction is indeed fantastic, but the imagination is involved more in its conjectural sense (Introduction C) than visually and poetically. The great exception is the sub-sub-genre of space fantasy, which is the special domain of the movies (and television). Perhaps it too has not much subtle fragrance, but there is a certain expansive sweetness about the homey all-American crews it features: the aging penitent computers expiating errors in self-sacrifice, star ships appearing like Manhattan hung upside-down to buzz highways and to glide into Wyoming, ugly extraterrestrial friendlies feeding off candy-coated chocolate drops, and a race of teddy bears beating the Evil Empire (*2001, Close Encounters, E.T., Return of the Jedi*). Here the mysticism is at a minimum and friendly skies are peopled by aliens rather than gods. It is good-natured countertranscendence for old and young alike.

Fantasy for children is generally, I suspect, written with more of a conscience and read less by way of diversion. I say "suspect" because the imagination of childhood is somewhat like the lost land of myth: To re-enter one must regain not so much a state of innocence (which a penitent heart might obtain) as a condition of ignorance (which requires nothing short of the reversal of life's processes). For children are not innocent. Why else would the forces and figures of evil in fantasy get such a soul-satisfying run for their money before their final defeat? But children are, as yet, ignorant of the habits of nature. They know very well, by and large, what is impossible—the impossible being the crucial category for fantasy—but they know it as a mere fact, not as a grounded necessity. They are ready to state that there are in fact no fairies well before they know explicitly why there are none. Their imaginative endowment of things and surroundings with fantasy life has a direct good faith, a sober objectivity, which is delightfully illustrated by the example told me of a little boy who, when taken out for a walk at dusk, tested the feel of the evening and pronounced: "No dragons here tonight." Children are generally not gullible believers who cannot distinguish what is and is not the case. They are simply less put off by nonexistence and less resistant to its actuality—less bound, in sum, by the rationalistic obligation to construe material reality and fantasy life as opposites.

Therefore, while the adult genre is a deliberate interlude in the ordinary realistic employment of the imagination, children's fantasy is more natu-rally integrated into imaginative life, just as children's play is more contin-uous with daily existence. It follows, incidentally, that juvenile literary fantasy ought to be the continual concern of adults, since it shapes the least reversible aspect of moral development, the imaginative sensibility.

I want to say a word about a fantasy dimension that seems to be especially germane to children's imagination, the miniature. Children—so much most of us do remember—like a book that "combines the lure of freedom with the snugness of security" (Fadiman 1983). Another way to put it is that they are easily enthralled by an opportunity for contemplating a microcosm combined with the practical power to dispose of it. Of course, the perpet-ually supervised child will enjoy being the overseer in turn. Yet the true shudder of content comes more from just surveying a well-appointed miniature world where the pine seedling is a tree, the pebble a boulder, the acorn cup a watering trough, the moss a lawn, and where the bug popula-tion scurries about its business, gently aided or diverted by the hand from heaven, and, where, joy of joys, a boat of bark sails over a puddle-pond with an impressed sailor-ant swarming up its twig-mast. What holds for tiny natural habitats and articles like model railroads and doll houses holds as well for literary microcosms: Although the peculiar magic of miniature worlds is elusive, a part of it is surely the chance to see into secreted corners and the delight in the delicately profuse detailing that is characteristic of miniatures (Stewart 1984). This old microcosmic magic is distinguishable from the microscopic fascination that invaded English adult literature in the later seventeenth century (Nicolson 1935) and to which Swift's Lilliput is the most memorable testimony. There is a world of difference between the dainty homunculi of fantasy discoverable by the naked eye and the crawly animalcules which have to be magnified by the microscope to become visible. The latter may be wonders to scientific curiosity but to human sensibility they are swarming vermin, the thought of whose invisible ubiquity holds a certain horror. The distinction is nicely illustrated by Swift's Lilliputians and their modern posterity. The microscope-inspired (if not actually microscopic) Lilliputians, "small-thinkers" according to their own name, with their horrid little vermiculate mentalities, bear witness, for all their meticulousness, to the skin-crawling sense that the human world has now lost its decent lower bound. On the other hand, their gallant fairy-tale descendants, the New Lilliputians of T. H. White's *Mistress Masham's Repose* (1946), abducted by Gulliver to England and rediscovered there by a little girl two centuries later, are very appealing. Unlike *Gulliver's Travels*, *Mistress Masham* was actually written for children, and its latter-day Lilliputians are *bona fide* fantasy creatures: inhabitants of a magically diminutive secret subcreation, which affords the child not only the masterful sense of surveying and perhaps protecting a world but the snug thrill of feeling that the environment is permeated with intimacy and companionship down to its tiniest recesses.

Finally, microcosms have, beside the magic of fantasy, another aspect traceable more directly to the faculty of the imagination itself, of which the fantasy is, after all, only a mode. It is the aspect of scale. I shall argue in the next part that easy changes of scale, from sublime hugeness down to dainty miniature, belong to the very nature of the image-making imagination (Ch. II A).

Children's fantasy, then, although it is like that of adults in being *ludus imaginationis*, play of the imagination, is yet more continuous with their life, just as their play time is a more integral part of their activities than "free time" is of adult business. Consequently, fantasy for children reaches deeper into the soul than the corresponding adult genre, and of this difference I want to give a last and particularly telling comparative example.

A thoroughly adult fantasy of sophisticated uncanniness and classic standing is Borges's "Tlön, Ugbar, Orbis Tertius" (1941). In this demonic tale the author comes on Volume XI of an encyclopedia written, it turns out, by a secret society of scientists and literati, describing a counterworld, Tlön: "To begin with, Tlön was thought to be nothing more than a chaos, a free and irresponsible work of the imagination; now it was clear that it is a complete cosmos." A postscript dated 1947 reports a "first intrusion of the fantastic world into the real one." Objects from the fantasy world are being disseminated in ours, which is disintegrating under its intrusion. For example, a fictitious past is obliterating traditional history.

Like all reflective fantasy, "Tlön" is primarily concerned with the problem of man-made unreality permeating the real world and with the possibility of imaginary being intruding on nature—be it by way of threat or of hope. Thus one hemisphere of Tlön is explicitly Meinongian (Part Three, Ch. III A), for here the nonexistent objects that fill it are brought into being through its literature. The encyclopedists turn the trick by producing just that intersection of a mass of adjectives which pushes words to the limit of visibility (a concretizing effect mentioned above—Ch. I B). By means of the laws of Tlön itself and through the very fact of its existence the trickiest problems are broached: idealism in philosophy, naming in linguisitics, nonexistence in logic, recursion in mathematics. They are broached, but all conclusions are left suspended. The story as well as its world are an unsettling, ghostly, cerebral game.

Now as it happens there is a children's book, one of the finest ever written, which similarly touches on the most alluring current intellectual problems. It is Michael Ende's *Neverending Story* (1979), a story about a fat and lonely little boy, a lover of apple strudel and a spinner of tales, who comes by a magical book about the land Phantasia. Phantasia is in the process of being literally annihilated for lack of human attention. As he reads, he realizes that he is chosen to bear the responsibility for saving the land of the imagination by entering the book. This he does, and after surviving terrific trials and making devoted friends he becomes in turn the deliverer, the tyrant, and the prisoner of Phantasia. He is finally restored to his father through the sacrifice of a severe and lithe young Indian brave, his bosom friend in fantasyland.

The book is packed with weird and vivid landscapes, heart-stopping trials, quests, adventures and scores of distinctively enchanting beings. Each and every one of these is unobtrusively the imaginative representation of a human perplexity or a philosophical problem. The inquiry begins with young Bastian, the hero, ruminating just before opening his book: "I would like to know what really goes on in a book as long as it is closed." Then are raised in turn, besides many ethical questions concerning the authorial power, all the most puzzling issues attendant on the exercise of the literary imagination: the role it plays in shaping the world and guarding it from grey foggy nothingness and the treadmill of recurrence; its own corruption and salvation; the standing of fictive worlds and their interrelations; the self-reference and recursion that occur when a story teller enters the story; the relation of lies to fiction and of memory to imagination, and the part both the latter play in the healing of the affective soul (Brann 1985).

The point here is that there seems to be a way to philosophy through Phantasia more viable than that afforded even by the sophisticated diversions of adult fantasy like Borges's. The difference is, I think, in the concreteness and continuity of the imaginative representations in the children's book. The perplexities are no more resolved in one than in the other, but rather than beginning and ending as uncanny, literary, intellectual constructs, in the *Neverending Story* they develop into human enigmas made imaginatively visible, vivid facts presented for reflection. To put it another way: Really fine children's fantasy is not really fantastic but imaginative, in the sense that the power of imagining is applied to turning mysteries of thought into marvels of vision—an eminently reversible effect.

Bibliography

Borges, Jorge Luis. 1941. "Tlön, Ugbar, Orbis Tertius." In *Ficciones*. New York: Grove Press (1962).

Brann, Eva. 1967. "The Music of the Republic." *AGON: Journal of Classical Studies* 1:1–117. [Reprinted in *The St. John's Review* (1989–90) 39: 1–104.]

———. 1972. "The Venetian Phaedrus." *The St. John's Review* 24:1–9.

———. 1976. "A Reading of the Gettysburg Address." In *Abraham Lincoln: The Gettysburg Address and American Constitutionalism*, edited by Leo Paul de Alvarez. Irving, Tex.: University of Dallas Press.

———. 1985. "Through Phantasia to Philosophy: Review with Reminiscences." *The Journal of Philosophy for Children* 6:1–8.

Brooke-Rose, Christine. 1981. *A Rhetoric of the Unreal: Studies in Narrative and Structure, Especially of the Fantastic.* Cambridge: Cambridge University Press.

Bulfinch, Thomas. 1855. *The Age of Fable; or, Stories of Gods and Heroes.* Boston: Sanborn, Carter and Bazin.

Campbell, Joseph. 1986. *The Inner Reaches of Outer Space: Metaphor as Myth and Religion.* New York: Harper and Row.

Carpenter, Humphrey, and Prichard, Mari. 1984. *The Oxford Companion to Children's Literature.* Oxford: Oxford University Press.

Cassirer, Ernst. 1925. *Language and Myth.* Translated by Susanne K. Langer. New York: Dover Publications (1946).

————. 1923–1929. *The Philosophy of Symbolic Forms*, Volume 2, *Mythical Thought*. Translated by Ralph Manheim. New Haven: Yale University Press (1955).

Cox, Harvey. 1969. "Fantasy and Religion." Chapter 5 in *The Feast of Fools: A Theological Essay on Festivity and Fantasy*. Cambridge: Harvard University Press.

Daedalus. Fall 1985. Miller, Jonathan, "The Mind's Eye and the Human Eye"; Shattuck, Roger, "Words and Images: Thinking and Translation."

Davenport, Guy. 1981. "Hobbitry." In *The Geography of the Imagination*. San Francisco: North Point Press.

Eliade, Mircea. 1960. *Myths, Dreams and Mysteries: The Encounters between Contemporary Faiths and Archaic Realities*. New York: Harper and Row.

————. 1975. *Myths, Rites, Symbols: A Mircea Eliade Reader*. Edited by Wendell C. Beane and William G. Doty. New York: Harper and Row.

Ende, Michael. 1979. *The Neverending Story*. Translated by Ralph Manheim. New York: Doubleday (1983).

Fadiman, Clifton. 1983. "The Child as Reader." In *Great Books Today*. Chicago: Encyclopedia Britannica, Inc.

Forster, E. M. 1927. "Fantasy." Chapter 6 in *Aspects of the Novel*. New York: Harcourt, Brace and Co. (1954).

Frank, Joseph. 1945. "Spatial Form in Modern Literature." Chapter 1 in *The Widening Gyre*. New Brunswick: Rutgers University Press (1963).

Frazer, James G. 1890. *The New Golden Bough*. Edited by Theodor H. Gaster. New York: Criterion Books (1959).

Friedländer, Paul. 1928. "Myth." Chapter 9 in *Plato: An Introduction* (Part I). Translated by Hans Meyerhoff. Bollingen Foundation LIX. New York: Pantheon Books (1958).

Frye, Northrop. 1957. "Archetypal Criticism: Theory of Myths." In *Anatomy of Criticism: Four Essays*. Princeton: Princeton University Press.

Goodman, Nelson. 1984. *Of Mind and Other Matters*. Cambridge: Harvard University Press.

Grey, Sir George. 1855. "Preface to Polynesian Mythology." In *Die Eröffnung des Zugangs zum Mythos: Ein Lesebuch*, edited by Karl Kerényi. Darmstadt: Wissenschaftliche Buchgesellschaft (1967).

Gronicka, André von. 1956. "Myth Plus Psychology: A Stylistic Analysis of *Death in Venice*." In *Thomas Mann: A Collection of Critical Essays*, edited by Henry Hatfield. Englewood Cliffs, N.J.: Prentice-Hall (1964).

Holländer, Hans. 1980. "Das Bild in der Theorie des Phantastischen." In *Phantastik in Literatur und Kunst*, edited by Christian W. Thomsen and Jens Malte Fischer. Darmstadt: Wissenschaftliche Buchgesellschaft (1985).

Huizinga, Johan. 1938. *Homo Ludens: A Study of the Play Element in Culture*. Boston: Beacon Press (1950).

Jaspers, Karl, and Bultmann, Rudolf. 1954. *Die Frage der Entmythologisierung*. Munich: R. Piper und Co. Verlag.

Jehmlich, Reimer. 1980. "Phantastik—Science Fiction—Utopie: Begriffsgeschichte und Begriffsabgrenzung." In *Phantastik in Literatur und Kunst*, edited by Christian W. Thomsen and Jens Malte Fischer. Darmstadt: Wissenschaftliche Buchgesellschaft (1985).

Kaufmann, Fritz. 1957. *Thomas Mann: The World as Will and Representation*. Boston: Beacon Press.

Kerényi, Karl. 1939. "Was ist Mythologie?" In *Die Eröffnung des Zugangs zum Mythos: Ein Lesebuch*, edited by Karl Kerényi. Darmstadt: Wissenschaftliche Buchgesellschaft (1967).

Lehnert, Herbert. 1965. *Thomas Mann: Fiction, Mythos, Religion*. Stuttgart: W. Kohlhammer Verlag.

Lévi-Strauss, Claude. 1962. *The Savage Mind*. Chicago: The University of Chicago Press (1966).

Lewis, C. S. 1955. *Surprised by Joy: The Shape of My Early Life*. New York: Harcourt, Brace, Jovanovich.

MacCormac, Earl R. 1976. *Metaphor and Myth in Science and Religion*. Durham, N.C.: Duke University Press.

MacDonald, George. 1858. *Phantastes*. London: Ballantine Books (1970).

Malinowski, Bronislaw. 1926. "Die Rolle des Mythos im Leben." In *Die Eröffnung des Zugangs zum Mythos: Ein Lesebuch*, edited by Karl Kerényi. Darmstadt: Wissenschaftliche Buchgesellschaft (1967).

Manguel, Alberto, and Guadalupi, Gianni. 1980. *The Dictionary of Imaginary Places*. Illustrated by Graham Greenfield, with maps and charts by James Cook. New York: Macmillan Publishing Co.

Manlove, C. N. 1982. "On the Nature of Fantasy." In *The Aesthetics of Fantasy Literature and Art*, edited by Roger C. Schlobin. Notre Dame: University of Notre Dame Press (1982).

Mann, Thomas. 1936. "Freud and the Future."

Molson, Francis J. 1982. "Ethical Fantasy for Children." In *The Aesthetics of Fantasy Literature and Art*, edited by Roger C. Schlobin. Notre Dame: University of Notre Dame Press (1982).

Nicolson, Marjorie. 1935. "The Microscope and English Imagination." Chapter 6 in *Science and Imagination*. Ithaca: Cornell University Press (1956).

Nodelman, Perry. 1988. *Words About Pictures: The Narrative Art of Children's Picture Books*. Athens: The University of Georgia Press.

Penning, Dieter. 1980. "Die Ordnung in der Unordnung: Eine Bilanz zur Theorie des Phantastischen." In *Phantastik in Literatur und Kunst*, edited by Christian W.

Thomsen and Jens Malte Fischer. Darmstadt: Wissenschaftliche Buchgesellschaft (1984).

Raglan, Lord. 1855. "Myth and Ritual." In *Myth: A Symposium*, edited by Thomas A. Sebeok. Bloomington: Indiana University Press (1965).

Searles, Baird, Meacham, Beth, and Franklin, Michael. 1982. *A Reader's Guide to Fantasy*. New York: Avon.

Shepard, Odell. 1956. *The Lore of the Unicorn*. New York: Harper and Row (1979).

Stewart, Susan. 1984. *On Longing: Narratives of the Miniature, the Gigantic, the Souvenir, the Collection*. Baltimore: The Johns Hopkins University Press.

Thurow, Glen E. 1976. *Abraham Lincoln and American Political Religion*. Albany: State University of New York Press.

Todorov, Tzvetan. 1970. *The Fantastic: A Structural Approach to a Literary Genre*. Translated by Richard Howard. Cleveland: The Press of Case Western Reserve University (1973).

Tolkien, J.R.R. 1947. "On Fairy Stories." In *Essays Presented to Charles Williams*, edited by C. S. Lewis. Grand Rapids: Wm. B. Eerdmans Publishing Co. (1968).

Verene, Donald P. 1981. *Vico's Science of the Imagination*. Ithaca: Cornell University Press.

Vico, Giambattista. 1725. *The New Science*. Translated by Thomas G. Bergin and Max H. Fisch. Garden City, N.Y.: Doubleday and Co. (1961).

Wolfe, Gary K. 1982. "The Encounter with Fantasy." In *The Aesthetics of Fantasy Literature and Art*, edited by Roger C. Schlobin. Notre Dame: University of Notre Dame Press (1982).

Wollheim, Richard. 1965. "On Drawing an Object." In *Philosophy Looks at the Arts*, edited by Joseph Margolis. Philadelphia: Temple University Press (1978).

Zaslavski, Robert. 1981. *Platonic Myth and Platonic Writing*. Lanham, Md.: University Press of America.

Part Five

Depiction: The Theater of Imaging

Depiction: The Theater of Imaging

Forming, harboring, and bringing forth resembling depictions is the aboriginal, primary—the *eponymous*—function of the imagination. This
straightforward and sturdy notion of the faculty of the imagination both as
a power of imaging and as a theater of images seems in the common
understanding to have survived the cavils of philosophers, psychologists,
logicians, and literary critics, which have been examined in order through
the previous parts of the book—as well as those of the aestheticians
presently to be considered.

In this, the penultimate part, the conditions and kinds of imaged depictions, natural and conventional, will be taken up, more or less as if their
existence had been granted, though the resemblance question is critically
reviewed in the third chapter. The verbal imagining considered in Part Four
required translation from the realm of denoting, discrete language to the
realm of ostensive, spatial visions. Depictive imaging, on the other hand, is
direct from visible sight to visible sight—from space to space. For space is
the primary medium of all sensory representation, but most manifestly of
vision. Whereas in Part Three the structure of images taken in themselves
was examined, here I consider the character of depictions insofar as they
are shaped in the medium of our imaging faculty (and by its functions) as
well as in external space. It is therefore the imagination *proper*—or rather,
the imagination in its proper element—which is finally the subject.

The traditional term "faculty" does not nowadays require as much
apology as it once did. Though proscribed for most of the century as a
pseudo-explanatory hypostasis, it has been resurrected in cognitive psychology, albeit in a technical context. It turns out to be very convenient to
postulate psychological mechanisms that have, along with other defining
properties, the characteristic of "domain-specificity." The term means that
these mechanisms work only on specific bodies of information—for example different aspects of space, such as color, shape, and solidity. Such

"vertical" faculties (in contrast to the more general "horizontal" mental processes, which operate across informational domains, as for example a general faculty of judgment) seem to play in cognitive studies the role of "interface systems" located functionally between the senses and the mind; they mediate between world and thought (Fodor 1984). So while the ensuing reflections on the imaging faculty make no pretense to cognitive cachet, it is a comfort to know that the ways converge on a complex faculty intermediate between sense and thought and having its own proper objects.

I have recalled as well another verbal exile, the word "soul" (Part One, Ch. V), since the power I shall be delineating is indeed a faculty of the soul. "Soul" is now nearly taboo in non-theological English (except in its Black sense), although admitted in the terminological guise of "psyche" and its compounds. It has been replaced in most contexts by "mind" (Bettelheim 1983). Now while the Philosophy of Mind assigns to this term features similar to those once belonging to the soul, including, besides rationality and unconscious processes, affective states and productive spontaneity, it admits no faculties. Cognitive psychology, on the other hand, does allow faculties, but employs the word mind with fairly strict cognitive connotations. Now the imagination is a faculty, but not a cognitive faculty exclusively. It is both passionate and productive; it is informed by feelings and brings forth fictions. Hence "soul" seems a fine word for the seat of the imagination, for it can accommodate it as a faculty and, moreover, as a faculty that is not narrowly cognitive.

To return to depiction: Since spatiality seems to be the underlying feature common to inner imaging and to outer picture-making, and since it presents mysteries even deeper than and prior to those concerning the figured resemblances that are achieved within it, this part will be organized as an inquiry into imaging space as a theater for the productions of the imagination.

Hence Chapter I will be concerned in a most fundamental way with the inner space of imaging, with its features and its officiating faculty. Chapter II will deal with that same space insofar as it receives inscriptions in accordance with mathematical thought and becomes geometric space. Chapter III discusses that same arena insofar as it submits to shaping by desirable sensory forms and becomes aesthetic space. Geometric and aesthetic imaging are each in its place treated under a double aspect, their internal as well as their external form. That is to say, they are considered as producing both images in psychic space and depictions in physical space— as functioning in both the theaters where imaging takes place.

Chapter I

The Space of Imaging

Every claim that there is a human capability for imaging, an activity having internal origins and external consequences, finally comes to speak of some sort of inner space, a space-like field in which the particular depictions take place. This chapter begins with a somewhat groping exposition of spatiality (A). For in order to say what space-likeness is, one first has to try to say what space might be like, to articulate the nature of space or spatiality—an endeavor complicated by the profusion of available attempts. Next something is said of the internal spatial faculty, namely intuition (B). And finally, grasping the nettle, an attempt is made to delineate the nature of the imaging field itself as actuated in inner space (C).

A. Spatiality: The Notion of Space

The notion I am trying to capture seems traditionally to have been pursued through five kinds of questions. The answers to these are naturally deeply enmeshed with one another and with the inquirer's world-view—a term somewhat less vacuous in this context than in most—since some perspectives on these questions are contiguous or complementary, others conflicting or incompatible. Is there some core insight they nonetheless share, such as might reveal spatiality itself?

The first question concerns the ontological standing of space: Is it a thing, real and intelligible (Descartes), or is it a no-thing, void and inapprehensible (the ancient atomists), or is it a bastard combination of these (Plato)?

The second question concerns its basic character: Is it a kind of primal opening, gap, or separation (Hesiod and *Genesis*), a receptacle (Plato), an envelope (Aristotle), the divine omnipresence (Jewish tradition), an absolute of locations (Newton), a relation of bodies (Leibniz), a form of sensibility

(Kant), a manifold of points and dimensions (Riemann), or an environment in which bodies are implanted and which human beings inhabit (the Phenomenologists)?

A third question concerns its various structural dispositions: With respect to bounds, is it a finite cosmos (Ptolemy), an indefinite extension (Descartes), an infinite universe (Newton), or an unbounded, self-reentering world (Einstein)? With respect to dimensionality, does the number of dimensions exceed three and include time? With respect to continuity, is it conceivable that it has missing locations and a discrete structure? With respect to orientability, can figures that differ from each other only as do our two hands be made to coincide by being moved about? With respect to inherent places and regions, is space homogeneous and isotropic or are there distinguishable locations and directions of motion? With respect to curvature, can one, two, or no parallels to a line be drawn through a point?

A fourth question concerns the original contents of space: Are these geometric elements (Plato, Galileo), impenetrable bodies related by force (Epicurus, Newton), a plenum of extended substances (Descartes), various ethers, or geometrical, or numerical fields?

The fifth question concerns our knowledge of space: Does it arise through experience (Locke), through intuition, or through rational construction? Are the mathematical spaces of geometry, the experienced space of physics, and ordinary lived-in space diverse or coincident, and which of these is primary?

(Buroker 1981, Jammer 1957, Koyré 1957, Čapek 1976.)

If the way to spatiality leads through all of these clusters of questions, it is the last which determines the beginning. For it intimates that we might have a special faculty for apprehending space aside from sense and particularly aside from reason. Now in the hierarchy of geometries it is only the lowest "metric" geometry that is immediately descriptive of the space to which the spatial faculty here in question would apply. For a geometry is metric if each of its points has to all the others a unique relation called their distance, realized by a straight line between them. The higher, non-metric studies, projective geometry and topology, being constructions of thought abstracted from the space of experience and imagination, are spatial only figuratively. Clearly, the spatiality I am seeking, the primary, naive spatiality of actual, experienced space, be it psychic or physical, involves distances. All the questions above have behind them that metric sense of space as distance.

(Russell 1897, Meserve 1955.)

That sense, in turn, is reducible to an intimation that the space about which those questions concerning its existence, character, structure, contents, and cognitive source are asked is always and ultimately some sort of connected separation, or spanned sunderance. One might also call it extensive exteriority: exterior insofar as it is the essence of the elements of space to be outside of, apart from, each other, and extensive insofar as there is a way extending from each such element to every other. Consequently, extensive exteriority is analyzable under two complementary aspects. First there are termini, pegs of distinction, differentiating here from there, this location from that, making by their mutual externality what we call "room," which means literally an opening, a wide place. Obviously, "exteriority" is meant to apply equally to internal and external space. Second, there are the extensions stretching through this opening, from each terminus to every other, as signified by the word "space" itself, which is cognate with "passage," as well as by all the metric terms signifying passing through from terminus to terminus, such as di-mension, di-stance, dia-meter.

These related aspects are nicely illustrated in the two stages of the first geometric theories of space on record, those of the Pythagoreans. In the earlier stage space is understood as arising out of two principles: an originating unit and a principle of limitless duplication. This second source, the cause of all "two-ness," all opening, stretching, apartness, or otherness, is what Plato later call the "indeterminate dyad" (Aristotle, *Metaphysics* 987b). Dimensional space thus arises when the duplicating principle draws out of the primal unit indefinitely many point-units, all mutually paired: "for 'dimension' is that which is conceived of as between two termini" (Nicomachus II 6). Between two point-units arises the dimension we call the first, the line; three determine the second dimension by the simplest linear plane figure, the triangle, and four points give the basic solid or three-dimensional configuration, the pyramid. However, in the later stage of theorizing, not the termini but the passages between them are emphasized. The point, by flowing continuously, produces a line, a line flows into a plane, and the flux of a plane makes the solid module of space, in this version a cube (Guthrie 1962). Some such understanding of space as externality and some such analysis of externality as a bonding relation between each and every pair of sundered terms is common to the few authors that care at all to ground their description of space in a notion of its essence, its spatiality. Among these are Kant (1787), Hegel (1830), and Russell (1897). Russell expresses this notion most incisively: Space is relativity, "the possiblity of relations between diverse things" (190).

Spatiality has its counterpart in whatever is monadic, discrete, item-like, digital—in sum, whatever is countable rather than scannable. The Pythagoreans who discovered dimensional space also tried to build space from discrete, countable units having position—from points—hoping to derive the visible world from countable elements. They failed, having discovered the scandal of ancient mathematics: the incommensurability of lengths in certain geometric positions, which betokened the fact that a line in space has more locations than there are articulable or "rational" numbers. Now there is a great modern construction of a line whose points are indeed numerable—by means of the real, or irrational numbers, not known to the ancients (Dedekind 1858). But here's the rub: Dedekind speaks of the point "of," not "on," a line. Stated explicitly this means that he understands the line as a set of point-elements whose continuity is exactly that defined for the reals. It follows that this reconciliation of space with number, this matching of what is now called the analogue with the digital realm, is here accomplished by the arithmetization of a geometric line. By this device its irreducible extensivity is bypassed; this line is not a distance but a "well-arranged domain" that meets a formal definition of continuity. But the spatial dimension I am after, the space of naive intuition, is a true extension, not a point-collection, a mathematical construction. It is that in experienced space which cannot be formalized away: its actual spread, the irreducibly non-digital.

It goes without saying that all this does not amount to a sharp, impregnable concept but only to a speculative attempt to articulate our sense of space. The object of this admittedly abstruse exercise is to lay the foundation for distinguishing a faculty essentially devoted to space-viewing, namely the imagination proper.

B. Intuition: The Faculty of Inner Vision

Intuition is the word at hand that best connotes certain generic features of that space-representing faculty by which —and, moreover, in which— imaging takes place. I shall in fact use it here for designating the mental place or medium which the imagination activates and in which it inscribes its figures—the field over which the faculty operates, so to speak.

I must now barge ahead without further agitating the perpetual question of the existence of such a capacity both for representation in general and for spatial representation in particular. For while there is simply no consensus on the concept itself, or on the relevance to it of experimental findings, or even about the possibility of framing the question, the accumulated experimental case for an imagery-medium and the emerging description of it are hard to dismiss. What is more, human beings persist, indefeasibly it seems, in speaking of imagining in their heads or souls and of seeing what they so imagine with the mind's eye. Mathematicians, painters, dreamers speak in this way, and this apprehension informs the whole tradition.

One more observation: Apparently undecidable arguments are usually those that touch the human condition most nearly, and this truth is exemplified by the imagination-controversy. Those who deny an inner space—of which the intuition in my sense is the condition—have characteristic standards for human cognition and an agenda embodying them: clarity, complexity, computability. Their opponents tend instead to cherish the facts of experience and do not shrink from entrenched enigmas, unplumbed depths, and anticipatory insights. The first group is more fertile in constructive projects, the second is more attentive to the contemplation of the way things are. I am speaking, of course, of the propositionalists and imagists of Part Two.

"Intuition" is a ubiquitous term with roughly four sets of uses: First it signifies a mode of knowing. This is a meaning, popular at present, which runs the gamut from instinctive and hunch-like to non-rational, non-rigorous, and informal knowing. The same discontent with rationality that animates the "imagery movement" has made the word in this application a term of praise and propaganda (Noddings and Shore 1984). Second, intuition means a kind of knowledge. This meaning, originating in classical philosophy, is the opposite of the first—it refers to a primary intellectual insight, not, to be sure, rigorous, but instead immediate, self-evident, certain, global, and vision-like. Third, as a special mathematical ability, it is a facility, which has become second nature through long familiarity, for "seeing" the structure of mathematical objects. It is applied even when these objects have been raised far beyond naive spatial imagination by a long process of abstraction and elaboration (Dieudonné 1975); practiced mathematicians in their element tend to confuse it with ordinary imagination.

There are, in addition, a variety of technical uses of the word in contemporary philosophy: unjustified but true belief, non-inferential knowledge of propositional truth, immediacy of conceptual knowledge, non-propositional knowledge of entities (Rorty in Noddings). But the meaning most suggestive in the present context is one whose elements are lifted from Kant (1787). As the form of all sensibility, that is, as the capability of being affected in general, Kantian intuition covers perception and imagination at once. I shall abstract from perception and attend only to imagination. It shows itself in two phases: as a "pure" geometric imagination, and again, when filled with matterless sensation, as the imagination of ordinary experience.

Here, then, is the fourth meaning of the word intuition: it is an inner sensibility, a receptive faculty before or in which representations are immediate, given, global, and spatial.

"Receptivity" describes this intuitive capacity insofar as we can, in Kantian terms, obtain representations in the mode of being affected by objects. This implies that there are actual objects that we receive to a certain degree passively and just as they present themselves to us, *in propria persona*, so to speak. "Immediacy" describes the same capacity insofar as the objects passively received are not—even unconsciously—reconstituted; in the language of cognitive psychology, there are no intermediate encodings. It is the possibility that there might be immediate presentations that is currently most strenuously denied in all disciplines from philosophy to aesthetics, but above all in cognitive science (with exceptions—Part Two, Ch. I C). All representations are said there to be mediated by mental processes beginning at the transducing organs. However, it is not cognitive immediacy that I mean here, but the immediacy of introspective experience. It is, after all, possible that intervening processes, like observational instruments, might occur simply so as to bring the object directly before us. An example that comes to mind is Galileo's delightful report on the first scanning of the heavens through his "new spy-glass," *The Starry Messenger* (1610). Surely a telescope mediates and preprocesses perceptions; yet for Galileo its wonderful property is precisely that it brings the moon "as near at hand as if it were scarcely two terrestrial radii away." The point is: We have no knowledge, only conviction concerning the question whether intermediate cognitive processes—and their neural counterparts—first constitute or in fact merely reconstitute the world for us. In the meantime, however, we have experiences of discursiveness and then again experiences of immediacy. It is a version of the latter that is the center of attention here.

"Givenness" refers to the way in which the objects come to be present: not as the conclusion of a conscious chain of inferences, but directly, self-evidently. "Globalism" refers to the all-at-once, as-a-whole apprehension of such representations. In the slightly off-beat language of the "imagery movement," they are "holistic" (a word in fact admitted into Webster's Dictionary in the early sixties), or in computer terminology, they are processed in parallel rather than serially (Kant 1787, B 33; Levinas 1930).

"Spatiality" is the result of all the preceding aspects—receptivity, givenness, globalism—taken together when the notion of extensionality as articulated above is added in. (Kant, of course, appears to hold that the intuition has two co-equal forms, temporality and spatiality, responsible for our experiencing things in time and space; but I have tried to show that he in fact treats spatiality as the primordial form—Part One, Ch. III D.) The intuition thus culminates in what Kant calls an "outer sense," but what is actually a sense of outerness, of externality taken in two ways, as extensive and as exterior: First, the outer intuition represents its contents as being spread out, having dimension, being self-external and extensional as described above. Such extension distinguishes the order of both spatial imagination and spatial reality from the temporal order (Ricoeur 1967). Second, the extensional intuition apprehends something as exterior to itself, since it is that faculty of the soul which is open to the world outside so as to represent it before, or to, the innermost thinking self. The two aspects together constitute the capacity that Kant calls "intuition," in German *Anschauung*, which means not a power of "in-sight," but a place for "at-sight." The intuition is both the theater of the soul and the viewer in it—where the thinking self becomes sighted and the understanding meets and molds sensation-filled space.

As such a meeting-ground it is a medium, a place, an inner space. That is why figures can be said to be "in" the intuition. It is within this space that the imagination in the ordinary sense, as "a faculty for having intuitions even without the presence of the object," does its work of either producing pure geometric structures (geometric intuition), or reproducing matterless appearances previously seen (memory), or reforming these immaterial appearances into new visions (imaginary imagination). From the present point of view, the theory of the transcendental imagination set out at length in Part One is simply an acute analysis of the conditions of the possibility for having an ordinary imagination at all. For that theory represents the intuition on the one hand as a "pure manifold" (1787, B 160 n.) modifiable by sense, and on the other as a place to be informed by the power of the imagination on all levels.

I must end this section with an admission and an avowal. The admission is that an intuitive medium, an inner space—that is to say, an internal externality—is an irresoluble contradiction in terms. "Inner space" should always be in quotation marks. The soul is at most space-*like*. But when all is said and done, what is space-like except space? The problem, under different perspectives, is perennial.

A little less than three quarters of a millenium ago it was a current question how the incorporeal angels actually occupied real places, that is, how spirits eventuated in space. My present problem, no less fascinating, is the inverse of Thomas's: How do souls encompass a representational space? It is a problem that can be blinked by ascribing it to mistaken manners of speech. One might, for example, claim that extension is literally and falsely attributed to consciousness because extended objects are metaphorically called "contents of consciousness" (Seifert 1979). Or one might attribute the perplexity to the equivocation of the phrases "inner space" or "quasi-space." But it is not the ways of speech that cause the problem. It is the perplexity that induces such manners of speech.

There are two real resolutions, real in the sense of facing the problem and resolving it. Both are extreme. One is, in fact, the Kantian. If spatiality is one and the same form of receptivity for all kinds of sensibility at once— for sensation, for pure geometry, and for imaginative play—and if space is its pure material, then the spatial field for perception and imagining are one. Hence the problem of a merely space-like representative space does not even arise. Inner and outer space are identical, both belonging to the subject, the soul. While using Kant's analysis of spatiality, I here make no commitment to its transcendental aspect, since it obviates my problem by the denial of extra-mental space. The effort here is, after all, to establish the imagination as an intermediary between world and intellect.

A diametrically opposed, fascinatingly eccentric, solution is that of Samuel Alexander (1916). Where in the Kantian hypothesis perceptual and image space are equally mental, in the Alexandrian system perceptions and images are equally in an extra-mental part of space. All space is one, but it falls into regions: "enjoyed" space and "contemplated" space. "Enjoyment" is Alexander's remarkable word for conscious activity: "The act of mind is an enjoyment; the object is contemplated" (perhaps as in the Presbyterian *Westminster Shorter Catechism*, where the first question "What is the chief end of man?" has the answer "to glorify God, and to enjoy Him forever"). The mind has a certain kind of "voluminousness," so that in enjoying the contemplated spatial objects it experiences, as it were, a mental simultaneity with them in space. The application to imagined space is that, as "contemplated," this space confronts the mind's perceptual space, which is "away from it," on an equal basis: "All images of external objects are themselves spatial in character," and "have position in the whole of space." "*Prima facie*, sense and images are on the same footing." What distinguishes images is only their lack of coherence and fit with veridical sensation: "They are rejected by the thing." Alexander's highly original struggle with the spatiality of imagery is unfortunately too deeply enmeshed in the cosmological system of *Space, Time, and Deity* to provide an independent solution to the perplexity concerning imaging-space for present purposes. But such extreme understandings illuminate the middling—and ultimately equally implausible—solutions.

So let me make the avowal intimated above: When all descriptions have been completed and all their conditions worked out, inner space remains an enigma. So be it. We have the choice of denying our central capacity or of talking on the edge of clarity. Well, on the ladder of significant discourse antiseptic negation stands below pregnant obscurity.

C. Inner Space: The Field of Inner Vision

The description of this inner space is the crux of the inquiry. It is, once again, a visual space. That is not to say that the imagination does not, somehow, work with all the sensory modes, or that the other major senses, touch and hearing, do not have their own relation to the distances and intervals of space (Introduction A). However, the spatiality of touch, for example, is rather curtailed, lacking the global aspect, though it is direct: congenitally blind children can make mental maps, including paths between objects they have separately reached from a third location, can grasp immediately the idea of a tactile map as an image of space, and can distinguish kinds of shapes (Gardner 1985). Yet these representations are neither panoramic nor color-filled. The spatiality of hearing, on the other hand, while so pervasive and rich as to make every aspect of music, including its peculiarly temporal features, very naturally representable in spatial notation, is nonetheless indirect, being evidently some sort of translation.

Therefore, as perceptual vision is the one sense that is fully and directly spatial, being receptive to the colored continua and configurations of extended space, so the inner space, if such there be, is primarily a visual space.

Moreover, only the imagination working in visual space effects images properly speaking, namely depictions that represent something. Of course, we have an auditory memory with which to reproduce images of perceived sound. But except for marginal effects, like metaphorical renditions of heights and depths, and direct imitations of birds or bells in music, neither perceived nor, consequently, imagined sound structures are properly representational. They might induce images of psychic and physical motions and shapes, but they do not stand for them with any determinate correspondence. It is no wonder: while space can contain representations both of itself and of the articulations of time, time has not the dimensions wherewith to image the shapes of space.

1. Denial and Affirmation. The urgent denial of the existence of an inner space does, after all, have to be taken up one last time. It is incited by what in the preceding section I called the externality of space, the fact that it is other than the reckoning and reasoning mind and escapes complete description and dominion by it. The proof adduced for the denial is usually to the effect that models of cognition can do without such a field, indeed have more explanatory virtue without it. Such proofs fail because they bypass the rock-bottom experience of inner extension and grapple only with the application of propositions to the spatial structure. But at the same time they also succeed, because whatever inner space may feel like, it eventually has to be spoken of, and then it is the propositionalists who produce the conceptual vocabulary for making its specifically spatial relations explicit (Part Two, Ch. II C) . Here is the briefest sketch of the procedure involved in such a cognitive approach, as set out by Olson and Bialystok (1983).

The hypothesis of this procedure does not start with an inner space that is, as above, a field or ground of spatial representations, but instead with a tacit description of spatial configurations: "An image is a set of propositions," that is, of predicates and their arguments. Such propositions are not, to begin with, verbally articulated, though the concepts involved may come to be named. The analysis has two phases. It begins by recovering this implicit structural description of spatial objects, a propositional representation of features which is constructed by the mind as perceptual spatial learning goes on. For example, the mental representation of a square consists of an implicit, evolving organization of its properties and relations, in this case the component points, lines, angles, and their nodes. The second phase recovers an aspect often psychologically prior, the assignment of meaning, when use and context come to be associated with the structure. For a structural description may have more than one meaning. An example is a circle with a vertical line hanging from it, which may depict a lollipop or a stop sign. Thus form–perception becomes separated from object-perception: Pure geometric figures are, along with all other images, structural descriptions made explicit, but they differ in being divorced from any object–identification.

In this geometry, the congruence of two figures would be the sameness of their propositional description. Consequently, the motive for a propositional theory of space is economy and perspicuity: "The trouble with images, simply, is that they may be useful as a theory of ideas but not for a theory of judgments" (Olson and Bialystok 1983). Since our business is eventually to make unavoidable propositional judgments of truth and falsity, "we may as well construct such propositions in the representational phase of the task." Thus images are dropped, being unnecessary hypotheses.

That lets some old cats out of the new bag. First and obviously, it seems to me, the purportedly tacit internal descriptions are, as far as one can tell, external explanatory constructions that in fact require a lot of ingenuity. Second, in converting spatial intuitions into propositions, their geometric arguments—points, lines, etc.—cannot help entering as undefined, or better, as unmeaning elements. That is fine in axiomatic geometry, which glories in the possibility and the process of formalizing spatial intuition.

But will it serve as a theory of unelaborated human knowledge? Is not propositionalism a false parsimony?

As it happens, we do externalize our experience of inner space in other than verbal propositional modes, in modes that seem moreover to render it more directly than do words, for instance, in pictures. It is hard to think of more persuasive testimony concerning the persistent activation of inner visual space than the watercolor landscapes painted by a woman who became blind when old enough to have accumulated the visual experiences that she later transferred section by section to the paper (Finke 1986). Of the general constitution of this essentially depictable space too, something can be said in words.

2. The Three Versions of Inner Space. To begin with, it comes in a perceptual (a), a geometric (b), and an imaginative (c) version, and the three are related to one another (d). In the following paragraphs, some fundamental features and unresolved questions will be set out.

a. A certain kind of imaging, vivid visual memory, is close to perception. It is the kind that can be studied through the recall of sharply curtailed perceptual stimuli in the laboratory. It is preeminently called "mental imagery" (Part Two). There is reason to think that such memory–imagery does share certain perceptual processes that occur at stages beyond the stimulation of the eye, since they behave in structurally equivalent ways (Part Two, Ch. VI A). For example, a real three-dimensional display can be mentally shifted so as to reveal to the imager the correct new configuration (Finke 1986).

It seems to be one and the same space of perceptual memory that is identified in a number of ways in psychology and philosophy. One such is Piaget's "representation space," into which images are inscribed mimetically in early childhood by means of a "translation of tactile into visual data." These images act to "signify" objects to thought (Part Two, Ch. IV B, Piaget 1948). Another is the cognitive space just set out, in which perceptions are structured by propositional processes.

The phenomenal field of the Gestalt theorists is another, very powerful version of perceptual space, whose properties are sharply distinguished from elementary geometric space. Thus, among other features, it is anisotropic: effectively different in various directions. For example, of equal vertical and horizontal motions, the vertical is, under certain conditions, experienced as faster (Koffka 1935). This formative perceptual space makes a bridge to the older philosophical representation spaces of Hume and Kant, which play host to perception and imagination at once. Thus for

Kant, as was pointed out above, the reproductive imagination, being a faculty for representing an object in intuition even without its material presence, takes its place in the same formative space that material perceptions occupy, although it lacks the reality belonging to lawfully related material objects.

This absence of physical responsibility is here taken to distinguish inner imaginative space from outer perceptual space. Memory tends to preserve the spatial aspect of things but to forget their temporal behavior. It is more likely to make light of the laws of motion than of shape. For example, inner motion preserves perspective but loses inertia (Part Two, Ch. II B). In this first of imaginative spaces the imagination therefore plays a labile and unreliable role. Out of the lawful physicality of perception it seems to retain only the mere appearance from which perceptual objects were first elaborated. Yet that job it does uniquely well; as Piaget expressed it: "Spatial images are the only images in which the symbolizing form tends to complete isomorphism with the symbolized content" (1963, 682).

There is one more consideration. Is the imaging of inner space done with eyes open or closed? Aristotle says that "we do not speak of remembering what is at present perceived" (*On Memory* 449 a), and Wittgenstein says that "while looking at an object I cannot imagine it" (*Zettel* 621). It does seem to be impossible to visualize a particular object while focusing strictly on it, probably because the same mechanisms are involved. On the other hand, it is quite possible to exercise visual memory while gazing into the world; most of the imagery experiments are done in that way. In fact, very vivid visual recall, like that of "eidetikers," requires projection onto an external field. Geometric and imaginative imaging, as well, are perfectly feasible, sometimes even more efficacious, with eyes open. Evidently only visual memory in the narrowest sense precludes simultaneous object-focused vision. A case will be made in the Conclusion that simultaneity of seeing and imagining are an essential work of the imagination.

b. Geometric space, the second imaging space, is, so to speak, perceptually attenuated where visual memory was high-toned. As mentioned above, I intend here that "naive" geometric intuition whose figures are internally visualizable and directly drawable in ordinary external space.

Perhaps the inner experience at issue wants some description, though it is familar to anyone who has ever, eyes glazed, tried to solve a problem by visualizing a geometric construction—who has mentally folded, pushed, or jumped its parts, drawn them on paper, and looked again into the distance, searching for the inspired auxiliary line. It is not, as a matter of fact, a crisp experience—it is hard to say whether the lines are "breadthless lengths" as defined by Euclid or only approximate that ideal, whether the figures are colorless or vapor-hued, whether shapes are perfect or only vague, have any size or no size, spontaneously appear in the field or are deliberately inscribed. Yet the sum of all these indefinites seems to make up the experience of elementary geometric visualization.

Just as the propositionalist-imagist debate concerns perceptual memory, so the long three-pronged quarrel among the empiricists, nativists, and logicists centers on geometric intuition: Are the dispositions of geometry built up from repeated perceptions of external space, are they intuited originally, or are they arbitrary, non-visual systems of pure relations? The next chapter is, in fact, an exposition of the middle possibility. In the meantime let me add an observation on yet a fourth theory, the idea that spatial insight develops in stages. In his studies of the development of spatial and geometric consciousness in children, Piaget (1948, 1960) maintains that not metric space but topological space has primacy. Before their fifth year or so, children's drawings of geometric objects ignore shape and size and preserve only order and position. However, it has been argued to the contrary that this fact proves little (Ninio 1979). The inadequacies of the child's externalizations are not necessarily revelations of the incompleteness of the child's inner representations. Furthermore, since Euclidean transformations are logically included among the topological transformations, these are "tautologically primary." What this phrase means is that if a drawn figure is to be recognizable as a figure at all it has to have certain features of order and position, but that fact does not make it topological. Indeed, any drawn figure is *ipso facto* metric, that is, measurable, though it might be messily so. Children might be careless about distance relationships, but the very fact of their drawing shows they are involved in them. So the developmental priority of topology is very doubtful.

"Grasped by a kind of bastard reason through non-sensation" in a kind of dim dream—that is how Plato mythologizes our hindered access to the receptacle that furnishes the geometric elements from which bodies are built (*Timaeus* 52). The reason that apprehends world-space is bastard because it is sired by the intellect upon a chaotic manifold that imposes its a-rational necessities on thought. It is non-sensory because it is a geometric space as described above, and it is dimly dreamt because it is imagined as vaporously as is that space. Although all coloration has been abstracted from the Timaean container of physical bodies, the sensibility is by no means absent in this and other classical treatments of geometry. Its figures are born of a somewhat mysterious congress between thought and sensation. Thus Plato, in his non-mythical treatment of geometry in the *Republic* (511), describes its apprehension as "something betwixt and between" (*metaxy ti*) thought and seeing; it is thinking implicated in extension: the *dianoia,* the power of "through-thinking" discussed in Part One (Ch. I A) is conceived precisely to effect that union. For him the study of geometry is a kind of practice-contemplation, which purifies the "eye of the soul" (527) from the contamination of sense without quite attaining pure intellection. Though he does not come right out and say it, the realm of geometry is all but an ideal sensibility—pure inner space as above defined.

Aristotle, and Thomas annotating him, have a lower opinion of mathematics, for they regard its objects not as belonging to a separable middle realm, but as arising by an act of abstraction from sensibles (Thomas Aquinas 1255, 1266). This is not to be taken for mathematical empiricism, since it concerns the intellectual genesis of mathematical objects in principle, quite apart from the progressive gathering of mathematical information. What abstraction yields are the geometric forms, with their individuating continuous quantity, their "intelligible matter" (1255, 29). This matter is perceived not by the external senses but "by means of the imagination alone, which is sometimes referred to as an intellect." The imagination receives just such "intelligible singulars" as designate the geometric forms (1266, on *Metaphysics* 1035). Retrospectively, we might see such singularized matter as bounded extension conceived in isolation from its field.

The inner sensibility becomes explicit under the denomination of "imagination-matter" (*hylē phantastikē*) in Proclus's Neoplatonic commentary on Euclid, where Platonic and Aristotelian elements are merged. What he adds to Platonic "in-between" intellection and Aristotelian spatial matter is the imagination—as a not entirely passive place of operation, part shaping power and part field-like medium. Into this imagery-medium the intellect projects its thoughts. The imagination, in receiving them, immattering them—so to speak—unfolds them, imparting to them extension and multiplicity. The following passage is the *locus classicus* of the geometric imagination:

> For the understanding contains the ideas but, being unable to see them when they are wrapped up, unfolds and exposes them and presents them to the imagination sitting in the vestibule; and in imagination, or with its aid, it explicates its knowledge of them, happy in their separation from sensible things and finding in the matter of imagination a medium apt for receiving its forms. Thus thinking in geometry occurs with the aid of the imagination. Its syntheses and divisions of the figures are imaginary; and its knowing, though on the way to understanding being, still does not reach it, since the understanding is looking at things outside itself. . . . But if it should ever be able to roll up its extensions and figures and view their plurality as a unity without figures,

then in turning back to itself it would obtain a superior vision of the partless, unextended, and essential geometrical ideas that constitute its equipment. This achievement would itself be the perfect culmination of geometrical inquiry, truly a gift of Hermes, leading geometry out of Calypso's arms, so to speak, to more perfect intellectual insights and emancipating it from the pictures projected in imagination. [Proclus 44]

I hesitate to start the exposition of the Kantian geometric imagination with a new paragraph, since it is in so many points like that of Proclus, its radically different context nothwithstanding. Kant's treatment is certainly not consciously derivative. I venture to say that it is the matter itself which speaks through both: spatiality is one of the two forms of intuition, but geometry requires that space itself be *"an* intuition" (1787, B 160). That is to say, space is the content of the receptive faculty, a content pure of all sensation. Within this space, the understanding functions to construct its concepts. There thoughts are inscribed or projected into the intuitive manifold, in extensional multiplicity, independent from experience (B 741). Again prior to all experience, the manifold, the extended medium, contributes its own determinations, which simply and brutely inhere within it: like Timaeus's "receptacle" it contains geometric traces (B 160). Some of these, such as "handedness" or "orientability," are very deep and encompassing. Others are somewhat more specific, above all, the Euclidean character, the "Euclideanism" of human space. For Kant the true science of geometry is the one discovered by the Greek mathematicians (B xi), and in it concepts and intuition cooperate. Thus the understanding represents the concept of a triangle as a rectilinear figure of three sides, the medium provides the determinative Euclidean property, that any triangle has an angle sum of two right angles, and—very much as in Proclus's text—the imagination as a mediating faculty produces the synthesis that brings together the concept and the pure intuitional space in a kind of general particular; presumably it can be multiplied and varied. This last is the imagined geometric figure, which signifies at the same time all sensible triangles in general and shows the particular intuited schema (B 180, Meerbote 1981). The notion of spatial matter as a pure substrate of geometric determinations recurs as late as 1897, in Russell's *Foundations of Geometry* (190).

In order to put Proclus's and Kant's theory back to back, I omitted a revolutionary step, the one taken by Descartes in introducing coordinate geometry (*Geometry* 1637). I am not at this moment thinking so much of the ultimate algebraicization of geometry, which was his explicit intention, as of the implicit effect the Cartesian revolution had on the geometric imagination. I have been speaking of it as a space. In truth, the term "space" is an anachronism in reference to pre-Cartesian geometry; what we mean by space is late in coming. In Euclid and Apollonius and the other ancient geometers there are extended figures, and all the attention is on them. Their spatial background never enters the system. Figures, triangles, cones, circles, are always defined as "contained" by their peripheries (*Elements*, Definitions); their unlimited exterior field is not the subject of attention. Nothing unreachable or uncontained ever is—one might almost say that that is what it means to be classical. In Cartesian (and Pascalian) geometry, the attention shifts from the finite figure to indefinite, even infinite, space. At the same time numerically determined locations, given by an arbitrary origin and directed dimensions, replace the locationless shapes of classical geometry which can be said to be in their place (*topos*) but not in a space. Consequently, Kant will regard geometric figures as delimitations of infinite space. Both geometric styles, classical and Cartesian, are "Euclidean." This turn from finite shape to infinite field does not yield a formally new geometric space, but it is more a quasi-aesthetic shift with far-reaching consequences to sensibility and understanding both. One might almost say that Cartesian geometry is the romantic foil to the classical view. For at all times, romanticism, as delineated in Part Four (Ch. II B), tends away from neat containments toward infinite extents, away from proper places to subjective origins, away from shaped figures toward spatial fields, and away from naive intuition to ever more sophisticated abstraction. And that, in sum, is the story of geometric space between antiquity and early modernity.

What all the authors so far mentioned have nonetheless in common is a faith in the fit of thought and space: the understanding adequately projects, inscribes, and functions in space. This harmony ends in the generation after Kant, with the publication of flawlessly thinkable yet quite unimaginable Noneuclidean geometries (Ch. II A). It turns out that the possibilities of geometric thinking are much wider than those of geometric intuition. This prospect, on top of the Cartesian algebraicization of geometry—the expression of figures in terms of equations satisfied by sets of numbers—opens the way to a more radical abstraction from visible geometry than Aristotle and Thomas could have dreamt of. The intuitive matter now simply drops out, except at the most elementary stage. Or if it does not drop out, it is systematically mismatched with its descriptive language, so that a dictionary is required to mediate between the intuitive picture and its verbal meaning. For example, a Noneuclidean plane may be modeled on a Euclidean sphere in such a way that one sees a great circle of the sphere while meaning a straight line in the plane.

Then follows a complex of consequences relevant to the inquiry concerning inner space. One is the project of formalizing geometry, realized by

Hilbert for Euclid (1898). Henceforth it becomes a purely logical system of relations of undefined elements. Its axioms are not spatial intuitions "worthy of being believed"—the literal meaning of the Greek term *axiōma*. For they do not refer to geometric intuitions but are arbitrary, though convenient, conceptual beginnings, which are not about space; if they are about anything they are about the concept of space—one remove from the imaginable.

Another consequence is that the old dilemmas pitting experiential science against innate geometric knowledge take on a novel, acute form, exemplified by Poincaré's "conventionalism" and its critics. Briefly stated: Kant had assumed both the actual applicability of geometric intuition to physical space and the unique fit of the functions of the understanding with the dispositions of the intuition. Hence his task was merely to find the faculties that would guarantee the applicability and the fit.

Poincaré, in contrast, had himself produced a proof that several conceptual systems of geometry were at least equally or "relatively" consistent (Ch. II A). Evidently, the mind can think of more valid possibilities than the soul can intuit. At this point, the geometric intuition (in the sense defined in B above) loses its standing as the source of geometry. The question becomes whether one or the other of these valid logical constructions can be proved true of physical space. A new kind of empiricism would seem to be called for, in which experience is expected not to teach the mind its geometric insights but to help choose among ready formal systems. Now Poincaré argues that this choice can never be made through experience because experiential terms can always be re-conceived so as to fit any geometry. He concludes that the choice must be made by a convention, and proposes Euclidean geometry as being simplest. His empirical critics reply that the required re-definition of terms is made effectively impracticable by the fact that physical definitions are coherently coordinated to natural objects.

(Poincaré 1905, Cassirer 1910, Reichenbach 1928, Sklar 1974, Nerlich 1976.)

In any case, for neither one side nor the other would the geometry be chosen on grounds of geometric intuition—not for Poincaré, because geometry is purely formal, and not for the new empiricists, because the world of physics has lost its immediacy. It is no longer the old world of direct human vision, which had its own, fittingly intellectualized, inner visualization in Euclidean geometry. "Intuitivity," as physicists will call it, is gone (Ch. II B).

Hence formal geometry and empirical space seem between them to effect the dispensability of the primary geometric imagination. Yet, though mathematical and physical systems have become vastly remote from ordinary insight, the straight and narrow gate to them—perhaps quickly passed through, but nonetheless utterly uncircumventable—is this same geometrical imagination: the first abstractions are made from its matter and the first advances take off from its axioms. Therefore it becomes of the most pointed, not to say poignant, importance that besides the unimaginable structures of higher and alternative spaces and the imageless symbols of formal reason, there is an intimate region in which the deliverances of direct vision and the insights of the intellect find each other. This region gains in human significance as it looses intellectual primacy, or so I will try to show below.

c. It is the third, the imaginative space, that might be said to *be* the imagination in its richest sense, as the space and place of an inner world. It is this psychic place of places we mean when we speak of scenes and figures as invented or transformed or harbored "in" our imagination—when, for example, Shakespeare bids his audience "In your imagination hold this stage a ship" (*Pericles* III, Gower 58). This imagination is really a space and a place at once. It is a space in being an illimitable field of possible places. And it is a place (to adapt the Aristotelian notion of *topos*) insofar as each region of the field, when brought into focus, becomes a containing abode, an enveloping atmosphere, proper home to the figures that fill it.

If perceptual memories are hard-edged, and geometrical figures are rarified, imaginative shapes are dyed, so to speak, with the magical colorations of inner space: this space is to the foregoing somewhat as painting is to drawing (Merleau-Ponty 1961). And yet, although quasi-sensory, this last of the spaces discussed is, along with its representations, in a curious way most remote from the space of perceptual memory, insofar as its images are often not at all referable to real-world originals for comparison. Yet this inner world, though it be of the soul, is not forever confined behind closed eyes. It is perfectly possible for imaginative space to cohabit with perceptual space and even to invest its figures. The first occurs when imagined visions are realized within the physical world and alongside its ordinary contents; paintings are prize examples (Ch. III B). The second takes place whenever figures of real space are seen in the light of imaginative vision or are invested with it; mythical re-enactments are a prime public instance (Part Four, Ch. IV A). In other words, there is both open-eyed and closed-eyed imagining. Inside or out, however, imaginative space is a space of meaning, for nothing within it is pointless; it is a space of significance, for nothing within it is isolated; it is a space of affectivity, for nothing within it is dull.

d. How, finally, are these three imaging spaces—memorial, geometric, and imaginative—related? Are they diverse working spaces for three sub-faculties of the intuition, or are they at bottom identical? All three alike can be variously activated: deliberately, spontaneously, incidentally, automatically, or involuntarily. The figures that so arise are all similarly exempt from the laws of motion while subject to the dispositions of space. Moreover the various contents are readily convertible into each other: The imagery fed by visual memory can be rectified and attenuated into geometric figures, and these can, in turn, become supple, tinged with color, and aesthetically appreciated. (The aesthetic fate of certain geometric figures, which accompanies, like a descant, the intellectual development of the West, offers examples of such transformations, cast, so to speak, into historical time; a prime case is the fascinating slow fall from intellectual and aesthetic grace of the canonical circle, and the ascent of the more variable ellipse at about the time when elliptical orbits are accepted in astronomy—Panofsky 1954, Santayana 1896, para 21.) Furthermore, the imaginative field is certainly peopled from memory, while perceptual memory is re-shaped by the imagination. Finally, the constructions of geometric space and the inventions of imaginative space can be realized in real space as diagrams and paintings, where they become in turn the source of fresh visual memories. And so each can go directly or derivatively into each.

It must be admitted here that Husserl dissents. His opinion on this question matters, since he was particularly interested in the transformations that bodies undergo under free imagining (Part One, Ch. IV A). He regards the "phantasy," with its mingling of memory and imagination as quite separate from the "ideal space" of pure geometric shapes. The latter, inasmuch as it is free of all sensibility and purely intellectual, is scarcely a space at all. However, the indispensable mediating notion of a "sensible ideality"—which describes the geometric space I have been at pains to delineate here—was broached but never worked out by him, probably because he never made the imagination thematic (Derrida 1974, 124).

Let me end with what seems to be the most fascinating transformation between two of these spaces. Investigators of perceptual-memory space agree that it is normally perspectival (Part Two, Ch. II B; imaginative space is often aperspectival—Part One, Ch. IV B). The objects in it are seen from a point of view: Parallel lines seem to converge to a vanishing point and circles appear as ellipses. Geometric space, on the other hand, tends to be absolute, in the sense that in it parallels are represented in their non-perspectival separation, and circles turn into ellipses not by a change of viewpoint, but if at all, only by a transformation of the figures themselves, through the convergence of the two foci. It is as if these plane figures were seen from a point beyond the space, an infinitely distant viewpoint. When in the *Optics* Newton calls his absolute space God's "boundless uniform *Sensorium*," he is in effect saying that for divine perception the infinite universe has the non-perspectival character of geometric space: such a space does not include the beholder's eye locally within itself and is consequently everywhere patent to its view. Now in its freedom from physical constraints, the human intuitive faculty shares this much of God's view: The mind's eye can zoom to a point of infinity and back home again in a trice. Thus absolute-geometric and perspectival-perceptual space are transformed into each other by the imagination with divine ease.

The space of our intuition, then, is surely one, though it is brought to life from three different sources: the senses, reason, and imagination; and, one might say, with three different intentions: perceptual recovery, visible intelligibility, and representational significance. I would denominate this unity one of the mysteries that this book is meant to save.

Bibliography

Alexander, Samuel. 1916–1918. *Space, Time, and Deity*, Volumes 1 and 2. London: Macmillan and Co. (1927).

Aristotle. 3rd quarter, 4th cent. BC. *Physics*, Book IV.

Berkeley, George. 1709. *A New Theory of Vision*. New York: E.P. Dutton and Company (1954).

Bettelheim, Bruno. 1983. *Freud and Man's Soul*. New York: Alfred A. Knopf.

Buroker, Jill. 1981. *Space and Incongruence: The Origin of Kant's Idealism*. Boston: D. Reidel Publishing.

Čapek, Milič, ed. 1976. *The Concepts of Space and Time: Their Structure and Their Development*. Boston: D. Reidel Publishing Co.

Cassirer, Ernst. 1910. *Substance and Function*. Translated by William C. Swabey and Marie C. Swabey. New York: Dover Publications (1953).

Charles, Annick. 1969. "L'imagination, miroir de l'âme selon Proclus." In *Le Néoplatonisme*. Paris: Éditions du Centre National de la Recherche Scientifique (1971).

Dedekind, Richard. 1858. "Continuity and Irrational Numbers." In *Essays on the Theory of Numbers*. La Salle: Open Court (1948).

Derrida, Jacques. 1974. *Edmund Husserl's Origin of Geometry: An Introduction*. Translated by John P. Leavey. Stony Brook: Nicholas Hays (1978).

Dieudonné, Jean. 1975. "L'abstraction et l'intuition mathématique." *Dialectica* 29:39–49.

Einstein, Albert. 1933. *Essays in Science.* New York: Philosophical Library.

Finke, Ronald A. 1986. "Mental Imagery and the Visual System." *Scientific American,* March, 88–95.

Fodor, Jerry A. 1984. *The Modularity of Mind: An Essay on Faculty Psychology.* Cambridge: The MIT Press.

Gardner, Howard. 1985. *Frames of Mind: The Theory of Multiple Intelligences.* New York: Basic Books.

Gruber, Howard E., and Vonèche, J. Jacques. 1977. *The Essential Piaget.* New York: Basic Books.

Guthrie, W.K.C. 1962. *A History of Greek Philosophy,* Volume 1, *The Earlier Presocratics and the Pythagoreans.* Cambridge: The Cambridge University Press.

Hegel, G.W.F. 1830. *Philosophy of Nature.* Translated by A. V. Miller. Oxford: Clarendon Press (1970).

Hilbert, David. 1898. *The Foundations of Geometry.* La Salle: Open Court (1950).

Hinckfuss, Ian. 1975. *The Existence of Space and Time.* Oxford: Clarendon Press.

Jammer, Max. 1957. *Concepts of Space: The History of Theories of Space in Physics.* Cambridge: Harvard University Press.

Kant, Immanuel. 1787. *Critique of Pure Reason.*

Koffka, K. 1935. *Principles of Gestalt Psychology.* New York: Harcourt, Brace and Co.

Koyré, Alexandre. 1957. *From the Closed World to the Infinite Universe.* New York: Harper.

Levinas, Emmanuel. 1930. *The Theory of Intuition in Husserl's Phenomenology.* Translated by André Orianne. Evanston: Northwestern University Press (1973).

Locke, John. 1688. *An Essay Concerning Human Understanding.*

Meerbote, Ralf. 1981. "Kant on Intuitivity." *Synthese* 47:203–228.

Merleau-Ponty, M. 1945. *Phenomenology of Perception.* Translated by Colin Smith. London: Routledge and Kegan Paul (1962).

———. 1961. "Eye and Mind." In *The Essential Writings of Merleau-Ponty,* edited by A. L. Fisher. New York: Harcourt, Brace, and World (1969).

Meserve, Bruce E. 1955. *Fundamental Concepts of Geometry.* Reading, Mass.: Addison-Wesley Publishing Co.

Nerlich, Graham. 1976. *The Shape of Space.* Cambridge: Cambridge University Press.

Nicomachus of Gerasa. c. 100. *Introduction to Arithmetic.* Translated by M. L. D'Ooge. Annapolis: St. John's College Press (1955).

Ninio, Anat. 1979. "On the Testing of Piaget's Hypothesis of Topological Primacy in Representational Space by Copying Geometrical Figures." *Human Development* 22:385–389.

Noddings, Nel, and Shore, Paul J. 1984. *Awakening the Inner Eye: Intuition in Education*. New York: Teachers College Press.

Olson, David R., and Bialystok, Ellen. 1983. *Spatial Cognition: The Structure and Development of Mental Representations of Spatial Relations*. Hillsdale, N.J.: Lawrence Erlbaum Associates.

Panofsky, Erwin. 1954. *Galileo as a Critic of the Arts*. The Hague: Martinus Nijhoff.

Piaget, Jean. 1963. "Mental Images." In *The Essential Piaget*, edited by Howard E. Gruber and J. Jacques Vonèche. New York: Basic Books (1977).

Piaget, Jean, and Inhelder, Bärbel. 1948. *The Child's Conception of Space*. New York: W.W. Norton and Co. (1967).

Piaget, Jean, Inhelder, Bärbel, and Szeminska, Alma. 1960. *The Child's Conception of Geometry*. Translated by E. A. Lunzer. New York: Basic Books.

Poincaré, Henri. Before 1905. *Science and Hypothesis*. New York: Dover Publications (1952).

Proclus [5th cent.]. *A Commentary on the First Book of Euclid's Elements*. Translated by Glenn R. Morrow. Princeton: Princeton University Press (1970).

Reichenbach, Hans. 1928. *The Philosophy of Space and Time*. New York: Dover Publications (1958).

Ricoeur, Paul. 1967. *Husserl: An Analysis of His Phenomenology*. Evanston: Northwestern University Press.

Russell, Bertrand A. W. 1897. *An Essay on the Foundations of Geometry*. New York: Dover Publications (1956).

Santayana, George. 1896. *The Sense of Beauty*. New York: Dover (1955).

Seifert, Josef. 1979. *Das Leib-Seele-Problem in der gegenwärtigen philosophischen Diskussion*. Darmstadt: Wissenschaftliche Buchgesellschaft.

Sherover, Charles M. 1971. *Heidegger, Kant and Time*. Bloomington: Indiana University Press.

Sklar, Lawrence. 1974. *Space, Time, and Spacetime*. Berkeley and Los Angeles: University of California Press.

Thomas Aquinas. 1255. *The Division and Method of the Sciences: Questions V and VI of his Commentary on* De Trinitate *of Boethius*. Translated by Armand Maurer. Toronto: The Pontifical Institute of Medieval Studies (1953).

———. 1266. *Commentary on the* Metaphysics *of Aristotle*. Translated by John P. Rowan. Chicago: Henry Regnery Co. (1961).

Wild, K. W. 1938. *Intuition*. Cambridge: Cambridge University Press.

Chapter II

Thoughtful Space: The Geometry of Imaging

Inner space, then, insofar as thought enters it to construct there the figures that reveal its intelligible structure, is geometric. It was observed long ago, and will be argued here, that the spatial medium not only supplies the matter for imaging but also exercises a normative function on the images by imposing its own constraints (Reichenbach 1928). These constraints—perhaps it is better to call them, more positively, qualifications of extension in general—determine the nature and even the very possibility of our capacity for imaging. Here I shall take up two of the most significant such spatial properties. The first is the felicitous Euclideanism of our geometric imagination (A). It is felicitous in this context because it is, I will argue, the necessary condition of our very existence as imaging beings (1). The second property is the dimensionality of human inner space which is in one respect plane-like and in another solid, but goes no further. The inability to imagine beyond three-space seems to be as accidental to our nature as our Euclideanism is necessary (2). Such reflections on the naive geometry of our souls elucidate our imaging capacity and vice versa: To look for the crux of our Euclideanism is precisely to come upon imaging, the eponymous activity of the imagination, the one it is named for; while, conversely, to consider imaging is to appreciate the nature of our naive geometric intuition.

Two kinds of imaging activity that go on in this human-geometric space in both its internal and its external manifestations and products will then be of special significance (B). One comprises the spatializations of thought and its operations (1). The other contains the modeling of the external world (2).

A. The Constraints on Human Geometric Imaging

Any being in the least like us, in whom the capacity to image both its own thoughts and the world confronting it is central, will have an intimate

603

geometry that is Euclidean. Not to keep the geometrically uninitiated reader in suspense: In Euclidean geometry alone is similarity, the preservation of shape across variations of size, possible—and similarity is the *sine qua non* of imaging. As a matter of fact, human beings regularly talk and behave, if not explicitly, then implicitly as if they were Euclideans.

1. Our Euclidean Geometry: A Necessary Fact. The claim expressed in this heading becomes significant only if we can conceive an alternative possibility, that of a Noneuclidean being. I propose to set out this fantastic alternative, confining myself to the elementary and synthetic—that is, picturable—facts, as opposed to analytic formulas (Wolfe 1945). Nothing more advanced anyway has much bearing on the ordinary imagination that is my subject. Moreover, in contravention of the famous notice over Plato's Academy, "Let no one without geometry enter here," I want to keep things simple for those who have not yet looked into this subject.

a. The Noneuclidean Sensibility: A Fantasy. What do I mean by our necessary Euclideanism? I mean that we have some beliefs, expressible in a rigorous axiom system, that we get from consulting, or "intuiting," our internal space and that we find corroborated in our immediate external space. For example, we believe that there are figures—in fact they dominate our constructed environment—whose four sides are straight and each of whose angles is a right angle. When we measure these rectangles with a protractor, we attribute deviations to an inexactitude in the instrument or the drawing and go right on believing that in principle there are such perfect figures and that in practice they are approachable. Here are three examples of what else we see and do in our mind's eye and expect to see and do in the world: There is, first, an unobvious fact which we continually use without necessarily knowing about it: All triangles have an angle-sum equal to a straight angle, that is, to 180 degrees; it is because of this property that we can cover floors with tiles in the shape of (isosceles) right triangles. Second, we expect that lines that start out being at the same time straight and equally distant from each other can continue to be so *ad infinitum*—that is to say, we can imagine what we call parallel lines, and we can realize stretches of them in the world, as in railroad tracks. Above all, we expect it to be possible to make scaled representations of anything we see—real pictures in the world or mental images in the imagination: Physical constraints apart, a shape can come in any size.

Geometrically this last property is, of course, the similarity mentioned above. In rectilinear figures geometric similarity means that the respective angles of two figures being compared are equal, and that while the sides are unequal, they are in proportion, which means that the ratios or size-relations of corresponding sides in each figure are the same. This—coloration apart—is the essence of spatial resemblance.

The triangles with a straight-line angle-sum, the parallels that are everywhere equidistant, and the possibility of drawing similar figures turn out to be equivalent axiomatic beginnings of Euclidean geometry. That is to say, if any one of these properties is among those postulated, the others follow, and the space will be the one in which we are at home.

Now to draw attention to our Euclidean propensities is to intimate other possibilities—Noneuclidean ones. It is, I think, no accident that these alternative conceptions lagged two millennia behind Euclid's systematic account. This belated genesis shows that a deep rupture in consciousness was required not only to incite the actual discovery of new geometries but even more to induce the willingness to entertain them. The term "Noneuclidean" signifies that this geometry is defined in opposition to a historically—and naturally—prior one. Hence the Noneuclidean world is best entered by way of its genesis, the account of which is here drastically telescoped (Bonola 1908).

Euclid's own beginning was by way of a postulate, his famous Fifth (*Elements*, c. 300 B.C.). In ancient mathematics postulates, "requirements," are distinguished from axioms by being a shade less self-evident; this distinction turns out to be significant. In a slightly tailored version, the Fifth Postulate says: Take a straight line as base. On it and at right angles set up an upright line, a perpendicular. Pick any point on the latter and through it draw another line, again perpendicular to this upright. The postulate now claims that if this last line deviates ever so slightly from the right angle it makes with the upright, it will cross the base line on the side toward which it is tilting and form a triangle with that base and its upright.

What students of geometry have always found less than obvious is not the truth of this postulate but its independence, namely its underivability from other, less pungent, axioms. And yet in over two thousand years all attempts to prove the postulate through more insipid axioms turn out to be flawed. They contain either outright mistakes or subtly circular reasoning, assumptions equivalent to the proposition to be proved. The postulate thus seems to be a genuine beginning—the sparest beginning in the neatest form as it happens, because other versions of this postulate and its alternatives assume a trifle more.

In 1733 a book was published by one Saccheri, partially entitled "Euclid Cleared of Every Flaw." It was an attempt to prove the Fifth Postulate by pursuing its denial through all its consequences to what, he hoped, would be an absurd conclusion. This indirect method of proof, ancient and fascinating, is called *reductio ad absurdum*, and its virtue (a vice to some mathematicians) is that with it one can work, so to speak, in the blind, avoiding intuition and entrusting the outcome to mere logic.

Leaving all the other explicit axioms of Euclid intact, Saccheri cranked out new theorems, which were flawless in their logic but bizarre to the geometric imagination. It turned out, for example, that no two straight lines are ever equally distant from each other throughout. He felt himself finally forced to conclude that the denial of the Fifth Postulate is plainly repugnant to the nature of a straight line. For such a line is simply unimaginable without the property of keeping itself equidistant from certain other straight lines. In other words, his final appeal jumps the logical track and returns to intuition. Yet he had irrevocably driven an entering wedge between mathematical form and intuited matter.

The conclusion, positively reinterpreted, is that Noneuclidean geometries—Saccheri discovered two—are perfectly possible. This conclusion was drawn independently and in short order by three mathematicians, first by Gauss, who long withheld his researches from publication for fear of the vulgar fracas they would cause, then by Lobachevski and Bolyai. It is the Lobachevskian format, made public beginning in 1826, that has entered elementary textbooks. He himself called it "imaginary geometry," but only because its analytic expressions involve imaginary numbers. Strictly speaking, it is precisely unimaginable.

Or nearly so. In setting out its elements one may, indeed, describe pictures, but they will be oddly related to the words and in crucial respects mismatched with them.

Saccheri, then, had discovered that two denials of the Fifth Postulate were possible. If in Euclidean geometry the slightest deviation of the top line makes a triangle, it follows quickly that there is only that one Euclidean parallel line through that point. The logically possible denials are therefore either that there are *no* such parallel lines, so that all lines intersect, or that there are at least *two* lines through that point parallel to the base. The former possibility was followed up later by Riemann and turns out to be even more radically divorced from intuition because it involves the denial of a second, implicit, Euclidean axiom, namely that a straight line, in being indefinitely extended, never returns on itself. Yet it is this alternative that turns out to be physically applicable to astronomical space.

Lobachevski had made his beginning by postulating the second of the two alternatives, that more than one line through a point is parallel to the base line. It turns out that there are two, one of those deviating lines inching toward the base at one side and its symmetrically situated counterpart at the other. Above these, passing through the same point on the upright, lie indefinitely many other non-cutting lines. But these are not so interesting as the first non-cutting lines; these alone are called the two "parallels" to the base line. I defy anyone to imagine or to draw this possibility without fudging the diagram, either by leaving off drawing when the inclined parallel line gets near the base, or by depicting the supposedly straight parallel as an asymptotic curve, a curve that approaches the base-line ever more closely without meeting it. All our depictions are hopelessly Euclidean.

However, if one takes that in one's stride, some remarkable results, given here without their derivation, follow very quickly. First, these parallels are obviously not everywhere equidistant but continually approach each other, coming as close as you please as you go further out from the upright. Second, the higher up on the upright you take the point through which the parallels are drawn, the sharper their initial inclination, the so-called "angle of parallelism," becomes; in fact this angle is a continuous (though not a linear) function of the height, and as the upright goes to infinity the parallel to the base will, strangely, tend to set off in the direction of the upright. At the hither end, near the base of the upright, the shorter the perpendicular height, the closer the angle comes to a right angle, so that for a vanishingly small figure everything is as in Euclid: very locally the geometry becomes Euclidean. A way to see this is to follow the pseudo-parallel (I mean the curve which is the Euclidean depiction of a Lobachevskian parallel) very far out as it continuously approaches the base-line, and then to drop a tiny upright between it and the base. The direction of the parallel will look to be nearly the same as that of the base-line. Third, and obviously related to all this, is the fact that the angle-sum of all triangles is less than two right angles and continuously decreases as their area increases. Consequently there is in the limit a strange maximum triangle with zero angle-sum. Also, no two triangles can be put together to make a rectangle, an equiangular rectilinear figure which is also right-angled. For if you put four Noneuclidean "pseudo-rectangles" together the angles around their common corner will not cover 360 degrees but will leave gaps. Noneuclidean houses built of equiangular bricks would be drafty.

But the fourth and, for present purposes, chief result, which one might guess from the fact that larger figures have smaller angle sums, is that figures cannot grow indefinitely large; moreover—and this is the real crux—figures cannot be of different size and yet preserve the same shape: there is no similarity.

I now come to the spectacular consequence for Noneuclidean visual perception, which must be wildly different from our own. The gist of visual perception seems to be this: Pointillistic light information passes along straight lines to the retina. Vision is thus mediated by space, light being a modification of space. If the object to be perceived, say, for simplicity, a notched stick, is upright and opposite the eye, the perceived pattern is identified as it is seen. If the plane of the figure angles away form the viewer, there is a geometric invariance, called the cross ratio, which connects the head-on notch configuration with the perspectival view (Adler 1958). Our perceptual apparatus appears to be able to make the identification automatically. A penny, for example, when seen obliquely is retinally sensed as elliptical but mentally "seen" as round. Similarly, railroad tracks can with equal truth be said to converge at a vanishing point and to appear as Euclidean parallels. In fact it usually takes a special effort to read a perceptual presentation literally so as to recover its uninterpreted basis (Murch 1973). Thus it is doubly erroneous to call perceptual space, as is often done, Noneuclidean. It is not Noneuclidean, because perspectival space obeys perfectly good Euclidean rules even when "parallel" lines converge at the vanishing point. For one thing, it is perfectly capable of including Euclidean parallels: a funny road that got proportionally wider as it stretched directly away from the viewer would appear to have parallel curbs. For another, as indicated above, the road does not even look Noneuclidean, since the completed act of perception has usually made the Euclidean interpretation.

What is the case is that our visual perception is indeed essentially projectival. This means that as the visual light rays converge on the eyes, shape relations are carried to them invariant but in diminishing format across distances. The fact that the looks of anything may be arrested as an image at a distance from the eye—by interposing a recording screen, say a canvas or a frame of film (Ch. III A 3)—is crucial to the human aesthetic constitution. The point here is to fantasize what perception would be like if it lacked that possibility.

First, going back to the notched stick, upright or slanting, the configuration cast by its notch pattern on a screen interposed between it and the Noneuclidean observer would preserve neither a simple proportion nor the only slightly more complicated cross-ratio. So the production of "images" on canvas, or their interpretation, would seem to be possible only if Noneuclideans came equipped with a terrifically complex perceptual-computation capacity, which would have to include a way of estimating remote distances very accurately, so as to compute the required associated "image"—if by image is meant the trace a figure farther off casts on a screen closer up.

In fact even that would not help. For as the visual rays reach the eye even the largest "image" shrinks, and when it is finally cast inverted onto the retina—recall that we are fantasizing Noneuclidean beings who have eyes like ours and are, like us, vanishingly small within their space—it will be relatively minute. Then what was perceptually processed would in fact be a Euclidean image. Now suppose such a being had an enormously long spindly arm with which to palpate distant space. In its world there might be a large pseudo-square, the rectilinear Noneuclidean figure analogous to a square, having four equal sides but angles the more acute the larger it got. The creature would see a blunt Euclidean square but it would touch a figure with corners sharp enough to draw green blood. Sight and touch would not jibe.

There is an old perceptual problem called "Molyneux's Question" after the man who proposed it to Locke: Could a blind man whose sight was suddenly restored recognize by vision immediately, without a period of practical experience, figures he had previously known only by touch? In our world the problem remains largely unsolved. In fact, it turns out that even its experimental formulation is increasingly controversial (Morgan 1977). In the Noneuclidean world the difficulty of the question would be vastly compounded, though one thing is likely: Intersensory transfer would certainly require much experience and would be very far from immediate, whereas in our world the newly sighted subjects seem to be able to make some identifications immediately (Gregory 1978).

In sum, the perception of such creatures is really, at least in our terms, only pseudo-visual. For Noneuclidean "vision" negates the essential property of our sight, which is that it brings general appearances to us unchanged through a distance: As Bergson pointed out (Part One, Ch. III K), we see not at the place of perception but at the place of the object. That fact contributes largely to the experience of the exteriority that was in the last chapter shown to define spatiality.

External images, the pictures of this Noneuclidean world, would be correspondingly pseudo-imaginal. Since for every kind of rectilinear figure the angles get blunter as the figure is reduced, the shape as we understand it continually changes. Therefore, no scaled images or models can in principle be made, quite aside from the aforesaid perceptual problems. The projection of a figure on a screen could scarcely be called its direct visual image, for it would require much computation to restore the original source behind it. All the trouble we have in trying to imagine a Noneuclidean figure, Noneuclideans would experience in visually comparing originals and copies in their own world: If they placed the reduced "image," say of a pseudo-square, next to its magnified original in the same plane, the two would look very unlike, though one would compute as a projection of the other. Since for them all figures that are shaped alike are of the same size, all their portraits had better be life-size and viewed close up: In other words, portraits could not function as they do for us, for example, as mementos carried in wallets.

Internal imaging, moreover, would be simply inconceivable. Noneuclideans might have a vast propositional-space memory containing multitudes of analytic formulas for magnifying or shrinking figures. But if they had a visual memory it would have to contain multitudes of multitudes of distinct shapes of different sizes. Now if there is one fact of our own internal imaging that there is agreement about, it is that our imagination does not so much permit scaling as prohibit absolute sizing: our images are indefinite in size, a fact which contributes to the blithe ease of our imaging. And that is a condition simply impossible within any determinate Noneuclidean world. (Such a world is determined when the so-called "constant of curvature" is chosen and all the distances become determinate.) *Mutatis mutandis*, what has been said about imaging holds for the other, Riemannian, class of Noneuclidean geometries. Only Euclideans can imaginably have a genuine imaging faculty.

It has been argued that our Euclideanism is natural in the sense of being evolutionary: Since our local physical environment is Euclidean, we have evolved a capacity for inner "first and second order isomorphisms," for representing spatial similarity (Part Two, Ch. II D). Evolutionary theory may well account for our present capacities, but like any genetic explanation, it attempts no speculation about their ultra-biological significance. A case will be made in Part Six (Ch. III) that it is among the distinguishing marks of humanity to exist in an intimate world set in a large space, to have a space-mediated perceptual mode such as vision, and to live largely through internal and external images.

b. Our Euclideanism is, then, necessary to our humanity. By the necessity I mean what was said above: Imaging belongs to human beings essentially, and an imaging being has to have the similarity-geometry. The fact, however, has to be further supported.

Proofs of mental fact are always dubious because, for one thing, they often have to appeal somewhat brazenly to common experience, over the heads of the dissenters. So suppose the claim is made—it is in fact sometimes made—that Noneuclidean space can be intuited. (This claim is distinct from the optical theory, beset with difficulties, that our visual space is itself Lobachevskian—Grünbaum 1973.) It is in principle uncontrovertable. At most we may choose to believe that the subject being tested is really doing something else (Pylyshyn 1981)—is in fact doing the same thing internally that geometers do externally when they want to present such geometries for visual consideration: They make a model.

Before considering models, another point has to be disposed of. It is often argued that even if internal representations were always Euclidean it would not prove that inner space is necessarily Euclidean but only that we lack visual knowledge, that is, external experience of the other spaces. With a little experience and much practice, it is claimed, we could get to be at home in other spaces. Our imagination, this implies, is not constitutionally Euclidean but it is a potentially Noneuclidean imagination exercised at the limit. We are vanishingly small in the world and use our capacities as small beings; were we to learn to take the larger view befitting the space age, we would find ourselves intuiting the geometry of outer space. It seems to me that this empiricist argument overlooks the circumstance urged here: An imaging faculty, any imagination in an imaginable sense, constitutionally requires an imaging geometry.

Now what about models? Helmholtz made a useful distinction between two kinds of geometric visualizations: external and internal. The latter has nothing to do with what I call inner space. It rather refers to considering a space from within, imagining the kinds of experiences we would have if we lived in a space, exactly as I have been doing in the previous section. Now internal imagining seems to me to exploit a certain indeterminacy of which our inner imagination is capable. We can, for instance, vaguely imagine two straight lines continually approaching each other as close as you please, together with all sorts of other Noneuclidean experiences. But as soon as we look more intently or try to render the indefinite inner visualization in a drawing, the inadequacy of our intuition to the space is exposed. This claim is easily tested by individual introspection. Hence "internal" modeling of Noneuclidean geometry does not seem to be possible. (Nerlich 1976, Reichenbach 1928, Salmon 1980.)

By external visualization Helmholtz meant model-making, the embedding of a representation of one space in another space. In theory each of the spaces can thus play host to models of the other, but the human interest is in the Euclidean accommodation of Noneuclidean space. Such modeling can take place without change of dimension, as in Poincaré's famous consistency proof for Lobachevskian geometry (B), in which all the points of the Noneuclidean plane are fitted into a circle whose circumference represents all the "ideal" points, the points at infinity, of the Noneuclidean plane. Or the modeling can be on a solid; thus part of the Lobachevskian plane is modeled on the surface of the solid of revolution generated from an indefinitely long curve called the tractrix; the solid is known as a pseudo-sphere and looks like a half-spindle. The surface of a sphere similarly models elementary Riemannian geometry, with the great circles standing for straight lines, which in this geometry all intersect each other not once but twice.

Now such models can be called reason-constrained visualizations, but never spaces in the proper, primary sense or direct visions of them. No one sees the modeled space as anything but Euclidean space. While looking at the Euclidean model we *think* the Noneuclidean space, which may be inferred but is never seen. What does evidently happen is that mathematicians become so practised at disregarding the Euclidean imaginal matter introduced by the nature of any model and focusing on the Noneuclidean relations, that they seem to themselves to be breathing in the Noneuclidean element. Actually they are only thinking there: hence "external" modeling is ineradicably Euclidean. So it turns out that arguments claiming that the three metric geometries are equally representable are at bottom arguments that geometry is essentially propositional—which taken as a formal science indeed it is.

If, however, one holds on to the intuitive aspect, then the sum of all the foregoing amounts to a fact, the fact that human beings have a Euclidean propensity that fits their environment and whose basic constructions they continually put to use in cultivating it.

The "how" (the constitutional mode) of our propensity is that we image perceptions or spatialize thinking in the imaging medium scalelessly. The inner space has magnitude, to be sure, but not determinate magnitude. The sizes of mental images can be compared but not measured, they can overflow the medium but the medium has only an angular, not an absolute measure (Part Two, Ch. II B). The mental eye can zoom in from far distances or back off with a sudden "blink transformation" that is part of the "physical irresponsibility" of the imaging capacity. There is no iridium meter deposited in a Paris of the imagination.

The "that" (the historical expression) of our imaging propensity is that all the mathematical and physical sciences have their historical and personal genesis in spatial intuition, whatever levels of abstraction they may eventually reach.

The primary practical use of this propensity is in constructing the second, human, re-worked nature in which we largely live. We lay out the surface of the land so as to make it subject to geo-metry, in particular to the areal unit, the square. We build pyramidal tombs, rectangular temples, oval huts, round tents, geodesic domes. We apply the carpenter's square to interiors and construct a "carpentered world" (Segal) for indoor living. We make rectification the symbol of soundness and, on occasion, of *ennui*: square meals, square deals, squared accounts and human squares. (The epithet "square" for a person of rectitude is, incidentally, antique, Aristotle—

Rhetoric III 10.) And, of course, we run neat roads and well-tied tracks straight to anywhere. The point is that we live this way not in a twilight of approximations as evanescently small denizens of a Noneuclidean world, but that we use the basic Euclidean figures as the decent-sized, exact, and perfect blueprints of our human environment. For above all, we begin our works by projecting the outcome in mental pictures and by imaging those visualizations in scaled external images, in models.

2. Our Solid Geometry: A Contingent Fact. If our Euclideanism is of the human essence, the geometric solidity of our bodily world and of our intuitive geometry is a mere fact—a merely contingent fact. This circumstance is brought home by the Pythagorean genesis mentioned above (Ch. I C). If a point flows without change of direction it traces a straight line; the line flows into a square plane; the plane, in turn, sweeps out a solid cube. There it stops; no further flux is imaginable. To put it another way: A point-element in each dimension can escape into a new setting. Thus a single point can double itself and mark out a line, a line can wander into a plane, a point in a plane can rise above it. But thereafter it is imprisoned—there is no ducking out of solid space. Since any point in space can therefore be located by its distance from three coordinate axes, our space is called three-dimensional.

(Guthrie 1962, Hinckfuss 1975. Paul Klee rediscovered the Pythagorean genesis in his Bauhaus lectures of 1921 as a way to inscribe an "ideal shape-structure" into a given space.)

Nevertheless, attempts to show the necessity of limiting the real world to three dimensions have been fascinating failures, appealing in turn to the magic of the number three, the topology of three-space, the topography of the cosmos (the earliest attempt was by Aristotle in *On the Heavens*), and above all, the nature of physical law. On the other hand, even Kant, that staunch Euclidean intuitionist, thought an n-dimensional space possible, and if possible, probably real (Jammer 1957).

A fourth dimension (for present purposes nothing higher need be considered) is, moreover, somehow more imaginable than a Noneuclidean structure. It is significant that the two old and well-loved dimension-romances, those of Abbot and Hinton (both of 1884), have no Noneuclidean counterparts. Abbot's *Flatland*, as sound as it is imaginative, shows how to a two-dimensional being there might come a three-dimensional epiphany: A sphere in passing through a plane leaves a moving trace, a point expanding into a growing circle that reaches a maximum and recedes. This event is not a model of one space embedded into another as described above, but an unfudged partial appearance of the solid itself. Hinton's long pseudo-mystical induction of non-mathematicians into the four-dimensional world is unfortunately not meant as fantasy: he takes seriously the notion of a "higher world." He even suggests that the passage from the cave of shadow images to the world of invisible ideas in the famous Platonic parable of the *Republic* is to be understood as an attainment of the fourth dimension. The first figure so reached, the hypercube, he calls a tesseract (a term appropriated by Madeleine L'Engle in her space-time fantasy for children, *A Wrinkle in Time*). The projected trace of a hypercube is an ordinary cube, and in general any of our polyhedra can be regarded as the outline thrown on a section of four-space obtained by passing through it a three-space, analogous to the way we obtain a section of a cube by passing through it a plane (Manning 1910, Hilbert and Cohn-Vossen 1932). My claim is that while a Noneuclidean imagination is a contradiction in terms, an n-dimensional imagination is perfectly conceivable—we just happen not to have one.

The sundry visions of the "fourth dimension" that entered popular literature in the last decades of the nineteenth century became in the early twentieth a preoccupation of avant-garde painters, above all the Cubists. They associated with the buzz-word of a fourth dimension the possibility of a new kind of pictorial space, an infinite universe released from the laws of perspective. Most of the talk about it was really only figurative hyperbole. Thus Apollinaire, in a 1912 essay on the Cubists, brought on the fourth dimension as representing "the immensity of space externalizing itself in all directions in any given moment. . . . It . . . endows objects with plasticity." What the fourth dimension, taken more soberly, did stand for was the possibility of painting not the appearances but their spatial analysis. Since the Cubists were seeking the truth behind the natural appearances, the figure of a fourth dimension was very congenial to them. However, they also made two other, more precise, uses of the added dimension, roughly corresponding to its spatial and its temporal interpretation: Poincaré (1905) had described a technique for visualizing a figure of four spatial dimensions by mentally running through its varying three-dimensional perspectives and making a composite of them. This fitted well with the conceptual orientation of Cubist art, in which the painter gained fuller knowledge of a form by mentally rotating it. In quite another way, Marcel Duchamp's once notorious paintings called "Nude Descending a Staircase" were meant to exemplify the temporal fourth dimension: the simultaneously recorded successive phases of her descent were to create higher-dimensional "virtual volumes." Nonetheless, these are spatial intimations, not intuitions. Indeed, most of what went for "a new conception of space" in 1900 was really a new and peculiarly talkative spatial sensibility.

(Henderson 1983, Kern 1983.)

These days everyone knows that we in fact live in a four-dimensional world. This half-information makes it necessary to touch for a moment on various meanings of four-dimensionality, aside from the fantasies of science fiction and that source of strange epiphanies, the vague Beyond of occultism. First of these legitimate meanings is the purely formal non-intuitive mathematical n-dimensional manifold introduced by Riemann. Second is the coordinate system sometimes termed "pseudo-Euclidean" space, a Euclidean three-space with an added dependent time-axis, one whose values are involved with those of the space coordinates; this kind of diagram is used in ordinary treatments of Special Relativity. And finally there is the spatialization of this time-axis in the Minkowsky diagram, which represents an atemporal "absolute" world picture. In it, given the appropriate laws of physics, every physical substance in space at every moment in its history can be geometrically located. This spatialization of time is the object of a lively philosophical debate, reminiscent of the ancient "battle between the gods and the giants," the defenders respectively of being and becoming. (Klein 1892, Einstein et al. 1923, Frazer 1966.)

Now, insofar as we live in the universe discovered by physics, we might, I suppose, be said to live in four-dimensional space-time, but we certainly do not often live with its properties. In fact our imagination particularly glories in contradicting its founding insight—that it is meaningless to call moments in places far apart simultaneous in the absence of a procedure for synchronizing clocks. Though the imagination is in physical fact probably limited by the speed of its mediating neural events, it appears to be everywhere at once and to travel instantaneously to the remotest regions, as do the ships, "swift as thought," of Homer's Phaeacians: "The mind passes in an instant from east to west," as Leonardo da Vinci says. We cannot overcome the sense that all the universe shares in our present moment of existence. Even Whitehead concedes in *Process and Reality* (1929), the most massive philosophical exploitation of Relativity, that metaphysics must take account of the "universal obviousness of conviction" that there is a temporal cross-section of the universe (191), a possible panoramic image of the whole at one moment (Brann 1983).

This instantaneous imaginative conveyance through the extension of space is all part of what I call the "physical irresponsibility" of the imagination. Moreover, while in it all places are reachable in and bound together by the same "now," the complementary case holds as well: To the imagination diverse regions of present space represent different slices of time, insofar as they are invested by different memories. Why else would we visit historical places—Jerusalem, Athens, Philadelphia? To wander on the site of Solomon's Temple, to stand within Phidias's Parthenon, to sit in Madison's chair in Constitution Hall (though, to be sure, all of these actions are—sign of the times—strictly forbidden nowadays) is to locate oneself in the time which pre-eminently shaped that place, be it 964 B.C.E, the 85th Olympiad or 1787 A.D. The imagination overcomes the physical necessities of space and time equally.

To return to our imaginative dimensionality: Although I conclude that it makes real sense to say that, though it might have been otherwise, we in mere fact neither perceive nor imagine four-dimensionally, that is, in more than three dimensions, it is not so clear that we do not normally imagine in fewer than three. The dimensionality of vision and of visual images is an old and tricky problem.

To begin with, imagery experiments have shown repeatedly that internal transformations can mimic depth relations. Shown a display of objects hung in a three-dimensional arrangement, subjects can rotate the display mentally and identify the new configuration correctly even when it is hard to guess (Finke 1986). While these results are remarkable in showing that the imagination possesses rules for perspective transformations, they do not really speak to the dimensional problem; rather they exemplify it. For granting that we interpret spatial displays as three-dimensional, are the images of these objects rotated in an inner three-space or are they projected on an inner plane?

It is an old and abiding claim that distance away from the viewer is invisible in the visible world: "It is, I think, agreed by all that *distance* of itself, and immediately, cannot be seen" (Berkeley 1709), for depth "quite clearly belongs to the perspective and not to things" (Merleau-Ponty 1945; Nerlich 1976). That is not to say that increasing depth does not emit "cues." Some of these are directly visible, such as thickening texture, atmospheric haze, and diminution of size. Some are indirect, such as the subconscious cues that come from the changing ocular convergence when the eyes fix on increasingly distant features. But, as Merleau-Ponty points out, there is an understanding not conveyed to us by mere visual observation: Each object in the world is distant from our own body with the same extension that separates it from the other bodies spread out frontally before us—depth is a dimension along with length and breadth.

One favorite notion from Berkeley on is that depth is primarily the deliverance of the tactile and the sensorimotor system, so that touch is the sense of three-dimensionality. Its preeminent organ is "the prehensile hand . . . the outer brain of man" (Kant in Merleau-Ponty). The tactile sensation of solidity, of muscular spanning, is thus considered to be the source of our consciousness of space as three-space. To be sure, this theory keeps losing ground as ingenious experiments with infants show that perception of depth—as indicated, for example, by the recognition of the size-constancy of receding objects, as well as by a preference for visually presented spheres over circles—is very early, probably too early to be the result of sensori-motor experience (Hamilton and Vernon 1976). But that does not mean that vision is not essentially a surface event. Rather it implies something much more interesting, that two dimensions can contain all the information necessary for a fairly direct impression of depth, the degree of inference involved being a matter of fierce current debate.

Now solidity, however vision comes by it, happens to be what the imagination in its gauzy lability lacks: as imagined motions are not inertial, so imagined bodies are not impenetrable. In dreams, for example, two bodily beings can easily manage to possess each other's place—"two in one" is a common oneiric mode. Yet impenetrability is the soul of solidity. It need not be the stiff resistance with which material macro-bodies repel material touch. It can be the merely ideal imprisonment of a space by geometric surfaces. But whether the barrier is physical or geometric, the idea is the same: Solidity essentially requires an enveloping surface protecting an indefeasibly inaccessible inside. The attempt truly to penetrate the surface of a solid always fails; it simply generates a new surface.

This impenetrable interiority seems to be lacking in our interior space: The figures of inner space have no impenetrability, no inaccessible last lair. They are all surface, all appearance. They are so through and through part of inner, psychic space that the interiority of the solid does not suit them. The human meaning of this circumstance is central to the most distinctive imaginative mode, the superimposition of images, which is taken up in the Conclusion of this book.

The geometric formulation of this observation is that the interior image medium is to be thought of as a two-dimensional surface for projections. Strictly speaking, as Thomas Reid observed two centuries ago, the visual field has a spherical curvature (Nerlich 1976), but it is for present purposes close enough to flat; the imagery field is similarly flat, and, as we know, recent experiments have shown that it has a roughly elliptical periphery (Part Two, Ch. II B). It is an arresting fact that the inner surface at any moment is no more a whole spherical surface than is the human visual field; the mental eye appears to be, as it were, fixed frontwards.

The following strange effect, which brings this fact home, can be easily induced: Have someone write an asymmetrical figure, like a 2, on your forehead with a blunt instrument. It will appear to your mind's eye reversed, as if it were painted on a glass through which you were looking out from behind. Now have the same done to the small of your neck. This time the figure will be unreversed, as if the inner organ, rather than swivel around, backed off behind the head, always "eyes front" to read the figure from the outside (Corcoran 1977). This frontal eye gazes, I am saying, at an imaginative space that is all facade. The aesthetic consequences, among them a certain primacy for painting among the visual arts, will be considered in the next chapter.

B. Model-Making: The Imaging of Soul and Thought

So far I have discussed the pure forms of our thought-directed imagination; now I shall give some examples of its most significant applied activities: figure-making and modeling.

It is part of the present assumption, as problematic as it seems unavoidable, that the human soul contains a field for spatial visualization, but the container itself is non-visible. Soul, self, mind, and thought are unextended if anything is. That hoary description is admitted in some version even by those who identify the mind with the brain: The functional architecture of mentation, at least, is non-spatial (Part Two, Ch. I A). So the aboriginal non-visibility of consciousness and its functions is assumed here. What I shall consider now is the visualization of the whole invisible soul itself in mythical figures and the imaging of its non-spatial activities in spatial models (1).

At the external end, the world that confronts consciousness is agreed to be—whatever else it is—spatial, visible, and imageable. As the imaging of the soul takes place from the inside out, so the world is imaged from the outside in: where the imaging of the soul is a spatialization of the invisible, the images of the world here to be considered are rational schematizations of already spatial appearances (2). Each is fraught with fascinating perplexities.

1. Mental Models. I am taking this term in two senses successively. In the now common use, explained below, a mental model is a schema, as opposed to a rule, of reasoning. But for the present, let it mean a model not of mentation or psychic activity as a process, but of the mind or the soul itself as a structure.

a. Soul and Mind: Images of the Invisible. No imaging is more poignant, more humanly revealing than the visible images we make of the seat of our most intimate life. There are all kinds of spatializations of the soul: geometric, topographic, and above all, corporeally figurative. The last kind is not so much a theoretical schema as a visible metaphor and therefore not strictly within the compass of this geometric chapter; besides, bodily metaphors for the soul have been noticed earlier (Part Four, Ch. III B). Yet they are too wonderful to pass over altogether. No text can compare with the Platonic dialogues as a treasure-trove for figurative psychology. The soul appears there as a many-headed monster (*Phaedo, Republic*) and as a barnacle-encrusted sea-god (*Republic*). In the grandest of all images, it is represented as a chariot drawn by two ill-matched horses, one dark and rapacious and lustful, the other light and modest and spirited, both reined in by a human charioteer standing for the rational power in the soul (*Phaedrus*). But chiefly the soul becomes visible as a human body, not only in the Platonic dialogues but also in Greek vase painting. On a black-figurerd oil jug, for example, the soul of the dying hero Sarpedon is seen as a little male figure issuing from his mouth, for the Greek word *psyche* literally means "breath." Later on, Psyche, personified now according to the gender of the noun rather than the sex of the corpse, is depicted as a maiden.

The representation of the soul as body is built into our psychic language: We are touched, wounded, moved (Part Four, Ch. III). Such metaphors obviously reflect the fact that psychic states are physically felt and find physical expression. Yet perhaps a deeper cause of our corporeal psychic language is our capacity for self-imaging, the awareness of ourselves as we appear to others, of our bodies as externalizations of our inner self (Kass 1985). In other words, we think that our soul is exposed to public view as a body. That is why so many corporeal psychic terms concern its vulnerability and violation.

However, the topic here is to be the theoretical imaging of the soul. Perhaps the most significant image in the context of the spatialization of the soul is the geometric image set out mythically in the *Timaeus* and developed by the Neoplatonists. Here the soul envelops the world in its sphere; as Plotinus puts it: "The soul is the place of this whole" (*Enneads* III 7, 11). Hence the world is *in* the soul, though the soul also extends through the world; the human soul is then derivative from this world-soul (Klein 1965). This spherical model of the soul is meant, I think, to represent not only the fact that spatial structures can be ensouled but also the remarkable capability of the human soul for "taking in" and imaging space—a capability that is, of course, *the* problem of the imagination as an inner space.

A not-so-remote descendant of the Platonic tripartite psychology is a Freudian structural model of the psyche. Freud sets it out in an "unassuming sketch" of a vertically oriented oval with the unconscious Id at the bottom, the Ego penned in the middle, and the Superego off to the side spanning the two; near the top is a Preconscious region and a sort of eye standing for the perceptual-conscious (Freud 1933). The regions of this model are not sharply demarcated but are to be imagined as colors melting into each other. Of course, Freud's modeling of the mind as "tinged with spatiality" goes much further than this plane sketch. Because for him sexuality is the meeting place of mind and body, the mind is assimilated to the body in its functions: "We are at home in our mind somewhat as in a body. This, we may say, is the mind's image of itself" (Wollheim on Freud 1974). Whether in philosophic myth or scientific psychology, it is hard to consider the soul without assigning it some figural extension.

The specifically cognitive part of the soul, the mind, is, of course, also imaged. Perhaps the most popular of all such representations are those introduced by Locke, in both the two- and the three-dimensional version: the "white paper" or *tabula rasa* to be painted with characters from experience, and the "empty cabinet" or "dark room" to be furnished or illumined through the senses (1690). The representations prevailing in contemporary cognitive science are, in contrast, not empty surfaces or cubicles, but spatializations of structures and processes, tables of organization and flow charts (Dennett 1978).

b. Reasoning: The Shape of Thought. The contemporary term "mental model" is, then, applied not to the representation of the cognitive faculties themselves but to their processes and products. Some are internal and others external.

Among such internal models are "cognitive maps," used to store spatial information and anticipate spatial experiences. Hence they are extremely pragmatic and colored with personal experience. Comfortably familiar locales take up large areas, while at their fringes looms *terra incognita*, filled with anxious conjectures, like those old maps that have written near the edges "Here be dragons." City dwellers, for example, carry in their heads— and tourist bureaus have actually provided for visitors—schematic maps marking the urban neighborhoods as safe or dangerous either by day or by night (Downs and Stea 1977, Neisser 1978). Though the "how" of it remains a mystery, the fact that the internal representations of the spatial environment are spatial is not very surprising.

However, spatialized representations can be and long have been made of subjects that are not intrinsically or necessarily topographic. They apparently facilitate learning and operating, usually moderately, sometimes even spectacularly. An old and often-cited example is the translation of unwieldy number names into the essentially spatial arabic numeral system, whose positional characteristics make calculation vastly more perspicuous than it is when done by name. More recently graphic and solid imagery for learning arithmetic, such as the color-coded Cuisinaire rods whose lengths are graded multiples of the unit, has gained attention (Lay 1982). For elementary mathematical learning in general, too, the importance of what Bruner called the "icon," the geometric picture, is regaining recognition. In his essay on "The Education of the Imagination" (1898), Hinton, who was mentioned in (A) above, had already made an issue of training the power of inward drawing and modeling "by having the small child engage in spatial play with solids, eschewing numerical calculations." It is an old issue, this repellent incomprehensibility—to amateur earners—of symbolic, that is, algebraic, as opposed to figural, representation; it is touched on in the intellectual autobiographies of Vico in the seventeenth century, of Rousseau in the eighteenth, and Darwin in the nineteenth. Rousseau says in his *Confessions* that "solving a geometric problem by equations seems to me like playing a tune by turning a handle." The consensus now is that beginners cannot really understand, for example, the significance of the formula for squaring the binomial, $(a + b)^2 = a^2 + 2ab + b^2$, until they geometrically see the large square on the length $(a + b)$ encompassing the two squares a^2 and b^2 plus the two rectangles $a \times b$ (Euclid, *Elements* II 4).

On the widest scale of conceptual imaging, there is the recent work on "spatial learning strategies," such as "net-working," "mapping," and "schematizing." These are specific techniques with their own symbolism for visually representing information in two-dimensional maps, especially information obtained from written texts (Holley and Dansereau 1984).

Behind these practical mappings of concepts and their complex properties, structures, orderings, and relations—behind any spatialization, topographical or mathematical—is a deep and remarkable fact. It is that logic quite naturally assumes a spatial form—*that thought can take shape*. Spatialization can even sometimes be crucial to the persuasiveness of a propositional proof. Recall that the first Noneuclidean geometry was a by-product of the search for an inconsistency in theorems that fell out of the denial of the parallel postulate (A above). Naturally, once the chief features of the system were established it became urgent to prove its consistency, to show that it did not contain self-contradicting propositions.

Since it turns out to be logically impossible to prove that a geometry is in itself consistent, the available practice is to use something like the Poincaré model to prove relative consistency—namely to show, in this case, that the Noneuclidean geometry is at least as free of contradiction as Euclidean geometry. The method is to model the former within the latter by assigning to all its axioms Euclidean meanings. For example, in the Euclidean interpretation Noneuclidean parallels are lines that meet on the circumference of the Poincaré circle. Since we have great faith in the consistency of Euclidean geometry, we are satisfied that if the consequences of the Noneuclidean axioms can co-exist in their Euclidean interpretation (as they indeed can), then the one geometry is at least as consistent as the other. Or: Noneuclidean geometry is consistent if Euclidean geometry is. So procedes the *formal* proof.

But whence comes the *faith* in the consistency of Euclidean geometry, the faith that, though not itself established in the proof, is essential to the conviction that the proof carries? It arises from the fact that Euclidean geometry is spatially intuitable—imaginable and imageable—for us. In Part Three, on the logic of images, it was shown that pictures and diagrams cannot contain contradictions—that only systems of propositions can be inconsistent. One way to sum up that argument was to say that whatever is concrete enough to exist in the sense of being present in our intuited space—as are geometric figures—cannot be affected with the fatal flaw of self-contradiction. Here then the spatial intuition belongs to the persuasive background of the logical system (Higginson 1982).

Next a word about the spontaneous use of mental spatialization, which is distinct from its use as a preferential learning strategy deliberately recommended. Spatialization occurs both in informal thinking and in solving logical problems. It is easy to illustrate the fact that almost any mental event, from a vague feeling to the most abstract of concepts, can be imaged in a depiction; the sketches people draw while "figuring" out a problem are prime evidence (Arnheim 1969).

The best test case for experiments in the spatializing of logic seem to be the premises of the linear or ordinary syllogism, a three-term series like "Alfred is older that Bertram, Bertram is older than Conrad." Such transitive inferences are ubiquitous in everyday cognition. There are eight different ways to state this relation. One of these is: "Bertram is older than Conrad, Bertram is younger than Alfred." Now it has been found that for the different versions there are different response- or latency-times.That is to say, the question "Who is oldest?" takes a little longer to answer for the second version than the first. The reason may well be that subjects try to make a spatial array, a visual line-up, and find this a littler harder to do for the second version. They begin with items in the first premise and then find that they cannot place those in the second premise without reversing direction, so that Alfred will again head or "end-anchor" the left-hand end of the series. Visualization, incidentally, is usually along a horizontal axis for adjectives like "wider" and "narrower" and along a vertical axis for "better" and "worse." Comparatives like "worse" are called "marked" because they convey not only relative but also absolute information: What is better may still be bad, but what is worse can never be good. Marked comparatives increase latency times, possibly because the usual placing of goodness-comparatives is from the top down, while "worse" (than x) has to be read from bottom up, contrary to the usual scanning direction. Other factors increasing the time required for answering are negatives, and, of course, the various alternate versions of a question. Experimental evidence seems to point to a mixture of linguistic and spatial representations in solving three-term inference problems. Subjects first decode the linguistic information so as to recode it spatially. Response-time seems to be increased by a mental scanning process, of the sort familiar in mental imagery-studies.

(Huttenlocher 1968, Sternberg 1980, Morris and Hampson 1983, Kaufman 1984.)

So much for examples of the credential importance and the psychological fact of geometric models and cognitive spatialization. What is really interesting is how and why it is possible to do such spatially extended imaging of thought.

The great mathematical metaphors of thought are apt to be classical, since in modern philosophical expositions mathematics usually comes on the scene as the subject of thought rather than as the figure for it. Again, above all, Platonic dialogues abound in illustrative mathematics (Brumbaugh 1954, Klein 1965). The geometry is usually used to indicate something about the intellectual realm which is hard to express in words. Sometimes it even represents that ineffability itself: In the famous demonstration in Plato's *Meno*, meant to show that the spontaneous "yes" or "no" responses to certain kinds of questions are brought up or "recollected" from within the soul, a mathematically uneducated young house slave is led to discover the line in a diagram of a unit square on which a square of double size can be erected; it is the diagonal, and it happens to be ineffable—"irrational," or inarticulate in terms of the given unit.

In the *Republic* the very reason that mathematical, particularly geometric metaphors are apt devices along the dialectic way is set out in a geometric metaphor, the equally famous "divided line" (509). The parts of this line are linked by a geometric proportion, reflecting the analogical relation of the cognitive realms for which they stand: Geometric figures are to purely intellectual forms as physical images are to their natural originals, and that is what makes geometry suitable for representing the pure ideas themselves. Here again is that "betwixt and between" character of geometry that gives geometric imaging its philosophical power (Ch. I C); it provides the most illuminating analogical account of the intellectual realm—an "intuitive" one.

The working complement to this mythico-philosophical geometry is the logic-diagram in which are spatialized not the insights into the essential nature of the intellect but the working patterns of thinking itself. Such diagrams have, of course, much more contemporary currency.

The formal thought-structures earliest recognized and still most often considered in studies of mental models are the figures of the class-syllogism. A syllogism is a pattern of connected propositions. Aristotle, who originated this formalism and its terminology in the *Prior Analytics*, himself speaks of *schemata*, "figures," but introduces no geometric or graphic layouts.

The invention of the current logic diagrams for representing syllogisms is attributed to Euler, who was inspired by Leibniz's habit of illustrating logical relations with geometric analogies (Kneale and Kneale 1962). Euler's diagrams, presented as pedagogical devices and published in *Letters to a German Princess* (1768), are simply circles representing the extension (the membership) of the classes. The circles are related to each other by inclusion, exclusion, or overlapping. These diagrams work beautifully for simple straightforward syllogisms, but they have drawbacks: There is no algorithm for knowing whether all the possible ways of representing the combination of the premises has been considered. For example, two overlapping circles standing for, say, human beings and animals may be taken to represent either "Some human beings are animals" (the overlap) or "Some animals are not human beings" (the remainder of the animal circle). People are probably influenced by the "atmosphere" of their particular problem in the reading they choose (Johnson-Laird 1983). In 1881, Venn, an admirer of Boole's symbolic logic, improved on this representation with a basic diagram of three mutually intersecting circles, pre-figuring all possible combinations, which are then neutralized by shading in null classes and null combinations.

It is very well to say that such figures are only illustrations. To be illustrative, it is agreed, the figures have to image the logical structure. But why should the spatial image be more perspicuous than the logical original? One might argue that the logic-diagram pictures logical extensions, the real membership of the classes that occur in the premises of the syllogism. If one were to round up all animals and all human beings, and then enclose them in fences by classes, using the minimum of fencing, the finished compound corral would have to look like Euler circles. However, that kind of membership imaging does not seem to be obligatory in reasoning. We do not necessarily envision classes as crowds.

One might diminish the problem by arguing, like Johnson-Laird (1983), that Euler and Venn diagrams are actually quite unnatural. Rather than being naive pictures, they are "sophisticated mathematical notations that depend on mapping sets of individuals into points in a Euclidean plane." And they have, to boot, a limited use, being incapable of handling premises with more than one quantifier, such as "Everyone loves someone." Hence he proposes another imaginative method for externalizing the mental process involved in syllogistic reasoning. Depict, he says, a kind of tableau in which persons take on different roles simultaneously: There is a group of Artists all of whom are also to play Beekeeper. Since the instructions do not say that only Artists are Beekeepers, there is clearly room in that imagined tableau for actors whose existence is undetermined (in the sense that they *may* exist) and who may be playing Beekeeper, but there is no reason to visualize them. Next, all the Beekeepers are instructed to play Chemist; clearly again instructions leave room for Chemists whose existence is uncertain. At this point the tableau, for all its indeterminacies, tells you clearly that each of the actors who plays Artists also plays a Chemist, and that is the desired inference. Note that this tableau is similar to the Euler corral above, except that the participants are listed and connected with their concurrent roles one by one. Behind this visualization stands a "mental model," a more abstract listing with tokens rather than role-takers. This mental model embodies a principle absent in the corral representation. The corral involves the presence of all members of the class, whether active in the reasoning or not, while the model shows that the totality of entities on the scene is irrelevant to the inference.

"Mental models" in this context are cognitive hypotheses standing descriptively between propositions and mental images. There is nothing necessarily intuitive about such models; their structures and processes are propositionally completely explicit. They are working replicas of physical or conceptual states of affairs, whose relational structures mimic the world, albeit in a simplified way; so far they refer to the world by corresponding to it. They differ from propositional strings of symbols in not requiring syntactical conventions and rules of inference; thus they can account for the fact that people do logic without knowing its rules.

Mental models are, furthermore, more determinate and specific than propositional systems need to be, and this distinction shows up in experiments. For example, if subjects are given two determinate propositions such as: "The knife is to the left of the spoon" and "The plate is to the left of the knife," they tend to remember not the words but the structural gist, a spatial model, the place-setting. Now, however, change the second proposition to: "The plate is to the right of the knife." Then the location of the plate becomes indeterminate insofar as it could be between the knife and the spoon or to the right of both. In that case the subjects' memory tends to do better with the verbal descriptions than with the mental model which requires determinacy (Johnson-Laird 1983, 162).

There is one specially pertinent advantage that the tableau-type of mental model seems to have over the older geometric diagram in accounting for syllogistic inference: it is finite. Mental models are discrete and work with finite sets of tokens, whereas the Euler and Venn diagrams are taken by Johnson-Laird to be mapping the individuals of ordinary natural classes into the infinitely many points of the diagram-plane.

But is that, I would ask, what they do? Do they actually and prodigally map the logical extension, the members of the class, into a spatial extension? Or do they instead depict the logical intension, the concept of the class, as an extended figure?

If they actually do the latter, the mental model may be a fine working hypothesis for ordinary syllogistic reasoning, but it does not explain away the diagrammatic possibility itself. For then this extensional representation of intension is not merely a sloppily extravagant kind of mapping. It is an unexceptionable realization of a strange capability of thought: the power to spatialize intellectual being and its relations, of imaging thought and its substance, of transmuting logical intension into spatial extension.

In general, although mental models seem at first to be the answer to the imagist's prayer, difficulties soon arise. In this theory of models, images are, to be sure, acknowledged and given a function: they are the views or visualizations of one particular type of model, the spatial type. There are said to be also several other non-spatial types—for example, the relational and the temporal mental models. If one begins to wonder which category the syllogistic model belongs to, the distinctions become blurred: surely its content is relational and its development is temporal. But it also has a visualization, the tableau, so it must be spatial. One begins to wonder whether mental models are not *ipso facto* spatial, and which way round it works: Are images views of models, or are models abstracted from images?

In cognitive theory the ultimate warrant for the concreteness of the model is its biological foundation, so far of an unknown configuration (Part Two, Ch. II A). It ought be be admitted that the spatial appearance of thought is, as a kind of incarnation, so far a mystery.

Up to this point I have discussed the mirroring in the imagination, in turn, of the soul, the intellect, and mental operations. Now I shall consider how the world is reflected within itself; I mean the modeling of the external, physical world in external, physical images.

2. Physical Models. In the beginning of natural philosophy among the Greeks, mathematical models image the visible heavens directly. Then in modern classical physics the mathematical pictures of all sorts of motions, while still to some degree intuitive, tend to represent physical quantities not depictively but symbolically. Finally, in the quantum physics of this century, imageability itself becomes problematic (though great biological models have come to the fore instead). The phase-out of physical imaging, with its attendant setting-aside of the imagination, will be sketched out below—with a hop and a skip and a jump, to be sure.

a. A Solid Model: The Cosmos as Copy. The first and grandest surviving description of a global mathematical model occurs, yet again, in Plato's *Timaeus*—it is identical with the soul-model discussed above. It is global in two senses: because it represents a coherent cosmic architecture and because the powers of its encircling first principles are diffused throughout the whole model. Dramatically, the dialogue of the *Timaeus* (perhaps) takes place on the day after the conversation about justice and its realization in a perfect political community that is reported in the *Republic*. In that conversation Socrates had been, as he says, "contemplating a beautiful living thing either composed in a painting or in fact alive but frozen in position." He means that he had set out his city as an intellectual scheme rather than an imaginative depiction. Since the mathematics suitable to that community is pure rather than physically applied, the astronomer within the city was told not to gape at the real heavens but to contemplate the true, invisible, figured motions of an ideal kinematic geometry. In the *Timaeus*, Socrates is to be entertained with a moving flesh-and-blood picture of the city and its cosmic site.

That cosmic setting is introduced by an epistemological apology and a mythical genesis. It is an apology and a genesis of epochal significance, for the former announces model-making as the mode of natural science and the latter gives the conditions under which the world is imageable.

The important sentence in the "prelude" to Timaeus's account is this: "Consequently it is appropriate to accept a likely story (*eikōs mythos*) about these matters and to seek no further" (29 d). As in English, so in Greek, the word "likely" means "highly probable" and also carries an undertone of likeness. The "likely myth" is the prototype of the grand scientific model. It is a best available rational conjecture; it is an intellectual construct intended to "save the appearances" by embodying certain intellectually appealing hypotheses; it is an image with the fewest possible distortions, the kind called "eikonic" in the *Sophist* (Part Three, Ch. I A).

The mythical account of its genesis intimates why the cosmos can be imaged to begin with: It can be copied because it is itself a copy. It is itself a sensible, spatial image made, according to the genetic myth, by a divine craftsman, an artificer working from a non-sensible, non-spatial, fully intelligible original, the model of models. Recall that we mean by "model" both the paradigm and its likeness. The cosmologist Timaeus in effect says that the divine intellectual model is the paradigm, that the world itself is the copied likeness, and that his own account, insofar as it is in turn derived from the latter, is only a likeness at second remove, though a likely one: a man-made mathematical image of the cosmos is possible because the world itself is a divinely made copy of an intellectual original.

So it is the rational prototype of the world that is conjecturally recovered in the likely account he gives. This account is naturally mathematical, since mathematics is the intellectual mode located between sure truth and mere faith, in accordance with its in-between standing set out above (Ch. I C). The marvelous model itself consists of the encompassing revolving starry sphere and the great oppositely moving chiastic circles, the horizontal Equator and the oblique Ecliptic with its planetary bands, both composed of intelligible stuff mathematically mixed. Within this containing cosmic geometry, in its middle and below the threshhold of visibility, the simplest plane figures, "traces" within the spatial stuff, combine variously into the regular solids, shaping and reshaping the primary elements of bodies. This geometrization of nature, astronomical and atomical, is what makes the Timaean Plato so congenial to physicists from Galileo to Heisenberg.

The Timaean model is in fact a description of an armillary sphere, a small-scale material stand-up model of the heavens. Again, the cosmos is thought to be copyable because it is itself an embodiment, an imperfect realization of a non-material model. In a word: We can represent to ourselves for contemplation the whole in which we live precisely because it *is* a well-joined whole, a *cosmos*, and because its genetic principle is the very principle that well-formed intelligible structures are imageable in space. That is the founding myth of physics.

Timaeus's model has remained the cosmic container for all geocentric astronomy. Within its cosmology are fitted the auxiliary hypotheses that account for the anomalies of planetary motion, such accounts being the chief task of astronomy proper as distinct from cosmology.

Again Plato was the man who, according to tradition, set the terms for this astronomy, asking: "What circular motions, uniform and perfectly regular, are to be admitted as hypotheses so that it might be possible to save the appearances presented by the planets?" (Simplicius, *Commentary on Aristotle's* On the Heavens, 6th cent. A.D.). The great ancient challenge, "to save the appearances," meant finding a mathematical undergirding that would rationally account for the points of light that wavered and wandered about in the heavens—the Greek word "planet" means "wanderer"—and would preserve the heavens for reason by interpreting the appearances as indicators of a mathematical substructure.

Now here's the rub. There are two alternative planetary hypotheses, the eccentric and the epicyclic, and planets other than the sun require a combination of these. The resulting diagrams are practically impossible to realize in a mechanical model. The problem arose: Was real imaging an epistemological requirement of astronomy? Some die-hards claimed that it was: "For Plato says that we would be engaging in futile labor if we tried to explain these phenomena without images that speak to the eyes" (Theon, *Astronomy*, 2nd cent. A.D. Of course Plato's own pronouncements in the *Republic* appear to be to the opposite effect).

The working astronomers, on the other hand, including Ptolemy, regarded the mathematical hypotheses as independent of physical-mechancial requirements. The planet's apparent complex motions—involving such strange loops that they were rarely drawn—are the resultants of these diagrammatic motions, which are chosen mainly according to criteria of simplicity; thus alternative explanations are tolerated if they too save the appearances. These hypothetical diagrams are also called "images," but they are contrivances "quite removed from likelihood" (Proclus, *Commentary on Plato's* Timaeus, 5th cent. A.D.). So the precise working geometry, while remaining eminently intuitive as geometry, grows away from the appearances it is intended to account for.

To leap over a millennium, modern physics appears to originate in refusal to tolerate that diremption, be it cosmological or astronomical. Copernicus believes that the heliocentric system is true, not merely geometrically convenient. (However, to save him from persecution, a friendly churchman wrote a preface to the *Revolution of the Heavenly Spheres* claiming that it set forth nothing more revolutionary than yet another likely hypothesis, albeit a particularly economical one.) Next, Kepler seeks a geometric expression not only of the shape but also of the physical causes of heavenly motions. Newton, finally, says outright that he "feigns no hypotheses," meaning in part that he no longer admits explanatory fictions—his diagrams represent real motions and the physical forces behind them. However, this realistic view of geometry as a part of universal mechanics expressed in the Preface to the *Principia*—what may be called the heavenly clockwork phase—is for all its power only an episode. As the infinite universe looks less and less like a copyable cosmos, the imaging of nature becomes more problematic than ever (c, below).

(Dreyer 1905, Duhem 1908, Koyré 1965, Taylor 1928.)

b. Diagrams: Graphs and Loci. The "New Science" of physics uses a new kind of diagram, one in which coordinate axes of space supersede the

cosmological place, and graphed trajectories replace global geometric figures. Galileo's great kinematic discoveries are set out in such diagrams, for
which Descartes was contemporaneously inventing his coordinate geometry. If these diagrams picture paths, they represent them not as holistic
shapes but as loci of points; for the most part, however, they do not *picture*
motions at all—instead they represent them symbolically (Claggett 1959,
Klein 1934).

One such Galilean discovery concerns in fact the shape of a path and its
analysis: the projectile parabola (1638, Fourth Day). Galileo thinks of the
body as rolling along a horizontal plane with a certain inertial motion and
maintaining that motion along a horizontal axis after dropping off the edge,
while also falling down the vertical axis according to the law of free fall.
The intersections of the distances from the two axes at every moment trace
out a locus which Galileo had probably previously observed to be a semi-
parabola (Drake 1978, 129). The two coordinate motions are *imagined* to
take place (Fourth Day, 274), while their composition, the parabola, physically appears. Hence the new diagram of terrestrial motions, besides displaying the locus of actual positions of the projectile, which is a simple
conic section, also separates it into coordinate rectilinear components that
symbolize a conceptual analysis. Galileo is close here to inventing the
parallelogram of forces.

This is a small but telling sample of the diagrammatic mode of the New
Science at its very origin. The diagrammatic modes of later classical physics
were discussed by the great Maxwell himself (1911). Both the representational ambiguities of such diagrams and the older, wider problem of the
status to be accorded to the mathematical constructs rationalizing the
phenomena remained at issue through the three and a half centuries after
Galileo. Eventually the problem became thematized as the question of
"intuitivity" in physics (c, below). In the last century the preference was
still for physical theorizing to stay as close as possible to imaging. Witness
Faraday's figures (Part Two, Ch. V A) and Boltzmann's pronouncement: "I
cannot really imagine any other law of thought than that our pictures
should be clearly and unambiguously imaginable" (1897, in Miller 1984).
In our century that expectation ceases.

   c. Beyond Physical Imaging. A macrocosm, the cosmic model of the
Timaeus, was the first physical image, and a microcosm, Bohr's model of
the atom as a planetary system in 1913, marked the end. "The thought that
the laws of the macrocosm in the small reflect the terrestrial world obviously
exercises a great magic on mankind's mind," but "the possibility of
considering the atom as a planetary system has its limits" (Max Born in

Miller 1984). With the establishment in the twenties of the insufficiency of that model for representing the discontinuities of atomic processes, there began a period of intense discussion concerning the role in physics of visualizability—a translation of the German key term *Anschaulichkeit*, literally "look-at-ability," also rendered "intuitivity" (Miller 1984). The question was whether the objects of quantum theory were in any sense visualizable—whether the "intuitive pictures" of classical physics could or should be imposed on quantum theory—and it involved the great physicists of the time: Born, Einstein, de Broglie, Pauli, Schrödinger, and above all Heisenberg, who especially wrote about the epistemology of the new physics along the following lines: Ordinary intuition relies on the indefinite divisibility of space and matter. In the past, electrons were understood as very small particles moving in the space and time complying with our intuition. This view turns out to be false; thus "the program of quantum mechanics has above all to free itself from these intuitive pictures" and "visualizable models." It must deal only with directly measurable quantities that are "so many numbers." Heisenberg then set about defining a new, highly abstract kind of intuition, in which the intuitivity of the physical objects is no longer associated with an imaginable residue abstracted from perception, but is entirely defined as intelligibility within the mathematical system and is known by a kind of intellectual intuition. Heisenberg compares these physical objects to the ideal archetypes of matter, those regular solids composed of plane-elements in Plato's *Timaeus* (Miller 1984). But of course, Heisenberg's objects lack the geometric intuitivity of the Platonic solids.

A recent, heroic attempt to draw the layman into post-classical physics displays the remoteness from ordinary imaging of the new "pictures" (Feynman 1985). The attempt to explain the quantum representation of the partial reflection of light from a sheet of glass involves imagining: the addition of vectors, whose lengths represent the square root of a probability, and whose directions are determined as parallel to the positions of a hand on a clock timing the light particle as it travels from its source and is reflected from the glass surface into a photomultiplier. This diagram is clearly nothing at all like a picture of the perceived world but is instead a symbolic representation of a sophisticated theory.

The visible surface and the intelligible substructure of nature are now twenty-five centuries' worth of theory apart from each other. The imaging faculty has ceased to be their mediator. However, the further science and mathematics in their levitations leave spatial intuitivity behind, the more urgent it is, if the project is to remain publicly accessible to all, that its roots in the imagination should not sink totally out of sight.

Bibliography

Abbott, Edwin A. 1884. *Flatlands: A Romance of Many Dimensions.* New York: Dover Publications (1952).

Adler, Claire F. 1958. *Modern Geometry.* New York: McGraw-Hill.

Arnheim, Rudolf. 1969. *Visual Thinking.* Berkeley and Los Angeles: University of California Press.

Berkeley, George. 1709. *A New Theory of Vision.* New York: E.P. Dutton and Company (1954).

Bohm, David. 1976. "Imagination, Fancy, Insight and Reason in the Process of Thought." In *Evolution of Consciousness: Studies in Polarity in Honor of Owen Barfield.* Middletown, Conn.: Wesleyan University Press.

Bonola, Roberto. 1908. *Non-Euclidean Geometry: A Critical and Historical Study of Its Developments.* New York: Dover Publications (1955).

Brann, Eva. 1983. "Against Time." *The St. John's Review* 34:65–104.

Brumbaugh, Robert S. 1954. *Plato's Mathematical Imagination: The Mathematical Passages in the Dialogues and Their Interpretation.* Bloomington: Indiana University Press.

Claggett, Marshall. 1959. *The Science of Mechanics in the Middle Ages.* Madison: The University of Wisconsin Press.

Corcoran, Derek W. J. 1977. "The Phenomena of the Disembodied Eye or Is It a Matter of Personal Geography?" *Perception* 6:247–253.

Dennett, Daniel C. 1978. "Toward a Cognitive Theory of Consciousness." In *Minnesota Studies in the Philosophy of Science*, Volume 9, edited by C. Wade Savage. Minneapolis: University of Minnesota Press.

Downs, Roger M., and Stea, David. 1977. *Maps in Minds: Reflections on Cognitive Mapping.* New York: Harper and Row.

Drake, Stillman. 1978. *Galileo at Work: His Scientific Biography.* Chicago: The University of Chicago Press.

Dreyer, J.L.E. 1905. *A History of Astronomy from Thales to Kepler.* Revised by W. H. Stahl. New York: Dover Publications (1953).

Duhem, Pierre. 1908. *To Save the Phenomena: An Essay on the Idea of Physical Theory from Plato to Galileo.* Translated by Edmund Doland and Chaninah Maschler. Chicago: The University of Chicago Press (1969).

Einstein, A., Minkowski, H., et al. 1923. *The Principle of Relativity: A Collection of Original Memoirs on the Special and General Theory of Relativity.* New York: Dover Publications.

Euclid. c. 300 BC. *The Thirteen Books of Euclid's Elements*, edited by Thomas L. Heath. New York: Dover Publications (1956).

Feynman, Richard P. 1985. *The Strange Theory of Light and Matter.* Princeton: Princeton University Press.

Finke, Ronald. 1986. "Mental Imagery and the Visual System." *Scientific American,* March, 88–95.

Frazer, J. T., ed. 1966. *The Voices of Time: A Cooperative Survey of Man's Views of Time as Expressed by the Sciences and by the Humanities,* 2d ed. Amherst: The University of Massachusetts Press (1981).

Freud, Sigmund. 1933. "The Dissection of the Psychical Personality." In *New Introductory Lectures on Psychoanalysis,* edited by James Strachey. New York: W.W. Norton (1965).

Galileo Galilei. 1638. *Two New Sciences.* Translated by Stillman Drake. Madison: The University of Wisconsin Press (1974).

Gregory, R. E. 1978. *Eye and Brain: The Psychology of Seeing,* 3d ed. New York: McGraw-Hill.

Grünbaum, Adolf. 1973. "Empiricism and the Geometry of Visual Space." Part I, Chapter 5 in *Philosophical Problems of Space and Time,* 2d ed. Boston: D. Reidel Publishing Co.

Guthrie, W.K.C. 1962. *A History of Greek Philosophy,* Volume 1, *The Earlier Presocratics and the Pythagoreans.* Cambridge: Cambridge University Press.

Hamilton, Vernon, and Vernon, Magdalen D. 1976. *The Development of Cognitive Processes.* London: Academic Press.

Henderson, Linda D. 1983. *The Fourth Dimension and Non-Euclidean Geometry in Modern Art.* Princeton: Princeton University Press.

Higginson, William. 1982. "Symbols, Icons, and Mathematical Understanding." *Visible Language* 16:239–248.

Hilbert, David, and Cohn-Vossen, S. 1932. *Geometry and the Imagination.* Translated by P. Nemenyi. New York: Chelsea Publishing Co.

Hinckfuss, Ian. 1975. *The Existence of Space and Time.* Oxford: Clarendon Press.

Hinton, C. Howard. 1884. *The Fourth Dimension.* New York: Arno Press (1976).

Holley, Charles D., and Dansereau, Donald F., eds. 1984. *Spatial Learning Strategies: Techniques, Applications, and Related Issues.* New York: Academic Press.

Holton, Gerald. 1978. *The Scientific Imagination: Case Studies.* Cambridge: Cambridge University Press.

Huttenlocher, Janellen. 1968. "Constructing Spatial Images: A Strategy in Reasoning." *Psychological Review* 75:350–360.

Jammer, Max. 1957. *Concepts of Space: The History of Theories of Space in Physics.* Cambridge: Harvard University Press.

Johnson-Laird, P. N. 1983. *Mental Models: Towards a Cognitive Science of Language, Inference, and Consciousness.* Cambridge: Harvard University Press.

Kass, Leon R. 1985. "Looking Good: Nature and Nobility." Chapter II, 13 in *Toward a More Natural Science: Biology and Human Affairs*. New York: The Free Press.

Kaufman, Geir. 1984. "Mental Imagery in Problem Solving." In *International Review of Mental Imagery*, Volume 1, edited by Anees A. Sheikh. New York: Human Sciences Press.

Kern, Stephen. 1983. *The Culture of Time and Space 1880–1918*. Cambridge: Harvard University Press.

Klee, Paul. 1921. *Das bildnerische Denken*. Basel: Benno Schwabe (1959).

Klein, Felix. 1892. *Vorlesungen über nichteuklidische Geometrie*. New York: Chelsea Publishing Co. [Reprint of 1927 edition].

Klein, Jacob. 1934. *Greek Mathematical Thought and the Origin of Algebra*. Translated by Eva T. H. Brann. Cambridge: The MIT Press (1968).

———. 1965. *A Commentary on Plato's* Meno. Chapel Hill: The University of North Carolina Press.

Kneale, William, and Kneale Martha. 1962. *The Development of Logic*. Oxford: Clarendon Press.

Koyré, Alexandre. 1965. *Newtonian Studies*. London: Chapman and Hall.

Lay, L. Clark. 1982. "Mental Images and Arithmetical Symbols." *Visible Language* 16:259–274.

Locke, John. 1690. *An Essay Concerning Human Understanding*, edited by A. S. Pringle-Pattison. Oxford: Clarendon Press (1960).

Lucas, J. R. 1973. *A Treatise on Time and Space*. London: Methuen and Co.

Manning, Henry P. 1910. *The Fourth Dimension Simply Explained*. New York: Dover Publications (1960).

Maxwell, James Clerk. 1911. "Diagram." In *The Encyclopedia Britannica*, Eleventh Edition.

Merleau-Ponty, M. 1945. *Phenomenology of Perception*. Translated by Colin Smith. New York: Routledge and Kegan Paul (1962).

Miller, Arthur I. 1984. *Imagery in Scientific Thought: Creating 20th Century Physics*. Boston: Birkhaeuser.

Morgan, Michael J. 1977. *Molyneux's Question: Vision, Touch and Philosophy of Perception*. Cambridge: Cambridge University Press.

Morris, Peter E., and Hampson, Peter J. 1983. *Imagery and Consciousness*. New York: Academic Press.

Murch, Gerald M. 1973. *Visual and Auditory Perception*. Indianapolis: Bobbs–Merrill Educational Publishing Co.

Nerlich, Graham. 1976. *The Shape of Space*. Cambridge: Cambridge University Press.

Neisser, Ulrich. 1978. "Perceiving, Anticipating, Imagining." In *Minnesota Studies in the Philosophy of Science*, Volume 9. Minneapolis: University of Minnesota Press.

Plato [4th cent. BC]. *Timaeus*.

Poincaré, Henri. 1905. *Science and Hypothesis*. New York: Dover (1952).

Pylyshyn, Zenon. 1981. "The Imagery Debate: Analog Media versus Tacit Knowledge." In *Imagery*, edited by Ned Block. Cambridge: The MIT Press.

Reichenbach, Hans. 1928. *The Philosophy of Space and Time*. New York: Dover (1958).

Russell, Bertrand A. W. 1897. *An Essay on the Foundations of Geometry*. New York: Dover Publications (1956).

Salmon, Wesley C. 1980. *Space, Time and Motion: A Philosophical Introduction*. Minneapolis: University of Minnesota Press.

Shepard, Roger. 1980. "The Mental Image." In *Human Memory: Contemporary Readings*, edited by John G. Seamon. Oxford: Oxford University Press.

Shibles, Warren. 1969. "Pictures of Reason." In *Philosophical Pictures*. Dubuque: Wm. C. Brown Book Co.

Sklar, Lawrence. 1974. *Space, Time, and Spacetime*. Berkeley and Los Angeles: University of California Press.

Sternberg, Robert J. 1980. "Representation and Process in Linear Syllogistic Reasoning." *Journal of Experimental Psychology* 109:119–158.

Taylor, A. E. 1928. *A Commentary on Plato's* Timaeus. Oxford: The Clarendon Press (1962).

Toulmin, Stephen. 1953. *The Philosophy of Science: An Introduction*. New York: Hutchinson's University Library.

Trimpi, Wesley. 1983. *Muses of One Mind: The Literary Analysis of Experience and Its Continuity*. Princeton: Princeton University Press.

van t'Hoff, Jacobus H. 1878. *Imagination in Science*. Translated by George F. Springer. New York: Springer-Verlag (1967).

Wilder, Raymond L. 1952. *Introduction to the Foundations of Mathematics*. New York: John Wiley and Sons.

Wolfe, Harold E. 1945. *Introduction to Non-Euclidean Geometry*. New York: Holt, Rinehart and Winston.

Wollheim, Richard. 1974. "The Mind and the Mind's Image of Itself." In *On Art and the Mind*. Cambridge: Harvard University Press.

Chapter III

Aesthetic Space: Pictures and Paintings

What distinction is more engaging to the intellect and more pervasive in life than that between something being so and something being appealing? This distinction shows up in our faculty of imaging: Image-making can be constrained primarily by truth; or it can be governed by beauty, in the sense well expressed in Findlay's two defining words "perspicuity" and "poignancy"—formal lucidity combined with arresting interest (1966).

The truthful kind of imaging, which is for the sake of correctly articulating the structure of space or truly modeling the underlying forms of the physical world, was the subject of the last chapter. In this chapter the faculty of imaging and its products will be the subject insofar as they give delight to the senses and express human meaning. I am not implying that geometric and physical models are not also delightful and expressive, perhaps even in a more lasting way. But their being so is a super-added grace granted to the intellect, whereas aesthetic imaging is immediately moved by considerations of beauty and meaning, whose relation to truth is a never-ending problem.

I call the space of this imaging "aesthetic" in the sense introduced by Baumgarten (1735), a sense that underlies the current usage of the word. In the original Greek "aesthetic" means "belonging to the senses," sensory. In the modern usage it means "belonging to the senses insofar as they are cultivated"—that is, belonging to the perfection of qualitative perceptual cognition (Baumgarten, 5).

The term is apt because this imaging space is certainly more sensory than is geometric space. For one thing, its figures, in contrast to the "beauty bare" of geometry, are usually colored, as is their ground. Coloration, atmosphere, and aura employ the eye to its fullest: as Berkeley observed, vision is primarily color vision, for in nature it is color that defines shape. And although aesthetic perception involves senses other than vision, such as the feeling of gravity and lightness, such as essences and fragrances, and, above all, sounds and voices, imaging is nevertheless primarily visual: visual images fill aesthetic space in its proper mode—that of containing extended figures; an argument has in fact been made that images are essentially visual (Introduction A, B).

Although I am trying to delineate not a formal aesthetic theory but the nature of an internal and a corresponding external representative space, still a reflection on aesthetic imaging, as evidencing a certain sort of a-practicality, if not the "pure disinterested pleasure" that is Kant's mark of aesthetic experience, cannot help figuring in the description. In this imaginative realm proper, considerations of getting, possessing, operating, and manipulating are at one remove—not always at a far remove, to be sure—but thoughts of purposeful intervention are somehow postponed. Though aesthetic imaging does often begin, and end, in its own kind of desire, still it is not a desire of the instrumental sort commonly associated with the sensory pointedness that means business: sniffing rather than smelling, grasping rather than touching, and, above all, inspecting rather than seeing. For concentrated practical intention causes temporary aesthetic blindness. The tool in hand, the black box in the laboratory, along with the world they belabor or measure, are invisible except as the instruments and locales of operation. Visionary contemplation and hands-on intervention are different—though also complementary—human modes: insofar as its products are externally realized, the aesthetic imaging space calls for practical focusing, but in its most intimate moments it invites a more receptive gazing.

This characterization of the imaginative space of course echoes Kant's understanding of the pure aesthetic pleasure we take in the beautiful. As was mentioned, he calls it "disinterested." Such pleasure has no relation to the existence of the object but is what has been called "autoaffection," an imaginative pleasing oneself in the object. Yet insofar as it is the object that pleases, this pleasure is—and here Kant admits a great difficulty—heteroaffection as well: "The most irreducible heteroaffection inhabits—intrinsically—the most closed autoaffection" (Derrida 1978). Now the simple thesis of the present chapter is that visual works of art come out of and are received into the aesthetic space of the imagination. As presences in the inner contemplative space their physical availability, their possessability, so to speak, is for the moment obviated: their enjoyment is already ours. But as images of the imaging faculty they inspire in us, as I have so often urged, an unquenchable interest in the being of their originals, a longing to know their actuality and, sometimes, to effect their existence: we may not want to possess imagined beauty but we do want it to be actual.

Aesthetic space, as roughly described above, will be studied primarily through two-dimensional works, because plane representations are, as was said before (Ch. II A) and as will be shown again, primary to the imagination. These, in turn, will be divided into pictures (A) and paintings (B), according to a distinction adapted from Gilson (1955). "Pictures" are depictions insofar as they invite consideration of resemblance to an original. "Paintings" are depictions insofar as they transmute the issue of verisimilitude into one of aesthetic truth, that is, candid beauty. These headings are chosen as leading straight to the principal imbroglio of the productive imagination: the copy theory. The copy or imitation problem is resolved in the most acute contemporary investigation in a way that "adds up to open heresy," for "resemblance disappears as a criterion of representation" (Goodman 1976, 230). I shall attempt to counter the heresy by an anti-iconoclasm: I shall try to rehabilitate "resemblance-representation."

A. Pictures: The Resemblance-Relation

The great question concerning aesthetic imaging is first *whether* artificial images resemble anything, and then *what* they resemble and *how* they achieve resemblance. To this compound question the European tradition gives a confident answer. It amounts to a doctrine of resemblance-representation (*1* a) that becomes problematic in our times (*1* b). With respect to plane images, the most powerful particular technique for achieving correct imitations is perspective (*2* a), and for making semi-natural replicas, photography (*2* b); both serve here to consider imaginal resemblance.

1. The Tradition of Mimesis. It is a fascinating fact that what the whole practical and critical tradition affirms is denied in contemporary aesthetics: the resemblance-relation of depiction or the genesis of paintings in imitation.

The mimetic tradition—*mimēsis* is Greek for "imitation"—which dominates ordinary opinion to this day, is that poetry and painting are imitative, that the fine arts are by gradations mimetic. In passing over from literature to music, where the imitation—if any—becomes less direct and less determinate, the mimetic claim becomes correspondingly less bold and therefore less vulnerable: Where there is no question of overt similarity, there is no invitation for an aggressive critique of imaging. For the premise of the mimetic theory is that an imitation is an image of a certain kind, a copy, the product of deliberate imaging.

The results of poll-taking, that contemporary way to truth by authority, may not be binding, but they are significant. A survey of what practicing painters say about the imitation question indicates how counterintuitive is the insurgency against imaging that dominates current aesthetic theory. The acute and careful analysis of logicians denies what people have naturally and for a very long time and in many places believed—the people who produce the work and the people who enjoy it. As far as the viewers are concerned, the reader is invited to ask around whether the following is not the normal view of the genesis and purpose of painting: The artist has particularly acute and revealing perceptual experiences of people and scenes. These, enhanced by memory and invention, become mental images or "pictures in the head." They in turn are projected by means of the painter's craft onto the canvas. Those images, imitations of reality, are, again, perceived by the viewer, who is then able to appreciate the original sitter or landscape as "seen through the painter's eyes." It seems to me salutary to keep this canonical account in mind, if only out of a decent respect for the opinion of mankind.

The painters tend to agree that the imitative representation of reality is the heart of the process. Perhaps it goes a little too far to say that they "see in their works nothing but the exact equivalent of the object" (Arnheim 1954), but one can furnish plenty of comment close to that opinion.

I begin with some ancient evidence about sculpture rather than about painting, to be sure, but too good and too close to the beginning of our tradition to pass up. Archaic Greek statues of the sixth century B.C. sometimes introduce themselves. They say on their body parts or on their pedestals: "I am the statue of so-and-so"—it is a felicitous fact that the Greek word for statue, *agalma*, literally means "pride and joy." They say what wonderful works they are and who made them and what mortal devoted them to what god. The thigh of a marble Apollo announces: "Mantiklos dedicated me to the god with the silver bow who strikes afar." Or the base of a group of marble women from the Ionian islands says: "Geneleos made us" (Lullies and Hirmer 1957, Richter 1953). Here, fully intended, is the paradigm of imitative re-presentation in a material more durable than flesh. It is representation to the point of impersonation.

The oriental tradition, albeit differing from the classical tradition in almost everything but its perfection, does share with it the re-presentative mode. Here is a fair example from master Kuo Hsi's essay on landscape painting (11th century A.D.):

> Having no access to landscapes, the lover of forest and stream, the friend of mist and haze, enjoys them only in his dreams. How delightful then to have a landscape painted by a skilled hand! Without leaving the room, at once, he finds himself among streams and ravines; the cries of birds and monkeys are faintly audible to his senses; light on hills and reflection in the water, glittering, dazzle his eyes.

The postclassical Western tradition of painting is soon embroiled in a tremendous fracas about the "iconic," depictive, nature of painting and the attempt to interdict it. This religious iconoclasm will be treated in Part Six (Ch. I A). Meanwhile I cannot resist the anticipatory comment: No species of beings could be seized by these occasional paroxysms of image-hatred to which we are subject if the imitation of world and its divinities were not a tantalizing possibility for it.

Moreover, the painters of the Renaissance and their successors consistently testify to their understanding of their art as eminently mimetic: Leonardo says that the correspondence of a painting with nature should be tested by mirroring the object represented and comparing the painted with the mirrored image. Michelangelo avers that to copy each object of nature is to imitate the work of God. Reynolds approves the universally cited rule "Imitate Nature," provided it is done not mechanically but with imagination. Cézanne says: "A minute of the world passes. To paint that in its reality!" Delacroix, Whistler, Braque, each speaks against the mere surface imitation of nature, but they do so in the interest of a deeper representational truth. Thus Braque says that one does not imitate appearances, for they are but the result; to be pure imitation, painting must forget appearance. Chirico similarly says that things have two aspects: the visible aspect seen by ordinary men and the metaphysical aspect visible only to rare individuals: The work of art must "narrate something that does not appear within its outline." Hopper says that his aim in painting has always been the most exact transcription possible of his most intimate impressions of nature (Goldwater and Treves 1945). That brings us by centuries into our time.

It is a notorious fact that in this century the question is complicated by the disavowal of natural forms in "abstract," "non-objective," and "non-representational" art. As for abstraction, Picasso, who takes the term literally, as a process of removal, says that "you must always start with something"; the further metamorphosis of the painting is then a revealing "sum of destructions." An example is given by his series of eleven lithographs entitled "Abstractions of a Bull" (1945–46), which begins with a detailed picture of a bull and ends with a figure of ten simple lines (Kahler 1968). But this procedure implies that abstract painting, being an abstractive project, acknowledges imaging as its beginning. So too for purely and aboriginally non-figurative painting: Mondrian says that this term is only approximate, "for every form, even every line, represents a figure: no form is absolutely neutral" (1937). Perhaps one should simply say that representational depiction comes in two degrees of specificity: It may image this or that particular figure or it may represent figurality in general; the former are objects seen in the world, the latter the building blocks of their visibility, their geometric elements.

There is, of course, painting that is by intention, at least, well and truly non-representational, but this extreme case shows why the non-representational movement is not determinative in the imaging question. The problem is not whether there can be paintings that do not depict anything, but whether picture-paintings that do depict something do so by imaging originals in some way.

In what way? That is the question. The philosophical reservations concerning the mimetic theory of painting are as old as its articulation.

The two great ancients who lead off the debate, Plato and Aristotle, agree that poetry, and painting *a fortiori*, are mimetic. However, their estimations and analyses of this mimesis differ in tandem with their views of knowledge. For the apprehension of a mimetic relation is essentially a cognitive act, though of course one with affective accompaniments. The difference between the two views is therefore a function of what might, with summary crudeness, be called Plato's top-down and Aristotle's bottom-up understanding of knowledge. Plato naturally emphasizes the dubiousness of the imitative arts, painting in particular, because they are at a second remove from the truth, copies of the visible copies of the intelligible originals (*Republic* 597). The more technically ingenious the imitation is, resorting to distortions of the image in the interests of effect, the less respectable it becomes, for it produces something even lower than a correct likeness or *eikon*: the mere appearance of a likeness, a phantom or *phantasma*.

For Aristotle, on the other hand, mimesis, which is the delight of children, is not only a powerful device for learning, but it enhances and illuminates the original. "Good portrait painters reproduce the distinctive features of a man, and at the same time, without losing the likeness, make him handsomer than he is" (*Poetics* 1453). So also poetry is closer to wisdom than history is, because poetry tells what ought to have been, not what was (1451; Hagberg 1984).

With these two views the terms of the intra-mimetic debate are given. On the one hand, quite aside from Platonic anti-imagist biases, there is the technical problem of imitative painting: on the premise that imitation *tout court*, iconic mimesis, is possible, is it or is it not the truest way to render appearances as appearances? Is the art of painting essentially *eikonic* or *phantastic*? This dilemma will be briefly taken up in (2).

On the other hand, there is the philosophical question raised by Aristotle's claim that the object of imitation is not the present appearance. What then is it, what is being copied? Painters and aestheticians who attack Aristotle's mimetic theory usually do so on the understanding that it considers the appearances of physical things to be the object of imitation. Schlegel in his *Doctrine of Art* (1801)—wrongly—accuses Aristotle himself of holding this view and exonerates him only from the most doctrinaire naturalism. But if not the appearances, then what? There seem to be three possibilities. One is that what is re-produced is a beautification, an idealization of the original (e.g., Croce 1901); a second view, currently ubiquitous, is that the artist expresses a personal vision of nature; the third view is that it is a truth behind the appearance that is imaged. The exalted philosophical expression of this last possibility—it is enough to make Plato turn in his grave—is Schopenhauer's theory that the original model (the *Vorbild* or "proto-picture") directly represented in painting and poetry is the Platonic idea, the invisible archetype itself (1818). However, others take the truth which must be reconstructed to be the geometry behind the appearance, or some primitive aboriginal shape or some visible heavenly reality above the mundane. Without here entering on the perplexities associated with the notion of imitating the internal, the invisible, and the hyper-real, the pertinent point to be made is that all three such realizations involve relations of verisimilitude: something is to be re-presented *truly*.

This long tradition now comes under sophisticated attack in our day. Paintings are never pictures in the Gilsonian sense cited above: Depicting, it is claimed, is never imaging.

2. The Possibility of Resemblance-Representation. That ubiquitous word "representation" has meant in turn the reflection of nature in the mirror of the mind (Part One), the symbolization of information by mental imagery (Part Two), the re-production of reality in images (Part Three), and the human reconstruction of the world in the imaginative mode (Part Four). In this section representation becomes the theme insofar as it involves figural resemblances, images whose similarity to their originals by shape or color is at issue.

The "representation" part of "resemblance-representation" is meant here in the most neutral possible sense: a "standing-for" relation, a function that coordinates elements or items that can be anything from incomparable to alike. A sign may represent without resembling at all, as "?" represents a question, or it may do so by a partial resemblance, as the blue lines on a highway map represent the minor highways, which are not usually blue, but look in fact sometimes like lines drawn on the land. But most simply— or so it would at first seem—a sign represents in the way of likeness, as a model represents a building. Such a resembling image may be apprehended by an immediate and global recognition as looking like the original. Alternatively, the similarity relation, the isomorphism, may require an intermediate process of identification. In other words, looking alike always involves some sort of isomorphism, but the converse is not the case: there are similarities that are not patent in the appearance of the copy (Part Two, Ch. II D).

One more word should be said in this context about the term symbol which suggests itself. A symbol is, historically, one thing that represents another through being attached to it by some sort of fit or likeness or convention. Thus the present question becomes: What sort of symbol is a picture? However, within the tradition of painting, the term "representation," literally a second presentation, is commonly used for similarity-symbolizations; and so in that context we might simply ask: Can pictures be representational? Yet there is something to be gained by holding on to the complete term "resemblance-representations," for to declare it redundant is to grant ourselves too much too soon.

"Resemblance" in general has a cluster of senses, most of them involving points of comparison or correspondence short of formal geometric similarity (Black 1972, Part Three, Ch. I B). But the meaning of interest here is simply that of likeness or ordinary similarity. It will not do to fix the criteria for these terms right off, since most of the resemblance-debate in fact turns about whether and how pictorial likeness can be achieved. Yet it would be perverse to deny that people do recognize the objects depicted, and do ascribe to the images degrees of similarity, even though they may mean, diversely, that the picture is strictly "realistic" or that it is somehow "true."

This is the moment to reiterate the motives behind this inquiry into the opposition to mimesis, so that they may be clear and up-front. The purpose of thought, it seems to me, is to find out about the human condition and to reflect on it, resolving perplexities when possible and, when not, learning to live with them. There is a certain logicistic mode of inquiry, currently powerful, which takes a chivying tone towards things as they are: It conducts some stretches of argument by the most stringent requirements of explicitness and then tacitly tele-transports through crucial junctures. It rejects as naive certain starting points, such as traditional wisdom, common opinion, and introspection, and proscribes as meaningless traditional accounts, from the "Platonic" to the phenomenological. While the purity and precision of this line is to be admired, resistance and critique are called for if it finally lands us where we cannot live. That opinion is behind the critical review of the attack on imaging about to be set out.

The naive notion that a picture represents something by resembling it can be questioned along the following lines: There are circumstantial difficulties posed by the occurrence of accidental similarities and by the fact that cultural conventions govern much image-recognition (a). There are logical and conceptual puzzles, such as the kind of reference involved in representation (b). There is in addition the special problem raised for a resemblance-theory by fictional depictions (c). Finally, however, it is possible to produce an argument that associates depicting with imaging in such a way as may save the resemblance theory after all (d).

a. Circumstantial Difficulties. Accidents ˙of resemblance will occur. In antiquity, Apollonius of Tyana took account of the things we see in the sky when the clouds are drifting, such as centaurs and stag-antelopes and wolves and horses. "Is God a painter?" he asks. No, is his answer—these shapes arise by pure chance and we interpret them (Gombrich 1960). Or suppose that an ant in our day, running about busily in the sand, traces out a trail that looks like a profile of George Washington. Can it be said to "represent" the Father of our Country? (The ant example comes out of Putnam 1981.) Such a circumstance seems to embarrass the resemblance-theory of representation, not because it in fact shows that there are resemblances that are not representations, but because it exposes an apparently extraneous criterion involved in resemblance-representation, namely intention. The accidental portrait of George Washington is the visual analogue of the aleatory typescript of *Hamlet* produced by those notorious monkeys pounding away for indefinite eons of time. Are the results respectively a picture or a play? The answer "yes" is somehow repulsive. And yet things do not stand well with resemblance if a criterion besides similarity has to be invoked, if we have to ask whether anyone intended the likeness or meant the words, or if we call on the history of the picture or the poem at all (Black 1972).

However, there are defenses that I want to marshall. First, it ought to count that accidental depictions happen not to occur often. Ant trails usually look like nothing at all. And when natural formations are suggestive, they tend to suggest anything and everything; they are inexhaustible because they are at most potential resemblances. Shakespeare's sky outdoes Apollonius's in profusion:

Sometime we see a cloud that's dragonish;
A vapour sometime like a bear or lion,
A towered citadel, a pendant rock,
A forked mountain, or blue promontory
With trees upon't, that nod unto the world,
And mock our eyes with air. [*Anthony and Cleopatra* IV 14]

It is a question-begging sort of attack on resemblance-representations that begins with a practically unlikely hypothesis. What ought to be significant is not that unintended portraits happen, but that they are so rare.

Moreover, when such resemblances do occur, when the profile of a mountain looks to all and sundry like Old Craggy-Face, the representational genre simulated is not that of portraiture, but of caricature. Caricature is specifically designed for quick symbolic identification. It is achieved by picking out and exaggerating a distinguishing feature—by a deliberate act of conventionalization with consequent toleration of broader limits of unlikeness (Gombrich 1960, 1972). Accidental depictions that go beyond caricature are rare enough to seem miraculous.

Another extenuating point is this: Though it seems to be a necessary condition for depiction to occur that someone have an intention, in the sense of meaning to image something (Gombrich 1960, Putnam 1981), yet the condition warrants only *that* something is a representation, not *what* it resembles. One might say that to intend is both to *mean* something and to mean *something*: It is the fulfillment of the motive-intention and not of the object-intention that is a necessary criterion for something to be called a depiction of anything at all. Thus it is possible to intend to depict an object and to fail to achieve a likeness for lack of technical know-how. However, this kind of intention-criterion touches the representational act of depiction but not the resembling nature of pictures—the activity, but not the outcome. Resemblance itself, I will argue, needs no external criteria but is self-revealing (d).

A second difficulty is that the recognition of pictures sometimes seems to be a function of cultural conventions rather than inherent likeness. As in the case of accidental depictions, it is not quite clear whether the argument is actually from experience or from principle. For in this argument partial real-life experience is universalized—evidently on principle—so as to lead to the claim, reviewed in (b), that all representation is relative to a conventional symbol-system. It is then a short step to the attack on the very possibility of imitation (Goodman 1976, 6). The gist of this attack is that even the most strenuous would-be imitation is aspectual and perspectival: the unavoidable choice of viewpoint hopelessly vitiates the notion of copying. This argument is so extreme and so interesting that it will be taken up below in (d). Meanwhile, it is hard to set aside the ordinary view that there are some depictions, like *trompe l'oeil* paintings, in which an imitation of an original is primarily intended and actually realized.

There is much conflicting evidence, systematic and anecdotal, about the time- and culture-bound nature of pictorial recognition, and, in general, about the necessity that the conventions of an art be absorbed as a precondition for appreciating it. As an example of culture-boundedness our inability to apprehend the meaning of non-Western music at first hearing is often cited (Huxley in Goodman 1976). Yet what is true of music cross-culturally may not be true cross-temporally within our own tradition. The most common development of individual musical taste is, after all, remarkably anachronistic, which suggests that not all conventions are equally conventional. Neither the Medieval antecedents of our tradition nor its Classical center nor its Contemporary epigenesis are the usual points of entry for untutored music lovers. In fact, adolescents still tend to appropriate the Romantic period, together with background Baroque, while Classical music is often discovered late in life. Don't these inversions of history by taste suggest that conventions of musical styles have their natural human connotations, and that people resonate to them according to their age and nature rather than their temporal acculturation?

In the visual arts, in contrast to music, even cross-cultural appreciation seems to come quite naturally. For example, to Western eyes the conventions for expressing human passion in Oriental art, and therefore their representations, seem fairly outlandish at first glance. Yet a rudimentary sense of both the significance and the verisimilitude of certain Oriental landscape paintings can, even at first sight, captivate a viewer who is quite ignorant of its subtle representational conventions or of, say, the weirdly wonderful land, the rocks about Guilin, for example, that it so faithfully depicts.

And then, what of the convention-inventing painter himself? There is the old chestnut about Picasso, who replied to a complaint that his portrait of Gertrude Stein did not look very much like her: "No matter; it will." If it is possible, as he was implying, to originate a way of seeing, within what convention do these convention-breakers and -makers operate? There is a kind of equivocality in the common use of the term "convention" in aesthetics: Are conventions established by arbitrary fiat, by rational invention, or by receptive discovery? Writers who propound the conventionality of art rarely accord it a role of pure randomness, and yet they rarely supply an account of the pre-conventional—one might even say natural—values that governed the choice.

So much is mere anecdote and opinion, but the psychological and anthropological evidence is equally inconclusive. On the perceptual level, for example with respect to the Müller-Lyer illusion (the two equal lines, one arrow-tipped and the other with the lines bent outward, which appear unequal—Part Two, Ch. I C), it turns out that certain groups of non-Western subjects were significantly less vulnerable to the illusion than a sample group of English children—but so were English adults. This result, although ambiguous, helps to explode an old theory that "primitive" people are more easily duped by optical tricks (Segall et al. 1966). There is limited evidence that in children the recognition of depictive images is not learned but develops naturally (this section, below). However, again there is contrary evidence that certain representational devices are not inter-culturally recognized. For example, bush women are reported to have turned a photograph this way and that, unable to make sense of the grey shadings on the paper (Herskovits in Segall et al. 1966), though again there are counter-reports of other natives looking at photographic images for the first time and displaying the terror or the delight of recognition (Deregowski 1980, 119). It appears, not surprisingly, that the representation of depth and perspective elicits the most equivocal reaction (*3* a). Above all, there does not seem to be much evidence about the speed and spontaneity with which alien picture conventions are learned. Yet such evidence would seem to be more important than signs of an initial disorientation that occurs, after all, not only in the viewing of contrived images, but also in the ordinary perceptual seeing of novelties. In sum, the experimental evidence is so far, at least, undecisive concerning the innate or universal recognition of resemblance-representations.

The foregoing arguments against resemblance-imaging in the arts took account of observable circumstances. Now some conceptual and logical objections will be considered.

b. Conceptual Cavils. The principal attack on the native and ordinary view of depiction, which persists in writings on representation in general and in the arts, will be reviewed in this section. It was mounted by Nelson Goodman in his *Languages of Art*:

> The most naive view of representation might perhaps be put somewhat like this: "A represents B if and only if A appreciably resembles B," or "A represents B to the extent that A resembles B." . . . Yet more error could hardly be compressed into so short a formula. [1976, 3]

Goodman directs a preliminary kind of argument against the possible coextensiveness of the two concepts: Resemblance is reflexive whereas representation is not; a being can resemble, but it rarely represents, itself. Also resemblance is symmetrical while representation is not: cars off an assembly line resemble but do not represent each other.

Now it is hard for me to see what general understanding of the respective terms this refers to, for self-representation is an important concept in law and sociology (Goffman 1959), though one rarely hears of self-resemblance. Again, we normally do not speak of the parents' resemblance to their children, while to say that a picture represents its subject but never the converse is not quite right either. It is a commonplace of art appreciation to think of a scene as representing a landscape painting: in some aesthetics nature imitates art (e.g., Croce 1901). Thus representation can be understood reflexively and symmetrically, while resemblance is often spoken of as unreflexive and sometimes as asymmetrical.

While that sort of analysis of usage does not seem to succeed in showing that such broad terms as representation and resemblance mean different things, grant nevertheless that they are not synonymous. If people thought they were, the naive view would be so absurd that one would not bother to attack it in the first place. In fact, any nation of voters knows, if it knows anything, that people and affairs do not always look like what they represent nor stand for what they resemble. Without possessing a logical analysis of the abstract concepts of resembling and representing, what people do think is simply that a picture brings on again, re-presents, some original in a particular way by means of its likeness.

But is that possible? Can even the particular kind of representation called a picture do its job by resembling? Any picture, Goodman argues, say a painting of Salisbury Cathedral, is more like another picture than it is like a cathedral, though it represents a cathedral and not a picture (5). This argument seems to assume that by a picture is meant a canvas covered with a thickness of oil-paint. Yet it would seem that what all paintings have in common may be a necessary condition for their being some picture or other, but it is by no means sufficient for a picture being this particular picture. This cathedral-picture surely strikes the receptive viewer more as an image of Salisbury Cathedral than as merely a picture.

There exists a pertinent phenomenological analysis of the structure of pictures into two factors, a real but pictorially suppressed bearer, the canvas, and an unreal but visually actual picture-world, the image (Fink 1930). As Gibson puts it:

A picture is both a surface in its own right and a display of information about something else. The viewer cannot help but see both, yet this is a paradox, for the two kinds of awareness are discrepant. We distinguish between the surface *of* the picture and surfaces *in* the picture. [1979]

It seems to me, furthermore, that a picture simply as a depiction can be apprehended on four levels of generality. The last of these is not representational; moreover, particular depictions may intentionally lack the first one or two levels. That said, any picture is, first, a document, a more or less faithful copy of a particular, identifiable person or a scene. It is, second, a representation of a generic, unidentifiable figure or landscape. It is, third, the intimation of an image in general, representing something in the most indeterminate sense. And fourth, it is of course always a mere material object, a picture in general. Thus one may recognize—or fail to recognize— a depiction as a resemblance in ascending levels of indefiniteness up to the vaguest sense of its being representational. In the Goodman argument it is the canvas that overbears the picture-world. Usually and appropriately, however, in viewing a painting interest is directed to the representation and the material substrate is "overlooked." It follows that a painting of a cat and a cathedral can rightly be called as unlike as a cat and a cathedral.

But these resoluble complaints against resemblance-representation are not the heart of the matter. The heart is the problem of "reference":

> The plain fact is that a picture, to represent an object, must be a symbol for it, stand for it, refer to it; and that no degree of resemblance is sufficient to establish the requisite relationship of reference. Nor is resemblance *necessary* for reference; almost anything may stand for almost anything else. A picture that represents—like a passage that describes—an object refers to and, more particularly, *denotes* it. Denotation is the core of representation and is independent of resemblance. [5]

The argument then is that pictures represent, representation involves reference, reference involves denotation, and denotation does *not* involve resemblance.

This chain, which Goodman pretty much takes for granted, gives the anti-resemblance argument the flavor of conclusiveness that attaches to reasonings through the logic of concepts rather than the nature of things. But is it obvious that representation involves reference and reference denotation?

First, then, what is denotation? It is the reference-relation between a word and what it labels. "The relation of a picture to what it represents is thus assimilated to the relation between a predicate and what it applies to." As it happens, denotation may be logically perspicuous but it is philosophically enigmatic: It is *at least* an open question by reason of what a word reaches its object and an object elicits its word (Part Four, Ch. I C). Is it not necessary, one might ask, to recognize an object before one can label it, be it with a word or by a picture?—not to speak of the fact that logicians are themselves by no means agreed on the denotation theory for words (Grayling 1982).

However, granting the denotational theory of reference for the moment, still the attaching of word labels seems to differ in at least two ways from the recognition of depictions. For one thing, a child whose attention has never been drawn to pictures, can, it seems, tell what pictures image, while there is agreement that no child can perform the naming function without specific language learning—notwithstanding a story recounted by Herodotus (II 2), which, though told tongue-in-cheek, happens to be the prototypical natural-language experiment: The Egyptians, in an effort to discover the oldest human race, isolated two infants allowing them only the company of some bleating goats for suckling. After two years the children were overhead crying "baa-kos." On inquiry this was found to be the Phrygian word for bread. Consequently the Egyptians conceded to the Phrygians the honor of speaking the aboriginal language.

The modern experiment supporting picture-recognition without learning is similarly conceived: A boy was raised (by his parents) from birth to nineteen months in an almost image-free environment and without pictorial training. At that time the child began to seek out pictures, and so the experiment had to be concluded. During the experiment the boy was tested and proved to be able to identify by name all sorts of outline drawings of familiar solid objects (Hochberg and Brooks 1962; naturally this experiment has been criticized for having a single subject and for failing to provide an absolutely image-free environment, since there were, for example, billboards on walks). A counterhypothesis to native image-recognition is that children learn the general "stand-for" relation first, from language, experience, and natural resemblances, and then look for further applications— hence their avidity for pictures (Sless 1981). Of course, this theory can claim only that children attend to natural similarities first, not that picture-recognition is necessarily learned as a convention. After all, not all cognitive development is acquisition of culture. For what it is worth, similar, and of course much more controlled, experiments on monkeys raised in isolation show that they recognize pictures of familiar objects. For example, they react appropriately to pictures of threatening monkeys (Walk 1976). In fact even fish "recognize" images: Male sticklebacks respond to strongly colored dummies of females and especially to caricatures that exaggerate the releasing features of the female appearance (Gombrich 1960). There is, however, no reason to think that animals recognize images *as* images. For all we know, they respond to the sameness of the image with its original, not also to the imaginal difference. That circumstance would, however, strengthen my point: that images are self-revealing.

The second difference between the denoting function and image-recognition has to do with the distinction in kind separating a pictorial representation from a description. Goodman certainly recognizes that pictures are differently constituted from paragraphs, though he does say that what may function as a picture in one system may function as a description in another—nothing is intrinsically a representation (226). The syntactic or inner-relational criterion of being representational is "density," the density that characterizes analog symbol schemes. For all practical purposes—if not formally—this comes to what is usually called continuity (137n). Pictures differ from words in their lack of discrete articulation. A consequence is that a thousand words can no more describe a picture than can a thousand pictures name one thing.

It also follows that a diagram and a painting, both being dense, are equally representations. Goodman imagines an electrocardiogram whose sawtooth outline is identical with a Hokusai woodcut of Fujiyama. (It seems to me significant that such coincidences simply do not happen, for reasons brought out above, but let that pass for the moment.) What makes only the woodcut a picture? The traditional view would be that an electrocardiogram is not a representation in the strong sense at all. For one thing, it is a symbolic spatialization of a temporal process, a graph, and for another it is not an intentional depiction but the artless automatic outcome of natural processes filtered through technology. In Goodman's understanding, however, the answer is that the distinction comes from the symbol-system: A diagram is "attenuated," while a picture is relatively "replete," meaning that everything about the line, every nuance of thickness, intensity, and curvature matters in the woodcut but is beside the point in the graph (229).

The point is, it seems to me, that electrocardiograms never do have anything to be replete with. In the first instance, the significant lines that make a picture replete are not accidental, though what matters about them is not so much that they are intended but that they are the realized intention. The repleteness of a picture is the consequence of trying to convey the volcano in its elegance and succeeding. How else could one tell that every least nuance does make a difference? (Danto 1979). In other words, why shouldn't the argument be turned around? Perhaps it is not that a picture is recognized because it fits into a symbol system requiring repletion, but that it ends up with certain symbolic features because it is meant to represent and succeeds in representing a snowy-sloped mountain.

"Pictures are not copied but achieved." Goodman is saying that the representational aspect of depicting is constructed through conventions. Here the semantic position tops a slippery slope. It easily slides into the claim that, since the recognition of likeness is not a given, primitive capacity of visual perception, anything can, by an act of creative and convention-setting seeing, come to resemble something else. The making of pictures then becomes a supreme didactic act, which teaches us to engage in creative reference, to take this as being like that (Wartofsky 1979). Here is a strong version of the contemporary creator-complex: It is the picture-maker who creates the organizing similarities of the world. This is not the old aesthetic notion that a painting teaches nature how to appear. It is instead a radical claim that the artist makes the world what it is. One might ask the obvious restraining questions: What guides this act of creative seeing and how does the painter persuade his public to accept this creation?

But the objection to the denotation-theory that supersedes all the others seems to me to be that depictive representation is not primarily referential at all. One thing literally re-fers to another by bringing one back to it: a symbol somehow directs the mind to what it stands for; a stop sign directs one to stop. But a pictorial representation does not really bring the imagination to the scene or person depicted. It is the other way around: A picture re-presents the object to imaginative sight in some actual aspect of itself, so that it achieves a second coming, as it were. A picture does not so much refer to its original as *reveal* it.

Again and again, Goodman emphasizes that his is a semantic theory of depiction, a theory that assimilates depiction to description; both help form and characterize the world by classifying its features through labels within a symbol system. Representation is finally subsumed under denotation (41). What I am suggesting is that representation is, on the contrary, wider than denotation, that it is not a kind of labeling (nor for that matter is speech), and that it is therefore not exclusively operative within a conventional system. Pictorial images are, so to speak, self-manifest, as explained below (d).

c. Likenesses without Originals. A great stumbling block to belief in resemblance-representation is the depiction of fictional beings. What on earth does a unicorn-picture resemble? Perhaps such monsters are composites culled from nature, as Leonardo recommends painters make (Goldwater and Treve 1945), and perhaps imaginary beings do have some sort of pre-existence (Part Three, Ch. III A)—but neither kind of answer is problem-free.

In the meantime, the denotational theory happens to have an ingenious solution. A picture of a rhinoceros is a picture denoting a rhino, but a picture of a unicorn cannot denote, since the class of unicorns is empty. Goodman's solution is that such a picture is a "unicorn-representing" picture, where "unicorn-representing" is an "unbreakable" one-place predicate (21). It is not possible to reach into such a predicate semantically; it does not have to be understood in its parts to be applied as a whole. For example, one does not have to know separately what a stag is and that horns are like antlers to pick out and label a staghorn beetle. So also, the argument goes, to sort out unicorn-representing pictures from, say, dinosaur-representing pictures one does not have to know, and in fact one cannot know, what "unicorn" denotes. For it and all other fictions denote the same, the null class. Nor, for that matter need one know what "representing" means. Under this theory it is perverse to object that we must know what a unicorn is in order to know how to apply the term "unicorn-picture," for we are able to learn well enough from samples where to apply the predicate.

Obviously, if a picture represents nothing it resembles nothing, and thus "the copy theory of representation," Goodman says, "takes a further beating here" (25). So it surely does, for the "unbreakable predicate" theory assumed to begin with that pictures are not sorted according to their originals, since they have none. But is the theory plausible? Perhaps not entirely (Scruton 1974, 194; Wollheim 1974a; Goodman 1984).

First of all, although it is not necessary for labeling a staghorn beetle to know that stags have horny antlers, it is certainly useful. It facilitates identification, improves memory, and might even enable us to arrive at the reference of the name independently of learning the convention. The enhancement of the naming relation through knowledge of the internal meaning of words is one of the benefits of etymological cultivation. Now why shouldn't a theory be required to take account of that circumstance? It seems that the way to do so is first to admit that "unicorn" means "one-horn" and "representing" means "resembling" so that a "unicorn-representing picture" is a picture that resembles a horse with a single horn—and only then to worry about whether the class of unicorns is utterly null. Certainly that proceeding has the great advantage of not making a special case of all the most fascinating representations, the fictions and fantasies. For in effect the denotation-theory fails to cover these, or covers them only through the special device of the unbreakable predicate—an odd limitation for a "unified aesthetic."

Another check to the "unbreakable predicate" solution is that it is so peremptory about what people are able to do. Surely it isn't satisfactory boldly and baldly to proclaim that they do in fact have the ability to sort out pictures of fictions while deriding the desire for an account of its plausibility. Surely a theory concerning so amazing a human feat should offer some explanatory lead.

d. Depicting as Imaging. Since neither fact nor logic is sufficient to settle the question of this chapter, what remains, as so often, is to speculate as reasonably as possible. That means that the answer should do the minimum violence to the matter of the question.

The questions, recall, are these: Should we assign to ourselves a capacity for recognizing representations insofar as they resemble their originals by imitating or imaging them? And, if so, what do fictional representations image? It is, finally, a matter of "assigning," because all theories of depiction at some point simply claim that we have the ability to do this or that: refer by denoting, sort out picture-kinds, see evident resemblances.

Certainly not all representations are resemblances; witness conventional symbols. Certainly not all resemblances represent; witness replicas (2 b). Certainly not all resemblances are imitations; witness twins. One might even argue that not all imitations are in every respect *bona fide* images— copies falling below their originals in seniority, dimensionality, duration, and significance. For an imitation may be a merely two-dimensional copy of a pre-existent person and may yet gain more fame, last longer and reveal more; witness great portraits of obscure sitters.

Therefore my attempted answer to the question above will be that depictions arise as the intersection, so to speak, of the class of representations with the classes of resemblances, of imitations, and of images. But what all these classes share is what I will call the pictorial imaging-function. Hence depiction is imaging. What does that mean? It means first of all that pictures can best be understood in terms of the functioning imagination.

A principal characteristic of functioning imaginatively is that every time we take in a picture, say of a lion, we see two things at once: a lion and a picture, a configuration and a representation. These are not alternative ways of seeing or speaking (Gombrich 1960, Wollheim 1974b, 1978)—they are complementary ways. For that is what an image does: It represents the thing itself in a second appearance in an alien material medium.

The relation of a depictive image to its original is not, I aver, one of reference, if by reference is meant an extrinsic relation, one that is fixed by a conventional symbol system. If there is reference at all it is what Putnam (1981) calls—derogatorily—"magical" reference. For example, "primitive" people think that a name is by its own power of necessity connected to its bearer. Putnam argues as follows: Suppose a picture of a tree is dropped by a spaceship on a planet that has people but no trees. Short of magic, it will be impossible for those people to puzzle out what the picture represents.

Of course it will be impossible for them to identify a picture in the absence of some acquaintance with the original. Such aquaintance is the condition of anything being a picture *to* someone. But that does not mean that some external relation between the two is needed any more than that a convention is needed to recognize a second tree, having seen a first (Part Three, Ch. I B). We do not know how we do it, but we do it, by nature. A picture might be self-revealing if the original were somehow right in it, presented there. And that presentation is just what an image accomplishes. Images *are* magical: the original appears *in* them.

It has not escaped writers, even if they have shrunk from the fact, that this perplexity about depiction mirrors the greater enigma just intimated: How are the originals themselves recognized? (Black 1972, 115). How do we know that something "looks like" a lion? There is an ancient attempt to answer this question: A lion displays its lionhood through its "looks" (*eidos*), its aspect, or form—faultily, for Plato, sufficiently for Aristotle. If these early tries at an explanation run into trouble, so do all subsequent ones, but it was only a foreseeable consequence that at some point writers on philosophy would deny that we can tell what things are by their looks. So my point about our picture-recognition ability really presupposes such a world-recognition ability. It turns out to be the implicit premise of this book.

Naturally not every picture has a recognizable original. That is because what it normally takes for something to be a picture is, as was said, both meaning-intention and object-intention; a picture must both be *meant* to depict and also meant to depict *something*. Now while there is no possibility of going wrong by *meaning* that something should be a picture, achievement of the object-intention can easily fail for lack of skill on the painter's part. Or recognition of the object can fail for lack of familiarity on the viewer's part. A notorious example is Duchamp's set of pictures, "Nude Descending a Staircase," a gabble of forms to a viewer unacquainted with his notion of "elementary parallelism" as a device for the "static representation of movement" (Henderson 1983; Ch. II A). Furthermore, there are pictures, perhaps better called designs, that have no object-intention. All the shapes of a design are what I called above "potential representations," where the objects are read into the canvas *ad libitum*, or where the recognition of an object is well and truly beside the point, as in the case of Mondrian's rectangles. (On the other hand, balancing these nonreferential works, there are *objets d'art* that are actually composed out of nothing but references, such as photographic collages.)

But in the long run—I make bold to prognosticate—these nonreferential cases are not central for the art of painting, which seems always eventually to return to depiction.

If paintings are imitations, then what are paintings of fictitious objects imitations of? What else would they be imitations of but imagination-images? Thus the whole burden of the argument rests on the existence of both imaginary objects and mental images—and those existences have been defended in Parts One and Three. If imaginary objects somehow exist and are seen in the imagination, then they are the obvious candidates for the originals that are imaged in pictures of fictions, a point that has already been argued in Part Three (Ch. III C).

★ ★ ★

I want to end this section with a brief reference to a mystery involving the imaging faculty most particularly. It is the one that first drove contemporary aestheticians into the resemblance-problem and that persists in some form through all solutions. The problem, or rather the thesis, set out by Gombrich in *Art and Illusion* (1960), is that "neutral naturalism" is impossible (critiques: Wollheim 1974b, Maynard 1978). Nature, he argues, cannot be captured in painting. First, nature's appearances are far richer than any painter's medium. Second, there is no "innocent eye"—no suppressing the importation of significances that modify appearances, and traditions that govern depicting. Indeed, there is no neutral perceptual field, for we never see mere colored patches. And third, there is our irrepressible capacity for what Gombrich calls "projection." The tradition concerning this capacity of our imagination for discovering likenesses in clouds, veined marble, and inkblots goes back to antiquity (A above). In this century the capacity has achieved a certain importance in psychology, particularly in Gestalt theory and in Rorschach tests. Though ordinarily the products of its exercise are too unstably fleeting to be worthy of much attention, the capacity itself is important evidence of the fact that it is the seeing subject who encodes fields of visual signals; in other words, the painter's marks are read by viewers. Nevertheless, Gombrich goes on to say, "naturalism" can be an ideal. It can be and is approached in the historical development of painting by successive approximations and enrichments of the image, by a process of making and matching. However, the ideal is not achieved through a correct realism, for that really is impossible in principle, but through the painter's cultivation of illusion—as opposed to "illusionism," which is the attempt to fool the eye into taking the copy for an original. In Platonic terms (Part Three, Ch. I A), the demand for "iconic" or faithful imaging is thus taken to be meaningless. All imitative painting is "phantastic" or illusion-employing. However, the devices of illusion are originally more like discoveries than like inventions. They become conventions only eventually.

Gombrich's revealing examples, showing that "faithful" paintings are illusion-constructions and that viewing is an interpretative exercise, again direct attention to the possibility of resemblance-representation. I would argue this: It is when such representation is accepted that *the* problem of the visual arts, that illusion should be the necessary way to visual truth, assumes its proper standing as a working mystery. I shall come back to this enigma (B).

3. Projection and Replication. I must stop a moment over the two devices most egregiously devoted to verisimilitude in imaging. One is the theory of perspective, which from its inception prided itself on being a science (a). The other is the technique of photography, which has long laid claim to being an art (b).

a. The Science of Perspective. Perspective is the primary artifice for making pictures look like perceived originals. Perhaps "artifice" is not quite the right word, for it is an open question in the resemblance-debate how artificial perspective really is. There are, at any rate, two ways of producing perspective. They might be denominated the empirical and the precise.

The empirical way was practiced in Greco-Roman antiquity, and it consisted of manifestly groping attempts to paint things as they look, freehand and without theory. The earliest phases of this determined search for the literal looks of things can be seen in paintings on Greek pottery, where the painters' pride in discovering devices for representing three-dimensional aspects is manifest. Thus the human and the equine body is first drawn in shadowy profile but given round frontal eyes; then a profiled eye is mastered, along with three-quarter views: "As Euphronios never could do" is the taunt written on a pot of the late sixth century B.C., painted by one Euthymedes who had just outdone his rival in the painting of three revelers in (red-figured) three-quarter view. Later on the apparent deformation of foreshortening is attempted successfully, and there are shy attempts to paint furniture and buildings in correct three-quarter aspect (Richter 1966).

Even the search for linear perspective can be documented at the very dawn of Attic figural painting. On funeral pottery of the eighth century B.C. biers are often shown. On one of these the two back legs are painted smaller than and between the forward ones; all four are connected by a trapezoidal top—an almost completely correct perspectival rendition of a table as it looks when the eye-level is somewhat below the ground. The corpse, however, is painted not visually but literally "on top" of the table surface—stretched on the top edge, in a combination of "cognitive" with visual realism. More than three quarters of a millennium later, in a few Roman wall-paintings parallel lines actually converge on a vanishing point. Yet it is more likely that the painter was rendering a visual phenomenon rather than an optical rule, though the rule for the visual diminution of objects at great distances was already known to Euclid (*Optics*, 3rd century, B.C.).

I would like to offer a wild surmise. Had the early Greek pot painters been shown the correct perspective technique, they would, first, have recognized it in a flash as the solution they had been searching for, and they would, second, have drawn back from it after all. They would have eschewed it as favoring the spatial organization of the painting over the salience of the figures, but even more as tastelessly bald and mechanical—much as over the centuries their descendants were to discover and to dismiss such theoretical and technical improvements as heliocentric astronomy and the steam engine. Not so for the later Roman wall-painters, who had become interested in "views."

The second, more precise way, which applies primarily to linear perspective, in turn includes two methods. One is the "legitimate" or mathematical construction, codified in complicated geometric schemes of which the main elements are these: First a viewing point is established, including an eye level that determines a horizon in the picture plane; seen from this point the picture becomes a unified whole. A complementary vanishing point, a point on the horizon to which all the straight lines in a given picture plane converge, is then fixed by the observer's distance and position *vis à vis* some rectilinear solid in the picture. This highly constructive replication of the visual scene through central perspective was discovered shortly after the first woodcuts had been produced in Europe, so that pictures could now be doubly faithful—true reproductions of the original designs and correct copies of the world (Arnheim 1954).

The other method is a practical kind of replication, which consists of projecting the model onto an upright grid directly by means of a sightline or a thread, and then transferring the point onto a tablet also prepared with a grid (Gombrich 1960), or even more simply, by "coincidence-tracing," that is, by directly marking it on glass (Gibson 1979).

These two methods, the mathematically correct construction of the phenomena and the direct observation of objects unmediated by cognition or convention, seem almost to prefigure the two conventionally recognized schools of modern science—the mathematical Cartesian, and the observational Baconian. However, what both of these schools have in common with both perspectival methods is "subjectivity," the viewer-centered standpoint, a deep characteristic of our civilization. One might say that the history of perspective exemplifies the development of the Western tradition: a viewing impulse of Greco-Roman antiquity elaborated into practical science in modernity.

What, more exactly, is perspective? What it means literally and originally is simply a close look (Latin, *perspicere*); thus it concerns the laws of careful viewing. What it does, in sum, is to provide devices for reducing depth to surface, for projecting a three-dimensional onto a two-dimensional space. Perhaps it might be better to say that perspective projects on a medium at a distance from the eye that momentary, stationary, surface aspect of the world on which visual attention has been fixed. Linear perspective, which has attracted the greatest body of theory, is, however, applicable only to rectilinear carpentered or built environments; the mathematical science of perspective was started by an architect, Brunelleschi (c. 1400). Consequently there are, besides linear perspective, other sorts, for example its counterpart for natural bodies, foreshortening. Landscape too has its perspectival tricks for showing depth and distance, in the Orient as well as in the West. There is diminishing size, and there is occlusion, when nearer objects overlap those farther off. There is the density gradient, which is the textural thickening that the markings on more remote surfaces undergo. And, above all, there is what Leonardo called aerial perspective, which takes into account the atmospheric changes in hue of more remote objects, producing the color analogue of size diminution in figural perspective. (Gibson 1969, Taylor 1957, Wilson 1980.)

As just described, perspective is the principal solution to the technical aspect of resemblance-representation. If the geometry of vision is indeed such that the plane picture (external or internal) is the natural imaging format of sight (Ch. II A), then the perspectivally plausible recording of depth is the chief task to be mastered, and that is what the art and science of perspective is for. One of the charms of city- and landscape-depiction, located somewhere between the reminiscence-pleasure of recognizing a picture and the aesthetic delight of construing a painting, is, after all, the imaginative penetration of its surface that perspective invites:

> We live in the picture, we walk about in it, we look into its depths, we are tempted to raise our heads to look at its sky. [Fromentin in Alpers 1983]

The sense is identical with that expressed in the anecdote of Wu Tao-tzu who walked off into his own painting (Introduction A).

Nevertheless it is, once again, argued that "the behavior of light sanctions neither our usual nor any other way of rendering space, and perspective provides no absolute and independent standard of fidelity" (Goodman 1976). The objections to a replicating science of linear perspective are these: The claim for correct perspectival depictions says that it supplies the eye with an array of light the same as would come from the object (Gibson 1966), so that the image may appear like the object and the object like the image by the natural laws of optics (Gombrich 1974). But, the criticism goes, to see this identical array, both object and picture image would have to be observed with one eye fixed through a peephole at one uniquely determined position. Yet this is a grossly abnormal requirement in which all sorts of attendant conditions are ignored. For example, the picture of a cathedral seen at six feet will give a different impression from a real cathedral seen at sixty. Moreover, a transfixed eye soon sees nothing at all, since scanning movements are necessary for vision. Furthermore, sense data received in this way could be interpreted as aspects of indefinitely many objects: Imagine four lines of sight converging on the eye and, fitted into them at different distances, quadrilaterals tilted at different angles; from the point of view of linear perspective all these can be superimposed for they all have the same representation; therefore conversely, the viewer is entitled to read one presentation in many ways. Finally, it is not even the case that the laws of optics are consistently applied in perspective drawings; for example, while horizontal railroad tracks are made to converge, upright telephone poles are usually and incorrectly drawn parallel. Thus perspective is not the natural science for making pictorial images of solids and their settings.

However, these criticisms take "too little account of circumstances" (Hochberg 1972). The eye, it turns out, is highly tolerant of inconsistencies. If a viewpoint is shifted too far either laterally or in terms of distance, there are visible distortions, but within limits they are not noticed; nor is the fact that some paintings embody several station-points easily observed. This is probably because the inconsistent parts of the picture are simply not compared. Sometimes, too, non-convergent solids that do not properly diminish toward the back may simply be read as divergent. Nor is a peephole required, since merely focusing attention on the picture may effectively serve the same purpose. The necessity for continuous scanning is not a condition peculiar to picture-viewing; it holds equally for looking at the original, and seems to be a necessary perceptual condition for seeing any integrated scheme. As for the multitude of objects being conveyed by the same bundle of light, that leaves out of account that even if the linear light information from several objects is the same, there are yet several kinds of additional perspective that flesh out the appearance of depth: I have mentioned the changing hue, the increasing haziness, and the thicker texture with more overlap, all of which mark not only increasing distance but differences of orientation. As for the apparently capricious use of the rule that parallels must converge, the inconsistency seems to dissolve if one remembers that the viewer's axis of sight is normally fixed as being into, not up the picture, so that only a relatively short part of the vertical is visible, too short for much convergence to appear. In any case, except for skyscrapers, in our world the horizonal lines tend to be far longer than the verticals. As for the different distances from which picture and original are usually viewed, this circumstance does remind us that a canvas and a cathedral are different objects; this difference is part of the pleasure of picture-seeing.

The sensible conclusion—and one usually reached by students of perception—seems to be that the perception of a scene and of its perspective rendering have enough in common to show that the "conventions" employed are sought-out discoveries, rather than arbitrary inventions. As usual, the question of inter-cultural picture recognition remains unsettled. The studies that seemed to show that the depth representation of Western depicting is not a *lingua franca* used pictures that were drawn in attenuated outline and therefore lacked the very variety of supplementary perspectival devices that usually give Western pictures verisimilitude (Deregowski 1972).

Perspective is, of course, not essential to achieving likeness when the subject is an isolated object, of which one revealing frontal or silhouette aspect or a composite of recognizable views can be shown. Such figures are common in Egyptian paintings, where the body is usually twisted to display part by part its most telling outlines: head in profile, shoulders frontal, hips and legs again in profile. What perspective does achieve is to unify the whole picture—not decoratively or informatively, but visually, so as to make it a "virtual space, . . . a self-contained total system" (Langer 1953), one unified view of the world. Thus the picture becomes, in Alberti's often cited definition, a window through which a viewer looks into a second world. This world may resemble a real or an imagined scene. The point is that looking at or into such a picture is in important respects like looking at a world, and the resemblance achieved with perspective is not so much for seeing the correct outlines of solid objects as for seeing deeply into an integral scene that yet appears on a surface. This aim brings the artificial representations of paintings particularly close to the natural space of the imagination.

b. The Art of Photography. If perspective is the insinuation of science into painting, photography involves an intermingling of art and mere replication. The ratio of the mixture is furiously debated. It is held at one extreme that photographs, just like laboratory-style memory-images, merely mirror experience mechanically, and at the other extreme that photography is fully as interpretative as painting (Singer 1977).

Being photogenic—capable of generating photographs—is a warrant of being there, of having one's place in the sun. Before turning to the issue relevant to this chapter, resemblance, I want to say a word about the place of photography in a book on the imagination in a wider sense. "Photography" means light-painting (*phōs*: light, *graphē*: a painting). The capability of blocking and reflecting light, of having a natural image, is a significant part of our existence. In the days before cameras were standard equipment around the Mediterranean, a Greek villager might produce for the traveling stranger his identity card, his *taftoteta*, literally his "selfhood," which bore his photograph. The fact that his face had cast its image on the film confirmed his existence as a somebody. What goes for the reflecting of light goes for the blocking of it: There is the eerie German story of Peter Schlemihl by Chamisso (1813). Count Peter allows the devil to cut out and carry off his shadow as if it were one of those old silhouette portraits, in return for a bottomless sack of gold. Shadowless, Peter is ostracized from love and human society. Unable to retrieve his shadow and his place in solid life, he ends his days in solitude as an explorer and scientist, an observer, not a part, of the world.

A consideration of photography is the obvious climax to the resemblance question, quite aside from the fact that photographic stills and moving pictures represent the largest set of artificial imaging-events in our world. An inventory of imaging-incidents would surely show that their bulk varies directly with the degree of their inadvertency: First in quantity must be the reflections and shadowings of nature by nature, as of mountains in a lake. Next comes half-intentional mirroring, the facile wizardry of re-creating the world by holding a mirror up to it, practiced in every bedroom and bathroom. Third, requiring more intricate equipment for its realization, is the taking of photographic pictures. Fourth, there is painting, in which the only inadvertency that is tolerated is the intentional one.

There is no difference of opinion whatever about the overwhelming bulk and power of photographic imagery in contemporary life. Witness articles such as the one entitled "The Photographer as God," which represents our world as created for us by photography (Dondis 1973). There is, however, incessant division about its benign or malign effects.

Thus photography is sometimes assigned the messianic mission of mass communication, of making effective the brotherhood of mankind, as in the massively attended "Family of Man" exhibition (mounted by Edward Steichen in 1960, Berger 1980). And at the other extreme, photography is identified as epitomizing the evil of modernity, the rapacious appropriation and thoughtless consumption of the world (Sontag 1973). Now, though the detailed and, if possible, deep analysis of the corruptions modernity is heir to seems to me a healthy enterprise, a generalized intellectual deprecation of the innocent uses we all make of our appliances seems to me unwarranted. Why should it be held against people that they use snapshots to "turn the past into an object of tender record"? No greater corruption should befall us! Photographs are memory-aids, and memory often functions amelioratively. By recording the present we acknowledge it as a past-to-be, and make up for our faithlessness in leaving it behind. I doubt that, as Sontag claims, photos are capable of the aesthetic chicanery of making a Russian dictator look huggable, even only as huggable as Gertrude Stein (70). But if they are, it is not so much photography that deceives as the mysterious opacity of the human frame: who can recognize human evil at a glance?

As there is a vigorous debate about the value of photography so there is much controversy about its nature. Clearly it participates both in the craft of replication and the art of depiction. Which prevails? But first, what is replication? It is a question of great interest, particularly because it is the mode in which the image most often confronts us in our contemporary tower of babble—image-babble. A construction entitled "Visual Tower" (1966) by Marcel Broothaers expresses this condition precisely. It consists of a column of seven tiers, each filled with glass jars containing the identical image of a woman's eye taken from an illustrated magazine. Here is an artist's ironic acknowledgment of the force of ocular replication in our day.

In the narrow sense, replicas are mechanically made products which are all on the same level of image-being (Part Three, Ch. I A). They are usually not made immediately from an original, though a prototype has to be at work somewhere. Instead they come from an inverse of some sort, like a mold for souvenirs or a photographic negative. Replicas in this sense are neither images of an original nor images of each other, if by image is meant a resemblance directly related to an original though inferior to it in status.

In the wider sense, however, replicating means any mechanical imaging. For example, any honest copying of a painting, by hand or by a process, is replication. This kind of reproduction has been the center of much recent debate. The *pros* point to increasingly faithful facsimiles and, when the originals are inaccessible, prefer them to having nothing at all. The *cons* argue both from the real and the ideal case: Painting is so subtle that even a good reproduction is a bowdlerization and worse than nothing; moreover, even a hypothetical perfect copy, a virtual second original, is unacceptable because the hand-made uniqueness and singular history of an artwork are a constitutional part of its being. This argument was apparently first made by Walter Benjamin in his essay "The Work of Art in the Age of Reproducibility" (1931). What distinguishes the genuine article, he says, is an "aura" that accrues to it as a unique work rooted in a tradition. Anatmospheric and overbearing mass-reproductions cause this aura to wither away and thereby simply obliterate pieces of history. Worse yet, replication is an invitation to the painter to paint for the camera, to betray his medium (Wind 1963).

Deliberately dishonest replication is, if anything, even more of a contemporary preoccupation. Fakes are usually not so much replicas of paintings as of styles. Their early acceptance and later exposure, as in the notorious case of the van Meegeren "Vermeers" painted in the thirties and forties, seem to provide an object lesson in a favorite topic of the times: the time-bound conventionalism of seeing in general and the consequences it has on the recognition of period and personal styles. What once looked like a genuine Vermeer is for scholars of a later time a manifest fake. Of course, in this case, the forger had confessed by then (in order to escape the charge of having sold Dutch national treasures to the Nazis—Mills and Mansfield 1982), so the lesson is a little less clear. It remains a wonderful fact that the nonexistence of permanently fool-proof forgeries is *ipso facto* undemonstrable.

From the present point of view, photography is replication *par excellence.* The production is left in a very direct way to optical laws and chemical processes. Anyone can point and shoot and let the light do the painting: the laws and looks of nature, not the artist's intuition, are primary. For that reason photography was not accorded full standing as an art in an anti-naturalist aesthetic: "The element of nature in it remains more or less unconquered and ineradicable" (Croce 1901). Because of that element photographs are indefeasibly faithful: be it evil-doers caught *in flagrante delicto* or age caught wrinkling up—nothing short of cropping or retouching can nullify the documentary exposure of what is the factual case. A painting, on the other hand, can easily incorporate information inconsistent with its title: Gombrich cites two views meant, according to their title, to be of the cathedral at Chartres, an engraving showing the west facade with the pointed arches this building might be expected to have, and a photograph revealing the rounded Romanesque arches that are in fact there (1960). This pair shows that it is indeed true that photography has relieved the graphic arts of an old responsibility for which they were ill-suited, that of preserving the factual looks of things for the record (Jean Cocteau in Gilson 1955).

The other side argues that faithful resemblance is a meaningless term; that all photographic imaging is conventional and therefore some of it is certainly artful. Moreover, photographs can indeed lie and manipulate and are therefore, if not artful, at least cunning. Photographic lying by omission and commission is richly documented. One can simply point the camera or crop the picture so as to report literally half the truth, which is untruth. Or one can tinge an innocuous newsreel red in order to raise the audience's passions. Or one can even use unedited, badly shot, war footage to give a false impression of official candor to civilian audiences. These are tricks of which the press of totalitarian countries has made a practice (Kracauer 1947).

Far more interesting in the long run is the faithlessness and the freedom inherent in photographic technique itself. The relation of a photograph to a scene can be described wholly in terms of its differences: Shots are squarely framed, as vision rarely is, and the world becomes a segmentable space rather than an environment. The size of our most popular camera-images is usually either disproportionally large, as in films, or small, as in snapshots. Whether black and white or colored, the hues are false; consequently the missing depth cues notoriously make photographed mountains into molehills. Honest photographers are as much editors as are lying propagandists, since half their art lies in the choice of place, frame, and moment. Moreover, truth itself must sometimes be gotten by trickery, as in the famous Karsh portrait of Churchill: this image of his indomitable pugnacity was really snapped during a moment of irritation at having his cigar snatched from his mouth by the photographer. Furthermore, the technical character of the camera is capable of imposing different ambiances on its subjects: Benjamin describes the composure of expression that characterized early portraits when the plates needed long exposures. The sitters grew into the picture, as it were, and lived in its extended moment; the casual snapshot, with its off-balance, instantaneous air, goes with the faster cameras of our day (Berger 1980).

All these factors together have led to a reinterpretation of photography as an original act of the imagination, an active imposition of form, a constructive technical process superimposed on the already constructive process of natural visual perception—photography does not render an image that is essentially similar to visual experience; it is not a resemblance-representation (Snyder 1974). This way of thinking, an extension of the conventionalist position, is once again characterized by a willingness to let attendant embarrassments overbear the central fact, that of photographic replication. Of course a photograph does not reproduce the visual experience of a freely viewed scene. However, it does seem to come close to replicating the experience of a scene as seen through a view-finder—a fairer comparison.

As the story of Peter Schlemihl reminds us, it is a fact of inexhaustible significance that a solid in the way of light, particularly the human body, casts shadows on the ground. The painting style that stands near the beginning of the ever-recurrent Western search for naturalism is the black-figure vase-painting of the sixth century B.C. On the pots of Athens the shades of great heroes are summoned from Hades to appear as black shadows cast on the brilliant orange clay used by Attic potters—to tremendous effect: For example, the great black kneeling figure of Ajax, painted by Exekias about 640 B.C., a concentratedly frowning Ajax fixing in a mound the sword on which he will impale himself, is the quintessence of isolated, manic desperation. In the next century the prevailing red-figure style will illuminate the human form itself. Reserved out of the black coat of glaze, though replete with black detail, it comes to the fore by reflecting the light (Beazley 1951). The point here is that shadows and reflections are from its founding a fascination of the Western depictive tradition, from the black-figure silhouettes on Attic pots through the magical views on the screen of the sixteenth century *camera obscura* (Snyder 1974) to the chemical recordings on modern film. Therefore "light-painting," precisely insofar as it does not actively seek to capture the looks of objects but simply allows them to cast their images on a recording ground, is really a longed-for consummation in Western painting, for the West is irresistibly attracted to mimicking replication.

It is unprofitable to take too extreme a position in these matters. The contemporary explanatory mode is to emphasize process and complexity, to favor the "how" over the "what." That operational approach does wonderfully subtilize the mind, while it simplifies ancient enigmas. It has more or less captured the day in our intellectual world, most successfully in the sciences. Long-lived reflections on the nature of visual similarity are now superseded by the claim that a picture is what maker and viewer between them say it is. The reason such positivism works fine for physics and is less profitable for aesthetics is that in physics the reasonable purpose is to solve problems, while in aesthetics it is to keep questions alive. It stands to reason that only if resemblance-representations, right down to mechanical replication, are accepted as human possibilities can the question of realism and truth in depiction arise in all its intricacy: What turns pictures into paintings?

B. Paintings: The Imaging of Images

This section will be brief in inverse ratio to the complexity of that question. I have called depictions "pictures" insofar as they are resemblance-representations. Hence the pleasure they give includes a strong strain of image-recognition: Here is a likeness! The same depictions might be called paintings, on the other hand, insofar as they induce delight through what I will make bold to call their beauty. Beauty in the classicizing sense of harmony or balance is a proscribed word in contemporary aesthetics; it is in any case not the notion I have in mind. That notion is also venerable, for it was first intimated in Plato's *Phaedrus* (250 b): Beauty is brightness. It is visible significance as opposed to representational signification; it is manifest meaning, poignant perspicuity, as was said earlier. Hence a picture is informative while a painting is revealing. The black-figure painting of Ajax described above is an example. The figure in the picture looks like a big nude bearded man, the shield like a large Homeric shield, the palm like a palm tree, and the sword stuck in a mound of earth just like a sword. Whoever knows the story can attach a name to the figure. The hero in the painting, on the other hand, is a large and grave man with a mind at once muscle-bound and vulnerable, now intent on falling onto his sword because Odysseus, a nimbler but smaller man, has been honored above him. Exekias has rendered at once the picture of Ajax and the painting of a tragedy.

Gilson's own distinction, from which mine is adapted, is, however, more like an antithesis. He says that a painting differs from a picture in having a purely internal, aesthetic, a-representational criterion of success; it is creative as opposed to imagistic. Though Gilson emphasizes the impossibility that human creativity should be a power to bring either matter or form into being, he nonetheless holds that a painting is a new being in the world—not a derivative image but an independent existence (1955, 242, 270). If there are such reference-less aesthetic existences—and certain contemporary painters do make that claim—they are clearly not within the compass of this chapter on visual imaging. For paintings in my sense are still pictures and images. As Ortega y Gasset puts it: A work of art is "an object with the double condition of being transparent and having what is seen through it be itself, not something else" (1914). Clearly a painting strains the limits of my definition of an image as a second and lesser presentation of the original. A painted image compensates for its diminished dimensionality and lesser substantiality by an accession of revelatory power.

This observation, as trite as it is true and as elusive as it is evident, issues in the problem of realism—not, of course, Realism as a multifarious historical school dealing in warts-and-all precision, humble-life-appreciation, unbuttoned sincerity, or, God forbid, tractor-worship. The subject is realism insofar as it presents the general claim that accurate imaging is the aim of painting. The problem is reflected in the great cluster of senses one finds attached to the term.

To begin at one extreme, even the currently prevailing conventionalist view of the arts makes room for something called "relative realism," the faithful adherence to the well-inculcated concerns of the symbol-system (Goodman 1976). One example of genuinely conventional-realist painting would be the Egyptian construction, achieved with the aid of a grid and maintained over millenia, of the human figure according to a fixed canon (Panofsky 1955).

At the other extreme is "naturalistic realism," the effort simply to transfer the visually perceived phenomena onto the canvas. This realism involves two articles of faith: the belief that there are what one might call absolute phenomena, ways things appear apart from the human interpretation; and the conviction that this replication is a grand mission because "the eye embraces the beauties of the world." Leonardo is the prime proponent—at least in theory—of this view that "the mirror is the master of painters," that "the painter's mind should be like a mirror" and that the canvas ought accurately to image this mental image because the world itself is beautiful and not in need of aesthetic enhancement (Alpers 1983, Leonardo, *Notebooks*). Perspective was studied precisely in the service of this kind of realism. The extreme of this extreme is *trompe l'oeil* illusionism, in which perceptual and pictorial seeing are to be for an instant indistinguishable.

Although the arguments against the extremes of conventionalism and realism as universal theories have been set out, let me refer to an additional one that is compelling against both of them. It is the history of painting itself, or better the very fact that it has a history. The slow, hesitant, but dogged pursuit of a right way in the earliest surviving paintings of the Western tradition, the relatively humble genre of pot-painting, which was sketched out above, is an example of a driving desire: to break out of convention and to achieve verisimilitude; it argues against an underlying "conventional realism." On the other hand, the very fact of a stylistic succession that makes each naturalism in turn look stylized speaks against a neutrally "naturalistic realism" as well. Leonardo himself, committed as he was to the beauty of all the visible realm, amended the mental-mirror-image idea of painting by introducing the corrective notion of the painter's mind as a mirror that reflects the "most excellent parts of the appearance which he sees."

Extremes aside, the vast center of meanings is occupied by what might be called the various "phenomenalistic realisms." Here the phenomena are regarded as having, so to speak, a literal or real version, to which the painters contribute "ways of seeing." Ways of seeing cannot be understood as narrowly perceptual idiosyncracies. For example, the old claim that El Greco painted elongated figures because he was astigmatic and literally saw them that way is not compatible with attributing to him a "way of seeing." (In any case, the claim has a logical flaw: Since he presumably saw normal figures astigmatically in life, to get the figures on canvas to appear elongated to him in just the right way, he would have had to paint life-like, undeformed shapes—Tormey and Tormey 1979.)

Phenomenalistic realism has two main versions. First and historically earliest is "cognitive realism," painting what one knows rather than what one sees. Cognitive realism is what is shared by children, some "primitive" painters, and, of course, their modern emulators. One extreme kind of cognitive device is to paint what one says rather than what one sees, as in the eighth-century Greek vase described above: The corpse is painted not visually centered in the bier's surface but literally on top of it, lying on its upper edge, "on" it. Another device is to display what is known to be present but visually hidden—to put, say, what is occluded in real space above or below its masking object in pictorial space. Yet another is to make a composite of aspects judged to be salient, as in the archaic Greek paintings already mentioned, where, until painters discovered the chevron-shaped side-view of the eye, the rule was: the face in profile but eyes frontal and almond-shaped.

The other version of phenomenalistic realism is the "illusion-realism" so impressively formulated by Gombrich in *Art and Illusion*: The painter's art lies above all in exploiting or inventing means for activating the viewer's pre-formed power of "projection," the visual imagination that seizes significance in adventitious shapes. Thus a painting must not so much simulate as manifest or indicate its subject—not only the painter's way of seeing the world but also the viewer's way of seeing the canvas contribute to this end. Here the term realism would seem to be pushed beyond the limit of its usefulness, except that painters themselves persist in using it. What they often seem to mean is that the painting, if successful, is faithful to the kind of non-propositional truth that is revealed in their mental images, and that its beauty derives from some sort of fidelity to them.

Almost all paintings—excepting those in some highly self-conscious modern styles—can be classified under one or more of these realisms. But the great occidental and oriental traditions seem to be at heart phenomenalistic. That is implicit in the claim above that paintings simulate and manifest their object simultaneously. If it is indeed so, then to think about the kind of imaging called painting is mainly to think about phenomenalistic realism. That granted, what is the perplexity? One level of the difficulty shows up in the phrase "phenomenalistic realism" itself, which is, though awkward, actually quite apt—not less so for being a contradiction in terms: "Realism" usually means a due regard for the material solidities of the world, while "phenomenalistic" implies attention to the experiencing of mere appearances. What the contradictory formula conveys is the old scandalous claim of all arts, and of painting in particular, that they manifest truth through illusion:

Painting is the most astounding sorceress. She can persuade us through the most evident falsehoods that she is pure truth. [Liotard in Gombrich 1960]

Without becoming embroiled in the details of technique or the depths of metaphysics, to either of which this claim leads with equal dispatch, I will seize on the one aspect most germane to this chapter. It begins with the circumstance that although the capture of a reality is the often-cited desideratum, it is to be achieved through the construction of appearances.

Now it is a commonplace of aesthetics that the reality to be captured for the viewers is in fact often not really "real" for them. That is to say, it is not necessarily a present, thing-like existence. In practice there often were no real originals, and if there once had been sitters or scenes, they are usually long dead or changed beyond recognition. Moreover, in principle, while it seems to me extreme to say that verisimilitude in portraits or places is of no consequence (Gilson 1955), especially in the past when painting still had the representational responsibilities that have now devolved on photography, it is not as a painting but as a picture that the canvas captures reality in that re-presentational sense. In other words, the conditions for naturalistic realism—literal mimesis—are rarely achievable for the viewer, who is, after all, the one who counts; and if they were achievable, they would produce pictures, not paintings.

If reality is elusive, the phenomena are formidable. After all, the painter's construal or the viewer's projection do not yield straightforward appearances in the normal perceptual sense. For reasons suggested above, it is not usually claimed that painters must literally, perceptually, see the world differently in order to produce a distinctive rendering on the canvas. Some small suggestion about how "a way of seeing" does come about will be made below. Meanwhile it seems to me that "seeing differently" should be carefully distinguished from "seeing something different"; different painters at different times are confronted with a different-looking world, with different objects and atmospheres. Aestheticians tend to ascribe the development of painting preponderantly to the painter's vision; but surely, all told, what the world happens to offer does as much or more to determine how the phenomena appear. Could painters have become interested in that most consequential way of seeing, linear perspective, if the carpentered and architectural environment had not offered long linear vistas on a flat ground? However, that observation does not help with the fact that, environments aside, there are genuinely different ways of envisioning the same "reality."

Moreover, the perplexity is not only that the painter "sees" in the world what is not there for prosaic perception, but equally that the viewer "sees" in the painting what does not and cannot perceptually appear there. *How* can greatness, isolation, intentness, and desperation lie in the lines and the color of that vase-painting of Ajax? Aristotle aptly observes that works of visual art "are not likenesses of character, but rather the shapes and colors produced are indications" (*Politics* VIII 5). One might say that real life offers the same quandary: How can a person "look" desperate? Yet that case is somewhat easier. We know from experience what particular people look "like" when they are being a certain way, since their looks find their exegesis in words and actions. A painted person, on the other hand, cannot be but can only look a certain way. So how can those looks be the warranted appearance of anything? How does a painting manage to be phenomenal in the sense of presenting appearances that reveal the inner character of things, their "moral nature" in the old, wide meaning of the term? (Part Six, Ch. III B).

It seems to me that the most sensible way is to throw the burden of the answer on the imagination. Let me begin by recalling that painting is a particular kind of imaging and that images have a peculiar double character.

Painting, I proposed above, is an imaging of images. That is surely not a novel notion, but it is one recently eclipsed. The general understanding that works of art are expressions of the imagination, is sometimes referred to as an "idealistic" aesthetics. It has a venerable history—the history of the "idea" in the visual artist's soul. Opinion about its source has undergone continual inflection. For Plotinus it comes from above as an intelligible form. For Thomas Aquinas it is an indwelling quasi-idea. For Dürer it is a treasure collected in the heart by drawing from life (Panofsky 1924; also Part One, Ch. II A). The present-day argument against such inner visions as first expressed in works of visual art, and then, in turn, incited by them, partly coincides with that brought forward against mental images as a whole: Internal images are supposed to be so private that it is pointless to speak of painter and spectator as having the same imaginative experience. The counter-argument would be that since such works of art are somehow experienced—internally apprehended—not only by the maker but also by the viewer, it is reasonable to think that the two have something in common. What they have in common is the painted image itself, which is the effect of the maker's successful effort to externalize an inner image and the cause of the viewer's receptive readiness in turn to internalize it.

Another part of the argument against painting as imaginative expression draws attention to the physical canvas as worth some attention. It is an artifact worth considering in its own right, a source of an independent, aesthetic perception. The defense grants this. There is no reason why any painting should not sometimes be viewed purely "aesthetically" in the original sense, as nothing but a visual-sensory value. Finally, the anti-image argument goes, although all paintings share the purely aesthetic element, their degree of representationality varies widely. Again, this is granted.

There are undoubtedly paintings that are as nearly as possible merely aesthetic physical objects and other paintings that are as nearly as possible mere images. The point here, as always, is not to lose sight of the middle for the extremes—kinds ought to take their characterization from the ordinary instance at its normal best.

In any case, my point here is that paintings are doubly images: They are physically based images of mental originals, which are in turn memory-images of real or fictional originals. (The thesis that mental images are themselves resemblance-images is established in Part Two, Ch. II.) Moreover, this duplex character permits the most straightforward account of the enigma of painting: that a loss in verisimilitude is often a gain in verity.

So the immediate originals of paintings are imagination-images, our cognitively informed, affect-filled inner visions. I say "our" because even people very poor at external image-making can be imaginative in this internal sense. (That fact is the despair of experimental psychologists, who know that depictions of mental imagery are usually inadequate representations of their highly imaginative originals.) This near-universal capability is a vital complement to the painter's efforts, since it makes possible that projection by which the ungifted viewer re-actualizes the painter's skillfully indicated intention: for one painter there are multitudes of grateful viewers. In other words, the art of illusion, phenomenalistic realism, requires a double realization: the initial, rare, and highly artful representation achieved by the painter, and the far more common, yet not undemanding, re-presentation just described, which is performed internally by the viewer. One partial proof is that a painting often has its maximum effect not when it is inspected on the spot but when it is re-viewed in memory.

So, just as I argued above that in the imagination resides the extension of the class of objects that a fictional picture images (Part Three, Ch. III C), here I am claiming that mental imagery—both memory and imagination-imagery—is manifested in those paintings that are not pure design. The mental images described in Part Two, released from the asceticism of the laboratory, are plausible candidates for this office (and, in fact, a scientist will speak quite unabashedly of their externalization—Ch. V A). They are credible because they display those pictorial properties that make them convenient originals from which to copy off the external pictures: they feature figure and ground, frame and format, perspective and aspect, two-dimensionality and freedom from physical law. Thus paintings show a sort of coincidence of the inner and the outer world. They effect this by being twice imaginal: they image mental images, which in turn image the world to some degree. (Of course, this notion of "imaginative originals" is perfectly compatible with an "interactive" theory of production, in which the painter continually re-views and reworks the image taking shape on the canvas.)

There is a kind of primeval documentation of this view of painting as the imaging of images. The earliest great paintings precede the historically continuous development of painting by some five hundred generations. These are the figures on the walls of the Old Stone Age caves, some two hundred of them, found in Southern France and Spain, the most famous among which are the caves of Lascaux and Altamira. They are the acme of phenomenalistic realism. This fact does not subvert the observation that early and primitive art is generally characterized by cognitive realism, since the major cave paintings are not archaic within the Paleolithic tradition itself, and so their makers were not "primitive," notwithstanding the fact that they used to be so classified. For example, Gombrich, in his *Story of Art* (1950), had applied that term to them, though not so much as a reflection on their art, but because he thought that they made images not for aesthetic contemplation but for magical protection, in the same utilitarian spirit in which they might have built shelters. However, an enchanting book, Pfeiffer's *Creative Explosion* (1982), proposes a purpose for the cave images that plausibly frees their makers and users from the imputation of magic and primitivism. It involves the imaging of the imagination in a most direct way.

A similar suggestion had been made long before. It was to the effect that the deep, winding cave at Lascaux might have represented to the painters the dark imaging space within their own heads, a cavernous inner court in which are stored the multitudes of beautiful and terrifying mental images that can be spotlighted in turn by the imagination (Lewin 1968).

The caves in Pfeiffer's vivid descriptions and haunting photographs appear in just this light. The paintings preponderantly represent animals: aurochs in procession, bison, a gravid cow, horses in various postures, a giraffe, a rhino, reindeer, bulls, deer, stock-still and in swift motion; some composite monsters, some animal parts, as well as some human figures. Nearly all the major figures are drawn with consummate elegance and masterly aplomb: they are at the summit of visual sophistication. More to the present point, they are most ingeniously placed on the weirdly configured limestone topography of the caves, which endows the great chambers with cumulus-like ceilings, corridors, crevices, shutes, and the simulacra of rushing underworld rivers.

The paintings are eminently phenomenalistic, "phantastic" in Plato's sense; they are modifications of a literal imitation for the sake of verity-in-appearance. For example, a horse might seem to have an overly elongated neck and a snouty head for a standing viewer, yet be in perfect proportion from a certain recumbent position (at Tito Bustillo Cave, 142).

If the figures are viewed under carefully contrived conditions, remarkable effects occur. The viewer is pre-positioned and subjected to an initiatory dark time; a torch suddenly produced provides a flash of spot-lighting. At first the viewer finds it hard to read the shapes. Then, abruptly, the animals spring to view, exactly as required by Gombrich's projection theory. They appear at once mysterious and brilliant, fleetingly momentary and permanently arrested. Above all, they appear simultaneously as fact and as fiction; they are " 'visibles' of the second power" (Merleau-Ponty 1961). The viewer beholds the bison in the light of the prairie-day while seeing the image in the cave. The live effect, I can attest, restores its original force to the word "fantastic."

Pfeiffer proposes that these painted worlds were used as panoramic illustrations of the mental encyclopedia recording tribal knowledge about the appearances of the animals and their effects on the hunters. In these caves the visual wisdom of the tribe was preserved and impressed on succeeding generations. They were a kind of memory-theater, as described above (Part Two, Ch. III B), a psychological training ground for the right responses to vital appearances by means of vivid visual imagery. If so—if it was in fact vital that these apparitions should live in memory—their unsurpassable beauty turns out to be of the essence. If beauty is indeed in essence memorable visibility, the magic of such visions is not primitive but primordial.

East or West, later landscape painters sometimes talk about the pleasure to be found in walking into their paintings—a complex imaginative exercise involving the three-dimensional mental rotations so exciting to cognitive psychologists. If the hypothesis just presented is right—and it rings true—the Paleolithic caves are externalized visions meant to be once again internalized as memory-landscapes in which to roam. They are the precursors, on a much higher aesthetic level, of the great memory-theaters of the Renaissance, which are similarly intended first to express, and then in turn to become, inner worlds. If for their makers the cave paintings conveyed and re-enforced the retention of vital information, for us they reveal the mimetic nature of a painting: it is a material image of a mental image. It invites not so much a recognition of resemblance as the apprehension of a twofold presence: the living original animal is there simultaneously with its painted double—the phenomenal quintessence of the beast in its most telling moments and motions, a magical apparition that reveals a being.

And that, in sum, tells the thesis of this section. On canvas—or rock—objects are imaged through the mediation of inner images. That is how external images can be at once imaging pictures and revealing paintings. As images they may approach realism; as revelations they are phenomenalistic—psychically revised appearances.

Bibliography

Alpers, Svetlana. 1983. *The Art of Describing: Dutch Art in the Seventeenth Century.* Chicago: The University of Chicago Press.

Arnheim, Rudolph. 1954. *Art and Visual Perception: A Psychology of the Creative Eye.* Berkeley and Los Angeles: University of California Press.

Baumgarten, Alexander Gottlieb. 1735. *Reflections on Poetry.* Translated by Karl Aschenbrenner and William B. Holther. Berkeley and Los Angeles: University of California Press (1954).

Beazley, J. D. 1951. *The Development of Attic Black-Figure.* Berkeley and Los Angeles: University of California Press.

Benjamin, Walter. 1931. "Kleine Geschichte der Photographie." In *Das Kunstwerk im Zeitalter seiner Reproduzierbarkeit.* Frankfurt am Main: Suhrkamp Verlag (1969).

Berger, John. 1980. *About Looking.* New York: Pantheon Books.

Black, Max. 1972. "How Do Pictures Represent?" In *Art, Perception and Reality,* edited by Maurice Mandelbaum. Baltimore: The Johns Hopkins University Press.

Chamisso, Adalbert von. 1813. *The Wonderful Story of Peter Schlemihl.*

Croce, Benedetto. 1901. *Aesthetic.* Translated by Douglas Ainslie. New York: The Noonday Press (1958).

Danto, Arthur. 1978. "The Artworld." In *Philosophy Looks at the Arts,* edited by Joseph Margolis. Philadelphia: Temple University Press.

―――. 1979. "Pictorial Representation and Works of Art." In *Perception and Pictorial Representation,* edited by Calvin F. Nodine and Dennis F. Fisher. New York: Praeger.

Deregowski, Jan B. 1972. "Pictorial Perception and Culture." In *Image, Object and Illusion: Readings from Scientific American.* San Francisco: H. H. Freeman and Co.

―――. 1980. *Illusions, Patterns and Pictures: A Cross-Cultural Perspective.* New York: Academic Press.

Derrida, Jacques. 1978. *The Truth in Painting.* Chicago: The University of Chicago Press (1987).

Dondis, Donis A. 1973. *A Primer of Visual Literacy.* Cambridge: The MIT Press.

Fiedler, Conrad. 1876. *On Judging Works of Visual Art.* Translated by H. Schaefer-Simmern and F. Mood. Berkeley and Los Angeles: University of California Press (1957).

Findlay, J. N. 1966. "The Perspicuous and the Poignant: Two Aesthetic Fundamentals." In *Aesthetics in the Modern World*, edited by Harold Osborne. New York: Weybright and Talley (1972).

Fink, Eugen. 1930. "Vergegenwärtigung und Bild." In *Studien zur Phänomenologie 1930–1939*. The Hague: Martinus Nijhoff (1966).

Furlong, E. J. 1961. "Art and Imagination." Chapter 9 in *Imagination*. New York: The Macmillan Co.

Gibson, James J. 1951. "What Is Form?" *The Psychological Review* 58:403–412.

———. 1960. "Pictures, Perspective, and Perception." *Daedalus* 89:216–227.

———. 1966. *The Senses Considered as Perceptual Systems*. Boston: Houghton Mifflin Co.

———. 1969. "The Stimulus Variables for Visual Depth Perception." In *Perception: Selected Readings on Science and Phenomenology*, edited by Paul Tibbets. Chicago: Quadrangle Books.

———. 1979. *The Ecological Approach to Visual Perception*. Boston: Houghton Mifflin Co.

Gilson, Etienne. 1955. *Painting and Reality*. New York: Meridian Books (1959).

Goffman, Erving. 1959. *The Presentation of Self in Everyday Life*. Garden City, N.Y.: Doubleday Anchor Books.

Goldwater, Robert, and Treves, Marco, eds. 1945. *Artists on Art from the XIV to the XX Century*. New York: Pantheon Books (1972).

Gombrich, E. H. 1960. *Art and Illusion: A Study in the Psychology of Pictorial Representation*, Bollingen Series XXXV 5. Princeton: Princeton University Press (1984).

———. 1972. "The Mask and the Face: The Perception of Physiognomic Likeness in Life and Art." In *Art, Perception, and Reality*, edited by Maurice Mandelbaum. Baltimore: The Johns Hopkins University Press.

———. 1974. "Standards of Truth: The Arrested Image and the Moving Eye." In *The Language of Images*, edited by W.J.T. Mitchell. Chicago: The University of Chicago Press.

Goodman, Nelson. 1976. *Languages of Art: An Approach to a Theory of Symbols*. Indianapolis: Hackett Publishing Company.

———. 1984. *Of Mind and Other Matters*. Cambridge: Harvard University Press.

Grayling, A. C. 1982. *An Introduction to Philosophical Logic*. Totowa, N.J.: Barnes and Noble.

Hagberg, Gary. 1984. "Aristotle's Mimesis and Abstract Art." *Philosophy* 59:365–371.

Henderson, Linda D. 1983. *The Fourth Dimension and Non-Euclidean Geometry in Modern Art*. Princeton: Princeton University Press.

Hochberg, Julian. 1972. "The Representation of Things and People." In *Art, Perception, and Reality*, edited by Maurice Mandelbaum. Baltimore: The Johns Hopkins University Press.

Hochberg, Julian, and Brooks, Virginia. 1962. "Pictorial Recognition as an Unlearned Ability: A Study of One Child's Performance." *American Journal of Psychology* 75:624–628.

Hopper, Edward. 1933. *Edward Hopper*, edited by Lloyd Goodrich. New York: Harry N. Abrams (1976).

Kahler, Erich. 1968. *The Disintegration of Form in the Arts*. New York: George Braziller.

Kracauer, Siegfried. 1947. *From Caligari to Hitler: A Psychological History of the German Film*. Princeton: Princeton University Press (1966).

Kuo Hsi [11th cent.]. *An Essay on Landscape Painting*. London: John Murray (1949).

Langer, Susanne K. 1953. *Feeling and Form*. New York: Charles Scribner's Sons.

Leonardo da Vinci. Early 16th cent. *The Notebooks*, edited by Edward MacCurdy. New York: George Braziller (1958).

Lewin, Bertram D. 1968. *The Image and the Past*. New York: International University Press.

Lullies, Reinhard, and Hirmer, Max. 1957. *Greek Sculpture*. New York: Harry N. Abrams.

Mast, Gerald. 1974. "Kracauer's Two Tendencies and the Early History of Film Narrative." In *The Language of Images*, edited by W.J.T. Mitchell. Chicago: The University of Chicago Press.

Maynard, Patrick. 1978. "Depiction, Vision, and Convention." In *Philosophy Looks at the Arts*, edited by Joseph Margolis. Philadelphia: Temple University Press.

Merleau-Ponty, Maurice. 1961. "Eye and Mind." In *The Essential Writings of Merleau-Ponty*, edited by Alden Fisher. New York: Harcourt, Brace, and World (1969).

Mills, John F., and Manfield, John M. 1982. *The Genuine Article: The Making and Unmasking of Fakes and Forgeries*. New York: Universe Books.

Mondrian, Piet. 1937–1943. *Plastic Art and Pure Plastic Art 1937, and Other Essays*. New York: Wittenborn, Schultz, Inc. (1947).

Ortega y Gasset, José. 1914. "An Essay in Esthetics by Way of a Preface." In *Phenomenology and Art*. New York: W.W. Norton (1975).

Panofsky, Erwin. 1924. *Idea: A Concept in Art Theory*. Translated by Joseph J. S. Peake. Columbia: University of South Carolina Press (1968).

———. 1937. "Style and Medium in the Moving Pictures." *Transition* 26:121–133.

———. 1955. *Meaning in the Visual Arts: Papers in and on Art History*. Garden City, N.Y.: Doubleday Anchor Books.

Pfeiffer, John E. 1982. *The Creative Explosion: An Inquiry into the Origins of Art and Religion*. Ithaca: Cornell University Press.

Putnam, Hilary. 1981. *Reason, Truth and History*. Cambridge: Cambridge University Press.

Rader, Melvin. 1974. "The Imaginative Mode of Awareness." Presidential Address, American Society for Aesthetics.

Read, Herbert. 1931. *The Meaning of Art*. London: Faber and Faber (1984).

Richter, Gisela M. A. 1953. *Handbook of the Greek Collection: The Metropolitan Museum of Art*. Cambridge: Harvard University Press.

———. c. 1966. *Perspective in Greek and Roman Art*. London: Phaidon.

Schlegel, August Wilhelm. 1801. *Die Kunstlehre*. Stuttgart: W. Kohlhammer Verlag (1963).

Schopenhauer, Arthur. 1818. *The World as Will and Idea*.

Scruton, Roger. 1974. *Art and Imagination: A Study in the Philosophy of Mind*. London: Routledge and Kegan Paul.

Segall, Marshall H., Campbell, Donald T., and Herskovits, Melville J. 1966. *The Influence of Culture on Visual Perception*. New York: The Bobbs-Merrill Co.

Singer, Irving. 1977. "Santayana and the Ontology of the Photographic Image." *Journal of Aesthetics and Art Criticism* 36:39–43.

Sless, David. 1981. *Learning and Visual Communication*. New York: John Wiley and Sons.

Snyder, Joel. 1974. "Picturing Vision." In *Art, Perception and Reality*, edited by Maurice Mandelbaum. Baltimore: The Johns Hopkins University Press.

Sontag, Susan. 1973. *On Photography*. New York: Farrar, Straus and Giroux.

Steichen, Edward. 1960. "On Photography." In *The Visual Arts Today*, edited by Gyorgy Kepes. Middleton, Conn.: Wesleyan University Press.

Taylor, Joshua C. 1957. *Learning to Look: A Handbook for the Visual Arts*. Chicago: The University of Chicago Press (1981).

Tormey, Alan, and Tormey, Judith F. 1979. "Seeing, Believing, and Picturing." In *Perception and Pictorial Representation*, edited by Calvin F. Nodine and Dennis F. Fisher. New York: Praeger.

Walk, Richard D. 1976. "Development of Spatial Perception." In *The Development of Cognitive Processes*, edited by Vernon Hamilton and Magdalen D. Vernon. New York: Academic Press.

Wartofsky, Max W. 1979. "Picturing and Representing." In *Perception and Pictorial Representation*, edited by Calvin F. Nodine and Dennis F. Fisher. New York: Praeger.

Wilson, Curtis. 1980. "Kepler and the Mode of Vision." *The St. John's Review* 32:1–15.

Wind, Edgar. 1963. *Art and Anarchy*, 3d ed. Evanston, Ill.: Northwestern University Press (1985).

Wölfflin, Heinrich. 1915. *The Principles of Art History: The Problem of the Development of Style in Later Art.* Translated by M. D. Hottinger. New York: Dover Publications.

Wollheim, Richard. 1974a. "Nelson Goodman's Languages of Art." In *On Art and the Mind.* Cambridge: Harvard University Press.

————. 1974b. "Reflections on *Art and Illusion.*" Ibid.

————. 1978. "Art and Its Objects." In *Philosophy Looks at the Arts,* edited by Joseph Margolis. Philadelphia: Temple University Press.

Part Six

The Worldly Imagination: Imaginary and Imaginative Visions

Part Six

The Worldly Imagination: Imaginary and Imaginative Visions

The imagination as a power for making and informing the world is the subject of this last part. This power is here termed "worldly" in this double sense: It makes worlds that do not exist and it invests the world that does with a second surface. I call the making "imaginary" and the investment "imaginative," with some support from literary criticism (Frye 1963). These two employments of the imagination are often reciprocal—one ebbs as the other flows—and sometimes simultaneous.

"World" is one of those wonderful, all-purpose words—more encompassing than "Earth" and more intimate than "Universe"—that introduce large meanings on short notice. In fact, the "The World of This-and-That," much like "The Such-and-Such Imagination" (Introduction C), is a favored form of book title. By a world I here mean, and I think most people mean, a humanly significant whole—in particular, a habitat that environs human life, a place in the psychic as well as the spatial sense.

The imagination, I shall claim, is the preeminently world-shaping power: Worlds are made and recognized, it is commonly said, by the vision of the imagination. I shall try to show, with some precision, what that means.

I should take note just once more, of a general objection to this way of talking. There are, it is argued, no fictive, no imaginary worlds established in and by the works of the imagination, for the simple reason that there *are* no nonexistent worlds. I have ventured to argue that there do seem to be in and behind works of fiction imagined worlds which have a certain actuality (Part Three, Ch. III). The complement to the denial of fictive worlds is the equally current denial that there is one unitary real world, on the grounds that there are many conflicting truths and incompatible contexts. That may be—though it is not yet the end of days, and who knows what ways may be found to make apparently hostile apprehensions nest within or nestle up

683

against each other, the lion with the lamb? What is important to the present enterprise is that some world be regarded exclusively enough as the everyday world to admit the interesting distinction between places seen *in* and places seen *through* the imagination. Not to talk in prepositional riddles: When the Apostle John writes in *Revelation* of

> that great city, the holy Jerusalem, descending out of heaven from God, having the glory of God, and her light was like unto a stone most precious [21:10]

he is seeing the visionary heavenly city *in* the imagination. On the other hand, when the poet Pindar sings a dithyramb to Athens as

> O the shining and the violet-crowned and the hymned bulwark of Hellas, Glorious Athens, miraculous city [Frag. 76],

he is seeing the real earthly citadel *through* the imagination.

These two possibilities will be the topics of Chapter II on the utopian, and Chapter III on the real, topography of the imagination. I begin in Chapter I with a review of the standing, high and low, accorded to the imagination's worldly work first in rationalism and then, and above all, in theology.

Chapter I

Theology: Contrary Estimations of the Imagination

The sharpest valuations of the imagination and its works in the world are to be found with respect to faith and religion. If in philosophy the traditional standing of the imagination is ambiguous—at once suspect and necessary—it is in theology that the faculty and its productions are most forcefully apprehended as evil (A) or as good (B).

A. Dimensions of Denigration

The strains of suspicion and contempt are not, however, exclusively theological. The secular objections to the imagination are usually not that it is evil, but that it is, in various ways, disreputable. Some of these have been taken up in the earlier parts: The imagination is held in low esteem for its pre-intellectual character and its ontologically low objects, as well as for its cognitive uselessness and its experimental elusiveness. The first set of objections forms the burden of the whole ancient and medieval philosophical tradition, where the imagination is cognitively and morally respectable but only so long as it is subordinated to reason. On its own it is emptily fantastic, willfully depraved, and susceptible to demonic invasion (Part One). The second set of objections form the tenor of some contemporary cognitive psychology (Part Two).

But the most pervasive modern secular attack is motivated by the sense, proper to men engaged in mastering nature by science, that the imagination is essentially childish and idle (*1*). The older theological resistances are much more pointed and correspondingly deeper. They concern the willfulness and the creative autonomy of imaginative life (*2*) and the moral dangers inherent in the very being of its specific material images (*3*).

685

1. Juvenile Thinking: The Rationalist Tradition and Spinoza. It is generally agreed that children are preponderantly imaginative beings. One could cite famous pedagogical pronouncements by the score, from Plato through Vico, Rousseau, and Whitehead, to the present (Part Two, Ch. IV). It may be a false emphasis—one could as truly say that children are born logicians—yet the imagination has been successfully branded as a juvenile mode, whose strength in an adult betokens an inferior sort of mind, a mind in which the intellectual part is weak and unprofitable for mature business.

The denigration of the imagination is hence quite naturally a standard topic of the rationalist tradition. Thus Macaulay says in his essay on Milton:

> Of all people children are the most imaginative. They abandon themselves without reserve to every illusion. . . . Such is the despotism of the imagination over uncultivated minds. [1825]

Of course the Romantics, in opposition, glorify the child's chief asset as the essential quality to be preserved by an adult human being (Plotz 1979).

One paradigmatic source of the rationalist attitude is Locke's works on education, *Some Thoughts Concerning Education* (1693) and *Of the Conduct of the Understanding* (1697). In the first he mounts a broad attack on the use of simile, a version of his anti-scholastic "to-the-things-themselves" realism: Figurative and metaphorical expressions make us "content ourselves with what our imaginations, not things themselves, furnish us with." In the later book he recommends that if a child "have a poetic vein . . . parents should labour to have it stifled and suppressed as much as may be . . . for it is very seldom that anyone discovers mines of gold or silver in Parnassus. 'Tis a pleasant air but a barren soil." A century and a half later the issue is still very much alive: In his *Idea of a University* (1858), Cardinal Newman finds it necessary to defend the classical education of the young against Locke and others who say that it "cultivates the *imagination* a great deal too much, and other *habits of mind* a great deal too little." He ventures to doubt that the study of classical authors is always an imaginative enterprise and claims that it is in fact useful, thus conceding Locke's criterion. Locke's utilitarian precepts had an especially great influence on American education, an influence first specifically and vigorously opposed on a large scale yet another century later, in our sixties and seventies.

In the rationalist spirit the vague and emotional imagination is opposed to the "solid and masculine parts" of the understanding. In this vein, novel-reading was in the last century a routine object of attack. It was said to inflame the imagination and to make the judgment effeminate. Since both readers and writers were so often women, parodies of these strictures found their comical, tongue-in-cheek way into the novels themselves—witness the take-off on the effects of reading gothic novels in Jane Austen's *Northanger Abbey*, or the following exchange between mother and daughter in Charlotte Brontë's *Shirley*:

> "Mutual love! My dear, romances are pernicious. You do not read them, I hope?
> "Sometimes—Whenever I can get them, indeed. . . . "

Nevertheless, the suspicion of the imagination as a faculty opposed to solid reasoning is very much endemic and very much in earnest for both sexes. In one of Jane Austen's late letters to the niece on whom she bestowed an almost passionate affection, she writes, seriously and astoundingly from one of the world's great imaginers:

> But how could it possibly be any new idea to you that you have a great deal of Imagination? You are all over Imagination. The most astonishing part of your Character is, that with so much Imagination, so much flight of mind, such unbounded Fancies, you should have such excellent Judgement in what you do! Religious Principle I fancy must explain it. Well, good bye and God bless you. [March 13, 1817]

The pitting of imagination against judgment is, in sum, an Enlightenment commonplace. Jefferson says of that calamitous imp, the ambassador of the French Republic, Genet, that he was "all imagination, no judgment" (1793).

This rationalist denigration of the imagination has its specifically modern origin in the Baconian sense that we moderns—as opposed to the youthful ancients—are the true adults of history, engaged in the serious business of progress through the mastery of nature. It eventually shrivels into a mindset, the preachy policy of pedagogues, imposed on hapless children but unregarded in adult art and life. In one application, however, contempt for the imagination has been of real consequence: biblical interpretation. I begin with a counter-instance.

Thomas Aquinas says that "to proceed by the aid of various similitudes and figures is proper to poetry, the least of all sciences" (*Summa Theologica* I 1, 9, also 51, 3). This ranking of poetry comes, of course, out of ancient philosophy (Part One, Ch. I A). Yet he feels entitled to defend the use of figurative language in the Bible because "it is natural to man to attend to intellectual truths through sensible things." Through figures of corporeal things even the simple may grasp intellectual things. "Besides, what is taught metaphorically in one part of Scripture is taught openly in others."

But poetry is not only for the naive; Thomas defends, most trenchantly, its philosophical use: "The very hiding of truth in figures is useful to the exercise of thoughtful minds."

This tolerant and even positive view is most influentially and extensively set aside by Spinoza in his *Theologico-Political Treatise* (1670). Whereas his predecessor Maimonides had allowed that prophets were receptive to the overflow from God both in their rational and in their imaginative faculty (*Guide of the Perplexed* II 37), Spinoza says that "prophets were endowed with unusually vivid imaginations and not with unusually perfect minds" (II). A careful reading of the sacred books shows that God's revelations can have been made to his prophets only either through real words and appearances or through imaginary evidence which they supposed they heard or saw. If the prophets' utterances are read so as to find nothing in them that they do not distinctly say, it emerges that only Moses really heard the voice of God. And Spinoza implies that even Moses is only imagining. For when summing up, he says that we may conclude that only "Christ received revelations of God without the aid of imagination" and "mind to mind" (I). So God adapts his communications to the capacity of the poetic but intellectually deficient prophets as they, in turn, speak to an imperfectly endowed multitude (Strauss 1952).

What makes the imagination inferior? In the *Treatise* it is said— obliquely—that the imagination has two drawbacks: It is always uncertain, lacking the self-evidence of clear and distinct ideas, and it is sometimes false, going beyond the boundary of the intellect (I, II). In the *Ethics* (1677) the cause is given. In ascending order the levels of knowledge are: "imagination," which is "cognition of the first [lowest] class," then reason, and on top [intellectual] intuition. The lowest level, the ideas of the imagination, arise as representations of corporeal affections caused by other bodies. They are passive, particular, and inadequate to the essence of their originals. They are, further, confused, especially insofar as the corporeal affections coalesce to form general, composite ideas which overload the body's receptive capacity (Sheldon 1979). Now inadequacy and confusion of ideas—the two deficiencies of cognition—are understood by Spinoza to define falsity. Hence the imagination-level of cognition is the source of error. Thus human beings must, above all, strive to transform their juvenile, corporeally confounded body into another that is appropriate to a soul, one in which the imaginative faculty is insignificant in comparison with reason (V, prop. 39). Spinoza furnishes a prime example of a certain intellectual contempt for the imagination. There are also those who regard it with whole-hearted moral fear.

2. Evil Imaginations: Willfulness and Hallucinogens. The following divine observation is both the cause of God's decision to blot out man in a great flood for his wickedness and the reason for His promise to be forbearing toward man forever, in consideration of the aboriginality of his evil:

> And God saw that the wickedness of man was great in the earth and that every imagination of the thoughts of his heart was only evil constantly. [*Genesis* 6:5, repeated at 8:21]

Here is the original text for the association of the imagination with human evil. It is not clear that the word translated as imagination in the King James Version refers to any sort of image, either of mind or heart: It is rendered as "plan" in Jewish versions (Plaut 1981), as *cogitatio* in the Vulgate, as *Dichten*, meaning "fashioning, imagining, making poetry," in the Luther Bible. The English wording evidently expresses the sense, by now traditional, that the imagination, as the agency of whatever mentation may have been meant in the original, is a source of evil.

Why should the imagination be peculiarly responsible for moral badness? We have only to consult our own souls to recover the numerous—and opposing—reasons given in the tradition: First, in a general way, the imagination is a disequilibrating power, a dis-easing capacity for projecting and remembering and consequently for inducing desire and fostering resentment; hence the Stoic injunction: "Wipe out the Imagination" (Marcus Aurelius, *Meditations* VII 29, 2d cent.). As in the biblical tradition just touched on, it is associated with the power for figuring and plotting, for plans and designs: it is the "designing" heart that the Old Testament passages denounce. Moreover, it has to do not only with ordinary lasciviousness but also, according to St. Bonaventure—one great warner against the bad imagination—with the exquisite concupiscence of forbidden knowledge and of manipulative magic: It is the cause of the swollen desire that leads Adam to commit the original sin (Kearney 1988). Actually it is, of course, Eve who initiates the Fall, and, accordingly, she is the one in Milton's interpretation, who has imagination and who is, from the moment of creation, image-prone: she falls in love with her own reflection (*Paradise Lost* IV 460).

However, just as there is danger in imaginal busyness and tumescence, so there is equal danger in idleness and languor. Thus Don Quixote artlessly says of a lady who has been playing foolish games with him that

> all the evil in that maiden arises from idleness, the remedy for which is honest and continuous occupation. She has just now informed me that they wear lace

in Hell, and since she must certainly know how to make it, let it never be out of her hands; for when she is busy working the bobbins the image or images of her desires will not work in her imagination.

And Isaac Watts versifies the commonplace:

For Satan finds some mischief still
    For idle hands to do. ["Divine Song" 1715]

It is a well-known, even an experimentally supported, fact that imagery activity increases with mental and physical idleness; thus it is often—and rightly—charged with what used to be called "wantonness." In the chapter of *Rasselas* entitled "The Dangerous Prevalence of the Imagination" (1759), Dr. Johnson paints a vivid picture of those who "indulge the power of fiction and send imagination out upon the wing." The "labour of excogitation is too violent to last long," and when the mind has no external business to divert it, it "riots in delights which Nature and fortune, for all their bounty, cannot bestow." Indeed, daydreaming, the half-deliberate, half-languid "inflaming of the imagination," which is most prevalent where the mind is most idle, namely in school, has ever been the bane of pedagogues, even into this century. How to control "reveries" and "indecent imagery" used to be a standard topic in books on educational practice (Part Two, Ch. V C). Thus the imagination's demi-passivity lends itself to manipulation and randomness equally, manifesting itself in both the calculating operator and the lascivious lounger. The Brazilian writer Machado de Assis reports a pertinent case, the serio-comic management of his fantasies by a young seminarian who is at once lewd and adroit:

When the evil returned later in the morning, I tried to conquer it, but in a way that would not wholly destroy it. Ye who are learned in the Scriptures may divine what it was. Even so. Since I could not cast out these pictures from me, I resorted to a treaty between my conscience and my imagination. These female visions would henceforth be looked upon as simple incarnations of the vices, and as such to be contemplated—as the best method of tempering the character and strengthening it for the rude combats of life. [*Dom Casmurro* 1899]

Second, besides being lewd, the imagination is inherently deceitful. As a faculty of illusion it is prone to the influence of the Deluder: Satan sits

Squat like a toad, close at the ear of Eve,
Assaying by his devilish art to reach
The organs of her fancy, and with them forge
Illusions, as he list, phantasms and dreams . . .
[Milton, *Paradise Lost*, IV 800]

Pascal devotes a whole sequence of thoughts to exposing the imagination as the "deceitful part of man; that mistress of error and falsity," dangerous because "being most generally false, she gives no sign of her nature, impressing the same character on the true and the false" (*Pensées* 1661, 82 ff.). She has, moreover, a greater gift of persuasion than reason, which she likes to dominate, having "established in man a second nature to show how powerful she is":

Imagination cannot make fools wise, but she can make them happy, to the envy of reason which can only make its friends miserable.

In fact, Pascal claims, the imagination is *the* worldly faculty; it makes the world go round by means of those social pretenses, such as robes and caps of office, that cause human beings to accept authority: The imagination is the motor of secularity, of worldliness.

Yet again and third, as imagination is the source of worldly conformity, so it is the cause of rebellion, or at least of the glorification of rebellion. The great English example is the dominating, gloomy splendor of Satan in *Paradise Lost*, which caused Blake to say of Milton that he was, as a true poet, of the Devil's party without knowing it. The imagination has an inherent longing for the extreme, the dark, the dangerous, for death and hell. There is a poem by Walter De la Mare, called "The Imagination's Price," which paints this propensity almost garishly:

Be not too wildly amorous of the far,
    Nor lure thy fantasy to its utmost scope.
            . . .
O brave adventure! Ay, at danger slake
    Thy thirst, lest life in thee should, sickening, quail,
But not toward nightmare goad a mind awake,
    Nor to forbidden horizons bend thy sail—
Seductive outskirts whence in trance prolonged
    Thy gaze at stretch of what is sane-secure,
Dreams out on steeps by shapes demoniac thronged
    And vales wherein alone the dead endure.
Nectarous those flowers, yet with venom sweet
    Thick-juiced with poison hang those fruits that shine
Where sick phantasmal moonbeams brood and beat,
    And dark imaginations ripe the vine.

From this brief sketch it emerges that two false relations of the imagination to other psychic faculties are the ground of its evils: First it is the seductive opponent of the rational faculty, and it is the part passive, part cunning servant of the will. The first flaw, the peculiar ir-rationality of the imagination, is to be distinguished from its a-rationality, which, as intimated above, ranks it as a childish rather than a vicious capacity. Its irrationality is a much-repeated theme that naturally comes to the fore just when the imagination is gaining independent stature. A typical early example comes from the Christian Humanist tradition. Pico della Mirandola in his work *On the Imagination* (Part One, Ch. II), written at the beginning of the fifteenth century, makes it an element of the dignity of man to rule by reason over phantasy if she errs; conversely, to obey the dictates of the deceitful imagination degrades him into a brute. To Pico the universal errors undermining Christian and philosophic life have their beginning in the vicious imagination: ambition, cruelty, passion, and false opinion (VII). Practically all later works on the imagination written in this vein of shocked fascination include similar observations. For example, the *Pleasures of the Imagination* by Akenside contains an almost identical catalogue of the evil that arises

> Where Fancy cheats the intellectual eye,
> With glaring colours and distorted lines. [29]

The corruption of the imagination through willfulness is the more specifically theological of these defects. It is very clearly set out by Augustine in *On the Trinity* (XI iii). Augustine is pursuing the multiple imitations of the Trinity in the patterns of human cognition (Part One, Ch. I G). One of these trinities consists of the corporeal form of a thing, its image as it informs a person's sense, and the will which fixes the senses on the thing to begin with. A second, inner, trinity arises when in the absence of the corporeal thing itself the will brings together memory and inner vision. Both outer and inner vision, sight and mental imagery, can move the imaginer's own body. Augustine mentions the physical effects of the mental fashioning of a female form which is near carnal. If the will toward the flesh is vehement enough, it is lust. Therefore those who live by these trinities live badly, for both are directed toward the use of things sensible and corporeal—the vehement will brings memories into the imagination not as purified from, but as compacted of, the flesh.

In these cases it is not the imagination in itself that is positively evil—it is the weakness of the reason and the perversion of the will that is at fault. Indeed, wickedness, which is theologically defined as evil sought for the sake of evil (Rahner and Vorgrimler 1965), is technically imageless, since it requires no concrete motive, no imaged object of lust, at all. However, some writers do consider that it is the imagination itself that is subject to vitiation, disease, and corruption. Thus Burton, in the *Anatomy of Melancholy* (1621), takes sides in what is apparently an old debate regarding the proximate cause of melancholy, by agreeing that the fault is "first in the imagination and afterwards in reason": It is the imagination that grows rank and reason that fails to do its work of correction.

In a most general way, the vices of the imagination are just the extremes of its virtue. Consequently, they show themselves at the two poles of excess and deficiency.

The imaginative deficit appears to be a peculiarly modern affliction: The imagination is dead or maunderingly moribund. The death or crippling of the imagination as the defining misery of the modern psyche is a dominant theme of twentieth-century literature. For example, the German novelist Jakob Wassermann, who was peculiarly sensitive to the atmospheric evils of the times, wrote that "in the majority of human beings the power of representation is degenerated and morbidly weakened"; the great incidence of depression and psychic debilitation is often the result of a flagrant defect, the stunting and crippling of the imagination (*Etzel Andergast* 1919). The objective correlative to this condition, the progressive annihilation of the imaginative world, is literally and vividly envisioned in the recent children's books of Michael Ende (Part Four, Ch. IV B). The failure of the imagination has been held responsible not only for the individual illnesses but also for the great atrocities of our century. It has been plausibly argued that the most acute symptom of a defective imagination is the "literalization of language" (Karl Kraus in Epstein 1985), the process of despoiling words of their figurative impact, so that metaphors are heard without the mitigation of what will later be called "semantic shock" (Part Four, Ch. III). As metaphors die, people become willing, even eager, to see figurative threats—as in the example of "holding someone's feet to the fire"—literally and blindly executed. What prepared the way for such a draining of the imagination, and the consequent craving for literal brutality, was its century-long abuse through sentimentality (Epstein 1985). It was the romantic-aesthetic penchant for images of suffering—the keeping of a "pet sorrow, a blue devil familiar" (Lowell 1884) in order to maintain a frisson of self-important "compassion"—that blunted many a sensibility and made it avid for literal strong stuff.

The most significant of the modern imagination's excesses, on the other hand, is, in Auden's bold phrase, her "promiscuous fornication with her own images," the rankly luxuriating self-referential play of disassociated romanticism (Part Four, Ch. II B). It is presented by Auden's speakers as a worldly evil with a theological cure: the acceptance of one unmediated union of meaning and appearance, that of the Incarnation:

> Because in Him the Flesh is united to the Word without magical transformation, Imagination is redeemed from promiscuous fornication with her own images. [Simeon in "For the Time Being" 1944]

The imagination is most excessively autarchic, most a world unto itself, without reference to reality or being, when activated by the hallucinogenic, the so-called "psychedelic" drugs. Aldous Huxley, a lesser De Quincey, speaks of being "transported by mescaline to some remote, non-personal region of the mind," a world that possesses "intrinsic significance." The images of the mescaline experience are not symbolic representations but self-sufficient events; they stand for nothing else: "The significance of each thing is identical with its being" (Huxley 1955).

De Quincey himself, unlike Huxley, understood the perilous gravity of his undertaking, and moreover had the imagination to give his opium dreams grandeur, the language to express their enormity, and the intellect to fathom their abysses. He speaks of the great melancholy of these bottomless significances, the "insufferable splendor that fretted my heart" ("The Pains of Opium," in Confessions of an English Opium Eater, 1822). Baudelaire, too, knew that the experience of an "artificial paradise" provided by hashish achieved but a paradis de la pharmacie, bought at the price of enslavement to a poison (Abrams 1971).

So in its gravest excess the imagination casts loose from its healthy function of imagining intentionally, in the sense of imaging some thing. Instead it produces reference-less "intrinsically significant" images—untethered image-monsters that are neither beings nor representations of beings. However, yet one more step is required to render the imagination absolute. That step is taken in that peculiar idolatry of the imagination which converts its rank excess into total defect. There is a strain of postmodern art that venerates "an imagination so engrossed in the potency and rapidity of its own operations that it refuses to descend into any finite image" (Albright 1981, 7). Its manifesto is Beckett's white-on-white fragment "Imagination Dead Imagine" (Part Four, Ch. II C). Thus the prideful perversion of the imaging function culminates in a sort of iconoclastic idolatry.

Fourth and finally, the imagination has a propensity for evil which stems from its most observed (and least studied) psychic relation (Part One, Chs. I G, IV B). It is the relation of the imagination to desire, be it to desire as a deliberately directed intention—the will, or as an unconscious energy—the libido. In some Christian and in almost all psychoanalytic understandings the imagination is thought to be aroused and informed by desire: Will or wish are originating causes behind the imagery, which is, as it were, only their shaped appearance. Yet, though this causal sequence undoubtedly holds for willful daydreaming (Part Two, Ch. V C), an old tradition, articulated by Aristotle (Part One, Ch.I B), recognizes the inverse order, which gives causal priority to the imagination as the faculty of representations. Just as the adventitious appearance of an external object arouses desire, so images spontaneously rising up from memory can induce moods and longings. This delicate and captivating problem, the intertwining of images and feelings, will be taken up in the last chapter.

Here is a coda of engrossing questions to this all too brief account of the evil imagination: Is the imagination really capable of evil? If so, is the power, so to speak, more fool or more knave? Does it go wrong passively insofar as it slips the grip of reason? Or does it originate evil by its own positive designs? To put it another way: Is the imagination a Manichean principle within us, a dual root of original good and original evil, or is it simply a neutral power of representation which takes its moral hue from desire?

As I intimated at the beginning, one need not be a rationalist or a theologian to agree that the imagination in fact assists in all sorts of harm. It stares, unmoved, at horrors, envisions sudden random mischief, revolves incessant images of resentment and revenge, brings up mephitic bubbles of graphic sadism, inflames itself with huge and thrilling visions, enjoys as spectacles the excruciating extremes of human experience, and conceives of human beings as the material for massive, emotive tableaux. These last vicious visions, the products of a politicised romanticism gone rampant, have been the backdrop of deeds it would be wrong to name merely in passing: Of the monstrous tyrants our century has spawned, two, at least, notoriously approached politics in terms of spectacular visual images (Johnson 1983). But if the imagination can undoubtedly be evil, how original is its badness?

It is, of course, not news that the imagination in turn leads and follows both the passions below and the reason above: Sometimes a mere flitting phantom of the imagination can rouse a turmoil of powerful passion; sometimes, on the other hand, obscurely deep drives can send up curiously well-wrought images. Again, obsessive imagery can resist all the dispersive efforts of sweet reason, while the designs of an unsound rationality can summon up banally grandiose visions. So if the soul has different powers, as I have argued (Part One, Ch. V), and if there is such a thing as depravity, which I take as given, all faculties would seem to share in its organization.

And yet: "ugly passions," "perverse will," "corrupt reason"—all these phrases sound to the ear somehow more in order than "evil imagination." Let me venture some guesses why. The imagination does have a saving measure of similarity with intellectual intuition. It entertains and cherishes its objects with a certain contemplative purity, welcoming those that illumine and resisting those that confound. Moreover, although it is not above having truck with badness, it is characteristically an unrealized badness. There is an old wisdom that one may dream and daydream of many things and deeds which it is shameful to stare at and criminal to do. But its innocence does not accrue to the imagination primarily from its privacy, from the public unreality of its designs. Even more fundamental is the neutralizing distance inherent in the power of imaging itself. Just as it is possible for participants in imagery experiments to visualize attentively and precisely pictures that do not have a ghost of a moral or emotional charge, so it is within the capacity of spontaneous imaginers to contemplate with disinterested absorption, with a kind of reserved passion, the theater without and within. In sum, I think that the imagination in itself and taken strictly, as the mere capacity for internal quasi-sensory re-presentation, is morally neutral, not a-moral but pre-moral. That is exactly why it functions as the place where good and evil apparitions from the world present themselves for review, and where, in turn, the dark and the bright impulses and counsels of the soul take on a shape and are judged.

3. False Images: Idolatry and Iconoclasm.

Thou shalt not make unto thee any graven image, or any
likeness of any thing that is in heaven above, or that
is in the earth beneath, or that is in the water under
the earth. Thou shalt not bow down thyself before
them, nor serve them: For I the Lord thy God am a
jealous God . . . [*Exodus* 20:4; also *Lev.* 26:1, *Deut.*
5:8, 16:22]

Thus goes the principal text against image-making in our tradition. The prohibition seems to be against all material representations. However, during the iconoclastic controversy an argument was advanced to the effect that the word "graven" restricted the prohibition to sculpture. Painting would thus be permitted, presumably because, lacking a dimension, it is that much the less a re-presentation of the creation, or a second creation.

That reading of the commandment as forbidding human world-making seems clear enough. Even so, the Second Commandment turns out to be anything but easy to interpret.

At its end the text itself intimates a reason for the proscription of images: It is to prevent idolatry, the worship of made images as real gods—such images as the golden calf of *Exodus* 32:8—in place of a God who is jealous of his status as the only God. But the universality of the prohibition seems to reach beyond idolatry, which is the abuse of images, to the mere attempt to image God. Yet why should the true God not be pictured? The question is implicitly acknowledged in *Deuteronomy* 4:12–19. Here Moses explains the commandment by the fact that God, though audible, has not been visible to his people: "Ye heard the voice of the words, but saw no similitude . . . Take ye therefore good heed unto yourselves . . . Lest ye corrupt yourselves and make you a graven image, the similitude of any figure, the likeness of male or female . . . . " In other words, the only God does not permit himself to be seen, and so much the less to be imaged as being of determinate gender.

The next perplexity would then be whether the imaging of God is prohibited because he is in his nature unimageable or because no image can avoid supplanting its original and becoming an idol. An idol, it should be said, is identified by three properties: First, it is made, or at least designated by human beings. Second, if it is made, it is shaped in the likeness of a being or a composite of beings in the created world:

> The idols of the heathen are silver and gold, the
> work of men's hands.
> They have mouths, but they speak not; eyes
> have they, but they see not;
>   . . .
> They that make them are like unto them; so is
> everyone that trusteth them. [*Psalm* 135:15; also
> 115:4]

Third and most important, this image of creation is worshiped not as a representation of a god but as the divinity itself.

Within the Old Testament, the questions just raised remain suspended. It gives no explicit theological reason why Yaweh should not be represented (von Rad 1957). But if the deep cause was his transcendent, invisible nature, it had fallen away in the New Testament with the Incarnation, a new and uniquely privileged imaging of God (B below). Consequently, there slowly arose a Christian iconography. By the seventh century of the Christian era the veneration of images, of Christ, of Mary, of the saints, had become part of the public liturgy. But hand in hand with image-worship came image-breaking: iconolatry incited iconoclasm. In 726 A.D. the theological issue turned into a political crisis, as an imperial edict against icons encouraged image-breaking. There ensued the often violent imbroglios of the Iconoclastic episode, which after more than a hundred years resulted in the victory of the Iconophiles. A moderated image-veneration is still an official part of the Catholic liturgy (Vatican II, 1963), and iconographic questions are most alive there (Nichols 1980).

The question of images and faith is understandably a passionate matter. The arguments on either side can be very refined, but the main issue was from the beginning whether image-veneration is of necessity idolatry. The defenders argue practically that the illiterate worshiper needs the visible word, the "pauper's bible," that the mystery of the Incarnation is more active in memory when there are visible images, and that things seen excite more feelings of devotion than things merely heard. But they also give reasons why image veneration is theologically permissible: The honor rendered to an image passes through to its prototype (St. Basil, *On the Holy Spirit*, late 4th cent.). And, according to Pope Gregory:

> It is one thing to worship a picture and another to learn from the language of a picture what that is which ought to be worshiped. [c. 600]

In other words, it is necessary to recall the imaginal nature of the image; what gives it its "aura of awful and blissful sacredness" is that it points beyond itself (Ladner 1953). From there on, however, the argument becomes divided: Some venerate the image as a symbol that only points toward God, others as a likeness that somehow actually shows him. A radical iconoclastic counter-argument is given by Philoxenes of Mabboug (5th cent.), who condemns the imagination as intrinsically perverse and images as evil by the mere fact of their re-presentational nature: They make a false claim to present spiritual truth with spatial and temporal immediacy (Kearney 1988).

The image-character and consequent imageability of the Christ in particular have several explanatory roots. One is the preparation in Judaeo-Platonic philosophy for an iconic intermediary between the highest being and the world. Thus Philo (first cent.) held that the Platonic forms, God's "very sacred ideas," are themselves "incorporeal images" (*eikones asōmatoi*). Consonant with this understanding, the Divine Logos, God's supremely rational thought, is also "the image of God."

Another rationale, also with classical antecedents, is in a distinction advanced in the full-blown iconophile writings of John of Damascus (eighth cent.): There are two sorts of images, those "according to nature" (*physis*) and those "according to art," "convention," or "imitation" (*technē, thesis, mimēsis*). Christ himself images God by nature; the images of art exist by a lesser imitation. The point is that the distinction, if firmly kept in mind, is a safeguard against idolatry and thus a legitimization of "mimetic" images, paintings, of Christ. However, the ultimate defense for such images derives from the mere fact that God appeared in the flesh, for what appears is veritably imageable. Thus the iconophile Fathers positively demand that symbols of Christ, such as the lamb, should be replaced by pictures of Christ in his truthful humanity. (Ladner 1953.)

Since it sets the Judaeo-Christian problem of images into strong relief, it is impossible to pass on without saying a word about the pagan Greek counter-tradition of visible gods, and registering a perplexity raised by it. (For a fine historical treatment, see the chapter "Seeing the Gods"" in Fox 1987.) The Homeric gods roam free and make only episodic epiphanies. It is not until much later that they are caught in sculpture and confined to sacred precincts. Are these later classical statues of divinities idols in the strict theological sense? They are certainly artifacts, even contrivances: The sculptor Phidias, for example, mounted the golden drapery of his Athena Parthenos, the center of the cultic life of Athens, so that it could be dismantled and weighed, should he be accused of stealing some of the gold—as indeed he was (Plutarch, *Pericles*). Did the ordinary worshipers who stood before the great gold and ivory form in her temple take it to be the goddess herself? I am conjecturing here concerning the unarticulated half-thoughts of people almost two and a half millennia dead. But is so naive an identification by these quick-witted Athenians likely, especially when another, larger statue by the same sculptor, the Athena Promachus, stood right outside the temple on the Acropolis? Is it not more plausible that the statue was to them indeed an appearance—one appearance—of the goddess, that it was, precisely, her image? What is astonishing in the present context is that image-worship was apparently neither the anxious problem nor the continual temptation for the Greek worshipers that it was for the Jews. Were these Hellenes simply light-minded? Or were they capable of a polymorphic vision which, like a suspended judgment, could accept, even see, the same goddess in all her images? Questions about pagan statue-worship are much harder to ask soberly than those about Christian iconophilia: the aesthetic presence of a Greek god-statue tends so disarmingly to overbear its re-presentational claims.

To return to the Christian tradition: In the earlier Renaissance the defense of sacred painting changes its tenor; it is now based on an enthusiastic praise of sight as the sense through which the perfect shape of Christ's body is known, the motions of the soul are revealed, and the delights of heaven and even divine wisdom are made manifest (Baxandall 1972). With the coming of Protestantism the argument against images again gains ground. The biblical prohibition against material images is extended to the interpretation of the Incarnation as a somatic imaging: It is not Christ's human body but his divine spirit that ought to be worshiped. Images represent the carnal aspect of Christ and are therefore unavoidably idols. Since they cannot possibly image what they pretend to image, Christ's spirit, they are inescapably worshiped for themselves, that is, idolatrously. As Hobbes (whose spirited attack on idolatry is, needless to say, directed against the Roman church) neatly puts it: "To worship God, as inanimating, or inhabiting such image, or place, that is to say, an infinite substance in a finite place, is idolatry" (*Leviathan*, ch. 45). Thus idols are doubly-false images, for in pretending to image the unimageable, they are also merely pretended images; sacred images are always twice-deceptive.

In our day, the wars pitting iconophiles and iconophobes against each other are dormant. Yet so vital is the image-question that it has a modern secular continuation, the one extendedly set out in the earlier parts of this book. It is fought on a score of fronts, but always between antagonists divided by a similar, crypto-theological fervor: those who want to break the idols so as to regain the purity of the word, and those who want, for all its perplexities, to save the manifestations of the image.

B. The Godly Imagination

While the Bible proscribes image-making as a human enterprise it also exalts it as the principal work of God (*1*). There is even a theological tradition, the mystic tradition, that centers on the Divine Imagination itself as the creative power of God (*2*). Finally the human imagination too is accorded an important place in the life of faith (*3*).

1. The Image of God: Icon and Imitation.

> And God said, Let us make man in our image, after our
> likeness. [*Genesis* 1:26; also 5:1, 9:6]

This is the prime text for the idea that human beings are themselves images. The word "image" (*tselem*) used in this passage occurs often in the Old Testament. Since in the other places it usually means statue, model, or picture, here it may mean a physical resemblance. On the other hand, the word "likeness" (*demuth*) may have been added to specify an image as bearing a nonsensory meaning (Porteous 1962): Man is like God not in shape but in his dominion over the created world (Berkouwer 1962). However, a theologian like Calvin, who considers that "the proper seat of the image is in the soul" (1559), regards the distinction as idle: both terms refer to spiritual imaging. In any case, all Old Testament image-terms— there is yet a third one, *temuna* (e.g., *Exodus* 20:4)—seem to carry the same double meaning of concrete and spiritual (Kearney 1988).

In the Greek New Testament, the word for image is usually *eikōn*. This word, however, is to be taken not as "mere image" but as a perfect reflection of an original, as already in *Hebrews* 10:1: "a shadow . . . and not the very image." To this shift in meaning corresponds a shift in application; it is now hardly ever man who is made in the image of God but Christ who is *the* image of God, simply: The "beloved Son" is "the image of the invisible God" (*Colossians* 1:15; cf. II *Corinthians* 4:4). Christ, it is explained by Irenaeus, a Church Father much concerned with this issue, is a recapitulator of mankind. *Recapitulatio*, meaning restoration as well as consummation, is a pervasive theme of his theology. (It has a great future in our century, as Heidegger's *Wiederholung*.) Thus Christ as a second Adam shows what the first Adam was meant to be; for in ancient times, although man had been told that he was created after the image of God, no image had actually been shown him. However, when

the Word of God became flesh he confirmed both image and likeness. For he showed forth the image . . . and the likeness he re-established unshakably by assimilating man to the invisible Father by means of the visible Word. [In Nichols 1980]

The direct opponent of this Irenaean "iconic" view is Origen, who considers the primary image of the invisible Father to be the pre-existent *invisible* Son, whose incarnation is only a passing pedagogical form. Here are the seeds of iconoclasm (Nichols, 64).

Insofar as human beings are made in the image of God, it follows that they should imitate either God or his prime image. That is to say man should actively approach the original in whose image he was passively created. Thus the iconophile Fathers thought of the imitation of God as a matter at once spiritual and intellectual, a way of being and an activity: The human being is already, by reason of his spiritual freedom and rationality, an image (*eikōn*) of God, but by means of active assimilation (*homoiōsis*) he can, by the grace of God, work to perfect himself. The fact of Christ's assumption of human form thus not only proves God's imageability by man in principle, but eases the task of assimilation in practice (Ladner 1953). Therefore, in contrast to the imitation of the pagan gods, which is less a matter of inner exertion than of ritual performance, the call to imitate God is a call to a way of life: "Be therefore imitators (*mimētai*) of God, as beloved children, and walk in love" (*Ephesians* 5:1). Similarly, the imitation of Christ is invited by his words "He that followeth me shall not walk in darkness" (*John* 8:12), words which significantly head the *Imitation of Christ* of Thomas à Kempis.

If the imaging of God in man is a deep mystery, and the imitation of God by man a great task, the two are obviated together in a work that marks the dawn of modernity: Pico della Mirandola's famous *Oration on the Dignity of Man*. In this manifesto of humanism, Pico tells a revised version of the Creation story, one which opportunely eliminates the notion of man as fixed in the divine image. The Supreme Maker had already filled all creation when at last he bethought himself of bringing forth man. All space and all properties having been distributed, he decreed that man, "this being of indeterminate image," should share in the gifts of all creatures, undefined by law, a "chameleon, a Proteus," a creature of metamorphoses and transformations. Thus Adam, having no visage or endowment properly his own, was enjoined by God to fashion *for himself* the form he prefers. "Oh wondrous and unsurpassable felicity of man, to whom it is granted to have what he chooses, to be what he will be." In such exaltation begins the familiar modern search for a self-image!

2. The Divine Imagination: Schelling and Ibn Arabi. If God creates images, it stands to reason that he does so through his imagination. The divine imagination is an idea pursued by the mystic rather than the mainstream writers of the Christian tradition. By "mystic" I mean here writers whose apparently figurative language is meant not to be rationally interpreted but to be apprehended by an immediate insight. Blake's imagination-theology has been touched on above (Part Four, Ch. II B); he was much influenced by Jakob Boehme, who began to publish in 1612: "The origin of all essential beings consists in nothing else than an Imagination of the Abyss (*Imagination des Ungrunds*). *Ungrund*, or Abyss, is Boehme's term for God (as it will later be that of the Romantics for the Unconscious). God shapes himself into imagehood (*Bildlichkeit*) and thus comes to self-contemplation. The divine imaging is mirrored in the human soul, who sets nature outside herself to serve as a mirror to her will (Hart 1968).

Schelling in his evolution toward mysticism assimilated Boehme's aboriginal imagination into his—continually reworked—philosophical system (particularly in its *Further Expositions* of 1802). In the fashion of the mystics he plays with imagination-words. The German word for imagination, *Einbildung*, is, in fact, a coinage of the mystics; the prefix *ein* refers to stamping or forming a picture *into* the soul, as in the word "impression." Schelling adds to this etymology the sense of *ein* as "one" (Part Four, Ch. II B). Thus he understands imagination as a power for uni-forming as well as in-forming its matter.

The "innermost secret of creation" is to be found in this forming-into-one of the "proto-imaginal" and the "counter-imaginal" (*das Vorbildliche— das Gegenbildliche*). The former is the infinite, essential, and general; the latter is the finite, formal, and particular. Their unity, or rather their identity, constitutes the Absolute (Schelling 1802, 446). But the Absolute can be seen under two aspects. Insofar as the proto-image is apprehended as "imaged into" (*eingebildet*) the counter-image, as is essence into form, there is reality or nature. Insofar as the converse aspect is emphasized there is ideality or God. The particular appearances are the "off-images" (as in "off-prints, *Abbildungen*) or copies of the first aspect, while the world of ideas images the second. However, as Hegel (1806) points out, this is figurative language with meager rational development.

There is a tradition in which the figure of the Divine Imagination, unencumbered by metaphysical speculation, evinces an imaginative immediacy and an ardent empathy into the condition of divine existence which silences dialectic caviling: The Sufism of Ibn Arabi. I have eschewed non-Western texts as beyond my competence, but his *Book of Revelations Received in Mecca* (1237), made accessible by Corbin's exegesis (1969), cannot be altogether omitted, since in it the Divine Imagination figures with equal splendor and complexity. Of course, the following sketchy culling of the high points cannot do the book justice.

In the beginning is the Sadness of the Divine Being unmanifest and alone: "I was a hidden Treasure, I yearned to be known" (184), but there is no one to name the Divine Names. The ardent desire for love issues in a Sigh of Self-compassion, which gives rise to a Cloud. This divine Exhalation is the primordial, subtile, existence-originating mass. In it all the forms are both made and received. Here takes place the original theophantic activity. Here the Divine Being shows itself to itself in an act of absolute, self-sufficient Imagination. Imaginative creation is essentially revelation, illumination, manifestation. It does not produce in the Western theological sense, *ex nihilo*, nor is it emanative in the Neoplatonic sense, as an overflow from a plenitude of being. Indeed, it does not issue outside the creator. Instead the Divinity clothes itself, as it were, in the creation. The world is its Appearance, a transparency in which it both manifests and veils itself.

The human imagination is a mediating faculty parallel to the Divine Imagination: As the Divine Imagination is to its imaginative space, that Cloud which arises between the hidden divinity and the world, so the human imagination is to the idea-images, the apparitional forms that are intermediate between the pure spirit and the visible world. In the latter, the human realm, there is a "science of the imagination." It is particularly concerned with imaginal refractions in surfaces like mirrors, where forms appear without being there; the same science also attains to paradisiacal contemplation; above all it meditates on God's theophanies. As for the worldly imagination itself, Ibn Arabi distinguishes an imaginative faculty conjoined to a subject and responsible for deliberate or spontaneous "subjective" images, and another power, separable from the individual soul, that produces externally subsisting images visible to mystics. Ibn Arabi admits that all this, known to believers and experienced by mystics, is by rational theoreticians accepted only reluctantly and as allegory.

Mystics are hard to approach: it would be supercilious to construe their figures as mere metaphor, and it is disingenuous to pretend to have a literal understanding. Yet alien as Ibn Arabi's intricate doctrines are, there is in them something that speaks very directly not only to mysteries often touched on in this book but even to those omitted as too grand: how the world of appearance originated, and why it presents itself as image-like and image-able. I do not say that Sufism resolves these enigmas for the non-mystic; I say only that it acknowledges them in terms at once apt, vivid and fervent.

3. The Religious Imagination: Visions and Interpretations. Parallel with open derogation there has always been implicit—and sometimes, as in Thomas Aquinas, an explicit—acknowledgment that the human imagination, far from merely betokening naiveté or a deficency of intellect, has a positive, even an essential role to play in religion. Recently this role has become an explicit topic.

Religious functions are assigned to the imagination both in non-theological and in theological contexts. Of the first, one example was given in Part Two, under "Near-Death Experiences" (Ch. V C). A far more influential case is Dewey's claim that "God" originates in human imagination and expresses its nature. In *A Common Faith* (1934) he takes Kant's reduction of God to a "regulative idea" a step further. The Kantian God is an ideal of reason, by means of which we can see our experience as having an ultimate unifying cause. Dewey now turns it into an ideal of the imagination:

> The idea that "God" represents a unification of ideal values that is essentially imaginative in origin when the imagination supervenes in conduct is attended

with verbal difficulties owing to our frequent use of the word "imagination" to denote fantasy and doubtful reality. But the reality of ideal ends as ideals is vouched for by their undeniable power in action. An ideal is not an illusion because imagination is the organ through which it is apprehended. For *all* possibilities reach us through the imagination. In a definite sense the only meaning that can be assigned the term "imagination" is that things unrealized in fact come home to us and have power to stir us.

So the imagination compounds values into a unitary representation which, although it reflects no real being, is yet not merely illusory, since it expresses the power of ideals to stir us to action: the pragmatist God is an expression of our imagination as the power of possibilities. A critique of the imagination as a possibilizing power was presented in Part One (Ch. IV B).

It is, however, in Christian theology that the powers commonly thought of as imaginative are called on for the most serious service and in a variety of ways, ranging from the strict imagery-function to the general cognitive mode.

First, then, since Christianity is a historical religion, it has at its center a concrete narrative that calls for imaginative absorption, indeed visualization (Dych 1982).

Second, since the sacred scriptures are full of sensory figurative language, their interpretation requires a peculiar power of metaphor. Metaphor therefore becomes a theological issue (Bevan 1938, Ricoeur 1960). In particular, parables, the teaching-metaphors of the Gospels are, it is argued, indispensably imaginative, in the sense that the meaning of a parable is not a literal and extractable moral point but an immanent force for bringing home the human condition: The parable testifies, through a "certain shock to the imagination," that everyday events have divine reverberations (McFague 1975). Perhaps the best example of a parable that requires an imaginatively receptive reading is the story of the prodigal son (*Luke* 15:11). This parable of parables surely presents a scandal to the rational sense of fairness: that the fatted calf should be killed for the return of the dissipated run-away while the dutiful son who stays put is taken for granted. Yet to the concrete imagination it might well serve as an epitome of the inexplicable rule of love.

Third, the imagination is the—carefully circumscribed—agency of "normal" religious visions in Catholic theology. The mystical doctors recognized three kinds of vision: corporeal, imaginative, and purely spiritual. Of these they regarded the imaginative kind as most valuable. It best fulfills the criteria of authenticity, which are designed to exclude both pathological hallucinations and normal internal imagery such as arises out of the personal subconscious. One criterion of authentic visions is that they be natural and divine at once: Both the psychical structure of the seer and the laws of nature must remain largely operative in the presence of a divine intervention that suspends them very discreetly (Rahner 1964).

The content of the mental image can be used as proof of a vision's genuineness only if it clearly exceeds the visionary's individual imaginative and intellectual capacities. Such a proof is so rarely available that authentication normally proceeds not from the content but from the source of the vision: whether it is indeed from God. However, the point at which God affects the soul is usually more interior than either sense or imagination. Hence the mystics, without denying visions, tend to downgrade their importance. They are only a superficial reflection of God's communication. I am reporting here on the most delicate subject in which the imagination is concerned. It is treated by Rahner with an open-minded judiciousness, which should abash too roughshod a scepticism.

To its narrative, metaphorical, and visionary functions, add, fourth and finally, the imagination as a cognitive mode of theology. The power of analogy, the capacity for apprehending similarity in difference, is largely the competence of the imagination; analogies of being, of existence, of relation, of participation, however, are central devices of speculative theology, both of the great medieval systems and of the various modern inquiries. Furthermore, when temporally affected, that is to say, when functioning as the power of memory and expectation, the imagination is indispensable to faith (Hart 1968, Tracy 1986). A contemporary issue is whether it is so as an originatively constructive power (Kaufman 1981), or whether it is so much determined by the historical context that it has to be regarded as a receptive capacity as well (Bryant 1989).

But the most distinct and powerful cognitive role is assigned to it in the imagination-based theology of Thomas. Since he teaches that knowledge requires the turning of the pure intellect toward the mental image (Part One, Ch. II B), human knowledge is essentially dependent on sensory—on spatial and temporal—intuition. From this cognitive constitution follows the theological position of human beings, who by nature desire to know: They are suspended between the eternal and the temporal, the incorporeal and the corporeal, their God and his world. Since the intellect has to turn— or in Thomas's word, to "convert"—to the "phantasm" of the imagination in order to know, it is the imagination that sustains humanity's essential world-dependence (Rahner 1957, 407). The imagination turns out to be nothing less than the faculty for worldliness: the human need and the human ability to be in the world.

Thus in the religious realm the imagination is a seat of this-worldly evil, a source of other-worldly knowledge, and a pivot between world and spirit. The next chapter will show it functioning in a secular mode to build the New Jerusalem.

Bibliography

Abrams, M. H. 1971. *Natural Supernaturalism: Tradition and Revolution in Romantic Literature.* New York: W.W. Norton Company (1973).

Albright, Daniel. 1981. *Representation and the Imagination: Beckett, Kafka, Nabokov, and Schoenberg.* Chicago: The University of Chicago Press.

Augustine. c. 417. *On the Trinity* (XI), edited by Arthur Haddan. Edinburgh: T. and T. Clark (1873).

Baxandall, Michael. 1972. *Painting and Experience in Fifteenth Century Italy: A Primer in the Social History of Pictorial Style.* Oxford: Oxford University Press.

Berkouwer, G. C. 1962. *Man: The Image of God.* Grand Rapids: Wm. B. Eerdmans Publishing Co.

Bevan, Edwin. 1938. *Symbolism and Belief.* Boston: Beacon Press.

Bryant, David J. 1989. *Faith and the Play of Imagination in Religion.* Macon, Ga.: Mercer University Press.

Burton, Robert. 1621. *The Anatomy of Melancholy.* New York: Everyman's Library (1964).

Calvin, John. 1559. *Institutes of the Christian Religion* (I xv 3). Translated by Henry Beveridge. Grand Rapids: Wm. B. Eerdmans Publishing Co. (1957).

Corbin, Henry. 1969. *Creative Imagination in the Sufism of Ibn Arabi.* Bollingen Series, Volume 91. Translated by Ralph Manheim. Princeton: Princeton University Press.

De Quincey, Thomas. 1822. *Confessions of an English Opium-Eater.* Garden City, N.Y.: Doubleday.

Dewey, John. 1934. "Faith and Its Object." Chapter 2 in *A Common Faith.* New Haven: Yale University Press.

Dych, William V. 1982. "Theology and Imagination." *Thought* 57:116–127.

Epstein, Leslie. 1985. "Atrocity and Imagination." *Harper's Magazine,* August, 13–16.

Fox, Robin L. 1987. *Pagans and Christians.* New York: Alfred A. Knopf.

Frye, Northrop. 1963. "The Imaginative and the Imaginary." In *Fables of Identity: Studies in Poetic Mythology.* New York: Harcourt, Brace and World.

Hart, Ray L. 1968. *Unfinished Man and the Imagination: Toward an Ontology and a Rhetoric of Revelation.* New York: The Seabury Press.

Hegel, G.W.F. 1806. *Lectures on the History of Philosophy* (Part III, Sect. 3 D).

Huxley, Aldous. 1955. "Mescaline and the 'Other World'." In *Moksha: Writings on Psychedelics and the Visionary Experience (1931–1963)*, edited by Michael Horowitz and Cynthia Palmer. New York: Stonehill Publishing Co. (1977).

Johnson, Paul. 1983. *Modern Times: The World from the Twenties to the Eighties.* New York: Harper and Row.

Johnson, Samuel. 1759. "The Dangerous Prevalence of the Imagination." Chapter 44 in *Rasselas: Prince of Abyssinia.*

Kaufman, Gordon D. 1981. *The Theological Imagination: Constructing the Concept of God.* Philadelphia: Westminster Press.

Kearney, Richard. 1988. *The Wake of Imagination: Toward a Postmodern Culture.* Minneapolis: The University of Minnesota Press.

Kroner, Richard. 1941. *The Religious Function of the Imagination.* New Haven: Yale University Press.

Ladner, Gerhart B. 1953. "The Concept of the Image in the Greek Fathers and the Byzantine Iconoclastic Controversy." *Dumbarton Oaks Papers*, Volume VII. Cambridge: Harvard University Press.

Locke, John. 1693. "On Languages." In *Some Thoughts Concerning Education* (XI c).

———. 1697. "Similes." In *Of the Conduct of the Understanding* (32).

Lowell, James Russell. 1884. "Rousseau and the Sentimentalists." In *Among My Books.* Boston: Houghton Mifflin Co.

Maimonides, Moses. Later 12th cent. *The Guide of the Perplexed* (II 36). Translated by Shlomo Pines. Chicago: The University of Chicago Press (1963).

McFague, Sallie. 1975. *Speaking in Parables: A Study in Metaphor and Theology.* Philadelphia: Fortress Press.

Moore, Albert C. 1977. *Iconography of Religions: An Introduction.* Philadelphia: Fortress Press.

Newman, John Henry, Cardinal. 1858. *The Idea of a University* (VII 4).

Nichols, Aiden C. 1980. *The Art of God Incarnate: Theology and Symbol from Genesis to the Twentieth Century.* New York: Paulist Press.

Pascal, Blaise. 1661. *Pensées* (82 ff).

Pico della Mirandola, Gianfrancesco. Before 1506. *On The Imagination*, translated by Harry Caplan. New Haven: Yale University Press (1930).

———. 1486. *Oration on the Dignity of Man.* Translated by Robert A. Caponigri. Chicago: Henry Regnery Co. (1956).

Plaut, W. Gunther. 1981. *The Torah: A Modern Commentary.* New York: Union of American Hebrew Congregations.

Plotz, Judith. 1979. "The Perpetual Messiah: Romanticism, Childhood, and the

Paradoxes of Human Development." In *Regulated Children/Liberated Children*, edited by Barbara Finkelstein. New York: Psychohistory Press.

Porteous, N. W. 1962. "Image of God." In *The Interpreter's Dictionary of the Bible*. New York: Abingdon Press.

Rad, Gerhard von. 1957. *Old Testament Theology*, Volume 1, *The Theology of Israel's Historical Tradition*, translated by D. M. Stalker. New York: Harper and Row.

Rahner, Karl. 1957. *Spirit in the World*. Translated by William S. J. Dych. New York: Herder and Herder (1968).

————. 1964. "Visions and Prophecies." In *Inquiries*. New York: Herder and Herder.

Rahner, Karl, and Vorgrimler, Herbert. 1965. *Theological Dictionary*. New York: Herder and Herder.

Ricoeur, Paul. 1960. *The Symbolism of Evil*. Translated by Emerson Buchanan. Boston: Beacon Press (1969).

Schelling, F.W.J. von. 1802. "Fernere Darstellung aus dem System der Philosophie." *Schellings Werke*, Supplementary Volume 1, *Zur Naturphilosophie 1792–1803*, edited by Manfred Schröter. Munich: C.H. Beck and Oldenbourg (1965).

Sheldon, Mark. 1979. "Spinoza, Imagination and Chaos." *Southern Journal of Philosophy* 17:119–132.

Spinoza, Benedict de. 1670. *Theologico-Political Treatise* (I, II).

————. 1677. *Ethics* (II, Prop. 40 ff).

Strauss, Leo. 1952. "How to Study Spinoza's *Theologico-Political Treatise*." Chapter 5 in *Persecution and the Art of Writing*. Glencoe, Ill.: The Free Press.

Thomas Aquinas. 1277. *Summa Theologica* (I 1 9).

Tracy, David. 1986. *The Analogical Imagination: Christian Theology and the Culture of Pluralism*. New York Crossroad.

Chapter II

No-Places and Past Times: Imaginary Worlds

If in theology the imagination serves the other world, it serves this world in politics: in a wide sense civic life is informed or deformed according to the quality of public vision (A). In a narrow sense, the visionary dreams of individual dreamers, shaped into imaginary communities, utopias or "no-places," are expressed in the genre of political fantasy (B). Finally, reflection on the source of political imagining, wide or narrow, soon comes upon the marked role played by the consummated past and its store-house, memory (C).

A. Practical Imaginations: Public Vision

Citizens at large, poets and image-experts, all employ the imagination in politically consequential ways. Poets and experts are here mentioned insofar as they constitute a subspecies of the citizens through which the imagination has become, as it were, professionally political.

1. A "private citizen" is a contradiction in terms (as a "public citizen" is a redundancy): a citizen in the wide sense is any human being who participates in the political community, whether through action, thought, or imagination. Thus the imagination of citizens is, one might argue, the deepest force of political life. Certainly its pathology, its excesses, and deficiencies, are responsible for those publicly orchestrated enormities, from the Right or the Left, that have turned history into a theater of tragedies. The romantic inflammation of the imagination causes war to seem more vivid than peace; the rational desiccation of the imagination prevents it from envisioning the mundane disasters implicit in millennial plans (Oakeshott 1962). The first, the way of eruption, is the way of the agitated young or pseudo-young. Having in any case a suspicion that the world is imaginary and therefore governed by the imagination, they have no use for the homely middle range: they long for immediate liberation from reality and eschew concrete views of life thereafter; they live by dreams of a distant city on a hill but lack a mental map of the road to it. Hence the revealing parole of the students of Paris: "Let the imagination seize power (graffito, May 1968). The second way, the way of radical rationality, is the procedure of those grey souls who become blindly absorbed in the neat constructs and calculations of reason. The young at heart lack the imaginative middle distance; the fanatical planners fail to envision concrete consequences at any range.

If the extremism of the imagination is the chief cause of political harm, a moderated employment is, of course, equally productive of civic good. This sort of imagination underlies the sound, unforced, large patriotism which has its roots in the love of the concrete and the local, in "all the many small images of the great country in which the heart found something which it could fill" (Burke, *Reflections on the Revolution in France* 1790): This imagination lies behind the practical projects that have an integral relation to an actual country. It is hardly necessary to expatiate on the fact that, after all, most considered worldly actions start by being envisioned, which is to say that they undergo a dry run within imaginative space. The soberly ardent—and above all specific—civic imagination is the first testing-ground of reform, where distant visions must show their close-up detail.

2. Yet poets, whose imagination tends to have these qualities, have always had an intense and strained relation to the world of politics; a citizen-poet is a contradiction in terms, suspect in life, even if celebrated in death. In antiquity a famous assault from the philosophical quarter was directed against the inherent civic irresponsibility particularly of the tragic poets. In modern times the attack on poetry and the arts is primarily economic: artistic production is not true, economically profitable production. Thus it is argued in classical political economy that imaginative products do indeed have worth, but unlike the value of other commodities, artistic value is not related to the investment of labor in its products; it "is determined by their scarcity alone . . . and varies with the varying wealth and inclinations of those desirous to possess them" (Ricardo in Heinzelman 1980); as it is humanly invaluable, so art is economically valueless. Consequently the artists are "economically disenfranchised." Hard though a poet work, Yeats says, he will

Be thought an idler by the noisy set
Of bankers, schoolmasters, and clergymen. ["Adam's Curse"]

And Auden in his "Poem In Memory of W.B. Yeats" confirms their opinion:

For poetry makes nothing happen: it survives
In the valley of its saying where executives
Would never want to tamper . . . . [1939]

Just how far this is admission, how far irony, is a subtle problem. That it is not everywhere thought that poetry makes nothing happen is proved by the various modern censorships. Unlike the ancient polis, a modern liberal polity such as ours has really no legitimate relation to the particular substance of imaginative production except to leave it be; consequently politics—usually—holds no danger for poets, and poets, do, in turn, rarely make things happen. Totalitarian states, on the other hand, use poetry or suppress it; thus they acknowledge that when the state is pervasive poetry is powerful (Brann 1985). The rancorous brutalities of the cultural purgations practised by the National Socialists (proclaimed in a language whose demi-rational vulgarity defies English translation), and the byzantine ideological rigors of the more prolonged communist *proletkult* purification are the supreme proof of the political force of poetry, which was nowhere stronger than in pre-glasnost Russia. The poet Mandelstam, who later died in a camp, used to say:

"Why do you complain? . . . Poetry is respected only in this country—people are killed for it. There is no place where more people are killed for it." [Nadezhda Mandelstam, *Hope Against Hope* 1970]

3. Finally those experts at image-making should be mentioned who use the imaging power neither as citizens-at-large nor as poets. They are, for example, the team of Disneyland designers, the "Imagineers," who construct vast imaginary environments for entertainment, or, less innocently, people who transmogrify live candidates into image-products in contemporary political campaigns. Their business is not part of this book (Introduction A 1), though its subtle calculations trade cleverly on the specific characteristic of visual images: the high retention-level of briefly viewed optical information, the apparent veridicality of visual representation, and the inherent manipulability of documentary photography. This new imaging profession has in turn induced a new field, "image-ethics."

One formulation of an image-ethic, though not in the narrow professional sense, is that of Kearney (1988). He sketches the possibility of an ethical imagination in the face of a dual fact: the postmodern deconstruction of the imagination as a truth-telling agency by philosophy and the banalization of the image as a commodity by the mass media (Introduction A 5). He advocates an ethic of discriminating responsibility, which insists that questions of imaginal epistemology be subordinated to the ethical issue. The image-viewer's responsibility is that of responsiveness, of remaining aware of the face of the Other in the mirror play of images, of extending sympathy. The complement of this sympathy is social activism, "the invention of an alternative *social* project" (370) to replace humanist willfulness, theological quietism, and capitalist consumerism. This ethics of the "postmodern" imagination tends to political activism. It is intended not to reestablish the veritable imagination but to teach resistance to illusionism.

There are, of course, myriads of other human functions through which the imagination injects its visions more or less incidentally into the public realm. These three have been salient examples. However there is one area in which politics co-opts the imagination—in the form of fantasy—purposefully and productively: in utopian writing.

B. Utopias: Political Fantasies

"Utopia" means literally "No-placia," the land without locale. The name was coined by Thomas More for the work of that name (1516); it is Greek: *Ou-topia*. More and Erasmus, who engaged in a jocose pre-publication correspondence about the book, also refer to it as *Nusquama*, "No-wheria." Another humanist friend later joined in with *Udepotia*, "Neveria," but that, I shall claim, was inept.

More's "Golden Booklet," as the title page calls it, not only gave its name to the utopian genre but still remains its model work. In acknowledgment of the debt, later works are often named after it—for example, Samuel Butler's retrograde *Erewhon* (1872) and William Morris's nostalgic *News from Nowhere* (1891).

Placelessness is of the utopian essence. More might have called his work *Mē-topia*, which would have meant *Non*-place or *Un*-place. But proper utopias are not simply incapable of taking place; they are not—or should not—contravene the laws of physical space and time. Therefore, if they fail to exist it is human, not material nature that prevents their realization. Thus the utopian type is a kind of fantasy, but one that differs from the sort treated in Part Four (Ch. IV B), the sort that thrives on magic and throws nature to the winds (Crossley 1982).

In fact one might say that utopias are not so much without locale as that they are unlocatable, are conceived as unreachable:

The swarm of thoughts, the swarm of dreams
Of inaccessible Utopia. [Wallace Stevens, "The Man
with the Blue Guitar" XXVI]

Travelers return from Utopia to tell their tale and spend the rest of their lives longing to recover it. At least they do so if they found it a good place: the early utopias are indeed good places. More's "Utopia" can also be read *eu-topia*, the "Good-place," as a poem prefixed to the text reveals. Utopia thus starts off as unattainable eutopia (*1*). In this century the inaccessible dream is paralleled by an inescapable premonition. The designation *dystopia* or "Bad-place" is accordingly introduced (*2*). The relation of the two fantasies is that of fugitive wish-dream to impending nightmare.

Eutopias are, then, not located in any patent place but they are—usually—represented as being in an accessible time, in the narrative present. That eutopias should abscond in space but be present in time follows from their nature as well-conditioned, perfect civic worlds. The clever title *Erewhon* intimates just that: It is not only "No-where" reversed but also "now here" in a two-word anagram. Were a utopia depicted in the mode of bygone history, this would betoken its decline and fall and imply that it had a fatal flaw in it, some deficiency or lack of adjustment. (To be sure, Plato's *Republic* is a supposedly perfect polity that does include as part of its description an account of the corruption inherent within it. But then it is precisely not a utopia, for it is an ideal conjecture of the intellect, not a visible fantasy of political desire.) On the other hand, the future does not lend itself to the eutopian mode either, and futuristic fantasies are by and large dystopias. I will argue that this fact follows from the deepest constitution of the imagination.

So utopia is nowhere in space, though present in time. Thus is determined its peculiar imaginariness: Utopia presents "prescription as description" (Schlanger 1973). It is a conception that appears concretely. A utopia presents itself primarily not as a political theory, or even as a well-designed blue-print, but as a place imagined pictorially. Utopias often include an elaborate rigmarole of protection against discovery precisely because they are presented as concrete earthly environments. They are delineated with depth and color: the accounts are in fact feigned guide-books. The reader of a novel is drawn into its places; the reader of a utopia is taken on a tour of inspection.

This is the character of the genre from the beginning. The title of More's

Utopia begins with the words: "On the Constitution (*Status*) of the Best Republic." Hence it appears at first as a work in the ancient tradition of inquiries concerning the best polity, above all, Plato's *Republic*. However, the same discerning person who composed the prefatory poem reading Utopia as Eutopia also intimates that *Utopia* betters the *Republic* not only in political ideas—which is, albeit most respectfully, pointed out in the work itself—but in mode of presentation:

> Utopia the ancients called me because of my isolation.
> Now I am rival to the Platonic city,
> Perhaps even victor, for what she outlined
> In *written words*, I alone *exhibit*
> In men and means and the best laws. [My italics]

The Platonic republic is, as its narrator Socrates says repeatedly, a city "in speech" only; it is an ideal "exemplar perhaps laid up in heaven for anyone who wants to see" (IX 592). More has invented instead an imaginary city that has the looks of this world in colorful detail. As a fiction that insists on its factuality it is in the most imaginary of imaginative modes. But insofar as it has a certain worldly concreteness, as it can be judged and savored in its sensible consequences, it escapes Bacon's famous dismissal: "As for the philosophers, they make imaginary laws for imaginary commonwealths, and their discourses are as stars, which give little light because they are so high" (*Advancement of Learning* 1605).

Conscientious imaginariness thus characterizes the utopian genre proper. However, the term utopian is often used more widely with denigrating intention. In the Baconian tradition (which in turn comes out of Machiavelli's *Prince* XV), any thought is called utopian that produces schemes perfect in theory but unattainable in large-scale or long-range practice (Mannheim 1929). For example, the voluntaristic communitarian societies of the sort that are occasionally and briefly realized, particularly in America, are always called utopian.

In fact, the word "utopia" has four uses: It means any theoretical scheme, universal or particular, for political and social perfection. It designates the actual community that undertakes to live by it. It is the name of More's book, which often recurs in later titles, and of the particular island community that the book delineates. And finally, it refers indiscriminately to all the other imaginary places, set down in books or imagined in passing, that are meant to display human life reformed. The three meanings particularly taken up here will be the literary genre—political fantasy; the imaginary place— the perfect city; and the image realized—the live utopian community.

1. Eutopia. As has been said, utopia is not political theory incarnate. Political theory analyzes human nature and the human condition and speculates on the control of the one and the reform of the other. Utopias, on the contrary, leap to an imagined ideal end. They are perfunctory about the possibility of real reform, not to speak of the procedure for attaining it—and sometimes even about its desirability. Utopias, especially eutopias, are thus fantasized secular eschatologies, dreams of "heavens on earth."

Hence true eutopias, those that are not political, economic or educational programs thinly disguised as fictions, are more a matter of ritual, mood and setting than of expedients, arguments, and principles (Frye 1965). The utopian rituals, the devices that embody the author's political and social imagination—imagination here in the sense of inventiveness—are what give eutopias such practical applicability as they may have. Utopia-books are, to be sure, also full of bright practical notions and trenchant critiques; these are not, however, my business here.

(Berneri 1950, Louberre 1974, Manuel and Manuel 1966, 1979, Mumford 1922.)

There are a number of typical utopian moods: playful-tart, amazed-worshipful, nostalgic-sentimental, and future-smug. The last is rare, since at least in this century futuristic utopias are usually dystopic. Some of the older projective romances make enjoyable but somewhat chastening reading—not so much when they display the pitfalls of prediction, as when their imaginations have been realized and their conjectures borne out. Last century's marvels turn out to be today's mild conveniences, and the wonders have lost their romance. For example, who can more than mildly admire the shopping malls, catalogue stores and credit cards forecast for Bellamy's Boston of the year 2000 in *Looking Backward* (1887, ch. X)?

The best example of the sentimental eutopia is probably Morris's *News from Nowhere*, whose partial subtitle is "a Utopian Romance." It is in date futuristic but in mood pre-Raphaelite, that is to say, medieval-revivalist; it is a future to return to. *News from Nowhere* is presented as a dream of England purified of industry, once more a green and pleasant land of leisurely crafts and regulated passions. Its mood is twice nostalgic, first in the romantic longing for the past enshrined in the utopia itself and again in the melancholy wish to return to his dream expressed by the dreamer when he awakes. Incidentally, a common feature of most eutopian romances is a frame story in which a character reports—often in the first person singular—a dream or voyage. This narrative device serves to emphasize that the nature of political fantasy is personal and individual and that its imaginary places are inaccessible without the author's guidance.

Many eutopian visitors engage in much worshipful ooh-ing and ah-ing, especially over the feats of science and technology their authors have dreamed up. But the first and most prescient of technological utopias, Bacon's revision of the ancient Atlantis, the *New Atlantis* (1624), is not written in this mood at all. This security-minded island, one big research-complex in feel not unlike Los Alamos, fends off the visitor's curiosity with sinister mystifications. There are quite a few utopias whose authors mix sarcasm with enthusiasm so as to leave it in doubt whether their conception is eutopic or dystopic. For example, in Butler's *Erewhon*, the anti-machine utopia, everything is as backwards and double-edged as the names.

No other utopia, however, is as subtly playful, as tartly delightful, as *Utopia* itself. I am thinking of the reflective depths opened up by its rivalry with Platonic philosophy and the daring of its non-Christian religion, by the ambivalence of its communism (the subject of much debate), the hilarity of its mores, the elegance of its word-play, and above all by its vividly imagined setting and shape—its speaking topography.

(Brann 1972, Vickers in Villgradter and Krey 1973.)

The setting is, after all, what principally distinguishes the utopian fantasy from the ideal state of political philosophy. When Socrates comes to explain the actual founding of his thought-experiment, he simply ejects all inhabitants over ten and starts his young citizens off in the old city (*Republic* 540). When, on the other hand, King Utopus founds Utopia, he begins by digging a great canal to turn the land of the Utopians into a new place, a moon-shaped island—Utopias tend to bring the heavens to earth; as Utopia is lunar, the town of Campanella's *City of the Sun* (1623) is an elaborate model of a heliocentric system. The internal topography of More's island and the lay-out of its fifty-four cities is also pleasantly depicted. In fact the early edition of *Utopia* came with pretty maps; imagine, by way of contrast, illustrating Plato's *Republic!*

In short, utopias, especially eutopias, are first of all "spatial play": "Utopia is first and foremost a spatial organization designed for complete human dwelling, an activation of a sort of dwelling fantasy" (Marin 1984, 203). From the largest to the least feature, these dwelling spaces are visually detailed. Wherever the author's fancy happens to alight, from the priests' feathery vestments in More's *Utopia* to the tea service in Skinner's *Walden Two* (1948)—tall, slender glasses in straw stockings with straps—we are shown utopia in loving detail.

Sir Philip Sidney, in his "Defense of Poesie" (1595) supports these observations when he expresses his preference for "the way of Sir Thomas More's Eutopia" over that of the philosophers. For utopia is a form of poetry, and poetry is, in the tradition of *ut pictura poesis* (Part Four, Ch. I

B), "a speaking *Picture*, with this end, to teach and delight." Here I have dwelt more on the delight than the dogma.

Utopias, then, at least of the eutopic sort, are, in sum, delineations of fantasy-communities, not physically impossible but humanly improbable. The pleasure and profit in these imaginary civic worlds is that they express not so much the authors', the private dreamers', theoretical ideas as their social sensibilities: from the encompassing setting to the least detail, utopias manifest the looks of a reverie-designed habitat—serene and handsome.

Yet eutopias are, all in all, oddly dim, imaginatively subdued, for works of fantasy. There are several reasons: First, obviously, those utopian novels that are perfunctory covers for social schemes will be as imaginatively thin as any literature with ulterior motives tends to be. Again, being at bottom literary daydreams, eutopias induce that faintly repelled tedium so often aroused by the exhaustive expression of other people's desire. Third, reading several utopias in a row has a satiating effect. Unlike the fictive places of great novels which never stand in each other's light, all their little spots of invention are oddly inadditive: they damp each other's distinctiveness, without summing into one intenser vision. But first and last, the utopian life they describe—even those works which have behind them a genuine envisaging impulse—is apt to be, for all its vivid detail, colored pastel to dull grey over all, because utopia inevitably requires the management of the passions, whether they be merely gentled or quite rooted out. This neutering of the human soul informs the whole community and occasionally gives it the feel of dim Hades. Max Beerbohm wrote:

So this is Utopia.
    It is? Well—
I beg your pardon;
    I thought it was Hell.

However, for literary utopias Hell is too hard a word. They approach neither the splendid pandemonium of Milton's *Paradise Lost* nor even the hermetic horror of Sartre's *No Exit*. They are just, somehow, faint: unfree and uninvigorated by what has been called by an anti-utopian the "right to unhappiness."

Utopia is, next, not only a literary genre but the vision of a living community. Utopian attempts occurred in antiquity, especially the misguided projects for realizing Plato's ideal polity in actual communities called *Ouranopolis*, meaning "Heaven-City," and *Platonopolis* (in Villgradter and Krey 1973).

But for really tenacious utopianism America was the chosen continent

(Eliade 1965). Here was a large and lovely land both fit and free for settlements in which

> to follow out one's day-dream . . . , though if the vision have been worth the having it is certain never to be consummated otherwise than by a failure.
> [*Blithedale Romance* 1852]

Thus Hawthorne writes in his novelistic account of the dissolution of Brook Farm, the most gracious of living utopias, nine miles out of Boston. It was an intellectuals' idyll gone the way intellectuals' dreams do go, the way of self-destruction. Hawthorne had the sense that the finer the utopian vision the more short-lived its realization. But fine or crude, fantastic or pedestrian, a similar fate overtook communities established during the great time for utopian foundation, the nineteenth century, especially the middle decades. They are all gone except for the Amana villages founded in Iowa in 1854. These converted their plan of communal property into a stockholders' corporation and are now, though not without problems, a thriving, cozy pastoral with a profitable refrigerator plant.

What made America the home of choice for all those "heavens on earth," these "pocket editions of the New Jerusalem," as the utopian socialists were sarcastically denominated in the *Communist Manifesto* (1848)? It was a fusion of millennial expectations with paradisiacal recollections. It was a sense that intellectual progress had brought close the possibility of perfecting human institutions, fused with antique dreams of such occidental realms as the Hesperides of the setting sun, the Western Elysium, and the lost Atlantis. But above all, the idea of progress was merged with the Christian vision of the Garden of Eden and the City on the Hill.

In this century, utopian foundations, ephemeral or longer-lived, go on sporadically all over the world. One need only to visit the more established among them to know that though theory may steer them and hard work drive them, it is the imagination that keeps them buoyant.

(Doig 1976, Holloway 1951, Roehmer 1981.)

2. Dystopia as a recognized type belongs preeminently to this century, for it represents an accommodation of the utopian form to the horrors of political totalitarianism combined with technological control. As eutopias are wishful daydreams so dystopias are "cities that menace in nightmares and maledictions," in the words of Italo Calvino's *Invisible Cities*, that compendium of city-essences (1972). Yet there is an exception: The earliest prose utopia is a *bona fide* dystopia, namely the ancient island of Atlantis, the predecessor of Bacon's research compound, whose horrid topography is minutely described in Plato's *Critias*. It is a geometrically designed island prison, originating in the violence done to nature by Poseidon, a stronghold inhabited by degenerate half-gods, stuffed with raw materials and technological devices and barricaded by concentric circles of alternating land and water diametrically sliced by a vaulted canal. Its inner temple is gigantic and has "something barbaric" about it. The Atlantan taste seems to prefigure the designs of Hitler's architect Speer.

The Platonic dialogue breaks off abruptly just as Zeus is about to speak in judgment of the Atlantans, but we are told that their island had sunk into the Western sea some nine thousand years before the narration. The evil is in the past—as is everything of significance among the ancients. Modern utopias differ on this crucial point: The horror is almost always set in the near or not so remote future. In fact a few dystopias, with specific locales and futures close enough, have been overtaken by real time so that the projected terror of totalitarianism is relieved by the actual fact. Above all there is Orwell's *1984,* published in 1949, the most distinguished of the English dystopias, whose non-realization was celebrated some years ago with expressions of gratitude for the fact that the waking had turned out to be better than the dreaming. But, of course, prevention is the purpose of dystopias—they are written so that they may not come true. So, it must be admitted, they serve an even more urgent need than do eutopias.

As all dystopias are not futuristic, so some future-utopias are not dystopic. The former case is rare: Plato's ancient Atlantis has been mentioned. There is also Swift's Lagado, to be read as "Lag-a-do," the floating island cruising around lat. 46N, long. 183, and visited by Gulliver in 1717; it is a hilarious monument to the civic inefficiency of theoretical science. Its modern descendant, however, Arno Schmidt's orientable island, the *Republic of Artists and Scientists* (1957), is set in a post-nuclear-war future. Located in the horse-latitudes, it rotates about itself at increasing speed because its American-Russian co-managers keep giving the engineers contrary orders.

Over the last three centuries there have indeed been a few futuristic utopias intended as eutopias. In the first of all future-utopias, Mercier's *L'An 2440* (1771), the protagonist walks forth into a beautified Paris where the Bastille has been leveled (an event that was in fact less than two decades off). Morris's *News from Nowhere* (1891) is set in an England of unspecified future time but the mood is idyllic. Wells's *A Modern Utopia* (1905), an international, scientifically planned welfare state, "an imaginary whole and a happy world," can no longer be envisioned, he explains in his "topographical" first chapter, as being a traditional utopia, a small, static, isolated "no-where"; it must be spread over the whole real earth, a world state. Wells glories in "liberties of steel," "stupendous libraries," and like modernisms. He emphatically means his utopia, the first realistic technological prognostication, to be eutopic in its fusion of rationalistic universalism with individual uniqueness. In his macro-views he manages to be remarkably prescient and yet without much insight. It has, however, been argued that his enthusiasm is much more complexly qualified than appears at first reading and that the mass of oppositional dystopic science fiction he spawned is by no means merely parodistic—that Wells himself intended to give his future-visions a dystopic cast (Hillegas 1967).

There are many other optimistic science fantasies, but more numerous and more heartfelt are the anti-technological warnings and wish-fulfillments (Morgan 1980). A trendy example is Callenbach's *Ecotopia* (1975), set in 1999, a generation after the supposed secession of the Western states from the Union. They have formed a self-isolated nation dedicated to the use of natural foods and fabrics, to acting out fantasies, and to universal hugging.

Nevertheless, the most serious works are, as ever, dystopic. A confirming example is the latest of the new line of feminist utopias, Margaret Atwood's *The Handmaid's Tale* (1985). It is the scary story, set in the near future, of the United States converted into an extreme fundamentalist theocracy, the Republic of Gilead, a bigoted society in which women are rigidly subordinate and ruthlessly exploited.

The eutopian fancy feels free to gather blooms in the meadow of memory as it follows its political predilections. The dystopic imagination, however, does not go to work with pleasure. While eutopia lightens present dissatisfactions by means of freely envisaged alternatives, dystopia dwells on present fears and follows them out to the worst-case conclusion. Dystopia is a *reductio ad finem* to which the imagination is driven, not drawn, except in horrified fascination.

As I shall argue (C), the future is that phase of time inherently inaccessible to the imagination, for in itself the future has no face and hence no image. It is mere unformed possibility. Consequently, certain modern mystic millennial utopias are entirely indeterminate and devoid of concrete images. There is, for example, the utopia of pure possibility pursued by "the man without qualities," the Protean hero of Musil's great novel-fragment by that name (begun c. 1924), a life without fixed qualities or commitments. Insofar as a future-utopia does assume an imagined shape, one that is not merely a nostalgic borrowing from the past, it is bound to be an inexorably magnified projection of presently looming dangers, for the utopian impulse is not often aroused—as it was in Wells—by faith in present trends. At any rate, future-utopias may be shaped in the image of a golden past or a dark present, but the future itself is essentially invisible.

Dystopia puts the imagination in the service of dread, and presents as the ultimate dread the extirpation of the imagination itself. This fact is exemplified in two of the best known dystopic works, Huxley's England-dystopia *Brave New World* (1932) and Vonnegut's United States-dystopia *Player Piano* (1952). In both, imaginative literature is persecuted as subversive. But the most explicit and poignant case is made in Zamyatin's One-State-dystopia *We* (1922). This powerful and subtle nightmare of the total, the crystal-pure, scientific state is the matrix of all twentieth-century totalitarian dystopias. It itself had as political inspiration the then nascent Soviet dictatorship, while its literary antecedent must surely be Dostoevsky's dystopian "palace of crystal which shall be forever unbreakable, . . . whereat no one shall put out his tongue" (*Letters from the Underworld* X). The mathematical hero of *We*, D503, the engineer of the space ship Integral, becomes incurably diseased: He develops a soul (Sixteenth Entry). This diagnosis is explained to him in as precise and inadvertently poetic a delineation of the imaginative memory as literature offers:

> . . . You are a mathematician, aren't you?"
> "Yes."
> "Well, then—take a plane, a surface—this mirror, say. And on this surface are you and I, you see? We squint against the sun. And here, the blue electric spark inside that tube, and there—the passing shadow of an aero. All of it only on the surface, only momentary. But imagine this impermeable substance softened by some fire; and nothing slides across it any more, everything enters into it, into this mirror world that we examined with such curiosity when we were children. Children are not so foolish, I assure you. The plane has acquired volume, it has become a body, a world, and everything is now inside the mirror—inside you: the sun, the blast of the whirling propeller, your trembling lips, and someone else's. Do you understand? The cold mirror reflects, throws back, but this one absorbs, and everything leaves its trace—forever. A moment, a faint line on someone's face—and it remains in you forever. Once you heard a drop fall in the silence, and you hear it now. . . . "
> "Yes, yes, exactly. . . . "

The attendant doctor then pronounces: "A soul? . . . We'll soon return to cholera if you go on this way . . . I told you, we must cut out imagination. In everyone . . . extirpate imagination!"

In sum, as in eutopia the passions are mollified and the imagination is damped, so in dystopia the passions are denatured and the imagination is rooted out. In either case, in all utopias, it is as if the imaginary community could not itself accommodate the imagination, for it subverts the perfect secular—as opposed to the transcendent—stasis of their design. Wish-fulfilling daydreams are notoriously reiterative and rigid. Political fantasies, it turns out, are members, albeit rather superior members, of that class.

C. Memories: Private Reveries

Spatial and temporal play are a standard feature of eutopias: "No-places" are more often than not placed in a minutely imagined nowhere; they are dated neither in the past nor in the future and, while often contemporary with the narration, are not represented as practically accessible in the present either. What phase of time feeds such civic dreams—and for that matter the whole universe of imaginary worlds, especially private reveries? It is, I claim, a kind of past (*1*). Moreover, since the past is present through remembering, it is the past characteristically filtered by memory (*2*).

1. The Phases of Time. Utopia and Faerie (the locale of fairy-tales, so named by Tolkien) share a spatial mode, the imaginary place (Crossley 1982). Together with dreaming and fantasizing they also share a temporal mode, that of "once upon a time": whatever the time of their existence, the mode of their narration is that of a remembrance. To show why in particular the past should be the setting and the source of all sorts of imaginariness, it will help quickly to review the three phases of time: future, present, and past (Brann 1983).

The future is, as was said, properly faceless. To attempt to face it, as we are so often urged to do, means to try to see pure possibility. One may speak of it (though the logic of such speech is problematic), but it is, by the very meaning of perception as sense-presence, invisible and, by the very nature of imagining as sense-representation, unvisualizable. One may, to be sure, conjecture about the future; the science of such conjectures is called futurology. It proceeds by the sophisticated extrapolation of trends and is therefore largely concerned with quantitative prognostications. It uses such notions as "standard worlds" and "surprise-free projections," and one needs only to read the conjectures published, say, in the sixties, to see how true is the verse of the German wit Wilhelm Busch:

a. it turns out different, b. than you would guess.

Yet it is not the difficulty in conjecturing the future correctly that makes it essentially invisible. After all, one might simply envision the future wrongly, as one visualizes people one has never met and places one has never been to. My claim is that if there is a genuine future, a state that is unreservedly yet to be, it is not so much invisible as non-visible. Literal foresight is a logical impossibility. We have no natural faculty for seeing what will be, as we *do* have vision for what is, memory for what was, and imagination for what neither was nor is nor will be.

From a global, impersonal, point of view one might say that the human future is all the states of affairs that are now possible and have never yet occurred—all those that, as soon as they start happening, will be called "new." The trouble is that not the future alone brings newness. As Harry Truman was fond of saying, "The only thing new in the world is the history you don't know." It is, moreover, not only the historical past that is, for the most part, new to us; our own memory, too, in its imaginative function produces novelty. So newness is not a unique mark of the future but belongs to whatever is news to us as individuals. Moreover, the future is in any case always experienced in the present when it has ceased to be about to be. Newness describes nothing determinate until it is a little old.

Yet, it might be objected, people do make images of the future—futuristic images. Well, aside from the fact that Futurism as a fashion was a period-style like any other—the attempt to exploit the force and aura of machines in the visual arts—one need only survey the futuristic illustrations of science fiction to see how present-bound they are (Morgan 1980). In fact, illustrators proceed analogously to the futurologists: They extrapolate from the present; they deform, magnify, conflate. But above all, they archaize: give wings to a galleon, shape a space ship after a Roman sarcophagus (the movie *2001*) and dress the minions of the Evil Empire as Teutonic Knights (the movie *Star Wars*). In sum, the imagery of the future is not essentially distinct from any other fantasy: just as all numbers but zero can be assigned either a positive or a negative value or be taken as absolute, so all imaginary images can be *thought of* as present, future, past, or atemporal. But they cannot all be so *seen*, for the future is without sensory content. Very correctly does H.G. Wells end his tome on human happiness (1931) with a paean to the future which makes the universe "bright with the presence of yet unimaginable things."

Next comes the present, which in the strict mathematical sense is not a phase of time but the limit between past and future. The properly human present is the "specious present" or moment, long enough to accommodate the very fast iconic processes of perception and the somewhat more extended retentions of short-term memory (Part Two, Ch. III A). This present is that phase of reality where things are immediately and materially perceived. From the common agreement that the present is the real it does not follow that it is the actual, in the sense that it is humanly most significant.

Those who hold that it is both tend to argue that the past is not only irrevocable but also irrecoverable—that it is essentially bygone (Mead 1930).

The senses most proper to functioning usefully *in medias res*, here and now, are touch and the other unmediated senses, aided by unreflective sight and hearing. There is an old argument, started by Aristotle, to the effect that it is impossible to imagine in the perceptual present. There is also a newer, apparently contrary, argument claiming that the imagination is in fact the faculty responsible for turning sensory data into perceptions. The latter function of the imagination is transcendental and takes place on a level beneath imagery. The former restriction on its use seems to me too absolute: It may not be possible to imagine the strictly perceptual present, but I will urge in the Conclusion that it is not only possible, it is the best part of imaginative life, to imagine what is present *in* the present. The point here, however, is that the present cannot be the source of imaginary worlds, for it is a brief state, not a full store.

By the past, finally, I mean here neither the factual nor the conjectural totality of events dated before the present here and now. Those form a past which belongs to everybody and nobody; it is as inaccessible to the imagination as the future is, though in a different logical mode. I do mean the remembered past, the appropriated part of the past. There are two sources of memory: eye-witness experience and second-hand report, whether verbal or imagistic. But once these have been absorbed into long-term memory they are often distinguishable only by the extraneous knowledge of their origin. There are, for instance, people to whom events that occurred early in the first century of our era are more vivid than anything in their own time. They know that their source is Scripture but they remember them as if they had been there.

The memorial past does not run into the present. It is a fact of both human experience and empirical psychology that the formation of long-term memory takes time. Extremely recent events are not properly past; they seem revocable to the psyche. Witness viewers' tolerance for instant-replay on television, which they are inclined to regard as "live." Or take a more serious instance, the way time oscillates at the moment of a catastrophe, when we live, in flashes, back before the impact, as if all were still well. Indeed experiments show that details of scenes that are not remembered immediately after viewing are recovered later, which means that memory takes time to develop itself. The remote past does not creep but leaps into present consciousness.

So also for the medium-range past. It is a common experience that for weeks or months or even years lost loves and painful episodes go underground and are unavailable to visual memory. It is partly because the person shrinks from looking within, but more because the imagery simply refuses to present itself even to the most longing inner eye. Especially in dreams is the memory recalcitrant. Just when a bereavement is most oppressive by day do the missing figures abscond, refusing the summons of daydreams and eluding rendezvous in dreams at night. The consolidation of memory takes time—and it takes forgetfulness. An accessible long-term memory is conditioned on the ability to forget. Indeed, for wrongs suffered the pagan cure of forgetting is probably more conducive to a just and clarified memory than the Christian virtue of forgiving.

The rule of the middle distance holds, interestingly enough, not only for the private but also for the common memory. Not only for painful episodes—witness the historiography of Vietnam—must distance be gained so that history may begin. For the passage of modes, too, the rule holds: Even the most fulfilling of styles go "out of style," and whatever social and economic factors may bring about their oblivion, there is usually also a particular inner condition that makes the passage possible. It is "aesthetic fatigue," the invisibility bred by familiarity (Kubler 1962). But let the stylistic shapes pass deep enough into the common past, and the time will come for a revival analogous to the eventual repossession of personal experience—the renascence in history. "At certain junctures, people are . . . capable of anamnesis" (Yerushalmi 1989). The prime example in our tradition is the periodic resuscitation of antiquity, especially in the Renaissance itself. It was, as it happens, preceded during the Middle Ages by a number of minor renascences; these were transitory "galvanizations" of a fairly recent, and in many ways still present, past. The great Renaissance, on the other hand, was not a renovation or refurbishing of a still half-present residue, but the recollection of a distant and dreamlike event, the rebirth of a true past (Panofsky 1960). In a true renaissance the past beckons from the future. There is no greater imaginable glory than that of living in the expectation of a *second* coming. By a "true past" I therefore mean the past perfect, a past remote enough to have undergone the transfigurations of memory.

It is assumed here, because it both seems sensible and has empirical support, that the memorial imagination working underground is some-how—the precise means remain an enigma—continuous; in other words, the past is carried forward and reworked over natural time. Bachelard (Part One, Ch. IV C) has indeed broached the opposite notion that the memory-image is not sent up as an echo of the past but "on the contrary: through the brilliance of an image, the distant past resounds with echoes." This must mean that imaginative memory works by reaching back into a past that has stayed in its temporal place—an intriguing but unintelligible notion.

Before I detail what the transformations of memory are, something should be said of the misprisions of remembering. Like all human capabilities, memory has its pathologies, not of the clinical but of the spiritual sort. By far the harshest is the bleak amnesia, the inner suppression, which desolates the psychic landscape. It has an external counterpart, the memorial "lobotomizing" practised by totalitarian regimes, through which they devastate the public space, destroying its traditional memories and filling it with official memorials, "the melancholy flowers of forgetting," as Milan Kundera calls them (*The Book of Laughter and Forgetting* 1979).

Another sickness is much gentler, not to say sweeter. It is nostalgia, literally "return-ache," first named in a treatise published in 1688 and there identified, in the form of homesickness, as a sometimes mortal disease. By the second half of the eighteenth century it had metamorphosed into a distinctive sensibility, a luxuriating melancholy for all things gone, be they in the personal or the historical past (Brandt 1978), a romantic missing of bygone "worlds" (Casey 1987). The essence of this characteristically romantic feeling is a vague longing for the past *as* past, often a past that was never a real present. It is a mark of this sentiment to venerate in traditions their age rather than their merit. It is, for example, a sign of nostalgia to love a ruin as a ruin rather than as a clue for recovery and reconstruction. This "ruin-sentiment," a "delicious disease" that became an epidemic in the Romantic period, is still to be met with (Macaulay 1953). Nostalgia is a—mildly—perverse sentiment partly because the places that make the most romantic ruins are those whose charms are mainly retrospective, places like medieval castles, to whose amenities in their own day no sensible person would want to be consigned. Good places, conversely, make bad ruins. For beauty wants to be seen intact, and its ravaging ought to induce an access of sharp privation rather than a sense of sweet nostalgia. That is why the pedantic measuring and cataloguing that preoccupies imaginative archaeologists studying great periods is so reminiscent of the obsessive busyness displayed by people trying to live with a loss—we wish the Greek temple whole, though we might savor a Roman bath as a romantic ruin.

Nostalgia-movements arise when a sound sense of the past has been disrupted. There is a shallower nostalgia for the fashions of the previous generation and a profounder nostalgia for the traditions of the past. Both movements are flourishing at present; the second is richly described in Lowenthal's *The Past Is a Foreign Country* (1985), a mine of all the modes of luxuriating in the historical past. At the worst they represent a self-indulgent substitute for the necessary effort of appropriating the past, though at best they do keep the past popular—and popularity is better than oblivion. There is, after all, something healthy in glamorizing the past in the face of the rush to eradicate it. In fact, the occasional sense of sorrow for all the souls and all the settings that have come and gone, for all the irrecoverable human charms and communal efflorescences lost to our view and withdrawn from our love by the mere accident of time, the impatience, now and then, with the fragmented visual testimony and with the sparse written record from which we reconstruct the worlds that have passed away—these are a healthy rebellion against the loss of human substance to time. And as it is with the common, so it is with the personal past.

For "genuine sanity," says Schopenhauer, "lies in perfect recollection" (*World as Will and Representation* III 32). Of course it does not lie in preserving all daily detail in memory. The memories of most days "cover each other, as it were" in such a way as to make them individually unrecognizable. In the routine of life, he must mean, one image stands for a myriad of mundane days. The repetitions of life are oddly fugitive; they add into one dim atemporal scheme. But special, significant events—say the first and last day of a personal epoch—ought to be recoverable in memory. To have lost the clue to these is to have lost one's temporal self (Brann 1983). Sanity, however, is not all this past supplies.

2. Past Perfect. For the past, which means, of course, the memory, is the source of imaginary worlds. The memorial past I have in mind here is not the inferred, intellectually reconstructed past that the discipline of history chiefly yields. History goes for the "longue durée" (Braudel 1958), the intellectual account of long-term developments. However, this passing past, this temporally elongated past, is only weakly imaginable. For the adequate imaging of long temporal passages must itself take time, and a human being does not have that sort of time or memory. In thought and speech one may summarize the eventful changes of a decade in a paragraph, but what would an imaginal abbreviation of a long passage—not of its inception, climax and conclusion, but of its extended passing—be? Adequately imaging the passage of a long, "real" time is a practical impossibility—the imagination does not belong to the school of annalistic history. The past I mean is therefore not the intellectually inferred but the personally envisioned past, what emerges

When to the sessions of sweet silent thought
I summon up remembrance of things past . . .

This past of the personal memory also includes, beside the remembered perceptions of the bygone presents which are its workaday matter, all sorts of imagery-experiences not integrally traceable to any identifiable sensory origin. The universally accessible experiences of this sort are dreams (Part Two, Ch. V C). They are often triggered by the day's events and always fed by the common objects of perception. All the imagery of dreams is generically the same as what the waking world provides. Thus it is namable: men, women, children, monsters, animals, cities, canals, oceans, mountains, caves. Yet often these objects have never before been seen: they are at once spell-bindingly novel and heart-breakingly familiar. How often does one find oneself of a night in one's hometown, the very city that daily presents its mundane sights to casual perception, but whose streets and circles, whose harbor and campus, have suffered a sea-change into something rich and strange—as rich in significance as they are strange in looks?

The existence of never-perceived imagery, is, then, a matter of common experience. Its assignment to the past may appear to be a manner of speaking suggested by the mere sense that the imagination-imagery seems to rise up from the same source as do memory-images. Coleridge called this source "the reservoir of the soul," the "confluence of our recollections in the twilight of the imagination and just at the vestibule of consciousness"; in fact, he intimates that the memory is nothing but the unconscious part of the imagination. This identification is generally seconded by poets and psychologists. It is to be understood in two ways at once. First, memory, as a reservoir or treasury, is, after all, nothing but the inferred psychic place in which a hypothetical stock of memories is present for re-presentation to consciousness as images: memory is the storehouse of the imagination. Second, since imagination-imagery often transmutes perceptions or casts loose from particular experience, it is supposed that the imagination is already active within the memory: Memory is the work-place of the imagination. As Henry James puts it with precision:

> I dropped it [the idea] for the time being into the deep well of unconscious cerebration: not without the hope, doubtless, that it might eventually emerge from that reservoir, as one had already known the buried treasure to come to light with a firm iridescent surface and a notable increase of weight. [*The Art of the Novel: Critical Prefaces* 1907]

And Dilthey says, summing up the thought:

> As there is no imagination which is not based on memory so there is no memory which does not contain within itself an aspect of the imagination. Recollection is simultaneously metamorphosis. [*Imagination of the Poet* 1887]

So we may say that the imagination is not incidentally but essentially nourished by the past—if the past is understood to be whatever has passed into and through the underground workshop of the soul. There exists, of course, a powerful psychoanalytic theory concerning the processes at work there: condensation, displacement, projection. What follows is, in contrast, not a hypothesis about the mechanism of the unconscious but a brief descriptive catalogue of the transmutations perceptions undergo as they are passed through memory (a) and a description of a most significant memory-event, the "moment of being" (b).

a. The Crucible of Memory: Stasis and Catharsis. Stand-still and purification are the two great works that the imagination effects in the memory.

Memory-images are essentially stills, vignettes, moments caught out from the passage of time and fixed, picture-like. "Capture a Maryland Memory" says a bumper-sticker invitingly. "You have painted the walls of my memory" says a fictional auditor gratefully to the Greek bard Simonides, the same who discovered memory-imagery (Mary Renault, *The Praise Singer* 1978). The primarily momentary, pictorial, static character of imagery, which will be emphasized one last time in the chapter on places (Ch. III A), is confirmed not only by introspection but by the arts and sciences of the imagination as detailed throughout this book. Psychologists in particular often refer to the instantaneousness of imagery and to its immobility (Part Two, Chs. II B, IV B).

I think that imagery is more likely to be conceived as static than as kinetic because the order of time is more easily abrogated in the imagination than the shape of space. Anecdotal evidence for the fact abounds. For example, Nadezhda Mandelstam describes in her memoirs the "distinguishing feature" of long-term memory: the ability to conjure up in the mind's eye moments, static like a clear snapshot, frozen rather than moving scenes (*Hope Abandoned* 1972, 600). And in that wonderful children's book about the relation of the imagination to forgetfulness, Michael Ende's *Neverending Story*, there occurs a figure named, emblematically, Yor the Miner, blind by day and sighted in the dark, who digs deep in the shafts of the earth looking for the fragile stained-glass tablets, delicate transparencies, that are the forgotten dreams and memories of mankind. These are only a small sampling of the many texts remarking on the picture-likeness of memory-images.

Ivan Doig, a memorialist of the American Northwest, tries to explain the fitful instantaneousness of the memories he finds to be essential to daily living:

Memory is a set of sagas we live by . . . . If somewhere beneath the blood, the past must beat in me to make a rhythm of survival for itself—to go on as this half-life which echoes as a second pulse inside the ticking moments of my existence—if this is what must be, why is the pattern of remembered instants so uneven, so gapped and rutted and plunging and soaring? I can only believe it is because memory takes its pattern from the earliest moments in the mind, from childhood. And childhood is a most queer flame-lit and shadow-chilled time.

The incident-riven vastness of childhood time spawns flashing, though fixed, pictures. Yet it seems that at bottom the stasis of memory has more to do with what might be called a quasi-metaphysical propensity of the imagination: its tendency to offer sudden archetypal configurations for brief contemplation, to reveal essence-in-appearance through the only approach to timelessness that the temporal soul possesses, that psychic *nunc stans*, the moment.

Complementary to their stillness is the fact that memories do not return in temporal sequence. By dint of special effort it is, to be sure, possible to reconstruct stretches of contiguous memories. Yet their natural association is not by time but by significance. The memory is not a diary, but what in Biblical studies used to be called a "harmony"—a collection of parallel passages. It is this very power of memory to escape from the time sequence that makes the thickening of perception into experience possible (Koselleck 1979). More to the present point, it allows the distillation of one essential picture from repetitious, routine sights. Moreover, just as by passage through memory the attenuating spread of time is condensed, so the distracting variety of things is leached out. The memories that survive are single-minded wholes with significant features. As Janet Lewis writes of Isak Dinesen's *Out of Africa*:

> It has been filtered through memory and suffused with longing. Details that have been filtered through memory have more truth in them than facts in general because they carry an emotional content.

And yet memory purifies its contents of the perturbations of passion:

> For pain must enter into its glorified life of memory before it can turn into compassion. [George Eliot, *Middlemarch*]

What these passages together bring out is not at all that memory weakens affect, but that, as it drains the past of emotion it invests memories with feeling. It replaces the roiled surface of emotion with limpid depths of feeling (Ch. III B below).

But above all, the crucible of memory perfects and consummates the past by removing its scenes from the ravages of time and purging them of the taint of mortal misery. Probably the best-known expression of this fact of memory is the encouragement Aeneas gives his comrades in their trouble:

One day perhaps even this will delight you in memory. [Virgil, *Aeneid* I]

It is not so much a matter of that famous "emotion recollected in tranquility," as of images returning tranquilized in recollection—stilled by "the hush of solemnity of incipient transfiguration" as Marilynne Robinson says in her gemlike novel about memory, *Housekeeping* (1981). More, it is a common experience that the places of the past, especially childhood, have a golden sheen and a bright vividness belonging to the transmutations of memory. This experience is tellingly described by Scott in the *Raj Quartet*. Sarah Layton returns to the India of her childhood, to Pankot and Rampur:

Their reality was only a marginally accurate reflection of the mind picture she had of them . . . . There was too much space between the particular places she remembered—places which were strongholds of her childhood recollections— and the strongholds themselves had a prosaicness of brick and mortar that did not match the magical, misty but more vivid impressions they had left on her when young. [*The Day of the Scorpion* I 1]

But if the laity of the memory casually accomplish such transmutations, its professionals, the writers, take them as their difficult mission: "To transmute the raw perpetual motion of life into the perfect immobility of art," to create "endless Edens, shapely worlds formed out of the terrible void and the deep blue darkness of endless frightening space"—that is the struggle of a novelist, evidently close to Scott's heart, portrayed in *The Corrida at San Felíu* (I 9).

One could fill a commonplace book with similar observations. The prime work of the imaginative memory is a past fixed, purified, intensified, and glorified into an age of gold.

Pathology sometimes puts the human norm into bright relief. The glorifying memory has a neuropathological instance, called by Sacks, who narrates some cases, "hyper-mnesia" and "incontinent nostalgia" (1987). These recurrent, forced, factual reminiscences are torture for some patients, but for others they come as a hauntingly beautiful return to a lost childhood. It appears that even the abnormally remembered past can be under the aegis of the transmuting imagination. That the life that has passed should tend to return as consummated seems to be not a trifling but a deep condition of human remembering.

b. Moments of Being: C.S. Lewis and Virginia Woolf. There are certain royal moments of memory, transfigured in the manner just described, yet so distinct that they are specially named by those who write of them: "spots of time," "moments bienheureux" or "privilégiés," "Joy." As they are moments of memory so they are high points of the imagination; therefore they are fittingly considered in this section on the intertwining of past, memory, and imagination.

The moment (from a presumed Latin *movimentum*) is a minimal of change in consciousness, the psychic analogue to the physical differential of motion: a pregnant stasis. The Germans call it, aptly, a "glance of the eye" (*Augenblick*), a temporally unitary vision. *The* moment, as a peculiarly rare and significant and memorable present, is a phenomenon that has been noticed in scores of ways (Thomsen and Holländer 1984). It plays a role not only in literature, but also in religion as *kairos*, "the fullness of time," in philosophy as "the existential moment," in history as "the historical moment," in the visual arts as "the pure moment of surrender" to the vision, in human affairs in general as the moment of culmination. The moment in my present sense, however, is most often named and pondered among the writers, poets, and novelists—not surprisingly for it can be vital to the making of poetry:

> For some reason impossible to explain or understand, the flash point in art comes through contact between what has been accumulated (or concentrated in the bloodstream) over the ages and something occurring at a single passing moment which, as a particle in the flow of time, is unique and never to be repeated, yet also eternal by virtue of having been stopped in its tracks. . . . The passing moment is eternal for him who halts it, and his reward for this brush with eternity is a sense of poetic rightness: "How to describe this roundedness and joy?" [Nadezhda Mandelstam, *Hope Abandoned* 1972, 492]

But above all the moment is crucial to the coagulation of consciousness, to the punctuation of life. Something has been said above of Wordsworth's "spots of time" (Part Four, Ch. II B), and Proust's "blissful moments" will be taken up below, under the "topography" of the imagination, since they are quintessentially panoramic. In the middle of our century Virginia Woolf and C.S. Lewis both put moments of vision at the center of their autobiographical accounts, and these will be considered here.

The dominating experience of his early life is denominated "Joy" by C.S. Lewis. It "is here a technical term and must be sharply distinguished both from Happiness and Pleasure." "It is not settled happiness but momentary joy that glorifies the past." Both pleasure and joy are desirable, but unlike the one, the other is not in our power.

It began in childhood, an "enormous bliss" like that of Milton's Eden, a bliss that took the form of desire and lasted only for a moment of time. When it was withdrawn the world turned commonplace again, stirred only by a longing for the longing that had ceased. In a sense everything that ever happened thereafter was insignificant in comparison. The first such event is described as a memory of a memory. When he was a boy, suddenly, as from a depth of centuries, arose the memory of an earlier event in the nursery, trivial in itself but filled with desire, a desire in part for his own past, but largely of something ineffable.

This intense desire might take the form of a shock, a trouble. What the child was troubled by in a second such episode, triggered by the Beatrix Potter book *Squirrel Nutkin*, was "the Idea of Autumn," a kind of ungratifiable longing for its possession. The desire for this desire is the defining characteristic of "Joy." Joy is the cause of a "poignant nostalgia" such as no memory of humdrum happiness can arouse. Like all nostalgia it is more a wish for a feeling than a primary passion.

Then follows a curious turn. Lewis's account of his life, which ends with his Christian conversion, closes with the admission that the subject of Joy has since lost its interest. Not that the visionary gleam has passed away— but he submits the experience to a critique in the light of true spiritual joy. The "dialectic of desire"—by which he seems to mean the infinite regress of longing for longing—has revealed its inadequacy. So also he has come to recognize in himself the "idolatry of images," the failure to understand that the "lower life of the imagination" is not of itself a beginning for the life of the spirit. There is indeed a resemblance, which is not entirely accidental, between the Christian and the imaginative experience. But that is only because all things, not excluding the imagination, reflect heavenly truth. The romantic images of "delectable mountains and western gardens" are, it is true, sheer fantasies, luring the visionary into erotic reverie and even squalid magic. Yet it is not the images that offend—they are only the "mental tracks left by the passage of Joy." What is at fault is the ardent concentration on these mere imaginal traces and the longing for the longing behind by the object of desire. Thus Lewis provides a vivid inside account of the imagination's moments as well as a critique of their abuse by romantics and a reflection on their place in spirituality. He exposes these sudden visions as image-residues of a passing Presence; their merely aesthetic contemplation is unfulfilling because their meaning lies beyond, in a heavenly original not accessible to desirous vision. Nevertheless, he cannot forget them.

It is exceedingly revealing for these momentous experiences to put Virginia Woolf's account in her essay "A Sketch of the Past" (1940) alongside Lewis's meditations. The temporality of the two experiences is alike: an overwhelming suddenness, fleeting in time yet dominating it. However, both the content and its interpretation are very different. For Lewis the moments of Joy bring into view an imaginary world, a realm of fantasy in which the imagination applies its inventive magic to the essentially hopeless task of imaging the world of the spirit. For Woolf the matter of these "moments of being" is not imaginary but something more serious. It is what, at the beginning of this part, I termed imaginative—not fantastic but world-revealing.

Again the origin is in childhood, in remembered picture-moments of great strength, in first impressions of the nursery—a painting in "pale yellow, silver and green. There was the yellow blind; the green sea; and the silver of the passion flowers. I should make a picture that was globular; semi-transparent." These pictures, or impressions mixed of sound and sight, were, she remembers, a rapture rather than an ecstasy; I think she means that it was this world that seized her, not another.

"Those moments—in the nursery, on the road to the beach—can still be more real than the present moment," she says. And then she touches on the very enigma of the image-experience, hesitantly broached in the present book (Part Three, Ch. III C):

> [In] certain favourable moods, memories—what one has forgotten—come to the top. Now if this is so, is it not possible—I often wonder—that things we have felt with great intensity have an existence independent of our minds; are in fact still in existence? And if so, will it not be possible, in time, that some device will be invented by which we can tap them? I see it—the past—as an avenue lying behind; a long ribbon of scenes, emotions.

The strength of these memories lies in their absorbed simplicity, their absence of self-awareness. That may account for their predominance in childhood; they do not, however, cease in later life. Indeed, "the liability to scenes" is, she conjectures, the origin of her writing impulse. For its essence is that "a scene has arranged itself: representative: enduring." "Scene making is my natural way of marking the past."

However, her moments differ from those of all the other writers mentioned in including also experiences of despair. Although they are felt as epiphanies of being, the being that is revealed is not of a divine order beyond but the world as it is in itself. The ordinary day, good, indifferent, or bad, consists of what in her "private shorthand" she calls "non-being" or "cotton wool." The real novelists, Jane Austen, Trollope, Tolstoy, can, she says, convey this sort of flat, arid being as well as the irruptions of true being. For her the accesses of being take the form of a shock:

[W]e are sealed vessels afloat on what it is convenient to call reality, and at some moments the sealing matter cracks; in floods reality; that is, these scenes—for why do they survive undamaged year after year unless they are made of something comparatively permanent?

The being that floods in comes as a pattern; the whole world is for her a work of art of which human beings are a part. Human works of art in turn reveal the truth of it.

There are, of course, many more reports of such memory moments. Esther Salaman has made a collection of them, relying partly on her own experience, partly on literary autobiographies, among them those of Asakov (a Russian memoirist), Darwin, de la Mare, De Quincey, Dostoevsky, Rousseau, and Tolstoy. Her thesis is that these moments, which are by no means confined to extraordinary natures, have remarkably common characteristics: They are involuntary memories out of childhood; they are "like scenes lit up by sheets of summer lightning as one speeds in the train through the night." Be they whole memories or "precious fragments," they are distinguished from the ordinary associative detritus of memory by having as their initial cause a shock or disturbance which imparts to each memory its intensity (1970). My foregoing examples seem, however, to show that these shocks may follow not from an external trauma but from the child's own sudden imaginative vision of the world.

There is, to conclude, yet another feature common to these reported moments. It seems to me that they are really memories twice over—memories of memories. They have been recalled, sometimes re-lived; thus they carry with them a temporally justified sense of remembrance or *déjà-vu*. But they also recover an originating moment in time, their first event; often it occurred in childhood. This original experience, one might wish to say, cannot be memorial, simply because it is itself that unprecedented, memorable first time. It naturally occurs in childhood because children's memories are largely unstocked; they receive rather than revive impressions. Yet the first event itself belies this notion, for it itself already comes in the mode of memory, as a recognition, a recall, even a return. It is an epiphany of something long waiting to appear, an evocation of something expecting to be called. Memory, it seems, has two ancestral lines, one stretching into the temporal past proper and the other into a depth that is both felt and named by analogy to that past. The imagination, one might say, has the power of crossing these two lines with each other. That is the birth of its royal moments.

Bibliography

Atwood, Margaret. 1985. *The Handmaid's Tale*. Toronto: McClelland and Stewart-Bantam (1986).

Bacon, Francis. 1624. *New Atlantis.*

Bellamy, Edward. 1887. *Looking Backward: 2000–1887.* Garden City, N.Y.: Doubleday and Co.

Berneri, Marie Louise. 1950. *Journey Through Utopia.* New York: Schocken Books (1971).

Brandt, Anthony. 1978. "A Short Natural History of Nostalgia." *The Atlantic Monthly*, December, 58–63.

Brann, Eva. 1972. "An Exquisite Platform: *Utopia.*" *Interpretation* 3:1–26.

———. 1983. "Against Time." *The St. John's Review* 34:65–104.

———. 1985. "Politics and the Imagination." *The St. John's Review* 36:10–18. [Abridged version: "Utopia—The Imagined Polity." *This World* (Fall 1984): 78–83.]

Braudel, Fernand. 1958. "History and the Social Sciences: The *Longue Durée.*" In *On History* (Part 2), translated by Sarah Matthews. Chicago: The University of Chicago Press (1980).

Butler, Samuel. 1872. *Erewhon.* Garden City, N.Y.: Doubleday and Co.

Callenbach, Ernest. 1975. *Ecotopia: The Notebooks and Reports of William Weston.* New York: Bantam (1977).

Campanella, Tommaso. 1623. *City of the Sun.*

Casey, Edward S. 1987. "The World of Nostalgia." *Man and World* 20:361–384.

Crossley, Robert. 1982. "Pure and Applied Fantasy, or From Faerie to Utopia." In *The Aesthetics of Fantasy Literature and Art*, edited by Roger C. Schlobin. Notre Dame: University of Notre Dame Press.

Doig, Ivan, ed. 1976. *Utopian America: Dreams and Realities.* Rochelle Park, N.J.: Hayden Book Co.

Eliade, Mircea. 1965. "Paradise and Utopia: Mythical Geography and Eschatology." In *Utopias and Utopian Thought*, edited by Frank E. Manuel. Boston: Beacon Press.

Frye, Northrop. 1965. "Varieties of Literary Utopias." In *Utopias and Utopian Thought*, edited by Frank E. Manuel. Boston: Beacon Press.

Hawthorne, Nathaniel. 1852. *The Blithedale Romance.* New York: W. W. Norton (1958).

Heinzelman, Kurt. 1980. *The Economics of the Imagination.* Amherst: The University of Massachusetts Press.

Hillegas, Mark R. 1967. *The Future as Nightmare: H.G. Wells and the Anti-Utopians.* Carbondale: Illinois University Press (1974).

Holloway, Mark. 1951. *Heavens on Earth: Utopian Communities in America 1680–1880.* New York: Dover Publications (1966).

Huxley, Aldous. 1932. *Brave New World, and Brave New World Revisited.* New York: Harper and Row (1965).

Jehmlich, Reimer. 1980. "Phantastik—Science Fiction—Utopie. Begriffsgeschichte und Begriffsabgrenzung." In *Phanstastik in Literatur und Kunst,* edited by Christian W. Thomsen and Jens Malte Fischer. Darmstadt: Wissenschaftliche Buchgesellschaft.

Jouvenal, Bertrand de. 1965. "Utopia for Practical Purposes." In *Utopias and Utopian Thought,* edited by Frank E. Manuel. Boston: Beacon Press.

Kahn, Herman, and Wiener, Anthony. 1967. *The Year 2000: A Framework for Speculation on the Next Thirty-three Years.* New York: The Macmillan Co.

Kearney, Richard. 1988. *The Wake of Imagination: Toward a Postmodern Culture.* Minneapolis: University of Minnesota Press.

Koselleck, Reinhart. 1979. *Futures Past: On the Semantics of Historical Time.* Translated by Keith Tribe. Cambridge: The MIT Press (1985).

Kubler, George. 1962. *The Shape of Time: Remarks on the History of Things.* New Haven: Yale University Press.

Lewis, C. S. 1955. *Surprised by Joy: The Shape of My Early Life.* New York: Harcourt Brace Jovanovich.

Louberre, Leo. 1974. *Utopian Socialism: Its History Since 1800.* Cambridge, Mass.: Schenkman Publishing Co.

Lowenthal, David. 1985. *The Past Is a Foreign Country.* Cambridge: Cambridge University Press.

Macaulay, Rose. 1953. *Pleasure of Ruins.* London: Thames and Hudson (1984).

Mannheim, Karl. 1929. *Ideology and Utopia.* Translated by Louis Wirth and Edward Shils. New York: Harcourt, Brace and World.

Manuel, Frank E., ed. 1965. *Utopias and Utopian Thought.* Boston: Beacon Press (1967).

Manuel, Frank E., and Manuel, Fritzie, P., eds. 1966. *French Utopias: An Anthology of Ideal Societies.* New York: Schocken Books (1971).

———. 1979. *Utopian Thought in the Western World.* Cambridge: Harvard University Press.

Marin, Louis. 1984. *Utopias: Spatial Play.* Translated by Robert A. Vollrath. Atlantic Highlands, N.J.: Humanities Press.

Mead, George Herbert. c. 1930. *The Philosophy of the Present.* La Salle, Ill.: Open Court (1959).

More, Thomas. 1516. *Utopia.* In *The Complete Works of St. Thomas More,* Volume 4., edited by Edward Surtz, S.J., and J. H. Hexter. New Haven: Yale University Press (1965).

Morgan, Chris. 1980. *The Shape of Futures Past: The Story of Prediction.* Exeter, England: Webb and Bower.

Morris, William. 1891. *News from Nowhere, or An Epoch of Rest, Being some Chapters from a Utopian Romance.*

Mumford, Lewis. 1922. *The Story of Utopias.* New York: Viking Press (1962).

Oakeshott, Michael. 1962. *Rationalism in Politics and Other Essays.* New York: Basic Books.

Orwell, George. 1949. *Nineteen Eighty-Four, Text, Sources, Criticism,* edited by Irving Howe. New York: Harcourt, Brace and World (1963).

Panofsky, Erwin. 1960. *Renaissance and Renascences in Western Art.* New York: Harper and Row (1972).

Roehmer, Kenneth, M., ed. 1981. *America as Utopia.* New York: Burt Franklin and Co.

Sacks, Oliver. 1970–1985. *The Man Who Mistook His Wife for a Hat and Other Clinical Tales.* New York: Harper and Row (1987).

Salaman, Esther. 1970. *A Collection of Moments: A Study of Involuntary Memories.* London: Longman.

Schlanger, Judith. 1973. "Power and Weakness of the Utopian Imagination." *Diogenes* 84:1–24.

Schmidt, Arno. 1957. *Die Gelehrtenrepublik: Kurzroman aus den Rossbreiten.* Frankfurt am Main: Fischer (1964).

Thomsen, Christian W., and Holländer, Hans, eds. 1984. *Augenblick und Zeitpunkt* [subtitle: Studies in Time-structure and Time-metaphorics in Art and Science]. Darmstadt: Wissenschaftliche Buchgesellschaft.

Villgradter, Rudolf, and Krey, Friedrich, eds. 1973. *Der utopische Roman.* Darmstadt: Wissenschaftliche Buchgesellschaft.

Vonnegut, Kurt. 1952. *Player Piano.* New York: Dell Books (1980).

Wells, H.G. 1905. *A Modern Utopia.* Lincoln: University of Nebraska Press (1967).

———. 1931. *The Work, Wealth and Happiness of Mankind.* Garden City, N.Y.: Doubleday, Doran and Co.

Woolf, Virginia. 1940. "A Sketch of the Past." In *Moments of Being: Unpublished Autobiographical Writings,* edited by Jeanne Schulkind. New York: Harcourt Brace Jovanovich (1976).

Yerushalmi, Yosef H. 1989. "Postscript: Reflections on Forgetting." In *Zakhor: Jewish History and Jewish Memory."* New York: Schocken Books.

Zamyatin, Yevgeny. 1922. *We.* Translated by Mirra Ginsburg. New York: Viking Press (1972).

Chapter III

Places and Passions:
The Imaginative World

Pleasure, contentment, happiness are all attendant on real time spent in the real world, on duration. But bliss, which is possible even for those whose lifetime is tainted by some dis-ease, is momentary—the distillations of the imagination are momentary. That was the evidence of the previous chapter. And just as the imagination is temporally discrete, so it is spatially discontinuous; as it has its "spots of time," so it has its places in space. "Place" (*topos*) is an anciently appropriate word for a spot of space, an enclosure circumscribed and colored by the imagination. From the memory-loci, the empty scenes waiting to receive their memory props (Part Two, Ch. III B) to the ensouled panoramas about to be described, the imagination is a setting of settings, a place of places. Landscape is a good word also. Originally *Landschaft* means a cluster of dwellings encircled by fields—a cultivated place, the comforting antithesis of a bewildering and terrifying wilderness (Stilgoe 1982).

Now is the occasion for saying something about this imaginative discreteness I have been delineating, namely that it is the condition of a certain rhythm of life which is not universal: the mundane continuum punctuated by high moments. There are ways of life that oppose such bunching, and value instead a seamless, unitary spread of significance. Buddhist teaching, especially, sets itself against the disequilibrium of strongly distinguished states of mind. But it is a deep characteristic of the Western tradition to distinguish life's extensions into plains and peaks, into the ordinary and the extraordinary, into longueurs and high moments. Not that day-by-day existence, concentrated on avoiding catastrophe and scrabbling for conveniences and comforts, is without contentment and exhilaration, felt in extensive stretches and expressible in poetry:

What a girl called "the dailiness of life"
(Adding an errand to your errand. Saying,
"Since you're up . . . Making you a means to
A means to a means to) is well water
Pumped from an old well at the bottom of the world.
The pump you pump the water from is rusty
And hard to move and absurd, a squirrel-wheel
A sick squirrel turns slowly through the sunny
Inexorable hours. And yet sometimes
The wheel turns of its own weight, the rusty
Pump pumps over your sweating face, the clear
Water, cold, so cold! you cup your hands
And gulp from them the dailiness of life.
[Randall Jarrell, "Well Water," in *The Lost World*]

Thus when Arthur Koestler, in looking for the truth of the imagination, locates it in a bridging between the two plains of our life, the Trivial and the Tragic, he is expressing somewhat too dramatically the Western mode (1977); I would say the Daily and the Festive conforms more to the way our life is actually lived. For even the most effectively busy, productively absorbed daily existence acquires an obscure malaise, a diffuse longing, if it is completely devoid of festivities of the spirit, whether they are private and unscheduled or seconded by a calendar of public celebrations. This necessity may betoken something about the constitution of the World, the Human Being, the Divinity—I am, indeed, sure it does. But my claim here is a more restricted one. It is that the working mode of our imaginative capacity itself underwrites the gathering, the clustering, the compaction of significance that punctuate our life.

In sum, the imagination invests certain places and marks them with passion. This final chapter takes up the power of the imagination for topographical shaping (A) and its capacity for affective saturation (B).

A. The Topography of the Imagination

"Topophilia," or the love of place, is a recurrent term in this context. Thus Bachelard calls his poetics of space a topophilia, and there is an academic investigation into the sensibility of places and spaces entitled *Topophilia* (Tuan 1974). The loving delineation of the lie of the imaginative land, with which this section is concerned, begins with the two writers who have dwelt on the subject most intensely, Proust and Bachelard (1) and goes on to general observations about topophile experiences (2).

But first, a most congenial phenomenology of "place memory" by Casey (1987) should be briefly noticed. Casey observes that *"Place is selective for memories,"* giving those that it chooses, in Shakespeare's words, "a local habitation and a name." And conversely, *"Memories are selective for place,"* adhering to the site that harmonizes with them. Behind that special mutual selection of memories and places there is a general affinity. It derives from the close relation of the "lived body"—the perceiving, psychically informed body, to place. For place, as opposed to the colorless Cartesian location or "site," is a container fit to be "in-habited," a location made intimate; as *lieu intime* it is the proper environment of the human body.

Then through what properties can place accommodate us in this way? Casey observes three, which among them establish the landscape character of places. Landscape is here taken in Straus's sense (*3*), in which "the space of the sensory world stands to that of perception as the landscape to geography." The first landscaping property of places is variegation, their plenitude of interest and promise. Second is their sustaining character, derived from the occluding peripheries that delimit the places above, below, and round-about, orienting us and putting us securely "in place"; a landscape is not infinitely extended but has horizons that encompass us. Last and most relevant to this chapter is their property of expressiveness—places are "sympathetic space." In particular, expressive places have visibility, a radiance and luminosity that cancel the ordinary confrontation between us and the world and let us merge with the landscape. The two following treatments will bear this phenomenology out.

1. Proust's Scenes and Bachelard's Spaces. Proust's fictional practice centers on scenic epiphanies; Bachelard's poetic theory investigates spatial intimacies.

a. Proust's enormous novel, known as *Remembrance of Things Past* (1913 on), bears the literal title "Towards the Search for Lost Time" (*A la Recherche du Temps Perdu*). In the final book, *Time Retrieved*, Proust at last finds the master key of memory toward which he has been moving, the key that opens the entrance from which his search can begin. This key releases in him the power to transform his recollective search into art, and to begin the writing of the very novel we are about to finish reading. But as he resolves the problem of lost time by becoming artistically productive, Proust abandons the reflective contemplation of the mysteries implicit in his scenic moments: The ardent meditations on the landscapes of bliss, the reflections that punctuate his life, are foreclosed as the moments become simply the catalytic incidents for the making of literature.

The Proustian problem of time—of psychological time, of course—is an acute version of the ancient perplexity about memory: The experienced past is not truly a past, a past with its proper sonority and fragrance, unless it has also been forgotten. An image held continuously in memory lacks the patina of the past: "The man with a good memory does not remember anything because he does not forget anything" (Beckett 1931). *Oubli*, oblivion, is of the essence of remembrance.

And yet the voluntary, intelligent recollection that proceeds like the inspection of a photograph album has little evocative power. For it retrieves only rationally formed schemata of the past with their freight of anxiety and ambition. Deliberate recollection does not resonate with the present; it is unsignificant. The problem of memory is, thus, the problem of access to that "unknown domain" where memory-images lie invisible, an access without resort to the continuities of recall or voluntary-intellectual recollection. Proust's purely theoretical meditations on the nature of time are to the last confusing and discouraging—for him and for us (March 1948). However, he resolves the practical problem memory poses for the creative artist through the conjunction of two devices named by critics: The Involuntary Memory and a Stereoscopic Optics. The latter works as follows:

> The *stereoscopic principle* abandons the portrayal of motion in order to establish a form of arrest which resists time. It selects a few images or impressions sufficiently different from one another not to give the effect of continuous motion, and sufficiently related to be linked in a discernible pattern. This stereoscopic principle allows our binocular (or multiocular) vision of mind to hold contradictory aspects of things in the steady perspective of recognition, of relief in time. [Shattuck 1962, 51]

In Proust's words: "Time has taken here the form of space" (*Against Sainte-Beuve*, 1908). The memory arches back to an arrested image of the past and projects it, as by a magic lantern, on the present. Thus different times, or rather the accumulated changes wrought between them, are simultaneously seen in space, so that an effect of depth is achieved precisely because the intervening continuum is lost. Proust's "localization" of time is a device much remarked (Poulet 1963). But when one comes to consider it: How *can* time gone by be retrieved except as an imaginatively shaped space?

It is, however, human beings who are—or used to be—most intimately affected by the passage of time. Hence the stereoscopic vision is applied very productively to the "recognition" of persons. The last two hundred pages of Proust's novel are full of images retrieved from memory and projected onto Marcel's aged acquaintances. It is thus that his literary life begins.

If spatialized time serves to give temporal depth to his literary characters, momentary scenes serve to take the narrator's soul out of time altogether. These instants are those famous "blessed," "privileged," "magical" moments (*moments bienheureux, privilégiés, fétiches*). They are often tabulated by scholars (Shattuck, 70): They occur in childhood, fall off, and finally return in a veritable electric storm at the beginning of the last book (XII, ch. 3) as the heralds of Marcel's literary vocation. At that moment they serve to prepare him for what he calls the "hard law" of simultaneity, which is precisely the stereoscopic principle. They assure him, moreover, of the possibility of a sustained involuntary memory that is concretely and spontaneously conjoined with the present. This experience is surely not a Proustian idiosyncrasy: the opening of a new epoch in one's life is often heralded by meteor showers of *déjà-vu*-like memory-images.

Such memorial moments have a clear structure in this novel. They are always triggered by a sensory experience that releases a sensory memory. The best known of these is the madeleine dipped in linden-tea which, at the beginning of the work, sets off Marcel's very first retrieval, that of his childhood home in Combray. These triggers release a sense of overwhelming bliss, from which arises, almost as its distillation, sometimes a diffuse aura of felicity, colored a deep, intoxicating azure, more often an identifiable landscape, fragrant with its own ineffably singular yet infinitely familiar feeling.

Three features are to be remarked: First, whereas Proust's persons are almost always given a scenic setting that lends them its atmosphere, his scenic moments never contain characters. Places that express the soul, I will conjecture later, are properly unpeopled (2).

Second, Marcel's visions are always of actual places. Some he has himself seen, like the steeples of Martinville near Combray, others he knows indirectly, like Venice. The scenes are therefore not imaginary but imaginative in the sense here assigned to that term: The imagination works imaginatively insofar as it invests the real world.

Third, these landscapes have a curiously inspissated topography (Poulet 1963). They belong together, they make one universe—since they are, after all, real places. But it is a universe whose extension is not a continuum; its densely packed places are not separated by neutral distances or approached by spatial passages. The imagination, Proust says, carries us from home into the places we desire; its miracle is not that it leaps over distances but that it makes psychically contiguous certain places that are separate on earth.

In *Time Retrieved* Proust muses ardently about the effect and meaning of these moments. As a connoisseur of bliss, he succeeds in analyzing their felicity: "The true paradises," he discovers, "are the paradises we have lost" (XII 215). Their air is purest because it offers a deep sense of renewal. But the perfection of happiness demands more than memory; it requires real, present existence, here and now: the moments fuse past and present timelessly, like the "standing now" of eternity. Their effect is not, as in recollection, the stereoscopic piling up of times, but the abolition of time. This atemporality, this fusion of past and present, accounts, to Marcel, for their felicity, the "enigma of happiness," which they bid him try to solve (211). He takes their *nunc stans* for a living now.

What they ultimately signify is a different matter. For though the moments of Marcel's later life are memories of an early bliss, these first moments are not themselves memory-images but, as was observed at the end of the previous chapter, they are original visions. Their felicity is not memorial but archetypal. To understand their meaning it is necessary to decipher their "hieroglyphic" character, "to penetrate to the full depth of [the] impression," to that "something more, . . . that luminosity, something which they seemed at once to contain and to conceal." This was the task which the spires of Martinville had early imposed on the author (I 247). Even then it had come to young Marcel "that what lay buried within the steeples of Martinville must be something analogous to a charming phrase"; in other words, at the heart of the vision is a literary impulse. The old Marcel finds a similar final relief from this importunate mystery by turning it to account in the creation of a work of verbal art.

So what we have is these psychologically meticulous, visually haunting reports of the imaginatively transfigured world; but the search into the meaning of such moments is aborted, superseded by their literary exploitation. Thus unpenetrated they are rightly called by Beckett "an accidental and fugitive salvation."

There is an understanding of Proust's failure worth citing in conclusion. In his book on "the telling of space" (1987) Reichel formulates the problem of every writer who means to duplicate life in art as that of allowing "time to unfold in space." "Time" is here a Kant-inspired locution for inner life, consciousness. Like his contemporaries, Reichel says, Proust fails to find a social space for the satisfying action of informing the earthly scene with life. In childhood Marcel's longing for adventure is turned inward by the protective confinement imposed by his family; later he retreats into the frozen spaces of his recollected paradises. In short, the moments are an ultimately melancholy refuge from a world that has no place for him.

I shall later argue that it is not being debarred from the world of adventure that is the cause of melancholy, but romantic adventuring itself, the paradoxical longing for mere eventfulness (Coda). What is doomed to yield a curtailed satisfaction is the purposeful fixation on states of the soul that ought to be sought only obliquely, being the incidental reward of absorption in practical life. In sum, Proust—or at least Marcel—forces the grace of the imagination.

b. Bachelard devotes a whole book to the spatial imagination, *The Poetics of Space* (1958). He calls it a "topoanalysis," a phenomenology and psychoanalysis of inhabited space. The technical terms that stud the analysis have been reviewed in Part One (Ch. IV C). They are not necessary to an appreciation of his lively insights—they becloud them. In fact, the "analysis of place" really circumscribes a sensibility of space. Bachelard observes the feeling we have not only for particular places of memory like the house of our childhood, but also for spatial configurations like chests, nests, and shells; he also considers spatial scales, like miniatures and immensities. Of these three topics I mean to touch only on the house and the extremes of scale.

The space Bachelard seizes on is exclusively "felicitous space," "the space we love." Repulsive, unprotective spaces do not lend themselves to his inquiry, since it is concerned with the "intimacy" of space. "Intimate" means close and personal, deep and inward: The verb "to intimate" means to communicate knowledge by signs; the related Latin *intimus* means "innermost"; all these significations reverberate in Bachelard's use. The thesis is, accordingly, that "there does not exist a real intimacy which is repellent," and that "the space of hatred and combat can only be studied in the context of impassioned subject matter and apocalyptic images." All intimate space is attractive. (Perhaps one might even say that imaginative spaces display affectively a logical feature of pictorial spaces pointed out in Part Three: their incapacity for negativity—Ch. I B.) Bachelard appears to be making the delicate observation that combative issues and ugly corruptions are alien to any dreamy dwelling in space, to its imaginative investment, since these latter modes imply a ready inclination to remember. It is a point trite and wonderful in equal parts: intimate space tends to repel what is repulsive. Moreover, if intimate space is not the arena of strife, neither is it an area of indifference, "subject to the measures and estimates of the surveyor": Human space is essentially not so much extended as possessed.

Bachelard's first preoccupation is with houses and in particular with the houses of childhood. Enchanting questions abound. He asks, for instance, "how can secret rooms, rooms that have disappeared, become abodes for an unforgettable past?" It is a question asked from the hearts of generations whose childhood habitations have been lost to the bombs of war and the wrecker's ball. For, as Rilke wrote, much of the world's irreplaceably intimate visible furniture has disappeared and must be replaced by the "invisible vibration" of our nature (Letter to von Hulewiez on the purpose of the *Duino Elegies*). But Bachelard is not, I think, only wondering how one can call lost places home; he seems to me to be pursuing a magical propensity such dwellings have for adding space. In dreams they develop doors through blind walls, passages into hidden apartments peopled by mysterious-familiar presences. These are the dream-spatial realizations of the childhood sense that the house encloses more than is visible. It is that sense of secret extension which makes the childhood home the first staging ground for our forays into imaginative space.

What is at the bottom of the intimacy of a house, besides the physical shelter and the "material paradise" it offers, its "comfort" and its "coziness"? (Rybczynski 1986). Bachelard has a lovely answer: The house is "the resting place of daydreams." Since poetry is for him at bottom interchangeable with daydreaming, one might say that the house is filled with poetry. That is why its topoanalysis is a poetics of space. The house harbors a diversified topography of intimacy, for "the values of intimacy are scattered." The house has nooks and corners of solitude, and a bed- and living-room "where the leading characters held sway." It has a "vertical being," the polarity of bright, rational roof and dark, irrational cellar, held together by its "central being," its nature as an inhabited refuge. Bachelard knows well that the intimate topography of daydreaming cannot be fully articulated: "All we can communicate to others is an *orientation* towards what is secret without ever being able to tell the secret objectively."

For knowledge of intimacy, "localization of spaces is more urgent than determination of dates." "Memories are motionless, and the more securely they are fixed in space, the sounder they are." "Here space is everything, for time ceases to quicken memory. . . . We are unable to relive duration—the finest specimens of fossilized duration, concretized as a result of long sojourn, are to be found in and through space." It has, of course, been a claim of this book also that the imagination is essentially spatial rather than temporal (Ch. II C above).

Bachelard also treats the intimacies of miniatures and immensities. I have argued in Part Four (Ch. IV B) that magnification and miniaturization are formally essential to our imagination. Bachelard deals with the affective inwardness of scaling.

Immensity, vastness, move the imagination in strange ways. Darwin, looking back on the voyage of the Beagle, is puzzled by the fact that images of Patagonia, a land of vast and arid wastes, preoccupy his memory more than the green and fertile Pampas. His explanation is that the boundlessness of space and time gives freer scope to the imagination. The feelings, which he finds hard to analyze, are those associated by Burke (*On the Sublime and Beautiful* 1756) and by Kant with "the sublime." Kant gives a critical grounding to the association of spatial vastness with feelings of awe and grandeur in the *Critique of Judgment* (1790, 23 ff.). Its crux is that the sublime is the incomparably or absolutely great. In it the "unlimited progress" of the imagination is joined to the idea of "totality" supplied by reason, the faculty for intellectual closure. (The sublime would seem to be the analogue in sensible space to the actual infinite in mathematics.) Hence the sublime is satisfying not as an object but as an enlargement of the imagination. For the feeling of sublimity is aroused by something—infinity in nature—that is "according to its form not suited to our judgment, not fitting to our faculty of representation, and doing violence, as it were, to our power of imagination." There is a simultaneous discomfort and pleasure in the vision of vastness. The discomfort arises because it brings home to us the limitation of our imagination, its inability to encompass spatial immensity. The pleasure occurs because while feeling our physical impotence before it, we recognize our moral invulnerability as persons possessing reason.

The *Poetics of Space* preserves some elements of Kant's deep analysis of the sublime as "reverence-inspiring magnitude" (*magnitudo reverenda*), but it is far more romantic—that is to say, aggrandizingly subjective. Again it is the intimacy of immensity that Bachelard investigates: Immensity belongs to the category of the daydream, of the type that bears the mark of infinity. Thus the immense is within, or rather it is through their immensity that these two kinds of magnified space—the space of intimacy and world space—blend. "When human solitude deepens, then the two immensities touch and become identical." The immense is not an image and has no specific images; it is the pure imaginative motion to the far and the further, accompanied by a consciousness of enlargement, of unlimitedness, of solitariness and mastery.

The intimacy of the miniature, on the other hand, is that of a compacted, "nucleized space." Spatial intensification can as much give greatness to the minuscule as spatial extension gives grandeur to the infinite. The cleverer one is at miniaturizing the world, the better one can possess it, not only because "miniature . . . allows us to be world-conscious at slight risk," but because the world's "values become condensed and enriched in miniature." Bachelard is evidently thinking of the intense delight to be taken, for example, in miniature detailing: What is delicious to the ordinary sight becomes magical on the brink of visibility; moreover, what is gross becomes droll and what threatens can be dominated. In this vein, too, the miniaturizing imagination creates a new and concealing world into which the daydreamer may abscond. Bachelard recounts a word-vignette by Hermann Hesse which is the escapist counterpart of the Chinese landscape painter who wandered off into the space projected by his own imagination: A prisoner paints a tiny train entering a tunnel on the wall of his cell. When they come for him, he shrinks himself to minuteness, climbs aboard, and departs into the wall. The imaginary territories receive us not only as pleasure-seekers but also as fugitives.

Besides the effect of scale on the experience of space, the *Poetics of Space* considers mostly the psychic significance of particular protective enclosures, such as roofs, cellars, chests, and corners—locales that invite psychoanalytic speculation. I want instead to pass on now to a closer consideration of imagination-invested places. Again, by "place" I mean something inbetween the blank volume of mere space and the unitary configurations found within it—what might be called, adapting Wordsworth's phrase "spots of time," "spots of world."

2. Imaginative Places. The one incident in Cervantes's huge novel that has become American folklore is Don Quixote's adventure with the windmills. As it happens, it contains, almost incidentally, the Don's own statement of the crux of his life, the credo that makes his world one of high adventure. He is moved by his knight errant's sense of duty to attack a band of thirty windmills which he sees as just so many monstrous giants. Thrusting his lance through one of the sails, he is dragged off his nag Rocinante and badly bruised. Sancho Panza trots up on his ass ready with his "I told you so"; it was always plain to him that these were nothing but windmills. But Don Quixote's world is not to be so easily disenchanted. Not so, he explains: An old enemy, a sorcerer wise in the black arts, wishing to cheat the Don of his glory, has turned the giants into windmills. It is Sancho Panza's prose, not Don Quixote's poetry, that is deluded.

The point, implicit but crucial, is that it is our mundane soulless world of flour-grinding windmills that is under a spell, a reverse or disenchanting spell cast by the enemies of glory. This spell is the common condition that Santayana calls the "normal madness;" it is the pervasive notion that the ordinary is the actual. Break it, and the monsters and marvels re-appear. The quixotic windmill-giants are the emblem of the restorative disenchantment that the imagination can work on the ordinary world when it reverses the spell of the prosaic. From the perspective of the unregenerate, spellbound world the real windmills are actually the ghosts, for "ghosts are the ambassadors of a landscape into geographic space" (Straus 1956). The imagination allows that landscape to reappear. That is its knight-errantry. Put less fancifully: The imagination turns space into place insofar as it is equally a propensity for projecting human feeling into space and a readiness to be affected by its local presences. "Here dwells a presence," says T.E. Lawrence of the valley of Rumm and the fort of ancient Azrak:

> Both were magically haunted: but whereas Rumm was vast and echoing and God-like, Azrak's unfathomable silence was steeped in knowledge of wandering poets, champions, lost kingdoms, all the crime and chivalry and dead magnificence of Hira and Ghassan. Each stone or blade of it was radiant with half-memory of the luminous silky Eden, which had passed so long ago. [*Seven Pillars of Wisdom* 1926, ch. LXXV]

This passage is one example of imaginative place-sensibility. But the topophile imagination apprehends places in several ways worth briefly delineating.

There is, first, the spatio-temporal magic that comes about wherever a place draws the past into the present. The imagination resonates to nothing so well as to burdens of backward-directed reference. An especially poignant acknowledgment of this effect is peculiarly American. It is displayed in the artless reminiscences of remote cultural roots and the unaffected nostalgia for distant origins that make traveling through the towns of the blue highways such a romance of recognition. In his essay on "The Geography of the Imagination" (1978) Guy Davenport traces with delightful pedantry dozens of such references in Grant Wood's image of Iowa, "American Gothic," from the diminutive Gothic spire in the distance, through the board-and-batten Gothic of the farm house, to the hieratically frontal pose of the Pharaoh-farmer holding the trident pitchfork of Poseidon, his severely dignified consort at his side, wearing a classical cameo as ornament. The painting is an epitome of a peculiarly American kind of place-making, the affixing of historical references as decorations upon the plainest homespun.

There are, next, the Edenic places themselves, such as the Azrak of the *Seven Pillars*. Some are historical and steeped in human memory. Others are hidden and imbued with a primeval *genius loci*. Such are the lost paradisiacal canyons, haunts of the Anasazi, discovered by the fugitive hero and kept secret against future settlement, which turn up in so many of Louis L'Amour's well-researched and immensely popular westerns; these spots give the books a touch of topophile beauty beyond their satisfyingly formulaic people and plots. Such places, of course, such worlds of safe loveliness, have a long ancestry. They go back into antiquity to the walled pleasure-parks of the Persians, whose Avestan name the Greeks heard as *para-deisos*; "paradise," literally "Beyond-fear." Their descendant is the

English "wilderness" garden, evoking a mood of primeval snugness. Andrew Marvell called it a "lesser *World . . . And Paradise's only Map*" (in Hunt and Willis 1975).

Or, again, there are the cities of the imagination, which rise behind the real places, their dreamy doubles, as it were, like Proust's Venice or Rose Macaulay's hypnagogic Trebizond:

> Then, between sleeping and waking, there rose before me a vision of Trebizond: not Trebizond as I had seen it, but the Trebizond of the world's dreams, of my own dreams, shining towers and domes shimmering on a far horizon, yet close at hand, luminously enspelled in the most fantastic unreality, yet the only reality, a walled and gated city, magic and mystical, standing beyond my reach yet I had to be inside, an alien wanderer yet at home, held in the magical enchantment; and at its heart, at the secret heart of the city and the legend and the glory in which I was caught and held, there was some pattern that I could not unravel, some hard core that I could not make my own, and, seeing the pattern and the hard core enshrined within the walls, I turned back from the city and stood outside it, expelled in mortal grief. [*The Towers of Trebizond* 1956]

Or there are the "landscapes of a Western Mind," the heavens of home remembered daily in the square of a city sky, which widens

> to become the blue expanse over Montana rangeland, so vast and vaulting that it rears, from the foundation-line of the plains horizon, to form the walls and roof of all of life's experience that my younger self could imagine, a single great house of the sky. [Doig 1978]

Or, if the home is lost and gone, these memories furnish "an exquisite simulacrum—the beauty of intangible property, unreal estate" (Vladimir Nabokov, *Speak, Memory* 1947). So overmastering can the power of such a home-space be, that its "rememory" may, standing in outrageous contrast to terrible fact, beautify hell; witness a passage from Toni Morrison's *Beloved*:

> . . . and suddenly there was Sweet Home rolling, rolling, rolling out before her eyes, and although there was not a leaf on that farm that did not make her want to scream, it rolled itself out before her in shameless beauty. It never looked as terrible as it was and it made her wonder if hell was a pretty place too. Fire and brimstone all right, but hidden in lacy groves. Boys hanging from the most beautiful sycamores in the world. It shamed her—remembering the wonderful soughing trees rather than the boys. Try as she might to make it

otherwise, the sycamores beat out the children every time and she could not forgive her memory for that. [1987]

Or sometimes the memory with uncanny precision precedes the perceived place, say an archetypal river:

> I thought of the happy impulse that had brought me here—and found myself faced with a conundrum. When I was a child of seven I thought that I was imagining the Mississippi. Yet seeing it now, in all its old pictorial clarity, I found it hard not to think that somehow I had remembered it. The fit was troublingly exact; and there were details in it that I could never, surely, have got from Huckleberry Finn. I had to remind myself that I have no belief whatsoever in ideas of precognition. [Jonathan Raban, *Old Glory: An American Voyage* 1981]

Or again, a place is invested with memories as vivid as they are impossible: as, looking over its rim, one might glimpse the bottom of a steep canyon filled with cotton woods and pinyons and the ruins of an Indian pueblo, and be overcome by an ineffable but powerfully haunting sense of having once lived there.

Historic reference, Edenic echoes, memorial doubling, unreal estate, *déjà-vu*—the interplay of perception, imagination, and memory, may take these and various other forms. But in every case it is this interplay that makes places in my sense imaginative rather than imaginary. The imaginative world—recall that by "world" I mean here not a logically closed universe but a humanly coherent environment—is thus neither exclusively internal nor external. For by themselves the inner scenes may go amorphously moody, and of course external spaces all too often present abstract and anatmospheric sprawls.

Some do claim that the imagination's highest and best activity is quite separable from those functions that are woven into ordinary psychic contexts, like daily wishes, dreams, and projections. There is, in Dilthey's words, that "action of the imagination in which it erects a world distinct from that world of our busyness" (1905). What it does unconsciously in the figures of dreams it does consciously, he claims, in daydreaming, at play, and above all wherever a "festive heightening of human existence" brings forth a world separate from daily life. Now it seems to me that one might readily admit that the imagination makes a second, high world, provided it is not thereby relegated to the status of a fantasy-life preserve. For the imagination in its fullest actuality should be thought of as continuous with reality, as having a sort of covering contact with the world of practical life—a reflection elucidated and reinforced in the Conclusion. Here, however, the primary topic is inner places and outer locales of reverie, not scenes of action.

But the imagination seems to me to have yet another sort of connectedness: As its world—scenes and figures both—is coherent with ordinary life, so, I want now to say, it is continuous with itself. The question whether all the places and persons of the imagination belong to one world, taken up so inconclusively under the logic of images (Part Three, Ch. III C), is decided differently by philosophers and poets. The philosophers tend to deny that the class including all imaginary or imaginatively seen places can be sited in a unitary space, for that space would be *ipso facto* identical with the one and only space there is, real space. The poets, who live, as it were, in the space of the imagination, generally speak of it, on the contrary, as all one: Proust's magical scenes are all contiguous. So also are the places of Calvino's *Invisible Cities*, a compilation of short sketches delineating the psychic gist of many humanly actual, though geographically imaginary, cities. The book is conceived as the imaginative complement of Marco Polo's collected descriptions of the real cities of Cathay, eye-witness reports which he made at the behest of the Khan and published in his *Travels* (Book II). Calvino's Kublai Khan, too, finally causes all the cities of the soul described to him by the explorer—actual, remembered, undiscovered, not-yet-founded, imagined, imaginary, utopian—to be collected into a single atlas. For, as Marco has told his lord, they are all of one world, and there is a way to them all; nay, they are all aspects of one city. He will sail, he says, taking his departure from the merest hint and his direction from

> an opening in the midst of an incongruous landscape, a glint of lights in the fog, the dialogue of two passersby meeting in the crowd. . . . I will put together, piece by piece, the perfect city. . . . If I tell you that the city toward which my journey tends is discontinuous in space and time, now scattered now condensed, you must not believe the search for it can stop. [1972, 163]

And in the children's novels of Michael Ende, the land of the imagination, whose extent is infinite and whose center is wherever occurs one of its myriad condensations into a magical locale, is yet subject to one fate: its impending annihilation through human forgetfulness and the failure of the imagination (Part Four, Ch. IV B). This unitary topography is not simply a loose-minded conceit but it conveys the sense that, in defiance of surveying reason and its boundaries, all that is imagined has squatters' rights within one intimate territory.

The life of the imagination, people are fond of saying, has its own—

paralogical—laws. The contiguity of apparent incomparables, as in the unitary imaginative space just proposed, would be an example. However, I doubt that even the most disciplined musings bring up very law-like results, as compared to those found through the study of perception. It is a temptation here, near the end, to venture a comparison between perceptual and imaginative scene-seeing. The analysis of a perceptual scene is a serious subject in cognitive studies and artificial intelligence. The "semantics" of an (artless) pictorial scene as taken in at a glance—presumably transferred to the picture from the experience of real scenes—have been analyzed and the factors that make any perceived space immediately apprehensible as a scene have been enumerated. Among these factors are, first, scaling: objects must be of appropriate size; then, supportedness: objects must be in likely places; next, interpretability: objects must occlude each other correctly; and last, probability: objects must not seem bizarre in the context (Biederman 1981). Internal, imagined scenes are no doubt amenable to these same rules; they too must show pictorial coherence, except that it is a vacuous demand. For what would be the purport of a semantically unsound, an unmeaning inner vision? Unlike adventitious external displays, inner scenes can never suffer disintegration as semantic structures because even the most disjointedly nonsensical image of the imagination is not *bona fide* nonsense—it is felt to have meaning, however recondite. The more telling traits that distinguish inner from outer scene-seeing intimate why internal scenes are so unamenable to semantic laws. These traits are, first, the contemplative receptivity of the inner eye: one is not tempted to tinker with one's own *moments fétiches*; then, the holistic nature of the vision: it is not furnished part by part with movable bodies but arises as one spontaneous whole; and finally, the absence of progressively inspectable detail in the image: one is not inclined to take a microscope to its surface, but rather to allow it some image-haze. In sum, inner images seem to be semantically spontaneous; they are not composed by the rules that safeguard the meaning of percepts.

Above all, spontaneous inner scenes are never dull or affectless. By the same token by which they are through and through appearance, having no impenetrable matter to them (Part Five, Ch. II A), they are core and center made apparent, visible: they show, or rather body forth, the spirit of the place, its manifest soul, Hopkins's "inscape"—the visibility of things that gives an insight into their inner being. It is for the same reason, their perfect non-opacity, that they are easily irradiated by all the affects of the soul.

All this, one might object, could be said of painting; these are just the aesthetic-imaginal characteristics of pictorial art—and indeed this parallelism has been argued in Part Five (Ch. III B). In the same vein, finally, inner images have in the highest degree the most tantalizing quality of painting: a kind of referring beauty. Walter Benjamin articulates the enigma of beauty in a definition of profound simplicity, a definition which all but identifies being beautiful with being an image. Beauty occurs when an object is experienced "in the mode of being similar" (1939). The landscapes of the imagination are experienced in this way; they seem to image a deep-lying original and to signify its meaning. In this trait of imaginality probably lies the most telling distinction between the imaginative place and the perceptual scene.

★   ★   ★

Let me end with an observation and a reflection. The places of the contemplative imagination—in Proust, in Bachelard, in our own experience—are curiously often unpeopled. They belong to the genre of the "landscape without figures." Why is that?

Actual environments and their inhabitants, given a chance, eventually grow to be each other's reciprocals. "Flesh becomes place," characters have their landscapes and conversely (Blythe 1982). As a place shapes its people so they shape it, physically by looking after it and psychically by looking at it. For scenes long regarded with attentive love do acquire a look of their own, the secure bearing of an appearance well confirmed in its significance. The study of the human shaping of places, of "topophilia" at work, comes upon wonderful facts: Tribal towns are formed as *imagines mundi*, as reflections of their cosmos (Trigger 1978). A steep solitary mesa in Attica is treated as the soaring pedestal of a majestic marble temple to the country's goddess. A Chinese landscape is cultivated so as to be the perfect site for human meditation (Tuan 1974, 1977). The imaginative investment and sacral apprehension of space is a vast and wonderful subject (Nabokov 1987).

The ways of seeing places are a study to match the ways of shaping them. Among the many varieties of topophile sight, perhaps none leads to such intimate familiarity as living and working in a land- or cityscape; but even the guided gaping of sight-seeing and the pedantic accretions of historical information can leave over time a transfigured scenic residue. As Blythe observes: Intuition and tuition, the magic and the facts, are the twin aspects of landscape consciousness (1982).

As a complement to the topophilia of such peopled environments, Paul Scott, in *The Love Pavilion* (1960), weaves a meditation on the engrossingly problematic contemplation of unpeopled scenes. The setting is the Far East. A young man's true and central soul and dream—words he is warned not to wince at—are interpreted to him by an older man. The young man has some family relics, watercolors of the Punjab painted by his grandfather, which he has brought back with him from Bayswater to Bombay. The older man musingly describes them: "Intimate distances preserved behind glass. Landscapes without figures . . . Don't you carry in your mind's eye a kind of perfection of landscape your actual eye is always searching to match?" The young man admits it, but it is a melancholic thought—the dream is lonely without people. Thereupon his mentor tries to show him that the addition of figures, say, of Englishmen sitting under peepul trees, driven to judge and govern by their sense of duty and their delusions of grandeur, would invade and confuse the vision. Some imaginative places, whether in inner or outer aesthetic space, are, he says, essentially settings, merely longing to be perfectly inhabited, backdrops of an exactingly searching love.

Yet even in moods less melancholy, memory-scapes, the places of the imagination, are more rarely populated settings than self-sufficient scenes. How often does a view briefly and incidentally glimpsed in the course of mundane business swim up, *sans* personnel, as a magical memory? How often does a place dimmed by the myopia of personal distraction return in reverie disencumbered of all the long-since-indifferent facts and faces of the affair but invested with the residue of its best feeling?

The explanation is, I think, along these lines: Unpeopled places, especially scenes of nature, are ready to receive the human being; they are, as it were, expectant—as the empty pavilions that turn up so often in all-animate Chinese landscapes seem to signify. We in the West, too, are ready to say—if more self-consciously and if only as a figure of speech—that the places themselves may be ensouled, that they may sport a *genius loci*. However that may be, the converse is a psychic fact: The soul can be emplaced. Human inwardness can take shape in the imagination as landscape. These unpeopled places of the imagination express the lie of the inner land, the disposition of the spirit: imaginative space tends to be a landscape without figures because it features the soul itself. I will amplify this notion in the next and final section.

B. The Investment of Feeling

The imagination is intimate with all the affects of the soul: passion, sentiment, emotion, mood, and feeling. This is, finally, the one proposition about the imagination universally acknowledged. The power of the imagination to be imbued by affects and in turn to give shape to the passions had been recognized long before it became the object of extended reflections in the later Enlightenment, in works such as Gerard's *Essay on Genius* (1774).

Gerard ushers in Romanticism by identifying the imagination as the source of "genius," which is a "peculiar vigour" of imaginative association. Imaginative association is promoted by the influence of the passions. Passion "excites and channels the imagination," and conversely the imagination conjoins and "blends thoughts and feelings" (in Engell 1981).

Testimonials would seem unnecessary where no one demurs. Nevertheless, by and large the subject of the passions eminently belongs among the "missing mysteries" of the imagination. The cause is not so much that there is a "conspiracy of silence" about the subject (Walker 1969)—why should there be?—but that people are paralyzed by its boundlessness. What follows in this final section barely tabulates and scarcely unfolds the mystery.

First, then, since the imagination is affective, it is necessary to try to say what the passions in question are and in what ways they and the imagination mutually arouse and inform each other (*1*). The next question is how the products of the imagination, images, are expressive of emotion (*2*). The final question is whether there is an affect specific to the imagination, a distinctive imaginative feeling (*3*).

1. Affective Imagination. The passions are enigmatic because affect, which is non-rational, and sometimes even irrational, naturally eludes rational cognition and articulation. Passions can be named, expressed, described, and specifically aroused by words, and yet their nature remains undisclosed, for it is essentially inward, inexpressible. An old theory takes its departure from the term "passion" itself: Passion is something the soul undergoes or suffers, both in the strong sense of suffering a passive affect and more generally as possessing a specific receptivity distinct from that of the intellect or of the senses. For the functioning intellect and the transducing senses give us objects objectively in their own proper rational or visible form; this observation holds whether the objects of cognition are regarded as conveyed from the outside or as internally constructed. The affective receptivity, on the other hand, suffers objects to arouse and move the soul not, as it were, in their own behalf, but in ours. Through the passions we acknowledge things not for what they are in themselves but for what they are *to us*. The normal way to say this is that affects are subjective. Sometimes the object strongly asserts and impresses its shape while arousing our correspondingly specific acknowledgment, sometimes it moves us diffusely, formlessly, to mere movedness. The images of the imagination, I shall later claim, move us in a mode in which the inner appearance and its affect are peculiarly melded:

What any image is as event for my "I," as an executant state of mine, we call a feeling. Keeping this name for states of pleasure and displeasure, joy and sorrow, is an enormous error that psychology has only recently acknowledged. Every objective image, on entering or leaving our consciousness, produces a subjective reaction—just as a bird that lights on or leaves a branch starts it trembling, or turning on and off an electric current instantly produces a new current. [Ortega y Gasset 1914]

Why human beings should be moved by anything at all is itself a mystery: being subject to affects is a principal meaning of being animate, of having a soul. The movement under discussion is of course here taken to be non-physical, psychic, though it often has unconcealable somatic concomitants (actually taken by Jamesian psychologists for its cause). This assumption—that there is non-physical motion—the finest of themes for friendly conversation, is the most unprofitable of theses for a rigorous debate. For, when all is said, there is no compelling evidence for our having a movable—a feeling—soul except from two witnesses who can never take the stand, much less be sworn in: our introspective sense of ourselves, and the long-run consequences for the human condition. I have made the soul a working assumption of this book, because without it almost everything said of the imagination is a figure of speech waiting to be reduced to a more rigorously literal terminology.

Affect or passion is not implausibly to be taken as the most general term, having three species: emotions, moods, and desires (Solomon 1976). There are, to be sure, many other classifications. For example, feeling, encompassing all psychic experience except *a priori* cognition, may be taken as the genus of which sense and emotions are concurrent species (Collingwood 1938).

Emotions are concentrated, specific, namable passions with determinate causes and constitutions, usually accompanied by physiological and physiognomic changes. Such theories as there are, old and contemporary, deal mostly with the emotions: with their enumeration and classification, their objects and functions, their controllability and truthfulness; above all, they deal with that puzzle for philosophers and poets alike, the relation between the emotions and rationality—and of both to the imagination:

Tell me where is fancy bred,
Or in the heart or in the head?
How begot, how nourished?
Reply, Reply. [*Merchant of Venice* III ii 63]

Furthermore the logic of emotions has been studied, and the results may have a bearing on the imagination, or at least on imagery, which has also been shown to have its logic (Part Three). For it would be illuminating if emotions and imagination had some formal similarity. There is in fact a certain parallelism to be observed with respect to logical contradiction: Images that have contradictory verbal articulation can coexist (Part Three, Ch. I B), and so can emotions, as we all know (Greenspan 1980). One might say that the attentive recording of emotional ambivalence all the way up to self-contradiction is one of the glories of the novel (particularly the Russian novel). Again, as far as the law of the excluded middle is concerned, Brentano attempted to show that emotions do not obey it, since besides emotional affirmation and denial there is a middle ground, indifference (Chisholm 1982). Now something somehow similar can also be said of imagery, since it too, taken formally, neither affirms nor denies but simply displays. But to press the analogies seems forced; in the end the features common to imagination and emotion only express the fact that neither is proposition-like.

In fact, the great question—Why are images so often affectively charged and emotions so productive of imagery?—has no present answer. There is, to be sure, the beginning of a neurophysiological explanation in terms of the interconnections of affective and imaginative structures or events, but this account does not reach the tantalizing specificity of the internal phenomena. One might simply say that all inwardness is *ipso facto* interpenetrative: every inner landscape absorbs the affective atmosphere of inner space. The images of the arts provide the external evidence of this psychic fact.

There are, of course, a number of more precise theories connecting the emotions with the imagination. Sometimes imagination is taken as synonymous with empathy; thus to imagine is to borrow or to mirror feeling, to pass through that sheet of crystal which separates one imaginative consciousness from the affective life of the other. Another view, under the influence of Sartre's theory of the imagination (Part One, Ch. IV A), regards the passions in general as the "power of possibilities." Since that is just what Sartrean imagination is, the two are all but identifiable; at the bottom of feeling and imagining alike lies the promise of pleasures or sorrows to come (Solomon 1976). A third theory again takes off from Sartre, though this time as a correction of his claim that the emotions are a magical "degradation" of the world (Sartre 1948). An emotion, Sartre claims, is incantatory behavior in which the world is transformed so as to make it more amenable to human need. For example, the faintness felt in passive fear acts as a refuge, a way of annihilating the object of fear. (Here the more plausible examples are all of the aversive emotions.) Only reflection can liberate consciousness from these passional superstitions. Casey suggests an emendation: If the notion of the "magical" is replaced by that of the "imaginative," then the transforming emotional consciousness, instead of "degrading" the real world by holding it off with self-deceptive conjurations, enhances its own self-awareness by ordering the pattern of its intentions imaginatively. Under this correction, liberation is not *from* the emotions but *by* their imaginative expressions (1984).

There is a set of questions, most relevant to the relation of the emotions to the imagination, that these theories do not explicitly consider: Are the emotions representational? Do they somehow come before consciousness as images come before the mind's eye, or are they, as I suggested, inherently amorphous, un-objective? Are they perhaps images of a sort, or are they the cause of images, or possibly their effect?

The case of representational emotion-images is hardly likely. Suppose that emotions were identical with, say, certain memory-images, which are indeed often highly affective. Then it would be, if not logically impossible, at least unlikely for remembered imagery to be as often affectively neutral, hard-edged, and unevocative as is, for example, the imagery used in psychological experiments; surely all memory, even short-term laboratory recall, would be at least mildly infected by emotions. Nor is it easy to see how the feeling in some images could be wholly leached out, as from photographs of old loves. Inversely, passions can be blind and moods can be sightless, a sallow sprawl. Emotions cannot simply be convertible with or subsumed under imagery.

But images do flash out from an emotion such as rage, or swim up from a feeling like meditative happiness. Similarly, the formal presentations of the arts tend to induce in listeners and viewers much extraneous affective imagery so habitually that such "feeling-immanent representations" are decried by aestheticians. For this adventitious imagery is so diffusely associative and luxuriatingly passive, that it may vitiate the formal attention necessary for aesthetic appreciation (Kainz 1948).

Conversely, inner images give rise to emotions just as do external appearances. The reply to the question asked by Portia's singer—"Tell me where is fancy bred, / Or in the heart or in the head?"—is, accordingly, that "It is engendered in the eyes, / With gazing fed." As psychologists tend to give the lead in passionate life to emotion and also to desire, so the philosophers, beginning with Aristotle, tend to give it to the image: Desire requires an inciting image. Another, extreme, example of this propensity is Hume, who counts the passions among the secondary or reflective impressions, that is to say, as proceeding from the impressions of sensation or from the images derived from these impressions (*Treatise* II 1 i; Part One, Ch. III C). In the chapter of the *Treatise* entitled "Of the influence of the imagination on the passions" he goes on to assert that "nothing, which affects the former, can be entirely indifferent to the latter."

Even the moral philosophers assign a certain priority to the imagination: For example, Adam Smith maintains that all the passions that do not have their origin in the body have it in the imagination (1759, I ii 1). This holds particularly for love, which is consequently always in some measure ridiculous to the onlooker. For "our imagination not having run in the same channel with that of the lover, we cannot enter into the eagerness of his emotions." Yet there are certainly also introspective experiences that speak for passion and imagination inciting each other reciprocally: As an Elizabethan analyst of the passions observes: "The passion increaseth the imagination thereof, and the stronger imagination rendreth the passion more vehement" (Wright 1604).

Wright is, of course, speaking of desire, the passion for possession, which although distinct from emotion often has it as its concomitant. Desire is, very much like the imagination, defined in terms of the absence of its object. Longing for what one has not and envisioning what is absent often occur in tandem; not only do desire and imagination engender each other, but the second sometimes satisfies the first. Desire is sometimes willing, even eager, to take the image for the object, sometimes for want of the real thing, but at other times because a longing for what is lacking is on occasion a desire for the lack itself: It is the image *per se* that is wanted. Here the image, instead of leading desire on, may allay it. That fact in itself of course indicates that image and passion are diverse, though mutually adapted.

This is the place to mention the first text in which the relation between desirous passion, *eros*, and the imagination is explicitly articulated in its complex reciprocities, Plato's *Phaedrus* (259 ff.; Griswold 1986). The love relation in question is, to be sure, a particular, asymmetric sort, but it is nevertheless paradigmatic. In it one partner is more mature and more in love (the lover) while the other is young and receptive (the beloved). Socrates describes the course of love as follows: The beloved is affected by the lover's passion and becomes receptive to it because his own beauty is reflected back to him from the mirror of the lover's soul; the boy thus sees himself through the lover's image of him; he is aroused, as it were, by his own exalted reflection and conceives a "counter-love." The older man, on the other hand, sees within the beloved a god; or rather, he "fashions for himself an image" of a god which fits his own character; it is in effect the being that he desires to become himself. Thus passion and image enter within each friend into a dialectic of self-discovery and self-elevation.

As a complement, a famous modern theory linking love and imagination reciprocally must be mentioned, Stendhal's "crystallization." It is named on the analogy of a bough found in the Salzburg mines about whose bare branches salt had crystallized like scintillating diamonds. So also a man's imagination crystallizes perfections about a beloved woman as about a twig. At first such imaginative coagulation occurs when the man is still relatively heart-whole and confident of his success. One might say that at this stage imagination leads desire. However, there is a second crystallization which takes place when the man has come to doubt his right of possession, so that his imagination is infected with insecurity. Now his longing and desire direct the imagination. In either case, the beloved serves merely as an armature, so to speak, about which the imagination constructs charms and beauties. Consequently, love is a "folly" of false attributions (*On Love*, chs. II-VI). Here is love's ultimate subjectivization.

In our time the question whether the imaginative representation comes psychologically behind or before its emotion has been taken up by Hillman (1960) through a theory based on Jungian notions: The image acts, so to speak, at the two extremes of the soul. On the conscious surface, the mental image—of a knife for example—serves as an efficient cause of the emotion of fear. But it can have that effect only because it is associated with an "instinctual image," an unconscious, deep-lying archetype. This second image acts as a deep formal cause so as to transform the mental picture into a symbol, informing it with dark significance and causing motivated fear. Jung can speak of instinctual images because he considers that "there are in fact no amorphous instincts, as every instinct bears in itself the pattern of its situation. Always it fulfills an image and the image has fixed qualities" (in Hillman, 172). Instincts are thus considered not blind impulses but forms, patterns, significant images stirring up action. In these terms, emotions can be said to arise from representations. In his very comprehensive review of theories of the emotions, Hillman includes some that, again, assert the converse: It is always the emotions that first energize imaginal representation. What speaks against this one-sided view is, as I intimated, the often-cited existence of isolated, affectless mental imagery; it indicates that the imagination can be, narrowly regarded, a pure, affectless power of visualization. Insofar as the imagination can be neutral and the passions imageless, it is safe to say that our representative power and our affective capacity are distinct. Yet they stand in a close relation of reciprocal incitement—not a new, but certainly a very mysterious fact.

This section on the general relation of the passions and the imagination should not close without distinguishing moods and feelings somewhat more particularly from emotions. Emotions are, as was said, namable passions intending definite objects; desires add a possessive element. Imaginative feelings, which I take here somewhat arbitrarily to be non-intentional affects without definite objects, are discussed below (*3*). What remains for the moment are the moods.

Moods are the diffuse dispositions out of which emotions can arise (Bollnow 1941). As distinct from emotions like fear and joy, moods such as anxiety and joyousness have no intentional objects; they have not coagulated about any definite item. They belong to the levels of existence where the sense of self and the feel of the world coincide in a kind of temperamental climate. This feature comes out in the German word for mood, *Stimmung*, meaning a musical tuning or adjustment. In Heidegger's understanding, moods disclose the relation a human being has to its own existence here and now (*Being and Time* 340). Moods are thus the affects most apt for informing space, because they are a way of being in and with the world.

The depressed moods like anxiety and despair, or general "moodiness," are often imaginatively blank. The shutting down of the imaginative workshop is a sign, perhaps even the essence, of those bad moods that make us so exigent toward the world because we are so unprovided in ourselves. The high moods, on the other hand, tend to teem with imagery. Particularly the moods of high solemnity and festivity are image-laden. From these are born the images—mythic scenes and grand tableaux—that take human beings out of themselves. And again, of course, the reverse holds: As moods coagulate images, so images induce moods, ranging from fragrant zephyrs of reminiscence to furious tempests of despair.

2. Expressive Images. The emotions are notoriously recalcitrant to the immediate control of the will, though it used to be believed that the will has a long-range power over the passions. The imagination, however, is agreed to be at least partly voluntary. One can will to activate the imagination, will it to summon an image of something. And the deliberate imagination can, in its turn, summon emotions and feelings not only as spontaneous accompaniments but even, to some degree, as intentional effects. So once again the imagination is an intermediary, here between will and passion. The claim is not that an emotion is, like an image, a representation that can be tagged and retrieved through the imagination, but that the affect can be commanded by certain images insofar as they "express" emotions.

Emotions, moods, feelings thus willfully and artfully imagined are called "aesthetic." Aesthetic feelings pose a peculiarly Meinongian problem, that is to say, a logical problem in nonexistence (Part Three, Ch. III A), which has in fact been formulated by him with particular care (Meinong 1910): Are such summoned feelings, feelings designedly induced by imaginary or remembered objects, actual feelings about unreal things, or imagined quasi-feelings about real, though nonexistent objects? The distinction may seem oversubtle. And yet it is a puzzle not unfamiliar to most of us, who have eagerly welcomed emotions induced by works of the imagination whose real-life counterparts we would exert ourselves strenuously to avoid. The tincture of serenity that qualifies most imaginative feelings gives impetus to the question: Are we deeply moved or deeply unmoved by fictional fates? My own inclination is to think that such emotions mirror very faithfully the image-nature of the images that induce them: They move the soul according to all the affect flowing from the object's form but without the burdens of its existence. Just as imagery, released from the laws of physical nature, is without gravity and without inertia, so aesthetically—artfully—induced feeling is rarely as grievous or as tenacious as that caused by psychic or material nature (though it has the privileged status of being deliberately cultivated and cherished). For aestheticians the same question presents itself as the problem of expression: Exactly what does the common experience, that works of art are indeed expressive, in fact contain?

The problem differs for the representational and the non-representational arts. Of the latter, music especially seems to manifest, or to arouse, the motions and emotions of the soul more directly and more decipherably than does, say, painting (as, inversely, painting arouses far more determinate imagery). If the process remains an enigma, the fact of the immediacy is admitted: doctrines of affects and even dictionaries of emotive tropes and musical gestures have sometimes been thought feasible (Allanbrook 1983). But the complementary notion of a visual "language of emotions" is doubly complicated. One factor is the intervening spatiality of images, at least of still images like paintings; visual stills are *ipso facto* less conformable to psychic movement than are the temporal passages of music. The other complication is in the representational element itself, which requires shape and color and composition to function simultaneously so as to produce the image of a particular object and to express the—visually indeterminate—affect.

The various theories of visual expressiveness thus have to deal with this problem: How can still, spatially determinate images express psychic, unfigured motions even as they represent objects? There are several theories of the expressive imagination. They naturally concern themselves with external images. The investment of inner images by feeling is left to the last (3).

Expressive images are either natural or artificial. The ancient propensity for seeing nature as art has taken an aesthetic turn in modern nature-lovers. Despite the critics' warnings against aestheticism and the Pathetic Fallacy, they persist in seeing scenic nature both "picturesquely," as a series of sets, of panoramic pictures through whose frame one enters to gain further perspective views, and physiognomically, as a set of ensouled scenic countenances which show emotion much as does the animate human body. Few can be found nowadays who entertain the possibility that the haunts of nature are literally inhabited by soul, ensouled. And if there were some who did so, it would not solve the problem of scenic expression, for the expressiveness of the animate body is itself the greatest problem (Wollheim 1966): It is a mystery, for example, how we, the expressees, so to speak, recognize an expression to begin with: Is it done by a "constant correlation" of looks with behavior, or by introspective comparison, or by direct empathy? Again, on the side of the expresser, what is occurring? Is it a deliberate performance or a spontaneous outbreak, a piece of ingrained behavior or an act of memory? The fact that nature, facial or scenic, wears an expressive face for us, that it renders itself as an expressive image, is still altogether enigmatic (Part Five, Ch. III B).

In artificial images, particularly in paintings, the enigma is on the one hand better fixed, since the expressiveness is deliberately achieved, but on the other hand it is complicated by the difficulty of saying what is meant here by "expression." Do the artists somehow express their own frame of mind—do they view a subject, say, serenely, observe it detachedly, treat it calmly, inveigh against it, portray, comment, present it? (Sircello 1972)— and then paint onto the canvas permanently the expression their faces wear temporarily? Do painters in fact express the commentary of their own affects, or do they instead capture the affective spirit of the scene itself, or do they perhaps merely instigate affects, "aesthetic emotions," in others?

It turns out that all the theories of expression are more alternative formulations of the problem than solutions. Thus Collingwood (1938), for whom imagination—as always a mediating faculty—is that point at which the life of thought makes contact with the life of purely psychical expression, regards expression in art as a "clarification." The artist does not arouse, describe, or betray emotion, but makes it clear and represents it to himself or the viewer as this particular, understood affect: The aesthetic character of the feeling is the alleviation that comes from specifying the oppressively shapeless passion. Of course, this theory does not explain *how* a picture can accomplish this result.

Goodman (1976) does grapple with the question of expressive representation. Expression is accomplished, he says, not by imitation, but by intimation; the depiction involves the "metaphorical possession" of the emotional property. By such a figurative possession the sea, for instance, possesses serenity in a manner of speaking and not literally. In this formal approach the problem of pictorial expression is reduced, or, better, translated, into the equally difficult problem of figurative attribution. For who knows how the sea achieves figurative serenity—why a flat expanse seems peaceful rather than god-forsaken?

A third version is the old theory of "correspondences" revived by Wollheim (1966): An element in nature or art will serve as a representational symbol affecting viewers by setting a resonance going within them, a corresponding feeling. The production of a facial expression could then be considered as analogous to expressively "making a scene"; both are symbols—somehow—correlated to feelings. A fourth view, set out by Scruton (1974), brings together the notion of the imagination as a capacity for aspect-seeing—that is, for seeing a configuration as an identifiable thing—with an understanding of the imagination as merely the mode of any psychic state insofar as it is unasserted, in this case an emotion (Part One, Ch. IV B). Thus in imaginative seeing, what appears in the picture as an aspect is an inactual emotion. Though both this and the previous theory seem admirably to articulate how expressiveness is experienced, they do not really tell *how* feeling gets into or issues from formed images.

What all the theories do ultimately say is this: In aesthetic experience an unfelt feeling appears as an invisible sight. The motions of the soul come out, are ex-pressed, "pushed out," not only as immediate physiological effects—a swelling of the heart or a raising of the hair—but as spatial, visible configurations. The essentially inward can be "objectivated," turned into an external form. That this can be done is the condition of art; how it is done is the content of craft; why it is possible is as yet among the enigmas of the imagination. Let me here file an *amicus curiae* brief for the aestheticians: It is because the "as yet" is for good that they do well not to let the matter rest—feeling-in-form is not a problem for resolution but a question for reflection.

3. Imaginative Feeling. The grand cognitive schemata of philosophical psychology are almost all triadic: The mind is constituted of sensation, imagination, and intellect (Part One). The first famous volitional scheme is also tripartite: The soul is composed of desirous passion, temperamental "spiritedness," and truth-seeking reason (Plato, *Republic* IV). In the Platonic psychology, then, spiritedness, schematically but significantly, corresponds to imagination in the cognitive schema. As the imagination mediates between outside and inside, so spiritedness stands between the gross desire for things and the love of the truth about them. The Greek word usually translated as "spiritedness," is *thymos*; like the German *Gemüt* to which it is related, it means temperament. It demarcates that psychic arena in which feeling is less driven by a want than drawn by a vision. It delineates the middle ground between passions that are possessively pointed at particular objects and thoughts that seek invisible truths. It connotes, in sum, feeling closely tied to the imagination. Whether enthusiastically or dryly, the tradition keeps taking account of a psychic preserve for feeling as separable and free from desire: Kant, for instance, distinguishes passions, which belong to the faculty of desire, from feeling and affects (*Critique of Judgment* 29 n.). That free-zone of feeling is the topic of this last section of the book.

Yet the expression of emotion, that is to say, the investment of external images with determinate affect, is a far better established and a far more likely topic of inquiry than internal imagery-feeling, although the second is, by a fair conjecture, the most pervasive experience of inner life. Not that people, particularly poets and most particularly Romantics, have failed to brood upon it extensively. For example, Jean Paul Richter, the eccentric paladin of the imaginative sensibility, uses his essay on the "natural magic" of the imagination (1796) to pose quite earnestly the question: "Seeing that the imagination is but the golden evening-reflection of our senses, whence now comes this *peculiar* charm which attaches to dreams, absences, loved ones, remote times and lands, to childhood years . . . ?" His answer, in the spirit of the times, is that the characteristic yet diffuse feel of images comes from the infinity—he means indeterminacy—of the affect inhabiting them: The feeling that invests memory-images particularly is the expansively melancholy sense of possibility. But romantic longing is not the only imaginative feeling.

Let me submit—hesitatingly—that two traits characterize the affective imagination, or the feeling that invests inner images. First, the affective life of inner vision is well levigated and free from impurities. Remembered or imagined sights even of horror, even of hell, are somewhere, somehow, sometimes serene. Nietzsche's observations about art in the *Birth of Tragedy* (1870) apply to ordinary imaginative life: Apollo, the most serene of gods, presides over the imagination, that "Apollonian dream state in which the world of day is veiled and a new world, more perspicuous, more understandable, more moving than the former and yet more shadow-like, is in continual changes born for our eye" (8). Wordsworth too, in "Tintern Abbey," gives similar testimony when, in the din of the city, he recalls his imaginative memory of a landscape, and:

> that blessed mood
> In which the burthen of the mystery,
> In which the heavy and the weary weight
> Of all this unintelligible world
> Is lighten'd: that serene and blessed mood
> In which affections lead us on,
> Until . . .
> We see into the life of things.

Second, what I intimated earlier about the dreaming imagination (Part Two, Ch. V C) seems to hold for the waking imagination as well: I would not say that inner images literally "express" emotion; rather they contain or are suffused or informed by feeling, somewhat, indeed very much, as a music or a fragrance informs space. Accordingly, the associative confluence of sight, smell, and sound are acutely feeling-laden. Hermann Hesse gives an accurate description of such synaesthetic imagery:

> Well, every human experience has its magic, and in this case mine consisted in this, that the coming spring, which had already filled me with a powerful feeling of felicity as I was walking over the moistly splashing ground inhaling the fragrance of the earth and the buds, was now concentrated and escalated in the fortissimo of the elders' scent to a sensual similitude and an enchantment. . . . But now there was added yet a second factor: . . . On the day of the elder walk or on the next, I discovered Schubert's spring song "The gentle airs have come awake," and the first chords of the piano accompaniment descended on me as a recognition: these chords had the same fragrance as the young elders, so bitter-sweet, so strong, so compressed, so full of fore-spring. [*Magister Ludi* ch. I]

This experience is charged with feeling rather than emotion because it has no object and no general name: it is in itself neither sorrow nor pleasure nor fear nor love. That is why the description in words of dreams and images is so distorting. Qualify as you will—specify the fading pastel figures of a melancholy, the pearl-grey space of a happiness—it is never enough to convey the intense yet delicate particularity of the feeling. It suffuses the inner space so often broached in this book: as an atmospheric wash, a coloration, an aura, an effluvium, a corona—as the visually fragrant essence of its articulated image-shapes. The vision and its effect are all but one— what the inner eye beholds is equally shaped feeling and feeling-fraught shape. For all that, the image-feeling is far from unstrung, diffuse dreaming. On the contrary, it excites the sedulous fascination, the laborious attention that is the due of any specific significance.

And that seems to be, in sum, the nature of the feeling peculiar to the imaginative state: It is the feeling of *that* image, be it figure or scene, and of no other; it is *its* soul or *genius loci*—at once unarticulable in its particularity and archetypal in its significance, fascinating in its familiarity and elusive in its candor.

To end, once again, with a reflection: To the external world we are the looks by which we appear, the passions that expose us, the actions by which we leave a mark. About these, our worldly manifestations, there is continual talk and much passing of judgment. Again, in our invisible depths we may have a core that is common to all humanity, be it a natural intellect or a created spirit or a spontaneous will or the possibility of a self-forged existence. About this, the ground of our moral life, there is endless debate and much positing of dogma.

But in the middle, between our appearance in the world and the invisible ground of our being, there is an arena, a space of places, an inner world, vast and intimate, that is less frequently the subject of declarative discourse. It is the quasi-visible topography of our individual, unique soul. Here we go when we withdraw from the physical frame which is our outer facade, yet stop short of the imageless center where our innermost humanity resides. Here we disappear as tensed, self-asserting selves, to reappear as ensouled image-scenes, expansive and serene. Here, in the middle space, where we are no longer quite individual and not yet quite essence, the soul takes shape and appears as a manifold panorama of memory and imagination. Here we are not the looks we manifest but the visions we see. I conclude that the distinctive feeling, which informs these inner landscapes intimately and inseparably, stems from the fact that they represent the affective soul itself: Receptivity and representation find common ground in the imagination.

Bibliography

Allanbrook, Wye J. 1983. *Rhythmic Gesture in Mozart: Le Nozze di Figaro and Don Giovanni.* Chicago: The University of Chicago Press.

Bachelard, Gaston. 1958. *The Poetics of Space.* Translated by Maria Jolas. Boston: Beacon Press (1969).

Beckett, Samuel. 1931. *Proust.* New York: Grove Press.

Benjamin, Walter. 1939. *Charles Baudelaire: Ein Lyriker im Zeitalter des Hochkapitalismus: Zwei Fragmente.* Frankfurt am Main: Suhrkamp (1959).

Biederman, Irving. 1981. "On the Semantics of a Glance at a Scene." In *Perceptual Organization,* edited by Michael Kubovy and James J. Pomerantz. Hillsdale, N.J.: Lawrence Erlbaum Associates.

Blythe, Ronald. 1982. *Characters and Their Landscapes.* New York: Harcourt Brace Jovanovich.

Bollnow, Otto F. 1941. *Das Wesen der Stimmungen.* Frankfurt am Main: Vittorio Klostermann (1968, expanded edition).

Butor, Michael. 1958. *The Spirit of Mediterranean Places.* Translated by Lydia Davis. Marlboro, Vt.: The Marlboro Press.

Calvino, Italo. 1972. *Invisible Cities.* Translated by William Weaver. New York: Harcourt Brace Jovanovich.

Casey, John. 1984. "Emotion and Imagination." *The Philosophical Quarterly* 34:1–14.

Casey, Edward S. 1987. *Remembering: A Phenomenological Study.* Bloomington: Indiana University Press.

Chisholm, Roderick. 1982. *Brentano and Meinong Studies.* Atlantic Highlands, N.J.: Humanities Press.

Collingwood, R. G. 1938. *The Principles of Art.* Oxford: The Clarendon Press.

Davenport, Guy. 1978. *The Geography of the Imagination: Forty Essays.* San Francisco: North Point Press (1981). [Title essay.]

Dilthey, Wilhelm. 1905. *Das Erlebnis und die Dichtung: Lessing, Goethe, Novalis, Hölderlin.* Göttingen: Vandenhoeck und Ruprecht (1965).

Engell, James. 1981. *The Creative Imagination: Enlightenment to Romanticism.* Cambridge: Harvard University Press.

Goodman, Nelson. 1976. *Languages of Art: An Approach to a Theory of Symbols.* Indianapolis: Hackett Publishing Company.

Greenspan, Patricia S. 1980. "A Case of Mixed Feelings: Ambivalence and the Logic of Emotions." In *Explaining Emotions,* edited by Amélie O. Rorty. Berkeley and Los Angeles: University of California Press.

Griswold, Charles L. 1986. *Self-Knowledge in Plato's* Phaedrus. New York: Yale University Press.

Hillman, James. 1960. *Emotion: A Comprehensive Phenomenology of Theories and their Meanings for Therapy.* London: Routledge and Kegan Paul.

Hunt, John D., and Willis, Peter, eds. 1975. *The Genius of the Place: The English Landscape Garden 1620–1820.* New York: Harper and Row.

Kainz, Friedrich. 1948. "Aesthetic States: 5. Representations (Images)." In *Aesthetics the Science.* Translated by Herbert M. Schueller. Detroit: Wayne State University Press (1962).

Koestler, Arthur. 1977. "The Truth of the Imagination." *Diogenes* 100:103–110.

March, Harold. 1984. *The Two Worlds of Marcel Proust.* New York: Russell and Russell.

Meinong, Alexius. 1910. *On Assumptions.* Translated by James Heanue. Berkeley and Los Angeles: University of California Press (1983).

Nabokov, Peter. 1987. *Architecture, Cosmology and Space: Preliminary Bibliography.* [Photocopy.]

Nietzsche, Friedrich. 1870. *The Birth of Tragedy.*

Ortega y Gasset, José. 1914. "An Essay on Esthetics by Way of a Preface." In *Phenomenology and Art.* New York: W. W. Norton (1975).

Poulet, Georges. 1963. *Proustian Space.* Translated by Elliott Coleman. Baltimore: The Johns Hopkins University Press (1977).

Proust, Marcel. 1913 on. *Remembrance of Things Past.* Translated by C. K. Scott Moncrieff. London: Chatto and Windus (1957).

Reichel, Norbert. 1987. *Der erzählte Raum* [subtitle: "On the inter-lacing of social and poetic space in narrative literature"]. Darmstadt: Wissenschaftliche Buchgesellschaft.

Richter, Jean Paul. 1796. "On the Natural Magic of the Imaginative Power." In *The Life of Quintus Fixlein* (1).

Rorty, Amélie O., ed. 1980. *Explaining Emotions.* Berkeley and Los Angeles: University of California Press.

Rybczynski, Witold. 1986. *Home: A Short History of an Idea.* New York: Viking.

Sacks, Oliver. 1987. *The Man Who Mistook His Wife for a Hat and Other Clinical Tales.* New York: Harper and Row.

Sartre, Jean-Paul. 1948. *The Emotions: Outline of a Theory.* Translated by Bernard Frechtman. New York: Philosophical Library (1975).

Scruton, Roger. 1974. *Art and Imagination: A Study in the Philosophy of Mind.* London: Routledge and Kegan Paul (1982).

Shattuck, Roger. 1962. *Proust's Binoculars: A Study of Memory, Time, and Recognition in* A la recherche du temps perdu. Princeton: Princeton University Press.

Sircello, Guy. 1972. *Mind and Art: An Essay on Varieties of Expression.* Princeton: Princeton University Press.

Solomon, Robert C. 1976. *The Passions: The Myth and Nature of Human Emotions.* Notre Dame: University of Notre Dame Press.

Smith, Adam. 1759. *The Theory of Moral Sentiments.* Indianapolis: Liberty Classics (1969).

Stendhal. 1822. *On Love.* Translated by H.B.V., under the direction of C. K. Scott-Moncrieff. New York: Grosset and Dunlap (1967).

Stilgoe, John R. 1982. *Common Landscape of America, 1580 to 1845.* New Haven: Yale University Press.

Straus, Erwin. 1956. *Vom Sinn der Sinne,* 2d ed. Berlin: Springer-Verlag.

Trigger, Bruce G. 1978. *Time and Tradition: Essays in Archaeological Interpretation.* New York: Columbia University Press.

Tuan, Yi-Fu. 1974. *Topophilia: A Study in Environmental Perception, Attitudes and Values.* Englewood Cliffs, N.J.: Prentice-Hall.

——. 1977. *Space and Place: The Perspective of Experience.* Minneapolis: University of Minnesota Press.

Walker, Jeremy. 1969. "Imagination and the Passions." *Philosophy and Phenomenological Research* 29:575–588.

White, Thomas. 1604. *The Passions of the Minde in Generall.* Urbana: University of Illinois Press (1971).

Wollheim, Richard. 1966. "Expression." In *On Art and Mind.* Cambridge: Harvard University Press (1974).

Conclusion.
Imaginative Projection and Thoughtful Penetration: Transparence and Transcendence

The moment has come to set out, by way of concluding, my sense of the peculiar place and the specific work of the imagination in our psychic economy. I say "by way of concluding," but the conclusions have, in fact, been drawn part by part. I really mean "by way of revealing the heart of this inquiry."

The facade of worldly appearances comes to us through sense perception. By thought these multifarious surfaces are penetrated and their depths are brought up. The imagination, an intermediate third, can neither transduce the external stimuli (for that is the function of the perceptual apparatus), nor can it expose their hidden core (for that is the office of our faculties of thought). What then does it do?

Imaginative Transparence

Here is a wonderfully germane observation—the perfect text for my lesson and the most apposite epigraph for this book:

The universe is an appearance corrected by a transparence. [Victor Hugo]

It intimates that the imagination helps to construe the world by means of corrections and transparencies.

773

In the philosophical part of this study I considered the productive function of the imagination in constituting a knowable world, and in the psychological part I reviewed its reproductive role in cognitively indispensable processes of visualization. I went on in the logical part to analyze the constitution of images, and in the literary and spatial parts I returned to the imagination as a power for picturing words and a capacity for shaping configurations. But the last part was largely devoted to the imagination as a world-making agency. This activity begins in an inner space with visitations rather than exertions; it is antecedent to the "labor by which reveries become works of art," in Baudelaire's words. To this internal, unlabored work of the imagination can be attributed our most specifically human mission: to remake the world imaginatively. An originary, world-constituting imagination plays its role in the blind, arcane abyss beneath consciousness. The artful, poetic imagination is embodied in overt, visible works before our eyes. But the world-revising, world-emending imagination of which I am here speaking projects an inner world onto the external environment and elicits a second appearance from the visible world. This imaginative world is neither so interior as to lack visibility nor so external as to be devoid of soul.

Now the notion of a pre-poetic projectible inner world requires the hypothesis of a merely mundane external world. Such a world—perhaps it should be called an unworld: a prosaic, opposing environment, as distinct from a human habitation—has been the subject of fascinated aversion in the literature of the last two centuries: Wordsworth recoils from the "cold inanimate world." Baudelaire is obsessed by *ennui*, the banality of all the appearances devoid of significance that constitute the modern managed environment. Thomas Mann, in his essay "Ocean Voyage with Don Quixote," speaks of the transmogrification that the ocean undergoes in use,

> a disenchantment that evidently comes from the sobering-down of the natural element and its conversion into a shipping channel and an ocean highway, whilst it loses its character as vision, image, dream, idea, as a spiritual prospect on eternity, and turns into an environment. An environment, it seems, is not aesthetic; that is achieved only by the image that confronts it. [1934]

And Robert Musil in *The Man Without Qualities*, distinguishes between the bald and the imaginatively projected world with gratifying appositeness:

> One could say that things remain the same, but that they now exist in a different space, or that everything has the coloration of a different significance. In such a moment one realizes that beside the world for everybody, that solid,

rationally investigable and manipulable world, there is yet a second one, an animated, singular, visionary and irrational world, which is only apparently coincident with the former. It is, moreover, a world which we do not, as is generally believed, carry only in our hearts or heads; on the contrary, it is exactly as external as the acceptedly valid world. This is an uncanny mystery, and like everything mysterious, no sooner is the attempt made to articulate it, than it becomes easily confused with everything that is most ordinary. [1930–43]

So the sense that the world is dual, now bare to the cold eye, and now clothed by an ardent imagination, is well attested in modern times. I hasten to say, however, that these plaintively rebellious manifestos against brazen reality have overtones of a maundering reaction to modern life which are not really a part of my meaning. The effects of modernity can be viewed under far fairer aspects: The technical manipulations that appear to disenchant and de-animate the human world are, after all, grounded in a world of science that is full of intellectual appeal, an unexpugnable sort of natural magic. Moreover, while many a practical person knows at heart that efficiency is only the incarnate hatred for the world's ordinary business, yet it is, in fact, a backbreaking and soul-wearing life that technical rationalization is meant to master. Furthermore, the environment is, to be sure, temporarily invisible to those who are belaboring it, but then again, without such close involvement no significantly visible world can come to light either; moreover, the aesthetic imaging of the world needs a workaday original that supports basic life. And finally, the second visionary world is, Musil notwithstanding, no more the land of irrationality than the base upon which it is projected is a particular province of reason. All the romantic oppositions, which pit a subjective, imaginary, humane world against an objective, rational, inanimate universe, seem to me misapprehensions. The worlds of the imagination are not at odds with the world of reason, and contempt for one is no qualification for citizenship in the other.

The antithetical base-world I am speaking of is therefore not a world to be complained of. It is just our world in one of its possible aspects: when it is significant neither to reflective thought nor to imaginative sight, precisely unsignificant, uninterpreted, unenvisioned. It is the mundane facade as it comes before our moodless, unfocused stare, a facade to which we bear a thin relation of unmotivated, fixed observation, the sort that takes an equally unblinking pseudo-interest in peeling plaster and polychrome sunsets. Beauty is an offense to the preoccupied mind as ugliness is a rebuff to the receptive soul—but the mere world I mean engenders neither of these affects: It is a "sad" world in the older sense of the word: neutral-tinted, anxiously dull, unstrung. It is simply and unresonantly here and now, merely existent. In one of Flannery O'Connor's stories there occurs this sentence: "The sun shed a dull dry light on the narrow street; everything looked exactly like what it was." That is the world I am speaking of: a world exposed but not revealed. In positing it, I am only admitting the implications of an experience acknowledged by all who have the courage of their depressions: the experience of the world untuned, including the cold comfort of having seen the world as it is in and by and for itself. Let me hereafter take the experience, if not the existence, as granted. Upon this quintessentially neutral scene, displayed to the staring eye, the imagination projects its visions.

Disengaged perceptual vision is one thing. It is quite another by imaginative sight to re-envision internally images derived from perception and stored in memory, and it is yet a third thing to summon forth from the phantasy scenes without sensory origin. These last two kinds of imaginative seeing have been amply explored in this book. Now comes a fourth activity: to receive the surrounding world with open eyes and simultaneously to project upon it the interior scenes of the mind's eye.

A commonplace of the literature has it that perception and imagination must displace each other: "While I am looking at an object I cannot imagine it," says Wittgenstein, and "One doesn't long for someone present," says Cowley. In a very precise, bare sense each claim is undeniable; it is only a piece of logic. But experientially speaking both are colossally false. Who has not felt the image-laden longing for an object of love—any object, be it thing, person, or scene, and any sort of love—that accompanies precisely its physical proximity? Who is unfamiliar with the sense that the object present to the corporeal eye is only the ghostly double of the one that appears before the mind's eye? Instead of claiming that vision and imagination must displace each other, one should say that casting a cold, image-free eye is a curtailed kind of seeing.

The ability to imagine while seeing is not even a special gift. There may be some people whose imagination is so absolutely jigged, so totally guided by perception, that it is always mere re-visualization, that the phantasy never gives depth to memory or a new dimension to the present scene. But most of us, certainly all the people I know well, cast imaginative transparencies on the colorless, fine-grained, screen of existence. Although the "homospatial" power, the ability to envision an overlay of images, may be particularly acute in poets and painters, the classical experimental finding in the psychology of the imagination, the Perky effect, shows that such superimpositions are quite ordinary. People do overlay real slides thrown on a screen with their own imagined projections, and so there is actually a

certain literal application to my transparency figure. If such double vision were not to be counted on, the most common imaginative device, the poetic metaphor, would most often misfire. For, as I have argued, a metaphor is realized when the reader recognizes the sameness of a conceptual element in a comparison, while visualizing, like a pictorial palimpsest, two disparate pictures simultaneously.

To give flesh to these bare assertions, let me now detail some six occasions and effects of this "imaginative projection"—the projection of the present upon the present, or of the absent upon the present, or perhaps some other permutation.

First. This projection is the source of the peculiar imaginative investment which is part of a full-blown grand love, as opposed to the lesser emotional immediacies: "There is no direr disaster in love than the death of the imagination," says Meredith in *The Egoist*, for the imagination does most of love's labor. It wreathes the real present figure in shadowy illuminations:

What is your substance, whereof are you made,
That millions of strange shadows on you tend?

It projects the image of an absent—or present—figure upon every receptive scene. That well-known magic worked by love—the transformation of the merely real into the vividly actual—is largely the blithe labor of the imaginative eye.

The core of the penumbra, the ghostly essence of love, is often first coagulated in sleep. Dreams transfigure the facts of life into truths of the soul. In particular, questions of love left unasked in the waking world are answered in dreams by gestures, gestures elusive and meltingly gracious. Thereafter, back in embodied life, we know what we know.

Second. The separations of space are reparable by the mere effort of locomotion, but no material labor can recover lost times. In compensation the memorial imagination is a space of time-places. These places are temporally contiguous, not continuous. Accordingly, the memorial continuum of deliberate, consecutive recollection and its material counterparts, for example, the candid home movie, are the sobering anaphrodisiacs of the imagination. These artlessly meticulous reprises of time disenchant the memories of persons and places—the places suffer from the shabbifying factuality of exact photographic exposure, and the persons suffer from the exact recall, the comic constancy, of their typical gestures: "Yes," one says without much sentiment, "that's them, all right."

The past places of memory are all next to each other. They are brought into proximity by the power of imaginative forgetting, which cancels the wastes of time, and they are called up not so much by the will of the person as by the summons of the present place. Memories overlie every moment of life that is more than a mere passage from now to now. They give it resonance and reference. "I found the world out there revealing," says Eudora Welty, "because . . . *memory* had become attached to seeing, love had added itself to discovery" (*One Writer's Beginnings* 1984).

Sometimes this projection is of shades and shapes proper to the place, so that the transparency nearly jibes with the material ground, adding only a pure dimension of time gone by. Sometimes it works a violent estrangement of the spatial sense, so that a city revisited appears as an oscillating triple veduta: the present city of concrete buildings, the past city of remembered haunts, the timeless city of dreamed essences; with time these coalesce into a rich enamel upon the topography.

Sometimes again—and this is perhaps its most magical effect—the imagination imposes on the appearances at hand not so much a memory of the same place or a recollection of its inhabitant figures, as a related reminiscence aroused by an affinity of spirit. So will the spare white grace of a wooden New England church attract to itself as a second vision the crisp ivory grandeur of a Greek marble temple, a vision that fuses with the first in a kind of fraternity of beauty. It is through the projective imagination that the consanguinity of all fine things works its associative effect.

Once more—and this is perhaps its highest occasion—the imagination sometimes projects behind the present moment a timeless memory, an unremembered archetypal background that brings the scene and its figures to their essential life: it transforms routine into ritual.

Third. Among our stored images is, of course, a large stock of what might be called secondary or artifact visions—memories of works of art, visual or auditory. The anecdote of the painter who blithely passed into his own landscape never to return is now to be cited for the last time. Poems too can be so entered. Eudora Welty, again, speaks of her own experience with Yeats's "Sailing to Byzantium":

> It seemed to me that if I could stir, if I could move to take another step . . .
> that I could move in it, live in it—that I could die in it, maybe.

The more pertinent event here is, however, the converse motion, more feasible and more frequent: it is to re-project the remembered painting—or word-scene—out upon the world. We view the flatly-lit spread of the environment through the high-lighting transparency of works that can tune and compose its languid, dull ordinariness. Here our pictorial memory overlays the perceived scene with reminiscences of other people's vision.

Fourth. Now I must say something more of dreaming, the preeminently imaginative activity. If the outer universe is an appearance awaiting correction by the imposition of a transparency, the inner world is that transparency itself, incorrigible because already through and through significant. Dreams are its purest appearances. Nietzsche—adverting, incidentally, to that sense of signifying surface which has been a preoccupation of this book—speaks of the dream world in exactly this way:

> We enjoy it in the immediate understanding of its shape; all forms speak to us; there is nothing that is indifferent or unnecessary. Yet through the highest vividness of this dream-actuality there shimmers a sense of *appearance*; at least such is my experience. [*The Birth of Tragedy* 1870]

Consequently, nothing confirms the daily world in its continual hope of gathering significance like its reappearance in nightly dreams: Here the childhood home by a genial magic lends its aura to the present habitation and corroborates a new rooting. Here a half-formed love is first fully and irretrievably affirmed. But as day enters night, so night invades day: Dreams flash into business hours as sudden reminders that pallidly ordinary scenes too can become the soul's terrain.

Fifth. All imaginative play requires double vision. My childhood recollections persuade me that the mode in question is not the "seeing-as" that particularly interests present-day philosophers; imaginative play was never seeing this *as* that, but rather seeing this *and* that: There is a dirt-filled ant-jar imprisoning a heap of acrid-smelling, crawly insects *and* there is a secret underground city of competent and purposeful little comrades.

Sixth. The ancients gave to the imagination the mediating work, performed well up-front, of bringing the appearances into the soul; the moderns have assigned to it the radical function, performed in the abyss, of constituting the world itself. Thus the imagination bears heavy cognitive responsibilities in modern philosophical speculation. But there is a role, closer to the surface and less speculative, that the imagination seems to play in articulating worlds within the constituted world. By reason of a characteristic mode of operation often remarked in this book—its inveterate discontinuity of scale and time, its "momentousness," as one might say—the imagination can cut into the continuum of appearances and establish the resulting cross-sections as separate imaginative communities. Take a garden:

From the small life of the red spider-mites under the holly leaf to the mounds and spires of green that give the gardenscape its larger lines, there is a continuum of viewable aspects. The practical, inspecting eye scans these without favor of distinction, envisioning destruction for the pests and pruning for the bushes. Meanwhile, the imaginative vision sometimes contemplates the Lilliputian world of busy, red, illicit life, and then again it dwells on the Edenic whole. In physical space the insects are within the garden and subordinate to it, as a trouble spot is to a community. But their imaginative places are coordinate and side by side. Hence the space of the imagination is an archipelago. By its scaleless, imaginative projection it defeats the homogeneous magnitudes of mere external extension: Its places are contiguous by significance and incomparable in size.

These, then, are the six works and ways of imaginative projection that have presented themselves: the investment of the bare armature of love, the superposition of discrete times and kindred significances, the retroprojection of remembered aesthetic designs into the bare geography, the injection of dreams into the day, the simultaneities of absorbed play, and the unpacking of spatially nested locales into equi-valent contiguous worlds. These are the corrective transparences of my epigraph.

★ ★ ★

But how does the appearing universe come to need correction? It has large outlines and small detail, variety and persistence—independent presence enough of its own. What it wants is an enhancing, second surface, an accumulation of acknowledgments to cover the bareness of its mere existence—though not, to be sure, impertinent attention. Objects that are much stared at acquire a protective miasma: In *The Last Gentleman* Walker Percy describes the paintings in a great museum as encrusted with public secretions, and the air about them as churned blue with ravening particles. But places that have been long and lovingly looked at through the eye of many imaginations do gather about themselves the mantle of an aura that impregnates the material substrate and renders it autonomously visible—that is to say, beautiful. The human universe requires such corrective seeing, to which remedial doing is then the spontaneous complement.

How, again, does the transparency that accomplishes the correction really, literally work? There is no answer, only this or that observation. At one extreme is the projection of actually perceived figures called hallucination, which is commonly counted as madness; at the other is the diffuse coloring of the world, from glowing gold to murky puce, which is usually referred to as mood. In between range all the degrees and kinds of imaginative seeing, from the vividness of hovering images to faintness of ghosting memories. I have used the metaphor of imaginative projection, but it *is* only a figure of speech, fertile for the description of an essential human experience, futile as a pretended theory. Hence the metaphor is negotiable—perhaps the imaginative transparency lies upon the world, perhaps behind the eyes. Theories of imaginative sight, some suggestive, all insufficient, have been reviewed throughout this book—it is an account of the *experience* of simultaneous imaginative and perceptual seeing that constitutes the veritable sum and substance of this inquiry.

Thoughtful Transcendence

If the imagination imbues the appearances with significance by casting a second surface over the world, thought goes to the meaning there signified by piercing through the looks of things to their intelligible center. It is as if the enhancing transparence upon the world served to engage the intellect and start it on its way of transcendence, its penetration of the appearing surface in search of a sightless substance. There is an ancient tradition that philosophy originates in salient visibility or beauty. Whatever modern exigencies may seem to make such a beginning doctrinally infeasible, it is still the human point of departure, this stirring of reason by perception in its imaginative mode.

Therefore, I want to conclude by considering the relation of imagination to thought, not in the technical detail that has been the concern of earlier parts, but under three reflective headings. The first of these is "the approaches of thought to the imagination"; the second is "the imagination as a mode of reason"; and the third is "the relation between imagination and intellect."

The first reflection, then, concerns thinking *about* the imagination. The faculty for forming images, the imagination proper, is responsive enough to the solicitations of subtle experimentation, but before the assaults of positivist logic, the "moves," "blocks," and "strategies" of the analytic mode, it turns tail and retreats into one last tenuous defense of its claim to existence: It calls on the common experience of introspection—a plea that is as analytically disreputable as it is humanly indefeasible. It is strange that every contemporary book on the visual imagination must devote itself primarily to the problem of its existence. In the course of its exposition all definitions will be proved defective, all generalizations false, and the question itself undecidable—undecidable, that is, in the terms of rigorously positive reason. For such rationality acknowledges no right to inquire into any psychic life whose operations cannot be tested and modeled. Now the imagination's vital signs wane under such severe treatment. It is a saving grace that there is a more forgiving reasonableness, both in experimental science and in philosophy, before which the existence of the representational imagination and its broad efficacy in human life may be considered as well and truly proved. That has been the sum and substance of the foregoing text. But behind existence and efficacy looms another, an unanswered question: How can such a power be?

Even a brief bout with romantic obfuscation or ideological skewing brings home the virtue of the demand that speech either be clear, literal, and decisive or fall silent. Yet there are junctures where the truth requires that a mystery should be declared—declared and fumblingly delineated. By a mystery I do not mean either a problem whose resolution is yet in the future, or one of those questions people assert—God knows by what insight—to be unanswerable. I mean an ever-attractive focus of wonder, the recognition of which comes through a *docta ignorantia*, a knowing kind of nescience. As Hazlitt observes, the motto of philosophers, poets, and critics is rightly not "I will lead you onto all knowledge," but "I will show you a mystery." Such a mystery is not subject to a jigged, methodical solution. If it is mechanically approachable it comes, in Oliver Sacks's words, "into the sphere of 'problems,' but not 'mysteries.'" It is amenable less to the demands of a severe rationality than to the kind of laborious worship called reflection. It is described to perfection by Marianne Moore:

A reverence for mystery is not a vague invertebrate thing. The realm of the spirit is the only realm in which experience is able to corroborate the fact that the real can also be the actual.

This is the case of the imagination exactly. It is of that psychic realm in which factual reality is transfigured into significant actuality; hence its mysteries allow—no, require—precise and vigorous pursuit. For the corroborating mark of a mystery is an experience so vital and well-formed that the continual failure of its rational explanations excites rather than fatigues thought. Thought about the imagination is continually incited by three such mysteries. One is the fact that visibility is separable from its material substrate in such a way that the appearances of extended, external space can reappear in psychic, inner space. The second is the fact that the treasury of imaginative appearances far exceeds the file of perceptual memories, and so the world of dreams and imaginations, though infinitely poorer in continuous detail than the observable universe, is far richer in significant scenes. The third mystery is the sense of significance itself: a beckoning intimation, as insuppressible as it is unspecifiable, of a manifestation about to eventuate.

The second reflection concerns thinking *as* imagination. One might say that the philosophical reason in confronting any mystery becomes itself imaginative. That is the thesis of Eric Unger's posthumously published essay, "The Imagination of Reason" (1953). All there is, he says, can be divided into three realms: the known, the temporarily unknown, and the eternally unknown. It falls to science to labor in the fields of the contingently unknown and to philosophy, properly conceived, to levitate itself into the realm of the never-to-be-known. For that realm, impenetrable by science, is amenable to imaginative reason or reasonable imagination. This hybrid faculty has the power of re-envisioning the givens of existence by means of recompositions, alternatives, extensions. Its philosophizing, which is philosophizing *par excellence*, is the exploration of the possible—not the formally possible of logic but the materially possible in the realm of content; it is the intellect concretely—imaginatively—at play. Such speculative thinking comes upon what David Norton, in an article on "Philosophy and Imagination," calls "foreign essences," possible beings not found in the real world which entail worlds of unactualized possibility (*Centennial Review* 1966). Philosophy so conceived serves our sense that there are more things in heaven and earth than are dreamt of in our philosophy. It tries to gather in one synoptic view all there is or might be, strives less to refute than to integrate speculations, tries harder to gain perspectives than to establish points, and is naturally much given to figures and myths. To forestall criticism, one might denominate this attractive enterprise amateur philosophy, well aware that "amateur philosophy" is a redundancy.

But, more precisely, what is meant by attributing to reason an imaginative mode? The imagination has these relevant features which have emerged in the course of this study: First, it is spontaneous, in the sense of being open to intimations that present themselves unbidden, of being free to jump the tracks along which "consecutive reason" is constrained to drive itself. It is the very element of material or real possibility—it has, on occasion, actually been defined as the power of the possible—insofar as within its space freely imagined phantasms fuse with perception-derived memories. Next, pictures repell negativity, for images cannot directly express non-being or contradiction. By the same token the construction of an object in the imagination serves the thing as a sort of possibility-proof. For, although not every formally possible state of affairs is visualizable, everything that can be imaged is in some minimal aspect materially possible, since space can contain it. Yet another useful feature is the ability of the mind's eye to recede to infinity so as to encompass the panorama of the whole and again to zoom back in order to take up any viewpoint within it. Finally, the imagination can render non-sensuous thought in vivid and visible figures.

Therefore, just as the imagination follows and serves reason when it spatializes its patterns and diagrams its concepts, so it can guide and inform thought in the imaginative modes of free spontaneity, material possibility, panoramic perspective, and figurative visibility.

The third and final reflection concerns thinking *and* imagination. Thought and imagination, it has been claimed throughout, are discernibly different faculties. One last testimonal in behalf of this old distinction is offered by the experience of psychology, or rather psychiatry, which once again confirms what the analysis of philosophy tends currently to impugn. For extreme, pathological, deficits throw into relief the normal complement of psychic powers, and it turns out that people who are mentally defective in respect to rationality often possess remarkable "concrete imagery." As Oliver Sacks has so movingly shown, conceptual cripples can have an imagination, above all a capacity for inner visualization, that is rich, deep, and imbued with meaning.

I have used the figures of projection and piercing to express my acceptance of the tradition that distinguishes imagination from reason by assigning different modes and actions to them—a distinction preserved in the terms of an impeccably contemporary study, cognitive psychology. In sum, the imagination doubles the appearances by representing them internally and informing them externally: through it the soul's empire becomes *extensive*, spread in space. Thought, on the other hand, penetrates the multifarious spread to find the simplicities supporting the worldly facade, be they the laws behind the natural scenery or the self behind the human face. Accordingly, the mind's dominion is *intensive*, collected, concentrated, a-spatial— whatever is antithetical to the latitude of the imagination.

No sooner are the two faculties distinguished than they are also invidiously opposed. In antiquity the intellect is, most sanguinely, placed first; in modernity reason and imagination are quite wrathfully in turn condemned. So Charlotte Brontë allows the chilliest and most lucid of heroines, Lucy Snowe, to burst out against "this hag, Reason," from under whose rod we are glad to rush out to give one truant hour to the imagination. Others, on the contrary, see themselves struggling from the swampy iridescence of the imagination toward the bracing pure air of rationality. The crux of these antagonisms is always the consignment of the imagination to the province of the emotions, while reason is supposedly passionless.

These divisions are at work today. There is a contemporary program for delivering the world entirely over to visionless rationality; it was reported in the first two parts, together with the parallel attempts to recapture it for an intellectually spineless imagination. Indeed this romantic reaction to the depredations of the rationalists, a resistance conducted along the path of least effort, is echoed in a mood so widespread as to constitute a contemporary movement. Yet the imagination does not take kindly to these reactive incantations, stimulative or relaxant.

While it is true that imagination and feeling are indeed closely—if not invariably—linked, that our imaginative life is a matter of mood, and that emotions both arouse and follow inner images, it is banefully false that thought is passionless. It is alight with more than one passion: not only with the generic desire to know, as expressed in the very word *philosophy*, "the love of wisdom," but also with the specific passion for the subject in question. In respect to the informing passion, philosophy is the inverse equal of poetry: In poetry the world's particularities are celebrated in concise speech; in philosophy they are surmounted in discursive speech; in both cases laborious love is the driving force, though oppositely directed.

Serious efforts to right the balance do exist. Among those not previously reported belongs *Die Macht der Phantasie* by Ernesto Grassi (1979), an attempt to recover for rhetoric, that is, for figurative language, the primary philosophical position that it had for the Italian humanists, particularly Vico. The "power of the imagination" in the title refers to the ability of pictorial language to preserve the particular human and historical context of an argument. But above all it refers to the power of images to provide an immediate and unresolvably ambiguous intuition of simultaneous significances, such as is anathema to disambiguating, univocity-demanding reason. These modes of speech, Grassi claims, are both more humanly moving and closer to a certain primeval, seminal attitude to the world that we ought to recover as a human possibility.

Now it seems to me that while the imaginative function is here rightly delineated, it would lose its force did not its double view in turn incite reason to point out the contradiction, to turn the flaccid "both . . . and" into a tensile "either . . . or," to penetrate the imaginative pictures in pursuit of their common intellectual point. The imagination has powers whose product is spoiled if ungathered by reason.

In truth, then, imagination and thought have a complementary relation of cooperation; imagination *and* reason together participate in philosophical inquiry. The contributions of the imagination have been studied throughout this book: The imagination provides a cognitive clearing, a middle ground between the source of perception, the external environment, and the agency of reflection, the innermost intellect. In this space, freed from the burden of impenetrable matter and the distraction of infinite detail, objects gain perspicuity. Here experience is consolidated out of the accumulation of sensory memories. Here possibilities are tested by free play with variable visualizations. Here human affairs can be rehearsed and feelings assayed, away from the pressures of immediate reality.

From early to late in the course of human inquiry, the most promising philosophical beginning has been a sense of amazement that our world appears to us *as* an appearance, as a visible facade that both hides and reveals depths. It is by reason of this fact of life that the dreaming, fantasizing, remembering imagination, the imagination in all its modes, can cooperate in the cognitive venture and take part in it twice over: First it represents the appearances, clarified, within its own space; it absorbs them, beautified, into its own visions; it projects them back as rectifying transparencies upon the world. And then it procedes to captivate thought, inciting it to pierce these imaginative panoramas and to transcend them in search of their unseen core.

Coda.
The Life of the Imagination

Long, loving absorption in questions concerning the imagination has led to a set of reflections that fall in between the arcane preoccupations where ideas germinate in uncomforming originality, and the formal studies where those ideas are normalized for public presentation. I might characterize these intermediate reflections as "intimate," since they revolve about the imagination insofar as it is both interior and communicable; they can be expressed in a pleasant discourse that is neither idiosyncratic nor conventional. They concern the specifically imaginative life, its dangers and its blessings, its malaise and its bliss. So, as in the Conclusion above I summed up the imaginative mode descriptively, in this postscript I finally draw the practical lesson: I delineate the life of the imagination, or rather the imaginative living of life, and I advocate it—with due caution and due warmth, I hope.

It is therefore not the productive imagination to which I devote these last observations. The imagination has its professionals—the published poets in all idioms. And again, it has its amateurs and dilettanti, its "inglorious Wordsworths"—most of us. These tacit lovers and silent delighters are acknowledged as living in a certain fraternal continuity with the productive practitioners:

Poesy alone can tell her dreams,
With the fine spell of words alone can save
Imagination from the sable chain
And dumb enchantment. Who alive can say
"Thou art no Poet—mayst not tell thy dreams?"
Since every man whose soul is not a clod
Hath visions, and would speak, if he had loved
And been well nurtured in his mother tongue.
[*Hyperion*]

Yet in his generous afflatus Keats surely overstates the case at both ends: Most of us learn during adolescence that no amount of literacy imparts to us the gift to preserve the fragrance of a vision by giving it utterance. Moreover, in resigning the public profession of poetry, we not only bring relief to our friends, but also, far from entombing our imaginations in dumb enchantment, we considerably improve the shapeliness and sharpen the precision of our silent introspective accounts. Perhaps the spontaneous inner world of mere dreamers—where all the forest is first growth—may even have a magic lost to the well-logged interior ranges of practicing poets. That will be the case especially when they are constrained by the poetics of the age to be at once severely verbal and learnedly connotative, while the naive imaginer is still at liberty to entertain intimately direct visions. Be that as it may, it is the expressively inchoate but experientially full-blown imagination—the common, not to say ordinary, imaginative life that I have in mind.

Moreover, not only the imaginative power but its contents are common, and common in two ways: I have made an effort to show that the provinces of each individual imagination are internally contiguous and belong to one realm. The different domains of distinct imaginations similarly harmonize and make one world. What people brusquely deny as logicians and critics, they affirm as human beings in the intimate conversations in which—as friends, not as experts—they congregate around the monuments extruded by the subterranean continent of the imagination—works of prose, poetry, painting, plastic art, architecture, and music. Here, on the common ground of the imagination, they point out to each other their discoveries: spots of delight and concealed signals and deft devices. Moreover they seem to regard all such communings as belonging within one universe of discourse and reference, as the latitude of their citations shows: I have heard Tolstoy's Natasha and Homer's Nausikaa quite casually compared. It is no wonder that there are no friendships more tenacious than those established on the territory of the imagination.

Although I have just referred to the imagination as a netherworld, since evidently most of its store is kept and much of its work is done beneath the consciousness in which images become manifest, I have eschewed theories consigning it to the psychoanalytic unconscious, be it individual or collective. The "Unconscious" is a technical term defined within particular psychic topographies. It is a schematically useful, if logically questionable, construct, intended to make the mysteries of the passionate imagination amenable to systematic psychological and literary investigation and control. In the face of actual imaginative experience it seems jejune. But if one forgoes these illuminations what is left?

It is a thesis—or anti-thesis—of this book that the imagination is actual enough not to require construal by a formal theory, that a trusting attention to its phenomena, and observations expressed in models and analogies, will better preserve its substance and its life. *How* things never seen by the corporeal eye, or heard by the physical ear, come to be in the individual imagination is simply unknown, though devoted introspection affirms *that* there are such originally imaginative beings and scenes. We are free to conjecture about their source (though perhaps not wise to publish our conjectures). How the imaginations of widely diverse human beings come, on occasion, to harmonize so wonderfully is equally a mystery. These inner worlds, are, I will admit, hermetically sealed from each other. They are neither continuous, contiguous, coincident nor even effectively contemporaneous, being outside that unitary space and universal time which impart to the external human environment a formal unity. It is an uncircumventable fact that no one has ever seen directly into another's imaginative space. And yet a thousand small convictions persuade us that we windowless monads do often vibrate sympathetically with another's psychic motions and, mirrorlike, represent within ourselves each other's interior landscapes—from our own center and perspective to be sure, but preserving a certain isomorphism of aspect. With willing attention we can watch another's world take shape within us and see into the other by looking within ourselves.

This harmonizing of inner worlds with insuperably distinct centers seems to me, as I just indicated, to characterize a type of friendship that is the most intimate relation this side of love and the most unclouded delight anywhere to be found: the friendship of the sensibility, the imaginative friendship. This sturdily delicate friendship, the particular friendship of the soul, is the one in which we open to each other's unintrusive gaze intermittent glimpses of our inner panorama. It is, I think, a manifestation of the imaginative life that is peculiarly modern. At least it is not—a fascinating fact—among the types distinguished by Aristotle, who wrote in his *Nichomachean Ethics* the book on friendship for all times, now, then, or hereafter. For him the finest friendship and the truest happiness are coupled through the notion of excellence. The best friends love each other for the very excellence upon which each friend's own happiness is also conditioned— for happiness is the active, thought-governed fulfillment of the soul in accordance with excellence. Such happiness is a sedate, stable habit of active life, not a momentary glory or an instant of bliss. Well-conditioned activity in each partner separately, and mutual respect occasioned by their common excellence—these are the foundations of antique friendship, and, I think, remain its basis in our day: Neither unfulfilled souls nor morally disreputable characters are likely to enter into a good friendship, whether it is based on a common fate, or task, or conviction.

That granted, there remains the fact that Aristotle omits the imaginative bond even from his class of lesser and least friends, such as boon companions and business partners. The reason is, I think, that for him to *be* fully, is to be *active*, to be thoughtfully engaged. But the imaginative life of the soul that has been my theme here, the life that falls short of poetic production, has a musing and even a somewhat passive, cast. For its visions often present themselves when the intellect is on holiday, and they arrive, for all their splendor, fitfully and in quick-fading formats. So friends of the imagination love each other not only for the steadfast activity of their soul but also for its store of fugitive visions, not only for what they staunchly do in the world, but also for what they intermittently see within, not only for the salient excellence of their active character but also for the capacious receptivity of their inner space.

In principle all the ways of human beings are, I believe, possible anywhere at any time. Yet the imaginative life probably needed behind it the passage of history to become a canonical mode. For first, the long recorded flow of time was required to fill that imaginative reservoir, that vast store of scenes, styles, works, figures, and auras, which distinguishes our latter-day memories (no matter how haphazardly supplied) from the sparely, if weightily, stocked minds of the ancients. And second, time, though the significant cause of nothing, is yet the necessary condition for a development whose ramified course is detailed throughout this study: that specifically modern consciousness in which the imagination is not the secure servant of the intellect but the vulnerably independent opponent of a manipulative rationality. This modern mode may, in sum, be called romanticism.

Now romanticism has been the *bête noire* of this book, because in that extreme spirit which is its norm, it divorces the imagination from thought and turns it into a capricious, moody god. So my praise of a life centered on the imagination—and particularly of a human relation within that life— might bring on me a charge of *tu quoque*. But if it is romanticism, it is romanticism of a very sober sort. In fact "sober romanticism" would be a perfectly acceptable term for the life I mean, a life in which the imagination is suspect except as it is seconded by reflection and fulfilled in action, a life in which the imagination is not worshiped as an autarchic source but understood as the enigmatic conduit of visions.

That view of the imagination as essentially receptive rather than creative, as marking human incompleteness rather than testifying to its self-sufficiency, raises a moderating, even humbling thought about the imaginative life: It is dependent, even parasitical, on physical well-being, material comfort, and psychic security. There are, to be sure, those strong souls to whose imaginative mill every suffering is grist, to whose unharrowable vision even hell appears in sombre brilliance—I do not mean those perverse romantics who extract voluptuous pleasure from mephitic effluvia, but the staunch spirits who find saving beauties in horrors faced without flinching. Ordinarily, however, interminable misery such as chronic pain, wearing poverty, and, above all, pervasive tyranny, may eventually close down and lay waste the imaginative space within. And once the necessity of favorable material and particularly of political conditions is acknowledged, a converse ought also to be admitted: The lucky fulfillment of these conditions imposes an obligation actually to live imaginatively and not to use the normal imperfections of society at large as a pretense for living provisionally, distracted betwixt the diffuse ills of society and the narrow pleasures of the individual. But where these minimal political conditions fail, the imagination will, unhappily but resolutely, join the resistance, for its own life is at stake. The evidence is clear: Tyranny and imagination are archenemies.

As the unforced imaginative mode is set off from the antique life of public action, so it can be contrasted to many current instrumental activities. All sorts of business is carried on in virtual imagelessness or with hard-edged, narrow-gauged utilitarian images only: hard-driving, bare-boned techniques requiring a tensed mental grasp, obstacle-resolving common sense spun tight into a cocoon of practical interest, physical, repetitive labor defensively done with a blank mind. Add to these all the imageless pleasures: immediate, close-up, contact-pleasures—enjoyments energetic and pointed, but without much affective resonance or imaginative residue. And include computational thinking, severe and essentially sightless (not less so for being carried on before a screen of luminous green characters). Activities of this description form the supporting exoskeleton of contemporary life. They turn out to have a tendency to suffocate the organic innards, the imaginative heart. And yet, if, as someone once said, the unexamined life is not worth living, neither is this unenvisioned life—at least not if it preponderates.

Consequently, the imaginative life could do with some itemized advocacy. I had already begun it by distinguishing as its first-fruit a certain kind of human bond. Before proceeding to praise it in paragraphs I want to set out certain specific vulnerabilities of the imaginative mode, both passive and active.

For just as reason has its theory and its practice so imagination has its dreaming and its doing. There are high strains of imaginative contemplation, serene, and self-contained, such as are caught in these lines of muted fervor from a Buddhist text:

Well-roofed and pleasant is my little hut,
And screened from winds:—Rain at thy will, thou god!
My heart is well composed, my heart is free,
And ardent is my mood. Now rain, god! rain.

But this same dreaming, inward, contemplative imagination, when too much or too deliberately or inopportunely indulged, has its specific nemesis: The forced imagination loses the courage of its convictions and is overcome by the melancholy of its unreality. When its sustaining energy is strained, the trust in its visions collapses and a kind of inner calamity, an imaginative devastation ensues; the insubstantiality of the pageant seems manifest, the fabric of every vision appears baseless, and all the spirits melt into thin air.

A trifling, though telling, example arises in the reading of those facsimile fables, historical novels, which represent a peculiarly modern indulgence of the nostalgic imagination. At moments, in the entrancing diversion of watching perfectly current passions played out against romantically distant vistas, it suddenly comes home how doubly illusionary is the spell: These worlds that are irretrievably bygone are—insult upon injury—also worlds that never were. When, however, imaginative vigor is restored, pastness and nonexistence have no sting. There is satisfaction in the fact that these redolent worlds were so recently born before the inner eye of a contemporary story-teller and are now being re-envisioned by companies of fellow-readers. I shall try below to tell as soberly as I can why this sort of faith in the actuality of imaginative worlds is more than a slackly willing suspension of disbelief in unrealities.

At the other pole of image-savoring contemplation is the image-driven longing for worldly eventfulness through which the imagination becomes the cause of deeds, but deeds that are unfulfilling and vulnerable to a peculiar malaise. This pseudo-active aspect of the imaginative life is epitomized in adventure-seeking which is, if truth be told, a more potent motive than either wealth or power. What follows is an inventory of the impulses to adventure. It is perhaps a curious undertaking, but one intended to expose the paradoxes and melancholy rebuffs inherent in the purposeful search for the imaginative life in action. Adventuring, it turns out, is a strangely hollow activity. The reason is that adventure is a subspecies of the accidental: the premeditated accident. The adventurer shuns the sedate course of events and instead seeks a galvanizing eventfulness.

First among adventures was, traditionally, war. But its glories have long since become obsolete—modern technicized total war has no place for splendid paladins flashing about the field. Its exhilarations, too, are notoriously short-lived; initial enthusiasm is soon reduced to turns of tedium and terror. Such war is not decently experienced as adventure.

Second in adventurous appeal used to be life near the centers of power and close to the foci of permanent crisis. But even as at the courts of old the heady air of intrigue unfailingly thickened into sordid murk, so in modern democracies the early exultations of power can be counted on, these days, to come to an ignominious end.

There exists, third, a nobler and sounder sort of political intoxication, the sort that comes from being present at high moments and great creations, at the liberation of the land or the founding of a country. But here too, after-life exacts a price: Those who have lived intensely through supremely exciting times are often afflicted with the melancholy that comes from having unmatchable memories. (There is, to be sure, a sturdy, viable political enthusiasm, the sober desire to preserve and protect one's community. Such politics, too, can make the heart beat high, but its mood is the antithesis of adventurism.)

A fourth traditional source of adventure is the exploration of the world and the discovery of exotic wonders. But even when the *terra incognita* of our globe was not yet exhausted, when a traveler might come on lost cities and thriving empires none of his kind had ever seen, when the differences among civilizations had not yet been subtilized and concealed beneath the common uniform, be it blue jeans or business suit—even then these adventures were often miserable, precarious affairs, driven by gold-greed and tainted by treachery. What is left for us moderns seems to be the image-poor penetration of all-but-empty space, a feat prodigiously rehearsed and controlled, though punctuated by sudden disaster. Our voyages of discovery will not be imaginative adventures so much as technical ordeals; data, not imagery, will be their gold.

There is, fifth and last, a kind of adventure that is nearest the stuff of poetry. It is the spiritual quest during which the secular geography takes on the nature of a moral topography. This mode of adventuring is surely less feasible on our earth, which no longer holds many far and secret places. But then, even in its day, the adventure's true grail proved to be within the soul, and the spatial voyage an embellishment and a digression.

What I am saying is that risky, real adventure has always been too much beset by the paradoxes of its very conception to be truly soul-satisfying—except in its telling—and now it is exceedingly inaccessible as well. Instead, we moderns have developed a sophisticated counterfeit of the imaginative adventure, an expensive diversion complete with controlled risks, high-tech support, immediate comradeship, and romantic morality: tourism. Though why call it counterfeit when it is, in fact, a practical acknowledgement of the paradoxes inherent in the active life of the imagination: the desire to behold strange lands without the anxieties of uprooted transience, and the longing to be captivated by the aura of a place without workaday inclusion in its affairs?

Who among us has not been party to these image-hunting assaults on points of certified interest, when the imaginative eye, put practically on the spot, gawks in stupefaction where millions have been to gaze. But there is also a choicer part of tourism: the wilderness experience. It is especially dear to my heart because of the peculiarly contemporary, complexly ambiguous notional melange that possesses its devotees, not the least questionable element of which is the very idea of putting oneself deliberately in the way of an "experience." Nonetheless, of imaginative projects it is among the richest both in melancholy resonances and in restorative beauties: What sinks more deeply into memory than rafting down a dark green river that flows through a deep red and gold canyon, floating gently after the brief frisson of a white-water passage, recumbently squinting through overhanging cottonwoods at the crenellated escarpment backed by a blue sky—and the sudden sense, for one heartbeat beyond belief or disbelief, that the winged gods of the place are about to make an epiphany up there. It is a sense quickly checked by a sobering caution: we latecomers should not trifle with the *genius loci*.

Though we seek adventure for a swarm of reasons—to be first or fastest in place and space, to galvanize a sluggish sensibility with well-secured scares, to collect anecdotes, to store images against our days of blind, imageless busyness—behind all those manipulative schemes, there looms, its seems to me, a pure yearning for an original, unimpugnable, unpassing, quintessential eventfulness. We long for significance-laden visions with which the imagination may resonate unreservedly. But to no avail, for the truth is, once again, that this sort of forced imaginative worldliness is self-nullifying, no way of life. It is essentially parasitical and paradoxical—mere diversion if divorced from an engaging task, mere aestheticism if cut off from a substantial purpose.

The imagination entertains purposes because of a truth, asserted with grand simplicity by G.E. Moore:

> We think that the world would be improved if we could substitute for the best works of representative art *real* objects equally beautiful. . . . We can imagine the case of a single person, enjoying throughout eternity the contemplation of scenery as beautiful, and intercourse with persons as admirable, as can be imagined; while yet the whole of the objects of his cognition are absolutely unreal. I think we should definitely pronounce the existence, which consisted

solely of such a person, to be *greatly* inferior in value to one in which the objects . . . did really exist just as he believes them to do. [*Principia Ethica* 1903, paras. 117, 119]

Because for ourselves who are awake and for others who might be dreaming we prefer—by and large—that the imaginary should be enhanced by real existence, our imaginative life is so often the prelude to actions and the obbligato to their execution: "In dreams begin responsibilities," and dreams attend their fulfillment. Nevertheless we must never think that this longing for reality impugns the actuality, here so tentatively and persistently brought forward, of imaginative being. On the contrary: What could testify better to its vitality than our active desire to see it realized?

So the imaginative life ought, finally, to be for mundane existence what grace is for goodness. It is the imagination superimposed on the working day that maintains our faith and makes us—somewhat—immune to melancholy and ready to act. What then are the ways in which the imagination can take the part, not, to be sure, of life's steady tenor, but of its levitating descant?

Well, to begin prosaically, there are first those experimentally corroborated, hard-edged uses so often taken into account in this study. The external environment, as people spontaneously know and investigators laboriously prove, is most economically and effectively manipulated by means of vigorous visualization, be it the superimposition of a visualized furniture arrangement on a room, the projection of an imagined figure on a canvas, or the mental siting of a city in its place. Any work in the world that does not begin with contemplative imagining is only blind, bungling tomfoolery, whatever perverse pragmatism philosophers of our age are pleased to uphold. We are not condemned to plunge banging away *in medias res*, exactly because we possess a power of projective visualization: visual contemplation precedes practice.

As in production so in performance: Inner visualization of bodily schemata has been shown to improve the execution of athletic movements. The solution of logical and mathematical problems often begins with inscriptions made in an interior space. The limits of likelihood for practical construction are found by the free variations of their imagined counterparts. All these effects have been detailed in the text above.

A somewhat different kind of imaging, the careful reconstruction of memory, is also indispensable to life. Such visual recollection may serve no grander use than the recovery of lost keys. But then again it may accomplish the revivification of lost loves and the re-presentation of those that would be out of view,

Save that my soul's imaginary sight
Presents thy shadow to my sightless view,
Which, like a jewel hung in ghastly night,
Makes black night beauteous and her old face new.
[Sonnet 27]

But here we have returned from the restrained, external projections of the applied imagination to the spontaneous, intimate configurations of the contemplative imagination. As we rework the outer world to our requirements, so we make for ourselves a home within. To this place of refuge we go to wait out the dead or anxious stretches between action and action—for the times to act do seem always to come inconveniently bunched. To this retreat we come to live down the unavoidable calamities of public life: shaming slips, indignities brought on ourselves. Here we hide to recover from exhaustion, to find a recreation of the spirit. Here we cultivate a fragrant enclosure, gardenlike because it flourishes spontaneously, while our effort is only to plant and prune—a place secluded, calm, stately, ample, significant.

But it is not only a place for recovery; it is also a space for the magnification of experience, where a little of the world goes a long way: Think of the passionate poetry and perspicacious novels written out of their practically unaided imagination by all the confined spinsters of the past century. The wisdom extracted from experience in the imagination is often in inverse relation to its quantity; the reflective sensibility tends to obtain its intensest insights from the most minimal material. More happens in the slow interior than at the whirling periphery.

These inner precincts are largely filled with memory-matter, not the myriads of flat, factual visualizations we reconstruct for use, but the spontaneous, surprising returns of sights we have drunk in with delight, such as Wordsworth records:

I gazed—and gazed—but little thought
What wealth the show to me had brought:
. . .
For oft, when on my couch I lie
In vacant or in pensive mood,
They flash upon that inward eye
Which is the bliss of solitude;
And then my heart with pleasure fills
And dances with the daffodils. ["Daffodils"]

But imaginative memory not only stores for us the passing moments of perception; it also transfigures, distances, vivifies, defangs—reshapes deformed impressions, turns oppressive immediacies into wide vistas, imbues drained scenes with color, loosens the rigid grip of an acute desire and transforms it into a fertile design. The imagination, one might say, scales our affairs to humane proportions; it makes us free. It sights the middle distance; its vision lies between the large abstract stare and the minute particular squint. The imaginative memory, while blurring the definite contours of experience, brings out its concentrated, pungent essence.

These visions and re-visions not only furnish the inner space itself with its pictures but ready it for service to the external world, and that in a multitude of specific ways. Here, for example, are stored all the illustrations to which novels are the texts, all the worlds to which paintings are windows, all the gestures of the soul for which music is the embodiment.

Imaginative memory further serves the external world by amplifying its point-like temporality. The outside world confronts us in the curtest of time-phases, the instant; it is the preeminent phase of existence here and now, of presence. From memory the present acquires a penumbra, the past, the framing aura that makes it significant. Out of memories, too, are shaped those projections for the future that give the present its purpose. From memory, finally, comes the power to withstand present trends, and to resist mere currency. As it apprehends the fugitive now, so memory sabotages the tyranny of the moment.

But memory serves the world not only as the power of recollection but also as the agency of forgetfulness. It protects the active present against obsessional replays and reprises, either resentful or sentimental. The well-conditioned imagination indulges in the temptations of nostalgia only during those slack interludes that betoken a temporary collapse of imaginative energy. The proper memorial participation of the imagination in action is not in the mode of nostalgia but of renascence. Imaginative memory sponsors rebirths, the recovery of vital origins and archetypes. Such originating images are behind most significant human activity. But I am thinking here not so much of the grand political myths discussed earlier in the book, as of more intimate arch-views of beauty. There are places that show the pristine patterns governing their communal life, but there are other spaces, mercilessly past-less, where the evidence of their presence is debased or forlorn—yet often so much the more poignant: a garishly primeval landscape on the rear window of a van, a feathery Japanese maple on a tract-house lawn.

Furthermore the very labor of attending to the inner scene that the active imagination exacts from us turns out to be of use for living in the external world. Not only does such introspection put us in a state of readiness for decisive action; but also the practice of giving precise, nuanced, accounts of our inner world is our one best protection against the exhausting psychic blight of not being at home with ourselves.

Finally and above all, the imagination serves our worldly existence by pulling us out of its dumb immediacy, distancing us from an oppressively close present and disqualifying the primacy of the merely real here and now, while according actuality to the absent and the nonexistent. For though the fact borders on the miraculous, I nevertheless feel a flat certainty that the inner world of the imagination is not exhausted by retrospective and prospective images—by memories of past perceptions and expectations of future fact. It has space for visible, audible, all-but-tangible images of things that never were and probably never will be seen in mundane time and ordinary space. All such sights may, to be sure, have been worked up from traces of perceptual material imported from the external world. But their integral aspect and aromatic essence comes, at least on certain wonderful occasions, from the inner world of the imagination alone, as their enigmatic significance seems to refer us to a realm yet farther inward than imaginative space. Such durability as these imaginative epiphanies have in our lives is that of recurrence rather than of persistence. But in compensation they convey at each return a coalescence of meaning and appearance that the ever-available external phenomena forever lack. To these all-but-substantial imaginative visions, this book has been one tenacious, if tentative approach: They above all shape the imaginative life as a prelude to action, an incitement to reflection, and an intimation of paradise.

Index

Nearly all subject-entries have the imagination or images as context. Only selected subject-references and authors quoted or discussed are indexed; general references are usually not indexed. Italicized page numbers indicate definitions, quotations, main passages, and extended treatments.